Commercial and Residential Service Charges

Commercial and Residential Service Charges

**Adam Rosenthal, Elizabeth Fitzgerald,
Nathaniel Duckworth, Oliver Radley-Gardner
and Philip Sissons**

Bloomsbury Professional

Bloomsbury Professional Limited, Maxwelton House, 41–43 Boltro Road, Haywards Heath, West Sussex, RH16 1BJ

© Adam Rosenthal, Elizabeth Fitzgerald, Nathaniel Duckworth, Oliver Radley-Gardner, Philip Sissons 2013

Bloomsbury Professional is an imprint of Bloomsbury Publishing Plc

A CIP Catalogue record for this book is available from the British Library.

ISBN   978 1 84766 985 8

While every care has been taken to ensure the accuracy of this work, no responsibility for loss or damage occasioned to any person acting or refraining from action as a result of any statement in it can be accepted by the authors, editors or publishers.

Typeset by Phoenix Photosetting, Chatham, Kent
Printed and bound in Great Britain by CPI Group (UK) Ltd, Croydon, CR0 4YY

Foreword

For long leaseholders of flats the payment of a service charge is the most significant item of annual expenditure attached to the leasehold interest. For tenants of multi-let commercial property it ranks only behind the rent.

The separation of responsibility for the provision of services or the carrying out of works on the one hand, and the responsibility for payment on the other is almost bound to lead to friction if not outright dispute. So the practitioner needs to have a thorough understanding of how service charge clauses are drafted, what they mean, how to operate them and what to do if things go wrong. In addition, since leases are, for the most part, wasting assets, the long-term interests of the leaseholder and the reversioner are misaligned. As Shakespeare put it in his famous question:

> 'Why so large cost, having so short a lease
> Dost thou upon thy fading mansion spend?'

It is now over 40 years since Parliament first began to regulate service charges in the residential sector. The legislation has changed many times. In each case the balance has been tipped further in the leaseholder's favour. Jurisdiction over most service charge disputes in the residential sector has been removed from the courts and entrusted to the tribunal system. A large body of caselaw has grown up within the tribunal system. Much of it is not readily obtainable in regular series of reported cases. The authors of this work have been assiduous in finding, explaining and commenting on this wealth of material.

Although the commercial sector remains largely unregulated, professional bodies have issued guidance on the drafting and operation of service charge clauses. This too is carefully explained and analysed.

It is difficult to imagine a more comprehensive treatment of all aspects of service charges. In short, the reader will find within these pages everything he or she ever wished to know about service charges, and a good deal more besides. I welcome this addition to the property practitioner's essential library.

Kim Lewison
Royal Courts of Justice
London WC2A 2LL

Preface

Although the service charge is a relatively recent innovation,[1] the apparent conflict between the paying party and the receiving party has produced a disproportionate amount of litigation. At the heart of the law on service charges is the contract to contribute a sum of money towards a fixed or recurring cost. In the non-residential context, contractual principles prevail, although establishing a coherent set of principles is not an altogether straightforward task. When considering service charges relating to premises which consist of or include dwellings, there is a mass of statutory material which is super-imposed onto the contractual framework, which makes consideration of and advising on service charges all the more challenging. It is these challenges and the application of seemingly contradictory principles which we have sought to tackle in writing this text.

The law and practice of managing property, especially residential property, covers a number of areas which stray beyond the subject matter of service charges. The purpose of this book is to analyse and explore issues and the size of the subject in hand (service charges) is such that it has not been possible to provide detailed coverage of such related topics as the right to manage under the Commonhold and Leasehold Reform Act 2002 or the power of the Leasehold Valuation Tribunal to vary leases under Part IV of the Landlord and Tenant Act 1987, which are therefore covered only to the extent that they affect consideration of issues relating to service charges.

The focus of the text is the ability of one party (landlord, estate owner) to recover from another (tenant, freeholder of property within estate) a contribution towards the costs incurred in managing the estate. That estate might be a house converted into a small number of flats, a large block of flats, a holiday park, an office building or an industrial estate. In each case, the contractual principles, which must be the first port of call for the legal adviser, are the same. After considering how the principles of contractual construction apply specifically to service charges (in Part I), we have sought to consider the application of those principles to the subject matter of the obligation (Part II) and the machinery which has to be operated to create the obligation (Part III). We then consider the statutory overlay which applies principally (although not exclusively) in the

---

1 At least in the long leasehold context: see **1-08** below.

residential context (Part IV) and finally, we have included detailed coverage of the remedies available to either party in the event of failures by the other (Part V).

The subject-matter is constantly evolving. So much so, we are grateful to our publishers for agreeing to put back the publication date to allow us to write about the recent decision of the Supreme Court in *Daejan Investments Ltd v Benson* [2013] UKSC 14. This is the first case at Supreme Court/House of Lords level whose subject matter is a 'pure' service charge issue. The issue in that case was, in one sense, a narrow one, in the context of the subject as a whole, concerning the circumstances in which the Leasehold Valuation Tribunal ought to exercise its discretion to dispense with the rather burdensome consultation requirements under section 20 of the Landlord and Tenant Act 1985 and the regulations made thereunder. However, the impact of these regulations is immense and the importance of this decision should not be underestimated in the residential sphere. The ambit of the decision is discussed in detail in Chapter 30, below.

In addition to the much-publicised *Benson* case, there have been other recent decisions of the courts to which we have given consideration. To mention but a few, *Phillips v Francis* [2012] EWHC 3759 (Ch) is a decision of the Chancery Division on the scope of section 20, *Edward & Walkden (Norfolk) Ltd v City of London* [2012] EWHC 2527 (Ch) relates to the provision for service charges in a new business lease under the Landlord and Tenant Act 1954 and *Campbell v Daejan Properties Ltd* [2012] EWCA Civ 5103 concerns the approach of the court to difficult questions of construction which arise when applying service charge provisions.

Litigation concerning residential service charges is now, almost universally, conducted within the tribunal system. First instance recourse for most challenges to service charge demands is to the Leasehold Valuation Tribunal, with appeals lying to the Upper Tribunal (Lands Chamber). The Lands Chamber of the Upper Tribunal is the reincarnation of the former Lands Tribunal, created in 2009 as part of the unified Upper Tribunal system. The Leasehold Valuation Tribunal has retained its existence, outside the unified first tier tribunal structure. However, this is shortly to change and the Leasehold Valuation Tribunal is to be amalgamated with a number of other property tribunals to form the First Tier Tribunal (Property Chamber). This transfer of functions was originally due to take place on 1 April 2013 and we were hopeful that we would be able to include references to the new procedural rules which are to apply to the newly created tribunal. However, for reasons to which we are not privy, parliament has put the date back to 1 July 2013 and at the time of publication, there is still no sign of the First Tier Tribunal (Property Chamber) Rules which will regulate the procedure of the new tribunal. Although a draft set of rules was published in 2012, this was for consultation purposes only and it is likely that the final version will differ significantly. We have therefore continued to refer to the present Leasehold Valuation Tribunal (Procedure) Regulations 2003 where relevant. Having considered the initial draft of the rules for the new first tier tribunal, we do not think that it is necessary or worthwhile delaying publication of the book. First, we are not wholly confident that the revised date of 1 July 2013 for the transfer of functions to the new tribunal will necessarily be met, the original date having already been put back. Secondly, this text is intended to deal, principally, with the substantive aspects of the law. That is not to say that we have not, where relevant, included commentary on specific aspects of Leasehold Valuation Tribunal and Upper Tribunal procedure, but this is not the focus of the book. Thirdly, where reference has been made to specific procedural rules, it is unlikely that the new rules will be fundamentally different to the present rules.

We have sought, where relevant, to cite decisions of the Upper Tribunal (Lands Chamber) and the Lands Tribunal where those decisions address points of principle. Apart from certain chapters relating to the statutory provisions which are considered most frequently by the LVT, we have not sought to cite extensively from decisions of the LVT throughout the text. The LVT is an extremely busy forum and all of its decisions are published online. Most turn on particular facts and even where points of principle are involved, they do not bind subsequent tribunals.

We should express our gratitude to our colleagues at Falcon Chambers, who have encouraged us to embark upon this project and have challenged us to address and even attempt to solve various problematic areas they have encountered in practice. We are also grateful to Eloise Morgan and Rupert Cohen, both pupils at Falcon Chambers, who have assisted us immeasurably at the proof-reading stage.

The law is stated as at 19 April 2013.

Adam Rosenthal
Elizabeth Fitzgerald
Nathaniel Duckworth
Oliver Radley-Gardner
Philip Sissons

Falcon Chambers
Falcon Court
London EC4Y 1AA

Contents

APPENDIX

Table of Statutes

References are to paragraph numbers.

Table of Statutory Instruments

References are to paragraph numbers.

Table of Cases

References are to paragraph numbers.

B

H

M

Q

R

S

1

li

T

Z

PART I

Introduction

CHAPTER 1

Introduction

1-01   Where only part of a building or estate has been let, someone has to maintain the building and its common parts, someone has to provide the essential services necessary to enjoy occupation and someone has to pay for all of this. Accordingly, leases of buildings in multiple occupation invariably contain provisions requiring a tenant to pay a proportionate part of the landlord's costs of maintenance and of providing necessary services, usually by way of a variable payment known as a service charge.

1-02   The term 'service charge' is accordingly used to refer to a charge levied against occupiers of multi-occupied property by way of contribution to repairs, maintenance, management and other services provided in respect of the property.[1] Services charges arise in both a non-residential context, for example in multi-let office blocks, shopping centres and industrial parks, and in a residential context.

1-03   Although most commonly encountered in a leasehold framework, service charges are not limited to leasehold property and can also apply to freeholds. For example, where the freehold of individual units within an estate have been sold (e.g. within an industrial park, a housing estate or a holiday park) the former freehold owner may incur expense in maintaining the retained common parts, such as communal roads, and in providing services, such as drainage, and will want to recover such expense from the other property owners within the estate.

1-04   This book is largely concerned with issues which arise in connection with leasehold service charges; however, service charges affecting freeholds are also considered in Chapter 26.

1-05   In view of the limited number of commonholds which have been created since the Commonhold and Leasehold Reform Act 2002 ('CLRA 2002') was enacted, the commonhold equivalent of service charges is not considered.[2]

---

1   For the statutory definition of 'service charge' see **28-01** below.
2   For a detailed explanation of the commonhold regime see Fetherstonhaugh, Sefton and Peters, *Commonhold* (Oxford University Press, 2003).

Residential Estate Management Schemes arising under the statutory provisions of the Leasehold Reform Act 1967 and the Leasehold Reform, Housing and Urban Development Act 1993 are also not considered in detail.[3]

1-06   Under the provisions of the CLRA 2002, tenants of dwellings can (in certain circumstances) establish a right to manage company ('RTM') to take over the management functions of residential flats. This right to manage is separate to the right to require a manager to be appointed under Part II of the Landlord and Tenant Act 1987. Although there are a number of service charge consequences arising as a result of these rights introduced by sections 71 to 113 of the CLRA 2002, this is a subject in its own right and, accordingly, this topic has not been considered in detail in this book. The 'fault based' right to appoint a manager is dealt with at **47-46** to **47-62**.

1-07   The question of how service charges and sinking funds fall to be taxed are also outside the scope of this book and the reader is referred to specialist works for guidance as to the issues concerning the taxation of service charges.

LEASEHOLD SERVICE CHARGES[4]

History

1-08   Traditionally, in England and Wales, houses were the principal form of privately owned accommodation. From the 1840s onwards, purpose-built flats for charitable housing trusts, such as Peabody and Guinness, started to be developed and the first non-charitable block of flats was built in 1853. Blocks of flats for the private rental sector started to be built in central and inner London from 1880 and the late 1930s saw a wave of flat-building take place in London and the South East. By the outbreak of World War II, around 1,300 new blocks of flats had been built in London, but flat development in the UK did not take place on a significant scale until after World War II.[5]

1-09   From the mid 1950s onwards, flats and maisonettes were developed for sale on long leases and, by the mid-1960s, landlords had begun to grant long leases at nominal rents in return for a premium.[6] The introduction of the fair rent system in 1965 by the Rent Act, together with tax changes introduced by the Finance Act 1965, gave property companies a motive to sell flats on long leases,

---

3   For more detailed treatment of these schemes see Radevsky and Greenish, *Hague on Leasehold Enfranchisement* (5th edn, 2009), Ch 35.
4   Service charges in a freehold context are addressed in detail in Chapter 26 below.
5   For more detail, see the *Report of the Committee of Inquiry on the Management of Privately Owned Blocks of Flats* (1985) ('the Nugee Report').
6   See the report of the Ministry of Land and Natural Resources, *Leasehold Reform in England and Wales* (Cmnd 2916, 1966) which led to the right to enfranchise houses. At para 8, the report noted that '[t]he system of long leases for flats has arisen only in recent years.' It was not until the Landlord and Tenant Act 1987 that long leaseholders had a right to acquire their landlord's interest or control his management of leasehold property.

individually or as blocks. Changes to personal tax relief on mortgage interest, accompanied by a change of attitude on the part of building societies towards leasehold flats as security, saw a rise in owner occupiers. By the early 1970s, the privately rented, purpose-built flat sector was established.[7]

1-10   Most early leases did not contain service charge provisions, but made provision for the recovery of an inclusive rent which was intended to cover the cost of any work which the landlord had to carry out to the property. Such provisions are now extremely rare. Before the 1950s, fixed service rents were sometimes encountered[8] but were not common[9] and it was not until the 1970s that variable service charge provisions were more routinely encountered.[10] By as late as 1972, the recovery of a variable service charge was referred to in *Hyams v Titan Properties*[11] as the 'modern practice' whereby the tenant was made liable 'for a proportion of the total costs incurred by the landlord in respect of the provision of services proportional to that part of the building occupied by the tenant'.[12]

1-11   Eventually, as building techniques developed and more complex buildings were constructed, tenants' expectations grew and the cost to the landlord of providing services increased. This, together with the effect of inflation, led to the evolution of the more modern, recognisable form of service charge provision.[13]

Statutory intervention

1-12   Protection for residential tenants originally appeared in the Housing Finance Act 1972.[14] Section 124 of the Housing Act 1974 inserted a new section 91A into the 1972 Act which gave long leaseholders who paid variable service charges the right to challenge the charge. Provision was also made for estimates

---

7   See the Nugee Report, Ch 2.
8   An example of such a clause may be found in *Cumshaw v Bowen* [1987] 1 EGLR 30. See also the *Encyclopaedia of Forms and Precedents*, Vol 7 (1st edn, 1905), p 432.
9   See Wonnacott, *The History of Landlord and Tenant in England and Wales* (2012), Ch 3. *Woodfall's Law of Landlord and Tenant* (27th edn, 1968) makes no mention of service charges in the table of contents or in the index.
10 For example, the *Encyclopaedia of Forms and Precedents* (4th edn, 1965) contained no precedent for the recovery of a services rent. But there is a precedent for the 'reservation of a rent in respect of a garden used in common with other householders' 'And paying on demand as additional rent such proportionate part of the costs of the said garden as is hereinafter covenanted to be paid by the tenant' (Vol 11, p 304). See also the absence of such provisions in *Foa's General Law of Landlord and Tenant* (8th edn, 1957).
11 (1972) 24 P & CR 359.
12 See Buckley LJ at p 361.
13 In *Hyams v Titan Properties*, Buckley LJ said (at p 361): 'It is, I think, evident that the reason for this new practice … is that in an age of rapidly fluctuating and increasing prices it is a fairer arrangement between landlord and tenant that the tenant should pay a proportion of the cost year by year than that an arbitrary figure should be fixed at the inception of the lease to continue in force throughout the term as the amount payable in respect of services.'
14 Sections 90–91 gave certain tenants who were liable to pay service charges the right to obtain a summary of costs which affected the amount of the service charge from their landlord.

to be obtained by the landlord and for consultation with tenants to take place.[15] In addition, section 91A(1) added an 'embryonic' requirement for consultation between landlord and tenants about service charge expenditure.[16] Although there was no express provision about the effect of a landlord's failure to conduct the consultation, the subsection provided that in any dispute about the recoverability of a service charge (which would have been determined by the High Court or the County Court), evidence of the views of the tenants obtained during the consultation should be admitted.[17] Since 1974, successive Governments have attempted to legislate (in the residential sector) to alleviate the problems to which service charges give rise. The legislation is largely biased in favour of the tenant and very few provisions can be said to be to the advantage of the landlord.

1-13   The main body of legislation is now found in the Landlord and Tenant Act 1985, as amended by the Landlord and Tenant Act 1987, the Leasehold Reform, Housing and Urban Development Act 1993, the Housing Act 1996 and the Commonhold and Leasehold Reform Act 2002.

1-14   The important statutory provisions affecting residential dwellings are considered in Parts IV and V. Most of these provisions affect all residential dwellings but some provisions affect only certain types of leases. For example, sections 35 to 39 of the Landlord and Tenant Act 1987 allows 'any party to a long lease of a flat' to apply to a Leasehold Valuation Tribunal ('LVT') to vary a long lease which fails to make satisfactory provision in certain respects.[18] Another provision which affects only long leases of dwellings is Part I, Chapter V of the Leasehold Reform, Housing and Urban Development Act 1993, which gives some tenants the right to call for an audit. There are also a number of special service charge considerations which affect only public sector tenants.[19]

1-15   There are also some statutory provisions which indirectly impact on service charges and which may affect all types of service charges. For example, the Landlord and Tenant (Covenants) Act 1995 contains provisions affecting the recovery of service charges from former tenants, guarantors and landlords, and affects both commercial and residential property. This is considered in detail in Chapters 40 and 41 below.

---

15 Section 124 introduced the concept of reasonableness (see below) and the new s 91A(1)(a) provided that 'A service charge shall only be recoverable from the tenant of a flat – (a) in respect of the provision of chargeable items to a reasonable standard ...'.

16 See *Daejan Investments Ltd v Benson* [2013] UKSC 14, *per* Lord Wilson in his dissenting judgment at para 103.

17 According to Lord Wilson, the purpose was to ensure that a tenant could also deploy a failure to consult in a dispute with the landlord as to whether the amount payable or the standard of a service was reasonable. However, this was replaced by the Housing Act 1980, Sch 19 which introduced, for the first time, a penalty for the landlord in that failure to comply with the consultation requirements or to obtain dispensation would preclude the landlord from recovering more than a prescribed amount through the service charge. See further, Chapter 30 below for the current consultation and dispensation rules.

18 See **24-02** to **24-09** below.

19 See Chapter 38 below.

1-16   The Unfair Contract Terms Act 1977 does not apply to leases.[20] However, it has been accepted that the Unfair Terms in Consumer Contract Regulations 1999[21] may apply to service charges.[22] The Supply of Goods and Services Act 1982 may also be relevant to consider.[23] These are considered in Chapter 37 and at **2-91** below.

CODES OF PRACTICE

1-17   Unlike the residential sector, the commercial sector is largely unregulated.[24] However, the Royal Institute of Chartered Surveyors ('RICS'), on behalf of various industry bodies, published a good practice guide 'Service Charges in Commercial Properties' to help alleviate the problem of bad management in relation to service charges. In 2007, this became an RICS Code of Practice and, in 2011, an updated code was published, with the endorsement of the British Council for Offices, the British Council of Shopping Centres, the British Property Federation, the British Retail Consortium and the Property Managers Association.[25] The 2011 Code ('the Commercial Code') is effective from 1 October 2011. Its aims and objectives are:

- To improve general standards and promote best practice, uniformity, fairness and transparency in the management and administration of service charges in commercial property.

- To ensure the timely issue of budgets and year end certificates.

- To reduce the causes of disputes and to give guidance to resolving disputes where these do occur.

- To provide guidance to solicitors, their clients (be they owners or occupiers) and managers of service charges in the negotiation, drafting, interpretation and operation of leases in accordance with best practice.

1-18   The Commercial Code has the status of guidance notes. It is not mandatory and has no statutory force. However, as the guidance notes to the Commercial Code explain:

---

20 *Electricity Supply Nominees Ltd v IAF Group plc* [1993] 3 All ER 372.
21 SI 1999/2083. The regulations apply to terms which have not been individually negotiated and are contained in contracts between a seller or supplier and a consumer.
22 See *R (Khatun) v London Borough of Newham* [2004] EWCA Civ 55; *Canary Riverside PTE v Schilling* [2005] EWLands LRX_65_2005.
23 But see *Havenridge Ltd v Boston Dyers Ltd* [1994] 2 EGLR 73 where Evans J (with whom the other judges of the Court of Appeal agreed) saw force in the argument that since the parties have agreed as to the allocation of risk and responsibilities with regard to the services to be provided, the Act is unlikely to apply, but there could be a case where it would be appropriate to hold that there was a 'supply of services' for the purposes of the Act. He therefore declined to express any concluded view since it was not necessary for the purposes of the decision in that case. See also **2-91** below.
24 But see **28-07** and **47-03** below as to the effect of statutory control on mixed commercial and residential property following the decision in *Ruddy v Oakfern Properties Ltd* [2006] EWCA Civ 1389.
25 The RICS has also published an occupier guide to service charges.

'When an allegation of professional negligence is made against a practitioner, the court is likely to take account of the contents of any relevant guidance notes in deciding whether or not the practitioner had acted with reasonable competence.'[26]

1-19   The Code is frequently referred to in courts and tribunals as a reference point for reasonable practice by managers of property.

1-20   There is a separate code for residential property, the 'Service Charge Residential Management Code' ('the Residential Code'). The second edition of this code was published in 2009.

1-21   Section 87 of the Leasehold Reform, Housing and Urban Development Act 1993 makes provision for the Secretary of State to approve codes of practice which appear to 'be designed to promote desirable practices in relation to any matter or matters directly or indirectly concerned with the management of residential property by relevant persons'.[27] The Residential Code was approved in England[28] as from 6 April 2009.[29] In Wales, the previous edition of the code remains the approved code.[30]

1-22   Section 87(7) of the 1993 Act provides:

'A failure on the part of any person to comply with any provision of a code of practice for the time being approved under this section shall not of itself render him liable to any proceedings; but in any proceedings before a court or tribunal –

(a)   any code of practice approved under this section shall be admissible in evidence; and

(b)   any provision of any such code which appears to the court or tribunal to be relevant to any question arising on the proceedings shall be taken into account in determining that question.'

1-23   A failure to comply with the Residential Code is a ground for the appointment of a manager under section 24(2)(ac) of the Landlord and Tenant Act 1987.[31]

---

26 See also the comments of the Lands Tribunal in *Forcelux Ltd v Sweetman and Parker* [2001] 2 EGLR 173 (a residential case): 'there are, in my judgment, two distinctly separate matters I have to consider. Firstly the evidence, and from that whether the landlord's actions were appropriate, and properly effected in accordance with the requirements of the lease, the RICS Code and the 1985 Act.'
27 Section 87(1)(a).
28 Save for Appendix III and the section of the code 'Additional advice to landlords tenants and agents'.
29 The Approval of Code of Management Practice (Residential Management) (Service Charges) (England) Order 2009 (SI 2009/512), which replaces the approval given to the previous edition of the Residential Code by the Approval of Codes of Management Practice (Residential Property) Order 1996 (SI 1996/2839).
30 Approved by the Approval of Codes of Management Practice (Residential Property) Order 1996 (SI 1996/2839). The new code has not been approved following the transfer of power from the Secretary of State to the Welsh Assembly in 1999.
31 See **47-54** below.

1-24   Two further codes have also been published:

1   'The Code of Practice for Private Retirement Housing', which relates to the management of private retirement housing, and which was approved in England from 2 January 2006[32] and Wales from 2 March 2007;[33] and

2   the 'Rent Only Residential Management Code', which applies where tenants pay rent only, and was approved in England from 10 August 2004[34] and in Wales from 1 February 2006.[35]

SERVICE CHARGE LITIGATION

1-25   Perhaps unsurprisingly, disputes between those who arrange for the provision of services and works and those who pay for it are common, both in the commercial and residential sector.[36] The evolution of service charges has been accompanied by an increase in service charge litigation.

1-26   There is an inherent and unavoidable conflict between the interests of a landlord and those of a tenant. A landlord will generally want to recover as much as he can from his tenants whereas a tenant will want to pay as little as possible. Depending on the length of a tenant's lease and the imminence of the landlord's reversion, there may also be very different views as to matters such as the appropriate standard of repair of premises.[37] A further problem arises when older leases do not reflect modern practice.[38] Attempts to modernise leases on renewal can create problems as leases often fall in at different times, leading to two or more different service charge regimes being in place within the same block or estate. In the commercial sector, a landlord is constrained as to how he can modernise service charge provisions on a lease renewal under Part II of the Landlord and Tenant Act 1954, as such lease renewals are not subject to market control.[39]

1-27   Service charge disputes frequently concern the correct interpretation of service charge provisions, the standard of repair works carried out and the reasonableness of cost. Across both the commercial and residential sector, service

---

32   The Approval of Code of Management Practice (Private Retirement Housing) (England) Order 2005 (SI 2005/3307).

33   The Approval of Code of Practice (Private Retirement Housing) (Wales) Order 2007 (SI 2007/578).

34   The Approval of Codes of Management Practice (Residential Property) (England) Order 2004 (SI 2004/1802).

35   The Approval of Codes of Management Practice (Residential Property) (Wales) Order 2006 (SI 2006/178).

36   See the grievances of residential tenants reflected in the Nugee Report. Little seems to have changed since 1985 when the report was published.

37   A landlord has more financial incentive to keep a multi-occupied building in repair where he receives a market rent than when he simply collects a low fixed ground rent.

38   Older form of service charge provisions are often brief and are restricted to repairs of walls, structures, pipes, etc.

39   See *O'May v City of London Real Property* [1983] 2 AC 726, at **24-10** to **24-18** below. See also *Edwards & Walkden (Norfolk) Ltd v City of London* [2012] EWHC 2527 (Ch).

charges are contentious. Statutory intervention in this sector, which is beset by complexity, has resulted in the management of residential properties becoming increasingly difficult, creating a fertile source of litigation. The essence of many service charge disputes can be summed up by the comments made by Jonathan Gaunt QC, sitting as a deputy judge of the Chancery Division, in *Princes House Ltd v Distinctive Clubs Ltd*[40] at first instance:

> 'this case contains many of the typical elements which cause and exacerbate disputes of this kind: first, a managing agent who did not regard it as part of his job to read the lease or give any consideration to whether the items, a contribution to the costs of which he was invoicing, properly fell within the service charge; secondly, a landlord who, despite earlier misgivings, appears to have decided to include all the costs of his project in the claim for service charges irrespective of the propriety of doing so, placing on his tenants the onus of challenging his demands if they were able to discover and disentangle the calculations on which they had been based; thirdly, a situation where the tenant had been led to expect a certain level of charge and then found himself being charged four times as much with no explanation being offered as to how this state of affairs had come about; leading, fourthly, to the tenant becoming so frustrated and alarmed that he dug in his heels, refused to pay and resolved to take every point going, good or bad, with a view to resisting what he regarded as his landlord's patently unjustified behaviour. A more potent recipe for expensive and unproductive litigation it would be difficult to devise'.

---

40 [2006] All ER (D) 117 (the case was appealed to the Court of Appeal and the appeal was dismissed: [2007] EWCA Civ 374).

CHAPTER 2

The construction of service charge provisions

INTRODUCTION

2-01   Service charge disputes often involve questions of construction of service charge provisions. Such disputes invariably turn not on general legal principles, but on the correct construction of the particular wording used in the relevant instrument. As Beldam LJ said in *Berrycroft Management Co Ltd v Sinclair Gardens Investments (Kensington) Ltd*:[1]

> 'It is elementary that the specific covenants in each case have to be construed in the context of the lease in which they are contained. Construction of a clause in one lease in a particular way is no guide to the construction of a clause in another lease couched in different terms and set in a different context.'[2]

2-02   Notwithstanding the fact that specific covenants must be construed according to the context in which they are found, there are a number of more general principles of interpretation which are of assistance when construing a document. This chapter summarises the general principles which apply to the construction of leases, before considering the specific ways in which these principles apply to service charge provisions.[3]

GENERAL PRINCIPLES

2-03   It is well established that the starting point when considering how to construe a document, including a lease, is the five principles set out by Lord Hoffmann in *Investors Compensation Scheme v West Bromwich Building Society*.[4]

---

1   [1997] 1 EGLR 47.
2   See also Tuckey LJ in *Leonora Investment Co Ltd v Mott MacDonald Ltd* [2008] EWCA Civ 857 at para 14: 'I have not found these cases particularly helpful for the simple reason that we are only concerned with an issue of construction, the rules of which are not in doubt. The leases in this case must be construed in accordance with their own terms.'
3   For a comprehensive commentary on the principles of contractual interpretation see Lewison, *The Interpretation of Contracts* (5th edn, 2011).
4   [1998] 1 WLR 896.

Lord Hoffman's 'modern approach to construction' refers to the 'common sense' principles by which documents are to be interpreted[5] and notes that:

> 'Almost all the old intellectual baggage of "legal" interpretation has been discarded. The principles may be summarised as follows.
>
> (1)   Interpretation is the ascertainment of the meaning which the document would convey to a reasonable person having all the background knowledge which would reasonably have been available to the parties in the situation in which they were at the time of the contract.
>
> (2)   The background was famously referred to by Lord Wilberforce as the "matrix of fact," but this phrase is, if anything, an understated description of what the background may include. Subject to the requirement that it should have been reasonably available to the parties and to the exception to be mentioned next, it includes absolutely anything which would have affected the way in which the language of the document would have been understood by a reasonable man.
>
> (3)   The law excludes from the admissible background the previous negotiations of the parties and their declarations of subjective intent. They are admissible only in an action for rectification. The law makes this distinction for reasons of practical policy and, in this respect only, legal interpretation differs from the way we would interpret utterances in ordinary life. The boundaries of this exception are in some respects unclear. But this is not the occasion on which to explore them.
>
> (4)   The meaning which a document (or any other utterance) would convey to a reasonable man is not the same thing as the meaning of its words. The meaning of words is a matter of dictionaries and grammars; the meaning of the document is what the parties using those words against the relevant background would reasonably have been understood to mean. The background may not merely enable the reasonable man to choose between the possible meanings of words which are ambiguous but even (as occasionally happens in ordinary life) to conclude that the parties must, for whatever reason, have used the wrong words or syntax: see *Mannai Investment Co Ltd v Eagle Star Life Assurance Co Ltd* [1997] A.C. 749.
>
> (5)   The "rule" that words should be given their "natural and ordinary meaning" reflects the common sense proposition that we do not easily accept that people have made linguistic mistakes, particularly in formal documents. On the other hand, if one would nevertheless conclude from the background that something must have gone wrong with the language, the law does not require judges to attribute to the parties an intention which they plainly could not have had. Lord Diplock made this point more vigorously when he said in *Antaios Compania Naviera S.A. v Salen Rederierna A.B.* [1985] A.C. 191, 201:
>
> > "if detailed semantic and syntactical analysis of words in a commercial contract is going to lead to a conclusion that flouts business commonsense, it must be made to yield to business commonsense."'

---

5   See also *Pink Floyd Music Ltd v EMI Records Ltd* [2010] EWCA Civ 1429; *Rainy Sky SA v Kookmin Bank* [2011] UKSC 50.

The factual matrix

2-04   The process of construction involves ascertaining what the parties intended their rights and obligations to be. This is an objective process, as Lord Bingham in *BCCI v Ali*[6] explained:

'To ascertain the intention of the parties the court reads the terms of the contract as a whole, giving the words used their natural and ordinary meaning in the context of the agreement, the parties' relationship and all the relevant facts surrounding the transaction so far as known to the parties. To ascertain the parties' intentions the court does not of course inquire into the parties' subjective states of mind but makes an objective judgment based on the materials already identified.'[7]

2-05   Lord Hoffman's fourth and fifth principles, above, emphasise the importance of the context in which words are used to the process of construction. In *Mannai Investment Co Ltd v Eagle Star Life Assurance Co Ltd*,[8] Lord Hoffmann explained what was meant by the background information which can be taken into account in construing a document:

'In the case of commercial contracts, the restriction on the use of background has been quietly dropped. There are certain special kinds of evidence, such as previous negotiations and express declarations of intent, which for practical reasons which it is unnecessary to analyse, are inadmissible in aid of construction. They can be used only in an action for rectification. But apart from these exceptions, commercial contracts are construed in the light of all the background which could reasonably have been expected to have been available to the parties in order to ascertain what would objectively have been understood to be their intention: *Prenn v. Simmonds* [1971] 1 W.L.R. 1381, 1383. The fact that the words are capable of a literal application is no obstacle to evidence which demonstrates what a reasonable person with knowledge of the background would have understood the parties to mean, even if this compels one to say that they used the wrong words. In this area, we no longer confuse the meaning of words with the question of what meaning the use of the words was intended to convey.'

2-06   It now appears that this formulation was too wide and in *BCCI v Ali*[9] Lord Hoffmann reformulated the test as follows:[10]

'The background is however very important. I should in passing say that when, in *Investors Compensation Scheme Ltd v West Bromwich Building Society* [1998] 1 WLR 896, 913, I said that the admissible background included "absolutely anything which would have affected the way in which the language of the document would have been understood by a reasonable man", I did not think it necessary to emphasise that I meant anything which a reasonable man would

---

6   [2002] 1 AC 251.
7   See also *Chartbrook Ltd v Persimmon Homes Ltd* [2009] UKHL 38, where Lord Hoffman revisited (again) the principles for construing contracts and the House of Lords confirmed the rule that evidence of pre-contractual negotiations is not admissible evidence.
8   [1997] AC 749 at p 779.
9   [2002] 1 AC 251.
10   At p 269.

have regarded as *relevant*. I was merely saying that there is no conceptual limit to what can be regarded as background. It is not, for example, confined to the factual background but can include the state of the law (as in cases in which one takes into account that the parties are unlikely to have intended to agree to something unlawful or legally ineffective) or proved common assumptions which were in fact quite mistaken. But the primary source for understanding what the parties meant is their language interpreted in accordance with conventional usage: "we do not easily accept that people have made linguistic mistakes, particularly in formal documents". I was certainly not encouraging a trawl through "background" which could not have made a reasonable person think that the parties must have departed from conventional usage.'

Relevant background factors

2-07   When interpreting service charge provisions, background factors which may be particularly relevant might include the statutory background against which the service charge provision was drafted. For example, in *Yorkbrook Investments Ltd v Batten*,[11] the Court of Appeal held that prompt payment by the tenant was not a condition precedent to the landlord's liability to provide services[12] and, in reaching this decision, the court had regard to the statutory background against which the lease had been granted. In *Leicester City Council v Master*,[13] the Lands Tribunal[14] construed a lease granted by the local authority under the right-to-buy legislation in the Housing Act 1985 and this was considered to be one of the background facts relevant to the process of construction.

2-08   Conversely, in *Frobisher (Second Investments) Ltd v Kiloran Trust Co Ltd*,[15] Walton J declined to imply a term into a lease to remedy a problem which had arisen as a result of statute (which had been enacted after the grant of the lease) intervening to alter the contractual terms agreed between the parties because the legislation was enacted after the lease and, therefore, was not a relevant fact to take into account in construing it.[16]

2-09   Other background factors which might influence the court's approach to the process of construction are whether the charge relates to commercial or residential premises and the identity of the original parties (e.g. a local authority landlord).[17]

---

11   [1985] 2 EGLR 100.
12   Notwithstanding the following provision: 'The lessor covenants with the lessee that subject to the lessee paying the maintenance contribution pursuant to the obligation under clause 4 hereof the lessor will [perform the services].'
13   Lands Tribunal, 12 December 2008, 2008 WL 5485783.
14   HH Judge Huskinson.
15   [1980] 1 WLR 425.
16   Walton J said: 'It seems to me that if there is a disturbance of contractual relationships because a statute intervenes, then it must be left to the statute to say what is to happen consequentially upon its intervention, and that one cannot foist upon the parties what some outside body thinks would have been what they would have agreed to in circumstances which neither of them can possibly have contemplated under any circumstances.'
17   See, for example, *South Tyneside Council v Hudson* [2012] UKUT 247 (LC).

2-10   In general, courts take a strict approach to the construction of service charge provisions.[18] As Mummery LJ said in *Gilje v Charlgrove Securities Ltd*:[19]

> 'The landlord seeks to recover money from the tenant. On ordinary principles there must be clear terms in the contractual provisions said to entitle him to do so.'

2-11   In *Wembley National Stadium Ltd v Wembley (London) Ltd*,[20] Sir Andrew Morritt C, referring to Mummery LJ's comments, said:[21]

> 'No doubt, too, it is appropriate for the interpretation to be more restrictive in the case of residential tenancies as opposed to a commercial transaction between two substantial parties.'

2-12   The fact that a landlord's management functions are exercisable by an RTM company ought not of itself be a reason which affects the courts' approach to construction, and in *Wilson v Lesley Place (RTM) Co (LW)*[22] the Lands Tribunal noted that:[23]

> 'The liability of the tenant to the landlord in respect of service charges is to be ascertained purely by reference to the terms of the lease, and the fact that the management functions are exercisable by an RTM company does not affect the construction of the lease under these provisions.'[24]

2-13   In an appropriate case, the court, as part of the relevant matrix of fact, has had regard to the fact that a landlord's functions are exercisable by a residents' association. In *Embassy Court Residents' Association Limited v Hilliel Lipman*,[25] the landlord had demised the whole of Embassy Court to a residents' association, Embassy Court Residents' Association Ltd, by an intermediate lease for a term of 99 years. The landlord had accordingly transferred all of his rights and obligations as landlord to the tenants via the residents' association. The tenants were asked to pay a management fee to cover the costs incurred by Embassy Court in the performance of the landlord's functions. The leases, however, did not provide for such a fee to be recovered. When deciding whether the tenants were obliged to contribute, the court had regard to the fact that the residents' association had no funds and only a limited ability to perform the services of the landlord. It held that, in order to give business efficacy to the lease, it was necessary to imply a term to the effect that the residents' association could properly incur expenditure to carry out the functions and obligations which were imposed on it and that such expenditure could be recovered from the tenants.

---

18   This principle is discussed fully at **2-44** to **2-54** below.
19   [2002] 1 EGLR 41.
20   [2007] EWHC 756.
21   At para 44.
22   [2010] UKUT 342 (LC); [2011] L&TR 11.
23   At para 13.
24   Since an RTM company is not an original party and events after the date of the instrument are, in general, not relevant to its construction.
25   [1984] 2 EGLR 60.

2-14   Lord Justice Cumming-Bruce noted that the lease was clearly designed to bring into existence a legal arrangement whereby each of the residents in the flats would have a common interest and each would enjoy the rights and privileges conferred by their leases. The relevant rights and privileges were only capable of enjoyment so long as each of the residents in the 14 flats participated in their common interest. He said:

> 'It is clear, in my view, that for a proper understanding and construction of the lease of 16th August 1971, it is right to take into account that the background and matrix of that transaction was the intention of each of the individual residents who became signatories to similar leases, to obtain a situation in which they, the residents, acting through the machinery of their corporate body, the Residents' Association, would be able to take their own decisions as to the management of the building insofar as management had obligations in respect of the common parts and garages and for the due performance of the landlord's covenants of repair. One can see, in a case of a small block such as this with 14 residents, that great advantages are likely to be derived by individual lessees because each of them, by becoming a member of the Residents' Association Company, is by the machinery of these two leases put in the position of being able to take part and have a personal right in the performance of the landlord's covenants for the benefit, not only of each individual lessee, but of all individual lessees. It is also quite plain that parties who enter into the kind of transaction contemplated by 16th August must realise that such a scheme, for its efficacy, will only be workable if a certain modicum of good neighbourliness and common sense is afforded by each of the individual members of the Residents' Association, and provided that each of the residents is prepared to act with ordinary common sense and courtesy, it is likely that the costs of the Residents' Association Company may be restricted to a negligible amount. But it is also clear that, if by reason of awkwardness and difficulty on the part of any lessee to reconcile him or herself to co-operation in an ordinary civilised way with the Residents' Association, in that situation the work that may have to be undertaken by the Association may become such a burden that it is necessary to spend quite a lot of money by procuring the performance of the functions which the Residents' Association is by its Articles and Memorandum under an obligation to perform.'

2-15   The Court of Appeal in *Bluestorm Ltd v Portvale Holdings Ltd* was again influenced by the status of the landlord, in this case a company controlled by the tenants.[26] Leases often contain a provision which links the landlord's obligation to provide services to the tenant's obligation to make service charge payments, as was the case in *Yorkbrook Investments Ltd v Batten*, discussed above.[27] This issue arose in *Bluestorm*. Although it was not necessary for the Court of Appeal to reach a conclusion as to whether or not the tenants' obligation to pay was a condition precedent, and accordingly its comments in relation to this issue were *obiter,* the court indicated that it would not be constrained to reach the same conclusion as the court had in *Yorkbrook*. Buxton LJ distinguished *Yorkbrook* and, having express regard to the fact that the landlord had no means of raising

---

26 See also *Warrior Quay Management Co Ltd v Joachim* [2008] EWLands LRX_42_2006 where the relevant factual matrix included the fact that the leases contemplated that the leaseholders would become members of the management company.

27 Conditions precedent are considered below at **16-19** to **16-21**.

finance and depended entirely for his ability to run the building on contributions from the tenants, held:

> 'I think that it may well be an acceptable approach to a provision such as that under consideration to say that it deprives the non-payer of the right to complain of the landlord's breach when there is a direct connection between the non-payment and the breach. Thus some, but not all, and probably not very many, defaults in payment would disqualify action by the tenant.'

2-16   It does not, however, follow from the *Bluestorm* decision that a landlord will always be justified in refusing to perform services where a tenant has not paid and a landlord would be putting itself at risk if it refused to perform its obligations because a tenant had not paid its service charge.

Business common sense

2-17   Lord Hoffman's fifth rule also makes it clear that the purpose of the contract being construed is important. In *Mannai Investment Co Ltd v Eagle Star Life Assurance Co Ltd*,[28] Lord Steyn said:[29]

> 'In determining the meaning of the language of a commercial contract, and unilateral contractual notices, the law therefore generally favours a commercially sensible construction. The reason for this approach is that a commercial construction is more likely to give effect to the intention of the parties. Words are therefore interpreted in the way in which a reasonable commercial person would construe them. And the standard of the reasonable commercial person is hostile to technical interpretations and undue emphasis on niceties of language.'

2-18   In *Norwich Union Life and Pensions v Linpac Mouldings Ltd*,[30] Lewison J said:[31]

> 'The language of the licence must also be interpreted in a way that makes commercial sense. Commercial commonsense is not merely a cross-check; it is an essential part of the process of interpretation. Commercial commonsense must also be considered from the perspective of both parties.'

2-19   The purpose of a service charge was identified by Mummery LJ in *Universities Superannunation Scheme Ltd v Marks & Spencer plc*,[32] who said:

> 'The purpose of the service charge provisions is relevant to their meaning and effect. So far as the scheme, context and language of those provisions allow, the service charge provisions should be given an effect that fulfils rather than defeats their evident purpose. The service charge provisions have a clear purpose: the

28 [1997] AC 749.
29 At p 103
30 [2010] EWCA Civ 395.
31 At p 117.
32 [1999] 1 EGLR 13.

landlord that reasonably incurs liability for expenditure in maintaining Telford Shopping Centre for the benefit of all its tenants there should be entitled to recover the full cost of doing so from those tenants and each tenant should reimburse the landlord a proportion of those service charges.'

2-20   In *Boots UK Ltd v Trafford Centre Ltd*,[33] Morgan J declined to have regard to the commercial purpose of a particular service charge provision in circumstances where it was unclear what the true business purpose was.

2-21   In many cases, the aim of a leasehold service charge provision will be to ensure that all of the landlord's costs in maintaining and managing the property are passed on to the tenant, so that the landlord has a clear lease (i.e. receives a clear rent).[34] Institutional landlords, in general, insist on clear leases in the commercial sector and, other than short-term residential lettings, clear leases have been the norm in both the commercial and residential sector. Recently, however, there has been a trend towards the grant of shorter commercial leases, often with a capped service charge.

2-22   Although it is perfectly proper to have regard to the purpose of a service charge provision when seeking to give effect to the parties' intentions,[35] there is no general rule or presumption to the effect that a landlord is entitled to recover the full amount of his expenditure, even in a commercial context.[36] In *Leonora Investment Co Ltd v Mott MacDonald Ltd*,[37] at first instance HH Judge Seymour QC, referring to Mummery LJ's statement above, said:[38]

> 'In my judgment the passage from the judgment of Mummery LJ in *Universities Superannuation Scheme Ltd. v. Marks & Spencer Plc* in which he considered the purpose of service charge provisions in a lease needs to be approached with caution. It is always necessary in construing a provision in a written agreement to have regard to its purpose. However, it would be wrong, as it seems to me, to view the passage in the judgment of Mummery LJ in which he was dealing with the purpose of service charge provisions as indicating that there was some sort of presumption that a lessee would pay service charges in all circumstances. Whilst

---

33   [2008] EWHC 3372.

34   A 'clear lease' was described by Lord Wilberforce in *O'May v City of London Real Property Co Ltd* [1982] 1 All ER 660 at p 671 as a lease in which the tenants bear all the costs and risks of repairing, maintaining and running the building of which their demised premises form part, so that the rent payable reaches the landlord clear of all expenses and overheads.

35   By way of example, in *Billson v Tristrem* [2000] L&TR 220, Chadwick LJ gave effect to the clear intention behind the service charge provisions in a residential lease which had been ineptly drafted: 'There is, in my view, little doubt that the landlord's intention in this lease was to ensure that this tenant – in common with the tenants of other flats, having leases in the building in similar form – should each pay a proportionate contribution to the cost of doing the works which the landlords would ordinarily do in maintaining a building of this nature. It is, to my mind, no coincidence that the percentage contribution is fixed at 20 percent in circumstances in which the building comprises five flats'. But c.f. *Campbell v Daejan Properties Limited* [2012] EWCA Civ 5103.

36   See **2-73** to **2-74** below.

37   [2008] EWHC 136 (QB). An appeal to the Court of Appeal was dismissed: [2008] EWCA Civ 857.

38   At paras 38 and 40.

service charge provisions are very common in commercial leases and in long leases of residential property in this country, they are not usually encountered in short leases of residential property. The significance of that is simply that there can be no universal assumption that a lessee under any lease will pay service charges. Whether the lessee is bound to pay service charge or not will depend on the terms of the relevant lease.

...

In the end, although it must be right to have regard to the purpose of having service charge provisions in a lease, that consideration may be of little assistance in construing provisions which are said to have the effect of amounting to conditions precedent to the liability to pay or as specifying the circumstances in which there is a liability to pay.'

2-23   Where the words of a contract are clear, business common sense will not allow the court to re-write a contract. In *Credit Suisse v Beegas Nominees Ltd*,[39] Lindsay J said:

'I thus approach the underlease having in mind that the arrangements likely to have been intended to have been made by business people will be business-like arrangements. But I do not see the notion as going further than that; it does not enable me to give other than a natural meaning to the words used, although, doubtless, where two natural meanings equally beckon I should, in this context, prefer the more business-like.'

2-24   The court must give effect to the words used, even if they have no obvious commercial purpose. As Lord Hoffmann LJ reemphasised[40] in *Co-Operative Wholesale Society Ltd v National Westminster Bank Plc*:[41]

'This ... does not, however, mean that one can rewrite the language which the parties have used in order to make the contract conform to business common sense. But language is a very flexible instrument and, if it is capable of more than one construction, one chooses that which seems most likely to give effect to the commercial purpose of the agreement.'[42]

CORRECTING MISTAKES

2-25   An important tool in the process of construction is the court's ability to correct obvious mistakes. Prior to the decision in *Investors Compensation Scheme v West Bromwich Building Society*,[43] rectification aside, it was generally

39   (1995) 69 P&CR 177.
40   Referring to Lord Diplock in *Antaios Compania Naviera SA v Salen Rederierna AB* [1985] AC 191.
41   [1995] 1 EGLR 97.
42   See also, *per* Chadwick LJ in *City Alliance Ltd v Oxford Forecasting Services Ltd, Advanced Transaction Systems Ltd* [2001] 1 All ER (Comm) 233.
43   [1998] 1 WLR 896.

thought that the court could not depart from the words used in the contract.[44] Lord Hoffman's fifth principle (**2-03** above) may be said to be a divergence from this strict approach as it may involve a departure from the natural and ordinary meaning of the words used by the parties where 'something must have gone wrong with the language'.

2-26   Where the words used by the parties do not reflect their actual agreement, the court addresses this problem by reading the agreement so that it does reflect what the parties intended to say. There is no doubt that a court can correct such errors by a process of construction and that this process (i.e. the process of 'correcting mistakes') is simply part of the process of construction itself.[45] In correcting an error, the court is not seeking to enforce the underlying agreement behind the contract but the contract itself.

2-27   There is, of course, a limit to what the court can do when construing a document. In *East v Pantiles (Plant Hire) Ltd*,[46] Brightman LJ summarised the court's powers of intervention by saying that the principle would apply where a reader with sufficient experience of the sort of document in issue would inevitably say to himself: 'Of course X is a mistake for Y'. In *Homburg Houtimport BV v Agrosin Ltd (The Starsin)*,[47] Lord Bingham of Cornhill said:

> 'I take it to be clear in principle that the court should not interpolate words into a written instrument, of whatever nature, unless it is clear both that words have been omitted and what those omitted words were.'

2-28   In *East v Pantiles (Plant Hire) Ltd*, Brightman LJ had said that two conditions must be satisfied to correct a mistake as a matter of construction:

1   there must be a clear mistake on the face of the instrument;[48] and

2   it must be clear what correction ought to be made in order to cure the mistake.

2-29   In *Chartbrook Ltd v Persimmon Homes Ltd*,[49] Lord Hoffman[50] accepted this statement, subject to two qualifications. The first was to explain that the

---

44   Thus in *L Schuler AG v Wickman Machine Tool Sales Ltd* [1974] AC 235 at p 263, Lord Simon of Glaisdale said: 'There is one general principle of law which is relevant to both questions. This has been frequently stated, but it is most pungently expressed in *Norton on Deeds* (1906), p 43, though it applies to all written instruments: "... the question to be answered always is, 'What is the meaning of what the parties have said?' not, 'What did the parties mean to say?' ... it being a presumption juris et de jure ... that the parties intended to say that which they have said." It is, of course, always open to a party to claim rectification of an instrument which has failed to express the common intention of the parties; but, so long as the instrument remains unrectified, the rule of construction is as stated by *Norton*. It is, indeed, the only workable rule.'

45   See *Chartbrook Ltd v Persimmon Homes Ltd* [2009] UKHL 38.

46   [1982] 2 EGLR 111.

47   [2004] 1 AC 715.

48   See, for example, *Campbell v Daejan Properties Limited* [2012] EWCA Civ 5103, where the Court of Appeal held that there was no clear mistake in the context of a tenant's obligation to contribute towards the costs of repairs.

49   [2009] UKHL 38.

50   See paras 23–24.

correction of mistakes by construction was not a separate branch of the law, a summary version of an action for rectification.[51] Lord Hoffman's second qualification related to the requirement that the mistake be clear from 'the face of the instrument'. Lord Hoffmann said:[52]

'As the exercise is part of the single task of interpretation, the background and context must always be taken into consideration.'

2-30   Lord Hoffmann summarised by saying:

'What is clear from these cases is that there is not, so to speak, a limit to the amount of red ink or verbal rearrangement or correction which the court is allowed. All that is required is that it should be clear that something has gone wrong with the language and that it should be clear what a reasonable person would have understood the parties to have meant.'

2-31   The court's power extends beyond simply correcting mistakes of spelling or grammar. The court can correct a misnomer or a mistaken reference to a party. For example, in *Littman v Aspen Oil (Broking) Ltd*,[53] a break option in a lease erroneously referred to 'Landlord' rather than 'Tenant' and the court simply read 'Landlord' as 'Tenant'. The court can also correct sloppy drafting. In *Skilleter v Charles*,[54] the landlord sought to recover interest and bank charges incurred because the tenant had not paid its maintenance charges. The lease provided for the landlord to recover '[a]ny interest charges payable by the lessor on his Bank Account or accounts in respect of any for the purposes of the Maintenance Charge'. As drafted, this provision made no sense and the court held that it was the plain intention of the parties that interest would be chargeable and inserted the word 'incurred' after the words 'in respect of any'.

CANONS OF CONSTRUCTION

2-32   In addition to the above general principles of construction, the courts have developed a number of rules or canons of construction. Although labelled rules of construction, the principles are no more than guides to the correct construction of a document. In *BCCI v Ali*,[55] Lord Clyde said:

'Such guides to construction as have been identified in the past should not be allowed to constrain an approach to construction which looks to commercial reality

---

51 As Carnwath LJ said in *KPMG LLP v Network Rail Infrastructure Ltd* [2007] EWCA Civ 363: 'Both in the judgment, and in the arguments before us, there was tendency to deal separately with correction of mistakes and construing the paragraph "as it stands", as though they were distinct exercises. In my view, they are simply aspects of the single task of interpreting the agreement in its context, in order to get as close as possible to the meaning which the parties intended.'
52 At para 24.
53 [2005] EWCA Civ 1579.
54 [1992] 1 EGLR 73. See further **12-05** below.
55 [2002] 1 AC 251.

or common sense. If they are elevated to anything approaching the status of rules they would deservedly be regarded as impedimenta in the task of construction. But they may be seen as reflections upon the way in which people may ordinarily be expected to express themselves.'

2-33   In *K/S Victoria Street v House of Fraser (Stores Management) Ltd,*[56] Lord Neuberger of Abbotsbury MR, giving the judgment of the court, said:

> '*rules* of interpretation such as contra proferentem are rarely decisive as to the meaning of any provisions of a commercial contract. The words used, commercial sense, and the documentary and factual context, are, and should be, normally enough to determine the meaning of a contractual provision.'

2-34   Canons of construction thus have a limited role to play in the modern approach to the interpretation of contracts. It would be wrong, however, to dismiss them completely. A full discussion is outside the scope of this work,[57] but in relation to service charges, two rules have particular relevance and are considered below.

The ejusdem generis principle

2-35   The *ejusdem generis* rule, or maxim, can be summarised as follows. Where a list of particular items, with common characteristics, is followed by more general words, the general words should be construed by reference to the preceding words and not as comprising things of a different nature.[58]

2-36   An illustration of the rule can be found in *Saner v Bilton (No 1).*[59] A lease contained a covenant to yield up all doors, locks, keys, etc., wainscots, hearths, stoves, marbles, and other chimney pieces, etc., and all other buildings, erections, improvements, fixtures and things on the demised property. It was held that the general words should be limited to things in the nature of landlord's fixtures and did not include machinery affixed by the tenant for the purpose of his trade.

2-37   It is common in service charge provisions to find a list of repairing obligations or services which the landlord must provide, and/or to which the tenant must contribute, followed by a more general expression (perhaps intended as a 'catch all' or 'sweeping-up' provision[60]).Where, however, expressions such as 'whether or not similar to the foregoing' or 'without prejudice to the foregoing' or 'whatsoever' are used, it may be that the general words were intended to have

---

56 [2011] EWCA Civ 904.
57 For a detailed explanation see Lewison, *The Interpretation of Contracts* (5th edn, 2011), Ch 7.
58 The classic formulation of the principle is as stated by Vaughan Williams LJ in *Lambourn v McLellan* [1903] 2 Ch 268 at pp 275–276: 'if you can find that the things described by particular words have some common characteristic which constitutes them a genus, you ought to limit the general words which follow them to things of that genus.'
59 (1878) 7 Ch D 815.
60 See below.

a general meaning.[61] In *Warwickshire Hamlets Ltd, B Woodward (Harborne) Ltd v Olive Gedden,*[62] HH Judge Huskinson said (in relation to a service charge covenant which referred to 'all out goings whatsoever'):

> 'I accept, of course, the well established principles ... that the word "whatsoever" is a word adopted by draftsmen to show that the greatest width is intended and to exclude argument, based on ejusdem generis principles, that a restricted width should be placed upon the expression in question.'[63]

Contra proferentem

2-38   One rule of construction which gained prominence following the decision in *Gilje v Charlgrove Securities Ltd*[64] is the *contra proferentem* rule.

2-39   In *Tam Wing Chuen v Bank of Credit and Commerce Hong Kong Ltd,*[65] Lord Mustill[66] described the maxim as follows:

> 'the basis of the *contra proferentem* principle is that a person who puts forward the wording of a proposed agreement may be assumed to have looked after his own interests, so that if the words leave room for doubt about whether he is intended to have a particular benefit there is reason to suppose that he is not.'

2-40   The maxim *verba fortius accipiuntur contra proferentem*[67] was introduced into English law by Coke (Co Litt 36a, 183a), Bacon (*Maxims of the Law*, Regula III) and Blackstone (2 Commentaries 23, 4) and was applied to unilateral documents, such as deed polls. The maxim originally had no application to indentures, which, having been executed by both parties were considered as the words of them both.

2-41   The maxim, however, came to be applied in a commercial context, initially to control the operation of exclusion clauses and is now said to be a rule of construction which applies to all forms of contracts.[68] But the maxim is not always easy to apply to contracts which have been individually negotiated between parties (and the courts have not always been consistent in the approach taken to its application). For example, it is not always clear who is the person putting forward the wording (i.e. the *proferens*).[69]

---

61   See Devlin J in *Chandris v Isbrandtsen-Moller Co Inc* [1951] 1 KB 240.
62   [2010] UKUT 75 (LC).
63   But see Evans J in *BOC Group Plc v Centeon LCC* [1999] 1 All ER (Comm) 970: 'with regard to the rule or maxim *eiusdem generis* ... The meaning of general words, even whatsoever, may be limited by the context in which they appear.'
64   [2002] 1 EGLR 41.
65   [1996] BCC 388.
66   At p 394.
67   Words are to be interpreted most strongly against he who uses them.
68   See *Oxonica Energy Ltd v Neuftec Ltd* [2008] EWHC 2127 (Pat).
69   See Lewison, *The Interpretation of Contracts* (5th edn, 2011), Ch 7.

2-42   Despite its inadequacies, the maxim still survives, although, as has been made clear in a number of cases, it is a maxim of last resort. In *C & J Clark International Ltd v Regina Estates Ltd*, Neuberger J said:[70]

> 'save in unusual circumstances, such presumptions and principles have little part to play in the modern approach to the construction of commercial documents, including Leases. In *Investors Compensation Scheme v West Bromwich,* [1998] AUER 98, Lord Hoffmann cast doubt on the value of these presumptions in the modern age. One is construing a commercial document, albeit one prepared by lawyers and relating to land, and is concerned to find out what the parties to that document intended.
>
> I accept that one can get help from how such documents have been construed in the past, where what is in issue is the meaning of a common form of expression. I also accept that one can get help where it can be shown that lawyers have a particular understanding of a particular provision. However, to impute to the parties an appreciation of principles such as the contra proferentem rule does not seem to me to accord with modern commercial life.
>
> …
>
> Far better to consider the words used in the particular covenants to be construed, the other provisions of the Lease, the surrounding circumstances, and commercial common sense.'

2-43   In the service charge context, the *contra proferentem* rule has often been deployed, but without any real consideration as to its proper role in the process of contractual interpretation. The maxim has often been conflated with the more general principle which appears to have been developed by the courts of construing service charge provisions restrictively.[71] It is not correct to say that service charge provisions always fall to be construed *contra proferentem* against the landlord. Nevertheless, relying on the decision of the Court of Appeal in *Gilje v Charlgrove Securities Ltd*,[72] this is often relied upon as a general principle in the service charge context.

Gilje v Charlgrove Securities Ltd

2-44   The issue in *Gilje v Charlgrove Securities Ltd* was the liability of an underlessee to pay service charges in respect of the rental value of the flat occupied by a resident caretaker employed by the lessor. The issue turned on the construction of the material provisions of the underlease and, in particular, whether the notional rent of the caretaker's flat, which was foregone by the landlord, fell within the expression 'expended by the lessor'. The Court of Appeal held that the notional cost of providing the residence was not 'monies expended' and was not recoverable by the landlord. Laws LJ said:[73]

70 [2003] EWHC 1622.
71 But note the comments of Morgan J in *Arnold v Britton* [2012] EWHC 3451 (Ch) at para 45.
72 [2002] 1 EGLR 41.
73 Paragraphs 27 and 28.

'The landlord seeks to recover money from the tenant. On ordinary principles there must be clear terms in the contractual provisions said to entitle him to do so. The lease, moreover, was drafted or proffered by the landlord. It falls to be construed contra proferentem. …

At the end of the day, I do not consider that a reasonable tenant or prospective tenant, reading the under-lease which was proffered to him, would perceive that paragraph 4(2)(1) obliged him to contribute to the notional cost to the landlord of providing the caretaker's flat. Such a construction has to emerge clearly and plainly from the words that are used. It does not do so.'

2-45   Mummery LJ said:[74]

'In expressing my agreement I would make two short points. First, I note what is stated in paragraph 55 on page 71 of the 5th edition of the Encyclopaedia of Forms and Precedents, Vol. 23 on Landlord and Tenant in the section relating to the drafting of provisions in leases for service charges. It is stated as follows: "The draftsman should bear in mind that the courts tend to construe service charge provision restrictively and are unlikely to allow recovery for items which are not clearly included."

Cited as authority for that proposition are three cases, all decided in the 1980s. They include decisions of this court. They are collected in footnote 1. The proposition is obvious. Mr Holbech did not dispute it in argument. Indeed, the proposition reflects a particular application of the general principle of construction in the contra proferentem rule.'

2-46   Although the Court of Appeal in *Gilje* referred to the *contra proferentem* rule, little consideration was given to the nature of this rule. Further, the three 1980s cases Mummery LJ referred to (as cited in the *Encyclopedia of Forms and Precedents*) were not expressly concerned with this rule. They do, however, illustrate the requirement that a lease needs to make clear provision if a landlord is intending to recover an item of expenditure and they illustrate the reluctance of the court to adopt a broad interpretation of service charge provisions. The three cases were as follows:

1   The first case was *Frobisher v Kiloran Trust Co Ltd*,[75] where Walton J decided that a landlord could not recover from the tenants the cost of borrowing in the financial market moneys required to meet the expenditure required by the lease. Walton J held that there was no provision in the lease which authorised the landlord to recover the cost of this from the tenants. The *contra proferentem* rule was not considered.

2   The second case was *Rapid Results College v Angell*.[76] Here, the lease demised the first and second floors of a building (the second floor being the top floor) together with the use of common parts, such as staircases, landing, entrance hall. The building had a flat roof which was surrounded by a parapet wall. The parapet wall was in disrepair and needed to be

---

74   Paragraphs 31 and 32.
75   [1980] 1 WLR 425.
76   [1986] 1 EGLR 53, CA.

rebuilt. The landlord tried to charge the cost of this repair to the tenant via the service charge.

The lease provided for the tenant to pay 50% of various expenses and outgoings, including maintenance of the exterior, incurred by the landlord in respect of the premises (described as the offices on the first and second floors forming part of the building and shown bounded by the red line on the said plan) and 25% 'of the following expenses and outgoings incurred by the landlords in respect of other parts of the building specified in the First schedule hereto of which the Tenants have the use in common with the landlords and tenants and occupiers of other portions of the building'. The landlord argued that because the tenant had been demised the top floor, maintenance of the roof was part of the maintenance of the exterior of the tenant's offices. The Court of Appeal held that the parapets on the roof could not be regarded as the exterior of the offices on the first and second floors, in the context of this case because the roof could not be regarded as part of the exterior of the second floor office. The cost was also not recoverable as an expense relating to the repair and maintenance of parts of the building used in common.[77]

This case is a good example of the need for clear contractual terms before a landlord will be permitted to recover the costs of works or services. The court was not willing to give a broad interpretation to the lease but construed the words of the lease without regard to the *contra proferentem* rule.

3   The third case was *Jacob Isbicki & Co Ltd v Goulding & Bird Ltd*.[78] This case is considered in detail at **2-58** to **2-60** below but is again an example of the court approaching the construction of the lease in a strict way and without express regard to the *contra preferentem* rule.

2-47   In *Earl Cadogan v 27/29 Sloane Gardens Ltd*,[79] a case concerned with collective enfranchisement, but where the question of the landlord's entitlement to recover a market rent for a caretaker's flat through the service charge fell to be considered, HH Judge Michael Rich QC[80] referred to the above passage of Laws LJ and Mummery LJ in *Gilje* and explained:

> '[18] I think that in these passages, unless read carefully, Laws L.J. may appear to be conflating two separate principles of construction. That is why I have underlined his use of the word "moreover" which indicates that he was not treating the requirement of clear terms as the same as the *contra proferentem* rule which as Mr Denyer-Green reminds me, by reference to the short judgment of Cairns L.J.

---

77 Dillon LJ said at p 55L: 'Looking at the lease and the parcels demised as set out in the first schedule, it is quite plain that the tenants are given the use, in common with the landlord and other tenants and occupiers, of the entrance hall, staircase, landings and passages leading to the demised premises and various ladies' and mens' lavatories; they also have free passage of water, soil and gas, electricity and other services through various pipes, wires and cables; but they do not, in the sense in which the word "use" is used in the parcels in the grant of the easements, have any use of the roof at all.'
78 [1989] 1 EGLR 236.
79 [2006] L&TR 18.
80 The judge at first instance in *Gilje*.

in *Killick v Second Covent Garden Property Co Ltd* [1973] 1 W.L.R. 658 at p.663, requires an ambiguity before it can be called in aid. Cairns L.J. referred to the rule properly so-called in Agavil as follows:

> "… it is a rule which only applies where, apart from it, considerations on one side or the other are evenly balanced, and I do not find that to be the position here."

[19] Although Mummery L.J., in his judgment in *Gilje*, also used the expression *"contra proferentem"* he did so in supporting an approach to the construction of these clauses which in effect raises a presumption against recovery of charges unless the provision is in clear terms.'

2-48   HH Judge Rich QC then went on to set out what he regarded to be the correct approach:

'(i)   It is for the landlord to show that a reasonable tenant would perceive that the underlease obliged him to make the payment sought.

(ii)   Such conclusion must emerge clearly and plainly from the words used.

(iii)   Thus if the words used could reasonably be read as providing for some other circumstance, the landlord will fail to discharge the onus upon him.

(iv)   This does not however permit the rejection of the natural meaning of the words in their context on the basis of some other fanciful meaning or purpose, and the context may justify a "liberal" meaning.

(v)   If consideration of the clause leaves an ambiguity then the ambiguity will be resolved against the landlord as "proferror".'

2-49   It is thought that HH Judge Rich QC's clarification of *Gilje* accurately sets out the correct approach to the question of construction of service charge provisions and the application of the principle of *contra proferentem*, where relevant. The *contra proferentem* rule is distinct from the requirement that the lease must state in clear terms what a tenant is obliged to contribute towards under a service charge and it will only have any relevance in the case of ambiguity. The maxim is likely to have a very limited role in the modern process of construction. In *Cahalane v London Borough of Wandsworth*,[81] the President of the Lands Tribunal referred to the circumstances when the *contra proferetem* rule applies and the need for ambiguity. He noted:

> '[14] It does not seem to me that to construe the provision contra proferentem would require that the obligation should be construed narrowly or that such narrow interpretation would necessarily be the one "most favourable to" the lessee.'

2-50   As a general rule, *Gilje* supports the proposition that service charges fall to be construed restrictively[82] in the sense that a landlord cannot require the tenant to contribute towards the costs of any particular service charge item

---

81 [2008] EWLands LRX_150_2007.
82 *Norwich City Council v Marshall* [2008] EWLands LRX_114_2007 at para 14; but c.f. *Arnold v Britton* [2012] EWHC 3451 (Ch) at para 45, *per* Morgan J.

unless the lease makes specific provision for it. By way of example, in *Riverlate Properties Ltd v Paul*,[83] the landlords' obligations were set out in a number of subclauses, (a) to (d). The tenant's covenant requiring him to contribute made no reference to (a), which was concerned with structural alterations. The court held that the tenant was not obliged to contribute to the landlords' cost of performing works.[84] *Gilje* should not, however, stand as authority for the proposition that service charge provisions always fall to be construed *contra proferentem* against the landlord.[85] In *McHale v Earl Cadogan*,[86] Rix LJ said:

> 'I readily acknowledge that it is the policy of the authorities not to bring within the general words of a service charge clause anything which does not clearly belong there. To put the matter another way, service charge provisions have been construed restrictively.'   .

2-51   In *Arnold v Britton*,[87] Morgan J expressed the view that service charges were not subject to any special principles of construction[88] and that there is no rule which requires service charge provisions to be construed restrictively. The general principles relating to the interpretation of commercial instruments apply to the construction of service charge provisions. He referred to what Rix LJ said in *McHale v Earl Cadogan*[89] and said:

> 'In that case, the Court of Appeal held that the ordinary meaning of the words used was in accordance with the submissions of the landlord and not with those of the tenant. The general remarks in that case no doubt mean that if a landlord wants to be entitled to charge for some particular work or service, it is reasonably to be expected that the landlord will specify that work or service in any list of recoverable matters and that general words will not be read in an extensive way to cover matters which could have been adequately specified.'

2-52   Where the Unfair Terms in Consumer Contracts Regulations 1999 apply to a lease,[90] the court may be obliged to apply a statutory rule of construction which is analogous to the *contra proferentem* rule.[91] Regulation 7 provides:

---

83 [1975] Ch 133, CA.
84 See also *Sella House Ltd v Mears* [1989] 1 EGLR 65, discussed below at **11-04** and **11-05** where the landlord was not entitled to recover legal costs as the service charge provision was not sufficiently clear.
85 However, the case has been relied on as authority for such a general proposition. For example, in *Leicester City Council v Master*, HH Judge Huskinson said: 'I accept that, as shown in *Gilje v Charlgrove Securities Ltd* [2001] E.W.C.A. Civ 1777, the lease was drafted or preferred by the Appellant, that it falls to be construed contra proferentem and that where (as here) a landlord seeks to recover money from the tenant there must, on ordinary principles, be clear terms in the contractual provisions which are said to entitle the landlord to do so.'
86 [2010] EWCA Civ 14.
87 [2012] EWHC 3451 (Ch).
88 See in particular paras 43 and 45.
89 [2010] EWCA Civ 14. See **2-50** above.
90 See **37-02** below and *R (on the application of Khatun) v Newham LBC* [2005] QB 37.
91 See **37-08** to **37-11**.

'7 Written contacts

(1) The seller or supplier shall ensure that any written term of a contract is expressed in plain, intelligible language.

(2) If there is doubt about the meaning of a written term, the interpretation which is most favourable to the consumer shall prevail but this rule shall not apply in proceedings brought under Regulation 12.'

2-53   In *Peabody Trust Governors v Reeve*,[92] it was held[93] that, when confronted with a lease containing two flatly contradictory provisions, the meaning of the lease was 'in doubt' for the purposes of regulation 7, so that the interpretation most preferable to the consumer (the tenant) should prevail. The Deputy Judge said:[94]

'Accordingly, given that there is "doubt" as to the meaning of cl.5 as a whole, and, in the light of the contradictory terms of the sub-clauses, as to the meaning of the sub-clauses themselves, I am obliged in terms of reg.7(2) to adopt the interpretation most favourable to the consumer, in other words the tenant in this case. That interpretation must in my judgment be that there can be no variation of the Tenancy Agreement without the agreement in writing of both parties.

This rule in the Regulation appears to be analogous to the domestic English law principle of contra proferentem which is normally to the effect that in the case of ambiguity a document is construed against the party putting it forward. As Lord Mustill observed in the Privy Council decision in *Tam Wing Chuen v Bank of Credit and Commerce Hong Kong Ltd* [1996] 2 B.C.L.C. 69 at 77, the cases show that the principle "... can have some weight, even today".

The present case is not the usual case of ambiguity, where one expression may have two different meanings, but a very unusual one of two flatly contradictory provisions immediately next to each other. Nevertheless, it seems to me that if there is no compelling reason to choose one sub-clause over the other, the contra proferentem principle does enable the court to break the deadlock and apply the provision less favourable to the party putting the terms forward. This would mean that in cases not covered by the Regulations or its predecessor, the principles of English domestic law achieve the same result.'

2-54   Where the 1999 Regulations apply, regulation 7, could, potentially, impact on the process of construction. However, it will only be a weapon in the hands of the consumer (usually the tenant) in cases of 'doubt' and, following *Peabody v Reeve*, it seems that the requirement for 'doubt' is comparable to the necessary 'ambiguity' which must exist before *contra proferentem* can apply. Regulation 7 cannot, therefore, be regarded as a shortcut which enables a court to bypass the usual process of contractual construction, nor is it a provision which falls to be applied in the relaxed way in which the *contra proferentem* rule has sometimes been applied following *Gilje*. Its proper role is limited to those cases of genuine doubt or ambiguity and the circumstances when the regulation will properly apply are likely to overlap with those cases where the *contra proferentem* rule would be taken into account.

92   [2008] EWHC 1432 (Ch), [2009] L&TR 6.
93   By Gabriel Moss QC, sitting as a Deputy Judge of the Chancery Division.
94   At paras 31 to 33.

SWEEPING-UP CLAUSES

2-55   It is impossible for the draftsman of a lease to foresee all potential items of future expenditure which may be incurred by a landlord. It is, therefore, common in a service charge provision to find a clause designed to cover unforeseen items of expenditure ('sweeping-up clauses'). Examples of such provisions are those that provide for 'other costs and expenses reasonably incurred', 'such costs or expenses as the landlord shall deem appropriate', 'expenses incurred for the benefit of the building' and 'expenses incurred in the interests of good estate management'.

2-56   An example of the principle that service charge provisions should clearly specify the work or services which are intended to be recovered and will not be construed in an extensive way is found consistently in the court's approach towards sweeping-up clauses.[95] The strict approach taken to these provisions means that they will not, in general, provide a means of curing a defective service charge mechanism and a landlord will not be permitted to rely on such a provision to remedy a clear omission from a lease. For example:

1   In *Mullaney v Maybourne (Croydon) Management Co Ltd*,[96] the cost of replacing wood-framed windows with double-glazed windows did not fall within the following provision: 'such further or additional costs which the Company shall properly incur in providing and maintaining additional services or amenities.'

2   In *Boldmark Ltd v Cohen*,[97] a landlord could not recover interest incurred as a result of borrowing to finance the provision of services pursuant to the following provision: 'There shall be added to the costs and expenses and outgoings and matters referred to in the preceding paragraphs of this schedule such sums as the Lessors may from time to time expend in respect of the general administration and management of the Block.'

3   In *Jacob Isbicki & Co Ltd v Goulding & Bird Ltd*[98] (considered in detail at **2-56** to **2-60** below), the landlord was not entitled to recover the cost of external works.

4   In *St Mary's Mansions Ltd v Limegate Investment Co*,[99] the 'cost of all other services which the lessor may at its absolute discretion provide or install in the said Building for the comfort and convenience of the lessees' did not enable the landlord to recover legal costs.

---

95   See, for example, *St Modwen Developments (Edmonton) Ltd v Tesco Stores Ltd* [2006] EWHC 3177, where Toulson LJ said: 'A proviso of this kind, which can be referred to both literally and metaphorically in the present context as a sweep-up clause, has to be approached with caution. I have been referred to a number of authorities on the subject, but it is enough for the principle to refer to a judgment of Mummery LJ, in *Gilje v Charlgrove Securities Ltd* [2001] E.W.C.A. Civ 1777'.
96   [1986] 1 EGLR 70.
97   [1986] 1 EGLR 47.
98   [1989] 1 EGLR 236.
99   [2002] EWCA Civ 1491.

2-57   The scope of sweeping-up clauses is often considered in the context of issues concerning the recovery of landlords' legal and other professional costs. This is considered in more detail in Chapter 11 below.

2-58   When construing sweeping-up provisions, it is particularly important not to consider such provisions in isolation but to construe such provisions in the context of the lease as a whole. See, for example, *Jacob Isbicki & Co Ltd v Goulding & Bird Ltd*,[100] where the landlord sought to recover the cost of sandblasting the external walls of a building. The lease, at clause 3(2), required the tenant to pay:

> 'a proportionate part of the expenses and outgoings reasonably and properly incurred by the landlord in the repair, maintenance and renewal and insurance of the building and the provision of services therein and the other heads of expenditure as the same are set out in the fourth schedule hereto'.

2-59   The fourth schedule to the lease made reference to various items, but not work to the external walls. Finally, paragraph 8 of the schedule stated:

> 'provided always the landlord may at his reasonable discretion hold, add to, extend, vary or make any alteration in the rendering of the said services or any of them from time to time if the landlord at his like discretion deems it desirable to do so for more efficient conduct and management of the building.'

2-60   Mervyn Davies J held that these two provisions had to be read together and that they did not provide for the payment of two separate items by the tenant, namely one in respect of the repair of the building as a whole and the other in respect of the provision of services as set out in the fourth schedule. The sweeping-up provision at paragraph 8 could not be used to alter the obligations of the service charge to include within its compass works to the external parts of the house. He said:[101]

> 'Surely, para 8 is simply a proviso saying that the landlord (and I use the words of para 8) "may add to, extend, vary or make any alterations in the rendering of the said services ... if the landlord at his like discretion deems it desirable so to do." That seems to me to mean that, within the limits of the work for which the landlord can recover, the landlord has a limited right to alter those works, but not, as I see it, wholly to extend and make the tenant liable for a kind of work that was never contemplated by clause 3(2).'

2-61   Although the function of a sweeping-up provision is to provide flexibility and a means by which a landlord can recover costs not expressly mentioned elsewhere in the service charge clause, courts are reluctant to allow costs to be recovered through a sweeping-up provision where they more naturally fall to be included elsewhere in a lease. Expenses may not be permitted to be recovered under a sweeping-up clause where provision has been made elsewhere in the lease for the type of expense sought to be recovered and the landlord is seeking indirectly to enlarge or broaden the scope of such express provisions.

---

100   [1989] 1 EGLR 236.
101   At p 237D.

2-62   In *Holding & Management Ltd v Property Holding & Investment Trust plc*,[102] the lease contained a detailed provision relating to repair of the property. The landlord was not entitled to recover the cost of repair works pursuant to a sweeping-up clause.[103]

2-63   This provision was subject to a requirement to act reasonably (see **2-97** to **2-121** below) and the works which fell within this obligation were those works which the maintenance trustee considered necessary to maintain the amenities and facilities which, from time to time are considered appropriate for a block of first class residential flats. Nicholls LJ said:

> 'As living standards rise, so this or that feature can be expected to be changed or added to the building. Examples might be high speed lifts or improved air-conditioning. But these words are not directed at maintaining the structure or exterior walls of the building. That is a subject directly addressed in paragraph 2 [the repairing provisions].'

2-64   In *Lloyds Bank plc v Bowker Orford*,[104] Neuberger J refused to construe 'any other beneficial services which may properly be provided by the lessors' as extending to matters dealt with specifically elsewhere in the lease. For example, the lease provided for the landlord to carry out external repairs, but did not provide for the costs of this to be recovered. The sweeping-up provision referred to matters which were discretionary and which the landlord was not already obliged to carry out.

2-65   In *Rettke-Grover v Needleman*,[105] the issue was whether the lease allowed the landlord to recover the cost of accountants' fees. Provision had been made in the lease for a management fee to be paid, which was 15% of the total amount expended by the lessor on insurance and in complying with the landlord's service charge obligations. The landlord relied on the general provision,

> 'To provide any other services and to carry out any other works of whatever nature as the lessor may from time to time deem necessary or expedient for the efficient management of the Building and the garden area forecourt and footpaths belonging thereto.'

2-66   The Upper Tribunal held that the engagement of professional managing agents did not fall within this provision (so that it could recover the cost of engaging the managing agents and then a 15% management fee on top). The

---

102   [1989] 1 WLR 1313; [1990] 1 EGLR 65.
103   'To carry out all repairs to any other part of the building for which the maintenance trustee may be liable and to provide and supply such other services for the benefit of the tenant and the other tenants of flats in the building and to carry out such other repairs and such improvements works and additions and to defray such other costs (including the modernisation or replacement of plant and machinery) as the maintenance trustee shall consider necessary to maintain the building as a block of first class residential flats or otherwise desirable in the general interests of the tenants.'
104   [1992] 2 EGLR 44.
105   [2011] UKUT 283 (LC).

clause had to be construed on the basis that the provision of professional management services for the efficient management of the building was not a type of 'other service ... of whatever nature' referred to in the sweeping-up provision. It would be open to the landlord to engage an accountant, rather than prepare accounts themselves, but they would not be entitled to recover the costs of doing so through the service charge.

2-67 Sweeping-up clauses have been successfully used by landlords in the following cases.

2-68 In *Billson v Tristem*,[106] the lease included a provision,

'Without prejudice to the foregoing do or cause to be done all such works installations acts matters and things as may in the absolute discretion of the lessors be necessary or advisable for the proper maintenance safety and administration of the Building.'

2-69 This provision assisted the court in concluding that it was the parties' intention that the tenant should contribute to the costs of works to all parts of the building, for which the otherwise ineptly drafted lease would not have made provision.

2-70 The sweeping-up provision in *Sun Alliance and London Assurance Co Ltd v British Railways Board*[107] allowed the landlord to recover the costs of cleaning windows:

'The costs of proving such other services as the lessor shall consider ought properly and reasonably to be provided for the benefit of the building, or for the proper maintenance and servicing of any part or parts thereof.'

2-71 Unlike *Mullaney v Maybourne*,[108] in *Sutton (Hastoe) Housing Association v Williams*[109] the cost of replacing wooden windows with uPVC windows could be recovered under the following sweeping-up provision:

'additional works considered necessary by the lessor in its absolute discretion.'

2-72 In *Reston Ltd v Hudson*,[110] the right to recover legal costs was held to fall within either a provision entitling the landlord to recover the costs of management of the estate or under the sweeping-up clause which provided for the recovery of:

'all outgoings, costs and expenses whatsoever which the lessor may reasonably incur in the discharge of its obligations under clause 4 of the Lease and not otherwise hereinbefore specifically mentioned.'

---

106 [2000] L&TR 220.
107 [1989] 2 EGLR 237.
108 [1986] 1 EGLR 70. See **2-56** above.
109 [1988] 1 EGLR 56.
110 [1990] 2 EGLR 51.

NO PRESUMPTION OF FULL RECOVERY

2-73   Given the general principle that service charge provisions are construed restrictively, it is, perhaps no surprise that there is no presumption to the effect that a landlord is entitled to recover the whole of his expenditure. An example of this can be seen in *Rapid Results College Ltd v Angell*,[111] considered at **2-46** above, where Dillon LJ[112] said:

> 'In the court below it was urged that the provisions for the calculation of service rent reflected, and should be construed so as to tie in with, and cover, the matters on which the landlords had covenanted to incur expenditure under the third schedule. Obviously there is a degree of echo in the provisions of the fourth schedule of what the landlords are to do under the third schedule, because the effective charging clause reserving the services rent describes it as a further sum on account of expenses and outgoings incurred by the landlords in compliance with the covenants on the part of the landlords contained in the third schedule; but it does not follow automatically, nor has it been urged in this court, that the services rent must necessarily cover everything that the landlords are to do under the third schedule. The lease is for a term of only six years; one would not automatically expect that a tenant at a rack rent of a suite of offices in part of a building for a term of six years would be undertaking responsibility for the cost of repair of the main structure roof and foundations of the building.'[113]

2-74   Referring to *Rapid Results College Ltd v Angell*, Jackson LJ in *Campbell v Daejan Properties Ltd* said:[114]

> 'It is not always the case that the landlord of a property with multiple tenants on historic leases recovers 100% of his expenditure through service charges. Obviously this is what the landlord desires, but there are many possible reasons why he may not achieve that. There is no presumption in construing a lease that the service charge provisions will enable the landlord to recover all of his expenditure.'

PRESUMPTION AGAINST PROFIT

2-75   It is sometimes suggested that there is a general principle to the effect that unless expressed in the clearest possible terms, a lease will not be construed in such a way as to enable the landlord to recover a profit element over and above the costs incurred in providing services. As a general principle, this is thought to be correct, where the lease specifically links the service charge to the 'costs' or 'expenses' incurred by the landlord. However, it would be wrong to say that a landlord will never be permitted to recover a profit element through a

---

111 [1986] 1 EGLR 53.
112 At p 55C.
113 See also *Boldmark v Cohen; Mullany v Maybourne Grange (Croydon) Management Co Ltd* (1986) 277 EG 1350; *Woodtreck v Jezeck* (1982) 261 EG 571; and *Frobisher v Kiloran Trust Co Ltd* [1980] 1 WLR 425.
114 [2012] EWCA Civ 1503 at para 56.

service charge provision or that there is any presumption or general principle of construction to this effect.

2-76 For example, in *Earl Cadogan v 27/29 Sloane Gardens Ltd*,[115] the lease contained very clear provisions which allowed the landlord to recover through the service charge a sum equivalent to a notional rent for the caretaker's flat.[116] The tenant claimed that because the provision of the flat by the landlord was not an actual expense which the landlord had to incur or an income which the landlord was foregoing (the landlord's headlease prevented him from using the flat other than as rent-free accommodation for a caretaker), the landlord could not recover any notional rent through the service charge. The Tribunal held that the provisions of the lease were clear and that the landlord could recover the notional rent of the caretaker's flat as part of the service charge, even if this might entitle him to recover a sum in excess of the cost of providing services.

2-77 A case which is often cited in support of the proposition that a landlord should not be entitled to profit over and above the costs which he has actually incurred is *Jollybird Ltd v Fairzone*.[117] In that case, the lease contained a very unclear and ambiguous provision which, on one construction, entitled the landlord to recover more than the actual cost incurred in respect of heating charges. The court rejected such an interpretation of the lease in favour of a conclusion which entitled the landlord to be reimbursed his actual costs.

2-78 A similar result was reached in *Rettke-Grover v Needleman*,[118] where the landlord could not recover via the service charge the cost of engaging managing agents when he was also entitled to recover a 15% management fee on top of the cost of services.[119]

2-79 In *Arnold v Britton*,[120] it was argued, in reliance on *Jollybird Ltd v Fairzone,* that there was a principle of general application that a service charge provision should not be construed (in the absence of clear words) so as to entitle the landlord to a profit over and above reimbursement of his costs. Morgan J rejected this submission and said:[121]

> 'As to the suggested principle that a service charge provision should not be construed (in the absence of clear words) so as to entitle the landlord to a profit

---

115 [2006] 2 EGLR 89.
116 The relevant provision was: 'The cost of employing maintaining and providing accommodation in the building for a caretaker … and including an annual sum equivalent to the market rent of any accommodation provided rent free by the Lessor and general and water rates and gas and electricity charges in respect of such accommodation.'
117 [1990] 2 EGLR 55, CA.
118 [2011] UKUT 283 (LC).
119 In relation to the recovery of insurance premiums, the question sometimes arises as to whether a landlord is entitled to retain loyalty payments or commission on top of the costs of placing the insurance. See *Williams v Southark LBC* (2001) 33 HLR 22 and **10-17** below.
120 [2012] EWHC 3451 (Ch). Permission to appeal against the decision of Morgan J has been granted by the Court of Appeal but, at the time of writing, the appeal has not been heard.
121 At paras 42 and 43.

over and above reimbursement of his costs incurred in providing the relevant services, counsel relied on the statement to that effect in *Woodfall on Landlord and Tenant*, Vol. 1 para. 7.175. The textbook refers in this context to *Jollybird v Fairzone* [1990] 2 EGLR 55. I do not think that this decision lays down any general principle, to the effect suggested in the textbook. In that case, the Court of Appeal had a choice between rival constructions of a service charge provision in a commercial lease. The landlord's construction produced an absurdity. The tenant's construction meant that a phrase in the clause was not strictly necessary and merely stated something that would have been the position in any event. The court preferred the tenant's construction in order to avoid producing an absurdity. The court applied an entirely conventional approach to the question of construction before it. The landlord's construction would have given the landlord a profit over and above reimbursement of the relevant costs but that was not the reason given for rejecting the landlord's construction.

The statement in *Woodfall* contains an element of truth where the clause which falls to be construed allows a landlord to recover a sum calculated by reference to the cost of services. In such a case, the word "cost" would not normally be construed to include anything by way of profit to the landlord in addition to reimbursement of the actual costs. Furthermore, a typical service charge clause does not provide for the landlord to make a profit in addition to the cost of services. Beyond that, where there is a dispute about a non-typical service charge provision, I doubt if the proposition in the textbook is of much help to a court asked to construe that provision. I do not see why a service charge clause in a lease should be subject to a special principle. If there were a special principle about charging for services, it should apply generally and not be confined to leases. I consider that what is required is that the court must examine the wording of the charging provision in its context and against all the admissible background and in the light of the apparent commercial purpose of the clause and then decide what the provision means and how it operates. In other words, the court applies the general principles summarised about as to the construction of commercial instruments.'

2-80   A presumption against profit-making would not, in any event, prevent a landlord from recovering more than 100% of the total costs incurred if the total proportions payable by the lessees exceeds 100% of those costs.[122]

IMPLIED TERMS

Introduction

2-81   The principles of construction discussed above emphasize the paramount importance of the express terms of the lease. However, in addition to the express terms, terms may also be implied into the lease. Implied terms can be divided into three main groups:

1   terms implied in fact, i.e. those which a court concludes, as a matter of construction, the parties must have intended to include in the lease;

---

122   But see Chapter 24 for the power of the LVT under the Landlord and Tenant Act 1987 to vary leases in such a situation and *Morgan v Fletcher* [2009] UKUT 186 (LT).

2   terms implied by statute or operation of law;

3   terms implied by custom, i.e. where there is a generally accepted custom accepted by those doing business in a particular trade.

2-82   In *Luxor (Eastbourne) Ltd v Cooper*,[123] Lord Wright explained the difference between two types of implied term:[124]

> 'The expression "implied term" is used in different senses. Sometimes it denotes some term which does not depend on the actual intention of the parties but on a rule of law, such as the terms, warranties or conditions which, if not expressly excluded, the law imports, as for instance under the Sale of Goods Act and the Marine Insurance Act ... But a case like the present is different because what it is sought to imply is based on an intention imputed to the parties from their actual circumstances.'

2-83   Many terms which are implied in law have been put into statutory form. An example of this is found in contracts for the supply of services (see section 15 of the Supply of Goods and Services Act 1982, which is considered at **2-91** below). Other terms might be imposed as a 'legal incident' of a particular type of contract or relationship. For example, in *Liverpool City Council v Irwin*,[125] the House of Lords held that it was an implied term of a lease of a maisonette in a council-owned block of flats that the landlord would take reasonable care to keep the common parts in a state of repair. Lord Cross of Chelsea said:

> 'When it implies a term in a contract the court is sometimes laying down a general rule that in all contracts of a certain type – sale of goods, master and servant, landlord and tenant, and so on – some provision is to be implied unless the parties have expressly excluded it. In deciding whether or not to lay down such a prima facie rule the court will naturally ask itself whether in the general run of such cases the term in question would be one which it would be reasonable to insert. Sometimes, however, there is no question of laying down any prima facie rule applicable to all cases of a defined type but what the court is being in effect asked to do is to rectify a particular – often a very detailed – contract by inserting in it a term which the parties have not expressed.'

Terms imposed by statute

2-84   As explained in Chapter 1, statute has intervened considerably in the residential sector. Perhaps the most significant statutorily implied term relating to service charges is section 19 of the Landlord and Tenant Act 1985. This provides, in the case of leases of dwellings, that costs incurred by the landlord are only recoverable to the extent that they are reasonably incurred and only if the relevant works or services are of a reasonable standard.

123   [1941] AC 108.
124   At p 137.
125   [1977] AC 239.

37

2-85   Section 19 of the 1985 Act is discussed more fully in Chapter 29.

2-86   The 1985 Act does not provide any guidance as to the meaning of 'reasonably incurred'. It has been said to mean more than simply requiring that the money recovered by the landlord must actually be spent on performing the relevant covenants. The court has imposed a two-stage test. For costs to have been 'reasonably incurred':

1   it must have been reasonable to carry out the relevant works (or perform the relevant services);[126] and

2   the quantum of the costs must also be reasonable.[127]

2-87   In addition, section 19(1)(b) also expressly requires that the standard of works or services be of a reasonable standard.

2-88   The 'reasonably incurred' test thus looks not just to the bottom line cost payable by the tenant, but also to the circumstances which led to the costs being incurred.

2-89   The concept of 'reasonableness' is not unfamiliar to lawyers.[128] Section 19, however, uses the expression 'reasonably incurred' and a distinction has been drawn between these two expressions. In *Forcelux Ltd v Sweetman and Parker*,[129] the Lands Tribunal held:

> 'The question I have to answer is not whether the expenditure for any particular service charge item was necessarily the cheapest available, but whether the charge that was made was reasonably incurred.
>
> But to answer that question, there are, in my judgment, two distinctly separate matters I have to consider. Firstly the evidence, and from that whether the landlord's actions were appropriate, and properly effected in accordance with the requirements of the lease, the RICS Code and the 1985 Act. Secondly, whether the amount charged was reasonable in the light of that evidence. This second point is particularly important as, if that did not have to be considered, it would be open to

---

126 For example, in *Continental Property Ventures Inc v White* [2006] 1 EGLR 85 costs were held not to have been 'reasonably incurred' where they could have been carried out under guarantee.
127 See, for example, *Wandsworth LB v Griffin* [2000] 1 EGLR 105; *Wilson v Stone* [1998] 2 EGLR 155; *Forcelux v Sweetman* [2001] 2 EGLR 173 LT; *Veena SA v Cheong* [2003] 1 EGLR 175 LT.
128 In *Ashworth Frazer Ltd v Gloucester City Council* [2001] UKHL 59; [2001] 1 WLR 2180 (which was concerned with a landlord's obligation not to unreasonably refuse consent to a proposed assignment), Lord Rodger of Earlsferry said: 'The test of reasonableness is to be found in many areas of the law and the concept has been found useful precisely because it prevents the law becoming unduly rigid. In effect, it allows the law to respond appropriately to different situations as they arise. This has to be remembered when a court is considering whether a landlord has "unreasonably withheld" consent to the assignment of a lease. In this context I would follow Viscount Dunedin's advice in *Viscount Tredegar v Harwood* [1929] AC 72, 78 that one "should read reasonableness in the general sense".'
129 [2001] 2 EGLR 173, LT.

any landlord to plead justification for any particular figure, on the grounds that the steps it took justified the expense, without properly testing the market.

It has to be a question of degree, and whilst the appellant has submitted a well reasoned and, as I have said, in my view a correct interpretation of "reasonably incurred", that cannot be a licence to charge a figure that is out of line with the market norm.'

2-90   In *Veena SA v Cheong*,[130] the Lands Tribunal said:

'The word "reasonableness" should be read in the general sense and given a broad, common sense meaning. It should be distinguished from the words "reasonably incurred" as used in section 19(2A)(a) of the 1985 Act. The question is not solely whether costs are "reasonable" but whether they were "reasonably incurred", that is to say whether the action taken in incurring the costs and the amount of those costs were both reasonable.'

2-91   There are other forms of statutory intervention which may impose a reasonableness requirement. For example, where a service charge provision falls within section 15 of the Supply of Goods and Services Act 1982,[131] there is an implied term that the party contracting with the supplier will pay a reasonable charge. It is unlikely, however, that this provision will apply in an ordinary landlord and tenant context, whereby a landlord agrees to provide services and the tenant covenants to pay. In *Havenridge v Boston Dyers Ltd*,[132] the Court of Appeal held that this provision did not apply to a landlord's obligation to obtain insurance.[133]

Implied terms based on imputed intention

2-92   In *Attorney General of Belize v Belize Telecom Ltd*,[134] giving the opinion of the Privy Council, Lord Hoffmann said:

'[16] Before discussing in greater detail the reasoning of the Court of Appeal, the Board will make some general observations about the process of implication. The court has no power to improve upon the instrument which it is called upon

---

130 [2003] 1 EGLR 175, LT.
131 This provision applies to a contract for the supply of services (i.e. a contract under which a person ('the supplier') agrees to carry out a service – s 12(1)) under which the consideration for the services is not determined by the contract, left to be determined in a manner agreed by the contract or determined by the course of dealing between the parties (s 15(1)).
132 [1994] 2 EGLR 73.
133 Evans J said at p 76K: 'In my judgment, where the parties to a lease reach agreement as to the allocation of risk and of responsibilities between them, with regard to the placing of insurance and otherwise, it is unrealistic to describe the arrangement as "the supply of services" by one party to the other, especially when the landlord undertakes that he will insure the premises either entirely or largely for his own benefit. But there could be a case where, in substance, one party did undertake to procure insurance on behalf of the other, and in such a case it might not be so difficult to hold that a supply of services was involved. For that reason I prefer not to express a concluded view on the question of whether the Act could ever apply to a lease of this sort.'
134 [2009] UKPC 10.

to construe, whether it be a contract, a statute or articles of association. It cannot introduce terms to make it fairer or more reasonable. It is concerned only to discover what the instrument means. However, that meaning is not necessarily or always what the authors or parties to the document would have intended. It is the meaning which the instrument would convey to a reasonable person having all the background knowledge which would reasonably be available to the audience to whom the instrument is addressed: see *Investors Compensation Scheme Ltd v West Bromwich Building Society* [1998] 1 WLR 896, 912–913. It is this objective meaning which is conventionally called the intention of the parties, or the intention of Parliament, or the intention of whatever person or body was or is deemed to have been the author of the instrument.

[17] The question of implication arises when the instrument does not expressly provide for what is to happen when some event occurs. The most usual inference in such a case is that nothing is to happen. If the parties had intended something to happen, the instrument would have said so. Otherwise, the express provisions of the instrument are to continue to operate undisturbed. If the event has caused loss to one or other of the parties, the loss lies where it falls.

[18] In some cases, however, the reasonable addressee would understand the instrument to mean something else. He would consider that the only meaning consistent with the other provisions of the instrument, read against the relevant background, is that something is to happen. The event in question is to affect the rights of the parties. The instrument may not have expressly said so, but this is what it must mean. In such a case, it is said that the court implies a term as to what will happen if the event in question occurs. But the implication of the term is not an addition to the instrument. It only spells out what the instrument means.'

2-93   Whether or not a term is to be implied into a document is accordingly part of the general process of construction. Lord Hoffmann referred to the factors which courts have employed when determining whether a term should be implied into a document, as summarized in *BP Refinery (Westernport) Pty Ltd v Shire of Hastings*[135] by Lord Simon of Glaisdale:

'for a term to be implied, the following conditions (which may overlap) must be satisfied: (1) it must be reasonable and equitable; (2) it must be necessary to give business efficacy to the contract, so that no term will be implied if the contract is effective without it; (3) it must be so obvious that 'it goes without saying'; (4) it must be capable of clear expression; (5) it must not contradict any express term of the contract.'

2-94   In *Belize,* Lord Hoffmann noted that the above criteria are not a series of independent tests but a collection of different ways of expressing the central idea that an implied term must spell out what the contract actually means.[136] When deciding whether some provision ought to be implied in a contract, the question for the court is:

---

135 (1978) 52 ALJR 20, PC at p 26.
136 At para 27: 'The Board considers that this list is best regarded, not as series of independent tests which must each be surmounted, but rather as a collection of different ways in which judges have tried to express the central idea that the proposed implied term must spell out what the contract actually means, or in which they have explained why they did not think that it did so.'

'whether such a provision would spell out in express words what the instrument, read against the relevant background, would reasonably be understood to mean. It will be noticed from Lord Pearson's speech that this question can be reformulated in various ways which a court may find helpful in providing an answer – the implied term must "go without saying", it must be "necessary to give business efficacy to the contract" and so on – but these are not in the Board's opinion to be treated as different or additional tests. There is only one question: is that what the instrument, read as a whole against the relevant background, would reasonably be understood to mean?'[137]

2-95   Lord Hoffmann emphasised that, when a term is implied, the court is not making an addition to the relevant instrument, but is simply stating the meaning of a document. A court is not improving the document, but spelling out what the instrument means. In *Liverpool City Council v Irwin*,[138] Lord Cross emphasised that the correct question was not whether a term was reasonable, but necessary:

'what the court is being in effect asked to do is to rectify a particular – often a very detailed – contract by inserting in it a term which the parties have not expressed. Here it is not enough for the court to say that the suggested term is one the presence of which would make the contract a better or fairer one; it must be able to say that the insertion of the term is necessary to give – as it is put – "business efficacy" to the contract and that if its absence had been pointed out at the time both parties – assuming them to have been reasonable men – would have agreed without hesitation to its insertion.'

2-96   An example of the principle that a term will not be implied simply to improve upon the instrument which the court is called upon to construe is found in *St Modwen Developments (Edmonton) Ltd v Tesco Stores Ltd*.[139] Here, the lease provided for a service charge certificate to be signed by the local authority's borough treasurer. The original landlord was the Enfield Borough Council but the reversion to the lease subsequently vested in St Modwen. The landlord's finance director had signed the certificate (in the absence of there being a borough treasurer) but the court held that the certificates had no contractual force. When considering an argument that it would be possible to imply an obligation on the parties in the circumstances to use their best endeavours to appoint somebody else to have the certification responsibilities, Toulson J said:[140]

'I do not think that one could properly imply into the lease a positive obligation on the parties to use their best endeavours to create some alternative machinery, under the guise of interpretation.'

Implied term as to reasonableness

2-97   One of the more thorny issues which arise in relation to service charges is whether a term should be implied into a lease to the effect that expenditure

137 At para 21.
138 [1977] AC 239.
139 [2006] EWHC 3177 (Ch), [2007] 1 EGLR 63.
140 At para 12.

must be reasonable either in amount or must be reasonably incurred. It is sometimes argued, although wrongly in the authors' view, that there is always general implication of reasonableness affecting service charges in all types of leases.[141] Many leases expressly provide that expenditure must be reasonable, but, in the absence of such an express provision, there is no general rule to the effect that a court will always imply a term as to reasonableness. This will always depend on the general criteria discussed above.

2-98   Following the decision in *Finchbourne Ltd v Rodrigues*,[142] there has been a tendency towards assuming an automatic implication of a reasonableness requirement, certainly as regards the nature or circumstances of the landlord's expenditure, although not, perhaps, as regards the amount payable by the tenant.

Finchbourne Ltd v Rodrigues

2-99   The issue which arose in *Finchbourne Ltd v Rodrigues* was whether the lessor was limited to recovering only fair and reasonable outgoings. On appeal, on the question of whether it was necessary, having regard to the terms of the lease, to imply a provision that the costs should be fair and reasonable, Cairns LJ said:[143]

> 'Taking the strictest of tests on that matter, I am of the opinion that such an implication must be made here. It cannot be supposed the plaintiffs were entitled to be as extravagant as they chose in the standards of repair, the appointment of porters etc ... In my opinion the parties cannot have intended that the landlords should have an unfettered discretion to adopt the highest conceivable standard and to charge the tenant with it.'

2-100   Browne LJ also thought that a term must be implied to the effect that costs should be fair and reasonable.

2-101   Although often cited in support of an all-embracing implied term as to reasonableness on the part of a landlord, the above comments of Cairns LJ were *obiter* and do not obviously appear to establish a general principle of universal application. The Court of Appeal certainly did not discuss the general principles for implying terms into a contract. The decision in *Finchbourne* was helpfully explained by Walton J in *Frobisher (Second Investments) Ltd v Kiloran Trust Co Ltd*:[144]

> 'the Court of Appeal had no hesitation in implying a term that various matters should be carried out fairly and reasonably in a lease and that maintenance of

---

141   By way of example, in *Firstcross Ltd v Teasdale* (1983) 8 HLR 112, McNill J said: 'In approaching this question, I am, as I understand it, bound as a matter of law to accept, on the authority of the decision of the Court of Appeal in *Finchbourne Ltd. v. Rodrigues*, that the operation of a variable clause is, in any event and as a matter of law, limited by a "fair and reasonable" condition.'
142   [1976] 3 All ER 581.
143   At p 587, *obiter*.
144   [1980] 1 EGLR 34.

the property should not be left to the landlords' discretion to adopt the highest conceivable standard of maintenance for the block of flats and to charge the tenant with the cost. It seems to me that that case, as it were, speaks for itself. Obviously, in order to give business efficacy to a block of flats leased in the Mile End Road, one assumes a Mile End Road standard of maintenance. It seems to me that the readiness of the Court of Appeal to adopt, as it were, the current standard for the block of flats in that particular case does not in any way assist me in this matter at all.'[145]

2-102　*Finchbourne* was also referred to in *Gleniffer Finance Corporation Ltd v Bamar Wood and Products Ltd*,[146] where the tenant was obliged to pay a sum equivalent to the amount which the landlord paid by way of premium for keeping the demised premises insured for the full cost of reinstatement. The court considered whether the duty of the landlord in relation to the projection used for arriving at the cost or the full cost of reinstatement was:

1　that the landlord should exercise his power *bona fide*, or

2　he should do what was fair and reasonable,

but Forbes J declined to decide what was the precise manner in which the land-lord should approach his power. In this context, there was, perhaps no difference between the two concepts.

2-103　In *Bandar Properties Holdings Ltd v JS Darwen (Successors) Ltd*,[147] which was decided prior to *Finchbourne*,[148] the court declined to imply a term into a lease requiring the lessor to act reasonably in placing insurance so as not to impose an unnecessarily heavy burden on the lessees, finding that the lease worked perfectly well without the implication.[149]

2-104　In *Havenridge Ltd v Boston Dyers Ltd*,[150] the landlord was required to insure in an office of repute and the tenant required to pay all sums properly expended. The court again declined to imply a term of reasonableness or to construe 'properly' as if it meant 'reasonably'.[151]

145　This is similar to the formulation of the approach taken in relation to a standard covenant to keep premises in 'good tenantable repair' in *Proudfoot v Hart* (1890) 25 QBD 42.
146　(1979) 37 P&CR 208.
147　[1968] 2 All ER 305.
148　And which is considered at **10-09** below.
149　Roskill J said: 'I said a moment ago that the question: "what is reasonable?" is not the test. It has to be necessary to make the contract work as well as reasonable before the court will make any implication of the kind contended for on behalf of the lessees. … It is axiomatic that a court will not imply a term which has not been expressed merely because, had the parties thought of the possibility of expressing that term it would have been reasonable for them to have done so. Before a term which has not been expressed can be implied it has got to be shown not only that it would be reasonable to make that implication, but that it is necessary in order to make the contract work that such a term should be implied. It has sometimes been expressed as "necessary for the business efficacy of the contract"; and it is against that well-known and established principle that I approach the determination of the crucial question in this case.'
150　[1994] 2 EGLR 73.
151　See the judgment of Evans J at p 75, which is considered in more detail at **10-12** below.

2-105 It is not, perhaps, surprising that no term was implied in *Havenridge* given the wording of the lease, which had clearly limited the landlord's right to recover sums which he had to 'properly expend or pay' and where there was also a requirement that the landlord insure in an office of repute. It is difficult to see why an additional reasonableness requirement should have been added.[152]

2-106 The question of implied reasonableness requirements has arisen in connection with the repair works a landlord is entitled to carry out when claiming the cost of the works as service charges. The general principle is that the party who has covenanted to do works can choose what method of works to adopt, provided that the work is such as a competent careful surveyor or other appropriate professional person would advise as being appropriate and it restores the premises to the standard contemplated by the covenant.[153] However, where the party carrying out the works is the landlord and he intends to pass the cost of works through the service charge, this general position can be said to be qualified by a requirement that any decision as to what method or works is to be adopted must be reasonable in all the circumstances. The principles which apply to the landlord's decision-making process in this situation are discussed in more detail in Chapter 4 below. However, the reasonableness requirements on the landlord in such cases can be explained by reference to the following three cases.

2-107 In *Plough Investments Ltd v Manchester City Council*,[154] Scott J put the landlord's obligation in the following terms:

> 'Provided proposed works of repair are such as an owner who had to bear the cost himself might reasonably decide upon and provided the works constitute "repairs" within the meaning of that word in the ... [lease] covenant, the tenant is not, in my judgment, entitled to insist upon more limited works or cheaper works being preferred. I agree with Miss Williamson that the landlord cannot be limited to a minimum standard of repair only.'

2-108 In *Holding & Management Ltd v Property Holding & Investment Trust plc*,[155] Nicholls LJ, when rejecting a particular scheme of works proposed by the landlord as going beyond what was sensibly needed to cure certain physical defects, said:

> 'A prudent building owner bearing the cost himself might well have decided to adopt such a scheme, despite its expense. But what is in question is whether owners of 75-year leases in the building could fairly be expected to pay for such a scheme under an obligation to "repair".'

2-109 Later, referring to the requirement of the lease that the maintenance trustee shall carry out 'such ... works ... as the Maintenance Trustee shall

---

152 See also *Berrycroft Management Co Ltd v Sinclair Gardens Investments (Kensington) Ltd* [1997] 1 EGLR 47 where the Court of Appeal, again, declined to imply a term.
153 See *Gibson Investments Ltd v Chesterton Plc* [2002] EWHC 19 (Ch) and generally Chapter 4 below.
154 [1989] 1 EGLR 244.
155 [1990] 1 EGLR 65.

consider necessary to maintain the Building as a block of first class residential flats', he said:

> 'I agree with Mr Price that this paragraph may embrace works which are not strictly repair. Where I have to part company with him is that I cannot read this paragraph as giving the plaintiff a free hand to require the residents to pay for all works, whatever they might be, which the plaintiff might consider necessary to maintain the building as a block of first-class residential flats. In my view, it is necessarily implicit in this paragraph that the plaintiff will act reasonably.'

2-110   In *Fluor Daniel Properties Ltd v Shortlands Investments Ltd*,[156] where the court had to consider whether certain works to an office building, which largely consisted of replacement of the air conditioning system, fell within the landlord's repairing obligation so that costs could be recovered through the service charge, Blackburne J considered *Plough Investments* and *Holding & Management*. He said, in relation to the standard of repair:

> 'In short the works – i.e. the standard to be adopted – must be such as the tenants, given the length of their leases, could fairly be expected to pay for. The landlord cannot, because he has an interest in the matter, overlook the limited interest of the tenants who are having to pay by carrying out works which are calculated to serve an interest extending beyond that of the tenants.'

2-111   These cases highlight the willingness of the court to imply a reasonableness requirement on the part of the landlord when deciding what works to carry out, but the relevant question to consider is whether, considering all of the terms of the lease, the parties can be taken to have contemplated that the tenant should be liable to pay for the relevant works. This echoes Lord Hoffman's test in *AG v Belize*, namely 'There is only one question: is that what the instrument, read as a whole against the relevant background, would reasonably be understood to mean?'[157]

2-112   Where a reasonableness requirement is imposed, the Landlord will not be obliged to select the cheapest method of repair but he must act reasonably, having regard to the tenant's limited interest in the premises, in particular the length of the tenant's lease. Reasonableness is not to be equated to the lowest cost: provided a landlord acts reasonably, he cannot be criticised by reason of the fact that the works or services could have been provided or performed at a lower cost. The practical implications of a reasonableness requirement are considered in Chapter 4 below.

2-113   The result of the above cases is no different to the approach taken by the Court of Appeal in *Finchbourne*. On the facts of that case, the parties could not have intended the landlord to have an unfettered discretion when deciding what works and services to carry out to a block of flats leased in the Mile End Road

---

156   [2001] 2 EGLR 103.
157   Lord Hoffman's judgment in *Attorney General of Belize v Belize Telecom Ltd* [2009] UKPC 10 at para 21. See **2-92** and **2-94** above.

and, in deciding what works could properly be carried out, a Mile End Road standard of maintenance was assumed.

2-114 A reasonableness requirement was also implied in relation to the question of legal costs incurred by the landlord in *Morgan v Stainer*.[158] The main issue in this case was whether the defendant was entitled to claim the costs of legal proceedings as part of the service charge. David Neuberger QC (sitting as a Deputy Judge of the Chancery Division) said:

> 'It must, in my judgment, be implied into para 5(b) that the "legal and other costs" referred to therein have to be reasonably and properly incurred before they can be the subject matter of a claim under the service charge provisions. In addition, it seems to me that the sums claimed must, not only with regard to their quantum but also with regard to their nature, be fair and reasonable as discussed in *Finchbourne Ltd v Rodrigues*'.[159]

Implied terms as to reasonableness: Conclusion

2-115 The question of whether there is any general implication of reasonableness affecting service charges is more likely to arise in a non-residential context,[160] given the implied reasonableness requirement imposed by section 19 of the 1985 Act. As a general rule, where a lease makes no express qualification to the effect that a landlord must act 'reasonably' or 'properly', it is likely that such a qualification will be implied but, as the above cases illustrate, it cannot be stated that, as a general rule, such a term must always be presumed to apply and whether or not such a term should be implied must always be a matter of construction of the lease in question. The context of the lease will also affect what is actually required by a requirement of 'reasonableness'.

2-116 The following conclusions can be drawn:

1   Where the lease already contains a safeguard for the tenant, there will usually be no scope for implying a further requirement that the landlord act reasonably; for example, where a landlord is required to place insurance in an office of repute or there is an obligation to negotiate at arm's length, or perhaps where there is an express obligation to obtain competitive tenders before carrying out works.

2   Where a lease has been carefully drafted and expressly requires the landlord to take account of certain factors, again it is unlikely that it will be appropriate to add to this list and require a further reasonableness requirement.

3   In other cases, the factual background to the lease in question might well

---

158   [1993] 2 EGLR 73.
159   See further, Chapter 11 below.
160   Although see **28-05**ff. below for examples of cases where leases granted for residential purposes were held not to be leases 'of a dwelling' (e.g. holiday homes).

influence the question of whether a reasonableness criterion will be implied (as in *Finchbourne*).

4   In circumstances where the lease confers a discretion on the landlord, for example as to whether to add to or vary the services[161] or to vary the proportions of service charge payable,[162] the landlord's discretion must not be exercised capriciously or arbitrarily, but the court or tribunal will not substitute its view as to what a reasonable decision would have been. Likewise, where the decision-making power is placed in the hands of a third party.[163]

5   Where a lease does not contain a variable service charge but rather requires the tenant to pay a fixed sum towards the cost of services, the question of reasonableness will not arise.

2-117   As well as considering whether or not a term should be implied, it may be appropriate to consider the nature of the term to be implied. In *Mahon v Sims*,[164] a restrictive covenant case which considered whether a term should be implied into a transfer to the effect that the covenantee could not unreasonably refuse consent to a proposed development, Hart J referred to 'a possible hierarchy of implied terms ranging from: (i) an obligation to use the power in good faith; through (ii) an obligation not to use the power arbitrarily or capriciously; to (iii) an obligation not to use the power unreasonably.' It can be seen from the insurance cases discussed above that it may in some circumstances be easier to argue for an implied term which obliges a landlord to act in good faith rather than a term which requires him to be reasonable.

2-118   Where a reasonableness requirement has been implied, this is not the same requirement as the statutory term imposed by section 19. As has been explained at **2-86** above, section 19 requires that costs are to have been reasonably incurred and this is a two-stage test which expressly considers whether the amount charged was reasonable. A reasonableness requirement imposed as an implied term in fact concentrates more on the conduct of the landlord and not on the actual quantum of the costs incurred. Further, there is no requirement that the standard of work/services must be reasonable. The above cases do not seek to imply any reasonableness in relation to the amount charged by the landlord, as distinct from the question whether it was reasonable for the landlord to act in a particular way or incur a particular expense. In many cases, it will follow from the fact that the landlord is required to act reasonably in relation to his choice of work, or his selection of services, that the actual costs passed on to the tenant will be lower. However, there is not necessarily a direct link between reasonableness and the cost which is passed on to the tenant.

2-119   For example, in *Havenridge*, some limit was placed on the landlord in that his premium must have been 'properly' paid and the insurance transaction

161 See **3-04** below.
162 See Chapter 21 below.
163 See Chapter 17 below.
164 [2005] 3 EGLR 67.

was one which was arranged in the normal course of business. But the landlord was not obliged to find the cheapest premium nor was he under a duty to shop around for the cheapest quote. *Finchbourne Ltd v Rodrigues* was not concerned with the quantum which the tenant was being asked to pay but the expenditure to be incurred by the landlord. The landlord had to be reasonable in relation to the standard of services provided. Similarly, in *Plough Investments Ltd v Manchester City Council* (and the other cases cited above), the landlord was under no obligation to select the cheapest method of repair and the issue addressed by the landlord concentrated on the landlords' process of selecting works, not to the question of whether those works were carried out to a reasonable standard or as to the bottom figure which the tenant would be required to pay.

2-120   Although in *Morgan v Stainer*[165] the Deputy Judge referred to quantum, he had earlier referred to *Holding & Management Ltd v Property Holding & Investment Trust plc*,[166] where management trustees had sought to recover costs from the tenants pursuant to a provision in the lease which provided that the maintenance fund could be applied to make provision for the payment of all legal costs incurred by the maintenance trustee. Nicholls LJ held that:

> 'Read fairly, this paragraph embraces legal costs *reasonably* or *properly* incurred by the plaintiff in the enforcement of covenants.'

2-121   The reference to sums claimed being fair and reasonable 'not only with regard to their *quantum* but also with regard to their nature' accordingly arose in relation to the question of the reasonableness of the landlord's actions in incurring the expenditure, rather than a requirement imposing reasonableness requirement as to the amount charged by the landlord because of the nature of costs.[167]

No implied obligation to provide services

2-122   Where the lease makes no provision for either party to carry out repairs or for the landlord to perform services and the landlord refuses to carry out works or perform services which are required, the question may arise as to the extent to which the court will imply an obligation on the landlord.

2-123   As explained above, no term will be implied into a document where this would contradict an express term.[168] Where the parties have made express provision for something to be done in a particular way, a court will not suppose that they intended to do it in another way. This is why, in most cases, no implied obligation to repair or provide services will be implied into a lease. Where the lease provides a mechanism for the allocation of repair between the landlord and tenant, there will be minimal or no scope to imply further terms.

165   See **2-114** above.
166   [1989] 1 WLR 1313.
167   *Morgan v Stainer* [1993] 2 EGLR 73, *per* David Neuberger QC.
168   See the five conditions expressed by Lord Simon of Glaisdale in *BP Refinery (Westernport) Pty Ltd v Shire of Hastings* (1978) 52 ALJR 20, PC (at **2-93** above).

2-124 For example, in *Duke of Westminster v Guild*,[169] the demised premises were served by a drain which was erected partly on the landlord's adjoining land and partly on the demised premises. Works were necessary to repair the drain. The lease provided for the tenant to repair the demised premises and included a covenant whereby the tenant covenanted to pay a fair proportion of the cost of repairing a number of specific items, including drains, belonging to or used by the demised premises jointly with adjoining occupiers. The landlord had no express obligation to repair the drain and it was argued, amongst other things, that such an obligation ought to be implied. When considering whether to imply such a provision on the part of the landlord, the court approached the question by considering the presumed intention of the parties. In doing this, it considered that there were too many factors which pointed against such an implied term, not least the fact that:

'clause 2 of the lease contains a number of careful and elaborate provisions defining the tenant's contractual obligations in regard to repair and maintenance. If it had been intended that other contractual obligations relating to repair should be placed on the landlords themselves, one would prima facie have expected this particular lease to say so.'[170]

2-125 The more comprehensive a code in a lease, the less scope there is for the implication of a term. In *Hafton Properties Ltd v Camp*,[171] the Official Referee said:

'Where it is sought to raise an implied term one matter to which the court should have regard is whether the lease provides a comprehensive code for the carrying out of repair and the payment of them. The more comprehensive the code the less room there is for the implication of a term.'[172]

2-126 In *Gordon v Selico Co Ltd*,[173] Slade LJ said:[174]

'Where a written tenancy agreement relating to a flat, forming part of a larger building in multiple occupation, manifestly does not embody the complete agreement between the parties the court may well be willing to supplement the written document by implying terms placing obligations on one party or the other. Such a case was *Liverpool City Council v Irwin* … The repair and maintenance

---

169 [1985] QB 688.
170 *Per* Slade LJ at pp 699–700.
171 [1994] 1 EGLR 67 at p 70.
172 See also *Adami v Lincoln Grange Management Limited* (1998) 30 HLR 982, where Sir John Vinelott said: 'In my judgment the contention that it was an implied term of the lease that the lessor would be liable to make good any damage to the structure of the block whatever might be the cause of the damage, is simply untenable. The lease contains an elaborate scheme under which exceptional damage to the structure is to be covered by insurance effected in the joint names of the lessor and the lessee and maintained at the expense of the lessee … Insofar as damage to the structure results from an insured risk, there is simply no ground for importing any implied obligation to do more than lay out any insurance moneys coming into the hands of the lessor in making good that damage.'
173 [1986] 1 EGLR 71.
174 Giving the judgment of the court.

scheme provided by this lease is a very cumbersome one and we agree with the
learned judge that, even if the lessors and their agents were duly to carry out their
obligations, the scheme might not always suffice to give the lessees necessary and
timely protection. ... Nevertheless, ... we feel little doubt that it was intended, by
all parties, to provide a comprehensive code in regard to repair and maintenance
of the block. We are by no means satisfied that the implication of any further
terms in this respect is necessary to give the lease business efficacy, or that the
lessor, assuming it to have been a reasonable person, would have "agreed without
hesitation" to the insertion of the suggested implied additional terms relating to the
repair and maintenance of the block.'

2-127   Thus, in general, a court will be reluctant to imply a repairing obligation
on a party to a lease, where the lease contains express provisions which rule out
the inference of any further implied term. Even where no express terms have
been provided, the correct inference may be that no liability for repair arises. In
Demetriou v Robert Andrews (Estate Agencies) Ltd,[175] Stuart-Smith LJ said:

'it is a phenomenon, certainly known at common law, that there may be situations
in which there is no repairing obligation imposed either expressly or impliedly on
anyone in relation to a lease.'[176]

2-128   Implied obligations relating to repair may be implied as an incident of
the relationship of landlord and tenant (e.g. *Liverpool City Council v Irwin*[177]),
although this will be rare; they may be implied by statute (e.g. section 11 of the
Landlord and Tenant Act 1985) and they may be implied into certain types of
letting (e.g. furnished lettings where it is often an implied condition of the letting
that it is fit for human habitation at the time when it is let). However, in general,
it has not been regarded as necessary to give business efficacy to a lease that the
landlord should be obliged to keep the premises in repair.[178] The same can be said
about the provision of other services.

2-129   Where, however, there is no obligation on the part of a landlord to
carry out repairs or perform services, but the tenant has a covenant to contribute
towards costs incurred by the landlord in doing so, there may be greater scope for
the implication of a term on the basis of an implied correlative obligation to the
express obligation. In *Hafton Properties Ltd v Camp,*[179] it was said:

'An obligation placed upon the tenant may require the imposition of a correlative
or corresponding obligation on the landlord. If it can be shown that a landlord

175 (1991) 62 P&CR 536, [1991] 1 EGLR 100 at p 104.
176 See also *Lee v Leeds City Council, Ratcliffe v Sandwell Metropolitan Borough Council* [2002]
EWCA Civ 6, [2002] 1 WLR 1488 at para 64. Section 35 of the 1987 Act gives right to vary
lease where it fails to make satisfactory provision for repair.
177 [1977] AC 239.
178 See *Duke of Westminster v Guild* [1985] QB 688 (**2-124** above) and *Tennant Radiant Heat Ltd
v Warrington Development Corporation* [1988] 1 EGLR 41 at 43, *per* Dillon LJ: 'It may well
be objectively sensible, or reasonable, that there should be such a landlord's covenant, with a
corresponding covenant by each lessee to contribute a proportionate part of the expense, but
that is not enough to warrant implying such covenants.'
179 [1994] 1 EGLR 67, *per* Fox-Andrews QC at p 70.

is taking the benefit of a covenant he may be under an obligation to accept a corresponding burden. If a lease is silent as to an obligation which necessarily falls on either the landlord or the tenant this may give rise to an implication that the obligation is that of the landlord on the one hand or of the tenant on the other'.

2-130 In *Barnes v City of London Real Property Co*,[180] the landlords had let various sets of rooms and, by the tenancy agreement, had imposed on the tenants the obligation to pay a stated additional rent specifically for the cleaning of rooms by a housekeeper to be provided for the purpose. The agreements placed no express obligation on the landlords to provide for the cleaning of the rooms, but Sargant J said (*obiter*) that such an obligation should be implied.[181]

2-131 In *Edmonton Corporation v WM Knowles & Son Ltd*,[182] a lease obliged the tenant to pay to the landlords 'the cost ... of painting ... in a workmanlike manner every third year of the term all outside wood and metal work and other external parts of the demised premises'. McNair J[183] held there was to be implied a matching obligation on the landlords to do the repairs.[184]

2-132 Commenting on these cases in *Duke of Westminster v Guild*,[185] Slade LJ held that the correct approach was to ascertain the presumed intention of the parties. He said:

> 'We do not question the correctness of these two decisions on their particular facts, or doubt that in some instances it will be proper for the court to imply an obligation against a landlord, on whom an obligation is not in terms imposed by the relevant lease, to match a correlative obligation thereby expressly imposed on the other party. Nevertheless we think that only rather limited assistance is to be derived from these earlier cases where obligations have been implied.

> The general rule is in our judgment correctly stated in *Woodfall, Landlord and Tenant,* 28th ed (1978), vol. 1, para. 1-1465, p. 618:

>> "In general, there is no implied covenant by the lessor of an *unfurnished* house or flat, or of land, that it is or shall be reasonably fit for habitation, occupation or cultivation, or for any other purpose for which it is let. No covenant is implied that the lessor will do any repairs whatever ..."

> On occasions special facts may no doubt justify a departure from the general rule. However, the decision of the Court of Appeal in *Sleafer v Lambeth Borough*

180 [1918] 2 Ch 18.
181 See pp 32 and 33.
182 (1961) 60 LGR 124.
183 At p 127.
184 See also *Barrett v Lounova* [1988] 2 EGLR 54, where the tenant had a monthly tenancy and had covenanted to carry out all internal repairs. The court found an implied obligation on the landlord to keep the exterior in repair on the basis that the tenant's obligation could only be complied with if the outside was in repair. In *Adami v Lincoln Grange Management Ltd* (1998) 30 HLR 982, Sir John Vinelott noted that the Court of Appeal was bound by this decision but said: 'However, in my judgment it must be taken as decided upon the special facts of that case and no principle can be discerned which requires the implication of an obligation on the part of the lessor to keep the structure of the block in good repair.'
185 [1985] QB 688.

Council[186] well illustrates that, though the provisions of a lease may indicate the parties' contemplation that in fact and in practice the landlord will do repairs, and indeed may confer express rights on him to enter the demised premises for this purpose, it does not follow that any contractual obligation to do the repairs is to be implied against him: see, for example, pp. 56–57, *per* Morris L.J.'

2-133   The ordinary principles applicable to the implication of terms must not be forgotten and it does not follow from the fact that a landlord is entitled to recover the costs of a particular item that he is automatically under a correlative obligation to provide the service. In *Russell v Laimond Properties Ltd*,[187] an issue arose as to whether the landlord was obliged to provide residential porterage services. The lease contained a provision obliging the landlord to:

'provide and use its best endeavours to maintain the services of such maintenance staff as the company shall consider necessary for the performance of the matters specified in the seventh schedule hereto.'

2-134   The seventh schedule included the costs of providing porterage services and maintenance staff and maintaining telephone services in the entrance halls, including the costs of providing, maintaining and repairing a flat or other suitable residence or residences for such staff as may be, from time to time, employed within the premises. The court concluded that the landlord could discharge its obligation by providing either a resident or a non-resident porter and the fact that the lease entitled the landlord to provide residential porterage did not require the landlord to do so.

2-135   Where a lease contains a provision whereby the tenant covenants to pay for services, there will be a basis to infer a correlative obligation but it will not always be the case that the landlord is obliged to do the work. If the tenant is obliged to pay a fixed regular sum, it is likely that a correlative obligation will be found (it would otherwise be unfair if the landlord could recover a sum of money and not provide the service). However, where there is simply an obligation to pay if work or a particular service is performed, it will be much harder to justify an implied corresponding obligation to provide the service.

2-136   Where it is necessary to imply a correlative obligation because the express obligation on one party cannot be performed without such a correlative obligation being implied, as a general rule such a provision will be implied (e.g. *Barrett v Lounova*[188]). In *Churchward v R*,[189] Cockburn CJ said:

'yet there are occasions on which you must imply – although the contract may be silent – corresponding and correlative obligations on the part of the other party in whose favour alone the contract may appear to be drawn up. Where the act done by the party binding himself can only be done upon something of a corresponding

186   [1960] 1 QB 43.
187   [1984] 1 EGLR 37.
188   [1988] 2 EGLR 54.
189   [1865] LR 1 QB 173.

character being done by the opposite party, you would there imply a corresponding obligation to do the things necessary for the completion of the contract.'

2-137   In *Credit Suisse v Beegas Nominees Ltd*,[190] referring to *Barrett v Lounova*, Lindsay J said:

'Barrett might assist a court in coming to a business-like conclusion and in filling a gap where the language of a lease can fairly be construed either to leave a gap or to fill it but it cannot be authority for a proposition that whenever one encounters what seems to be an unbusiness-like gap then the court is able or obliged to fill it.'

2-138   Just as there may be no implied obligation on a landlord to provide a particular service, there may be no implied obligation on the tenant to pay.[191] *Bratton Seymour Service Co Ltd v Oxborough*[192] concerned a residential development which had been subdivided into units and conveyed freehold. The vendor covenanted to maintain various common parts and the purchaser covenanted to pay a percentage towards the costs of maintaining such parts. It was envisaged that a management company would be set up which would hold the common parts, the members of which would be the residents of the various units within the estate. The claimant was the management company. The company argued that in order to give business efficacy to the scheme which the promoters of the company had in mind, it was necessary to imply into the articles of association an obligation to contribute a reasonable sum, determined by the company, towards the cost of maintenance of the utility and amenity areas of the Bratton House development. The fact that the defendant was a member of the claimant company could not be used to imply a term into the company's particulars of association, which obliged him to make a contribution towards the cost of maintenance of the utility and amenity areas of the Bratton House development.

---

190   (1995) 69 P&CR 177.
191   See **2-38**ff. above as to the general principle that clear terms are required to enable a landlord to recover the costs of a particular service and the absence of a presumption that a landlord is entitled to recover the full cost of his expenditure.
192   [1992] BCC 471.

PART II

Services

CHAPTER 3

The Services: Overview

3-01   This section considers the specific items for which a service charge might be payable. Generally, this will be the starting point in any service charge dispute. The landlord must always ensure that the head of cost which is being charged to his tenants falls within the ambit of the tenant's service charge covenant.[1] Typical heads of service charge are the following:

1   Repairing/maintaining/renewing those parts of the building not demised.[2]

2   Heating and lighting the building/common parts.[3]

3   Cleaning and refuse collection.[4]

4   Compliance with legislation.[5]

5   The costs of management and employing managing agents.[6]

6   Employing caretakers/porters/other staff.[7]

7   Insurance.[8]

8   Legal costs incurred in managing the estate/building.[9]

9   The cost of borrowing to fund the management of the estate/building.[10]

10   Promotion and advertising costs.[11]

---

1   See Chapter 2 above in relation to the construction of service charge provisions.
2   See Chapter 4 below.
3   Chapter 5.
4   Chapter 6.
5   Chapter 7.
6   Chapter 8.
7   Chapter 9.
8   Chapter 10.
9   Chapter 11.
10   Chapter 12.
11   Chapter 13.

11   Setting aside funds in a reserve or sinking fund for irregular items of capital expenditure and/or regular or routine items of maintenance.[12]

3-02

These categories are used for analytical purposes only. There may well be overlap between them. For example, management fees might be recoverable in connection with a particular scheme of work which the landlord has undertaken, but it is only if the cost of that scheme of work is recoverable as service charges that the management fees associated with carrying out those works will be payable by the tenants.[13]

3-03   In addition to the specific 'services' usually listed in a properly drafted lease, there will almost invariably be a 'catch-all' provision[14] intended to cover types of 'service' which do not fall within one of the specific heads listed. Such 'catch-all' or 'sweeping-up' clauses are dealt with in Chapter 2 above.

3-04   It is not uncommon for leases to give the landlord the power to add to or vary the services for which a service charge is payable. Such provision will usually be framed in such a way as to confer a discretion on the landlord with regard to withdrawing and/or adding to services to be provided, for which he will then be entitled to recover the costs from the tenants as service charges. Where the landlord exercises such a discretion, the scope for the tenants to challenge it is limited because, necessarily, the decision-making power is conferred on the landlord rather than on some third party. However, such provisions will be construed strictly[15] and it will be necessary for the landlord to comply with any conditions precedent to the exercise of such discretion, e.g. giving notice to all tenants, consulting with the tenants (where such consultation is required by the terms of the lease).

3-05   Once the landlord has exercised such a discretion, the court (or tribunal) will only intervene in very limited circumstances. In *Unique Pub Properties Ltd v Broad Green Tavern Ltd*,[16] Warren J considered a number of authorities relating to the circumstances in which a court will intervene in the decision-making process. He summarised the position as follows:

> 'What I conclude from those authorities is this principle, namely that a contractual discretion must be exercised honestly and in good faith and must not be exercised arbitrarily, capriciously or unreasonably, unreasonableness being assessed in the sense that no reasonable person would exercise the discretion in the manner proposed. Sometimes the courts appear to approach these restrictions by way of implication. In others, they appear to approach the matter of one of construction. It

---

12   This is covered in Part III, Chapter 22 below.
13   See Chapter 8 below in relation to management charges, generally.
14   Often described as a 'sweeping-up' clause.
15   As to construction of service charges generally, see Chapter 2 above.
16   [2012] EWHC 2154 (Ch).

does not matter which approach is more accurate, especially as the implication is, in any case, a facet of construction as explained by Lord Hoffmann.'[17]

3-06   Therefore, the landlord must exercise a discretion to vary the services to be provided in the best interests of estate management rather than for personal gain and the decision must be one which is within the range of decisions which a reasonable landlord in that position would make. In the residential context, the courts are perhaps more likely to intervene to set aside a decision to withdraw or add to services to be provided by a landlord where the decision is not in the best interests of the estate as a whole. However, the above principles apply equally to commercial leases and, therefore, landlords should be astute to ensure that their decision-making process is open and fair and that the tenants are kept informed (even if this is not required by the terms of the lease), so that the scope for later challenge is reduced.

3-07   In addition to contractual rights to vary the services provided, the landlord can negotiate variations to the leases with all of the tenants. However, where a system of service charges is in place, all tenants must agree to a proposed variation in the services, otherwise it will not be possible to implement the variation across the board, so that consensual variations become more problematic the larger the estate. Alternatively, in the residential context, Part IV of the Landlord and Tenant Act 1987 gives the LVT power to vary long leases of dwellings in certain circumstances in relation to the provision of services and the computation of service charges.[18]

---

17 Referring to the speech of Lord Hoffmann in *Attorney General of Belize v Belize Telecom Ltd* [2009] UKPC 10 (see **2-92** above).
18 See Chapter 24 below.

CHAPTER 4

Maintenance and repairs

4-01   This category of service charge often proves to be the most contentious, for a number of reasons. First, it sometimes involves large sums. Secondly, charges in relation to this head of services sometimes involve one-off costs of a 'capital' as opposed to a 'revenue' nature.[1] Thirdly, the question of whether the tenant is liable for particular charges in this category can give rise to numerous and overlapping thorny issues which stray into the related field of dilapidations.

4-02   There are three broad questions which will usually have to be considered in determining whether tenants are liable to contribute towards particular maintenance or capital costs:

1   Is the tenant obliged to contribute towards the cost of remedying the particular problem which has arisen? This turns, principally, on the terms of the service charge obligation.

2   If the tenant is liable to contribute towards the cost of remedying the problem, is the landlord entitled to charge for the remedial work which he has chosen to carry out? This will often require expert evidence as to the different ways of addressing the problem.

3   Is it reasonable for the landlord to claim, as service charges, the cost of work which is being undertaken and is the cost of that work reasonable?

4-03   It will be readily apparent that there is some degree of overlap between these three categories (especially 2 and 3). The question of whether a landlord is entitled to charge for a particular type of work (e.g. replacing a roof, rather than patch repairs) is likely to be informed by the reasonableness of the landlord's decision to carry out the relevant work. Moreover, in many cases, the distinctions between these questions becomes particularly blurred or confused and that makes analysing reported cases on this head of service charges far from straightforward.

---

1   Such larger, capital items might not fall so easily within the scope of the service charge obligations and might well attract more scrutiny under the Landlord and Tenant Act 1985, s 19. See also *Lloyds Bank Plc v Bowker Orford* [1992] 2 EGLR 44 at p 46G–H for the view that the difference between capital and revenue items, which is well known to revenue law, should not be applied slavishly to the interpretation of service charge provisions in leases.

IS THE WORK WITHIN THE SCOPE OF THE SERVICE CHARGE OBLIGATION?

4-04 The question here is no different to the question which arises when a repairing covenant is construed to determine whether a particular scheme of works to remedy a defect falls within the scope of a covenant. Reference is made to *Woodfall: Landlord and Tenant*[2] and more specialist works on dilapidations.[3] What follows is a brief outline of the principles which apply.

The subject matter of the obligation

4-05 First, one must ask whether the particular part of the building on which the landlord intends to incur expenditure is within the subject matter of the repairing or other obligation. A well-drawn service charge scheme will ensure that all parts of the building which are not demised, or which the tenants are not liable to keep in repair, are subject to a service charge obligation, so that any maintenance or repair works needed can be charged to the tenants.[4] Sometimes, however, there will be ambiguities.[5] In *Rapid Results College Ltd v Angell*,[6] the demised premises consisted of second-floor offices in a three-storey building. The landlord covenanted to repair 'the external walls and structure and in particular the roof … of the building'. The tenant covenanted to contribute towards the cost of the maintenance of the exterior, by reference to the offices on the first and second floors. The question which arose was whether the tenant was obliged to contribute towards the cost of replacing a parapet wall on the flat roof of the building. The Court of Appeal held that 'the exterior' here meant the exterior of the first and second floor offices only.

4-06 It might also be relevant to consider whether the service charge obligation extends to additions to the buildings or to other premises which are subject to the service charge liability. Again, ultimately, this will be a question of construction of the relevant leases. This issue might arise in a whole host of scenarios. For example, additional buildings might be constructed in the grounds: a car port, garage facilities, storage facilities, which are used in common by some or all tenants, either with or without the landlord.[7] It is likely that comprehensively drafted provisions will extend to such additions. Equally, the building in which

---

2 Volume 1, Ch 13.

3 Such as Dowding & Reynolds, *Dilapidations, The Modern Law and Practice* (4th edn, 2010).

4 For a not so well-drafted provision, see *Billson v Tristrem* [2000] L&TR 220. See also *Hallisey v Petmoor Developments Ltd* [2000] EGCS 14, where Patten J held that a roof terrace was included in the landlord's repairing covenants and the service charge obligations because to hold otherwise would mean that the landlord had intended to cede control of a small part of the exterior fabric of the building to one of the tenants who may or may not comply with his obligations, a conclusion which was considered to be 'an unlikely scenario'. See also *Ibrahim v Dovecorn Reversions Ltd* [2001] 2 EGLR 46 and **4-40** below.

5 See **2-127**ff. above as to implied obligations to repair.

6 [1986] 1 EGLR 53.

7 See the comments of Nicholls LJ in *Holding & Management Ltd v Property Holding & Investment Trust Plc* [1989] 1 WLR 1313.

Maintenance and repairs **4-08**

the demised premises themselves are located might be extended (e.g. by the landlord constructing additional units in the roof space) and it will be a question of construction as to whether, and if so to what extent, the tenants' service charge obligations extend to such construction.[8] This issue might, however, be resolved by varying the proportions of the total expenditure payable by the individual tenants.[9]

Whether the subject matter is in a condition which requires the landlord to carry out remedial work to it

4-07   In short, where the service charge is payable in relation to 'repairs', if the subject-matter of the service charge obligation is not damaged or has not deteriorated from its original condition, there can be no disrepair. This principle is seen at its most stark in the decision of the Court of Appeal in *Quick v Taff-Ely BC*.[10] The landlords covenanted to keep in repair the structure and exterior of the house. The house in question suffered from severe condensation, such that it was described, at times, to be unfit for habitation. However, there was no damage as such to the metal windows or the lintels, which were in more or less the same condition as when the house was built. It was held that the landlord was not liable to replace the window frames with a more appropriate material (e.g. wood or uPVC) because they were not in a state of disrepair. Similarly, in *Post Office v Aquarius Properties Ltd*,[11] the tenant of an office building covenanted to keep it in repair. The basement became ankle-deep with water as a result of the defective 'kicker' joints installed between the walls and floor. However, since the joints were in the same condition as when constructed, there was no disrepair to remedy.

What needs to be done to remedy the defective condition?

4-08   Where there are various ways of remedying a defect, the usual rule is that the covenanting party must adopt such method of repair as the reasonable

---

8   See, for example *Hannon v 169 Queen's Gate Ltd* [2000] 1 EGLR 40, where the question for the court was whether a freeholder and landlord of a block of flats was entitled to construct additional flats in the airspace above the roof of the existing block. It was held (distinguishing *Devonshire Reid Properties Ltd v Trenaman* [1997] 1 EGLR 45) that the landlord was not pre-cluded from building additional units. One of the arguments in support of a construction of the lease which prevented the landlord from constructing the additional units was that the building work would result in additional service charge expenditure by the lessees. However, this point was not specifically addressed by the Deputy Judge.

9   In *Hannon*, the tenant's proportion was a 'fair and reasonable proportion' and therefore the leases themselves had sufficient machinery to effect this variation. If the proportions are fixed, it might be necessary to rely on the Landlord and Tenant Act 1987, Pt IV to vary the leases: see Chapter 24 below. If the lease is of commercial property, this will not apply and the fixed proportions payable by each of the tenants towards the service charges might be a factor which leads to a construction of the leases which prevents the landlord from adding to the existing building in a way which will materially increase the service charge burden with no obvious way of sharing the cost.

10   [1986] QB 809.

11   [1987] 1 All ER 1055.

surveyor would advise as being appropriate in all the circumstances.[12] Where the choice is between patch repair and replacement, the covenanting party will only be liable to replace it if patch repair is no longer considered a reasonable means of dealing with the problem.[13] However, this principle is modified where, as in most service-charge situations, the covenanting party is not the paying party.[14]

4-09   As explained by Scott J in *Plough Investments Ltd v Manchester City Council*,[15] in a service charge context, the landlord's repairing obligation is also, in one sense, a right. It entitles the landlord to carry out work which will protect his reversion at the tenants' expense. One area which a landlord might stray into is the rather fine line between remedial work and preventative work. Where a landlord carries out work which is required to remedy a deterioration in the condition of the subject matter, i.e. work in the nature of repair, the fact that the work includes measures to prevent future deterioration will not mean that the work ceases to be repair.[16] Conversely, however, it is unlikely that a standard covenant which requires the subject matter to be kept in repair would entitle a landlord to carry out purely preventative work where the subject matter is not in a state of disrepair.[17]

4-10   Often, a landlord's covenant includes verbs other than repair, which appear to go further than repair, such as 'renew' or 'rebuild'. This generally means that the remedial work required to remedy the deteriorated condition might go further than repair, strictly so called.[18] Nevertheless, it remains necessary for the landlord to show that there has been a deterioration or that the item in question is in disrepair.

4-11   Whilst a covenant to keep the subject matter in repair requires a deterioration in the subject matter from its original condition, a covenant to

---

12 See *Gibson Investments Ltd v Chesterton Plc* [2002] EWHC 19 (Ch), *per* Neuberger J.
13 *Riverside Property Investments Ltd v Blackhawk Automotive* [2004] EWHC 3052 (TCC). See also *Scottish Mutual Assurance Plc v Jardine Public Relations Ltd* [1999] EGCS 43.
14 See **4-21**ff. below.
15 [1989] 1 EGLR 244.
16 See *Holding & Management Ltd v Property Holding & Investment Trust Plc* [1989] 1 WLR 1313 and *Postel Properties Ltd v Boots the Chemist* [1996] 2 EGLR 60, where the landlord decided to replace the roof of a shopping centre on the advice of its surveyors, in phases. The landlord's surveyor had decided that a phased replacement was more economic than continuing with patch repairs. The landlord was entitled to look to the future and given that the life expectancy of the roof was no more than around five years, it was held that the landlord was entitled to implement a phased replacement. See also *Carmel Southend Ltd v Strachan & Henshaw Ltd* [2007] EWHC 1289 (TCC).
17 *Mason v TotalFinaElf UK Ltd* [2003] 3 EGLR 91. Blackburne J commented that merely because a piece of equipment is old and there must come a time when it will need to be replaced, preventative works can be required to prevent the consequences of the equipment failing even though, in the meantime, it continues to perform its function.
18 *Norwich Union Life Assurance Co Ltd v British Railways Board* [1987] 2 EGLR 137; *New England Properties Ltd v Portsmouth New Shops Ltd* [1993] 1 EGLR 94; *Gibson Investments Ltd v Chesterton Plc* [2002] 2 P&CR 494.

keep in good (or some other, e.g. tenantable) condition is arguably of a different nature. In *Credit Suisse v Beegas Nominees Ltd*,[19] Lindsay J said:

> 'whilst I accept the inevitability of the conclusion of the Court of Appeal in *Aquarius* that one cannot have an existing obligation to repair unless and until there is a disrepair, that reasoning does not apply to a covenant to keep (and put) into good and tenantable condition. One cannot sensibly proceed from "No disrepair, ergo no need to repair" to "no disrepair, ergo no need to put or keep in the required condition" ... all that is needed, in general terms, to trigger a need for activity under an obligation to keep in (and put into) a given condition is that the subject matter is out of that condition.'

4-12   In practice, however, it is difficult to see how an obligation to keep in good condition can require (or entitle[20]) a landlord to carry out work where the subject matter is not in a deteriorated condition such that some sort of repair work is required.[21] The contrary view was expressed in *Fluor Daniel Properties Ltd v Shortlands Investments Ltd*,[22] where Blackburne J considered that such an obligation extends beyond works that might fall within the scope of repairs, strictly so called, but considered that the obligation presupposes that the item in question suffers from some defect (i.e. some physical damage or deterioration, or, in the case of plant or machinery, some malfunctioning) such that repair, amendment or renewal is reasonably necessary.[23]

4-13   It will only be in rather exceptional circumstances that work will fall within the landlord's covenant to keep an item in good condition where that item has not suffered from some sort of deterioration, or malfunction. Moreover, where the landlord has the right to recoup the cost of the work as service charges, and that right is subject to the charges having been reasonably incurred, the criterion of reasonableness may well provide an additional barrier to the landlord's attempt to require the lessees to pay for an improvement in the subject matter of the covenant where it was not previously damaged.

4-14   At one time, it was considered that there was a doctrine of 'inherent defect', according to which a want of repair which arises because of an inherent

---

19 [1994] 1 EGLR 76.
20 See **4-09** above.
21 See Dowding & Reynolds, *Dilapidations: The Modern Law and Practice* (4th edn, 2010) at para 8-12 where it is noted that in *Credit Suisse v Beegas Nominees* [1994] 1 EGLR 76, Lindsay J purported to require that in order to engage a covenant to keep in good condition, all that is required is that the condition of the premises should fall short of what would reasonably be required by the reasonably minded tenant, the covenant will be broken even where there is no damage or deterioration in the subject matter. However, he then went on to find that on the facts, there had, in fact, been a deterioration in the subject matter and therefore, strictly, the judge's comments on this issue were *obiter*.
22 [2001] 2 EGLR 103.
23 In *Alker v Collingwood Housing Association* [2007] EWCA Civ 343, it was held that a landlord's covenant to keep a house in good condition did not require the landlord to put the front door of the house into a safe condition by replacing a glass panel with toughened glass where the glass panel was not in disrepair and there had been no failure to maintain it.

defect or design fault will not be subject to the covenant to repair.[24] However, in *Ravenseft Properties Ltd v Davstone (Holdings) Ltd*,[25] Forbes J considered the relevant authorities and concluded that there exists no such doctrine. Rather, it is always a question of fact and degree whether the work in question is within a repairing covenant.[26]

4-15   Where a landlord has an obligation to keep the building in repair and a corresponding right to recover the cost from the tenants, the cost of carrying out those repairs will include the cost of obtaining advice as to the means of remedying the defects.[27] This is to be distinguished from the cost of obtaining advice as to the condition of the building generally (which will only be recoverable if there is a specific right to recover such costs) and advice as to the method to be adopted of repairing a defect which exists and which falls within the scope of the repairing covenant.[28] Where a large scheme of works is involved, this element of the 'preliminary costs' could involve extensive surveys and reports from structural engineers and other relevant construction professionals.

4-16   The RICS Residential Code provides[29] that managers of residential property should notify tenants of how and to whom repairs should be reported and should have an established procedure for dealing with urgent repair work. It goes on to make the following suggestions with regard to the management of residential property:

1   Repairs should be arranged to be undertaken to completion in a reasonable time and, if necessary, to a pre-agreed programme.

2   Repair work should be cost-effective taking into account its durability and expense.

3   Proposals should be made to the tenants for a cyclical maintenance regime which should reflect a realistic cost of maintenance, including periodic redecoration work.

4   Consideration should be given to the use of experienced or qualified building consultants/specialists, having regard to the size and complexity of the project.

---

24 The doctrine originated in a statement of Lord Esher MR in *Lister v Lane* [1893] 2 QB 212: 'If a tenant takes a house which is of such a kind that by its own inherent nature it will in the course of time fall into a particular condition, the effects of that result are not within the tenant's covenant to repair.'
25 [1980] QB 12.
26 This has since been approved in a number of Court of Appeal decisions: *Quick v Taff Ely BC* [1986] QB 809; *Post Office v Aquarius Properties Ltd* [1987] 1 All ER 1055; *McDougall v Easington District Council* (1989) 58 P&CR 201. For the 'fact and degree' test, see generally Dowding & Reynolds, *Dilapidations: The Modern Law and Practice* (4th edn, 2010) at para 11-04ff and *Brew Brothers Ltd v Snax (Ross) Ltd* [1970] 1 QB 612.
27 See *Plough Investments Ltd v Manchester City Council* [1989] 1 EGLR 244 at p 249M.
28 See the RICS Service Charge Residential Management Code, para 13.12 with regard to the need for residential property managers to obtain specialist advice wherever necessary.
29 In Pt 13.

THE CHOICE BETWEEN ALTERNATIVE METHODS

4-17   Frequently (although not exclusively), service charges are drafted in a way which produces bilateral rights and obligations. On the one hand, the landlord covenants to keep parts of the building which are used in common by different tenants or occupants in a particular state of repair and condition. On the other hand, the tenants covenant to reimburse the landlord's costs. This can produce a tension between the usual rule, whereby the covenanting party is entitled to choose what work it intends to carry out to comply with its obligations, and the fact that ultimately, it is not the covenanting party (the landlord) who will be paying for the work.

4-18   This issue arose in *Plough Investments Ltd v Manchester City Council*.[30] The claimant landlords of an office building brought claims for various declarations relating to their proposals to remedy defects to the steel frame of the building. One of the issues which arose was whether the landlords, who had a choice between two methods of remedying the rusting of the external steel frame, were entitled to carry out the more expensive of the two methods and recover the cost from the tenants. Scott J said:

> 'The landlord's fifth schedule repairing obligation is, although nominally an obligation, in a sense also a right. If it were simply an obligation, then, presumably, the three tenants of the building could choose to release the landlord, in whole or in part, from that obligation. But the provision is not, in my view, simply, or even mainly, for the benefit of the tenants. It is also a provision for the benefit of the landlord. It enables the landlord to keep its building in repair at the tenants' expense. If the repairing obligation had been imposed on the tenant, the tenant would have been entitled to decide on the manner in which it would be discharged. Provided remedial works were sufficient to discharge the obligation, the landlord could not require a different type of repair to be effected. Under these leases, however, the relevant decisions regarding repairs to the exterior are to be taken by the landlord. If reasonable remedial works are proposed by the landlord in order to remedy a state of disrepair for the purposes of its fifth schedule obligation, the tenants are not, in my judgment, entitled to insist that cheaper remedial works be undertaken.'

4-19   He went on to accept the landlord's submission that providing the proposed works of repair are such as an owner who had to bear the cost himself might reasonably decide upon and provided the works constituted 'repairs' within the meaning of the landlord's covenant, the tenant was not entitled to insist upon more limited works or cheaper works being preferred. The landlord was not limited to a 'minimum standard of repair'.[31]

4-20   This approach was distinguished in *Scottish Mutual Assurance Plc v Jardine Public Relations Ltd*,[32] where the lease was a short one (three years). In that context, the Deputy Judge said:

30   [1989] 1 EGLR 244.
31   See also *Credit Suisse v Beegas Nominees Ltd* [1994] 1 EGLR 76 at p 85F–H.
32   [1999] EG 43 (CS).

'In my judgment in the context of this short lease, the provisions relating to service charges were inter alia to enable the landlord to comply with his repairing obligations (partly) at the tenant's expense. Those obligations were to use his best endeavours to provide the services of inter alia *"maintaining and repairing etc. the structure of the building including the roofs"* during the short (i.e. three year) period of the term. In my judgment this lease does not entitle the landlord to charge to the tenant the cost of carrying out works suitable for the performance of his obligations over a period of twenty or more years when such works are not necessary for the fulfilment of those obligations over the actual period to which they relate.'

4-21   In *Fluor Daniel Properties Ltd v Shortlands Investments Ltd*,[33] it was submitted, on behalf of the tenant, that where the obligation is imposed on the landlord, but it is the tenant who has to pay for the works, the normal rule as between covenantor and covenantee (that the covenantor has the right to choose the mode of performance, providing the choice is a reasonable one[34]) does not apply. It was submitted that either *Plough Investments v Manchester City Council* did not decide the contrary, or that if it did, it was wrongly decided.

4-22   The submission (that the ordinary rule as to the choice of the mode of work is that of the landlord as covenanting party is reversed) was rejected. In this case (as in *Plough Investments*), the repairing obligation was equally for the benefit of the landlord, who also had an interest (separate from the interest of the tenants) in ensuring that the building is properly serviced, thereby helping to maintain the attractiveness of the building to tenants. On that basis, the principle is the same as applied by Scott J in *Plough Investments*, namely that it is for the landlord to decide what method of work is required to address the defects and, provided the landlord acts reasonably, the tenants cannot complain, even if the landlord could have adopted another cheaper method of work.

4-23   However, in *Fluor Daniel*, Blackburne J applied a different nuance to the ambit of the landlord's discretion in determining the work which can be carried out. He said:

'Where I agree with Mr Dowding is in his questioning of the standard of work that, acting reasonably, the landlord should be free to carry out at the tenants' expense. In the passage from his judgment referred to above, Scott J. accepted as the appropriate standard "proposed works of repair ... such as an owner who had to bear the cost himself might reasonably decide upon." In *Holding & Management*, Nicholls LJ, in rejecting a particular scheme of works as going beyond what was sensibly needed to cure certain physical defects in the leased premises said in that case at p.69A:

A prudent building owner bearing the costs himself might well have decided to adopt such a scheme, despite its expense. But what is in question is whether owners of 75-year leases in the building could fairly be expected to pay for such a scheme under an obligation to "repair".

---

33 [2001] 2 EGLR 103.
34 See **4-17** above.

In short, the works – ie the standard to be adopted – must be such as the tenants, given the length of their leases, could fairly be expected to pay for. The landlord cannot, because he has an interest in the matter overlook the limited interest of the tenants who are having to pay by carrying out works that are calculated to serve an interest extending beyond that of the tenants. If the landlord wished to carry out repairs that go beyond those for which the tenants, given their more limited interest, can be fairly expected to pay, then, subject always to the terms of the lease or leases, the landlord must bear the additional cost himself.'

4-24   The effect of the authorities discussed above is that the landlord does not have an unfettered choice between different schemes of work, each of which will address the problem. In particular, the landlord must have regard to the limited interest of the tenant and the duration of his lease. It is considered that this means the length of the term as originally granted rather than the unexpired term at the time when the issue arises.[35]

4-25   The duration of the lease will be relevant at each of the three stages in determining whether the tenants are liable to contribute towards the cost of a particular long-term scheme of works. However, this is simply one of a number of factors which will be taken into consideration and if clear words are used to impose a liability on a tenant to contribute to the cost of works of replacement or renewal, the court must give effect to those words. So, in *New England Properties v Portsmouth*,[36] the tenant covenanted to contribute to the costs incurred by the landlord in renewing and replacing the premises or any part of the premises, where necessary. The tenant argued that these words (which followed on from the general repairing obligation of the landlord) should be construed as merely particularising the general obligation to keep the component parts in repair and did not extend to renewing the whole of the premises (if it is necessary to do so). The tenant relied on the fact that the lease was for 25 years, rather than a longer term and that it is inconceivable that the parties could have intended to impose such an onerous obligation on the tenant. As noted by the judge, there was nothing inconceivable about such a construction from the landlord's point of view. From the tenant's perspective, the words used were clear and there may have been reasons for taking the risk of having to lay out a significant sum notwithstanding the tenant's limited interest or there might have been other concessions from the landlord (in relation to the rent, for example). It is not for the court to investigate the strength or otherwise of a particular bargain.

4-26   Conversely, in *Scottish Mutual Assurance Plc v Jardine Public Relations Ltd*,[37] in deciding between short-term patch repairs to a roof and longer term

---

35 See Dowding & Reynolds, *Dilapidations: The Modern Law and Practice* (4th edn, 2010) at para 10-08. This sits with the principle that the lease must be construed at the time it is granted. Otherwise, the lease might permit the landlord to recover the cost of a particular scheme if the problem presents itself earlier in the term, whereas if the same problem were to arise later, the landlord might be precluded, by reference to the same covenant, from recovering the costs of the works. However, it is considered that the remainder of the unexpired term might be relevant to the question of reasonableness (see **4-28**ff. and Chapter 29 below).

36 [1993] 1 EGLR 84.

37 [1999] EGCS 43.

replacement, it was held that the tenants under a three-year commercial lease were not liable to contribute towards the significantly higher costs of replacement. However, this decision was premised on a finding that both types of work were sufficient to 'repair' the roof. Replacement would only be justified as a 'long-term solution' and was not, for this reason, within the scope of the tenant's service charge liability. It also appears to have been significant that the landlord, having embarked upon the replacement scheme of works, was anxious to complete the works before the short-term lease expired, with a view to recovering as substantial a proportion as possible from the tenants.

4-27   The decision in *Scottish Mutual v Jardine* more clearly reflects the nuanced approach adopted by Blackburne J in *Fluor Daniel Properties Ltd v Shortlands Investments Ltd.*[38] In the extract from the judgment cited at **4-23** above, Blackburne J accepted most of what was decided by Scott J in *Plough Investments* as to the extent of the landlord's discretion in determining the nature of the works to carry out to address a particular problem, but subject to the qualification that this discretion must have regard to the limited interest of the tenant. Clearly, the more limited the tenant's interest (in terms of duration), the less scope the landlord has for implementing what was described in *Scottish Mutual v Jardine* as a 'long-term solution'.

IS IT REASONABLE TO RECOVER THE COSTS?

4-28   Although the question of whether a particular charge has been reasonably incurred features predominantly in relation to leases of dwellings because of the statutory restrictions in section 19 of the Landlord and Tenant Act 1985,[39] similar restrictions will sometimes be either expressed or implied in leases to which these statutory provisions do not apply.[40]

4-29   Ordinarily, where the costs relate to work which (a) falls within the relevant service charge provisions[41] and (b) is considered to be a method of work which the landlord is entitled to carry out and charge to the tenants, in principle, the resultant costs will be held to be reasonable.[42]

4-30   Where a landlord carries out work which, for whatever reason, is outside the scope of the tenant's service charge obligations, but the premises are in need of repair and work of some sort is required, it may be relevant to consider whether

---

38 [2001] EGLR 103. See **4-23** above.
39 See Chapter 29 below.
40 See **2-97**ff. above.
41 See **4-04**ff. above.
42 See, for example, *Wandsworth LBC v Griffin* [2000] 2 EGLR 105, where the Lands Tribunal held that the cost of the landlord's works carried out to replace certain flat roofs with pitched roofs and to replace metal-framed windows with uPVC double-glazed windows were reasonably incurred for the purposes of the Landlord and Tenant Act 1985, s 19. There was no issue before the Tribunal as to whether the works were necessary: it was agreed that the roof needed renewal and that the windows needed to be repaired.

the landlord is entitled to recover the reasonable cost of the more limited work, if that falls within the tenant's service charge obligations. This issue arose in *Crane Road Properties LLP v Hundalani*.[43] The claimant claimed the cost of resurfacing a private road pursuant to an obligation under a freehold transfer to contribute towards the cost of 'maintaining and repairing' the road, over which the transferee was granted a right of way. It was held that the works actually carried out went some way beyond the nature of the work which fell within the covenant. The claimant therefore argued that it was entitled to recover a contribution towards the cost of whatever works would have been required to maintain or repair the road as opposed to the improvements carried out which rendered such repairs unnecessary. It was held, as a matter of construction,[44] that such notional costs were not recoverable. According to the Deputy Judge, the liability to contribute arose only if the cost of works within the scope of the covenant had been actually incurred, not merely where other work has been carried out which avoids the need to carry out 'repair and maintenance' work.[45]

4-31   Although the cost of the works in *Crane Road Properties LLP v Hundalani* was disallowed because the works were held to be outside the scope of the transferees' obligation to contribute, there is no reason why this principle should be applied any differently where the costs are disallowed for some other reason. So, for example, if a landlord undertakes work to the roof of a building which is considered to be too extensive to fall within the tenant's service charge obligations, the landlord will not, ordinarily, be entitled to recover the notional cost of patch repairs. Similarly, if it is held that it is unreasonable for the landlord to replace the roof (for whatever reason), but that it would have been reasonable to carry out patch repairs, it is unlikely that this would entitle the landlord to the lesser cost.[46]

4-32   Where this principle will not apply is in relation to the requirement that the cost of the works itself be reasonable.[47] If it is held that the cost of the work which was actually carried out was unreasonably high, the landlord will be entitled to the lower, reasonable cost of carrying out the same work.

4-33   The question of whether it is reasonable for the cost of works to be charged to the tenants might also take account of the manner in which the landlord intends to carry out a particular scheme of works. In *Garside v RFYC*

---

43 [2006] EWHC 2066 (Ch).
44 See also *Scott v Brown* (1904) 69 JP 89.
45 The claimant sought to rely on *Fluor Daniel v Shortlands* [2001] 2 EGLR 103, *Postel v Boots* [1996] 2 EGLR 60 and *Scottish Mutual Assurance plc v Jardine Public Relations Ltd* [1999] EGCS 43 (as to which, see **4-23** to **4-26** above). Although the judgments in those cases spoke of the landlord having to bear the additional costs of works which were outside of the covenant, there was no question of the landlord charging a lower, notional sum for works which were not carried out.
46 Whether under the Landlord and Tenant Act 1985, s 19 or by virtue of an implied condition of reasonableness.
47 See, in relation to the Landlord and Tenant Act 1985, s 19, Chapter 29 below and implied terms, **2-97**ff. above.

Ltd,[48] the Upper Tribunal considered the reasonableness[49] of the cost of major works carried out to a residential estate, where the works followed several years of neglect and therefore resulted in a sharp increase in the service charges payable. It was held[50] that there is nothing in the 1985 Act to limit the ambit of what is reasonable so as to exclude considerations of financial impact on the tenants. Although the Upper Tribunal did not reach any conclusion on the facts of the case (but rather remitted the case to the LVT for further consideration of the effect of the increased charges on the lessees), some guidance was given as to whether phasing of works might be considered reasonable. In particular, it is necessary to take account of the degree of disrepair and urgency of the work. Moreover, it was stressed that if repair work is reasonably required at a particular time, carried out at a reasonable cost and to a reasonable standard, and the cost of it is recoverable under the relevant lease, the tenant cannot escape liability to pay by pleading poverty.[51]

4-34 In *Continental Property Ventures Inc v White*,[52] the Lands Tribunal held that it was unreasonable for a landlord to incur a cost in carrying out damp-proofing and redecorating works where those costs could have been recovered under a guarantee in respect of earlier damp-proofing work. Since the landlord adduced no evidence as to why it was reasonable to incur a cost without claiming on the guarantee, there was no escape from the conclusion that the entirety of the costs was unreasonable under section 19 of the Landlord and Tenant Act 1985 and therefore irrecoverable.

4-34A Another issue which sometimes arises where reasonableness comes into play is the timing of a landlord's claim for the cost of works. Where a landlord carries out a large and costly scheme of works close to the end of the term and seeks to pass the cost on to the tenants whose interest in the property is soon to end, the question arises of whether it is open to the landlord to recover the full cost of the works notwithstanding the fact that the work otherwise falls within the scope of the service charge provisions.[53] The onus will be on the tenants to satisfy the court or tribunal that the costs claimed are unreasonable and therefore irrecoverable. The shorter the length of the original term, the more likely it is that such an argument would succeed. It is considered that unless the evidence suggests that the landlord is being opportunistic in squeezing a program of major works into the timescale required purely to enable recovery from the tenants, it is unlikely that the landlord would be precluded from recovering the costs on the ground that they have been unreasonably incurred. However, every case must be considered on its particular facts and the closer the works to the term dates of

---

48 [2011] UKUT 367 (LC).
49 Under the Landlord and Tenant Act 1985, s 19.
50 By HH Judge Alice Robinson, disagreeing with the reasoning of the LVT and therefore allowing the appeal.
51 See *Southend-on-Sea Borough Council v Skiggs* [2006] EWLands LRX_110_2005, where it was emphasised that the LVT cannot alter a tenant's contractual liability to pay.
52 [2006] 1 EGLR 85.
53 See **4-24** above.

the leases and the more extensive the works, the more scope there will be for the tenants to challenge the costs claimed.

4-35   The RICS Residential Code provides guidance to property managers with regard to the carrying out of works which are chargeable to the tenants as service charges. Paragraph 12.1 suggests that the landlord or management company should be the employer under any contract rather than the managing agent and any financial or other connection between a contractor and the appointing managing agent should be declared to both landlord and tenants. It is also suggested that contractors should, where possible, be members of a relevant trade organization, which has published a code of practice for the assessment of its members. Contractors' duties should be defined and property managers should take all reasonable steps to ensure that contractors carry out their duties promptly and to a reasonable minimum standard, e.g. 'by use of competitive tender, written contracts with detailed provisions, arrangements for stages payments and liquidated damages'. There should also be in place a procedure for instructing contractors. Managers should ensure that contractors have in place appropriate public liability insurance. Importantly, managers should ensure that there are sufficient funds prior to instructing contractors[54] and that the method of payment has been agreed prior to work commencing.

APPLICATION OF THE PRINCIPLES: EXAMPLES

Windows

4-36   *Mullaney v Maybourne Grange (Croydon) Management Co Ltd*,[55] is an example of a case where the landlord replaced old, rotten wooden framed windows with modern double-glazed windows in a block of flats. The court considered that it was very desirable, in terms of good-housekeeping and in everyone's interests, to replace defective and unsatisfactory windows with something more durable and calling for less maintenance. However, the court was constrained by the restrictive terms of the leases to hold that the work did not fall within the relevant service charge provisions, which were limited to maintenance and the provision of 'additional amenities'.

4-37   This decision may be contrasted with the case of *Sutton (Hastoe) Housing Association v Williams*,[56] which also concerned an estate which comprised blocks of flats, houses and maisonettes, all constructed with wooden window frames which had rotted. The housing association landlord replaced the windows with modern uPVC windows and sought to recover the cost of the replacement works as service charges. *Mullaney v Maybourne Grange* was distinguished because

---

54   See Chapter 12 below as to whether a landlord is entitled to recover borrowing costs from the tenants.
55   [1986] 1 EGLR 70.
56   [1988] 1 EGLR 56.

of the limited scope of the service charge provisions. The leases in this case required the tenants to contribute towards the cost of (inter alia) 'repairs and maintenance'.[57]

4-38   It may be relevant to consider whether skylights are 'windows' for this purpose. In *Easton v Isted*,[58] it was held that the 'glazed top of a conservatory' was a 'window' for the purpose of the repairing covenant. In *Taylor v Webb*,[59] the landlord covenanted to repair 'the outside walls and roofs'. It was held that skylights were part of the roof. This conclusion (whether a skylight is a window or part of the roof) is more easily reached where the skylight forms part of the common parts, but if it lights part of the premises demised to a tenant, the issue might be more finely balanced. It is suggested (subject always to the wording of the lease or other deed in which the obligations are contained) that where the service charge liability extends to all windows in the building, it is more likely that it will extend equally to skylights, even if they lie above demised premises rather than common parts.

Roofs

4-39   If replacement of a roof is within the scope of a landlord's covenant and/ or the tenant's service charge obligations, it will be a matter for experience and judgement as to when the time has come to renew the roof. In *Postel Properties Ltd v Boots the Chemist*,[60] the court was concerned with the question of whether the tenants of the Milton Keynes Shopping Centre were obliged to contribute towards the cost of replacing the roof covering. The tenants argued that the replacement works were premature. The court was required to balance the cost of replacement against the likely increasing cost of patch repairs. This is a matter for expert evidence and there can be no hard and fast rule which applies across the board. However, providing a respectable professional opinion supports replacement over continuing patch repairs, this will normally be accepted. Contrast *Scottish Mutual Assurance Plc v Jardine Public Relations Ltd*,[61] where there was no suggestion that more limited patch repairs could not be done or were not practical. Rather, the landlord argued that this would not provide a long-term solution (viewed from the perspective of a prospective purchaser of the building), but this was held to be outside the obligations of the tenant under a

---

57 See also *Sutton LBC v Drake* [2007] EWLands LRX_69_2004, where the Lands Tribunal allowed an appeal against the decision of the LVT which concluded that the installation of new PVC double-glazed windows was outside of the scope of a landlord's repairing covenant on the ground that the old Crittall windows were not shown to be sufficiently out of repair, with only limited buckling having been evidenced and no corrosion being apparent. According to the Lands Tribunal, this failed to take account of the fact that the overall scheme of works included replacement of the cladding and window sub-frames and that this would require the existing Crittall windows to be removed and replaced with a modern equivalent.

58 [1903] 1 Ch 405.

59 [1937] 2 KB 283 (not appealed on this issue).

60 [1996] 2 EGLR 60.

61 [1999] EGCS 43.

short-term lease (of three years) and the landlord would not have been in breach of covenant if it had opted for the short-term repairs rather than the long-term solution of a full replacement.

4-40 Difficult issues can sometimes arise where there are balconies or roof terraces demised to the tenants of flats. It will be a question of construction in any particular case whether (a) any part of the terrace or balcony is demised and/or (b) whether the landlord is entitled/obliged to keep the surface or other parts of the balcony or roof terrace in repair and recoup the costs via the service charge.[62]

Mechanical and electrical plant and equipment

4-41 A tenant's service charge liability is likely to extend not only to the fabric of the building and the grounds, but also to plant and equipment contained in it. This might include electrical installations, lighting, water supplies, heating and cooling apparatus and lifts. The principles set out above[63] are applied in the same way to such equipment as they are to the building itself, although it is always necessary to ascertain whether the service charge obligation does, indeed, extend to the particular item to which work is required. Sometimes, there will be specific reference to particular items of equipment. However, where the obligation to repair applies to 'the demised premises',[64] that will extend to all fixtures[65] and therefore will usually be apt to apply to most items of plant and equipment.

4-42 It is even more relevant, when considering items of mechanical and electrical plant and equipment to consider whether the item in question is in a state of disrepair.[66] Services and machinery tend to have a shorter life than the fabric of a building. The fact that there exist more modern equivalents which might be more efficient or powerful does not enable a landlord to replace the existing equipment at the tenant's expense. An old piece of machinery may

---

62 See, for example, *Petersson v Pitt Place (Epsom) Ltd* [2001] EWCA Civ 86, where it was held that the roof terrace was demised, in its entirety and therefore outside of the landlord's repairing obligation. Conversely, in *Hallisey v Petmoor Developments Ltd* [2000] EGCS 124, Patten J held that the whole of a roof terrace used with a flat was within the landlord's obligation to keep in repair 'the main structure of the building ... and the roof'. He concluded that the 'main structure' should be construed to include not only the bare concrete shell but also whatever additional surfaces were created by the landlord in order to make that shell a complete and effective structure for the purpose of maintaining the physical integrity of the flats within the development, rather than the landlord ceding control of part of the exterior fabric of the building to one of the tenants. See also *Ibrahim v Dovecorn Reversions Ltd* [2001] 2 EGLR 46 and *Marlborough Park Services Ltd v Rowe* [2006] EWCA Civ 436.

63 At **4-04** to **4-16**.

64 Or similar description which does not limit the obligation to a specific part of the building, e.g. the structure or the exterior.

65 A fixture, as the name suggests, is an item which has become fixed to the demised premises. The distinction between a chattel and a fixture depends on the degree of annexation and the purpose of its annexation: see *Elitestone v Morris* [1997] 1 WLR 87; *Botham v TSB Plc* [1996] EGCS 149.

66 Or, putting it another way, whether it has 'malfunctioned': *per* Blackburne J in *Fluor Daniel Properties Ltd v Shortlands Investments Ltd* [2001] 2 EGLR 103 at p 110D.

continue to perform its function and work adequately, in which case there will be no deterioration which engages a covenant to keep it in repair or good condition.[67]

4-43   Often, reliance is placed on published tables as to the likely lifespan of similar plant or equipment.[68] However, even if a particular item of plant or equipment is 'at the end of its useful economic life' by reference to those tables, that, itself, is not a reason for replacing it if, notwithstanding the data in the tables, it continues to perform its function adequately. Conversely, if the item in question is defective, the fact that it is nearing the end of its useful economic life might well be a good reason for replacing it rather than continuing to carry out patch repairs.[69] In *Fluor Daniel Properties Ltd v Shortlands Investments Ltd*,[70] Blackburne J said:[71]

> 'Plant is not in disrepair, nor is replacing it "repair" simply because it is at the end of its age range in the CIBSE tables. Plant that works satisfactorily and does so near to its maximum efficiency is in repair, even though it may be close to the end of its working life. The obligation to "amend" adds nothing because it means no more than to "mend", thereby implying a state of disrepair. "Renew" presupposes that the physical condition of the plant or item in question (or of any part or parts of it) is such that renewal is reasonably necessary. The standard to apply is that laid down by *Proudfoot v Hart* (i.e. having regard to the age, character and locality is the condition of the subject matter of the dispute reasonably acceptable to a reasonably minded tenant of the kind likely to take a lease of the building?). The landlord is not entitled to replace plant, or any part of it, that is in proper working order, is in a satisfactory physical condition and is capable, to all intents and purposes, of performing as well as it did when new. The position is the same as regards the landlord's obligation "to keep in good and substantial condition". While this may require the carrying out of works going beyond straight repair, the obligation is only triggered where, as a matter of fact and degree, the subject matter is not in good and substantial condition. Where it is triggered, the *Proudfoot* standard applies. The obligation does not require or entitle the landlord to carry out works that go beyond what is sensibly needed to remedy the defective condition in question.'

4-44   Section 8 of the RICS Commercial Code[72] relates to the 'Initial provision, replacement and improvement of fabric, plant and equipment'.[73] The Code states that service charge costs 'may include improvements or enhancement of the

---

67 See, for example, *Mason v TotalFinaElf UK Ltd* [2003] 3 EGLR 91; *Ultraworth Ltd v General Accident Fire & Life Assurance Co Ltd* [2000] 2 EGLR 115.
68 Such as those produced by the Chartered Institute of Building Services Engineers ('CIBSE').
69 So data such as the CIBSE tables might well assist in determining what a reasonable incoming tenant might require in order to remedy the defective plant. If the plant has malfunctioned, such that repair of some sort is required and the plant is at the end of its useful economic life according to industry-accepted statistics, that might well lead to a conclusion that it should be replaced rather than repaired. See also *Westbury Estates Ltd v The Royal Bank of Scotland Plc* 2006 SLT 1143.
70 [2001] 2 EGLR 103.
71 At p 109F.
72 See **1-17**ff. above.
73 This is not addressed specifically in the RICS Residential Code.

fabric, plant or equipment where such expenditure can be justified following the analysis of reasonable options and alternatives and having regard to a cost benefit analysis over the terms of the occupiers' leases'.[74] It goes on to suggest that managers of commercial property should provide the facts and figures to support and justify such a proposal. Where a landlord contends that equipment should be replaced rather than repaired, the question of whether the equipment is approaching the end of its economic life should be determined by an inspection by an experienced engineer and a review of service records and records of the occurrence and frequency of failures.[75] It is also recommended[76] that any proposals to include the cost of upgrades or improvements in the service charge should be communicated to occupiers before any expenditure is committed, to ensure agreement.[77]

74 This follows the various authorities discussed above.
75 RICS Commerical Code, para 8.2.
76 At para 8.6.
77 In the commercial context, there is no equivalent mandatory statutory consultation requirement as exists under the Landlord and Tenant Act 1985, s 20 in relation to dwellings: see Chapter 30 below.

CHAPTER 5

Heating and lighting

5-01   A tenant will usually be obliged to contribute towards the cost of heating/lighting the common parts of a building. Absent any specific limitation, this will usually extend to all parts of the building retained by the landlord and used by one or more tenants.[1] In *Elmcroft Developments Ltd v Tankersley Sawyer*,[2] the landlord covenanted to light the 'entrance hall, stairs and passages' and this was held to apply to the external access to a basement flat from the exterior common parts.

5-02   In *Lloyds Bank Plc v Bowker Orford*,[3] the service charge liability of the tenants of commercial premises was based on the cost of providing certain 'services' which included providing hot water to the communal lavatories, lighting the common parts and 'other beneficial services',[4] which was held to include heating the common parts. The provision of these services entitled the landlord to recoup a due proportion of capital expenditure in respect of heating and lighting the common parts. The Deputy Judge saw no reason to distinguish between 'capital' and 'revenue' items in the provision of these services. Providing the replacement of lighting/heating equipment was necessary, the landlord was entitled to recover the cost. Similarly, in *Yorkbrook Investments v Batten*,[5] the landlord covenanted to provide a 'good sufficient and constant supply of hot water and an adequate supply of heating in the hot-water radiators'. It was for the landlords how this should be achieved, but the antiquated system in place at the date of the lease having broken down, the landlord was obliged to replace it in order to comply with its obligation.[6]

---

1   Subject to any more restrictive definition of 'common parts' in the lease.
2   [1984] 1 EGLR 47.
3   [1992] 2 EGLR 44.
4   As to 'sweeping-up' clauses, see **2-55**ff. above.
5   [1985] 2 EGLR 100.
6   The 'service' which the landlord covenanted to provide in each of these cases was not based on an obligation by the landlord to keep in repair the system installed to supply heating and hot water or to maintain it, etc. Where a landlord or property manager seeks to replace the whole system under a repairing (or similar) obligation, it will be necessary to consider whether the extent of the works proposed falls within the scope of the covenant: see **4-04**ff. above.

5-03   In *Levitt v Camden LBC*,[7] the landlord was entitled to claim the cost of installing a new boiler and communal heating system from those tenants who relied on the communal heating.[8] This included the applicant tenants who argued that they should not have to contribute because they replaced their own flat's heating system themselves, before the landlord replaced the system serving the building. Since the tenants always intended to connect to the communal system once it was ready, it was held that they were subject to the same liability as the other tenants.

5-04   Most comprehensive service charge provisions enable the landlord to recover the cost of gas/electricity used to heat/light the common parts of the building. The onus will be on the landlord to prove the amount of electricity and gas used for this purpose and usually the prudent course will be to install a separate meter for those installations which are the subject of the tenants' service charge liability. A potential problem arose for the landlord in *OM Property Management Ltd v Burr*,[9] where the gas supplier undercharged for a number of years and presented a large, back-dated invoice to the landlord which the landlord settled and then sought to pass on the one-off payment to the tenants. It was argued that the landlord was precluded from recovering these costs because of section 20B of the Landlord and Tenant Act 1985, under which a landlord cannot recover costs which were incurred more than 18 months before the tenant is notified of them or a demand is made for their payment. It was held, by the Upper Tribunal, that the costs were not 'incurred' for this purpose until the landlord was invoiced by the utility company and therefore the landlord was entitled to recover the costs from the tenants.[10]

---

7   [2011] UKUT 366 (LC).
8   In this case, the local authority landlord had agreed that those tenants who did not benefit from the communal provision of heating and hot water (because they had their own independent supplies) were liable to contribute towards these costs. It is not inconceivable that such a liability could arise where the leases are appropriately worded.
9   [2012] UKUT 2 (LC); [2012] L&TR 17.
10   See also **19-12** and **31-11** below.

CHAPTER 6

Cleaning and refuse collection

6-01   It is not uncommon for a service charge scheme to require the tenants to contribute towards the cost of keeping the common parts of a building clean.[1] In *St Modwen Developments (Edmonton) Ltd v Tesco Stores Ltd*,[2] the tenant, Tesco, argued that it should not be liable to contribute towards the landlord's costs of collecting and disposing of the refuse of other tenants of the shopping centre, since Tesco arranged its own refuse collection. The landlord argued that refuse collection fell within the scope of the obligation to keep the common parts clean. The fact that Tesco arranged for its own refuse to be collected without relying on the landlord did not absolve Tesco from the liability to contribute towards the cost of collecting the refuse left by other tenants.

6-02   It is important that the lease defines precisely which areas the landlord is to clean. For example, in *Embassy Court Residents' Association Ltd v Lipman*,[3] the services to be provided by the landlord included 'cleaning outside windows'. This was held to relate to all windows in the building, not just those in the common parts. In a multi-tenanted block, it is more likely that the lease would be construed (if permitted by the drafting) as requiring the landlord to arrange for the exterior surfaces of all windows to be cleaned (including those serving parts of the building demised to tenants), but only the interior surfaces of those windows in the common parts.

1   In *Barnes v City of London Real Property Co* [1918] 2 Ch 18, a lease reserved a weekly rent which included an element for cleaning and Sargant J said (*obiter*) that gave rise to a correlative obligation on the part of the landlord to clean the demised premises.
2   [2007] 1 EGLR 63.
3   [1984] 2 EGLR 60.

CHAPTER 7

Compliance with legislation

7-01   It is a fact of modern life that many aspects of the use and enjoyment of property are regulated by statute. There are numerous examples, such as complying with the appropriate building regulations when carrying out works to the fabric of the building, fire safety regulation, anti-discrimination legislation, and health and safety legislation. It is not appropriate to explore the numerous extensive statutory regimes which could conceivably apply to the use and management of commercial and residential premises in this work and reference should be made to more specialist works on the particular legislation which might be in issue. The purpose of this chapter is to consider how and in what circumstances costs incurred by a landlord or manager solely in connection with complying with a legislative requirement can be passed on to the tenants as service charge.

7-02   It is necessary to distinguish between those costs which are required as a result of works and other expenditure which relates to the premises demised to a particular tenant. It is not uncommon for leases (both residential and non-residential) to contain a standard provision by which the tenant covenants to comply with statutes and statutory instruments and most works or other adjustments required to the demised premises will fall within the scope of that obligation. The concern, here, is with works or other items of expenditure required in relation to common parts, to which the service charge regime attaches. More modern leases tend to include an equivalent obligation on a landlord to comply with statutes in relation to the common parts with a corresponding right to recoup the cost from the tenants.

7-03   Where there is no such general obligation, numerous aspects of statutory compliance might well be covered by other service charge provisions. So, for example, if a landlord is required to carry out works to the common parts under a repairing or maintenance obligation and as a result of the latest building regulations, additional expenditure is required (e.g. the use of fire-proof materials), it is likely that the reasonable cost of complying with the obligation to maintain or repair will include whatever is required by the relevant regulations.[1] However, a landlord cannot rely on an obligation to repair/maintain the building

---

1   See, for example, *Lurkott v Wakeley* [1911] 1 KB 905.

to recover the cost of providing something new where its provision does not result from a defect or the condition of the existing building.[2] Alternatively, a landlord might seek to rely on a sweeping-up provision in order to recoup the cost of making adjustments to the common parts.[3] Sweeping-up clauses are dealt with in Chapter 2 above.[4] They are generally construed restrictively,[5] but where a landlord is required by statute to incur expenditure in relation to the common parts enjoyed by all of the tenants, it is likely that such expenditure would fall within a comprehensive sweeping-up clause as a 'service' to be provided to the tenants for the purposes of good estate management.

7-04   The provisions of the Landlord and Tenant Act 1985 apply equally to service charges which result from a statutory duty on a landlord or property manager relating to residential premises. If a landlord is required to incur a cost in order to comply with a statutory duty, it is difficult to conceive of circumstances in which it might be said that the cost has not been 'reasonably incurred',[6] but the requirement that the cost itself should be reasonable will be applied in equal measure to those costs where there is no statutory duty. The existence of a statutory (as opposed to a contractual) duty on a landlord to provide a service does not give the landlord a blank cheque for the provision of that particular service.

7-05   The remainder of this chapter considers some of the more topical examples of statutory compliance which might feature in a service charge account. However, it should be stressed that these are merely examples and there are numerous instances of regulation which might require a landlord or manager to incur expenditure which is then passed on to the tenants as service charges and it is necessary to consider the nature of the regulation and the charge incurred in order to determine whether, as a matter of construction, the tenants are required to pay.

HEALTH AND SAFETY

7-06   The Health and Safety at Work Act 1974 and the extensive regulations made under it contain a detailed labyrinth of duties imposed on employers with regard to the workplace. Where the workplace is tenanted, some of the duties may well fall on the landlord, as the person with responsibility for the maintenance or repair of the workplace. A typical example is the statutory regime for the control of asbestos in non-domestic premises. The Control of Asbestos Regulations 2012[7] came into force on 6 April 2012 and impose numerous duties on the person responsible for the maintenance or repair of the building. In a

---

2   See **4-07** above.
3   See **7-12** below.
4   See **2-55**ff.
5   See **2-56** above.
6   Under the Landlord and Tenant Act 1985, s 19. See Chapter 29 below.
7   SI 2012/632.

tenanted office or other non-residential premises,[8] this will frequently be the landlord. In these circumstances, the landlord is required to take reasonable steps to find out if there are materials containing asbestos in the premises and if so, the amount and condition of the asbestos. There is a presumption that materials do contain asbestos unless there is strong evidence that they do not. A record must be kept of the location and condition of asbestos-containing materials and risk assessments must be carried out followed by a risk-management plan which must then be implemented. This will not, necessarily, require the removal of asbestos-containing materials. In some circumstances, it is safer to leave it in place and to manage it.

7-07   Any works required to be carried out in order to implement a management plan under the regulations might fall within more conventional aspects of a service charge, but a significant element of the landlords' compliance with these statutory duties requires investigations to be carried out and reports to be produced. Whether those investigations and reports can be charged to the tenants is likely to turn on whether there is specific provision for the landlord to pass on the cost of statutory compliance generally or, alternatively, on whether this can be charged via a sweeping-up clause.

DISABILITY DISCRIMINATION

7-08   Formerly, property managers were subject to duties with regard to the management of premises under the Disability Discrimination Acts 1995 and 2005. These have now been subsumed within the Equality Act 2010.

7-09   Under section 20 of the 2010 Act, certain duties are imposed to make 'reasonable adjustments' to premises. The duty will require the removal or alteration of physical features, fixtures and fittings of a building in circumstances where the physical feature puts a disabled person at a substantial disadvantage in relation to a relevant matter in comparison with persons who are not disabled. A 'disability' is defined as any physical or mental impairment which has a substantial and long-term adverse effect on the person's ability to carry out normal day-to-day activities.[9] At present, these duties apply to:

(a)   a controller of let premises;

(b)   a controller of premises to let; or

(c)   a commonhold association.[10]

7-10   By section 36(3), a 'controller of let premises' is a person by whom premises are let or a person who manages them. There is no further definition

---

8   The duty applies to all 'non-residential premises' which can include offices, shops and industrial premises. It will also apply to the common parts of a mixed-use building.
9   Section 6.
10   Section 36(1).

of 'management' for this purpose. However, this is to be distinguished from the duties imposed on 'a person responsible in relation to common parts' under section 36(1)(d). Common parts are defined by section 36(6)(a) as:

> 'the structure and exterior of, and any common facilities within or used in connection with, the building or part of a building which includes the premises'.[11]

7-11   The duties imposed on a person responsible in relation to common parts, under section 36(1)(d) have not yet been brought into force.[12] When they come into force, these duties will apply only to buildings which contain residential premises, either as mixed-use buildings or solely residential.[13]

7-12   The duty (when it is brought into force) in relation to common parts will require the manager of the common parts to make reasonable adjustments in the same way as a 'controller of let premises', under section 20. Alterations to a physical feature will only be required where the physical feature puts a disabled resident at a substantial disadvantage in relation to his/her use of the physical feature. Typical examples might be the installation of a stair lift or the installation of Braille signage. Where this duty arises, however, the manager has a duty to consult 'all persons who might be affected by' the proposed works. That will include all others who use the common parts. This consultation will, no doubt, overlap with the consultation required by section 20 of the Landlord and Tenant Act 1985 (where the cost of the reasonable adjustments exceeds the statutory limit).[14]

7-13   Until the wider duty in relation to common parts is brought into force, there is only limited scope for the duties imposed under the relevant provisions of the Equality Act 2010 to give rise to service charge expenditure.

FIRE SAFETY

7-14   The Regulatory Reform (Fire Safety) Order 2005[15] imposes duties on a 'responsible person' in relation to all premises except private dwellings (but including common parts of two or more dwellings). In relation to a workplace, the 'responsible person' is the employer, but in all other instances, it is the person who has control of the premises in connection with his trade, business or other undertaking or if there is no such person, 'the owner',[16] who is the person who receives a rack rent (on his own account or as agent for a third party) or who

---

11 In relation to commonhold land, s 36(6)(b) defines 'common parts' as every part of the commonhold land which is not for the time being a commonhold unit in accordance with the commonhold community statement.

12 No equivalent duty was imposed under the Disability Discrimination Acts 1995 and 2005.

13 See Sch 4, para 5(4), by which it is provided that a reference to a disabled person, to whom the duty is owed, is to a person who occupies premises as his only or main home.

14 See Chapter 30 below.

15 SI 2005/1541.

16 Regulation 3.

would receive a rack rent if it were payable. In relation to common parts of multi-let buildings, therefore, the duties under the regulations will, most likely, fall on the person responsible for managing the common parts.

7-15   The duties are extensive. As with numerous other health and safety regulations, the regulations impose duties to undertake risk assessments, and then to make arrangements to eliminate or reduce the risks. There are further duties to provide sufficient means of escape, alarms, fire detectors and to train management personnel to act efficiently in the event of fire. Other duties require the provision of fire-fighting equipment and emergency routes. Some of these duties will involve items of capital expenditure (e.g. the provision of suitable means of escape). Others will involve recurring expenditure (e.g. undertaking risk assessments, obtaining suitable advice from appropriately trained personnel). Again, the extent to which these items can be charged to the tenants will turn on the scope of the service charge provisions in the lease. It is generally considered, however, that provisions entitling the landlord to charge for the 'management' or 'provision of services' will cover expenditure on most of the duties under this and similar health and safety legislation.

ENERGY EFFICIENCY

7-16   Under Chapter 2 of the Energy Act 2011, the Secretary of State is given power to make regulations to prevent landlords of domestic and non-domestic property from letting property unless they achieve a minimum energy efficiency rating.[17] Current indication is that the threshold will be an 'E' rating.[18] Although no regulations have yet been made, the Act requires such regulations to be in force by 1 April 2018. It is quite possible, therefore, that regulations which will be made in the coming years, will require landlords to carry out works to improve the energy efficiency of buildings which contain domestic and non-domestic property for letting and this will almost certainly give rise to questions of whether such works to common parts of a building can be charged to the tenants as service charge. The scope for such regulations to impact on a domestic service charge regime is more limited. This is because the definition of 'domestic private rented property'[19] is limited to a property which is let under an assured tenancy[20] or a regulated tenancy[21] and does not include long tenancies at a low rent, such as are more likely to be encountered in a multi-let building with common service charge provisions.[22] Until the Regulations are published, it is only possible to speculate as to the impact which they might have on a service charge regime, but it is likely that there will be instances where a landlord will seek to charge

---

17   Section 42 (domestic property) and s 49 (non-domestic property).
18   On a scale of A to G. See the Department of Engery and Climate Change website.
19   In s 42.
20   Under the Housing Act 1988.
21   Under the Rent Act 1977.
22   However, the definition includes such other tenancy as might be specified in the regulations to be made by the Secretary of State: s 42(1)(a)(iii).

for the cost of increasing a building's energy efficiency in compliance with this legislation to its tenants. It will also be necessary to have regard to the 'green deal' by which a funding mechanism is to be provided to assist with compliance with the regulations, under Chapter 1 of the Act.[23]

---

23 The possible implications of this legislation in the non-domestic context are considered in an illuminating article by Nicholas Dowding QC and David Gilbert, 'The Energy Act: A Wolf in Sheep's Clothing?', Estates Gazette (24 November 2012).

CHAPTER 8

The costs of management and managing agents

8-01 Charges for management have become a common feature of service charge claims, in both residential and commercial contexts. These charges underpin the other 'services', the cost of which makes up the service charge account. Repairs, maintenance, cleaning, gardening, administration of such matters as insurance and the preparation of the service charge accounts all require the investment of time and some degree of experience to implement. This chapter considers the extent to which tenants are liable to make payment in respect of that personnel time and experience by way of service charges. First, it is necessary to consider the nature of 'management charges' in general terms. It is then necessary to look at the identity of the people who are entitled to charge for this service. Thirdly, the type and extent of management for which charges can be made must be considered and finally, it is necessary to have regard to the level of charges which can be levied.

MANAGEMENT CHARGES: GENERAL

8-02 The most recent, authoritative exposition of the nature of management charges and their recoverability as service charges is that of Sir Andrew Morritt C in *Wembley National Stadium Ltd v Wembley (London) Ltd.*[1] There, the defendant, the owner of the site of the old Wembley Stadium, sold the stadium to the claimant and granted a 125-year lease to the claimant of much of the surrounding land, comprising parking and access routes. The lease required the defendant, as landlord, to carry out certain works and services, including maintenance, traffic control and maintaining insurance. There was express provision entitling the lessor to employ 'such suitable and reputable staff and/or contractors to perform or carry out the Lessor's obligations'. The service charge was payable in respect of 'Expenditure' which was defined as 'all costs fees expenses and outgoings whatsoever properly incurred by the Lessor in complying with its obligations in respect of the Lessor's Services'.

---

1   [2007] EWHC 756 (Ch), [2008] 1 P&CR 3.

8-03   It was argued by the claimant that the defendant was not entitled to charge for 'in house' management in circumstances where the relevant services were not provided by a third party contractor, but rather by the defendant's own employees. This argument was rejected. Morritt C said:

> 'At all events I can find nothing in the wording of this lease in general and the definition of "Expenditure" in particular to confine the relevant services to the actual service to the exclusion of any management cost incurred in its provision. Why, for example, should the wages of the employee who actually applied the tarmac to the surface of the car park be included but the salary of he who arranged for the employee to do it and for the tarmac to be available for such application be excluded. In my judgment the wording of the definition embraces both."

8-04   The management charges in issue in that case included what were described as 'indirect' costs of management and corresponding 'overhead' expenses and all such costs were held to be recoverable, providing they were incurred 'in' complying with the lessor's obligation to provide services. Such costs included the provision of office accommodation, training, medical insurance and pensions.

8-05   The same principle is echoed in the earlier decision of the Court of Appeal (in a residential context) in *Embassy Court Residents' Association Ltd v Lipman*.[2] There, the claimant was a company whose members were the lessees of all of the flats in a block. The company had no other assets and had been granted a headlease of the block in order that it should undertake all of the management responsibilities involved in running the block. Cumming Bruce LJ (with whom Parker LJ agreed) said:

> 'There was necessary expenditure on printing, stationery and postage and various other administrative expenses. It was necessary in order to comply with the Companies Act to give an annual return accompanied by audited accounts for which purpose it is necessary to employ a professional auditor and there were manifestly innumerable small items which were liable to arise in any year pursuant to and necessary to the due performance by the Residents' Association Limited of the obligations that it had undertaken. If there is no power pursuant to a proper understanding of the lease of 1971 and the subsequent lease of 1972 for the Residents' Association Ltd to recover *pro rata* from the lessees a share of such administrative expenses, the whole scheme of the tripartite agreement becomes completely unworkable after such point of time as it is impracticable for all the work to be done by the individual members of the Association.'

8-06   Cumming Bruce LJ went on to consider whether it was open to the residents' association company (as landlord) to employ managing agents to carry out this administrative work. He made it clear that if a landlord intends to recover the costs of engaging managing agents, he must include 'explicit provision' in the lease. However, having made that comment, he went on to find that in the context of the arrangement whereby the landlord was effectively the collective alter ego of the tenants, the lease should be construed (notwithstanding the absence of

2   [1984] 2 EGLR 60.

'explicit provision') as entitling the landlord to recover this expenditure. The court therefore found that this was an implied term of the lease.[3] He was clearly influenced by the fact that if a decision to employ agents was excessive or if the cost of those agents unreasonable, the recoverability of the cost of those agents would be challengeable under the statutory predecessor of section 19 of the Landlord and Tenant Act 1985.[4] In a commercial context, although the statutory scheme does not apply, it is likely that an implied term as to the reasonableness of charges which a landlord seeks to recover from tenants as service charges will have the same effect on the recoverability of the cost of employing agents, where this is considered to be excessive.[5]

IDENTITY OF MANAGING AGENTS

8-07   Usually, where managing agents are appointed, they will be unconnected to the landlord, in which case it is unlikely that any issue as to their identity will arise. However, sometimes, a landlord will be connected with a particular management vehicle (perhaps another company in the same group, or where a company which manages the estate is the alter ego of an individual landlord). In such situations, whilst the court or tribunal must be astute to ensure that the arrangements are genuine and that the management functions are being carried out properly and in accordance with the obligations under the lease, the connection between the landlord and the manager will not, necessarily, preclude the landlord from recovering the costs.

8-08   In *Skilleter v Charles*,[6] the landlord claimed, as service charges, the cost of employing a company to manage the property. The company was wholly owned by the landlord. It was argued that the company had been incorporated by the landlord solely to recover expenses to which the landlord was not entitled. That argument was rejected because the evidence showed that the landlord's company had, in fact, been incorporated to manage a number of properties. The question was whether the device of the company was a sham.[7] It was held that it was not. Since the lease permitted the landlord to recover the cost of employing a manager, the costs of employing the landlord's company were recoverable. This was contrasted with *Finchbourne v Rodrigues*,[8] which concerned the identity of the agent who

---

3   But see **2-92** above and *Attorney General of Belize v Belize Telecom Ltd* [2009] 1 WLR 198 for the view that the implication of terms in contracts is part of the overall process of construing the contract.

4   As to which, see Chapter 29 below. In the context of a local authority letting, see the decisions of the Upper Tribunal in *Palley v Camden LBC* [2010] UKUT 469 (LC) and of the Lands Tribunal in *London Borough of Brent v Hamilton* [2006] EWLands LRX_51_2005.

5   As to the circumstances in which such a term might be implied, see **2-97** above.

6   [1992] 1 EGLR 73.

7   A 'sham' exists where the acts in question (here, the incorporation of a company for the purpose of managing the property) is intended to create a different impression and to confer rights and liabilities which are different to those which it purports to create: see *Snooks v London West Riding Investments Ltd* [1967] 2 QB 786.

8   [1976] 1 EGLR 51, [1976] 3 All ER 581. See **17-16** below.

was required to provide the annual certificate of service charge expenditure. It was held that the agents were required to be someone different from the landlord and the so-called managing agent was, in fact, no more than the landlord's nominee.[9]

8-09   *Skilleter v Charles* was applied by the Upper Tribunal in *Country Trade Ltd v Noakes*,[10] where the LVT was criticised for casting implied aspersions on the probity of management arrangements between the landlord company and a company with common ownership and directorship. HH Judge Gerald said:

> 'Unless, which is not the case here, it is asserted that the management arrangements were a mere "sham" i.e. an arrangement which disguised the true relationship or agreement between the parties, there is nothing in principle objectionable to a management company such as the Appellant employing a company it owns or is involved in to provide services: see *Skilleter v Charles*.'

8-10   Similarly, where management is provided 'in house' by a landlord (rather than by employing a third party company which is connected to the landlord), providing the charges for that management are genuine, in principle, there is no reason why the landlord cannot recover the costs of such internal management (subject to scrutiny as to the reasonableness of those charges).[11]

NATURE OF THE MANAGEMENT SERVICES

8-11   It is not necessarily the case that the tenants are required to pay for all aspects of management costs incurred by the landlord. For example, in *Lloyds Bank v Bowker Orford*,[12] it was held that a provision requiring the tenant to pay for the 'total cost to the lessors … of providing the services specified in section 2 of this Part of the Schedule and defraying the costs and expenses relating and incidental to such services' entitled the landlord to recover the management costs associated only with those matters set out in the relevant part of the schedule. This did not include the landlord's obligation to repair the common parts/structure (which was not, in that case, a service charge item). The landlord's management costs associated with any such work, as well as collecting rent and service charges, were held to be irrecoverable.[13]

8-12   Similarly, in *Norwich City Council v Marshall*,[14] the President of the Lands Tribunal held that the local authority landlord was entitled to recover a

9   See also *Parkside Knightsbridge Ltd v Horwitz* [1983] 2 EGLR 42, where the landlord company charged the tenants in respect of management services provided by its parent company. See **8-16** below.
10   [2011] UKUT 407 (LC).
11   *Embassy Court Residents' Association v Lipman* [1984] 2 EGLR 60. See **8-05** above.
12   [1992] 2 EGLR 44.
13   See also *Rettke Grover v Needleman* [2011] UKUT 283 (LC), where a lease entitled the landlord to charge a management charge of 15% of the cost of the services provided and it was held that the landlord was not entitled to recover any additional management costs associated with administering the service charge account (including the cost of employing accountants to audit the annual accounts).
14   [2008] EWLands LRX_114_2007.

sum equal to the management costs it had incurred (internally) in managing the various services for which the service charge was payable.[15] However, this did not include the costs incurred in dealing with breaches of covenant and enforcement of leases, rent collection and such like.

8-13   In *Wilson v Lesley Place (RTM) Co Ltd*,[16] the Upper Tribunal held that costs associated with the incorporation and running of a right to manage ('RTM') company were not recoverable as service charges under standard provisions entitling the landlord (or RTM company) to the costs of managing the estate. The LVT had concluded that, since the RTM company is set up and operates for the sole purpose of the management of the block of flats, such costs were recoverable, but the Upper Tribunal disagreed. The effect of sections 96 and 97 of the Commonhold and Leasehold Reform Act 2002 is to transfer to the RTM company the management functions of the landlord under the lease and to make the tenant liable to the RTM company rather than the landlord in respect of the tenant's obligations under the lease. These provisions do not modify those rights and duties and they do not create new rights and duties in favour of the RTM company against the tenants. The fact that the management functions are exercisable by an RTM company does not affect the construction of the lease.

8-14   Paragraphs 2.4 and 2.5 of the RICS Residential Code[17] set out numerous items of work which a managing agent ought to carry out as part of an agreed annual fee[18] and might be expected to carry out outside an annual fee.[19] These duties of a managing agent are, of course, subject to the terms of the contract between the agent and the landlord and, in any particular case, the LVT or court would have regard to the nature of the services provided in order to determine whether a particular fee payable by the tenants as part of their service charge is reasonable. However, if the agents are providing the services listed in the RICS Residential Code, that is a good starting point for the landlord's contention that the charges for such agents have been 'reasonably incurred' for the purposes of section 19 of the Landlord and Tenant Act 1985.[20]

LEVEL OF MANAGEMENT FEES

8-15   Sometimes, the lease itself will make provision for the level of fees to be incurred. In *Thames Side Properties Ltd v Brixton Estate Plc*,[21] a lease provided for management fees to be paid at the rate set out in a scale laid down by the RICS which, subsequently, had been abrogated.[22] The issue came to a head

15   Applying *Wembley London Ltd v Wembley National Stadium Ltd* (see **8-02** above).
16   [2010] UKUT 342 (LC).
17   2nd edn.
18   In para 2.4
19   In para 2.5.
20   See Chapter 29 below.
21   [1997] NPC 5.
22   As a result of a determination by the Monopolies and Mergers Commission that such scales operated against the public interest.

because the reversion was sold by landlords who had used third-party agents at a commercial rate to a landlord which engaged a subsidiary company as its agent and sought to charge the rate payable under the RICS scale immediately, before it was abolished (which was considerably higher than the market rate for such services). Lightman J construed the lease by considering the purpose of the provision for management fees, holding that it was to provide a yardstick or benchmark of what is a reasonable fee for the services in question. Applying that construction, he held that since the reference to the scale was no more than a convenient machinery for determining a reasonable cost to the landlord of obtaining management services, the lacuna created by the abrogation of the scale should be filled by a provision that the tenant should pay an equivalent percentage of the gross internal rental of the building as would be paid in the market from time to time after arm's length negotiations with a managing agent. In other words, 'the going rate for the job'.[23]

8-16   In *Parkside Knightsbridge Ltd v Horwitz*,[24] the landlord employed a parent company to manage the building. Although there was no cash payment, the payment charged to the lessees was reflected in the account running between the two companies and although this was the subject of criticism by the tenant, the Court of Appeal rejected this criticism, holding that the mechanism was a perfectly genuine one.[25] The court determined that the charge in question was a reasonable one by reference to a comparison with the charges made by other firms of managing agents. A similar approach was adopted in *Forcelux v Sweetman*,[26] where the Lands Tribunal considered the reasonableness of the management fees included in the service charge accounts by asking not whether the expenditure was necessarily the cheapest available, but rather whether it was 'reasonably incurred' and, on the evidence, it was held that the fees charged were in accordance with market rates.[27]

8-17   In *South Tyneside Council v Hudson*,[28] the Upper Tribunal had to determine whether it was open to the local authority landlord to recover management costs incurred by an 'arm's length management organisation' ('ALMO'), which it had employed to manage its entire housing stock, including properties subject to long leases (acquired under the right-to-buy legislation) and the remainder of its portfolio which was subject to short-term leases at rack rents. The management functions of the ALMO were provided in relation to a stock of around 16,000 flats, of which (by 2008, when the application was made to the LVT) 702 had been sold off under the right to buy legislation. Following criticisms of the flat rate of £25 per annum applied to each of the long leases by

---

23 *Per* Lightman J.
24 [1983] 2 EGLR 42.
25 See also *Skilleter v Charles* [1992] 1 EGLR 73 at **8-08** above.
26 [2001] 2 EGLR 173.
27 See **29-04** below for the meaning of 'reasonably incurred'. A similar approach has been taken in relation to the tenant's contribution towards the cost incurred by the landlord in placing insurance where the tenant cannot avoid paying merely by showing that a cheaper premium might have been obtained. See Chapter 10 below.
28 [2012] UKUT 247 (LC).

the Audit Commission,[29] the landlord created a dedicated 'leasehold team'[30] with responsibility for the properties subject to long leases. The local authority leases contained express provision entitling the landlord to appoint managing agents, to recover the cost and to delegate any of its management functions to any firm or company whose business it is to undertake such obligations.

8-18   There was no issue about the right of the landlord to recover the costs of an external manager appointed to manage its properties. The dispute concerned the method of apportionment of the costs of the ALMO, whose employment extended to the whole of the landlord's housing stock. First, the global fees payable to the ALMO each year were apportioned to 15% relating to management of the leasehold properties. Secondly, of that 15%, a further deduction was made to account for the costs incurred in relation to specific properties, e.g. requests for consent to an assignment/pursuing arrears of breaches of covenant. Since those costs were recoverable from individual lessees,[31] they were excluded. Thirdly, the balance was divided amongst the 702 leasehold owners.

8-19   The LVT, whilst 'sympathetic' to this method of apportionment, held that it was not open to the landlord to charge the resulting costs to the lessees under the terms of the leases, which required specific management costs relating to the building/estate in question to be ascertained. The council's appeal was allowed. The broad right to delegate its functions on such terms and conditions and for such remuneration as it thinks fit was held to entitle the council to provide management of the relevant building as part of its residential property portfolio. It was held that the apportionment of the ALMO's fees was 'careful and reasonable' and obtained a 'fair and reasonable assessment of the cost and expenses incurred or to be incurred by the [council] in managing the relevant buildings'.

8-20   This decision turned on the broad right for the council, as landlord, to recoup the cost of management and delegation of its management functions and also the detailed evidence as to the mode of apportionment of the costs of the ALMO. Although not stated expressly, it is likely, also, that the context of a local authority letting gave some additional weight to the reasonableness of the method of apportionment. That is not to say that the same result would not be reached in respect of a similarly apportioned management charge across a large private estate. However, it would be wrong to take this decision as carte blanche to adopt a less rigorous mode of apportionment where a particular landlord employs agents to manage a number of properties for a flat fee.

8-21   The RICS Residential Code provides that managing agents should enter into written management contracts and that the basis of fee charging and

---

29   The criticism was that this underestimated the actual cost of managing the leasehold properties, so that the tenants paying rack rents were, in effect, subsidising the long leasehold owners (as the local authority was required to ring fence its housing budget under the Local Government and Housing Act 1989).
30   Which involved the employment of two additional members of staff by the ALMO.
31   As an administration charge under the Commonhold and Leasehold Reform Act 2002, Sch 11.

duties should be set out clearly in such a contract.[32] So far as the level of fees is concerned, the code provides that charges should be 'appropriate to the task involved'. Fixed fees are considered to be preferable to percentages of outgoings or income, so that tenants can budget for annual expenditure.[33] That said, if the lease specifies a different form of charging for management costs, that will take precedence.

8-22   The RICS Commercial Code is more explicit on the question of management fees. It provides:

'**1.3.1 Total Cost of Management**

The management charge is the reasonable price for the total cost of managing the provision of the services at the location, and relates only to work carried out in managing and operating the services and administering the service charge.

The management charge might comprise two elements:

- The fee charged by the manager for the management and supervision of the services to a site (the management fee).

- The cost of site specific management staff, whether based on-site full time or part time (the site management costs).'

8-23   The Commercial Code goes on to emphasise that no two buildings are the same in the way they need to be run. The management fees charged ought to be a reasonable cost and overhead in relation to the operation and management of the services and should reflect the work necessary to fulfil the principles of the code. It is also recognized that whoever is providing the service is entitled to cover their costs and overheads and to recover a reasonable profit. As with the Residential Code, the Commercial Code provides that fees should be based on a fixed price rather than calculated as a percentage of expenditure, which is considered to be a 'disincentive to the delivery of value for money'. Rather, the fee should be fixed and subject to annual review or indexation.

---

32 Paragraph 2.1.
33 Paragraph 2.3.

CHAPTER 9

Employing caretakers/other staff

INTRODUCTION

9-01   Sometimes, landlords are required to employ staff to assist with the maintenance/running of the building or estate. Typically, such staff might include porters, caretakers, cleaners etc. The salaries of staff employed by the landlord will only be recoverable if they fall within the scope of the relevant service charges provisions and will be subject to the requirement of reasonableness.[1] In some circumstances, a landlord's obligation to employ staff might extend to housing the caretaker/porter, etc. within the building. The issue of resident staff has produced a number of disputes regarding the question of whether the landlord is entitled to recover, as service charges, the notional rental value of the accommodation occupied rent-free by the employee.

PROVISION OF IN-HOUSE PORTER/CARETAKER

9-02   *Hupfield v Bourne*[2] concerned a block of flats described as a 'luxury block', where the leases of the flats contained a covenant by the landlord to employ such persons as 'shall be reasonably necessary for the due performance of the covenants on [the landlord's] part ... and for the proper management of the block'. Initially, the landlord provided a resident caretaker, but then ceased to do so, employing, instead, managing agents who, it was contended, provided the same service. The court did not accept this contention, holding, on the evidence, that the substitutes did not provide the same level of service and that the services of a resident caretaker were reasonably necessary. Although the lease did not provide that the staff who were to be employed pursuant to this covenant were to be located 'in-house', the court granted an injunction restraining the landlord from selling the caretaker's flat, holding that it was reasonably necessary that the caretaker reside in the block.

---

1   Under the Landlord and Tenant Act 1985, s 19, in relation to residential accommodation and (possibly) by virtue of an implied term in relation to non-residential premises (see **2-97** above).
2   (1974) 28 P&CR 77.

9-03   In *Posner v Scott-Lewis*,[3] the landlord of a block of flats was subject
to a covenant to employ a 'resident porter'. The landlord dispensed with the
services of the porter who resided in the building and sought to dispose of the
porter's flat. Having granted an interim injunction to restrain the sale, the court
considered whether the landlord was entitled to replace the resident porter with
an employee who lived outside of the block, albeit only 'one minute away'.
The landlord argued that all of the duties which the leases required the resident
porter to perform would be performed by the replacement. However, this was
not enough. An obligation to provide a resident porter was just that: it required a
porter to live in the building.[4] Mervyn Davies J said:

> 'Clause 3(11) indicates that (a) there will be a porter in residence and (b) that he
> will perform certain functions. To arrange for his functions to be carried out by a
> non-resident cannot in my view discharge the defendants from their duty to keep a
> porter in residence. There is, to my mind, a world of difference between living in
> a block with a porter in residence and living in a block where there is no porter in
> residence. A tenant of a block of flats understandably attaches great importance to
> the presence of a resident porter. While the tenant no doubt appreciates the manual
> work that the porter may perform, he equally appreciates the feeling of security
> (and the opportunities to ask for help) that arises from the presence of a resident
> porter. In other words, a resident porter is valued not only for the duties which he
> is expected to perform but also for his very presence.'

9-04   The court went on to consider whether it would be appropriate to make
an order for specific performance of the landlord's obligation to employ a resident
porter and held that it would.[5]

9-05   Conversely, in *Veena SA v Cheong*,[6] there was no obligation on
the landlord to provide any sort of porterage services, but the service charge
provisions required the tenants to contribute towards the cost of 'the maintenance
of the services of a porter or porters'. The landlord had employed a full-time
(non-resident) porter and part-time cleaners. The Lands Tribunal held that these
costs were unreasonably incurred and therefore irrecoverable under section 19 of
the Landlord and Tenant Act 1985. The block comprised only seven flats and it
was considered reasonable in all the circumstances to require the tenants to pay
for a part-time porter only.

9-05A   In *Carey-Morgan v de Walden*,[7] the landlord held a head lease of the
building from Cadogan Holdings Ltd which contained a tenant's covenant to
provide a full-time in-house caretaker for the building, to reside rent-free in the
basement flat. Until around 2008, the landlord did not employ a resident caretaker
and Cadogan, the superior landlord sought to enforce the head lease covenant.

3   [1986] 1 EGLR 56.
4   Contrast *Russell v Laimond Properties Ltd* [1984] 1 EGLR 37.
5   Distinguishing *Ryan v Mutual Tontine Westminster Chambers Association* [1893] 1 Ch 116.
6   [2003] 1 EGLR 175.
7   [2013] UKUT 134 (LC).

In response, the landlord employed a full-time resident caretaker and housed her in the basement flat as required by the head lease. The landlord then sought to recover the costs of the caretaker's salary and the notional rent for the flat as service charges, pursuant to the terms of the underleases of the flats. The strange feature of this case was that both the landlord and the tenants of the individual flats agreed that it would not be appropriate to employ a full-time resident caretaker for the building in question. For that reason, the LVT held that the costs of doing so were not 'reasonably incurred' within section 19 of the Landlord and Tenant Act 1985.[8] This was reversed on appeal, by the Upper Tribunal, holding that the LVT ought to have given decisive weight to the possibility of the superior landlord forfeiting the head lease for breach of the covenant to provide a full-time resident caretaker. In the context of this case, it was wrong for the LVT to approach the question of what was reasonable under section 19(2) on the basis of what was reasonably needed for the day-to-day running of the building. The LVT ought to have taken into account the fact that it was reasonable to provide a resident caretaker in order to avoid potential forfeiture proceedings in respect of the head lease and this led to the conclusion that such costs were, indeed, reasonably incurred.

COSTS OF ACCOMMODATION

Whether recoverable

9-06   As noted above, a fertile area of dispute is the question of whether the cost to the landlord of housing a resident porter or caretaker is recoverable as service charges. Usually, the landlord will retain a flat in the building for the use of the porter or caretaker and will seek to charge a 'notional' rent (in the sense that it is the rent which would otherwise have been recovered for the occupation of that flat) from the tenants as service charges. At first blush, it seems natural that a landlord who provides accommodation for a caretaker ought to recover the lost rent which would have been recoverable for that accommodation had it not been used for that purpose. However, as will be seen below, clear terms are required to impose such an obligation on the tenants and this is justified on the assumption that the premium paid by the original tenants for the leases included the right to a resident porter/caretaker without the recurring obligation to contribute towards the cost of housing him.

9-07   In *Agavil Investment Co v Corner*,[9] the Court of Appeal held that the cost of providing the accommodation for a resident caretaker was recoverable under the service charge provisions which entitled the landlord to recover the 'costs, charges and expenses incurred in employing a caretaker for the buildings whether resident upon the premises or otherwise'. It was held that the notional

---

8   See Chapter 29 below.
9   Unreported, 3 October 1975.

rent of the accommodation provided by the landlord could be recovered as a 'cost'.

9-08   Similarly, in *Lloyds Bank v Bowker Orford*,[10] the landlord was entitled to recover the notional costs of the accommodation provided for a caretaker. There, the tenants covenanted to contribute towards the costs of providing certain services, which were defined by reference to the landlord's obligations, which included employing and housing a resident caretaker. David Neuberger QC[11] said[12] that the reference to the caretaker being 'housed' supported the contention that the cost of such housing should be part of the service charge. Although that cost was, in a sense, a notional cost, it was a cost 'in the sense of money foregone, as opposed to money spent'. The Deputy Judge relied on the decision in *Agavil*. It was not considered to be relevant that *Agavil* concerned a block of flats, whereas *Lloyds Bank v Bowker Orford* related to office premises. It was argued that *Agavil* ought to be distinguished on the ground that the landlord in that case had the option of housing the caretaker elsewhere (in which case there would be a stronger argument for recovering the accommodation costs), but that argument was also rejected since this was not a reason for the conclusion reached in *Agavil*.

9-09   These cases were both cited to the Court of Appeal in *Gilje v Charlgrove Securities Ltd.*[13] There, the service charge covenant was subtly different. The tenants were required to contribute a proportion of 'all monies expended by the lessor in ... providing the services and management and administration called for under clause 5(4)'. Clause 5(4) contained a covenant on the part of the landlord to maintain, etc. the building in accordance with the fourth schedule, which, in turn, contained a list of 'services' in respect of which the tenants were to contribute. These services included the provision of a resident housekeeper or porter.

9-10   The question for the court here was whether the notional rent foregone by the landlord could be described as 'monies expended'. Whilst notional rent could be a 'cost' (as in *Agavil*), according to Laws LJ, it did not fall within the rubric 'monies expended'. Mummery LJ also considered the absence of any machinery for computing the notional rent for the porter's accommodation to be a factor which was telling against the landlord's argument, although it is right to note that in none of the cases where it has been held that such notional rent is recoverable has any such machinery existed. Accordingly, this case fell on the other side of the line and it was held that the accommodation cost was not recoverable as service charge.

---

10   [1992] 2 EGLR 44.
11   Sitting as a Deputy Judge of the Chancery Division.
12   At p 47C.
13   [2002] 1 EGLR 41.

9-11   A more difficult case is *Cadogan v 44/46 Lower Sloane Street Management Co Ltd and McHale*.[14] There, the landlord was entitled to recoup, as service charges, the 'expenses and outgoings incurred' as set out in the third schedule to the relevant lease, which provided for the cost of employing a housekeeper/caretaker[15] and, in respect of any accommodation provided in the building, the cost of outgoings for such accommodation and the cost of providing such accommodation, including the loss of rack rent thereon. Notwithstanding this apparently clear reference to a loss of rack rent, it was held that this provision did not entitle the landlord to the loss of a notional rent for the caretaker's accommodation. It was considered by the Lands Tribunal that such a construction should only apply if it was 'unavoidable'. Since the service charge provision referred to the cost of such accommodation 'if any', it was possible that the words could have meaning (even if only theoretical) even if they refer only to a loss which has actually been suffered (by reason of the landlord having to pay rent for accommodation outside the building). Since this alternative (theoretical) meaning existed, the words would not be consigned to mere surplusage by holding that the notional loss (as opposed to actual loss) in relation to the accommodation within the building did not fall within the service charge provision.

9-12   The service charge covenant in *Cadogan v 27/29 Sloane Gardens Ltd*[16] required the tenant to contribute towards the 'costs expenses outgoings and matters incurred in connection with the management and running of the building', with specific reference to the matters listed, which included the cost of 'employing, maintaining and providing accommodation for' a caretaker. It was held that this clearly entitled the landlord to recover the notional rent for the caretaker's accommodation. It was clearly a 'cost' or a 'matter', applying the decisions of the Court of Appeal in *Agavil* and *Lloyds Bank v Bowker Orford*.[17] The disappointed freeholder applied for permission to appeal[18] and this application was dismissed.[19]

---

14 Lands Tribunal, unreported, 30 July 2004, LRA/29/2003. This case, together with a number of the authorities which follow, was a decision in the context of a collective enfranchisement under the Leasehold Reform, Housing and Urban Development Act 1993. The issue for the tribunal was the price payable by the nominee purchaser for acquiring the freehold of the building. The tribunal is required to determine the value of the landlord's interest if sold on the open market, subject to the rights and burdens with and subject to which the conveyance to the nominee purchaser is to be made. If the otherwise vacant flat used to house a caretaker is required to be used for that purpose without any right to recoup the cost, this will depress the value of the landlord's interest (here, a head leasehold interest). It is therefore necessary for the tribunal to resolve the disputed question of the right to recoup such expenditure.
15 In fact, the head lease referred to a caretaker, but the occupational underleases referred to housekeepers, but it was held that nothing turned on this distinction.
16 [2006] 2 EGLR 89.
17 [1992] 2 EGLR 44; see **9-08** above.
18 As with many of these cases, this was a decision in the context of a collective enfranchisement, where there was a head lease in place, in which case it was the freeholder who was arguing that the notional rent was irrecoverable by the mesne landlord, in order to increase the freeholder's share of the marriage value.
19 [2006] EWCA Civ 1331.

9-13   These two cases were cited by the Court of Appeal in *McHale v Cadogan*,[20] an appeal from a decision of the Lands Tribunal as to the apportionment of the price payable on a collective enfranchisement. The relevant service charge provisions were materially identical to those considered by the Lands Tribunal in *Cadogan v 44/46 Lower Sloane Street Management Co Ltd*.[21] The freeholder submitted that the Lands Tribunal's *obiter* comments in the earlier case were wrong (to the effect that if the provision for the cost of the housekeeper's accommodation referred only to the caretaker's flat in the building, the only possible conclusion was that the reference to 'loss of rack rent' entitled the freeholder to recover a notional rent).[22] It was argued that there could be no loss of rack rent where the caretaker's flat was required to be licensed to the caretaker rent-free (by the terms of the head lease). This was rejected by the Court of Appeal. According to Rix LJ, since the clause in question expressly included the loss of rack rent as being within 'the cost of outgoings for such accommodation', it was impossible to say that the loss of rack rent was not included in circumstances where the flat was required to be provided to the caretaker rent-free. Therefore, in contrast to the earlier Lands Tribunal case, the Court of Appeal held that notional rent was recoverable.

9-14   In *Hildron Finance Ltd v Greenhill Hampstead Ltd*,[23] there were two sets of leases for consideration. The first set of leases contained a covenant by the tenants to pay a proportion of the 'cost of employing maintaining and providing accommodation in the Building for a porter or porters'. The second set provided for payment of a proportion of the costs which included 'an annual sum equivalent to the fair rent of any accommodation owned by the Lessors and provided by them rent free to [caretakers, porters, etc.]'. Unsurprisingly, it was held that the second set of leases clearly provided for the recovery of a notional rent for caretakers' accommodation. However, the first set of leases was less clear. The covenant was to pay a proportionate part of the 'expenses and outgoings'. Following *Gilje*, it was held that notional rent was neither an 'expense' nor an 'outgoing'.

9-15   Drawing the above authorities together, the following conclusions can be drawn:

1   It is a question of construction, in each case, as to whether the landlord is entitled to recover a notional rent for the provision of accommodation for a caretaker/other staff.

2   In construing the leases, the courts held that such notional rent was recoverable in *Agavil Investment Co v Corner*,[24] *Lloyds Bank v Bowker*

---

20   [2010] 1 EGLR 51.
21   Lands Tribunal, unreported, 30 July 2004, LRA/29/2003; see **9-11** above.
22   These comments were *obiter* because, as explained at **9-11** above, the Lands Tribunal went on to hold that the provision could equally refer to some other accommodation and therefore that it did not entitle the landlord to recover a notional rent for the caretaker's flat.
23   [2008] 1 EGLR 179, [2008] 4 EG 168 (CS).
24   Unreported, 3 October 1975; see **9-07** above.

Orford,[25] *Cadogan v 27/29 Sloane Gardens Ltd*[26] and *McHale v Cadogan,*[27] but not in *Gilje v Charlgrove Securities,*[28] *Cadogan v 44/46 Lower Sloane Street Management Co Ltd and McHale*[29] or *Hildron Finance Ltd v Greenhill Hampstead Ltd.*[30]

3   The same rules of construction applicable to all service charge provisions apply.[31] In general, it is necessary for the lease to make it clear that such notional rent will be payable.

4   An obligation to contribute towards 'expenses', 'expenditure', 'monies expended' or 'outgoings' is less likely to be held to include a notional sum foregone (as opposed to an actual sum incurred). Conversely, an obligation to contribute towards 'costs' will more readily be construed as applying to a notional rent payable for staff accommodation.

Calculation of accommodation costs

9-16   Where the landlord is required to pay rent to a third party for accommodation for a caretaker, there is no difficulty in ascertaining the cost to be passed on to the tenants. This cost might well be subject to a test of reasonableness,[32] but, otherwise, it is readily apparent what cost is to be the subject of the tenants' contribution.

9-17   On the other hand, where the tenant is being charged a 'notional rent' for accommodation which is retained by the landlord, the absence of an actual cost paid by the landlord potentially makes quantification more difficult.[33] As noted above,[34] in *Gilje v Charlgrove Securities Ltd*, Mummery LJ considered that the absence of machinery for computing the notional rent for staff accommodation was a factor which counted against construing the lease as

25 [1992] 2 EGLR 44; see **9-08** above.
26 [2006] 2 EGLR 89; see **9-12** above.
27 [2010] 1 EGLR 51; see **9-13** above.
28 [2002] 1 EGLR 41; see **9-09** above.
29 Lands Tribunal, unreported, 30 July 2004, LRA/29/2003; see **9-11** above.
30 [2008] 1 EGLR 179, [2008] 4 EG 168 (CS); see **9-14** above.
31 See Chapter 2 above.
32 Under the Landlord and Tenant Act 1985, s 19, in relation to residential accommodation and (possibly) by virtue of an implied term in relation to non-residential premises (see **2-97** above). See, however, *Carey-Morgan v De Walden* [2013] UKUT 134 (LC), where the landlord argued that a notional loss of rent was not a 'cost' within the expression 'relevant costs' under s 19. It was not necessary for the tribunal to decide this point. However, HH Judge Huskinson commented (*obiter*) that since the lease deemed the lessor to have incurred a 'cost' in respect of the flat, it might not be open to the landlord, in claiming this head of service charge, to then go on to argue that it was not a 'relevant cost' under s 19.
33 See **9-08**.
34 See **9-10**.

including such costs. However, it is extremely rare for any such machinery to be included in leases.[35]

9-18　　The notional rent will usually be market-based. If the lease specifies a 'market rent' or 'rack rent', open market evidence should govern the parameters of an appropriate sum to be paid by the tenants. A reference to a 'fair' rent for the caretaker's flat, particularly where the lease was entered into before the coming into force of the Housing Act 1988, might raise the question of a discount for scarcity, as required under the Rent Act 1977.[36]

35　Although this is clearly desirable, from a tenant's point of view, when drafting such provisions. In *Cadogan v 27/29 Sloane Gardens Ltd* [2006] 2 EGLR 89 (see **9-12** above), the lease required the payment of the equivalent of a 'market' rent which, at least, gives some guidance to the court in the event of dispute.

36　Under the Rent Act 1977, which applied to qualifying lettings of dwellings prior to the introduction of the Housing Act 1988, a discounted fair rent was payable. This was changed to a market rent by the Housing Act 1988 in relation to assured tenancies.

CHAPTER 10

Insurance

10-01   It is commonplace in multi-occupied buildings for the landlord to be subject to an obligation to obtain an appropriate policy of insurance against various risks in respect of the building and for the tenants to be required to reimburse the cost of that policy. Although usually covered as another 'service' to be provided by the landlord, the landlord's and tenant's obligations with respect to insurance differ in some ways from the other 'services',[1] although in relation to leases of dwellings, the statutory regulation of service charges defines 'service charge' to include an amount payable by a tenant for insurance. Moreover, most service charge clauses (both residential and commercial) include the tenant's obligation to contribute towards the insurance premium with the other service charge obligations.

10-02   Whilst most discussions focus on buildings insurance, it is worth noting that a landlord might also be entitled to charge the tenants for other types of insurance, such as insurance against damage to mechanical or electrical plant or equipment (e.g. lifts, air conditioning etc.).[2] The principles discussed below will apply equally to insurance policies other than buildings insurance.

10-03   This chapter will consider the following issues:

1   What are the circumstances in which the tenant becomes liable to pay towards the insurance policy?

2   To what extent can the tenant challenge the landlord's choice of policy or its cost?

3   What sums is the landlord entitled to recover?

---

1   *Property Holding & Investment Trust Ltd v Lewis* (1969) 20 P&CR 808 was an appeal to the Court of Appeal in respect of a decision of a Rent Assessment Committee, determining a 'fair rent' under the Rent Act 1965, in which it was held that buildings insurance was not a 'service' provided by the landlord to the tenants and therefore that it was not part of the 'cost of services' provided by the landlord.
2   Which, incidentally, was held to be within the 'services' provided by the landlord in *Property Holding & Investment Trust Ltd v Lewis* (1969) 20 P&CR 808 (see above).

WHEN IS A TENANT LIABLE TO CONTRIBUTE TO THE COST OF INSURANCE?

10-04   As with all heads of service charge, the tenant will only be liable to contribute towards a particular cost if the lease so requires. However, as with all other heads of service charge, this point is easy to make but sometimes difficult to apply in practice. In the case of insurance, the difficulty often arises because the landlord's obligation to insure will usually be circumscribed by reference to numerous factors, such as the type of risk to be covered by the policy, the level of cover (e.g. reinstatement value of the buildings) and the type of (or even identity of) the insurer. Usually, the tenant's obligation to contribute will extend only to those policies of insurance which fall within the landlord's covenant and if the landlord does not comply with his covenant in obtaining insurance, he might be at risk of being unable to recover the cost from his tenants.

10-05   A striking example can be found in the decision of the Upper Tribunal in *Green v 180 Archway Road Management Co Ltd*.[3] There, the landlord's covenant was to keep the building insured in the joint names of landlord and tenant. The policy obtained by the landlord did not name the tenant in this instance. The landlord relied on the 'general interest' clause under the policy under which the interests of 'all leaseholders' of parts of the building were deemed to be noted on the policy. The LVT determined that the tenant was liable to contribute, because the insurance policy obtained by the landlord afforded her sufficient protection in the event of a claim. This decision was reversed on appeal to the Upper Tribunal. The LVT was considered to have asked the wrong question. Rather than considering whether the policy provided adequate protection for the tenant, the tribunal ought to have asked whether the landlord had insured the building in accordance with the terms of his obligation, which required insurance to be in the joint names of the landlord and tenant (thereby entitling the tenant to make a claim under the policy). Since the insurance was not in joint names, it was not obtained pursuant to the landlord's obligation and therefore the costs were irrecoverable.[4]

10-06   The Upper Tribunal case of *Mihovilovic v Leicester City Council*[5] involved a challenge by the tenant under a right-to-buy lease, under which the local authority was landlord, to the sums claimed by the local authority for insuring the building. The list of 'services' to which the tenant was liable to contribute included 'the costs and expenses of insuring the Premises and the Building'. Rather than purchasing a policy of insurance, the council included an amount in the service charge in respect of their costs of bearing the risks themselves. The LVT upheld the council's claim for these costs. This was reversed on appeal to

---

3   [2012] UKUT 245 (LC).
4   In that case, the tenant's obligation was to pay one quarter of the cost expended for insuring the building 'in accordance with' the landlord's covenant. Some leases might not make the express link between the tenant's liability to contribute and the landlord's covenant to insure. In such circumstances, the more general question asked by the LVT (which, in the circumstances of this case, was held to be the wrong question) might be appropriate, although in each case, the starting point must be to consider the express terms of the service charge obligations.
5   [2010] UKUT 22 (LC).

the Upper Tribunal. It was submitted on behalf of the council that the council's insurance obligation should be construed broadly in accordance with the wide powers of housing management enjoyed by the council. This was rejected. The tenant was liable to contribute towards the cost of insurance, not the cost of reinstatement. The costs attributed to the risk borne by the council landlord were not costs of the service of insuring but rather the services of rebuilding and reinstatement in the event of damage or destruction. Whilst the council may well have had the statutory power to bear these risks itself, under the standard wording of the tenant's covenant, the council was not entitled to levy a charge to the tenant based on the council's assessment of this risk as this was not a 'cost and expense of insuring'.

10-07   These two (rather extreme) examples demonstrate the importance to the landlord of obtaining an insurance policy which falls squarely within the scope of the tenant's service charge obligation. Where the tenant's obligation relates back to the landlord's covenant to insure, the landlord must insure strictly in accordance with that covenant. If the policy obtained is not a policy which complies with the landlord's covenant, the landlord may well find himself having to bear the expense without any right to reimbursement by the tenants.

FETTERS ON A LANDLORD'S ENTITLEMENT TO RECOVER THE COST OF INSURANCE

10-08   If a landlord obtains an insurance policy which complies with the landlord's covenants, to what extent can a tenant challenge the landlord's choice of insurer or policy and/or refuse to contribute towards the cost? What if the tenants have evidence that an appropriate policy of insurance could have been purchased for significantly less than the cost incurred by the landlord? In general terms, the courts have been astute to avoid construing a lease in a way which enables the tenants to scour the market to find a cheaper policy than the one to which they are being asked to contribute and to refuse to pay for the more expensive policy obtained by the landlord.[6]

10-09   In *Bandar Property Holdings Ltd v JS Darwen (Successors) Ltd*,[7] the landlord covenanted to insure the demised premises 'in some insurance office of repute or at Lloyds'. In accordance with that covenant, the landlord obtained cover and the tenant obtained a quote for similar cover at a lower cost. The tenant argued that its obligation to reimburse the landlord should be capped at the lower cost because the landlord was in breach of an implied term to act reasonably in placing such insurance and not to impose an unnecessarily heavy burden on the tenant. This implied term was rejected by Roskill J.[8] Moreover, there was no suggestion that even in accordance with such an implied term, the landlord could be subject to an obligation to obtain the cheapest rate.

6   See also **2-103** to **2-105** above.
7   [1968] 2 All ER 305.
8   See **2-103** above.

10-10   This issue was raised in *Gleniffer Finance Corporation Ltd v Bamar Wood Ltd*,[9] where the principal issue was the reinstatement value for which insurance should be obtained by the landlord. In addressing that question, counsel for the landlord had submitted, based on *Finchbourne Ltd v Rodriguez*,[10] that the landlord's duty is to act in a way which is 'fair and reasonable'. Alternatively, the landlord was to exercise his power to insure in good faith. Forbes J did not see the need to resolve this apparent conflict. He was satisfied that the landlord's approach in that case satisfied either test.

10-11   The question did, however, arise for decision by the Court of Appeal in *Havenridge Ltd v Boston Dyers Ltd*,[11] where the tenants of commercial premises argued that there was an implied term in the leases in question that the insurance premiums demanded by the landlord should be 'fair and reasonable'. There, the covenant required the tenant to pay such sums as the landlord should 'properly expend' in insuring the premises. The discussion centred on the ambit of the word 'properly'. The tenant's submission was that where the sum claimed by the landlord is unreasonably high or unreasonably incurred, as a result of evidence that the landlord, acting reasonably, could have obtained the insurance from an insurer 'of repute' at a lower cost than he has paid for it, this will be a good defence to the claim by the landlord.[12] The court, however, accepted the landlord's submission that 'properly' means that the landlord must show that the insurance was placed with an insurer 'of repute' in respect of the defined risks and otherwise in accordance with the contract, that the insurance was negotiated at arm's length and that the premium was no greater than 'the going rate'. That is not the same as requiring the landlord to pay a 'reasonable rate' (which would enable the tenants to shop around in the market for a lower premium, which would cap the amount that the landlord could recover). Rather, this reinforces the requirement that the landlord's negotiation with the chosen insurer should be an arm's length one and that the rate charged should be that chosen insurer's going rate for the policy in question.

10-12   Evans LJ considered both *Bandar Property Holdings Ltd v Darwen*[13] and *Finchbourne v Rodriguez*.[14] He did not consider that these two cases conflicted. Rather, *Finchbourne* was a decision on the particular words of the lease before the court and did not require the court to accept the tenant's argument in this case. He reconciled the authorities in this way:

> 'But the question remains, what limit should be placed upon the tenant's obligation to indemnify the landlord, so as to preclude an exorbitant claim or what Cairns LJ described in *Finchbourne Ltd* as an "outlandish" result? In my judgment, it matters

9   (1978) 37 P&CR 208.
10   [1976] 3 All ER 581. See **2-99** above.
11   [1994] 2 EGLR 73.
12   It was accepted by the tenants that this did not necessarily mean that the landlord could not recover more than the lowest amount which could be described as 'reasonable' in the circumstances.
13   [1968] 2 All ER 305; see **10-09** above.
14   [1976] 3 All ER 581; see **2-99** above.

not whether the limit is expressed as the meaning or true construction of "properly pay" or as an implied restriction on the landlord's right of recovery under clause 2(6)(a). The limitation, in my judgment, can best be expressed by saying that the landlord cannot recover in excess of the premium which he has paid and agreed to pay in the ordinary course of business as between the insurer and himself. If the transaction was arranged otherwise than in the normal course of business, for whatever reason, then it can be said that the premium was not properly paid, having regard to the commercial nature of the leases in question, or, equally, it can be supposed that both parties would have agreed with the officious bystander that the tenant should not be liable for a premium which had not been arranged in that way.

If this is the correct test, as in my judgment it is, then the fact that the landlord might have obtained a lower premium elsewhere does not prevent him from recovering the premium which he has paid. Nor does it permit the tenant to defend the claim by showing what other insurers might have charged. Nor is it necessary for the landlord to approach more than one insurer, or to "shop around". If he approaches only one insurer, being one insurer of "repute", and a premium is negotiated and paid in the normal course of business as between them, reflecting the insurer's usual rate for business of that kind then, in my judgment, the landlord is entitled to succeed. The safeguard for the tenant is that, if the rate appears to be high in comparison with other rates that are available in the insurance markets at the time, then the landlord can be called upon to prove that there was no special feature of the transaction which took it outside the normal course of business.'

10-13   Peter Gibson LJ considered that the landlord's concession that 'properly' might require the premium to be that obtained in an arm's length bargain between landlord and insurer might go too far. So, where, for example, the insurance company is the landlord, if the policy is obtained from an associated insurance company, it would not be improper if it was no more than a payment at market rate. However, he agreed with Evans LJ's ultimate conclusion that the landlord is not required to 'shop around'.

10-14   Whilst this decision gives some helpful guidance as to what the parties meant by 'properly' pay in the context of that lease, this should not be followed slavishly in relation to all insurance covenants. The Court of Appeal's approach, rejecting the submission that a landlord is required to shop around for the cheapest policy in the market, is one which reflects a theme in these cases.[15] However, the starting point must always be to consider the express restrictions in the lease before looking to apply this guidance.

15 See also *Berrycroft Management Co Ltd v Sinclair Gardens Investments (Kensington) Ltd* (1996) 75 P&CR 210, where the Court of Appeal rejected the argument that the landlord's right to nominate an insurer should be subject to an implied term that the nomination is a reasonable one or that the tenant should not be required to pay a substantially higher sum than he could himself arrange with an insurance office of repute. The tenant relied on *Finchbourne v Rodriguez* [1976] 3 All ER 581. The landlord relied on *Bandar Property Holdings Ltd v Darwen* [1968] 2 All ER 305 and *Havenridge Ltd v Boston Dyers Ltd* [1994] 2 EGLR 73. The court held that the express requirement that the insurance office should be 'of repute' provided sufficient protection for the tenant and that it was not necessary to go further. See also *Ustimenko v Prescot Management Co Ltd* [2005] EWLands LRZ_65_2004.

10-15   In light of the clear trend against an obligation on a landlord to shop around for the cheapest premium in the market, it is difficult to see what role section 19 of the Landlord and Tenant Act 1985 can play in circumstances where a landlord has obtained a policy from an insurer of repute as a result of an arm's length bargain. In *Berrycroft Management Co Ltd v Sinclair Gardens Investments (Kensington) Ltd,*[16] it was argued that section 19 applied to introduce an additional layer of reasonableness. The actual decision on that point was that section 19 did not apply because the contributions to the insurance policy were payable to a management company rather than the landlord.[17] It is likely that where there are no express contractual fetters on the landlord's choice of insurer or policy, section 19 would enable a tenant to adduce evidence that the policy was not obtained from an appropriate insurer ('of repute'[18]) or that the bargain struck by the landlord was not made at arm's length. Beyond that, it is unlikely that an argument by a tenant of a dwelling that the landlord could have obtained a cheaper policy will fall foul the requirement that the cost of the insurance be 'reasonable'.[19] It is relevant to go back to the decision of Roskill J in *Bandar Property Holdings Ltd v JS Darwen (Successors) Ltd,*[20] where it was held[21] that even if (contrary to the decision) a term had been implied that the landlord should act reasonably in obtaining insurance cover, it was still not suggested that this required the landlord to obtain the cheapest policy available. It is therefore suggested that in cases concerning dwellings, tribunals should not be astute to accept evidence from tenants who have conducted a survey of the insurance market and have managed to find an insurer who would provide a similar policy at a lower cost and, as a result of such evidence, to hold that the cost incurred by the landlord was unreasonably high. First, there will always be a difficulty of comparing 'like for like'. Even if the terms of the policy are the same, there are other factors which are more difficult to compare, such as the reliability and strength of the insurer in question. Secondly, it is suggested that in light of the authorities cited above, this is the wrong approach to take under section 19 where a tenant argues that the cost of insurance is unreasonable.

10-16   Other factors that might be relevant in a challenge to a landlord's claim for contributions to an insurance premium might focus on the policy itself. Where the landlord is allowed latitude by the terms of the lease as to the risks to be insured or the reinstatement value/loss of rent to be covered, for example,

---

16   (1996) 75 P&CR 210.
17   Since 'relevant costs' are defined to mean costs incurred by or on behalf of a landlord and the management company was considered not to incur the costs of insurance on behalf of the landlord. See **28-23** below. The same point applied in *Ustimenko v Prescot Management Co Ltd* [2005] EWLands LRZ_65_2004.
18   Even this term is limited: providing the insurer offers policies in the market, it is difficult to see how the choice of insurer can be challenged.
19   See, for example, the decision of the Upper Tribunal in *Redendale Ltd v Modi* [2010] UKUT 346 (LC) where it was argued that the landlord had not obtained competitive quotes for the relevant years. The tribunal accepted the landlord's evidence that it took 'all reasonable steps to effect insurance covenant in accordance with the covenants under the lease and in a cost effective manner'. There had been difficulties in obtaining insurance on favourable terms because of the history of the building and these difficulties were taken into account.
20   See **10-09** above.
21   At p 789.

it would be open to a tenant to argue that the cost of the insurance was not 'reasonably incurred' to the extent that the landlord included unnecessary risks,[22] or insured to an unreasonably high value.[23] The RICS Residential Management Code provides[24] that regular valuations should be undertaken for insurance purposes. Moreover, it states that where a property manager is selecting an insurance company, regard should be had to experience of that company's handling of claims as well as the premium.

RECOVERABLE COSTS: COMMISSION

10-17   Often, landlords are able to negotiate discounts with insurers for bulk purchases where they insure a number of properties with the same insurer. It will be a matter of construction, in each case, of whether the landlord is required to pass on this discount to the tenants. In *Williams v Southwark LBC*,[25] the local authority landlord obtained a 25% discount on the premium payable for insuring the building. Of that 25%, 5% was attributable to a 'loyalty bonus' or commission. It was conceded that this ought to be passed on to the tenants. The remaining 20% was consideration for the local authority handling and administering the policies. It was held that this need not be passed on to the tenants. The latter point ultimately turned on the terms of the rather odd arrangement between the local authority and the insurer. Under the policy, the local authority was obliged to pay the full premium and the insurer agreed to assign to the council responsibility for claims handling and to pay the council 20% of the premium in return for those services. Therefore, on analysis, the premium was not, actually, reduced by the further 20% and therefore it was held that this was payable by the lessees.

10-18   Although the issue as to the loyalty bonus or commission was based on a concession, it would require very plain terms before a tribunal or court would allow a landlord to retain a commission received for bulk insurance purchases.[26]

---

22   In *Re 80A Bolton Crescent*, Lands Tribunal (LRA/140/2007), the President of the Lands Tribunal said (*obiter*) that if a landlord insured against risks additional to those normally insured against under a householder's comprehensive policy, the cost associated with those additional risks would not be a cost reasonably incurred (para 13).

23   The level of the reinstatement value was in issue in *Gleniffer Finance Corporation Ltd v Bamar Wood and Products Ltd* (1978) 37 P&CR 208. The circumstances were unusual. The insurance was effected at a time of rapid inflation. The landlord obtained a policy of insurance which estimated the cost of reinstatement at a date some two years after the beginning of the year in which the policy is to take effect to account for the delay between the possible damage or destruction during that year and the eventual reinstatement of the building. This was held to be the correct approach, as a matter of construction of the lease (since this related to commercial premises and therefore there was no statutory gloss to consider): the parties must have contemplated delay between damage being caused by an insured peril and eventual reinstatement to be covered by the policy.

24   At para 15.16

25   (2001) 33 HLR 22.

26   A concession to the contrary was made in the leasehold enfranchisement case of *Castlebeg Investments (Jersey) Ltd v Lynch* (1989) 57 P&CR 493, where the Lands Tribunal was determining the price payable on enfranchisement of a house and took into account the capital value of the commission receivable by the landlord on insurance premiums. See also *63 Perham Road Ltd v Manyfield Ltd* [1995] 2 EGLR 206. It is not considered that these cases would influence the decision as to the treatment of such commission if it were directly in issue.

STATUTORY INTERVENTION

10-19   Under section 30A and the schedule to the Landlord and Tenant Act 1985, tenants of dwellings are given rights to obtain information about the insurance policies held by landlords and to notify the insurer of a claim under the policy. These provisions are considered in detail in Part IV, below.[27]

---

27   See **33-36**ff. below.

CHAPTER 11

Legal costs

INTRODUCTION

11-01 It is necessary to distinguish between three discrete issues which arise. First, the question of whether a landlord is entitled to recover legal costs (e.g. solicitors, counsel) arising out of disputes with other tenants in relation to their leases. The disputes might relate to the collection of service charges or they might relate to other aspects of the leases, e.g. other breaches of covenant by tenants. It is this question which is the subject of this chapter. Secondly, and following on from the first issue, there is the question of whether the landlord of a dwelling should be precluded from recovering legal costs as service charges by virtue of section 20C of the Landlord and Tenant Act 1985.[1] This is covered in Chapter 29, in relation to statutory provisions concerning service charges. Thirdly, questions might sometimes arise as to whether a landlord is entitled to recover costs, contractually, against a recalcitrant tenant in relation to that tenant's breaches of covenant under the lease. This sometimes raises a further issue of the correct basis of assessment of costs which are recovered from a tenant pursuant to a contractual right.[2] This final issue is outside the scope of a text on service charges.[3]

11-02 As with most of the heads of service charge, ultimately, the question of whether a landlord is entitled to recover legal costs incurred in relation to the management of the estate/proceedings against other tenants, turns on the true construction of the lease and the nature of the costs which have been incurred by the landlord. It is clearly preferable for such an entitlement to be spelled out in clear language. The reported cases tend to focus on arguments that more general covenants to contribute towards the costs of management of the estate include a right to recover legal costs. In this context, as in relation to the other aspects of this section where specific items are held to fall within or outside the service charge provisions of a particular lease, the courts are not held to a

---

1 There is no equivalent jurisdiction in relation to non-residential premises.
2 See, for example, *Gomba Holdings (UK) Ltd v Minories Finance (No 2) Ltd* [1993] Ch 171 (where the basis of the payment of costs pursuant to a mortgage was considered); Church *Commissioners v Ibrahim* [1997] 1 EGLR 13; *Forcelux Ltd v Binnie* [2009] EWCA Civ 854.
3 See *Woodfall: Landlord and Tenant*, Vol 1, Ch 7.

particular conclusion as a result of a previous decision, in relation to a different lease, concerning a different property, with a differently worded service charge provision.[4]

11-03   A landlord will usually seek to recover litigation costs or costs arising out the enforcement of covenants against a recalcitrant tenant from the tenant himself. It is only if either that tenant is unable to pay or there is a shortfall in the costs recoverable from that tenant, that the landlord will need to have recourse to the service charge provisions in order to recover the costs or the shortfall from the other tenants.[5] In the residential context, this issue also arises, which is in relation to the costs of proceedings for the determination of the tenants' liability to contribute to service charges in the LVT where the tribunal's powers to award costs are limited by Schedule 12, paragraph 10 to the Commonhold and Leasehold Reform Act 2002 to a fixed sum[6] and only in circumstances where the tenant has acted 'frivolously, vexatiously, abusively, disruptively or otherwise unreasonably in connection with the proceedings'. However, where the leases contain a sufficiently broad provision for the landlord to recover the costs of recovering rent/service charges from other tenants, that will entitle the landlord to recover the costs of proceedings before the LVT from the tenants as service charges.[7]

CASES WHERE COSTS IRRECOVERABLE

11-04   In *Sella House Ltd v Mears*,[8] a landlord sought to charge to the tenants costs incurred in recovering rent and service charges from other tenants. The relevant provisions under which the landlord claimed to be entitled to recover these costs as service charges entitled the landlord to the costs associated with employing 'a firm of Management Agents and chartered Accounts to manage the buildings ... including the cost of computing and collecting the rents and service charges' and 'all such surveyors builders architects engineers tradesmen accountants or other professional persons as may be necessary or desirable for the proper maintenance, safety and administration of the building'.

---

4   See, for example, *Iperion Investments Corporation v Broadwalk House Residents Ltd* [1995] 2 EGLR 47 (**11-13** below), where Peter Gibson LJ said that he was unable to derive any assistance from what appears, at first glance, to be a similar clause in *Sella House Ltd v Mears* [1989] 1 EGLR 65; *St Mary's Mansions Ltd v Limegate Investment Co Ltd* [2003] 1 EGLR 41 at paras 64–65, where Ward LJ rejected the analogy with *Iperion Investments*.
5   Such costs can include in-house legal costs, e.g. *OM Property Management Ltd, Re 36 Culpepper Close* [2012] UKUT 102 (LC).
6   Currently £500: para 10(3)(a).
7   This will be subject to the Landlord and Tenant Act 1985, s 20C; see Chapter 29 below. See also *Freeholders of 69 Marina, St Leonard-on-Sea v Oram* [2011] EWCA Civ 1258, where it was held that the service charge obligation was too narrow to encompass LVT and County Court costs incurred against non-paying tenants, but the Court of Appeal also held that such costs were recoverable contractually from the tenants in question under the covenant to pay the landlord's costs incidental to the preparation and service of a s 146 notice. See also **45-38**ff. below.
8   [1989] 1 EGLR 65.

11-05   So far as the first of the two limbs was concerned, it was argued that where the managing agents instructed solicitors and/or counsel (on the landlord's behalf) in relation to 'collecting the rents and service charges', such costs fell within the first limb. As for the second limb, it was argued, for the landlord, that the costs in question related to the 'proper ... administration of the building'. These arguments were both rejected. Dillon LJ confessed to having had 'certain hesitation on this point', especially in light of the argument about solicitors instructed by managing agents, but, in the end, concluded that the costs were not recoverable under either limb. Taylor LJ said:[9]

> 'Nowhere in clause 5(4)(j) is there any specific mention of lawyers, proceedings or legal costs. The scope of (j)(i) is concerned with management. In (j)(ii) it is with maintenance, safety and administration. On the respondent's argument a tenant, paying his rent and service charge regularly, would be liable via the service charge to subsidise the landlord's legal costs of suing his co-tenants, if they were all defaulters. For my part, I should require to see a clause in clear and unambiguous terms before being persuaded that that result was intended by the parties.'

11-06   *St Mary's Mansions Ltd v Limegate Investment Co Ltd*[10] was an appeal against a number of declarations made concerning aspects of the service charge provisions in the leases of flats in Maida Vale. One of the three issues on appeal was whether legal costs were recoverable under two service charge provisions. The first entitled the landlord to the costs of 'all other services which the lessor may at its absolute discretion provide or install ... for the comfort or convenience of the lessees' and 'the reasonable and proper fees of ... the Lessor's managing agents for the collection of the rents of the flats in the said Buildings and for the general management thereof'. In the County Court, the parties had distinguished between different types of legal costs (e.g. proceedings for recovery of service charges, proceedings for recovery of ground rent and obtaining legal advice in relation to the covenants in the leases). On appeal, it was held that no category of legal costs was recoverable as service charges. Ward LJ (with whom the other members of the court agreed) relied on the dictum of Taylor LJ in *Sella House Ltd v Mears*.[11] He agreed with the trial judge who concluded that expenditure on legal fees was not 'the provision of a service in the said buildings' and concluded that the other covenant relied upon by the landlord provided for the costs of the managing agents and rejected the submission that this might extend to costs incurred by the managing agents in obtaining legal advice/incurring other fees in connection with its management of the building. To this extent, the decision followed *Sella House Ltd v Mears*.

11-07   A rather different issue arose in *Holding & Management Ltd v Property Holding & Investment Trust Plc*.[12] There, the court held that the legal costs in question were irrecoverable, notwithstanding an express provision that litigation costs were payable as service charges. The claimant was a trustee of the

---

9   At p 68E.
10   [2003] 1 EGLR 41.
11   [1989] 1 EGLR 65.
12   [1989] 1 WLR 1313.

maintenance fund and was a party to the leases. The obligation to carry out the matters for which the service charge was payable was that of the trustee and the trustee had the right to recover the service charges from the tenants. The service charge fund was held on an express trust. An issue arose with regard to major works required to the building. A number of schemes were proposed and the trustee selected the most extensive, the cost of which was to be over £1 million (divided between 47 flats). The tenants obtained their own advice and put forward an alternative scheme. A third, mid-way scheme was then suggested by the landlord's engineers. At trial, the tenants' engineers and the landlord's engineers managed to agree a fourth scheme. The trial judge held that the leases did not permit the trustee to implement the original scheme of works and therefore disallowed the trustee its costs.

11-08 The trustee appealed, relying on the principle that a trustee is entitled to an indemnity for costs it incurs in seeking the court's directions in the execution of the trust, under section 30(2) of the Trustee Act 1925. The trustee relied on its position as being independent from the landlord. Apart from its remuneration as trustee, it was argued that the claimant had no interest and therefore ought to be paid its costs of the proceedings out of the trust fund in accordance with the principles applicable when a trustee seeks the assistance of the court. This was rejected because although the maintenance trustee was a trustee of the maintenance fund, this was not a case where there was a dispute between the beneficiaries.[13] The tenants were all represented by common counsel and the landlord accepted the position adopted by the tenants. Therefore, the trustee brought proceedings of an adversarial nature and was not entitled to recover its costs as a matter of course. It was considered that the trustee's stance was unreasonable and that it could not take advantage of the rules applicable to trusts where it was, equally, relying on the tenants' covenants to reimburse the cost of works carried out. According to Nicholls LJ, the effect of the claim to reimbursement was to 'get through the back door what has been refused at the front', the trial judge having decided that on the merits, the most appropriate order was no order as to costs.

11-09 *Morgan v Stainer*[14] was also a case where there was an express provision in the lease that the legal costs of proceedings for the recovery of service charges could be charged as service charges.[15] A number of tenants brought proceedings against the landlord seeking declarations and other relief in relation to service charges. Those proceedings resulted in a consent order whereby the tenants agreed to pay some £85,000 (out of a total of £130,000) towards the landlord's costs. Subsequently, the landlord sought to recover the balance by way of service charges. The Deputy Judge[16] held that such costs could not be recovered under the covenant. First, it was considered that the proceedings in question were

---

13 Such as, for example, *Reston Ltd v Hudson* [1990] 2 EGLR 51, which was not cited in *Holding Ltd v Property Trust Plc*.
14 [1993] 2 EGLR 73.
15 The lease provided that service charges were payable in respect of 'all legal and other costs that may be incurred by the landlord in obtaining payment of maintenance contributions from any tenant in the building.'
16 David Neuberger QC.

not proceedings for the recovery of service charges. They were brought by the tenants to determine various disputed issues. The recovery of service charge arrears might have been a bi-product of the proceedings, but that did not lead to the conclusion that the costs fell within the covenant.[17] Further, the Deputy Judge said that the consent order amounted to a contract between the parties under which the tenant agreed to pay the landlord's costs and therefore, there was no scope for the operation of the covenant. He also considered that it would be implied that any costs which the landlord seeks to recover would be just and reasonable[18] and that it would be presumed, as a result of the consent order, that the additional costs were not reasonably incurred.

CASES WHERE COSTS RECOVERABLE

11-10   In *Reston v Hudson*,[19] the landlord discovered, in redecorating the exterior of a block of flats, that a number of window frames were defective and needed to be replaced. Although only some were defective, the landlord took the view that they should all be replaced at the same time, for aesthetic reasons. They canvassed opinion amongst the tenants and some argued that the replacement of the window frames did not fall within the service charge provisions of the lease. The landlord therefore applied to the court for a declaration. In the end, although a number of tenants were joined as defendants (presumably, those who had objected to the proposals), none of them appeared at the hearing or took any active part in opposing the claim.

11-11   The lease entitled the landlord to recover the costs of 'management of the estate' and 'all outgoings, costs and expenses whatsoever which the lessor may reasonably incur in the discharge of its obligations under clause 4 of the lease'. The latter provision was said to include matters other than the actual works of repair. It was held that, in view of the obvious difficulties concerning the interpretation of the lease and the difficulties which would flow if the landlords went ahead without resolving the legal obstacles, the landlords had reasonably incurred the costs of the application and those costs fell 'fairly and squarely' within the relevant service charge provision.

11-12   In *Skilleter v Charles*,[20] the lease contained a broad right for the landlord to recoup 'all legal and other proper costs' incurred in the running and management of the property and in the enforcement of the tenants' covenants,

---

17   Again, it was considered that a provision of this sort ought to be given a narrow or restrictive construction (without reference to the judgment of Taylor LJ in *Sella House Ltd v Mears* [1989] 1 EGLR 65).

18   Applying *Finchbourne v Rodrigues* [1976] 1 EGLR 51 (see **2-99** above). This tends to suggest that the Landlord and Tenant Act 1985, s 19 was considered not to apply to the leases in question. The only description of the demised premises is 'various suites in a substantial building'. It is not clear whether these suites were residential or commercial suites, but, even if used for residential purposes, they might have been considered not to be 'dwellings'.

19   [1990] 2 EGLR 81.

20   [1992] 1 EGLR 73.

in so far as not recovered from the tenant in breach. This was, unsurprisingly, held to cover the costs of recovering rent and other sums from some of the tenants. However, Parker LJ thought that the existence of a right to recover via the service charge brought about a corresponding duty on the part of the landlord to endeavour to recover the expenses from the defaulting tenants. In principle, this seems sound, but its application could well give rise to problems of degree. What level of endeavour is required? How far must a landlord go to recover from the tenant in question? This is not a question which has arisen, squarely, for decision in any reported cases. In theory, if this duty exists, it would operate as an implied pre-condition to the landlord's right to recover the legal costs (rather than a free-standing obligation owed to the tenants, breach of which would sound in damages). It is also considered that this would be relevant to the question of whether legal costs have been reasonably incurred for the purposes of section 19 of the Landlord and Tenant Act 1985.[21]

11-13 Legal costs were also held to fall within the relevant service charge covenant in *Iperion Investments Corporation v Broadwalk House Residents Ltd*.[22] There, the landlord incurred costs in defending what was ultimately determined to be an unlawful physical re-entry[23] and resisting an ultimately successful application for relief from forfeiture. The defendant tenant was ordered to pay only half of the landlord's costs (to reflect the fact that the landlord was unsuccessful on some of the issues). Peter Gibson LJ (with whom the other members of the court agreed) held that the landlord was entitled to recover its costs of the proceedings, providing those costs were properly incurred in managing the property. That would not be the case if the landlord incurred costs (whether in bringing or defending proceedings, or otherwise) improperly or unreasonably. Subject to that qualification, however, the costs were clearly costs of managing the property. However, the landlord was ultimately deprived of the right to charge these costs to the defendant tenant via the service charge under section 20C of the Landlord and Tenant Act 1985.[24]

11-14 In *Staghold Ltd v Takeda*,[25] it was held, in the County Court, that the costs incurred by a landlord in proceedings before the LVT in which the tenant's challenge to certain aspects of the service charges failed, almost in its entirety, were recoverable under a covenant to contribute to the cost of:

> 'employment of … legal or professional advisors … for the collection of rent of the flats in the block of flats or in connection with the general management or maintenance thereof or to estimate, carry out or supervise or arrange for the

---

21 Consider the analogy with the Lands Tribunal decision in *Continental Property Ventures Inc v White* [2006] 1 EGLR 85, where it was held that the cost of works was not 'reasonably incurred' in circumstances where the landlord could have recovered the costs by claiming on a contractor's guarantee.
22 [1995] 2 EGLR 47.
23 Because, unbeknown to the landlord, a housekeeper was in residence.
24 See Chapter 29 below.
25 [2005] 3 EGLR 45.

estimation, carrying out, execution or supervision of all or any of the above services or any or all of the Landlord's rights or obligations hereunder'.

11-15 It was also argued by the tenant that the landlord was precluded from recovering the costs by virtue of of Schedule 12, paragraph 10 to the Commonhold and Leasehold Reform Act 2002[26] and this argument was rejected. The landlord had a contractual right to recover the costs as service charges and the court accepted the landlord's argument that paragraph 10 cannot have been intended by the legislature to extinguish a contractual right to recoup costs.

11-16 In *Plantation Wharf Management Co v Jackson*,[27] the Upper Tribunal reversed a decision of the LVT and held that legal costs of proceedings to recover service charges (which were subsequently transferred by the County Court to the LVT) were recoverable. HH Judge Mole QC said:

> 'Therefore, to put it all together, the lease says that the service charge includes "the fees charges ... and expenses ... of professional advisers" engaged in "the enforcement ... of any covenants ... relating to any unit ... in the interests of good estate management". Clearly the enforced collection of the covenanted service charges from tenants who are refusing to pay them may be "in the interests of good estate management" because otherwise there will not be enough money to manage the estate properly. A primary, if not the only, proper method of the enforcement of covenants against a tenant is by bringing legal proceedings. It is extremely difficult to contemplate the bringing of legal proceedings, in most circumstances, without also contemplating the employment of lawyers, whether solicitors or counsel and whether advising, drafting, or acting as advocates. Although it is true that the words "legal costs" or "the costs of legal advisers" do not appear in the lease, it seems to me to be overwhelmingly clear that such costs are indeed included, on any fair construction. I find the provisions of the lease "clear and unambiguous" (to borrow Taylor L.J.'s words in *Sella*) that a tenant is liable, via the service charge, to subsidise the landlord's costs of suing defaulter tenants. (Certainly, in my view, those words are clearer than the provision that the Court of Appeal considered sufficient to include legal costs in the case of *Iperion*.)'[28]

11-17 It has also been held in an appeal to the Lands Tribunal in *Canary Riverside PTE Ltd v Schilling*[29] that the landlord's costs of resisting an application made by one of the tenants to the LVT for the appointment of a manager under section 24 of the Landlord and Tenant Act 1987[30] were recoverable as 'the fees of ... solicitors, counsel, surveyors ... employed or retained by the Landlord for or in connection with the general overall management and administration and supervision of the Building'. HH Judge Rich QC said that incurring fees in resisting an application to change the manager of the building is clearly in connection with the management of the building and, if the fees are proper and

26 Which limits the extent to which the LVT can make an order for costs in service charge proceedings.
27 [2012] L&TR 18.
28 See also *Re Shinereach Ltd* [2006] EWLands LRX_94_2005.
29 [2005] EWLands LRX_65_2005.
30 As to which, see **47-46**ff. below.

reasonable, they fall within the costs chargeable to the service charge.[31] He went on to explain that such costs are recoverable in the same way as costs incurred in collecting service charges from tenants who fail to pay. Whilst, ordinarily, such costs will be recoverable from the unsuccessful tenant, providing the landlord has reasonably incurred those costs, in so far as they are not recoverable from the complaining tenant, they can be charged to the service charge as costs of management. It was further held that Schedule 12, paragraph 10(4) to the Commonhold and Leasehold Reform Act 2002 does not preclude recovery of such costs.[32]

---

31 At para 13. See also para 15 where he said: 'Resisting such challenges is part of the ordinary cost of management, just as is the cost of collecting the service charge from tenants who fail to pay on demand.'
32 See also *Staghold v Takeda* [2005] 3 EGLR 45 (County Court); **11-14** above.

CHAPTER 12

The cost of borrowing

12-01   Most well-drawn leases contain a comprehensive system for payments on account to be made by tenants so that the landlord has a sufficient cash-flow to pay for ongoing matters which arise and form the subject matter of the service charge budget.[1] Additionally, it is common for provision to be made for payments into a reserve fund to provide for larger or one-off items of expenditure which might arise.[2] Reserve funds are usually intended, primarily, for the benefit of the tenants, to avoid significant items of expenditure in a particular year. However, they are also of benefit to landlords, avoiding the need to take steps to recover larger sums and to meet the shortfall in the meantime.

12-02   However, even where there is both a system for payments on account and provision for a reserve fund, it is not uncommon for landlords to be required to fund the provision of services. Sometimes payments on account are insufficient and, usually, it is only after the end of the relevant service charge year that the landlord is able to claim a balancing payment from the tenants. Sometimes, larger items of expenditure do not fall within the scope of the matters on which the reserve fund might be spent or the reserve fund is insufficient to cover the cost of a significant item of expenditure. In these circumstances (which are not uncommon, especially in relation to larger estates/centres), the landlord will find itself in a position where it is required to provide funds itself, pending recovery from the tenants.

12-03   This gives rise to the question of whether the landlord can include, as an additional service charge item, the cost of funding the shortfall. That cost might reflect the actual cost to the landlord, where the landlord borrows the money, or it might be in the nature of a notional cost (where the landlord draws on his capital resources). However, therein lies the problem, as explained by Slade LJ in *Boldmark Ltd v Cohen*:[3]

> 'If in any particular year the lessors, without the necessity to borrow, have sufficient liquid resources to pay for the paragraphs 2 to 6 items and choose to

1   See **16-01** below.
2   See Chapter 22 below.
3   (1985) 19 HLR 135.

121

pay for them out of such resources, they will be deprived for the time being of the use of the monies concerned. Yet there will be no question of their being able to claim reimbursement from the lessees in respect of lost interest. Mr. Weeks (in my opinion rightly) expressly conceded that the crucial phrase in paragraph 7 would not on any construction be wide enough to include a claim for interest on notional borrowing. If the construction urged on behalf of the lessors were correct then, as Mr. Wood pointed out on behalf of the appellants, the extent of the lessee's liability for service charges would depend on the personal circumstances of the lessors or their policy in arranging their financial affairs. If in any particular year of the tenancy they were impecunious, they would have to borrow, and the lessee's liability for service charges would be correspondingly increased. If, on the other hand, they had sufficient resources to render borrowing unnecessary, the extent of the lessee's liability would depend on whether the lessors chose, as a matter of financial policy, to borrow. It would, of course, be perfectly possible for parties to a lease by clear words to contract in terms which subjected the tenant to a liability for service charges which would vary according to circumstances of this nature, over which he had no control. For my part, however, I would be slow to construe general phraseology of uncertain import (such as the crucial phrase in paragraph 7) in such a way as to produce these potentially anomalous results.'

12-04   Thus, in that case, the court held that in the absence of specific provision entitling the landlord to recover interest on borrowing, the landlord was not able to do so. Similarly, in *Frobisher (Second Investments) Ltd v Kiloran Trust Co Ltd*,[4] it was held that interest was irrecoverable in the absence of express provision.[5] The landlord's entitlement to recover the costs of 'general management and administration' and 'other outgoings payable … in respect of the property' were considered to be insufficient.

12-05   Conversely, however, in *Skilletter v Charles*,[6] there was express provision for the recovery of interest incurred for the purpose of the maintenance charges. Although there was a drafting error, the court readily held that such interest was recoverable. Parker LJ went on to say that if the express provision could not be construed in the landlord's favour, a term could be implied that interest should be chargeable to the tenants, on the basis that such a term is necessary to give business efficacy to the contract or, alternatively, on the basis of the officious bystander test. The question of whether such a term could be implied was addressed in *Frobisher (Second Investments) Ltd v Kiloran Trust Co Ltd*[7] and this argument was rejected by Walton J. It does not appear that this was argued in *Boldmark Ltd v Cohen*[8] in the Court of Appeal. However, notwithstanding Parker LJ's *obiter* comments, it is likely that in the absence of an express provision as

4   [1980] 1 WLR 425.
5   That case concerned the impact of the Housing Finance Act 1972, s 91A, which made provision restricting the recovery of residential service charges to those which were reasonably incurred. However, in doing so, it was held by Walton J that the legislation prevented residential landlords from recovering payments on account (which was changed by subsequent legislation). Therefore, the landlord found itself in an impossible position, which was not catered for by the lease (which predated this legislation).
6   [1992] 1 EGLR 73.
7   [1980] 1 WLR 425.
8   (1985) 19 HLR 135.

to interest, the combined authorities of *Frobisher* and *Boldmark* would preclude any such argument from succeeding.

12-06   In *Skilletter v Charles,* Parker LJ said, in relation to interest, that 'no question of reasonableness can arise'. In the context of that case, the comment was probably intended to mean that no question of reasonableness arose or, alternatively, that no question of whether it is reasonable to pay interest could arise (given that the interest was only incurred because of defaulting lessees leaving a shortfall in the service charge account). However, at least in a residential context, a tenant would be entitled to challenge an interest charge as being unreasonable, under section 19 of the Landlord and Tenant Act 1985.[9] If a loan was negotiated by the landlord at commercial rates, it might well be difficult for the tenant to challenge the rate payable, but it is not inconceivable that the landlord might accept a loan at an unreasonably high rate for purposes which otherwise suit the landlord, which is held to be an unreasonable amount for the tenants to pay by way of service charges.

---

9   See Chapter 29 below.

CHAPTER 13

Marketing and promotion costs

13-01   This head of service charge is often found in leases of units in retail centres where it is important for both the landlord and the tenants to attract members of the public to the centre. For the tenants, it is important to boost trade in order to maximise income. This has a knock-on effect for the landlord because tenants whose income stream is flowing represent a stronger and more secure covenant than tenants who struggle to make a profit. If such costs are to be recoverable as service charges, the leases must make clear provision to that effect. It is unlikely that this would fall within a sweeping-up clause.[1]

13-02   An example of a dispute about a provision entitling a landlord to recover the costs of 'promotion' can be found in *Boots UK Ltd v Trafford Centre Ltd*.[2] The lease of a unit in the Trafford Centre in Manchester entitled the landlord to recover the costs of 'promotion' which was defined to include 'advertising and other forms of promotion of the centre intended to bring additional custom to the Centre'. The court rejected the tenant's submissions that this impliedly excluded any activity (whether or not related to advertising) within the centre, rather than outside it, and the submission that this was limited to one-off, rather than regular, activities was also rejected.

13-03   It is usual for the leases of units in a centre, which require the landlord to undertake promotion and advertising and give the landlord the right to recoup the cost from the tenants, to prescribe the nature of the activities to which the tenants are liable to contribute, with a view to ensuring that the advertising or promotional activities are genuinely for the benefit of all tenants. In *Boots UK Ltd v Trafford Centre Ltd*, the clause expressly provided that 'Promotion' excluded any advertising in relation to letting individual units.

13-04   Paragraph 10.1 of the RICS Commercial Code contains guidance as to the best approach for a landlord to take with regard to the recovery of marketing and promotional costs, with specific reference to shopping centres (which is

---

1   See **2-55** above.
2   [2008] EWHC 3372.

where such provisions are most likely to be found). The following points are worthy of note:

1   'Joint funding' (by landlord and tenants) may well cover not only actual marketing and promotions, but also providing specialist staff and accommodation, etc.

2   It is best practice for marketing plans (including promotions) to be prepared and presented to occupiers in advance of the period to which they relate. Marketing plans should be reviewed regularly with occupiers to analyse their effectiveness. Any pedestrian flow data should be issued to the tenants as a matter of course.

3   Costs incurred in relation to the initial promotional launch or rebranding of a scheme are to be borne by the owner and are not to be considered as service charge recoverable costs.

4   The cost of entertainments, attractions, Christmas and other seasonal decorations and events within a centre are not usually to be considered a marketing and promotional cost but are to be regarded as amenities or facilities.[3]

5   The marketing of vacant units is not a service charge item.

13-05   Generally, as with any specific points made by either of the RICS codes of practice relating to service charges, these comments must yield to the terms of the lease in question, which may well limit or even extend the type of charges which are recoverable by the landlord.

---

3   This reflects the decision in *Boots UK Ltd v Trafford Centre Ltd* [2008] EWHC 3372. It should be borne in mind, however, that that case turned solely on the wording of the lease before the court and was not setting any general precedent in relation to the recovery of such costs.

PART III

Service charge machinery

CHAPTER 14

Overview of machinery

14-01 The details of service charge machinery naturally vary from lease to lease and how such machinery operates will involve construction of the terms of a particular lease, bearing in mind the commercial objectives of such clauses and the specific principles of construction discussed in Chapter 2 of this book. Despite the variance in structure and detail, some common issues can be identified, which are addressed in this Part of the book.

14-02 This Part considers the following issues:

1   The most common types of management structure, their implications for the rights and responsibilities of the parties and the ways in which a management structure can be changed.

2   The procedural requirements for and preconditions to a liability to pay service charges.

3   Third party certification.

4   Accounts.

5   Demands.

6   Apportionment.

7   Sinking and reserve funds.

8   Particular problems with service charge machinery.

9   Variation of service charge provisions.

10 Machinery relating to freehold service charges.

CHAPTER 15

Types of management structure

BI- AND TRIPARTITE LEASES

15-01 Commonly, service charge structures are either bipartite (landlord-tenant) or tripartite (landlord-tenant-manager). In the former case, it is the landlord who agrees to provide services in exchange for payment of service charge. In the latter case, the right to collect service charge, and the correlative obligation to provide services, is vested in some form of manager. It is a matter of construction of the terms of a particular lease as to whether there are any residual obligations to provide services resting on the landlord which may be invoked when the manager is in default of his obligations. However, in that regard, it must be borne in mind that the point of tripartite structures is for landlords to insulate themselves from the responsibilities and liabilities of managing a building, so that such residual obligations may be difficult to establish.[1]

15-02 Some leases permit a switch between a bipartite and tripartite structure, so that even if there is no manager appointed at the inception of the lease, there may be a contractual right for the landlord to delegate functions to a manager at some later point. Additionally, some tripartite leases provide that, in the event that a manger becomes insolvent or otherwise incapable of discharging its functions, then those functions revert to the landlord (under a so-called 'step-in provision') who may then be able to appoint a further manager. It is therefore essential to have regard not just to what the lease says, but also to the status of the parties to it and whether or not the parties have exercised any contractual rights to vary the scheme set up at the start of the lease.

THE NATURE OF THE MANAGER

15-03 The status of the service provider can be significant. If, for instance, services are provided by a management company which is tenant-owned, then, in their capacity as shareholder members of that company, the tenants may be called upon pursuant to a resolution to make a contribution to boost that company's

---

1 *Hafton Properties Ltd v Camp* [1993] EGCS 101.

capital reserves to fund proposed major works. As payments of this kind are not made under leases, and are not in the nature of service charge, they are not subject to the same statutory controls and defences as a service charge claim under the lease.[2] Difficulties may, however, arise in holding the landlord to account in the event of a default by the management company.[3]

15-04 Sometimes, leases provide that the third party manager is to hold service charge funds and provide services in a trustee capacity (and is then usually called a 'maintenance' or 'management' trustee).[4] As a 'true' trustee, fiduciary duties will be owed, the statutory provisions applicable to investments and other trustee functions will apply (subject to the terms of the contract),[5] equitable remedies will be available against the trustee and third parties either receiving trust assets or interfering with the trust, and beneficiaries of the trust will enjoy greater security in the event that the trustee becomes insolvent.[6] Additionally, it appears that costs and other rules applicable to litigation by trustees will then also apply.[7]

15-05 A further significant point may be the effect of the impecuniosity of the service provider where it is acting in a trustee capacity. While the courts have in general declined to allow a landlord to argue that a lack of funds excuses him from provision of services,[8] the position of a maintenance trustee might be different. A trustee with a mere power to apply the trust fund to provide services under the lease is not required to top up the service charge funds with its own reserves where it transpires that the costs of services provided are in excess of

2   *Morshead Mansions v Di Marco* [2008] EWCA Civ 1371. There is no reason why the same should not occur where the landlord is to provide the services and collect service charge, and is tenant-owned. Further consequences were considered in *Morshead Mansions v Mactra Properties Ltd* [2006] EWCA Civ 492.
3   *Hafton Properties Ltd v Camp* [1993] EGCS 101; *Alton House Holdings Ltd v Calflane (Management) Ltd* [1987] 2 EGLR 52 (where a maintenance trustee sought to set off contributions it had made out of its own reserves against rent which it had collected for and was obliged to pass to the landlord).
4   Examples of such a structure may be found in *Nell Gwynn House Maintenance Fund Trustees v Customs and Excise Commissioners* [1999] 1 All ER 385; *Gordon v Selico Co Ltd* [1986] 1 EGLR 71. As to the circumstances in which a trust relationship might be found, see **22-10** to **22-22** below. In residential cases, the person holding the service charge funds is a trustee of those funds by reason of the Landlord and Tenant Act 1987, s 42, as to which see Chapter 36 below.
5   See generally *Lewin on Trusts* (18th edn, 2008), Pt IV.
6   *Ibid.* pp 766 *et seq.*
7   One potential difference is the extent to which a maintenance trustee may be entitled to recover the costs of litigation from the trust fund, which is governed by ordinary trust principles: see *Holding and Management Ltd v Property Holding and Investment Trust Plc* [1989] 1 WLR 1313 (though in that case the trustee, engaged in adversarial litigation, was not so entitled). See too *St Mary's Mansions Ltd v Limegate Investments Co Ltd* [2001] 1 EGLR 41, where the issue is addressed but not decided. For a discussion of the trustee's right to an indemnity from the trust fund, see *Lewin on Trusts* (18th edn, 2008), pp 710–762.
8   *Marenco v Jacramel Co Ltd* (1964) 191 EG 433; *Francis v Cowliffe* (1977) 33 P&CR 368; *Yorkbrook Investments v Batten* [1985] 1 EGLR 71; though note the *obiter* observations in *Bluestorm v Portvale Holdings Ltd* [2004] 2 EGLR 38 at paras 36, 41 and 49; it is apparent that the Lords Justices considered *Yorkbrook* not merely distinguishable, but potentially requiring reconsideration. A different approach is taken in the context of covenants for quiet enjoyment: see *Taylor v Webb* [1937] 2 KB 283.

what it has collected from tenants.[9] Where, however, a trustee has acted in breach of trust, he will be ordered to execute the trust and account by way of restitution to the trust estate.[10]

CHANGING PARTIES TO THE LEASE

15-06 In addition to any contractual rights to vary the identity of the service provider under a particular lease, Parliament has intervened in a number of respects to protect tenants from unwilling or inadequate service providers, and also in cases where there is no person left capable of providing the covenanted-for services.

Powers of the LVT

15-07 Residential tenants who wish to appoint their own manager may rely on two distinct statutory regimes:

1   Under the provisions of Part II of the Landlord and Tenant Act 1987, they are able to apply to the LVT for an order to appoint a manager,[11] including on an interim basis,[12] on the statutory grounds specified within section 24 of that Act.[13] The manager appointed will have such functions in connection with the management of the relevant premises or such functions of a receiver, or both, as the tribunal may order.[14] The order may relate not just to the building containing the leased units, but to other land having a connection with the manager's functions, such as amenity land.[15] If a receiver is appointed pursuant to the provision of that Act, then his rights and obligations are the result of an order by the tribunal, and do not arise under the terms of the leases. This means that tenants do not have the same rights against such a manager as they would have had against their landlords, such as the right to set-off.[16]

---

9   *Alton House Holdings Ltd v Calflane (Management) Ltd* [1987] 2 EGLR 52 at p 53. It appears that, in this case, the problem may have arisen due to a misunderstanding of the effect of the Landlord and Tenant Act 1985, s 19(1)(a).

10 *Gordon v Selico* [1986] 1 EGLR 71 (CA). In that case, however, the lease was particularly elaborate and the landlord had a duty to procure the execution of the trust.

11 Sections 21–23.

12 Once an interim order has expired, it cannot be renewed and a fresh application must be made: *Eaglesham Properties Ltd v Jeffrey* [2012] UKUT 157 (LC).

13 Specified in s 24(2).

14 Section 24(1), (4). There is a right to apply to the tribunal for further directions. An example of that jurisdiction at work can be found in *Howard v Midrome Ltd* [1991] 1 EGLR 58 (decided at a time when the power to appoint was still vested in the High Court); *Re Moreshead Mansions Ltd* [2003] EWLands LRX_49_2002.

15 *Cawsand Fort Management Co Ltd v Stafford* [2007] EWCA Civ 1187; *Schilling v Canary Riverside Estate Management Ltd* [2008] EWLands LRX_41_2007.

16 *Maunder Taylor v Blaquiere* [2002] EWCA Civ 1633; *Taylor v Joshi* [2006] EWLands LRX_107_2005.

2   Under the complex and imperfectly drafted provisions of Part II, Chapter
     1 of the Commonhold and Leasehold Reform Act 2002,[17] an application
     may be made to the LVT for the transfer of management functions relating
     to 'premises'[18] on a 'no fault' basis. The right is exercisable by an RTM
     company[19] incorporated by 'qualifying tenants'.[20] The right is exercised by
     the RTM company inviting non-member qualifying tenants to participate.[21]
     Provided that there is a sufficient proportion of qualifying tenants who
     become members of the RTM company,[22] then the company can give[23]
     a notice of claim ('claim notice')[24] to acquire the right to manage any
     'premises'.[25] The notice must be given to the landlord, other parties to a
     lease who are neither landlord nor tenant and any manager appointed under
     the 1987 Act.[26] All qualifying tenants are also to be given a copy of the

---

17 For anti-avoidance provisions, see s 106.
18 Defined in s 72 as meaning a building or self-contained part of a building comprising more than
    two flats, with no fewer than two thirds of the flats being occupied by 'qualifying tenants'. A
    part of a building cannot be the subject of the right to manage if it is not vertically divided from
    the rest of the building: *London Rent Assessment Panel v Holding and Management (Solitaire)
    Ltd* [2007] EWLands LRX_138_2006 (where an underground car park interrupted the vertical
    severance of the part of the building). For a discussion of the meaning of 'appurtenant property'
    within s 72(1)(a), see *Gala Unity Ltd v Ariadne Road RTM Co Ltd* [2012] EWCA Civ 1372. For
    consideration of the question of what proportion of a property is non-residential, see *Gaingold
    Ltd v WHRA RTM Co Ltd* [2005] EWLands LRX_19_2005 and *Connaught Court RTM Co Ltd
    v Abouzaki Holdings Ltd* [2008] EWLands LRX_115_2007. Certain premises are excluded by
    reason of Sch 6 even if they satisfy the s 72 requirements. For Crown premises, see s 108.
19 Defined in ss 73–74 and with further prescribed information contained in the RTM Companies
    (Model Articles) (England) Regulations 2009 (SI 2009/2767) and the RTM Companies (Model
    Articles) (Wales) Regulations 2011 (SI 2011/2680). For a (failed) attempt to recover, through
    the service charge, the costs of incorporating and then running an RTM company, see *Wilson v
    Lesley Place (RTM) Co Ltd* [2010] UKUT 342 (LC).
20 Defined in s 75 as tenants of a flat under a long lease. 'Long lease' is defined in ss 76 and 77.
    Further definitions relevant to construing Pt II, Ch 1 are to be found at ss 112 and 113.
21 Section 78. On the need to serve new notices to participate on withdrawal of an earlier claim
    notice, see *Gateway Property Holdings Ltd v 6–10 Montrose Gardens RTM Co Ltd* [2011]
    UKUT 349 (LC). Where the qualifying tenant is a trustee, see s 109.
22 Section 79(4) and (5).
23 As to when a notice is 'given', see *Plintal SA v 36–48A Edgewood Drive RTM Co Ltd* [2008]
    EWLands LRX_16_2007.
24 The requirements for the contents of claim notices are set out in s 80, and the Right to Manage
    (Prescribed Particulars and Forms) (England) Regulations 2010 (SI 2010/825) and the Right
    to Manage (Prescribed Particulars and Forms) (Wales) Regulations 2011 (SI 2011/2684). A
    failure to set out the registered office of the RTM company is fatal: see *Assethold Ltd v 15 Yonge
    Park RTM Co Ltd* [2011] UKUT 379 (LC), and is not curable under s 81(1) (supplementary
    provisions are to be found in s 81 relating to validity and other matters). A failure to state the
    correct date for a counter-notice is also fatal: *Moskovitz v 75 Worple Road RTM Co Ltd* [2010]
    UKUT 393 (LC). The President revisited *Moskovitz* in *Assethold Ltd v 14 Stansfield Road RTM
    Co Ltd* [2012] UKUT 262 (LC) and disapproved his earlier reasoning, though stated that the
    outcome would have been the same in any event. For notices under the Act generally, see s 111.
25 Section 79(1).
26 Section 79(6). It has been decided that this extends to the mortgagee if appointed as landlord's
    attorney and, therefore, the mortgagee may serve a counter notice: see *Alleyn Court RTM Co
    Ltd v Abou-Hamdan* [2012] UKUT 74 (LC). In a case where the premises already have a 1987
    Act manager, the relevant court or LVT which made that order must also be given the notice: s
    79(9). Persons specified in s 79(6) who are missing are dealt with by s 85.

claim notice.[27] The persons to whom the claim notice must be given (but not qualifying tenants, who are merely given a copy) may serve a counter-notice objecting to the exercise of the right to manage.[28] The RTM company has rights to disclosure and inspection during this process.[29] If a person served with a claim notice wishes to object, then the sole basis for objection is where the formal criteria for exercising the right to manage have not been met. Any difference has to be resolved by the LVT.[30] Whether or not the matter goes to the LVT, a person who was served with a notice under section 79(6) is entitled to costs.[31] The right to manage, if ultimately acquired, is acquired on the 'acquisition date', the calculation of which depends on whether or not the claim notice was objected to, and how that objection was resolved.[32] There is a procedure to ensure that parties to existing management contracts are notified of the fact that the right to manage has been acquired.[33] There is also a duty on the part of the person holding the service charge under the pre-right to manage arrangements to pay to the RTM company a sum equal to the amount of accrued, uncommitted service charge which is held as at the acquisition date.[34] The Act then makes provision for the transfer of management functions to the RTM company,[35] though it does not spell out what happens to any subsisting long-term contractual relations which have already been entered into by the former person with management functions. It has been assumed that they are frustrated, or perhaps impliedly terminated by statute, but the position is far from clear. In certain circumstances, the right to manage may cease.[36]

---

27 Section 79(8). A failure to do so where this causes the omitted qualifying tenant no prejudice does not invalidate the claim notice: *Sinclair Gardens Investments (Kensington) Ltd v Oak Investments RTM Co Ltd* [2005] EWLands LRX_52_2004, following *R v Immigration Appeal Tribunal, ex parte Jeyeanthan* [1999] 3 All ER 231; see too *Alleyn Court RTM Co Ltd v Abou-Hamdan* [2012] UKUT 74 (LC).

28 Section 84. See also *Alleyn Court RTM Co Ltd v Abou-Hamdan* [2012] UKUT 74 (LC).

29 Sections 82 and 83.

30 Section 84(3)–(8). Withdrawal and deemed withdrawal of a claim notice are dealt with by ss 86 and 87. As to the question of what information the LVT should have in order to determine an application, see *Gateway Property Holdings Ltd v 6–10 Montrose Gardens RTM Co Ltd* [2011] UKUT 349 (LC).

31 Section 88. Different sub-sections deal with costs incurred with or without an LVT determination to deal with objections. There is a right to apply to the LVT in relation to s 88 costs: see subs (4). Where the claim ceases, costs are dealt with under s 89. Section 88 is considered in *Plintal SA v 36–48A Edgewood Drive RTM Co Ltd* [2008] EWLands LRX_16_2007. Costs can include the costs of an in-house solicitor: see *Fairhold Mercury Limited v Merryfield RTM Co Ltd* [2012] UKUT 311 (LC).

32 Section 90.

33 Sections 91–93.

34 Section 94, meaning uncommitted sums which have actually been collected and are held by the landlord or manager under the relevant leases: *OM Ltd v New River Head RTM Co Ltd* [2010] UKUT 394 (LC). A tenant who has paid to the original landlord sums after the date of acquisition may not set those off against the charges payable to an RTM company: *Wilson v Lesley Place (Maidstone) Ltd RTM Co Ltd* [sic] [2010] UKUT 139 (LC).

35 Sections 95–103.

36 Section 105.

Powers of the High Court

15-08   The High Court retains a general jurisdiction to appoint a receiver under a lease where it appears just and convenient to do so.[37] The appointment may be on an interim basis, or it may be on a final basis.[38] The jurisdiction tends to be exercised in cases where there is a missing landlord,[39] where a landlord has no apparent interest in carrying out its repairing obligations,[40] or where the landlord was doing some, but not all, of the things that it had covenanted to do under the lease.[41] The power extends to a management company as well as a landlord,[42] but not to a public body which is subject to its own specific statutory duties.[43] The receiver appointed under this power is an agent of the Court, and is able to claim service charges under the terms of the lease or an indemnity from the tenants, but he is unable to claim funds from the landlord.[44]

37 However, where a tenant has a right to apply for a manager under the Landlord and Tenant Act 1987, Pt II, he may not apply to the High Court: see the Landlord and Tenant Act 1987, s 21(6).
38 The Senior Courts Act 1981, s 37(1). As stated above, a tenant who has a right to apply for a manager under the Landlord and Tenant Act 1987 has no right to apply to the High Court.
39 *Hart v Emelkirk* [1983] 1 WLR 1289.
40 *Blawdziewicz v Diadon Establishment* [1988] 2 EGLR 52; *Howard v Midrome Ltd* [1991] 1 EGLR 58.
41 *Daiches v Bluelake Investments Ltd* [1985] 2 EGLR 67.
42 *Hafton Properties Ltd v Camp* [1994] 1 EGLR 67.
43 *Parker v Camden London Borough Council* [1986] Ch 162.
44 *Evans v Clayhope Properties Ltd* [1988] 1 WLR 358.

CHAPTER 16

Common service structures

MODERN LEASES

16-01   Most modern leases set out machinery and a timetable for tenants to make payments. Usually, the term granted to the tenant is divided into 'service charge years' or 'accounting periods' for accounting and payment purposes,[1] and the tenant will ordinarily be obliged:

1   To pay an amount (or usually periodic amounts payable half-yearly or quarterly) on account of anticipated expenditure in the following service charge year. Such amounts are usually calculated by reference to a prior certified estimate, ideally given to the tenant before the commencement of the relevant period,[2] or by reference to the costs incurred in the preceding year with an adjustment.[3]

2   To make a balancing payment at the end of the relevant accounting period if there is a deficit, calculated on the basis of accounts showing actual expenditure in that year.[4] A shortfall may be recoverable on demand, or simply becomes payable on the next quarter on which an interim charge falls due after the presentation of the relevant end-of-year accounts, without any further demand. If the accounts show a surplus, then this is usually either credited back to the tenant or retained and set off against the next year's on-account charge.

---

1   These are often fixed, but sometimes variable at the discretion of the landlord: in *Wembley National Stadium Ltd v Wembley (London) Ltd* [2007] EWHC 756 (Ch) at para 74, the Chancellor rejected the submission that a late notification of a change of financial years was ineffective, but left open the question of what the result might be where the tenant had acted on the basis of the unchanged financial year.

2   For a discussion of late provision of documentation, see **16-15** to **16-18** below; for the effect of such provisions as conditions precedent to liability, see **17-03** to **17-12** below.

3   As to demands, see Chapter 20. For reasonableness controls over the amounts demanded, see **2-97** to **2-114** (implied reasonableness term at common law) and Chapter 29 (statutory control of reasonableness of residential service charges).

4   For a discussion as to how costs are to be apportioned if incurred over more than one year, see *Barrington v Sloan Properties Ltd* [2007] 3 EGLR 91. For the question of late provision of accounts, see **16-15** to **16-18** below.

16-02   It is to be noted that the entitlement to on-account payments is entirely separate from an entitlement to claim end-of-year payments. So, if only interim charges are claimed, then a failure to set out the year's expenditure and thereafter to claim an end-of-year balancing payment does not mean that the on-account amounts must be returned.[5] Similarly, a failure to claim any payments on account of service charge does not mean that the right to do so is waived by a subsequent claim for end-of-year payments.[6]

16-03   Supplementing the above machinery, there may also be provision for contributions to a 'reserve fund' and/or a 'sinking fund', which are considered below.[7]

DIFFICULTIES WITH OLDER LEASES

16-04   Older leases (for reasons already explained in the first part of this book)[8] create their own problems. In many older leases, no provision was made for the payment of service charges at all, the provision of necessary services being regarded as a cost payable out of the rent received by the landlord. When provision was made, it was often in the form of either a fixed or an index-linked sum.[9] Occasionally, leases simply permitted the recovery of service expenditure in arrear, but made no provision for recovery of on account service charge.[10]

16-05   Fixed or indexed-linked charges are clumsy ways of funding services in a building, as they are unresponsive to fluctuating costs and hence create a risk of (usually) under-funding of services, producing ever-increasing service charge deficits. The more modern variable charge is a significantly better approach.[11] It may still prove deficient if there is a failure to provide for on-account payments, resulting in cash-flow difficulties, particularly when the provider of services is an under-capitalised, tenant-owned management company.[12] That difficulty can be acute, as one line of authority suggests that even where the provision of services

---

5 *Gilje v Charlgrove Securities Ltd* [2002] 1 EGLR 41 (High Court).
6 *Wembley National Stadium Ltd v Wembley (London) Ltd* [2007] EWHC 756 (Ch), paras 59, 63–65.
7 See Chapter 22.
8 See **1-08** to **1-11** and Chapter 23.
9 Examples of such a clause may be found in *Coventry City Council v Cole* [1994] 1 All ER 997; *Cumshaw v Bowen* [1987] 1 EGLR 30.
10 See for instance *Capital and Counties Freehold Equity Trust Ltd v BL Plc* [1987] 2 EGLR 49; *Brent LBC v Shulem B Association* [2011] EWHC 1663 (Ch).
11 As discussed in *Edwards & Walkden (Norfolk) Ltd v Mayor & Commonality & Citizens of the City of London* [2012] EWHC 2527 (Ch) at para 83.
12 Contrast the case law on management companies and maintenance trustees at **15-03** to **15-05** above. The problem is sometimes addressed by giving service providers the power, not the duty, to provide services; see *Russell v Laimond Properties* [1984] 1 EGLR 87. However, the courts have also been prepared from time to time to imply a duty to provide services from the right to receive payment: see *Barnes v City of London Real Property Co* [1918] 2 Ch 18. As in all cases, the wording of a particular lease will be crucial.

is expressly 'subject to' payment of service charge by tenants, services must nonetheless be provided even in the absence of such funds.[13]

OPERATING THE CONTRACTUAL SCHEME

16-06 Rehearsing counsels' arguments, the Court of Appeal in *Leonora Investment Co Ltd v Mott MacDonald Ltd*[14] distinguished between:

> 'whether terms in a lease are conditions precedent to obligations to pay, substantive procedural provisions which have to be followed to the letter before a liability to pay is triggered, or mere mechanics which do not have to be insisted on regardless of the circumstances'.[15]

16-07 This section considers the court's approach to:

1 procedural provisions; and

2 preconditions.

16-08 Whether or not a particular provision falls within the third category, and amounts to 'mere mechanics',[16] and is hence not to be insisted upon, is a question of pure construction and, in practice, it appears that the courts have treated this third category as of little significance.[17]

Procedural steps

16-09 Where a lease prescribes a contractual path to recover service charges, then that path should be followed. It has been repeatedly emphasised that the parties to a lease will be held to the procedure which they have agreed.[18] This seemingly strict approach is, however, tempered by the fact that, unless the lease provides to the contrary or statute inhibits this, more than one attempt can be

---

13 *Yorkbrook Investments v Batten* (1985) 52 P&CR 51. A contrasting approach was suggested (but did not arise for consideration) in *Bluestorm Ltd v Portvale Holdings Ltd* [2004] 2 EGLR 38. For cases considering management trustees with powers to provide services, see above, **15-03** to **15-05**. See the discussion in Chapter 2 at **2-15** to **2-16**.
14 [2008] EWCA Civ 857.
15 At para 14.
16 Reynolds QC and Fetherstonhaugh QC, *Handbook of Rent Review* (Looseleaf), para 3.4.3, discuss the term 'machinery' in the context of rent review clauses.
17 Instances where steps to be taken (in each case certification) were mere machinery which were not pre-conditions for liability are *Universities Superannuation Scheme Ltd v Marks and Spencer Plc* [1999] 1 EGLR 13 and *Scottish Mutual Assurance Plc v Jardine Public Relations Ltd* [1999] EWHC 276 (TCC).
18 The importance of compliance with the terms of the lease has particularly been emphasised in relation to reserve fund payment demands: *St Mary's Mansions Ltd v Limegate Investment Co Ltd* [2003] 1 EGLR 41 at paras 32–39; *Mohammadi v Anston Investments* [2004] EWCA Civ 981; *FCH Housing and Care v Burns* [2007] EWLands_LRX_9_2006 at para 16; *Redendale Ltd v Modi* [2010] UKUT 346 (LC).

made to satisfy the contractual requirements, and generally time for taking the procedural steps prescribed is not of the essence. In short, the courts will adopt a 'businesslike' approach and will avoid construing service charge machinery as a series of traps for the landlord to avoid.

16-10   This approach can be clearly seen in two decisions of the Court of Appeal. The first is that in *Universities Superannuation Scheme Ltd v Marks and Spencer Plc*.[19] That case concerned a tenant's liability for year-end balancing payments. The scheme of the particular lease (of a retail store) provided that such payments were to be calculated by reference to the rateable value of the premises. Separately, it was provided that the total amount of expenditure in any given year was to be calculated and certified by the landlord's managing agent. That certificate was not expressed to be conclusive, and was to be served 'as soon as practicable' at the end of the relevant financial year. The landlord's managing agent went further than the lease required, and calculated the actual proportion of the overall costs which the tenant was liable to pay. However, too small a rateable value was applied and the amount claimed was in fact too low. The tenant argued (successfully, at first instance) that the landlord was tied to the lower amount that had been specified in the certificate. Allowing the appeal, however, the Court of Appeal held that the starting point was that the tenant had covenanted to pay a service charge by reference to the true rateable value of the premises. Payment of a lesser amount was not a discharge of that obligation. Additionally, all that the certificates were required to show was the total amount of expenditure in any year; there was, in fact, no requirement that the certificate further showed the sums due from a particular tenant. Those certificates were also not stated to be conclusive in any event. Accordingly, the landlord was entitled to the higher, correct amount.[20]

16-11   The second Court of Appeal decision is that in *Leonora Investment v Mott MacDonald Ltd*.[21] There, the court emphasised that while landlords had to comply with the contractual procedures to trigger tenants' liabilities to pay,[22] such procedural requirements should not be applied in an overly technical way so as to deprive the landlord of a right to recoup where there had been a mistake. In that case, commercial leases of offices in a block provided that the landlord should provide to the tenant estimated service charge in relation to the coming service charge year, with that sum being apportioned to the tenant and then to be paid quarterly. The lease then went on to provide that the landlord would provide a statement of actual costs as soon as practicable at the end of the relevant year, whereupon the tenant was required to pay a balancing payment on demand. The landlord carried out certain works during the service charge year ending December 2002. Both the estimated charge and the year-end statement omitted

19   [1999] 1 EGLR 13.
20   At p 14L–M.
21   [2008] EWCA Civ 857.
22   And see too *Jacey Property Co Ltd v De Sousa* [2003] EWCA Civ 510; *Barrington v Sloane Properties Ltd* [2007] EWLands LRX_31_2006. *Brent LBC v Shulem B Association Ltd* [2011] 1 WLR 3014 is a further instance of the court declining to allow a landlord to recover monies where the demand machinery under the lease had not been observed; see para 51.

to mention those works and the landlord apparently treated those works as a sum due from the tenant entirely outside the framework of the service charge machinery, and raised an entirely separate invoice, in a form which was not provided for in the lease. The landlord did not argue that this invoice ought to be treated as a demand for the purposes of the lease, but instead argued that the machinery under the leases was non-exclusive and that it remained free to levy additional charges outside the contractual machinery.[23] The Court of Appeal rejected that argument. Tuckey LJ stated[24] that:

> 'I do not see this as a case in which the leases contain a condition precedent to the landlord's right to recover. Rather they prescribe the contractual route down which the landlord must travel to be entitled to payment. The prescribed route in this case is, we are told, a very familiar one and it is obviously not difficult to follow. The statement will be of considerable importance to the tenant. It gives him information about the actual service costs for the past year, which only the landlord will know, and how they have been apportioned to him so that he can make an informed decision as to whether to pay or not in the knowledge that the landlord may acquire a right to forfeit if he does not. [Counsel for the landlord] had to accept in argument that the logic of his submission was that the landlord can make a demand for service charge outside the part 2 regime in any form, for any service cost for up to six years. This would be contrary to what sensible commercial parties would contemplate in a relationship carefully defined by the terms of a commercial lease.'

16-12   He went on to observe[25] that:

> 'The conclusion I have reached may seem harsh or over technical, but if so it results from what I consider to be the proper construction of the leases. No one has challenged the judge's conclusion that it was open to the landlord to issue a revised statement. Nor would I. Provisions of this kind should not be seen as procedural obstacle courses. Businessmen dealing with one another often make mistakes and there is no scope for saying that the provisions in this clause only gave the landlord one opportunity to get it right. I say nothing about the landlord's prospects of being able to get it right even now, because we have not heard argument about this.'

16-13   As to that last observation, it is to be noted that the *Leonora* case was one in which the end of year statement had to be furnished 'as soon as practicable'. The landlord, therefore, could potentially have served a second, lease compliant statement to supplement the first which had failed to include proper amounts. Such an approach is, however, statutorily restricted in residential service charge cases.[26]

---

23 It is suggested that such an argument is in any event difficult to maintain. Absent a contractual right, express or implied, to recoup, the landlord would only be able to recover sums under the law of restitution. Apart from that, it is correct that costs of repair were recoverable in tort (in that case, nuisance) from a squatter who had acquired the upper floors of a building by adverse possession in *Abbahall Ltd v Smee* [2002] EWCA Civ 1831, but the facts of that case were peculiar, and that would not provide an actionable remedy to landlords in an ordinary case.
24 At para 22.
25 At para 24.
26 See Chapter 31 below.

16-14   The courts have further regularly rejected technical arguments that a failure to provide year-end accounts should deprive the landlord of its entitlement to retain and expend on-account service charges for the year in respect of which the failure occurred.[27] The argument that such a term should be implied has also been rejected.[28] By the same token, where a landlord had failed to claim interim service charges, but then brought a claim (subsequently abandoned) for the actual costs incurred at year-end, bringing that claim did not waive any entitlement to uncollected interim service charge.[29] The latter point is, it is submitted, plainly right as the right to collect on-account amounts and to claim year-end payments are complementary and not inconsistent contractual rights, so that invoking one cannot be said to be an election inconsistent with the other and, on the facts of that particular case, there was no potential issue of double recovery.

Time for compliance

16-15   As already explained above, in general and apart from statute, time is not of the essence for the provision of end-of-year accounts or for the taking of other steps under service charge procedures. Usually there is no specific time stipulated for compliance as a matter of contract and compliance is merely required 'as soon as is reasonably practicable', or words to that effect. Further, where there is no stipulated time for compliance, a reasonable time for compliance will be implied as a matter of general contract law.[30] Therefore, it is generally permissible for landlords to be late in calculating on account service charge demands[31] or to provide end of year accounts late.[32] It is considered that, in principle, a tenant could make time of the essence by service of an appropriate notice.[33]

16-16   Evidently, if the time limits imposed by a lease are (unusually) of the essence, then the landlord may find himself limited to any demands served within that particular time limit. Such strict clauses are not, however, encountered in practice. If the service charge relates to a dwelling, then considerations under section 20B of the Landlord and Tenant Act 1985 might come into play,[34] however

---

27   *Gilje v Charlegrove Securities Ltd (No 2)* [2003] 3 EGLR 9; *Warrior Quay Management Co Ltd v Joachim* [2008] EWLands LRX_42_2006; *Redrow Homes v Hothi* [2011] UKUT 268 (LC).
28   *Redrow Homes v Hothi* [2011] UKUT 268 (LC), para 26.
29   *Wembley National Stadium Ltd v Wembley (London) Ltd* [2007] EWHC 756 (Ch), paras 59, 63–65.
30   *Redrow Homes v Hothi* [2011] UKUT 268 (LC).
31   *Ibid.*
32   *West Central Investments v Borovik* [1977] 1 EGLR 29; *Mohammadi v Anston Investments Ltd* [2004] EWCA Civ 981; *Bhambhani v Willowcourt Management Co (1985) Ltd* [2008] EWLAnds_LRX_22_2007; *Warrior Quay Management Co Ltd v Joachim* [2008] EWLands LRX_42_2006; *Akorita v Marina Heights (St Leonards) Ltd* [2011] UKUT 255 (LC) (relating to both interim and final payments).
33   *Barclays Bank Plc v Saville Estates Ltd* [2002] EWCA Civ 589.
34   As to which see *Gilje v Charlgrove Securities Ltd (No 2)* [2003] 3 EGLR 9; *Holding & Management (Solitaire) Ltd v Sherwin* [2011] 1 EGLR 29; see further Chapter 31 below.

it must be borne in mind that the time limit for recovery imposed by subsection (1) is qualified by subsection (2), which disapplies the time limit where a written demand has been made in relation to amounts that had been incurred.[35]

16-17   Non-compliance or late compliance may not be entirely without sanction, however. Faced with a landlord who is not operating the machinery properly, a tenant may be entitled to an injunction or specific performance[36] for a failure to comply with a certification or accounting requirement, or may be entitled to exercise a set-off.[37] If a tenant is required to seek relief from the court for a failure to provide relevant documentation within a reasonable time or at all, then the defaulting party might find that it faces a costs sanction.[38] Finally, a failure to provide required documents may also operate to a landlord's detriment on an application to the LVT under section 27A of the Landlord and Tenant Act 1985.[39]

16-18   It follows from the fact that time is generally not of the essence, and that the courts will generally adopt a 'businesslike' approach to service charges, that there is no objection in principle to supplemental demands being made,[40] though those further 'corrective' demands must themselves comply with the contractual requirements imposed by the relevant lease.[41] It is considered that, in an appropriate case, the payment of a lesser amount on the basis of an incorrect demand might estop the landlord from claiming further amounts.[42] The circumstances in which the parties are free to go behind a certificate which is stated to be conclusive are considered at **17-31** to **17-45** below.

Conditions precedent

16-19   The above section considered the court's approach to procedural machinery. Leases often contain express provisions which make liability under service charge (or other) covenants subject to a precondition which must be satisfied in order for liability to arise in the first place. In some cases, it is obvious and inherent in the nature of the obligation imposed that an event must occur before liability arises. For instance, where service charge is payable in arrear, the

---

35 A point that was relevant in *Akorita v Marina Heights (St Leonards) Ltd* [2011] UKUT 255 (LC), see para 15; and see too the detailed discussion of this provision in *Brent LBC v Shulem B Association Ltd* [2011] 1 WLR 3014 at paras 52–69. Section 20B is discussed in more detail in Chapter 31 below.
36 See *Morshead Mansions Ltd v Mactra Properties Ltd* [2013] EWHC 224 (Ch) where the claimant tenant obtained specific performance of the landlord's obligation to produce accounts.
37 *Wembley National Stadium Ltd v Wembley (London) Ltd* [2007] EWHC 756 (Ch) at para 67.
38 *Gilje v Charlgrove Securities Ltd (No 2)* [2003] 3 EGLR 9.
39 *Warrior Quay Management Co Ltd v Joachim* [2008] EWLands LRX_42_2006 at para 25.
40 *Universities Superannuation Scheme v Marks and Spencer Plc* [1999] 1 EGLR 13.
41 *Leonora Investments v Mott MacDonald Ltd* [2008] EWCA Civ 857.
42 For the general law on part payment of a debt, see *Chitty on Contracts* (31st edn, 2012) at paras 3-115–3-136.

landlord must be able to point to some actual expenditure which it is seeking to recoup.[43]

16-20   In relation to whether a provision operates as a condition or not, the Court of Appeal in *Yorkbrook Investments Ltd v Batten*[44] adopted the following as a proper statement of the law:

> 'The proper approach for the court is set out in *Foa's General Law of Landlord and Tenant* (8th ed), at p 119: "The question whether liability in respect of one covenant in a lease is contingent or not upon the performance of another is to be decided, not upon technical words, nor upon the relative position of the covenants in the case, but upon the intentions of the parties to be gathered from the whole instrument."'

16-21   Leases commonly require certification of accounts (or other matters).[45] That requirement is often found to be a true precondition to liability,[46] but not always,[47] though it is fair to say that cases in the latter category are the exception. It is suggested that they will ordinarily be true conditions because, absent compliance, a tenant will not be able to know how much must be paid to the landlord. Detailed consideration of what certification entails, whether certification is a true condition precedent and challenges to certificates are considered in Chapter 17.

---

43   *Quirkco Investments Limited v Aspray Transport Ltd* [2011] EWHC 3060 (Ch). For consideration of the word 'incurred' and similar terms, see **19-07** to **19-15** below.
44   [1985] 2 EGLR 100, at p 104.
45   As to the related of topic of estimates, see Chapter 18 below.
46   *Woodfall's Law of Landlord and Tenant*, Vol 1, para 7-180; the statement in *Woodfall* was approved by the Upper Tribunal in *Akorita v Marina Heights (St Leonards) Ltd* [2011] UKUT 255 (LC). In addition to the cases discussed below, see also *Mohammadi v Anston Investments Ltd* [2003] EWCA Civ 981; *Crampton v Park Place 96 Ltd* [2009] EWLands LRX_100_2007. Where the landlord must comply with such requirements to build up a reserve fund, the position appears to be that compliance will be a strict pre-condition to an entitlement to do so: *St Mary's Mansions Ltd v Limegate Investment Co Ltd* [2003] 1 EGLR 41 at paras 32–39; *FCH Housing and Care v Burns* [2007] EWLands_LRX_9_2006; *Redendale Ltd v Modi* [2010] UKUT 346 (LC).
47   See, for example, *Universities Superannuation Scheme Ltd v Marks and Spencer Plc* [1999] 1 EGLR 13. *Scottish Mutual Assurance Plc v Jardine Public Relations Ltd* [1999] EWHC 276 (TCC). The position is more open in the related area of certificates issued under building contracts: Furst *et al*, *Keating on Construction Contracts* (9th edn, 2012) at para 5-011.

CHAPTER 17

Certification

17-01   Leases frequently contain a provision whereby a specified person, such as an accountant or surveyor, is to determine and certify, for example, the level of estimated or actual service charge expenditure in a particular service charge year or the tenant's proportion of service charge payable. Quite separately, experts may also be appointed to fulfil a dispute resolution function. This chapter is principally concerned with the former question, though many of the cases on experts are derived from cases where their function has been quasi-judicial.

17-02   It is to be noted at the outset that the appointment of an expert to determine issues relating to service charge is ousted in the residential context by the powers conferred on the LVT by section 27A(6) of the Landlord and Tenant Act 1985.[1]

CONDITIONS PRECEDENT

17-03   In *Finchbourne Ltd v Rodrigues*,[2] the tenant of a flat was required to pay a fixed percentage of expenditure incurred by the landlord in relation to the block of flats. The amount to which the percentage was to be applied was to be ascertained and certified by the managing agents of the landlord, acting as experts and not arbitrators. In answer to the question of whether the ascertainment and certification of that amount was a condition precedent to liability to pay the charge, the trial judge said succinctly: 'Of course the answer is yes. Otherwise the tenant could not know what sums they have to pay'. There was no challenge to that finding on appeal.

17-04   In *Rexhaven Ltd v Nurse and Alliance & Leicester Building Society*,[3] the management company under a 999-year lease of a dwelling was required, on each quarter day, to provide a certificated estimate of expenditure for the ensuing quarter, setting out the tenant's proportion. The certificate was stated

---

1   Reference should be made to the discussions of that section in Chapter 42 below.
2   [1976] 3 All ER 581.
3   (1996) 28 HLR 241.

to be binding and conclusive. The management company sent two letters which cumulatively set out the amount of on-account charge that would be claimed. One letter was sent on 29 September 1993 and the more detailed explanation was set out in a letter sent on 27 October 1993, that is, after the quarter day had passed. HH Judge Colyer QC (sitting as a Deputy Judge of the Chancery Division) accepted that those letters constituted a certificate on the true construction of that particular lease and that the condition precedent to liability for an on-account charge had been satisfied.

17-05 Similarly, in *Wagon Finance Ltd v Demelt Holdings Ltd*,[4] a case relating to end-of-year balancing payments, the Court of Appeal accepted that a certification provision under a lease was a condition precedent to liability for the payment of the balancing charge, at least for the purposes of defending an application for summary judgment under what was RSC Order 86.

17-06 In *Jacey Property Co Ltd v De Sousa*,[5] the tenant agreed to pay the 'proper and fair proportion as determined by the landlord's surveyor of the expense of repairing renewing rebuilding' various items. There was no issue in that case as to the manner of apportionment or the reasonableness of the costs. However, what was disputed was that it was the solicitor for the landlord who had undertaken the exercise. Arden LJ stated[6] that:

'I see no escape from the proposition that the parties have submitted to the arbitrament of one person, that is the landlord's surveyor, and that is one person only. It is not open to the landlord to substitute another person, however well qualified in other respects, and even though he is appointed to act in a surveying role. As I see it, that is outside the fair construction of the clause.'

17-07 She distinguished the decision of *Scottish Mutual Assurance Plc v Jardine Public Relations Ltd*.[7] In relation to that, she said as follows:

'That case was very different. In this case the court makes no determination of the due amount payable by the tenant, whereas in Scottish Mutual the court made that determination. Moreover, it was not in issue in that case that some person other than the landlord's surveyor or the court could make the determination. That is the issue in the present case. As I see it, the machinery in the clause must be followed. It is not a situation where it is impossible to use the machine for which the parties have clearly provided'.[8]

17-08 If the lease requires, not certification, but 'determination' of a question or 'resolution' of a difference, then those requirements will be treated as preconditions. The Upper Tribunal decision in *Rigby v Wheatley*[9] dealt with a tenant's obligation to pay insurance rent. The insurance rent payable was a 'fair

4 Unreported, 19 June 1997, Court of Appeal.
5 [2003] EWCA Civ 510.
6 At para 48.
7 [1999] EWHC 276 (TCC), discussed at **17-12** below.
8 At para 50.
9 [2005] EWLands LRX_84_2004.

proportion (to be determined by the Lessor's surveyor for the time being)' of the amount to be expended by the landlord on insurance of the building, payable on demand. The tribunal rejected the argument on behalf of the landlord that the right to demand insurance rent was independent of the requirement for a determination to be made by the surveyor. Rather, that determination was a precursor to a valid demand. The tribunal noted that, without such determination, there was no basis on which a tenant would be able to know the amount of his liability.[10] The tribunal did not accept the view expressed in the decision of the LVT below that, for determination to be conditional, more emphatic language would be required.[11] Further, the tribunal did not accept the LVT's attempt to distinguish between certification and determination, stating that the distinction made was one of pure form over substance.[12] However, the role of such an expert in the residential setting is somewhat unclear, given that such decisions will probably be susceptible to review under section 27A(6) of the Landlord and Tenant Act 1985 in any event, and it would seem to be the more practical outcome that the requirement for a prior expert determination would be superseded by a determination of the amount of service charge payable by the LVT in the event that the requirement remained unfulfilled by the date of the determination.[13]

17-09 In *Wembley National Stadium Ltd v Wembley (London) Ltd*,[14] a lease required accounts to be prepared as soon as practicable after each year end. The quarterly on-account service charge was then to be calculated by the lessor's accountant. In default of the latter, the lease provided that on-account charges were to be made at the same level as the last quarter's instalment, paid in the preceding year. The landlord complied with neither the account nor the calculation requirements for a number of years. Instead, a claim was brought (and then abandoned) for actual expenses incurred in the relevant years. The ultimate claim was instead for payment of the advance service charges, payable by reference to the amount due on the last preceding quarter. The tenant argued that the landlord was no longer entitled to claim sums on account of historic years. The tenant argued that the issuing of a claim for actual costs incurred waived any entitlement to on-account costs. This submission was rejected by the Chancellor, who stated that no such waiver had occurred and that a contingent liability to

---

10 At paras 37–38.

11 At para 40.

12 At para 42.

13 In *London Borough of Brent v Shulem B Association Ltd* [2011] 1 WLR 3014 at para 39, Morgan J stated that: 'It may be that this reference to the finality of the surveyor's decision is no longer contractually effective in view of section 27A(6). I did not hear specific argument on that point.' Contrast the position of the Lands Tribunal in *Warrior Quay Management Co Ltd v Joachim* [2008] EWLands LRX_42_2006, where it stated (at para 25) that: 'The absence of any proper certificate is a matter which may weigh against WQMC and may result in the LVT deciding that a lesser sum than hoped for by WQMC may be decided to be the amount payable. Also the absence of the certificate should result in the position being that the amount which is decided by the LVT to be payable by way of shortfall will not be payable until a proper certificate (certifying that at least this amount is payable) is provided by WQMC's auditors or accountants.'

14 [2007] EWHC 756 (Ch).

pay on-account charges remained.[15] Further, the non-provision of accounts had nothing to do with liability for on-account charges. Under the structure of the lease in question, the preparation of accounts followed the payment of on-account sums and was an independent obligation. Therefore, a mere breach of the obligation to provide accounts in that case was not a defence to a claim for on-account service charges.[16]

17-10   In *Akorita v Marina Heights (St Leonards) Ltd,*[17] certification was found to be a condition precedent to liability. There, the appellant tenant argued that no interim or final service charge was due because of a lack of end-of-year certification. No document constituting a valid certificate was provided by the respondent. Such certificates as there were had been prepared by accountants, not the contractually required surveyor, and it was also plain from the face of the documents that no expertise had been applied to the contents of those documents.[18] The Tribunal concluded that the lease did make the certificate for interim and final charges a condition precedent to liability. It considered that the wording was plain and that this conclusion was in line with the general position recognised by a leading textbook.[19]

17-11   An important gloss on the above position, as far as residential service charges are concerned, is to be found in the decision of the Upper Tribunal in *Warrior Quay Management Co Ltd v Joachim.*[20] The Upper Tribunal decided that it could partly fulfil the certification function where no certificates had been issued by the landlord. There, a dispute arose between tenants of residential units and the management company. The lease included an obligation that, at least once a year, there should be sent out to the tenants a certificate relating to various actual items of service charge expenditure, following which certification process, the tenants were liable to pay any balance due to the management company. The LVT determined that, as there had been no service of certificates at the end of the year, there was no balancing payment due at all, and further that there was no proof of expenditure, so that all of the interim payments made had to be returned to the tenants. The Tribunal reversed that decision.[21] While the provision of a proper certificate was potentially a precondition to the tenant becoming liable to make payment, the tenant had the power to circumvent a landlord's intransigence by approaching the LVT to carry out the task of determination under section 27A of the Landlord and Tenant Act 1985. However, the Tribunal still considered that liability to make the payment would not be triggered until the (now academic) paper formality of providing a written certificate had been gone through.[22]

---

15   At paras 65–66. See also **16-01** to **16-03** above.
16   At para 67. The Chancellor noted that the tenant would have access in any event to other remedies in order to compel compliance, particularly where such delay would perpetuate a liability to pay balancing payments.
17   [2011] UKUT 255 (LC).
18   See paras 20–21.
19   Referring with approval to *Woodfall's Law of Landlord and Tenant,* Vol 1, para 1-780.
20   [2008] EWLands LRX_42_2006.
21   See **16-14** above for this aspect of the decision.
22   But contrast the view expressed by Morgan J in *London Borough of Brent v Shulem B Association Ltd* [2011] 1 WLR 3014 at para 39.

17-12   As stated at the outset, certification has not always been found to be a true precondition. In *Scottish Mutual Assurance Plc v Jardine Public Relations Ltd*,[23] a tenant of offices challenged a service charge liability on a number of grounds, including that the landlord had failed to abide by the lease machinery and had not complied with certification requirements. The service charge under that lease was payable annually on demand, being a fair proportion of expenditure determined by the landlord's surveyor. It was further provided that a certificate should be provided by the landlord showing the amount of the service charge, which certificate was stated, for the purpose of this covenant, to be conclusive evidence of the amount so to be paid (save in the case of manifest error). Mr David Blunt QC (sitting as a Judge of the Technology and Construction Court) accepted the submission that, on the terms of the instant lease, the requirement for a certificate was purely 'machinery' and that the 'absence of such a certificate would not prevent the Plaintiff from recovering service charges', at any rate where the clause in question contained a primary obligation to pay, with the certification requirement being merely a subsidiary part of that payment obligation. The certificate's sole function was to be conclusive evidentially, but not to be a precondition for liability. The document purporting to be a certificate was, in any case, bad and did not comply with the content requirements under the lease. It was, therefore, open to the court to undertake the relevant determination of sums due.[24]

ATTRIBUTES, QUALIFICATIONS AND INDEPENDENCE OF THE CERTIFIER

17-13   It may be that the characteristics of the original contractual certifier, or the post-contractually specified certifier, are so important that an assignment of the reversion has the effect of rendering the certification machinery inoperable and placing the determination of disputes into the hands of the courts.[25]

17-14   Usually, however, the certifier is not so specifically identified, and rights to certify are given to some identified professional or person with a relevant skill, such as the landlord's accountant, auditor, surveyor, or managing agent. Evidently, the expert must be appointed in accordance with the instructions set out in the contract.[26] Beyond that, what qualities must the appointee have? This commonly gives rise to two subquestions:

---

23 [1999] EWHC 276 (TCC). See, however, the discussion of *Jardine* in *Jacey v De Sousa* at **17-06** above.
24 Compare the comments as to the ability of the LVT to do so in *Warrior Quay* at **17-11** above.
25 *St Modwen Developments (Edmonton) Ltd v Tesco Stores Ltd* [2007] 1 EGLR 63, where the certifier was the borough treasurer of the local authority landlord.
26 *Epoch Properties Ltd v British Home Stores (Jersey) Ltd* [2004] 3 EGLR 34 (Court of Appeal: Channel Islands), paras 28–30; *Jacey Property Co Ltd v De Sousa* [2003] EWCA Civ 510 (where the certification was done by a solicitor and not by the landlord's surveyor as provided for in the lease); *Akorita v Marina Heights (St Leonards) Ltd* [2011] UKUT 255 (LC) at paras 20–21.

1   Must the person charged with certifying have formal expertise or will 'life experience' suffice?

2   What happens if the person charged with certifying is in some way connected with the landlord?

17-15   Both of those questions arose for consideration in *New Pinehurst Residents Association (Cambridge) Ltd v Silow*.[27] In that case, the landlord was a tenant-owned residents' association. Originally, the landlord was the developer. Under the terms of the relevant leases, there was a power to appoint managing agents in the management of the building. The managing agent was to certify annual service charge contributions and, in that role, they were to act as experts and not as arbitrators. The residents' association decided to elect a committee of six of its members to fulfil the role of managing agents. The evidence showed that, though not formally qualified for that role, the committee was composed of experienced individuals who acted conscientiously and independently. The appellant tenant challenged the appointment of shareholder members of the residents' association as managing agents, suggesting that they were neither qualified, nor independent.

17-16   In relation to the question of independence, the appellant in the *New Pinehurst* case relied on *Finchbourne Ltd v Rodrigues*.[28] In that case, the landlord, in reality an individual named Mr Pinto, appointed a firm, Pinto & Co, as managing agents for certification purposes under the relevant leases. Pinto & Co was, in fact, Mr Pinto himself. As there was no meaningful practical separation between the landlord and managing agent, the essential arbitral function of certification could not be fulfilled.

17-17   Distinguishing *Finchbourne*, Kerr LJ stated that:[29]

> 'I think two principles are to be derived from [Finchbourne]. First, it is quite clear that the managing agents must be legally distinct from the lessors. Second, since they are to act as experts and not arbitrators, I must accept from the judgments that a measure of expertise is to be required from them; but I would not accept that they have to be professional persons with professional qualifications.'

17-18   Kerr LJ concluded that the appointment of the management committee was not precluded by the first of the principles, pointing out that the management committee was legally distinct (in the sense that it was comprised of persons separate from the landlord) and, secondly, that they were found to have been appointed on the basis that they could and would have exercised independent judgment. The mere fact that they happened to be tenants was not enough to impugn their independence. As to expertise, Kerr LJ concluded that it was sufficient that the appointed persons were able to show the requisite competence to discharge the task of applying expertise, whether that expertise was derived from real world experience or from a formal qualification.

27   [1988] 1 EGLR 227.
28   [1976] 3 All ER 581.
29   At p 229.

17-19   The *New Pinehurst* case makes clear that, as a general rule, it is not necessary for the expert to be entirely independent from one of the parties, though it is necessary for the expert to reach an independent judgment.[30] The mere fact that the certifier has some form of relationship with the landlord is not, therefore, of itself enough. So, in *Skilleter v Charles*,[31] it was acceptable for a landlord to appoint as its managing agent a landlord-owned company. The court noted that this arrangement was acceptable unless it could be shown that the arrangement amounted to a 'complete sham'.

17-20   A case falling on the wrong side of the line, but concerned with resolution of a dispute and not certification, as such,[32] was *Concorde Graphics v Andromeda Investments SA*.[33] In that case, the lease provided that the landlord's surveyor was to resolve any difference arising out of the determination of costs and expenses incurred in managing the subject premises and in apportionment of those costs. A difference arose, in that a tenant, following an escalation in costs, challenged certain fees which were being claimed. The managing agent, who had been appointed under the lease and who had levied the demands for service charge, was also appointed as the surveyor for the purposes of determining any difference. That, Vinelott J decided, was impermissible on the grounds that the person who had made (and sought to justify) the disputed claim could not then determine the difference arising out of the claim.

17-21   Finally, it must be noted that it is not often the case that one can discern from a bare certificate what sorts of skills have been applied and how, and given that there is no general duty to give reasons,[34] it will not be easy to impugn a certificate because the expert has not carried out any exercise involving his expertise. However, where it is plain from the document and/or evidence that the expert has not, in fact, carried out any expert function, then a certificate will be held not to satisfy the requirements of the lease in question.[35] An expert who has negligently certified may be liable in negligence.[36]

FORM OF THE CERTIFICATE

17-22   Whether a certificate must satisfy any particular requirements of form is a question of construction of the document said to be a certificate and the requirements

---

30 See Kendall, Freedman and Farrell, *Expert Determination* (4th edn, 2008), paras 8.7.1–8.7.3. A further example of a failure to certify independently is to be found in *Hickman v Roberts* [1913] AC 229.

31 [1992] 1 EGLR 73; see too *Parkside Knightsbridge Ltd v Horwitz* [1983] 2 EGLR 42 (certifier was parent company of landlord).

32 It may be that the demands for independence of the parties are tighter where the function of the expert is to resolve disputes, rather than to certify amounts: Kendall, Freedman and Farrell, *Expert Determination* (4th edn, 2008), pp 134–135, 230–234.

33 [1983] 1 EGLR 53.

34 *Bernard Schulte & Co KG v Nile Holdings Ltd* [2004] EWHC 977 (Comm); *Vimercati v BV Trustco Ltd* [2012] EWHC 1410 (Ch) at para 21.

35 *Akorita v Marina Heights (St Leonards) Ltd* [2011] UKUT 255 (LC), para 20–21.

36 *Sutcliffe v Thackrah* [1974] AC 727.

of the lease in question. Where all that is required is a 'certificate' without more, however, it is considered that usually the substance and intent of the document are what matters and not the form it is in.[37] What matters is that the document is an expression of judgement, opinion or skill on the part of the appointed certifier.[38] Use of the word 'certify' is not a pre-requisite for a valid certificate.[39] Given that the purpose of a certificate is to inform the intended recipients of the information which it contains, it must ordinarily be issued to them.[40] Experts are not, however, under any duty to give reasons or to observe the rules of natural justice.[41]

17-23 Some further guidance was given in the decision of HH Judge Colyer (sitting as a Deputy Judge of the Chancery Division) in *Rexhaven Ltd v Nurse and Alliance & Leicester Building Society*.[42] The case concerned forfeiture of a lease for failure to pay service charge and the question was whether the charges had been properly certified so as to fall due under the terms of the particular lease. He explained as follows:[43]

'The lease gives no definition of what is meant by "a certificate". So what is a certificate for the purposes of this clause? Has the word any established meaning, so that if a draftsman used it without defining the word, the reader would know what the term means? "Certify" and cognate expressions deriving therefrom, are widely used terms. Extracts of documents at title are certified every day of the week by solicitors as true copies. Facts are certified as correct, and so on. But in final analysis the word is usually otiose and adds little, if anything, to the recital of the extract or the facts and the verifying signature of the party who provides it. Use of the word sometimes makes it clear that that party warrants the truth of what is certified – a somewhat otiose concept where the landlord is certifying its own estimate. Clearly however, "a certificate" is a document. It has to be written out. Mr Neuberger adopts Chambers' definition of the word:

"Certificate – a written definition of fact". The Concise Oxford English Dictionary, I observe, has a slightly different definition. "A document formally attesting a fact." Mr Neuberger submits that as to the certificate, to require a person to provide a certificate of its own estimate, that is as opposed to a certificate of an actual expenditure, is no more than to require that person to provide a statement in writing of the estimate and that the letters of September 29, 1993 and October 27, 1993, which I have read, taken together comply with the provision of the lease. He says that the purpose of the provision in the lease is to ensure that the tenant has knowledge of the total estimate of expenditure and the proportion that is payable by her. The purpose was more than met by those two letters.

I accept that the plaintiff's case here derives some assistance from *R. v. St. Mary's Vestry, Islington* 25 QBD 523, especially the observations on pages 527 and 529. I derive some assistance, although of course that authority is only persuasive since

---

37 *Token Construction v Charlton Estates* (1973) BPR 48 at p 52; *Minster Trust v Traps Tractors Ltd* [1954] 1 WLR 963; *Cantrell v Wright & Fuller Ltd* [2003] EWHC 1545 (TCC).
38 *Token Construction v Charlton Estates* (1973) BPR 48 at p 52.
39 *Ibid.* at p 57.
40 *London Borough of Camden v Thomas McInerney* (1986) Const LJ 293.
41 *Bernard Schulte & Co KG v Nile Holdings Ltd* [2004] EWHC 977 (Comm); *Vimercati v BV Trustco Ltd* [2012] EWHC 1410 (Ch) at para 21.
42 (1996) 28 HLR 241.
43 At pp 249–250.

I am construing a document from the observations that were made in that case. I accept, however, the propositions that Mr Neuberger has relied upon and in these circumstances I find that the letter of October 27, which of course was precise as to its figures, did satisfy the requirement for "a certificate", by which word I see the draftsman of this lease was requiring nothing more or less than a formal statement in writing of the precise amount or amounts. I would observe, but this is *obiter dicta*; that if the figures had been scribbled on the back of an envelope and handed in a highly informal manner to the tenant, in my view that would not be enough. Some degree of solemnity or formality is needed for a document to satisfy the requirement of this lease. It is not enough that it be scribbled down casually. It has to be written down and it has to be written down with precision; but here it was. I therefore see no hope of success in the defence that there was no good certificate in this case.'

17-24   A similar view – that the question was one of substance, and not of mere form – was taken by the Court of Appeal in *Wagon Finance Ltd v Demelt*,[44] in which a tenant's argument that a document which failed to state that the landlord 'certified' expenditure was not a certificate failed. The document was plainly intended to be a final statement of account and provided a reasonable amount of detail. In substance, therefore, the function of a certificate was fulfilled.

WHETHER A CERTIFICATE IS CONCLUSIVE

Certificates not expressly stated to be conclusive

17-25   The question which sometimes arises is whether or not a certificate issued pursuant to the terms of a lease is conclusively binding upon the parties. If a certificate is not stated by the terms of the lease to be 'conclusive' or 'binding', or words to that effect, then it may be capable of being re-opened by the parties for the purpose of challenging the contents of that certificate,[45] though it may still be that the context of the contract requires, even absent express words, that the determination of the expert be treated as final and binding to the exclusion of the court.[46] As has already been explained, no certificates are of themselves binding as to specified amounts in the residential context, due to the intervention of statute, though it remains open to doubt whether the need for such certificates in the residential context has been entirely ousted by statute.[47]

Can certificates be conclusive on statements of law?

17-26   Whether or not it is possible to challenge a decision of an expert which has been arrived at on the basis of an error of law has not been conclusively

---

44   Unreported, 19 June 1997.
45   *Universities Superannuation Scheme Ltd v Marks & Spencer Plc* [1999] 1 EGLR 13.
46   See, for example, *Regent Holdings Incorporated v Alliance* (unreported, 23 July 1999, Court of Appeal); *Homepace Ltd v Sita South East Ltd* [2008] EWCA Civ 1 at para 28, *per* Lloyd LJ. It is said that strong words are required to achieve this result: *Beaufort Developments (NI) Ltd v Gilbert-Ash (NI) Ltd* [1999] 1 AC 266.
47   See **17-11**.

settled. The decided cases generally draw a distinction between errors committed by an expert as to his jurisdiction (e.g. answering a question he was not in fact asked) and errors committed in answering the question which the expert was asked. Whether or not an expert who has committed an error of the latter kind has made a void decision has been the more vexed of the two questions. It is considered that the general tenor of recent cases has been to allow errors of law to be reviewed by the court.

17-27   There is authority for the proposition that an expert's certificate cannot be conclusive on matters of law (which include questions of construction).[48] In *Re Davstone Estates Ltd's Leases*,[49] a lease provided that a surveyor's certificates were conclusive as to the level of contribution payable by a tenant towards costs of repairs. A tenant challenged the certificates on the basis that they were based on works to remedy defects in design and other defects which did not fall within the ambit of a covenant to repair. The landlord relied on the fact that the certificates were expressed to be 'final and not open to challenge in any manner whatsoever'. The landlord argued that, for the certificate to be conclusive as to the amounts charged, it also had to be conclusive as to the underlying works of repair, that is, as to the construction of the lease's repairing covenant.[50] Ungoed-Thomas J concluded that, as a matter of pure construction of the particular clause in that case, the expert clause excluded from the surveyor's conclusive decision questions of construction. His expertise was confined to the question of determining the relevant expenses alone. He did, however, go on to consider the alternative submission by the tenant, that the true construction of the repairing covenant was a question of law, and that, therefore, it was contrary to public policy and void for an expert determination clause to seek to be conclusive on such questions.[51] Ungoed-Thomas J found that it would be and that, as it could not be severed from the rest of the clause, the clause was void.[52]

17-28   A different approach has been taken in another line of cases. In *Nikko Hotels (UK) Ltd v MEPC Plc*,[53] the issue arose in the context of an expert determination of a rent review. The rent review was to proceed on the basis of an average room rate during a period preceding the review date. The tenant's auditor was then required to certify (amongst other matters) that average rate. The tenant produced a certificate which gave the average occupancy rate which the rooms, in fact, received in that period, requiring detailed examination of any special discounts that had, in fact, been given, and so on. The landlord contended that the figure that should have been used was the average occupancy rate at

---

48 No public policy objections arise where the question is one of fact: *Baker v Jones* [1954] 1 WLR 1005 at p 1010. Such a decision may be challengeable for fraud or perversity: see *West of England Shipowners Mutual Insurance Association (Luxembourg) v Cristal Ltd (The Glacier Bay)* [1996] 1 Lloyd's Rep 370.
49 [1969] 2 Ch 378.
50 Reliance was placed on *R v Ayton ex parte Cardiff Corporation* [1935] 1 KB 225.
51 Relying upon *Scott v Avery* (1856) 5 HL Cas 811; *Lee v Showmen's Guild of Great Britain* [1952] 2 QB 329.
52 A similar result was reached in *Rapid Results College v Angell* [1986] 1 EGLR 53, though the parties agreed that the certificate in that case was not binding on points of law.
53 [1991] 2 EGLR 103.

which the rooms were exposed to the general public. The lease provided that a dispute was to be referred to a chartered accountant, sitting as expert, to resolve. The expert determined that the rent should be calculated on the basis of the landlord's construction and awarded the landlord a higher rent. The tenant issued proceedings, arguing that the expert's determination could not be conclusive on construction issues and that the expert had erred in his construction.

17-29   Knox J decided, having reviewed the conflicting earlier authority (including the unreported Court of Appeal decision in *Jones v Sherwood Computer Services Plc*[54]) that there was no bar on experts determining questions of construction as part of the proper exercise of their expertise. Further, he concluded that *Re Davstone* had been decided on too wide a basis.[55] He went on to note that:[56]

> 'The result, in my judgment, is that if parties agree to refer to the final and conclusive judgment of an expert an issue which either consists of a question of construction or necessarily involves the solution of a question of construction, the expert's decision will be final and conclusive and, therefore, not open to review or treatment by the courts as a nullity on the ground that the expert's decision on construction was erroneous in law, unless it can be shown that the expert has not performed the task assigned to him. If he has answered the right question in the wrong way, his decision will be binding. If he has answered the wrong question, his decision will be a nullity.'

17-30   The observations in *Nikko Hotels* relating to the true scope of the rule of public policy have subsequently been approved in a number of cases in the Court of Appeal.[57] *Nikko Hotels* cannot be treated as having settled the question, however. It is to be noted that the Court of Appeal has left open the question of whether any error of law within the expert's remit will always be reviewable by the court,[58] though the point has yet to be definitively settled. It is considered (subject to what is said below in relation to manifest errors and material departure from instructions) that the present attitude of the court is that it is likely to be more receptive to challenges founded purely on errors of law and that the pendulum has swung back away from the *Nikko Hotels* position.

54   Now reported at [1992] 1 WLR 277.
55   And see in particular the critical comments at p 109. In the same place, he rejected the submission that *Jones v Sherwood* could be distinguished on the basis that that case was only about the skill of the expert accountant and not about construction.
56   At p 108.
57   *Brown v GIO Insurance Ltd* [1998] Lloyd's Rep IR 201 at p 208 (where Chadwick LJ expressly stated that there was no rule of public policy against referring to a third party 'some issue which involves questions of construction or of mixed law and fact'); *West of England Shipowners Mutual Insurance Association (Luxembourg) v Cristal Ltd (The Glacier Bay)* [1996] 1 Lloyd's Rep 370 at p 377; *Mercury Communications Ltd v Director General of Telecommunications* [1996] 1 WLR 48; *British Shipbuilders v VSEL Consortium* [1997] 1 Lloyd's Rep 106; *National Grid Co Plc v M25 Group Ltd (No 1)* [1999] 1 EGLR 65. See also *Inmarsat Ventures Plc v APR Ltd* (unreported, 15 May 2002, High Court).
58   See *Barclays Bank Plc v Nylon Capital LLP* [2011] EWCA Civ 826, paras 35 (*per* Thomas LJ) and 63–72 (*per* Lord Neuberger MR, who expressly questioned the safety of relying on the cited passage from *Nikko Hotels*); *Persimmon Homes Ltd v Woodford Land Ltd* [2011] EWHC 3109 (Ch); *Ackerman v Ackerman* [2011] EWHC 3428 (Ch) at para 291.

Challenging a 'conclusive' certificate

17-31   There have been a number of cases setting out the bases on which an expert's determination might be attacked. The general principles governing such challenges are set out in the following principles provided by Lightman J in *British Shipbuilders v VSEL Consortium:*[59]

'(1) Questions as to the role of the expert, the ambit of his remit (or jurisdiction) and the character of his remit (whether exclusive or concurrent with the jurisdiction of the court) are to be determined as a matter of construction of the agreement;

(2) If the agreement confers upon the expert the exclusive remit to determine a question (subject to (3) and (4) below), the jurisdiction of the court to determine that question is excluded because (as a matter of substantive law) for the purposes of ascertaining the rights and duties of the parties under the agreement the determination of the expert alone is relevant and any determination by the court is irrelevant. It is irrelevant whether the court would have reached a different conclusion or whether the court considers that the expert's decision is wrong, for the parties have in either event agreed to abide by the decision of the expert;

(3) If the expert in making his determination goes outside his remit, e.g. by determining a different question to that remitted to him or in his determination fails to comply with any conditions which the agreement requires him to comply with in making his determination, the court may intervene and set his decision aside. Such determination by the expert as a matter of construction of the agreement is not a determination which the parties agreed should affect the rights and duties of the parties, and the court will say so;

(4) Likewise the court may set aside a decision of the expert where [...] the agreement so provides if his determination discloses a manifest error;

(5) The court has jurisdiction ahead of a determination by the expert to determine a question as to the limits of his remit or the conditions with which the expert must comply in making his determination, but (as a rule of procedural convenience) will (save in exceptional circumstances) decline to do so. This is because the question is ordinarily merely hypothetical, only proving live if, after seeing the decision of the expert, one party considers that the expert got it wrong. To apply to the court in anticipation of his decision (and before it is clear that he has got it wrong) is likely to prove wasteful of time and costs – the saving of which may be presumed to have been the, or at least one of the, objectives of the parties in agreeing to the determination by the expert.'

17-32   It is considered that, unless the expert's appointment itself can be challenged (for lack of independence, and so on), or unless the court can be persuaded (in line with some of the *dicta* in *Barclays Bank v Nylon*, discussed at **17-30** above) that it retains a supervisory jurisdiction over all errors of law, then the only bases of challenge to a conclusive certificate are:

---

59 [1997] 1 Lloyd's LR 106. See too the discussion in *Aviva Life & Pensions UK Ltd v Kestrel Properties Ltd* [2011] EWHC 3934 (Civ).

1   An expert acting outside the scope of his instructions so that he is not doing what the parties have contractually agreed that he should do (called a 'material departure from instruction'); and

2   A challenge based on fraud or collusion, or one based on 'manifest error' where the contract permits a challenge to a conclusive certificate on such basis.

'Material departure from instructions'

17-33   It appears that, save perhaps in the case of a particularly widely drafted expert determination clause,[60] it will generally be open to the parties to challenge an expert's determination where he has materially not done what the contract required him to do. It is important to note that the challenge here is not on the basis that he has done something badly within the scope of his instructions. Rather, the challenge is on the basis that he has misunderstood his instructions in the first place and has, therefore, not resolved the dispute in accordance with the instructions given to him by the parties, on the basis of which instructions jurisdiction was conferred upon him.[61]

17-34   An illustration of this can be found in *National Grid Co Plc v M25 Group Plc*.[62] In that case, relating to a rent review by expert determination, the independent expert was asked to determine the rent on review having regard to, amongst other matters, the terms of the lease relating to user. Those were contractual directions and instructions in accordance with which the expert was required to act and the parties had not, therefore, conferred upon the expert the sole exclusive right to determine the meaning of certain provisions of the lease, as had been done in (for instance) *Norwich Union Life Insurance Society v P&O Property Holdings Ltd*.[63] Accordingly, if, on the true construction of a particular lease, the question of the meaning of a provision of the lease goes to the scope of the expert's instructions, then it would seem that those questions remain capable of determination by the court.[64]

17-35   The question was reconsidered in some detail in *Veba Oil Supply & Trading GmbH v Petrotrade Inc*.[65] This case related to a contract for the sale of

---

60   *Barclays Bank v Nylon Capital LLP* [2011] EWCA Civ 826 at paras 23, 28 (*per* Thomas LJ, pointing out that in an expert determination, particular issues are referred to the expert, whereas arbitration clauses operate more widely) and 63–73 (*per* Lord Neuberger MR). A clause may delegate the interpretation of the scope of the expert's instructions to the expert too: see *Dixons Group Plc v Murray-Oboynski* (1997) 86 BLR 16.

61   See the discussion in *Ackerman v Ackerman* [2011] EWHC 3428 at paras 258–263 and 274.

62   [1999] 1 EGLR 65. See too *Homepace Ltd v Sita South East Ltd* [2008] EWCA Civ 1, in which case a surveyor was to provide a certificate confirming that minerals had been exhausted. The contract did not, however, confer on him the power to determine what 'minerals' were for the purposes of the contract. See too *Level Properties Ltd v Balls Brothers Ltd* [2007] EWHC 744 (Ch).

63   [1993] 1 EGLR 164.

64   See too *Director General for Telecommunications v Mercury Communications Ltd* [1996] 1 WLR 48 at pp 58–59 (agreeing with the dissenting judgment of Hoffmann LJ in the Court of Appeal (unreported, 22 July 1994) on this point).

65   [2001] EWCA Civ 1832.

gasoil. The mutually appointed independent expert under that contract was to determine the density of the gasoil by reference to a prescribed testing method, such determination to be conclusive save for fraud or manifest error. The expert used a different test, producing a different result, as a result of which the buyers brought a claim for losses they had suffered. The sellers applied for summary judgment on the basis that the court's jurisdiction had been ousted. The Court of Appeal determined that, in not following the contractual direction as to the type of test to be used, the expert had departed from his instructions. The next question was whether that was a *material* departure or not. Having considered the authorities, Simon Brown LJ pointed out that there was a conceptual difference between misunderstanding one's instructions and not following what the contract required one to do, and making a mistake, albeit within the instructions set out by the contract. While a mistake made by an expert in executing his properly understood instructions could only be vitiated by a 'material mistake' (as to which see **17-38** to **17-40** below), when an expert was mistaken as to his instructions, the threshold was not so high. The reason for that was that, in the latter case, he was not carrying out what he had been instructed to do badly; he was not carrying out what he had been instructed to do at all. In a case in the latter category, he stated that:

> 'Given that a material departure vitiates the determination whether or not it affects the result, it could hardly be the effect on the result which determines the materiality of the departure in the first place. Rather, I would hold any departure to be material unless it can be truly characterised as trivial or de minimis in the sense of it being obvious that it could make no possible difference to either party'.[66]

17-36   The test, therefore, is better described as 'non-trivial departure from instructions'.

17-37   It is suggested that the earlier authorities, arguably including *Jones v Sherwood Computer Services Ltd*,[67] *Nikko Hotels (UK) Ltd v MPEC Plc*,[68] but also *Pontsarn Investments Ltd v Kansallis-Osake-Pankki*,[69] approached the question of 'departure from instructions' in a manner which is different from the way that question is understood in the cases following *Mercury Telecommunications*.[70] So, the earlier cases appeared to regard the 'instructions' as being the general, overarching question the expert was asked to determine and regarded the legal questions that needed to be answered 'along the way' as subsidiary questions lying within the expert's contractual jurisdiction (and hence outside the court's supervision).[71] The newer cases, however, appear to regard the subsidiary legal

---

66   See para 26; see too *Shell UK Ltd v Enterprise Oil Plc* [1999] 2 All ER (Comm) 87.
67   [1992] 1 WLR 277.
68   [1991] 2 EGLR 103.
69   [1992] 1 EGLR 148.
70   And in particular the judgment of Lord Slynn at pp 58–59. Note also the approach of Timothy Lloyd QC (sitting as a deputy judge of the High Court) in *PosTel Properties Ltd v Greenwell* [1992] 2 EGLR 130 (a case in which a declaration was sought before an expert had determined the question and an application to strike the proceedings out was dismissed).
71   See, for example, *Nikko Hotels (UK) Ltd v MEPC Plc* [1991] 2 EGLR 103 at p 109.

questions as cumulatively amounting to the instructions of the expert, so that, if the expert answers one of those questions wrongly, he is not in fact acting in accordance with the parties' bargain as it was intended by them to operate.[72] The latter approach permits a broader range of challenges to expert determinations, as this approach allows one to argue that any error of law committed by an expert in the course of his deliberations (provided the error is capable of being established from his reasoning (if available)) would allow one to argue that he had stepped outside the ambit of the instructions of the contract.

Challenging a decision made within the scope of instructions

17-38   An expert's determination may be impeached on other, limited grounds:[73] naturally, fraud and collusion remain invalidating grounds.[74] However, beyond those grounds, it is accepted that, in accordance with the policy of encouraging parties to resolve disputes without recourse to the court, the court should be slow to find that a certificate ought to be set aside for other reasons.[75]

17-39   An expert determination may be set aside for 'material' or 'manifest error', meaning 'oversights and blunders so obvious and obviously capable of affecting the determination as to admit of no difference of opinion'.[76] This avenue of challenge may however only be open to the parties if the contractual terms provide for it.[77] Absent such an express term, the parties may remain saddled with the decision, no matter how wrong, unless it can be attacked for some other ground.[78]

---

72 See for instance *Barrington v Sloane Properties Ltd* [2007] EWLands LRX_31_2006 at para 51.
73 In addition to any grounds which go to the validity of that expert's appointment in the first place, which are separate issues and are discussed at **17-13** to **17-23** above.
74 'Fraud and collusion unravels everything': *Campbell v Edwards* [1976] 1 WLR 403, *per* Lord Denning MR; *South Eastern Railway v Warton* (1861) 2 F&F 457.
75 *Toepfer v Continental Grain Co Ltd* [1974] 1 Lloyd's Rep 11 at p 14 (*per* Cairns LJ, adding 'fundamental mistake' to the list of grounds).
76 *Veba Oil Supply & Trading GmbH v Petrotrade Inc* [2001] EWCA Civ 1832.
77 The issue was argued but left open in *Alliance v Regent Holdings Inc* (unreported, 23 July 1999, Court of Appeal). Gage LJ there stated that, absent an express term, he would not have implied one on the facts of that case. In *Veba Oil Supply & Trading GmbH v Petrotrade Inc* [2002] 1 All ER 703 at para 33, Simon Brown LJ apparently considered that it was necessary to have an express clause to that effect, relying on the departure from the law as stated in *Dean v Prince* [1954] Ch 409 at p 427 in subsequent cases. Reynolds QC and Fetherstonhaugh QC, *Handbook on Rent Review*, para 11.12.5, state that an express provision to this effect is required. The latter view is supported by *Clemence v Clarke* (1880) HBC (4th edn), Vol 2, paras 54 and 65.
78 In *Alliance v Regent Holdings Inc* (unreported, 23 July 1999, Court of Appeal). Gage LJ left open the possibility that a manifest error might have allowed the argument that the expert had not followed his instructions, or had stepped outside his authority; as to whether a plain error can amount to a vitiating ground for other reasons; see *Conoco (UK) Ltd v Phillips Petroleum Co* [1998] ADRLJ 55 at p 70. The proposition that the mere fact that there is a manifest error means something has gone wrong with the expert's compliance with his instructions was, however, doubted in *Pontsarn Investments Ltd v Kansallis-Osake-Pankki* [1992] 1 EGLR 148 at p 151.

17-40   Given the nature of most of the provisions with which this book is concerned, which often will involve a simple certificate not backed up with reasons, and given that there is no general duty for experts to give reasons absent contractual requirements to do so, errors will be difficult to detect in the first place. Further, however, it is clear that the threshold for making out an error of the appropriate degree of obviousness, and with the required effect on the certificate, is a very high one and it will be difficult to do this in the usual case.[79]

When are certificates a nullity?

17-41   It has been said that a certificate issued outside the scope of the parties' instructions is of no effect.[80] The Lands Tribunal has, however, stated that a certificate which is not, on its face, plainly invalid, takes effect as a valid certificate, but subject to any right to challenge, and would seem, therefore, to be voidable rather than void on that analysis.[81]

Can a court fulfil the function of a certifier?

17-42   It is not yet settled whether a court will intervene where the parties have agreed that a dispute or decision should be referred to an expert, and it may be that the court's readiness to do so will depend on whether or not a reference has in fact already been made, and what indications the expert has given as to what he proposes to do. It may be that where, for instance, the court has formed the view that the expert is intended to proceed on an erroneous basis, then it would exercise its discretion to grant declaration as to the meaning of provisions which the expert is to apply. Where, on the other hand, there is no sign that the expert is about to 'go wrong', the court may decline to exercise its declaratory jurisdiction as a matter of discretion.[82] In *Concorde Graphics Ltd v Andromeda Investments SA*,[83] a lease of commercial property provided that service charge, payable in arrear to the landlord, was subject to conclusive determination by the 'landlord's surveyor' in the event of a dispute. The Court of Appeal left open the question of the whether it could determine the amount itself under such a clause, or if a determination by a suitable surveyor was a condition precedent for liability to arise in the event that there was a 'difference' which had arisen.

17-43   In circumstances where the expert determination machinery has broken down so that there is no longer a person who can properly fulfil the contractually specified expert function, it would seem that the court will step in and substitute

---

79   *Invensys Plc v Automotive Sealing Systems Ltd* [2002] 1 All ER (Comm) 222.
80   *Veba Oil Supply & Trading GmbH v Petrotrade Inc* [2001] EWCA Civ 1832 and *Homepace Ltd v Sita South East Ltd* [2008] EWCA Civ 1 at para 54.
81   *Barrington v Sloan Properties Ltd* [2007] 3 EGLR 91 at para 45.
82   As to this, see *PosTel Properties v Greenwell* [1992] 2 EGLR 130; and the discussion in Reynolds QC and Fetherstonhaugh QC, *Handbook on Rent Review*, para 11.11.11.
83   [1983] 1 EGLR 53.

its own decision to ensure that the contract remains operable.[84] Further, the court will, in an appropriate case, not allow experts to frustrate contractual machinery by refusing to issue certificates.[85]

17-44 A case which seems somewhat at variance with the above, and appears to signal a greater preparedness on the part of the court to substitute its own judgment for that of the expert, is *Scottish Mutual Assurance Plc v Jardine Public Relations Ltd.*[86] There, the court was faced with a case in which the relevant lease provided that service charges were recoverable only on certification, such certificate to be binding save for manifest error. David Blunt QC, sitting as Deputy Judge of the High Court, determined that the certification requirement was merely procedural and that he could, therefore, proceed with assessing the payable charges himself and it did not matter that certification had not been undertaken. If the underlying premise, that the certification requirement was purely procedural, is correct, then the case is unexceptionable. However, it is suggested that the underlying premise is open to question, as (a) certification is usually a precondition to liability and not mere machinery, and (b) the case appears to go significantly further than the cases considered above in allowing (in effect) the court simply to override a contractual expert determination provision. It is considered that *Jardine* cannot be considered authority for the proposition that, without more, a court can obviate the contractual requirement that a particular issue be determined by an expert.

17-45 One must distinguish from the above the position where the LVT or the Upper Tribunal is asked to determine the reasonableness of service charge. As it is not possible to oust those tribunals' jurisdiction by agreement,[87] a lack of certification is not a bar to a determination, though it may be a bar to a landlord recovering the determined amount before the formality of a certificate is gone through, even if that is rendered a rather academic exercise in light of the determination under section 27A.[88]

---

84 *St Modwen Developments (Edmonton) Ltd v Tesco Stores Ltd* [2007] 1 EGLR 63.
85 *Henry Boot Construction Ltd v Alstom Combined Cycles Ltd* [2005] 1 WLR 3850 at p 3861.
86 [1999] EWHC 276 (TCC).
87 Landlord and Tenant Act 1985, s 27(6).
88 *Warrior Quay Management Co Ltd v Joachim* [2008] EWLands LRX_42_2006.

CHAPTER 18

Consultation, estimation, information and consent requirements

18-01 The statutory consultation requirements (and the machinery for dispensing with the need to comply with them) for residential service charges are considered in Chapter 30. In this chapter, consideration will be given to contractual requirements of that nature and related obligations to provide costs estimates and other 'information' conditions. Again, it is considered that, where a contractual obligation is drafted for the purpose of ensuring that the tenant has an opportunity to comment on a proposed amount to be charged, then that opportunity ought to be afforded before the demand is levied, so that such requirements ought, as a rule, to be preconditions to liability.

18-02 The first question which has been considered is: Will the courts imply an obligation to consult or to provide prior estimates absent an express contractual requirement to do so?[1] As to prior consultation obligations, on the one occasion that the court has considered the question, it has refused to imply such a term.[2] It also does not appear that the court would imply a term that the provider of services under a lease should obtain estimates before carrying out works,[3] though it does appear that the court might be willing to read such an obligation into a lease where service charge is charged in advance.[4]

18-03 Express consultation provisions have, however, been considered by the courts. In *CIN Properties Ltd v Barclays Bank Plc*,[5] it was provided by an underlease of commercial premises that CIN, as successors to the original landlord, would not carry out certain works to a building without first obtaining estimates or tenders on the open market and would not accept any tender or estimate, or place a contract, without providing them (with supporting documentation) to Barclays for approval, not to be unreasonably withheld or delayed. In order urgently to cure falling masonry from the building, CIN engaged contractors without seeking

---

1   In the residential context, see the guidance in the RICS Residential, Pts 8 (budgets and estimates) and 18 (consultation).
2   *Walker v Badcock* [1997] 2 EGLR 163.
3   See the commentary in *Woodfall: Landlord and Tenant*, Vol 1, para 7-165.
4   *Gordon v Selico Co Ltd* [1985] 2 EGLR 79, affirmed on this point by the Court of Appeal, [1986] 1 EGLR 71. For the position of the RICS on consultation, see the RICS Commercial Code at pp 18–19.
5   [1986] 1 EGLR 59.

prior approval from Barclays. Despite reservations as to the merits of Barclays' position, the Court of Appeal decided that, on its true construction, the provision was not a mere piece of machinery designed to allow Barclays to have input in the decision-making process, but was a true condition precedent capable of enforcement against CIN. Accordingly, Barclays were not liable to contribute to the works undertaken. CIN's alternative argument, based on waiver and estoppel, failed on the facts.

18-04   Similarly, in *Northways Flats Management Co (Camden) Ltd v Wimpey Pension Trustees Ltd*,[6] Wimpey held a commercial unit in a mixed block under an underlease of which Northways was the landlord. The underlease provided that in the event of 'major or substantial repairs the Landlord shall before carrying out such works submit a copy of the specification of works and estimates obtained upon such specification to the Tenant for consideration', after which the tenant had 21 days to object. If the tenant failed to object, he was deemed to have agreed the specification and estimates as reasonable and proper and had no right to make any further objection. If there was an objection, the matter was to go for expert determination. Northways had not complied with that procedure. Following *CIN*, the Court of Appeal found that this covenant did not merely set out machinery for the tenant to be informed of intended works, but created a true condition precedent to being charged for works carried out. Fox LJ considered that the following matters were significant, which provide helpful guidance as to how the court approaches the contractual obligation to consult:

'(1)   There is a specific obligation upon Northways that, before it carries out works, it will submit a copy of the estimates and specifications to the tenant for consideration. The obligation, in my view, derives from the word "shall", which I read as peremptory.

(2)   The obligation is an essential part of the mechanism whereby disputes between the parties regarding the works can be resolved, if necessary, by the disputes procedure specified in para 7(ii).

(3)   It is reasonable to assume that the parties intended the contractual provisions which they have entered into should be effective and should be subject to some sanction to that end.

(4)   If Wimpey is bound to pay for the works whether or not Northways complies with its obligations under para 7(ii), then the obligations are largely worthless to Wimpey. It is difficult to believe that the parties can have intended such a result. I accept, as did Oliver L.J. in the CIN case, that it is unfortunate that the landlord should have deprived itself of the right to contribution by what may have been just an oversight. But the alternative is that the paragraph is largely deprived of value to Wimpey.'

18-05   What degree of accuracy is required of an estimate? At first instance in *Princes House Ltd v Distinctive Clubs Ltd*,[7] a question arose as to what the effect would be if a landlord's estimate, which the learned trial judge found to be a pre-

---

6   [1992] 2 EGLR 42.
7   Unreported, 25 September 2006 (Jonathan Gaunt QC, sitting as Deputy Judge of the High Court). This aspect of the decision was not appealed to the Court of Appeal.

condition for liability, turned out to include non-chargeable items. The learned judge stated:[8]

> '(1) One is dealing with estimates, the amount of which is subject to checking and adjustment when the expenditure for the accounting year is determined and certified; a degree of inaccuracy not only of costing but of specification is to be expected and tolerated at this stage;
>
> (2) The estimate is made by the Landlord and the onus is therefore on him to ensure that the estimate only includes costs which are included in and not excluded from his entitlement to charge;
>
> (3) A tenant can nevertheless (and often does), if he suspects that he is being wrongly charged, ask for a breakdown of the landlord's estimate, from which he will be able to form a view what proportion of it is attributable to non-chargeable items;
>
> (4) The point of a service charge regime which provides for on account instalments is to ensure that the landlord is funded for the cost of providing services; he is not expected to provide the services and recover the cost a year later;
>
> (5) If however, a landlord seeks to recover pro tanto, i.e. if he is to recover that part of his estimate attributable to chargeable items if it be found that part related to non-chargeable items, then he must at least provide the court with clear evidence of what his estimate would have come to had the non-chargeable items not been included.'

18-06   This led him to conclude that:

> 'In my judgment, therefore, if it is possible on the evidence to identify with some precision that part of the cost which has been incorrectly included in an estimate upon which an on account demand for service charges has been based, then the Court can determine the extent to which the estimate was reasonable and hold the tenant liable to make a payment on account of that amount'.[9]

18-07   The learned judge also determined that, where a lease required service rent to be apportioned by reference to net internal floor areas, those proportions did not have to be recalculated whenever the reversion changed hands.

---

8   At para 88.
9   At para 89. For similar considerations applied to progress or interim certificates in construction law, see *Secretary of Sate for Transport v Birse-Farr Joint Venture* (1993) 62 BLR 36 and *Henry Boot Construction Ltd v Alstom Combined Cycles Ltd* [2005] 1 WLR 3850, which are discussed in detail in Furst *et al*, *Keating on Construction Contracts* (9th edn, 2012) at paras 5-009–5-010.

CHAPTER 19

Accounts

THE ROLE OF ACCOUNTS

19-01   As discussed at **16-01** above, in the usual case, a landlord who operates a standard service charge scheme will need to prepare accounts at the end of the year to show what monies were incurred or expended in a particular year, so that any shortfall is recoverable from the tenant and also, potentially, in order to estimate the next year's on-account service charge. If the contractual scheme of the lease requires the preparation of year-end accounts in order to render shortfalls recoverable, then such accounts will need to be prepared and served.[1] The RICS has given detailed guidance on the procedures for producing accounts, to which reference should be made in addition to the matters set out below.[2]

LATE OR NO ACCOUNTS

19-02   The question of late provision of accounts, or a failure to provide them at all, has been dealt with at **16-15** to **16-18** above. The special rules applicable to residential service charges are considered in Chapter 31 below.

FORMAL REQUIREMENTS OF ACCOUNTS

19-03   The observations already made in relation to compliance with contractual requirements, certification (if required) and the need to ensure that an appropriately qualified person prepares the accounts, are clearly applicable in relation to accounts.[3]

---

1   See **16-09** to **16-14** above, although note the gloss on this rule which is applied in *Warrior Quay Management Co Ltd v Joachim* [2008] EWLands LRX_42_2006.
2   RICS Commercial Code at pp 22–28; RICS Residential Code, Pt 4 (record keeping), Pt 10 (accounting for service charges), Pt 11 (audits).
3   See *Barrington v Sloane Properties Ltd* [2007] EWLands LRX_31_2006 at para 44.

CONTENT OF ACCOUNTS

'Costs', 'expenses', 'incurred', etc.

19-04   The meaning of 'costs', and sums 'expended' or 'incurred', by a landlord during a particular service charge year, can give rise to difficulties of construction. One question which arises is whether or not that is limited to sums expended, or the presentation of an invoice for payment, or whether it also extends to expenditure which the landlord is committed to under a contractual provision, but has not yet in fact paid. Some examples of how various courts and tribunals have approached the question of interpretation are considered in this section.

19-05   In *Marenco v Jacramel Co Ltd*,[4] a tenant covenanted to pay 'a fair proportion of the cost' of cleaning and maintenance of the reserved parts of the building. The landlord had failed to provide any services, and the tenant's interest had thereby been damaged. Danckwerts LJ stated (in what is only a summary of the judgment) that the tenant's 'contribution could occur only after the landlords had repaired the premises'. Accordingly, this case is understood in one subsequent authority to stand for the proposition that 'cost' means 'money expended', but is also said by that same authority to be inadequately reported.[5]

19-06   The question arose again on the special facts in *Capital & Counties Freehold Equity Trust Ltd v B L plc*.[6] There, identical leases of different parts of a building provided that the tenant was in each case obliged to pay, on demand, a fixed percentage of 'all amounts sums costs and expenses of each and every kind whatsoever which may from time to time during the said term be expended or incurred or become payable by the Landlord'. There was no service charge period by reference to which expenditure could be demanded and no machinery for recovery of on-account charges. A contract for extensive building works was placed shortly before the end of the term and, though no sums were paid, the landlord argued that the service charge provisions were sufficiently wide to allow him to recover accrued, but unpaid, liabilities. HH Judge Paul Baker QC (sitting as a Deputy Judge of the High Court) rejected that submission and decided that the landlord was confined to recovery of monies actually spent. While he accepted that the wording was wide under this particular lease clause, the construction contended for by the landlord, if applied to a lease under which the tenant was not liable for service charges in relation to a particular period of time, exposed the tenant to the risk that it would be saddled with large liabilities incurred by the landlord, without being able to spread that cost over service charge periods.

19-07   In *Gilje v Charlgrove Securities Ltd*,[7] in the context of residential leases, the landlord was entitled to recover 'monies expended' on certain items under

---

4   [1964] EGD 349.
5   *Barrington v Sloane Properties Ltd* [2007] EWLands LRX_31_2006 at para 37.
6   [1987] 2 EGLR 49.
7   [2001] EWCA Civ 1777.

a general management and administration clause. What it did was to provide a caretaker's flat in the building, for which it sought to charge a notional rent. The Court of Appeal decided that 'monies expended' did not include a notional cost, but actually involved the landlord parting with money.[8]

19-08   *Hyams v Wilfred East Housing Co-op Ltd*[9] was concerned with the question of the meaning of the word 'payable' in the context of the right to buy legislation contained in Part V of the Landlord and Tenant Act 1987. The President of the Lands Tribunal decided that 'the amount in each invoice became payable on the date stated in that invoice, and I cannot see on the evidence before me how it could fail to constitute costs incurred at that date'.[10]

19-09   The meaning of 'cost' was considered in *Barrington v Sloane Properties Ltd*.[11] There, building works were carried out by a contractor in two contractual phases. There was a series of interim certificates issued during the life of the contracts, which entitled the builders to payment for the works to which the certificates related. One question which arose was whether the landlord was entitled, under the terms of its leases, to demand, by way of service charge, sums which had been certified under the building contracts but not yet paid. He decided that 'once that certificate has been issued, and the 14 day period has expired, then the liability exists and is to be regarded as a cost. I do not consider that it is prevented from becoming a cost before it is actually paid'.[12]

19-10   In *Wembley Stadium Ltd v Wembley National Stadium Ltd*,[13] the Chancellor decided that use of in-house staff was a cost that was 'incurred', at any rate in commercial leases.[14]

19-11   In *Holding & Management (Solitaire) Ltd v Sherwin*,[15] on-account service charge had been collected and expended. A shortfall arose in relation to some years, and a demand for a balancing payment was made. The question arose whether these demands were too late, as some of the service charge year to which the demand related was more than 18 months before the demand was made. The tenant argued that deductions should be made from the balancing payments to reflect that fact. The Lands Tribunal rejected that submission. For the purpose of computing the 18-month period under section 20B(1) of the Landlord and Tenant Act 1985, costs were not 'incurred' until the on-account payments had been exhausted. It was only thereafter that section 20B(1) was engaged, having regard to its underlying policy.

---

8 For a discussion of the problem of recovery of notional rent for staff accommodation, see Chapter 9.
9 [2006] EWLands LRX_102_2005.
10 At para 30.
11 [2007] EWLands LRX_31_2006.
12 At para 37.
13 [2007] EWHC 756 (Ch).
14 At para 47. Contrast *Mihovilovic v Leicester City Council* [2010] UKUT 22 (LC) (council not entitled to recover cost of choosing to self-insure).
15 [2011] 1 EGLR 29.

19-12   In *Brent London Borough Council v Shulem B Association Ltd*,[16] Morgan J held that 'expenses' connoted actual expenditure and the clause in that lease (dating from 1974) related only to monies spent by the lessor, but 'possibly' monies which the lessor is under a present liability to expend. While some comments of Morgan J on the meaning of 'incurred' appear to suggest that he would have been minded to allow contracted-for liabilities to be included, on this issue his observations were *obiter*.[17] The same view of the meaning of the word 'incurred' in section 20B was taken in *OM Property Management Ltd v Burr*.[18] HH Judge Mole QC stated that 'A liability does not become a cost until it is concrete, either by being met or paid or possibly by being set down in an invoice or certificate under a building contract'.[19] He went on to reject the submission that, in section 20B, a cost was incurred simply when a liability arose under a contract.[20]

19-13   The President of the Upper Tribunal (Lands Chamber) further considered the meaning of 'incurred' in *Jean-Paul v London Borough of Southwark*[21] in the context of section 20B of the Landlord and Tenant Act 1985. In order to avoid the time limits imposed by that section, the council argued that costs were only incurred in relation to construction works when the final account was rendered by the contractor, which was obviously the latest date possible. The President stated in that context,[22] that:

> 'in my judgment, however, costs are only "incurred" by the landlord within the meaning of section 20B when payment is made. There is clearly a distinction between incurring liability (i.e. an obligation to pay) and incurring costs, and it is the latter formulation that is used in the provision.'

19-14   The Lands Tribunal has subsequently observed that any tension between this statement and the earlier statement in *Hyams*[23] was not material and can be explained by the different facts in each case, and that in neither case was it necessary for the Lands Tribunal to draw a distinction between invoicing and payment.[24]

19-15   It is considered that the approach which the cases support most strongly is that costs will be incurred when they have either been paid or have been invoiced.[25]

---

16 [2011] 1 WLR 3014 at para 41.
17 At para 58.
18 [2012] UKUT 2 (LC).
19 At para 21.
20 At para 23.
21 [2011] UKUT 178 (LC).
22 At para 17.
23 See **19-08** above.
24 *O M Property Management Ltd v Burr* [2012] UKUT 2 (LC) at para 22.
25 See also the decision of Warren J in *Morshead Mansions Ltd v Mactra Properties Ltd* [2013] EWHC 224 (Ch), a claim by a tenant for specific performance of a landlord's obligation to provide year-end accounts in respect of the service charges. It was necessary to consider the meaning of the word 'expenses' which were required to be reflected in the accounts. This was defined to include 'costs paid or incurred ... during the year in question'. The judge held that costs were incurred when the obligation to pay arises (rather than when a contract is entered into under which a sum of money may become due in the future).

CHAPTER 20

Demands

IS A PRIOR DEMAND NECESSARY?

20-01   It is of course a matter of construction of each lease as to whether and when service charge falls due. While there is a general principle of contract law that uncertain sums must be demanded so that the debtor knows what he owes,[1] in practice in leases certainty may be ensured by some other mechanism, such as ensuring that a prior estimate is served, or some other mechanism is put in place to allow the tenant to know what it owes, and a demand specifying that amount may be unnecessary.[2]

FORMAL REQUIREMENTS FOR A DEMAND

20-02   A lease may specify what amounts to a valid demand[3] and the RICS has given its own guidance in relation to residential service charge (and other) demands.[4] It is also common for any demand to be in writing.[5] If there are such requirements, then those need to be abided by.[6] However, absent anything special required by the relevant contract, the ordinary rule is that any communication which makes it clear that payment is required will suffice.[7] What matters is that

---

1   The general principle in contract law is that demands are necessary where amounts due are uncertain: see *Brown v Great Eastern Rly Co* (1877) 2 QBD 406. Of course, the principle would not apply to fixed or inclusive service charge, where the sum payable is not indeterminate.
2   Hence the tendency for prior certificates and estimates to be preconditions for liability: see Chapters 17 and 18 above.
3   *Brent London Borough Council v Shulem B Association Ltd* [2011] 1 WLR 3014, para 40.
4   RICS Residential Code, Pt 6.
5   The question may arise whether or not an email is a demand for those purposes. See *E.ON UK Plc v Gilesports Ltd* [2012] EWHC 2172 (Ch) for a recent discussion of that question in a different context.
6   *Manni Investment Co Ltd v Eagle Star Life Assurance Co Ltd* [1997] AC 749 at p 776.
7   *Re A Company* [1985] BCLC 37; *Bank of Credit and Commerce International SA v Blatner* (unreported, 20 November 1986, Court of Appeal); in relation specifically to service charges, see the comments in *Paddington Walk Management Co Ltd v Governers of the Peabody Trust* [2009] 2 EGLR 123 (CC); *Quirkco Investments Ltd v Aspray Transport Ltd* [2011] EWHC 3060 (Ch) at para 47.

the document conveys the fact that payment is to be made, so that an accountant's certificate or 'information' document was not a 'demand' for the purposes of section 20B of the Landlord and Tenant Act 1985.[8] As discussed in greater detail below, it may further be the case that as a condition of its validity, the demand must relate to matters in respect of which the tenant is properly liable under the lease and not matters for which he has no liability, though it may be that, in a case where the demand includes amounts under both headings, it is only valid to the extent that it demands sums for which the tenant is in fact liable.[9]

20-03   For the special requirements for demands relating to residential service charges, see Chapter 32.

MUST THE DEMAND STATE AN AMOUNT AND MUST IT BE THE RIGHT AMOUNT?

20-04   If a demand is required, what must it state? While there is authority from other contexts that a general demand for payment without specifying an amount will suffice,[10] it is considered that in the context of service charges, unless the amount payable is certain from an earlier certificate or account, the demand ought to state what the sum is that is due. There is authority for the proposition that an excessive amount in a demand does not invalidate it,[11] however the question, specifically as it relates to service charges, has been considered in greater detail in *Brent London Borough Council v Shulem B Association Ltd.*[12] There, in relation to a clause (referred to below as clause 2(6)) which required the tenant to pay a rateable amount of expenses incurred by the landlord, Morgan J stated as follows:[13]

> '40.   What are the minimum requirements of clause 2(6) as to the form and content of such a demand? In my judgment, it is clear that a demand must specify a figure which is to be paid by the lessee. Clause 2(6) simply will not operate if

8   *Brennan v St Paul's Court Ltd* [2010] UKUT 403 (LC); see too *Gilje v Charlgrove* [2004] 1 All ER 91 at para 24 (though in both cases there was a surplus from the on-account charges and there was nothing to 'demand' in any event). An email sent for information purposes was found not to be a demand in *Paddington Walk Management Co Ltd v Governers of the Peabody Trust* [2009] 2 EGLR 123 (CC) for s 20B purposes. In *Leonora Investment Co Ltd v Mott MacDonald Ltd* [2008] EWCA Civ 857 at para 23, the landlord expressly did not contend that an invoice which did not comply with the requirements of the lease could be construed as a demand under its contractual terms.

9   *Brent London Borough Council v Shulem B Association Ltd* [2011] 1 WLR 3014 at paras 41 and 42.

10   *Bank of Baroda v Panessar* [1987] Ch 335. This case and the authorities it considered may be explicable on the basis that they relate to 'all monies' clauses under mortgages and associated guarantees, which may be a special context different from the present one.

11   That the demand is a valid one appears to be supported by, for example, *Fox v Jolly* [1916] 1 AC 1; *Bank Negara Indonesia 1946 v Taylor* [1995] CLC 225. It is seemingly also the basis for the decision in *Phillips v Forte* [2004] All ER (D) 436, though the decision is inadequately reported and is, at any rate, simply an appeal from an application for summary judgment.

12   [2011] 1 WLR 3014.

13   At paras 40–41.

all that the landlord does is to ask the lessee to pay a proportion of the lessor's expenses without notifying the lessee of the figure which is said to be payable. As a matter of form, the demand must relate to the specified matters for which a charge may be made and a demand which on its face relates to other matters will not be valid in point of form, quite apart from the lessor having no entitlement to charge for those other matters. I can illustrate this point with an example. The specified matters include works to the building of which the flat forms a part. Accordingly, the specified matters do not included works to another building. If the lessee of a flat in building 1 was served with a demand to pay a proportion of the lessor's expenses of repairing building 2, in my judgment, that would not be a valid demand pursuant to clause 2(6) of the relevant lease and, in addition, the lessor would not be entitled to recover the expenses of the works to building 2 from the lessee of a flat in building 1.

41.   Clause 2(6) entitles the lessor to charge the lessee with a proportion of the lessor's expenses. "Expenses" refers to monies which the lessor has spent or, possibly, monies which the lessor is under a present liability to expend. The word does not include anticipated future expenditure. Accordingly, if the lessor served a demand on a lessee that the lessee should contribute a proportion of sums which the lessor expected to expend in the future, that demand would not comply with clause 2(6). In my judgment, the form and content of the demand would not satisfy the requirements of clause 2(6) and, in addition, the lessor would not be entitled to recover a proportion of anticipated future expenses.'

20-05   It appears that Morgan J, therefore, considered that demands which, on their face, deal with irrecoverable matters are not formal demands under the terms of the lease. It does not appear that the irrecoverable amounts were considered severable once they were shown to be irrecoverable.[14] Where, however, there is an undifferentiated sum sought which is too high, then the position appears to be different. In relation to '[a] demand which is for a specified amount which is in excess of the lessor's true entitlement under clause 2(6)', the position was considered to be as follows:[15]

'The amount demanded by a lessor may be too high for any number of reasons. The landlord may have made a mathematical error in computing the amount of its expenses or the due proportion or the result of multiplying one by the other. The lessor may have included costs which are not recoverable under clause 2(6) although that fact does not appear on the face of the demand. If, for whatever reason, the figure specified in the demand is in excess of the lessor's underlying entitlement, is the demand formally invalid? This type of problem is likely to arise frequently. A typical case would be where a lessor serves a demand for a specified sum, the lessee does not pay all or any part of the demand, the lessor sues for the sum stated in the demand, the matter is investigated in court proceedings as a result of which it emerges that the lessor's entitlement is to a smaller sum. In such a case, does the court dismiss the lessor's claim because there is no prior demand for the smaller sum as determined by the court or does the court give judgment for the smaller sum? In my judgment, the court should give judgment for the smaller sum on the basis that the original demand was formally valid but cannot entitle the

14   A different approach appears to have been taken in relation to estimates founding interim demands: see **18-05**.
15   At para 43.

lessor to recover the specified sum unless the lessor has an underlying entitlement under clause 2(6) to that sum.'

20-06   In the event that a difference arose between the parties on, for instance, questions of apportionment leading to a reduction in the demand, it appears that no fresh demand is required to be served:[16]

> 'In the case of a difference between the parties, the proportion is to be settled by the lessor's surveyor. These provisions give rise to two possible questions. The first is whether the demand must specify the amount of the expenses and the amount of the proportion separately or whether it suffices for the lessor to demand a specified sum stating that it is a due proportion of the expenses. In other words, must the demand be for x% of £y or can a simple demand for £z suffice? It can certainly be argued that the demand must specify the amount of the proportion to enable the lessee to understand the proportion which is claimed and to be in a position to dispute it so that it can be referred to the lessor's surveyor for decision. On balance, I prefer the construction which requires the lessor to state the sum which he demands (as a due proportion of its expenses) without separately stating the amount of the proportion and the amount of the expenses. The second point concerns a possible case where the landlord demands a sum of money under clause 2(6), the lessee challenges the proportion which has been used by the lessor, the matter is referred to the lessor's surveyor who determines that the proportion used by the lessor was too high and specifies a lower proportion. Is the original demand formally valid but operates as modified by the surveyor or is the original demand formally invalid so that a further demand needs to be made using the proportion determined by the surveyor? In my judgment, there is no real difficulty in holding that the original demand was valid as a matter of form but it takes effect in the way modified by the surveyor's determination. On that basis, it is not necessary to serve a further demand.'

20-07   Unless (possibly) the mistake is such as to render the demand formally invalid in the sense used by Morgan J in *Shulem B*,[17] it is considered that an excessive demand for service charge is nonetheless a valid demand. Cases which hold the contrary do so in the context principally of guarantees, where it is suggested different considerations apply.[18] In an appropriate case, any mistake or lack of clarity in the drafting of a particular demand may, in any event, be curable on ordinary principles for curing defective notices.[19]

---

16   At para 42.
17   [2011] 1 WLR 3014 at paras 42–43.
18   *Dow Banking Corpn v Mahnakh Spinning and Weaving Corpn and Bank Mellat* [1983] 2 Lloyd's Rep 561 at p 566; see also the cases cited in *Halsbury's Law of England* (8th edn, 2008), Vol 48, Financial Services and Institutions, para 1105; *Brent London Borough Council v Shulem B Association Ltd* [2011] EWHC 1663 (Ch) at para 44.
19   *Mannai Investment Co Ltd v Eagle Life Assurance Co Ltd* [1997] AC 749; specifically in relation to demands, that authority was considered in *Brent London Borough Council v Shulem B Association Ltd* [2011] EWHC 1663 (Ch) at para 45. The point appears to have arisen in *Phillips v Forte* [2004] All ER (D) 436, but there is no proper transcript available in relation to this appeal from a summary judgment decision.

CHAPTER 21

Apportionment

WAYS OF FIXING PROPORTIONS

21-01   There are a number of ways in which service charges can be apportioned.[1] It may be that a fixed percentage is applied per unit, or a division of costs by reference to floor areas (perhaps 'weighted'[2] to take into account certain characteristics) is undertaken, or that cost is divided by reference to relative rateable values.[3] Alternatively, a landlord may reserve the right to apportion in a manner which he considers to be 'fair and reasonable', or some other such form of words. Naturally, the certainty of the former methods is at the expense of a lack of flexibility. The flexibility of the latter approach generates the risk of multi-party disputes as to the most appropriate basis of apportionment from year to year. It is to be noted that, in the event of a unit being vacant, tenants ought to require, in line with best practice, that the landlord bears the service charge costs attributable to the vacant unit(s).[4]

21-02   Frequently, in mixed use blocks, separate service charge regimes apply to the commercial and residential parts. Further, different kinds of services may be treated differently to reflect the fact that they are unevenly shared between different classes of tenants.[5] The RICS has given particular guidance as to how service charges are to be dealt with in such developments.[6]

FIXED PERCENTAGES

21-03   A lease may fix a percentage contribution for which the tenant is liable. It may be that one percentage is applied to some shared facilities, and a different

---

1   RICS Commercial Code at p 5, paras 4–6, and pp 14–16.
2   A method particularly relevant to shopping centres: see the RICS Commercial Code at p 39.
3   Other, less popular, methods include apportionment by volume, on a comparative rent basis, or by proportion of area occupied on the entire site.
4   RICS Commercial Code at p 15, para 1.5.3.
5   For an example of an older lease with a 'profusion of different obligations on the lessee' with different proportions being payable for different services, see *Campbell v Daejan Properties Ltd* [2012] EWCA Civ 5103. This gave rise to a difficult question of construction in relation to the extent of the service charge obligations. See **2-74** above.
6   RICS, 'Managing Mixed Use Developments' and 'Apportionment of Service Charges in Mixed Use Developments'.

percentage is applied to others. Where the percentage contribution has been fixed contractually, then that is the percentage which a tenant must pay subject to the court's (it is suggested) very limited jurisdiction to intervene to 'update' a contract to take into account radical changes in circumstances.[7] In the residential setting, contractually stipulated percentages are not open to review by the LVT.[8] Further, a tenant will not be able to dispute contractually-fixed proportions under the provisions of Part IV of the Landlord and Tenant Act 1987, unless the percentages exceed or do not amount to 100% of the overall cost.[9] Many leases are, however, drafted with an appreciation that percentages calculated at the outset of the lease might need to be reconsidered to meet new circumstances on the ground and, therefore, contain a clause to that effect.

21-04   Particular problems may occur where the freeholder grants a headlease. In *Adelphi (Estates) Ltd v Christie*,[10] a lessee of a flat was required to pay 2.9% of the service charge incurred by his landlord. Subsequently, the freeholder granted a concurrent lease of the flat to another company. Under that lease, the intermediate lessee became liable to pay 2.9% of the cost incurred by the freeholder. The tenant claimed that, by reason of the insertion of a new intermediate reversionary interest, she was only liable to pay 2.9% of that amount. The Court of Appeal rejected that argument on the ground that the lease ought to be construed so as to mean that the 'lessors' to whom service charge was to be paid included not merely the immediate reversioner, but also the ultimate freeholder.

FLOOR AREA BASIS[11]

21-05   Tenants may be liable for service charges on the basis of the floor area of the units they occupy, expressed as a percentage of total lettable area.[12] While this method may be responsive to development, it may inadequately take into account variations in the quality of accommodation.[13] It may also penalise tenants of large units for particular services – like the cleaning of common parts – which are

---

7 *Pole Properties v Feinberg* (1982) 43 P&CR 121, discussed further at **23-11** below. The RICS Residential Code, Pt 14 deals with this specific problem in the residential context.

8 *Canary Riverside v Schilling PTE* [2005] EWLands LRX_65_2005; *Southern Rent Assessment Panel v Rowner Estates Ltd* [2007] EWLands LRX_3_2006; *Warrior Quay Management Co Ltd v Joachim* [2008] EWLands LRX_42_2006.

9 *Morgan v Fletcher* [2009] UKUT 186.

10 [1984] 1 EGLR 19. For a case in which there was a construction question as to what was meant by 'the building' in respect of which service charge was payable, see *Stapel v Bellshore Property Investements Ltd* [2001] 2 EGLR 7.

11 RICS Commercial Code at p 15.

12 For a case in which the tenant extended his unit, see *Mehra v CityWest Homes Ltd* [2011] UKUT 311. For a case discussing methods of measurement, see *Kilmartin SCI (Hutlon House) Limited v Safeway Stores Plc* [2006] EWHC 60, [2006] 1 EGLR 59, where the measurement was to be carried out in accordance with the RICS Code of Measuring Practice, by reference to 'usable area'.

13 For a case in which deterioration of commercial elements of an estate rendered a floor area basis inappropriate for the fair apportionment of service charges, see *Southern Rent Assessment Panel v Rowner Estates Ld* [2007] EWLands LRX_3_2006.

not directly related to floor area, but rather, for instance, to length of frontage. Further, it might be that some plant, such as lifts, are of benefit only to certain parts of the building. This is particularly so in shopping centres, where the so-called 'weighted floor area' basis is often to be preferred.

RATEABLE VALUE BASIS

21-06 Difficulties can arise when the draftsman has used rateable values as his basis for calculating the proportions and the latest RICS guidance is that this method is no longer recommended as an appropriate method for commercial property.[14] Domestic rateable values have been prospectively abolished.[15] It is, however, incorrect to say that domestic rateable values no longer exist. They have been specifically retained for some purposes.[16] Where the draftsman has simply used rateable values as at the date of the lease as an expression of the relative values of one unit to another at that particular date, then the scheme may well remain workable as the prospective abolition of rateable values makes no difference to that exercise.[17] Further, there probably will also not be a problem where, though expressed to be the rateable value from time to time,[18] the premises are purely residential. This is because, though prospectively abolished, residential premises will retain rateable values, albeit frozen as at 31 March 1990. Real problems may, however, arise in mixed residential and commercial buildings. As commercial rateable values have not been abolished and continue to be updated, the rateable values of the domestic premises will become increasingly historic and residential tenants' proportions will become more out of kilter with the proportion payable by commercial tenants. In a case of the latter kind, it may be that only *Pole Properties v Feinberg* will assist,[19] unless it can be shown that the contractual machinery has become entirely spent.

FAIRLY AND REASONABLY

21-07 What is a fair and reasonable apportionment? The answer to this may depend on the service in question. In the case of heating, for instance, the Court

14 RICS Commercial Code at p 15, para 1.5.6.
15 Local Government Finance Act 1988, s 117(1), stating that 'The General Rate Act 1967 shall not have effect as regards any time after 31 March 1990'.
16 For example, the Local Government and Housing Act 1989, s 149; see too the discussion in *Camden v Sainsbury* (LON/00AG/LSC/2004/0168). This apportionment basis was applied in *Levitt v London Borough of Camden* [2011] UKUT 366.
17 See also the discussion in *Camden v Sainsbury* (LON/00AG/LSC/2004/0168). If for some reason there remains a problem, consideration can be given to an application to vary the leases under the Landlord and Tenant Act 1987, Pt IV; see **15-07** above.
18 As was the case in *Moorcroft Estates v Doxford* (1979) 254 EG 871. The relevant rateable values were those obtaining when the expense was incurred and not the date of the demand for payment. This means that a later and backdated reduction in the rateable value of a property will not mean that the tenant ought to have service charge credited back to it: see *Universities Superannuation Scheme v Marks & Spencer* [1997] 11 CL 370 (an aspect of the case which was not appealed to the Court of Appeal).
19 See **23-09** to **23-11** below.

of Appeal decided that (in the case of a defectively drafted lease) a fair proportion for such a service would be a floor area basis.[20] Amongst other factors that the court ought to take into account is the length of the tenant's term. A tenant with only a short term remaining might not to be expected to pay for replacement of a service charge item, the economic life of which is well in excess of the remainder of his term.[21] Further, changes in circumstance – for instance the deterioration of unlettable commercial units – may make it reasonable to remove the commercial units from the service charge regime, thereby reducing the absolute cost of estate services, but increasing the proportion payable by tenants of residential units of that lesser overall amount.[22]

20 *Jollybird Ltd v Fairzone Ltd* [1990] 2 EGLR 55; see too the discussion in *Pole Properties v Feinberg* (1982) 43 P&CR 121.
21 *Scottish Mutual Assurance Ltd v Jardine Public Relations Ltd* [1999] EWHC 276 (TCC).
22 *Southern Rent Assessment Panel v Rowner Estates Ltd* [2007] EWLands LRX_3_2006.

CHAPTER 22

Sinking funds and reserve funds

DEFINITIONS AND TERMINOLOGY

22-01   Reserve funds and sinking funds are devices for spreading the cost of services over the term of a lease and to even out 'spikes' and 'troughs' in expenditure.[1]

22-02   Although the terminology is now used more loosely and interchangeably,[2] a reserve fund strictly refers to sums accumulated in order to even out fluctuating regular expenditure. For instance, the costs of repairs or decoration may vary from service charge year to service charge year and a reserve fund can be used to ensure that there are no unexpected escalations in expenditure which tenants have not anticipated.[3] A sinking fund, on the other hand, is a fund accumulated over the term to meet the cost of the repair or renewal of a particular item, usually costly plant or machinery.

22-03   It is a question of construction whether accumulated funds are held on a kind of purpose trust, held on a purely contractual basis, or held as a stakeholder by a third party. Whether such funds, and indeed service charge funds generally, are held on trust is discussed at **22-10** to **22-13** below in a separate section, though it should be noted that Parliament has intervened in the residential context and imposed a statutory trust in that setting (as to which see Chapter 36 below).

22-04   A related but distinct technique for dealing with cost fluctuations is to ensure that the list of services under a lease includes an entitlement to recover depreciation allowances, which device is considered below.[4] It may well also be

---

1   RICS Commercial Code at p 33 and see the comments on service charge provision for maintenance, replacement and repair at pp 34–36; for relevant considerations in the context of residential leases, see the RICS Residential Code, Pt 9.
2   See, for example, *Princes House Ltd v Distinctive Clubs Ltd* [2007] EWCA Civ 374 at para 21; *Redendale Ltd v Modi* [2010] UKUT 346 (LC) at para 50. However, the terms are sometimes used in their technical sense: see *Bagley v Bagley* [2004] EWHC 426 at para 38; *Leicester City Council v Master* [2008] EWLands LRX_175_2007.
3   *Solitaire Property Management Co Ltd v Holden* [2012] UKUT 86 (LC).
4   Such a charge may be found in *Secretary of State for the Environment v Possfund (North West) Ltd* [1997] 2 EGLR 56.

that the terms of the lease permit the taking of monies on account of accrued, but unsatisfied, liability, which is not strictly the same as setting up a reserve or sinking fund, but may replicate some of its effects.[5]

ENTITLEMENT TO ACCUMULATE IN A FUND

22-05   Whether or not a landlord may accumulate monies under one of the two fund devices under consideration is a question of construction. It is, however, unnecessary for the wording in the service charge machinery to refer to a right to accumulate in a fund in express terms. It is sufficient that the wording is wide enough to allow the landlord to accumulate funds for expenditure over the term.[6] By the same token, however, the mere use of the word 'reserve' does not mean that a reserve fund will have been created.[7] In the context of a lease which entitled the landlord to retain monies for a sinking fund, but contained no machinery to demand it, the Lands Tribunal held that there was no right to build up a sinking fund: see *Southall Court (Residents) Ltd v Buy Your Own Freehold Ltd.*[8]

22-06   The kind of wording which a court might find creates a reserved fund is illustrated by the relevant clause in *St Mary's Mansions v Limegate Investment Co Ltd,*[9] where leases included the following definition:

> 'The expression "the expenses and outgoings incurred by the lessor" as hereinbefore used shall be deemed to include not only those expenses, outgoings and other expenditure hereinbefore described which have been actually disbursed, incurred or made by the lessor during the year in question but also such reasonable part of all such expenses, outgoings and other expenditure hereinbefore described which are of a periodically recurring nature (whether recurring by regular or irregular periods) whenever disbursed, incurred or made and whether prior to the commencement of the said term or otherwise including a sum or sums of money by way of reasonable provision for anticipated expenditure in respect thereof as the lessor or its accountants or managing agents (as the case may be) may in

---

5   See the definition of 'incurred' at **19-04** to **19-15** above.
6   As was found to be the case in, for instance, *Ustimenko v Prescot Management Co Ltd* [2005] EWLands LRX_65_2004 and *Leicester City Council v Master* [2008] EWLands LRX_175_2007. For a case where the clear wording was against the finding of a reserve fund, notwithstanding the resultant inconvenience, see *Crampton v Park Place 96 Ltd* [2009] EWLands_LRX_100_2007 (with a follow-up decision [2011] UKUT 57 (LC)).
7   *Brown's Operating System Services Ltd v Southward Catholic Diocesan Corp* [2007] EWCA Civ 164 at paras 29–30, though it does appear that the Court of Appeal there found that the arrangement was a reserve fund, in the strict sense, in substance. It would appear that this decision is explicable on the basis that the Court of Appeal considered that classification as a reserve fund meant that the monies contained in that fund were non-returnable at the expiry of the lease, though it is considered that there is no principle of law that requires that result; the issue of returnability appears to be one solely of construction (see **22-14** to **22-22**).
8   [2008] EWLands_LRX_124_2007. Whether it is right that no obligation to pay could be implied seems debatable, though it would appear that the leases were subsequently varied by the LVT: see discussion of this aspect of the case in *Southall Court (Residents) Ltd v Tiwari* [2011] UKUT 218 (LC).
9   [2002] EWCA Civ 1491 at para 19.

their discretion allocate to the year in question as being fair and reasonable in the circumstances and relates pro rate to the demised premises.'

22-07   The practice of the landlord had been to credit year-end surpluses from the on-account service charge to the reserve fund. The question was whether it was entitled to do so, a question which the Court of Appeal, noting the above definition, answered affirmatively.[10] However, the Court of Appeal went on to emphasise that it was a requirement under the lease that there be appropriate certification of the amount to be carried over into the reserve and that there would be no entitlement to do so where the procedure was not followed. The need for compliance with procedural requirements set out in a lease has been subsequently re-emphasised by the Upper Tribunal.[11]

22-08   Naturally, the funds accumulated may generally only be applied to the stated purpose in the lease, whether that is in the nature of a contractual limitation of the use of such funds or a stated purpose of a trust fund. Again, in the residential setting, the purposes of the statutorily imposed trust are as set out in section 42(3) of the Landlord and Tenant Act 1987.[12]

22-09   Apart from any contractual requirement a lease might impose in the residential context, the level of contribution recoverable from tenants is regulated by section 19 of the Landlord and Tenant Act 1988. See Chapter 29 below.[13]

CAPACITY IN WHICH FUNDS ARE RETAINED

22-10   There are a variety of bases on which service charge funds might be retained. It appears that, as a rule, service charge funds are beneficially owned by the person entitled to them, rather than impressed with a trust, though it is possible also for the sums to be held in a stakeholder capacity.[14] In the residential context, service charges of multiple-tenant buildings are deemed by statute to be held on trust.[15]

22-11   It was once thought that concepts of trusts ought not to be imported into commercial relationships, including those of landlord and tenant. It was stated

---

10   *Per* Ward LJ at para 34.
11   *FCH Housing and Care v Burns* [2007] EWLands LRX_9_2006 at para 16; *Redendale Ltd v Modi* [2010] UKUT 346 (LC) at paras 52–53.
12   See Chapter 36 below.
13   For the operation of the jurisdiction, see, for example, *Ustimeko v Prescot Management Co Ltd* [2005] EWLands LRX_65_2004; *FCH Housing and Care v Burns* [2007] EWLands LRX_9_2006; *Hyde Housing Association Ltd v Lane* [2009] UKUT 180 (LC). The existence of a sinking fund may also bear on whether a particular course of action chosen by the landlord is reasonable: see *Southall (Residents) Ltd v Tiwari* [2011] UKUT 218 (LC).
14   *Frobisher (Second Investments) Ltd v Kiloran Trust Co Ltd* [1980] 1 All ER 488.
15   Landlord and Tenant Act 1987, s 42, discussed further in Chapter 36.

in *Frobisher (Second Investments) Ltd v Kiloran Trust Co Ltd*,[16] that 'one does not import the question of trust into a matter of this nature, which is a purely commercial matter, unless one has to do so'.[17]

22-12   However, that statement must be revised in light of later statements to the contrary effect, noting that the trust has a number of commercial applications which create desirable results. For instance, in *Target Holdings Ltd v Redferns*,[18] Lord Browne-Wilkinson expressed the more modern view that:[19]

> 'In the modern world the trust has become a valuable device in commercial and financial dealings. The fundamental principles of equity apply as much to such trusts as they do to the traditional trusts in relation to which those principles were originally formulated. But in my judgment it is important, if the trust is not to be rendered commercially useless, to distinguish between the basic principles of trust law and those specialist rules developed in relation to traditional trusts which are applicable only to such trusts and the rationale of which has no application to trusts of quite a different kind.'

22-13   Accordingly, it will generally be possible to argue that service charge funds are held on a trust basis by the landlord, though whether or not a particular arrangement will constitute a trust will be a question of pure construction. It is no longer necessary that there be any particular verbal formula for the courts to find that a trust exists. The courts will look at, for instance, the question whether or not the funds are to be held in a separate bank account[20] and how they are to be dealt with (and in particular whether they have been held separate from the funds of the recipient and treated as a discrete fund), and so on. Further, it is no objection to there being a trust that the trust is primarily for a purpose, such as to discharge a particular debt or fund a particular scheme of works, rather than for a certain class of beneficiaries.[21] The significance of finding that the funds are held on such a trust is that the tenants will be protected as secured creditors in the event of the insolvency of the holder of the trust fund and also that, on the failure of the purpose of the trust, the funds will be returnable on a secondary resulting trust.[22] Further, the result of a trust being found will be that the holder of the funds holds them in a fiduciary capacity, so that equitable remedies might be available against him, as well as third parties liable for dishonest interference or knowing receipt, or the holders of traceable proceeds of the trust fund. The incidences of

16 [1980] 1 All ER 488 at p 493. See too *O'May v City of London Real Property Co Ltd* [1981] Ch 216 at p 226 (per Brightman LJ): 'The service rent so collected from the tenants, though gauged by reference to actual or estimated expenditure, becomes in the hands of the landlord its absolute property to deal with as it pleases'.
17 *Secretary of State for the Environment v Possfund (North West) Ltd* [1997] 2 EGLR 56 is another example where such an argument was not accepted.
18 [1996] AC 421.
19 At p 435.
20 *Re Chelsea Cloisters (in liquidation)* (1981) 41 P&CR 98; *Re Kayford Ltd* [1975] 1 WLR 279.
21 *Quistclose Investments Ltd v Rolls Razor Ltd* [1970] AC 567; *Twinsectra Ltd v Yardley* [2002] UKHL 12. In the context of s 106 agreements, it was conceded, and the concession was accepted, that s 106 funds were held on trust: *Patel v London Borough of Brent* [2003] EWHC 3081 (Ch).
22 *Westdeutsche Landesbank Girozentrale v Islington London Borough Council* [1996] AC 669.

trusteeship and of finding that a sum is held on trust are not further explored in this section, and reference should be made to the relevant specialist textbooks.[23] However, the capacity in which the funds are held will be extremely important in determining what is to happen with any surplus funds, and how the funds are to be dealt with in the interim.

RETURN OF SURPLUS AT END OF TERM

22-14   When a lease comes to an end by effluxion of time, or is brought to an end by the operation of a break option, forfeiture or surrender, then the question may arise on what basis, if at all, the landlord is permitted to keep any surplus service charge funds.[24]

Relevance of a contractual or trust basis for retention of funds

22-15   If the service charge funds are found to belong to the landlord beneficially, i.e. they are not, on receipt, impressed with any purpose trust but are to be dealt with under the terms of a contractual web of lease provisions (albeit with the landlord or manager owning them for the duration subject to the strictures of the lease provisions), then (applying, by analogy, conventional rules relating to unincorporated associations) a tenant who ceases to be a tenant during the currency of the service charge scheme is no more entitled to claim his service charge back than a member who leaves an unincorporated association.[25] It may, however, be the case that (by the same analogy) any excess funds held under the leases fall to be distributed at the end of the contractual scheme as between any remaining tenants unless the contractual arrangement requires otherwise.[26]

22-16   If, on the other hand, it is found that the funds are held on trust for the purposes of providing services under the terms of a lease, and all of the leases in the block come to an end, then it might be that the effect of this is that the purpose of the trusts is at an end and the contributing tenants are entitled to their surplus back under a resulting trust implied by operation of law.[27] However, it is (it is suggested) unlikely that a single tenant whose lease comes to an end (where others remain on foot) could claim a pro rata share in the unexpended service charge funds held by the landlord or manager at that time. In those circumstances, it might be said that the funds should be retained, as the trust as a whole remains in operation, even if to the exclusion of the former tenant.

---

23   For example, *Lewin on Trusts* (18th edn, 2008).

24   For an unusual case on what is to happen if there is a deficit, see *Estate and Agency Holdings Plc v Giltagent Ltd* [2003] EWHC 1247 (QB).

25   See the discussion of this in *Hanchett-Stamford v HM Attorney-General* [2009] 2 WLR 405 at para 47.

26   By analogy with the contract-holding theory applicable to unincorporated associations: see *Re Bucks Constabulary Fund* [1979] 1 All ER 623; *Re GKN Sports Club* [1982] 1 WLR 774; *Hanchett-Stamford v HM Attorney-General* [2008] EWHC 330 (Ch) at para 48.

27   In line with the position in *Re Bucks Constabulary Benevolent Fund* [1978] 1 WLR 641.

Contractual analysis as the dominant approach

22-17   While the distinction between funds held on contract and funds held on trust for specified purposes has been considered in cases relating to unincorporated associations, the existence and implications of trusts of service charge funds (outside the statutory trust imposed by section 42 of the Landlord and Tenant Act 1985) have not been fully considered in the cases, and the courts have generally approached the question as one of pure contract law. Under the latter approach, the starting position is that the recipient of service charge funds is entitled to retain them beneficially at the end of the term (or earlier determination of the lease), unless on the true construction of the lease an obligation to repay can either be found, or one can be implied.

22-18   A case in which the landlord was entitled to keep funds at the end of the term is *Secretary of State for the Environment v Possfund (North West) Ltd.*[28] Regard ought to be had to the facts of that case, however. The landlord had collected service charges during the currency of a lease (which had come to an end by effluxion of time) which had been earmarked to fund replacement air conditioning plant. By the time the lease had expired, none of the money had been used for that purpose. The earmarked fund was then transferred to the new landlord and a fresh lease was negotiated with the tenant under the former tenancy. The tenant argued that the earmarked fund ought to be repaid to him on the grounds that the money could now no longer be used to satisfy the landlord's obligations under the expired lease. Rimer J rejected that argument, finding that the funds which had passed to the landlord had become his, absolutely. He pointed to the fact that the tenant had covenanted to pay a contribution towards the annual depreciation of the plant and that the provision of funds towards the eventual replacement of the plant was justified by that provision. He considered, therefore, that the payment of the earmarked funds was not a true payment in advance, but was instead an indemnity of an actual cost – the depreciation of the plant – incurred by the landlord. The tenant's argument, that monies ought to be repaid, was in his view not a commercial one and would even require repayment in the event, for instance, that the lease was forfeited for breach. He did not consider that it made any difference when the funds collected were expended. Further, Rimer J decided that, in the event that an excess of funds had been accumulated, then in such a case 'the answer might well be that the landlord can keep the excess' and that this result would be a justifiable one in light of the fact that such matters were likely to be discussed, and compensated for, in negotiations for any new lease with a new tenant, or, as in the instant case, upon renewal by the former tenant.

22-19   The decision in *Possfund* was distinguished in *Brown's Operating System Services Ltd v Southwark Roman Catholic Diocesan Corp.*[29] In that case, a surplus of service charge had been accumulated by a landlord. The tenant argued that it ought to be given a service charge holiday in light of that surplus. The landlord refused and served a break notice. The tenant withheld its service charge. Smith

---

28   [1997] 2 EGLR 56.
29   [2008] 1 P&CR 7.

LJ decided that the *Possfund* decision should not be treated as having laid down any legal principles of general application (and should not be read as authority for the proposition that service charge excesses were non-returnable at the end of the term unless kept in a true reserve fund), but, rather, that the decision turned on the terms of a particular lease.[30] She pointed in particular to the fact that in *Possfund*, there was a mechanism for the landlord to recover sums which related to capital depreciation. Smith LJ, in construing the lease before her, decided that, although the landlord had been entitled to make provision for future expenses by demanding monies on account, on the true construction of the service charge machinery in that lease, the funds were only expendable on liability incurred on services provided during successive years of the term, meaning that the money could not be retained thereafter. She stated that it made no difference whether the lease was terminated by effluxion of time, or by the exercise of a landlord's break option.

22-20   On the question of forfeiture, Smith LJ stated as follows:[31]

> 'I can see that, if the lease were forfeit on account of the tenant's breach of covenant, the landlord might well be aggrieved if it had to return money it had been holding in anticipation of works to be carried out at a later date but during the currency of the lease. Of course it would be open to a landlord to make express provision that sums held should remain its property or to make a provision such as appeared in the *Possfund* lease, where there was held to be a special depreciation fund allocated to cover a specific replacement whenever it took place, whether before or after the termination of the lease. No such provisions were made. It is possible (and it is not necessary to consider the point in this appeal) that, if the lease were terminated by forfeiture on account of the tenant's breach of covenant, the landlord might be able to recover, as damages, the money it was holding in anticipation of works to be carried out during the currency of the lease.'

22-21   While the comments of Smith LJ, that *Possfund* was a decision on the terms of a particular lease and not one of general principle, are to be noted, it is considered that the decision in *Brown* signals that, as a matter of construction, unless there is a strong indicator that the landlord is entitled to retain any surplus, the surplus will be returnable to the tenant.

22-22   A different problem arose in *Scottish Mutual Assurance Plc v Jardine Public Relations Ltd.*[32] There, a service charge provision contained no clear machinery for the tenant to pay balancing payments which fell due after the expiration of the lease term. It was found that, as a matter of construction, the date for payment could be identified as the next quarter date on which rent would have fallen due under the lease, but that in any event the court would have been prepared to imply a term that the parties in such a case ought to 'account to each other within a reasonable time'.[33]

---

30   At para 30.
31   At para 33 and the concurring remarks of Longmore LJ, at para 41.
32   [1999] EWHC 276 (TCC).
33   At p 36.

CHAPTER 23

Problematic machinery

23-01   This chapter will consider some problematic aspects of service charge machinery which are to be found in the cases and the arguments deployed in respect of those problems.

NO ADVANCE PAYMENTS PROVIDED FOR

23-02   If there is no specific wording in a lease entitling the landlord or manager to recover monies on account, then it is generally considered that the courts will not wish to imply such an obligation.[1] One possible way of meeting, or at least mitigating, the omission of a right to on-account payments is to argue that the wording of the lease should be construed in such a way as to permit recovery not just of sums which have actually been expended on services, but also of amounts which, though not yet paid, the landlord or manager has become liable to pay (such as liabilities under a contract). Whether or not the court will allow service charge provisions to be interpreted in this way is a matter of construction, which will be considered in detail below: see **19-05** to **19-15**.

23-03   A second way in which the hardship of not being able to recover payments on account can be mitigated is if the lease can be construed as to provide that a landlord or other service provider who has covenanted to provide particular services, but must borrow money to meet the costs of providing them until he has been reimbursed by a tenant, is entitled to recover the costs of borrowing those funds through the service charge. The landlord was held entitled to do so

---

1   The case usually cited in support of this view is *Daiches v Bluelake Investments Ltd* [1985] 2 EGLR 67, though the issue arose at an interlocutory hearing and the court expressed only a tentative view on that question in the context of specific lease provisions. It is to be noted that the issue there was not whether there was a general right to interim payments on account of all service charge expenditure in a particular period, but merely whether a contribution could be demanded in relation to specific and necessary works of repair. *Capital & Counties Freehold Equity Trust Ltd v B L Plc* [1987] 2 EGLR 49 may also be cited as an instance of the court being reluctant to allow a landlord to recover payments for future anticipated expenditure, though that case is discussed in more detail at **19-06** above.

in *Skilleter v Charles*,[2] though in that case the court considered that the wording of the lease, though defective, indicated strongly that borrowing costs were to be recoverable. By contrast, in *Frobisher (Second Investments) Ltd v Kiloran Trust Co Ltd*,[3] the court declined to construe a lease, nor to imply a term into it, to the effect that borrowing costs were recoverable, though that was in circumstances where the lease had, in fact, made contractual provision for on-account payments, but that part of the service charge scheme was unlawful due to the operation of section 91 of the Housing Finance Act 1972 (as amended). The submission that 'costs' under a lease of a flat should include interest on borrowings by the landlord to fund works was similarly rejected in *Boldmark Ltd v Cohen*,[4] though in that case, the Court of Appeal found that it was not possible to read the service charge provisions of the leases in question as extending to borrowing costs.[5]

NO PROVISION FOR A SINKING FUND

23-04 A problem which a landlord might face is that the lease does not provide for the accumulation of funds over the term to reflect the fact that some large infrastructure or structural items – like lifts, air conditioning units or roofs – are depreciating over the term of the lease. One option for the landlord is to wait until the condition of the item entitles him to replace it, though, from the tenant's point of view, that may well be unsatisfactory and inconvenient. In *Regis Property Co Ltd v Dudley*,[6] in construing certain provisions of the Rent Act 1957, Pearce LJ explained that:[7]

> 'it seems to us that, once it is conceded (as it must be and is in this case) that the plant in question is necessary in order to provide the services, some provision for its depreciation or replacement must be included in any computation of the reasonable charge for those services. In 1956 the landlords spent £5,000 in renewing the boilers; in 1955 they spent £3,500. They have not brought these sums into account since, in their view, it would be capricious and unscientific to take particular years; they prefer to put forward an item representing an average annual allowance for depreciation, or sinking fund for replacement, calculated on the estimated life of the plant. In our view, no computation of a reasonable charge can be made without taking some such item into consideration. The life of plant used in providing a service is one of the important matters to be considered in finding out both what the provision for the service costs and what is a reasonable charge for it.'

23-05 The difficulties caused by the absence of a sinking fund may therefore be mitigated somewhat by claiming an annual depreciation allowance, if that is properly recoverable under the terms of the lease in question.

---

2   [1992] 1 EGLR 73.
3   [1980] 1 All ER 488.
4   [1986] 1 EGLR 47.
5   See generally, Chapter 12 above.
6   [1958] 1 QB 346.
7   At p 360.

UNSATISFACTORY PAYMENT PERIODS

23-06 In *Tingdene Holiday Parks Ltd v Cox*,[8] the question arose whether or not tenants of leases of chalets on a holiday park were obliged to pay an advance service charge annually or quarterly. The leases in question provided for an annual payment, but later leases provided for a quarterly basis, and, as a matter of practice, the landlord charged the advance charge on a quarterly basis. The LVT decided that (a) because the older leases spoke of 'interim charges' (plural), more than one annual payment was contemplated, or, alternatively, (b) that an estoppel by convention had arisen. The President of the Upper Tribunal (Lands Chamber) reversed the decision of the LVT. There was no basis for implying a quarterly advance payment. Further, whatever the convention that had arisen by demanding and paying quarterly payments, the estoppel by convention that was found to have arisen did not operate prospectively. The alteration of service charge machinery in this way may cause problems when the landlord seeks to exercise the remedy of distress.[9]

OBLIGATIONS TO REPAY SURPLUSES AT THE EXPIRATION OR EARLY DETERMINATION OF THE TERM

23-07 The courts have from time to time considered the question of the status of service charge funds where the lease has come to an end, so that any surplus funds cannot be applied in performance of the landlord's covenants under the lease (which no longer exist). This topic has generated divergent judicial opinions and is dealt with at **22-14** to **22-22**.

CHANGED CIRCUMSTANCES SINCE THE GRANT OF THE LEASE

Change of parties

23-08 Usually, a mere change in the identity of the landlord will make no difference. The assignee simply steps into the shoes of his predecessors. However, workable service charge machinery can also be affected by assignment of the landlord's interest where the service charge machinery is predicated on certain attributes of the original landlord which are highly personal to him. It may be, for example, that the service charge machinery (and in particular the certification requirements under it) is drafted with a specific kind of landlord in mind. If the reversionary interest is assigned, questions arise as to how that machinery is to operate. The problem arose in *St Modwen Developments (Edmonton) Ltd*

---

8 [2011] UKUT 310 (LC); see too *Fernandez v Shanterton Second Management Co Ltd* [2007] EWLands LRX_153_2006, where a landlord mistakenly believed that there had been a permanent variation of the terms of a lease informally, though the Lands Tribunal did not have full arguments on the point and no authority was apparently cited.
9 *D'Jan v Bond Street Estates Plc* [1993] EGCS 43.

v Tesco Stores Ltd.[10] A lease originally granted by Enfield London Borough Council contained service charge machinery which required certification by the council's treasurer. Their interest was then sold to the claimant, St Modwen. St Modwen decided that the certification process should be undertaken by their finance director, whose position in the company was broadly similar (it was thought) to that of the council treasurer. Toulson J, accepting the submissions of the defendant, rejected that argument,[11] observing that a public official, such as the treasurer, was not analogous to a finance director in a private company. He determined that the public status of the treasurer was crucial, and that, therefore, the certification by the claimant's finance director was insufficient. Because there had been a change which meant that the contractual certification machinery could no longer be carried out by such a person, it was spent and of no further effect. Absent a certification process, the landlord had (in the event of a dispute as to the amounts charged) to go to court to have the matter determined; all that the certificates, if produced, could do from then on was to start the ball rolling for discussions between the landlord and the tenant.[12]

Changes in circumstances generally

23-09 Some leases anticipate that circumstances might change over the term of a long lease and make express provision, for example, for the variation of the services to be provided[13] or the alteration of the tenant's contributions. However, such clauses are by no means standard and the court may therefore be asked to intervene to give the lease meaning and effect. As the *St Modwen* case demonstrates,[14] the court may be prepared to intervene to declare part of the service charge machinery simply spent where it no longer applies in light of (as in that case) a change in parties by assignment.

23-10 There are, however, cases which appear to support the proposition that a court will intervene more generally to allow a contract to respond to changed circumstances, though the basis for this power is doubtful and appears to be founded on cases which dealt with a much more specific issue, namely whether or not the courts ought to imply into a perpetual contract a right to terminate where none was expressly provided for. It is considered that is difficult to support the more general power – that contractual provisions which have been overtaken by developments can be derived from the latter line of authority.

23-11 The narrower line of cases begins with *Staffordshire Area Health Authority v South Staffordshire Waterworks Co.*[15] In that case, a historic agreement for the supply of water, containing no termination provision, bound a water supplier to supply a hospital's water at highly historic rates. Goff and

---

10 [2007] 1 EGLR 63.
11 At para 9.
12 At para 12.
13 See also **3-04** to **3-06** above.
14 See **23-08** above.
15 [1978] 1 WLR 1387.

Cumming-Bruce LLJ were simply prepared, in the specific context in which the agreement had arisen, to imply a right to terminate the agreement. Lord Denning MR was prepared to go further and apparently suggested that the court would not simply be confined to implying a termination right, but could 'take hold' of the contract and make fair and reasonable changes to meet the new situation.[16] Although the majority reasoning was more limited, Lord Denning MR developed his own *dicta* further in *Pole Properties v Feinberg*.[17] That case concerned the effect of an extension of a building on the proportions of cost payable for central heating by tenants whose proportions had been calculated on the basis of the building in its prior, unextended condition. Lord Denning MR considered (with the other judges concurring) that the court had the power, where there was a 'radical change in circumstances' since the inception of the contract, to 'do what is fair and reasonable in the new situation',[18] which inherent jurisdiction extended to varying the terms of the bargain and was not confined merely to implying a right to terminate an open-ended agreement (which had been the issue in the *Staffordshire* case). It is considered that the approach of Lord Denning MR in *Pole Properties* goes well beyond the more limited problem (i.e. that of a perpetual contract incapable of termination) identified in the *Staffordshire* case and the cases preceding and following that decision. While *Pole Properties* has never been overruled, it has not, apparently, been followed as authority for the broader proposition that the court can update contracts more generally where unforeseen, radical changes in circumstances arise.[19] It is suggested that, in light of the statutory powers to vary residential leases,[20] there is little or no room for the continued operation of what appears to be an overly broad extension of the *Staffordshire* principle in that particular context.[21] It is noted that, while *Pole Properties* has from time to time been cited in argument, no case has been discovered in which that decision has been successfully applied by either a court or the Upper Tribunal and it may be that the general proposition for which that case stands, though it has never been formally rejected by the courts, should be regarded as a bad one.

16 See p 1395.
17 [1981] 2 EGLR 38; the other judges agreed with his approach. It will be noted that, in *Pole Properties*, it was common ground that the service charge provisions were not fit for purpose as drafted and neither side was contending that the original bargain should proceed on the assumption that the building was unextended.
18 At p 40.
19 It was considered in the Scottish case of *Lloyd's TSB Foundation for Scotland v Lloyd's Banking Group Plc* [2011] CSIH 87 at para 29. In that decision, the Court of Session determined that there was no 'doctrine of equitable adjustment' in Scotland and it was noted that *Pole Properties* proceeded on the basis that both parties acknowledged that the scheme for payment of service charge was 'no longer operable'.
20 See **24-02**ff. below.
21 It is considered that cases such as *Jollybird Ltd v Fairzone Ltd* [1990] 2 EGLR 55 or *Stapel (Ernst) v Bellshore Property Investments Ltd* [2001] 2 EGLR 7 are not instances of a court varying a contract, but simply cases of the court dealing with difficulties on a construction basis.

CONDUCT AND REPRESENTATIONS AT VARIANCE WITH THE PROVISIONS OF THE LEASE

23-12   It is very common for the parties to ignore, or forget, what the lease requires and to arrange their affairs, or to make statements, on a basis which is at variance with the strict terms of what the contract requires.[22] Naturally, as in the case of any contract, the rights of parties might be varied by what they say or do. Familiar doctrines such as waiver, election, or the various common law and equitable forms of estoppel, may assist on the facts of a particular case. Reference should be made to the relevant texts in relation to the detailed rules of those doctrines.[23] In what follows, some of the doctrines are considered in the specific context of landlord and tenant relationships.

Promissory estoppel

23-13   Promissory estoppel clearly operates in the context of leases to restrict the rights of a party where a clear and unequivocal promise or representation is made by one party to a pre-existing relationship to another, upon which representation the other party acts to his detriment making it unconscionable for the representor to go back on what he has represented.[24] Where the promise is supported by consideration, that might give rise to a collateral contract.[25] It has been frequently invoked in the landlord and tenant context, usually by tenants seeking to defend against a landlord seeking to rely on the letter of an agreement which he had previously promised not to enforce in accordance with its strict terms:[26]

1   *Hughes v Metropolitan Railway*[27] was a case in which a landlord's six month notice to repair was served on the tenant. Rather than rectify the disrepair, the tenant instead offered to sell his interest to the landlord, at the same time proposing to defer repairs to allow negotiations to proceed. The landlord entered into negotiations with the tenant on that basis. The House

22 See, for an example of how these doctrines might operate in the service charge context, *Minster Chalets Ltd v Irwin Park Residents Association* [2001] EWLands LRX_28_2000; *Bhambhani v Willowcourt Management Co (1985)* [2008] EWLands_LRX_22_2007.

23 See generally *Snell's Equity* (32nd edn, 2010) for an overview of the relevant principles, at Ch 12.

24 As to the question of whether it operates not merely as a shield, but also as a sword, see the discussion in *Riverside Housing Association Ltd v White* [2005] EWCA Civ 1385 at paras 59–67 (reversed for other reasons by the House of Lords: [2007] HLR 31); *Bhambhani v Willowcourt Management Co (1985)* [2008] EWLands_LRX_22_2007. It is doubtful that the doctrine can be used to extend a party's rights: see *Chitty on Contract*, Vol 1, para 3-099 and the cases there cited.

25 See *Chitty on Contract*, Vol 1, para 3-105. If there is a contract, then, depending on its terms, it may also benefit third parties under the provisions of the Contracts (Rights of Third Parties) Act 1999. For collateral contracts and leases, see *Woodfall's Law of Landlord and Tenant*, Vol 1, paras 4.047, 4.055 and 11.055.1. For an illustration, see *Malt Mill Developments Ltd v Davis* [2002] EWCA Civ 440.

26 Though sometimes it is the tenant who is estopped: see *Smith v Lawson* (1998) 75 P&CR 466.

27 (1877) 2 App Cas 439.

of Lords made clear that the landlord did not enter into those negotiations with any intention of lulling the tenant into a false sense of security. When negotiations failed, the landlord sought to rely on the original six-month period under the notice. The House of Lords found that the effect of negotiating with the tenant on the basis proposed by the tenant was to suspend the effect of the notice, so that time under it could not be computed until negotiations were broken off.

2 *Brikom Investments Ltd v Carr*[28] was a case in which the landlord of blocks of flats had entered into agreements for lease exhibiting draft leases. Under those leases, the landlord covenanted, at the expense of the tenants, to repair the roof. The landlord assured the tenants, in some cases in writing, in others orally, that it would not pursue tenants for service charges in relation to the roof and, on the basis of that assurance, the tenants entered into their leases. The landlord subsequently sought to charge the tenants for the works when they were carried out four years later. The majority of the Court of Appeal (Roskill and Cumming-Bruce LLJ) decided that the landlord had entered into a collateral contract not to seek service charge, which contract was enforceable by all representees who remained tenants. In those cases where the leases had been transferred to successors in title, the majority found that the landlord had waived, once and for all, any rights to claim service charge in respect of the roof, and therefore there was no right left to assert against assignees of individual flats.[29] Lord Denning MR preferred the analysis that the landlord's representation and the tenant's reliance had created a promissory estoppel, the benefit and burden of which passed to each party's successors in title. Roskill LJ was not prepared to accept the promissory estoppel analysis, with the proprietary effect on successors in title for which Lord Denning MR contended.

23-14 The distinction between, on the one hand, being prevented from asserting a specific claim under a contract and, on the other, a contract being permanently varied, was blurred in *Central London Property Trust Ltd v High Trees House Ltd.*[30] In that case, the defendant company was liable to pay a ground rent to the claimant freeholder under a headlease of a block of flats. The difficulty which arose was that the prevailing wartime conditions made it difficult for the defendant to let the flats. By 1945, the rental market had recovered and the flats were let. Prior to the September quarter day, the claimant demanded the full rent be paid from that date. The claimant and the defendant issued 'friendly' proceedings to determine the rent payable by the defendant to the claimant. Denning J decided that the effect of an oral promise acted upon (which he declined to characterise as an estoppel, or at any rate as an estoppel by representation) had the effect of varying a deed under seal and operated as an extension of the rule that a lease by deed could be varied by written contract.[31] However, on the facts of *High Trees*,

---

28 [1979] QB 467.
29 In relation to questions as to the scope of such waiver, see *Broomleigh Housing Association Ltd v Hughes* [1999] EGCS 134.
30 [1947] KB 130.
31 At pp 133–135 and the cases there referred to.

it was not necessary to find that the lease had been varied permanently, as the expectation underlying the estoppel was that the reduced rent would only be payable while wartime conditions obtained, which had ceased to be the case by September 1945. Hence the estoppel was satisfied and spent by that date.

23-15   However, a permanent variation was found to have occurred in *Mitas v Hyams*,[32] where the landlord and the tenant agreed that, instead of rent being payable on the quarter days originally agreed, the rent would be payable on the usual quarter days. This revised arrangement was operated for some years, until the landlord brought an action for rent arrears, relying upon the originally agreed rent days. Denning J, relying on *High Trees*, found that it was not open to the landlord to argue for the original rent days. It appears accepted by the leading textbooks that promissory estoppel may (depending on the nature of the representation on which it is founded) effect a permanent variation of the rights of parties under a lease.[33] However, in light of the *dicta* of the majority of the Court of Appeal in *Brikom*, it remains unclear whether such a representation can run with the lease or the reversion so as to benefit successors in title. It may well be that a distinction needs to be drawn between those with the benefit of a promissory estoppel and, on the other hand, those who are burdened by promissory estoppels made by third parties.[34]

Estoppel by convention

23-16   Where two parties to a transaction proceed on an assumed state of facts or law, whether because they share the assumption or one party acquiesces in the other's understanding of the situation, then the parties are prevented from acting contrary to that assumption if it is inequitable to do so. This operates as a species of equitable estoppel called estoppel by convention.[35] As *Tingdene Holiday Parks Ltd v Cox* makes clear,[36] estoppel by convention is fragile in that it only lasts until the parties are disabused of their assumption.[37] While, therefore, estoppel by convention may justify past conduct which proceeded on an erroneous basis, the estoppel will not effect a permanent change to the legal relationship of the parties once the true facts are understood.

---

32 [1951] 2 TLR 1215.

33 See *Chitty on Contracts*, Vol I, para 1-115; *Woodfall: Landlord and Tenant*, Vol 1, para 7-118.

34 Statements that support the position that it might can be found in two boundary dispute cases, *Hopgood v Brown* [1955] 1 WLR 213 and *Valentine v Allen* [2003] EWCA Civ 915. This question is debated in the 2004 Blundell Debate between Lord Justice Neuberger and Mr Justice Lewison (as they were then), 'Estoppel and Third Parties' (unpublished).

35 *Amalgamated Investment & Property Co Ltd v Texas Commerce International Bank Ltd* [1982] QB 84; *Troop v Gibson* [1986] 1 EGLR 1. This doctrine is specifically discussed in the 2008 Blundell Lecture given by Professor Hugh Beale QC and Jonathan Gaunt QC, 'Estoppel by Convention – When, How and For How Long'.

36 [2011] UKUT 310 (LC); see too *Fernandez v Shanterton Second Management Co Ltd* [2007] EWLands LRX_153_2006, but the point was not fully argued in the latter case and the precise estoppel at play was not identified.

37 Relying on *Hiscox v Outhwaite (No 1)* [1991] 3 All ER 124.

Proprietary estoppel

23-17   Proprietary estoppel[38] is potentially significant as it is beyond doubt
for registered land, and appears now to be widely accepted for unregistered
land, to be capable of burdening successors in title of the representor.[39] Further,
proprietary estoppel can clearly be used to found a cause of action. In that regard,
the doctrine does not simply operate to give rise to property rights, but can also
operate so as to release the representee from some right, where the representor has
made a representation to that effect upon which there has been reliance rendering
it unconscionable for the representor to assert that right.[40] Additionally, unlike
promissory estoppel, the courts will permit general and imprecise representations
to found a proprietary estoppel claim.[41] Finally, however, it must be borne in mind
that the court retains a remedial discretion when deciding how (if at all) to satisfy
the equity to which the proprietary estoppel has given rise and, undoubtedly,
such factors as (a) whether the parties intended the arrangement to be permanent
or temporary, or (b) what hardship giving effect to the representation might result
to the landlord and other tenants, are factors that must be weighed in the scale.
That discretion notwithstanding, it may nonetheless be more advantageous from
a number of points of view for the tenant to cast his argument in the form of a
proprietary estoppel claim, if the facts allow.

---

38 For a general discussion of the ingredients of this doctrine, see Harpum, Bridge and Dixon,
    Megarry and Wade: The Law of Real Property (8th edn, 2012), Ch 16.
39 For registered land, the position was clarified by the Land Registration Act 2002, s 116.
40 *Jackson v Carter* (1800) 5 Ves 688 (landlord injuncted from asserting right to enter and cut
    timber on tenant's land).
41 Contrast **23-13**.

CHAPTER 24

Variation of service charge schemes

24-01   There are a number of ways in which problematic service charge machinery can be tackled. The cases considered above which illustrate some reported instances of deficient machinery show that problems may be alleviated by construction arguments or the implication of terms into the lease.[1] Defective machinery may also be susceptible to rectification in an appropriate case.[2] There are, however, other ways in which service charge provisions might be varied or corrected which do not depend on those particular doctrines. This section will consider, first, statutory rights to vary service charge machinery in leases and, secondly, the ability of the parties to vary, by agreement or conduct, the effect of service charge machinery.

STATUTORY VARIATION OF THE LEASE DURING THE TERM: RESIDENTIAL PREMISES ONLY

24-02   The powers that exist to vary the identity of the person with management functions under leases have already been considered at **15-07** above. This section is concerned with the powers that exist for varying the content of the rights and obligations which managers have by statute. Specifically, under Part IV of the Landlord and Tenant Act 1987,[3] the LVT is able to vary long leases[4] of flats[5] on application[6] by a party to such a lease (section 35(1)). The respondent to such an application may require the other relevant leases to be amended too (section 36). The grounds on which such a variation might be made are (section 35(2)) (so far as relevant to the present section):

> 'the lease fails to make satisfactory provision with respect to one or more of the following matters, namely –

---

1   See Chapter 2 above.
2   See, for example, *Westvilla Properties Ltd v Dow Properties Ltd* [2010] EWHC 30 (Ch).
3   Which also applies to Crown land: see the Commonhold and Leasehold Reform Act 2002, s 172. RICS Residential Code, Appendix I.
4   Defined in ss 60, 59(3) and 35(6).
5   Defined in s 60 and see *Hong Kong Resort International Ltd v HKR Management Ltd (Lavender Dock)* (unreported, 4 June 2008, LON/00BE/LVT/2006/0004).
6   The application is governed by the Commonhold and Leasehold Reform Act 2002, Sch 12.

...

(d)   the provision or maintenance of any services which are reasonably necessary to ensure that occupiers of the flat enjoy a reasonable standard of accommodation (whether they are services connected with any such installations or not, and whether they are services provided for the benefit of those occupiers or services provided for the benefit of the occupiers of a number of flats including that flat);

(e)   the recovery by one party to the lease from another party to it of expenditure incurred or to be incurred by him, or on his behalf, for the benefit of that other party or of a number of persons who include that other party;

(f)   the computation of a service charge payable under the lease'.

24-03   In *Gianfrancesco v Haughton*,[7] the Lands Tribunal considered the meaning of the term 'fails to make satisfactory provision' and stated (at paragraph 21) as follows:[8]

'Before it can make an order under section 38 of the 1987 Act the tribunal has to be satisfied that the lease fails to make satisfactory provision with respect to one or more of the matters specified in section 35(2) and referred to in the application. I am not sure that the language used creates a lower threshold of qualification than that in section 57(6)(a) of the 1993 Act, which refers to remedying a defect in the lease, but that is not a matter that needs to be decided. Whether the lease fails to make satisfactory provision is one for the tribunal to judge in all the circumstances of the case. A lease does not fail to make satisfactory provision, in my judgment, simply because it could have been better or more explicitly drafted. For instance the need to imply a term is not necessarily, or even probably, an indication that the lease fails to make satisfactory provision for the matter in question.'

24-04   As to section 35(2)(d) (also applicable to (c), not referred to above), the Act further provides in subsection (3) that:

'For the purposes of subsection (2)(c) and (d) the factors for determining, in relation to the occupiers of a flat, what is a reasonable standard of accommodation may include –

(a)   factors relating to the safety and security of the flat and its occupiers and of any common parts of the building containing the flat; and

(b)   other factors relating to the condition of any such common parts.'

24-05   As to section 35(2)(e), subsection (3A) further provides that:

---

7   [2008] EWLands LRX_10_2007.
8   See too *Stapel v Bellshore Property Investments Ltd* [2001] 2 EGLR 7 and the decision of the LVT in *Re 90 Wigmore Street* (unreported, 27 June 2011, LON/00BK/LVL/2010/008), where the tribunal held that it did not have power, under these provisions, to substitute a management company incorporated by the lessees for the original management company which was responsible for providing the services under the relevant leases and which had also been owned by the original lessees, but which had been dissolved.

'For the purposes of subsection (2)(e) the factors for determining, in relation to a service charge payable under a lease, whether the lease makes satisfactory provision include whether it makes provision for an amount to be payable (by way of interest or otherwise) in respect of a failure to pay the service charge by the due date.'

24-06   Under section 35(2)(e), it has been decided by the LVT that the provision cannot be used to exclude a tenant from liability for services which are of no benefit to him.[9] The provision might be used, however, where the service charge scheme as drafted does not permit the landlord to make 100% recovery.[10] The Lands Tribunal has upheld a decision by the LVT that, under section 35(2)(e), the words 'on demand' and 'in advance' could be inserted into a lease where they were patently omitted from the original drafting. In another case, the Upper Tribunal varied a lease to supply an obligation to make payments of service charge which it was clearly contemplated that the tenant would pay, but where there was nothing in the lease requiring him to do so.[11]

24-07   Under subsection 35(2)(f) (computation of service charge), further reference has to be made to sub-section 35(4). This states that:

'For the purposes of subsection (2)(f) a lease fails to make satisfactory provision with respect to the computation of a service charge payable under it if –

(a)   it provides for any such charge to be a proportion of expenditure incurred, or to be incurred, by or on behalf of the landlord or a superior landlord; and

(b)   other tenants of the landlord are also liable under their leases to pay by way of service charges proportions of any such expenditure; and

(c)   the aggregate of the amounts that would, in any particular case, be payable by reference to the proportions referred to in paragraphs (a) and (b) would [either exceed or be less than] the whole of any such expenditure.'

24-08   The ground in subsection 35(2)(f) is concerned with computation of amounts only.[12] The Lands Tribunal has further explained in *Morgan v Fletcher*[13] that the purpose of the section is to enable 100% of service charge to be recovered and that residential service charge ought be operated on a not-for-profit and a not-for-loss basis.[14] Under this subsection, it is possible for fixed-percentage contributions to be varied to a 'fair and reasonable' basis where changes in the building necessitated such a change.[15]

24-09   In addition to the above powers, a majority application can also be made for the updating of leases, under section 37. In order to make a variation order

9   *Hong Kong Resort International Ltd v HKR Management Ltd (Lavender Dock)* (unreported, 4 June 2008, LON/00BE/LVT/2006/0004).
10   *Hammersmith and Fulham Housing Management and Services Ltd v Hyde* (LON/00AN/ LVL/38/0005). It is considered that this is more properly a concern under subsection 35(2)(f).
11   *Mawhood v Sinclair Gardens Investments (Kensington) Ltd* [2008] EWLands LRX_59_2007.
12   *Cleary v Lakeside Developments Ltd* [2011] UKUT 264 (LC).
13   [2008] EWLands LRX_81_2008.
14   See **2-75** above for further consideration of a presumption against profit.
15   *Mehra v Citywest Homes Ltd* [2011] UKUT 311 (LC). See **2-75** to **2-80** above for the presumption against making a profit, which operates independently of the statutory scheme.

under section 37, the tribunal must be satisfied, first, that where the application is in respect of less than nine leases, all or all but one of the parties concerned has consented, or where more than eight leases are concerned, the variation is not opposed by more than 10 per cent of the total number of the parties concerned and at least 75 per cent of that number consent to it.[16] Secondly, in all cases, the tribunal must be satisfied that the object to be achieved by the variation cannot be satisfactorily achieved unless all the leases are varied to the same effect. Therefore, where there is a significant majority in favour of a particular variation, it is open to the landlord or any of those lessees to apply for the leases of the minority to be varied, providing it is satisfied that this is necessary in order to achieve the object of the variation. In order to determine an application under this section, the tribunal must, first, establish what that object is.[17]

24-09A In all cases, whether the application is made under one of the grounds in section 35 or under the 'majority' provisions in section 37, the tribunal must consider whether the variation would be likely substantially to prejudice any respondent to the application or any person who is not a party to the application and that an award of compensation under subsection (10) would not afford him adequate compensation, or that for any other reason it would not be reasonable in the circumstances for the variation to be effected.[18] The tribunal, therefore, has a wide discretion to reach a fair and just result in any case. Under section 38(10), the tribunal has power to award compensation to any party 'in respect of any loss or disadvantage that the tribunal considers he is likely to suffer as a result of the variation'. There is no significant authority as to how compensation might be assessed under this provision. In *Cleary v Lakeside Developments Ltd*,[19] the President of the Upper Tribunal said (*obiter*) that 'loss or disadvantage' was not limited to diminution in value of the lessee's interest in his lease. In that case, the variation proposed (to require those lessees who had not contracted to contribute towards a management fee to do so) would have involved additional expenditure for which the lessees had not contracted. The President said that 'on the face of it', it was difficult to see how such a requirement would not be a loss or disadvantage requiring the payment of compensation.[20] The phrase 'loss or disadvantage'

---

16 Section 37(5).
17 *Shellpoint Trustees Ltd v Barnett* [2012] UKUT 375 (LC), where HH Judge Gerald explained that although the object might well be self-evident from the content of the variation itself, that will not always be the case and it is for the applicants, rather than the tribunal, to identify, with evidence, what object or purpose is intended by the variation. It must then go on to consider whether the variations do, indeed, achieve this purpose and secondly, whether it is necessary, in order to do so, that all of the leases be varied.
18 Section 38(6).
19 [2011] UKUT 264 (LC).
20 In *Brickfield Properties Ltd v Botten* [2013] UKUT 133 (LC), HH Judge Huskinson said that he did not consider that a back-dated variation requiring the tenants to pay a higher proportion of service charge (so that the total costs would equal 100 per cent after one of the blocks within the estate had been taken out of the service charge regime following a collective enfranchisement) would attract compensation. He considered that the loss of an 'unintended windfall' (caused by the de facto reduction in their service charges because of the reduction in costs to which they were required to contribute) was not a 'loss or disadvantage' within the meaning of subs (10).

is also used in section 84(1A) of the Law of Property Act 1925, by which the Upper Tribunal has power to award compensation for the discharge or modification of restrictive covenants, and decisions on the assessment of compensation under that provision might provide some assistance in determining the proper basis of compensation under section 38(10) of the Landlord and Tenant Act 1987.

24-09B In *Brickfield Properties Ltd v Botten*,[21] the Upper Tribunal (Lands Chamber) held that in an appropriate case, the LVT has power to back-date a variation.[22]

STATUTORY VARIATION OF THE LEASE ON RENEWAL: BUSINESS AND RESIDENTIAL TENANCIES

Business tenancies

24-10 When a tenancy is renewed under the provisions of Part II of the Landlord and Tenant Act 1954, it is open to either party to request that the court should depart from the terms of the original tenancy. The question of whether the service charge scheme can be altered on renewal has been considered on a number of occasions.

24-11 The leading case on changing terms on renewal is a case about service charge: *O'May v City of London Real Property Co Ltd*.[23] In that case, the tenant contended that his renewal tenancy should follow the terms of the expired tenancy and require him only to pay the costs of heating and lighting the common parts of the building in which they had an office. The landlord contended that the lease should be modernised to be a 'clear lease', requiring the tenant to contribute service charge for the service and repair and redecoration of the interior and exterior of the entire building (with the effect of reducing the rent payable under the renewal tenancy). The decision appears to have been particularly informed by the fact that the tenant was taking only a five-year lease term, and would not expect to be liable for contributions towards capital depreciations of the kind that the landlord was seeking to impose, such as the costs of repairing the structure and exterior. Accordingly, it remains open whether a court would take a similar view in the case of a longer renewal tenancy. It appears that a proposal which does

21 [2013] UKUT 133 (LC).
22 It was considered appropriate in that case where the variation was sought under s 35(2)(f) on the ground that one of a number of blocks in an estate had been taken out of the service charge regime following a collective enfranchisement, so that the lessees in the remaining blocks were paying the same proportion as before, but for a lower cost (because the landlord no longer incurred costs in relation to the enfranchised block). However, for the landlord, there was a shortfall because those who remained in the service charge regime paid fixed proportions which no longer added up to 100 per cent. The LVT held that it did not have power to back-date the variation. This was reversed by the Upper Tribunal and the tribunal exercised its power to back-date to avoid a windfall to the lessees.
23 [1983] AC 726.

not make a tenant liable for capital costs of replacements and costs of extensive repairs and maintenance will be more acceptable to the court.[24]

24-12   The courts are therefore not automatically opposed to altering service charge machinery on renewal. In *Hyams v Titan Properties Limited*,[25] decided before *O'May*, the Court of Appeal decided that a trial judge had been wrong, on a renewal application, simply to increase by £25 the annual amount payable by a tenant towards services provided at the building in which he had a tenancy. Instead, the Court of Appeal decided that the correct term to impose was the 'generally accepted' practice of paying a proportionate service charge. The extent to which *Hyams* is consistent with *O'May* insofar as the Court of Appeal were prepared to allow the insertion of a clause that made the tenant liable, on a variable basis, for repairs and capital items, is debatable and, arguably, *Hyams* is not consistent with the *O'May* approach.

24-13   *O'May* was applied in *Edwards & Walkden (Norfolk) Ltd v The Mayor and Commonality and Citizens of the City of London*.[26] In around 1981, leases were granted of shop, office and stall premises in the East and West Markets at Smithfield. A variable charge was payable by the majority of tenants,[27] as a separate and distinct charge on top of rent. In 1987, however, the payment structure was changed and the tenants paid service charge in a fixed, not variable, amount, in anticipation of disruptive planned refurbishment works. The evidence before the court suggested that this switch was an interim measure, however, the tenants refused to enter into fresh leases under which a separate variable charge was payable. As a compromise, the leases permitted the payment of a fixed inclusive charge, but with a clause stating that the basis of the service charge was to be determined at a future date and containing provision (albeit inoperative) for the payment of a separate variable charge.

24-14   Sales J found that tenants tended to take longer term lettings and, in the instant case, were seeking the maximum renewal period which the court could order under section 33, that is, 15 years. Sales J further found that:[28]

> 'This is not a case where there is a high turnover of tenants, where the interest of the landlord in the fabric of the building which is let can more readily be regarded as entirely distinct from that of the tenants.'

24   *Leslie & Godwin Investments Ltd v Prudential Assurance Co Ltd* [1987] 2 EGLR 95; a more generous approach may also be detected in *Amarjee v Barrowfen Properties Ltd* [1993] 2 EGLR 133 (County Court), though the reasons for the decision are not clear.
25   (1972) 24 P&CR 359.
26   [2012] EWHC 2527 (Ch).
27   It is to be noted that there were two other groups of leases in the market. There was the 'main group of Poultry Market tenancies', which had been granted at a variable service charge from the outset (though various *ad hoc* agreements had been made with tenants to pay an inclusive rent from time to time, which was agreed to be a temporary measure in each case). They wished to switch to a fixed charge with the majority. In relation to two units in the Poultry Market (the Unit 207 and 221 tenancies), the tenancies granted were always at a simple, all-inclusive rent. Those tenants wished to keep their tenancies in that form on renewal.
28   At para 52.

24-15   The market, therefore, had a very stable body of business tenants. Further, while the City of London wished tenants to be liable for any future maintenance costs in relation to the market, it was accepted by the City that any existing disrepair ought to be its responsibility and it appears that the proposed lease terms provided for an independent expert to undertake an investigation into the market to prepare, as it were, a 'schedule of condition' for which the tenants would not be responsible. The effect of the City's proposals would, therefore, not be to visit on the tenants historic disrepair. Further, Sales J noted that the tenants at the market (and at Billingsgate Market, which was comparable before the court) had been prepared to countenance a variable charge historically. While Sales J acknowledged that tenants had an interest in knowing with certainty what their future outlay would be in relation to their trading premises, tenants running small businesses did not have an absolute right to the certainty of fixed outgoings, including those by way of service charge. Finally, Sales J rejected the suggestion that the City's management of the market was susceptible to criticism. Most significantly, Sales J also recorded that the tenants and the City accepted as common ground the principle that the tenants ought to be liable for the costs of provision by the City of all services at the market.

24-16   Those factors led Sales J to distinguish the facts of the *Smithfield* case from *O'May* and find that a separate variable charge was appropriate. He noted that the basic position was that 'the Court should not generally exercise its discretion under section 35 to change the parameters of the commercial arrangement between the landlord and the tenant'.[29] He decided, having reminded himself of that position, that the City of London had established good reasons for switching the service charge structure to an exclusive rent with variable service charge under the East and West Market tenancies. It was critical to this finding that (a) there was no 'clear' deal struck at the outset as to how risks were to be apportioned between the parties under the 2001 leases, and (b) that both sides were entirely agreed on the principle (already referred to) that the cost of provision of services ought to be borne by the tenants.[30] The only point of difference between them was how that ought to be achieved. Accordingly, the court was not being invited to find that there should be no service charge payable at all. Those two facts set the Smithfield case apart from *O'May*. Given that the court was therefore simply being asked to find service charge machinery which best allowed the landlord to ensure that its costs were covered, Sales J considered that the best way of arriving at that result was to impose a variable charge, rather than a 'crude' index-linked fixed charge. That approach was further supported by *Hyams v Titan*,[31] as well as common current market practice. While those were the main grounds of his decision, it is also obvious that the stable tenant base at the market and the length of the terms being sought on renewal supported such a conclusion. Sales J's decision in relation to the East and West Market had a 'knock on' effect on the other leases in the Poultry Market. It will be

---

29   At para 80.
30   See paras 83 and 87.
31   See **24-12** above, but it is to be noted that this was a pre-*O'May* decision.

remembered that the main group of Poultry Market leases were at a variable service charge, so that it was the tenants arguing for a change in the terms of the renewal tenancies. Unsurprisingly, they failed. Notably, Sales J also determined that Units 207 and 221, which had always been at an inclusive rent encompassing a fixed service charge, should be switched to a variable service charge in the interests of uniformity across the market as a whole.

Residential properties

24-17   In addition to the powers of the court under the Landlord and Tenant Act 1987, the LVT may, when a new lease is sought by a tenant of a flat, alter the terms in limited circumstances under section 57(6) of the Leasehold Reform, Housing and Urban Development Act 1993.[32] The circumstances are where it is necessary to change the terms to cure a defect in the lease, with necessity being given a narrow meaning. The prevailing view is that this aspect of the subsection does not justify modernisation on grounds of convenience.[33] The other limb applies where modification is required in light of changes arising since the date of the commencement of the original lease, which means that again defects in the original drafting, or inherently inconvenient but workable provisions, are not curable. However, in relation to service charge specifically, section 57(2) provides that:

'(2)   Where during the continuance of the new lease the landlord will be under any obligation for the provision of services, or for repairs, maintenance or insurance –

(a)   the new lease may require payments to be made by the tenant (whether as rent or otherwise) in consideration of those matters or in respect of the cost thereof to the landlord; and

(b)   (if the terms of the existing lease do not include any provision for the making of any such payments by the tenant or include provision only for the payment of a fixed amount) the terms of the new lease shall make, as from the term date of the existing lease, such provision as may be just –

(i)   for the making by the tenant of payments related to the cost from time to time to the landlord, and

(ii)   for the tenant's liability to make those payments to be enforceable by *distress, re-entry or otherwise* [re-entry or otherwise (subject to section 85 of the Tribunals, Courts and Enforcement Act 2007)] in like manner as if it were a liability for payment of rent.'

---

32   As to the general effect of which, see Radevsky and Greenish, *Hague on Leasehold Enfranchisement* (5th edn, 2009) at para 32-05.

33   Though Lord Neuberger expressed the view that the powers of the LVT under this subsection were 'relatively wide' in *Howard de Walden Estates Ltd v Aggio* [2009] 1 AC 39 (at para 49).

24-18   There are similar provisions in relation to lease extensions of houses under section 15(3) of the Leasehold Reform Act 1967.[34] Where an extended lease is sought under that Act, it is provided that:

'Where during the continuance of the new tenancy the landlord will be under any obligation for the provision of services, or for repairs, maintenance or insurance, the rent payable in accordance with subsection (2) above shall be in addition to any sums payable (whether as rent or otherwise) in consideration of those matters or in respect of the cost thereof to the landlord; and if the terms of the existing tenancy include no provision for the making of any such payments by the tenant, or provision only for the payment of a fixed amount, the terms of the new tenancy shall make, as from the time when rent becomes payable in accordance with subsection (2) above, such provision as may be just for the making by the tenant of payments related to the cost from time to time to the landlord, and for the tenant's liability to make those payments to be enforceable by *distress, re-entry or otherwise* [re-entry or otherwise (subject to section 85 of the Tribunals, Courts and Enforcement Act 2007)] in like manner as the liability for the rent.'

---

34   See Radevsky and Greenish, *Hague on Leasehold Enfranchisement* (5th edn, 2009), para 7-41.

CHAPTER 25

Effect of destruction of premises

25-01   Leases sometimes contain abeyance clauses, though these often relate only to 'rent'. Such clauses can give rise to a number of difficult questions of construction. The most obvious is the meaning of the term 'rent'. An illustration of the difficulties this can give rise to is shown by the judgment of Neuberger J (as he then was) in *P&O Property Holdings Ltd v International Computers Ltd*.[1] The facts arose out of the IRA bombings of the Arndale Centre in Manchester in 1996. The relevant lease in *P&O* provided that, on occurrence of any of the insured risks, 'the rent hereby reserved or a fair proportion thereof' was to be suspended. During the period in which the tenant's unit was damaged, the landlord sought to recover the costs of refurbishment of the air condition system.

25-02   Under the lease, the tenant had been obliged to pay as additional rent the service charges or insurance during the period in which his unit in the shopping centre was unusable. The landlord was continuing to provide services in much the same way as before the bomb (indeed costs incurred by the landlord, to be recovered as service charge, were higher in light of the exceptional circumstances obtaining). The tenant argued that, as his service charge was reserved as 'additional rent', it fell within the terms of the rent abatement clause. Rejecting that argument, Neuberger J determined that the abeyance clause should not be read as also referring to the additional rents (i.e. the service charge and insurance premiums). The reddendum of the lease distinguished between 'rent' and 'rents' on the one hand, and 'additional rents' on the other. Secondly, to permit a tenant to refrain from paying service charge for the relevant period was commercially unfair on the landlord. Finally, it was a strange result that the tenant ought to be able to escape liability for contributions towards lasting works from which it could ultimately hope to derive benefit at some future time when the unit was reinstated.[2] As to other services, such as gas and electricity, from which the tenant would not be deriving any practical benefit while the unit was unusable, that question was regulated by the terms of the lease itself.

---

1   [2000] 2 All ER 1015.
2   See p 1021.

25-03   If a tenant has a right to a rent suspension on the basis of (for instance) storm damage, this may amount to an equitable set off against a lessor's claim for rent which can be raised to prevent a lessor from levying distress for that rent: *Fuller v Happy Shopper Markets Ltd.*[3]

---

3   [2001] 1 WLR 1681.

CHAPTER 26

Enforcement of service charges between freeholders

26-01   As explained in Chapter 1, this book is predominantly concerned with leasehold service charges. Issues concerning the recovery of the cost of services relating to freehold properties are less commonly encountered in practice. When they do arise, it is often in relation to the sale of freehold houses within an estate, where the purchaser agrees to pay, in addition to the purchase price, an annual sum towards the maintenance of estate roads, drainage, etc. Industrial estates and retail parks may also comprise freehold units which are served by common areas and where the individual freehold owners have covenanted to contribute towards the costs of maintaining those areas.

26-02   Freehold service charges present a unique problem because of the rule that the burden of a positive freehold covenant requiring something to be done by the owner of land for the time being cannot, as a general rule, be made to run with the land so as to bind the owner of the land from time to time. A covenant to perform services or to carry out work is a positive obligation, as is a covenant to pay money. No such problem exists with leasehold covenants as the burden of a positive covenant may run with a leasehold estate.[1]

ENFORCEABILITY OF POSITIVE COVENANTS

26-03   At common law it has always been the case that the benefit of a covenant will run with the land.[2] However, the same is not true of the burden of a covenant. The rule at law is that the burden of a covenant will not pass with freehold land. This rule can be traced back to 1834 and the decision in *Keppell v Bailey*,[3] which

---

1   In the case of a lease granted prior to 1996, covenants which 'touch and concern' the land are enforceable by the landlord against successors in title to the tenant. In the case of a lease granted after 1995, the Landlord and Tenant (Covenants) Act 1995 provides that all covenants between landlord and tenant are enforceable by and against successors in title, save for personal covenants.
2   At law, this applies equally to negative covenants and positive covenants (such as a covenant to pay a service charge). However, for the reasons which follow, this is largely academic because in equity, only negative covenants can run.
3   (1834) 2 My&K 517, 39 ER 1042.

settled that although positive leasehold covenants ran with land, positive freehold covenants did not.[4]

26-04   In equity, subject to certain conditions, the burden of a restrictive covenant (i.e. a covenant which is negative, such as a covenant not to carry on a particular activity on land) can run with land and bind successors in title to the original covenantor[5] but as the House of Lords explained in *Rhone v Stephens:*[6]

> 'Equity cannot compel an owner to comply with a positive covenant entered into by his predecessors in title without flatly contradicting the common law rule that a person cannot be made liable upon a contract unless he was a party to it. Enforcement of a positive covenant lies in contract; a positive covenant compels an owner to exercise his rights. Enforcement of a negative covenant lies in property'.

26-05   The problem created by the rule that the burden of a positive covenant does not run at law is crying out for reform and there have been many proposals to reform this rule.[7] The introduction of commonhold as a new system for freehold ownership provides a partial solution to the problem but it will not always be appropriate to create a commonhold property and, as explained in Chapter 1, commonhold has not been widely adopted.

The significance of this rule for freehold service charges

26-06   In practice, the prevention of the transmission of the burden of a positive covenant means that an obligation on a freeholder to maintain or carry out repairs, for example to estate roads, will not be enforceable against a successor in title. Similarly, an obligation on a freeholder to pay a service charge to the owner of the common parts of an estate will not be enforceable against a purchaser of the freeholder's land. This presents significant problems for enforcement of service charges and it has been necessary to seek to achieve performance of a positive covenant by indirect methods.

Indirect methods of enforcing positive covenants

26-07   The following indirect methods provide a solution, albeit an imperfect solution to the problem of enforceability.

---

4   See also *Austerberry v Corporation of Oldham* (1885) LR 29 Ch D 750, also regarded as authority for this rule.
5   See generally Harpum, Bridge and Dixon, *Megarry and Wade: The Law of Real Property* (8th edn, 2012), Ch 32.
6   [1994] 2 AC 310, at p 318, *per* Lord Templeman.
7   See *The Report on the Committee on Positive Covenants Affecting Land* (1965) Cmnd 2719; *The Law of Positive and Restrictive Covenants* (1984) Law Com No 127; *Commonhold: A Consultation Paper* (1990) Cmnd 1345; *Making Land Work: Easements Covenants and Profits à Prendre* (2011) Law Com No 327.

Chain of covenants

26-08   A, the freehold owner of land enters into a positive covenant with B to pay a service charge in respect of services provided by B. When A comes to sell his land, he enters into a contract with his successor in title, C, whereby C covenants to pay for the services and to indemnify A for any loss arising from C's failure to do so. A remains liable on his contractual promise as a matter of simple contract law. If C comes to sell to D, C will enter into a similar contract with D whereby D agrees to pay for the services and indemnify C against the consequences of not doing so. This solution to the problem of enforcement is straightforward, but is cumbersome and has a number of shortcomings. As time goes by, it is relatively easy for the chain of covenants to get broken, either by the failure to obtain a covenant of indemnity from a successor in title or by the insolvency or disappearance of one of the links in the chain.

Benefit and burden principle

26-09   Where acceptance of the burden of the covenant is made a condition of enjoyment of the benefit, it may be possible for the burden to effectively pass to successor in title (for example, making the use of a road conditional on payment of a proportion of the cost of maintenance). This principle was confirmed by the decision in *Halsall v Brizell*.[8]

26-10   In *Halsall v Brizell*, the defendant's predecessor in title to a house on an estate had been given a right to use roads and sewers on the estate and had covenanted to pay a proportionate share of the cost of the maintenance of these facilities. The court held that the defendant, even though he was a successor in title, was liable to contribute to the cost of maintenance while he made use of the roads. Upjohn J referred to *Elliston v Reacher*[9] and the 'ancient law that a man cannot take a benefit under a deed without subscribing to the obligations there under'.[10]

26-11   *Halsall v Brizell* was approved in *Rhone v Stephens*.[11] In *Rhone v Stephens*, it was argued that a successor in title was bound by the burden of a positive repairing covenant because she enjoyed the benefit of having her roof supported by the adjoining cottage. Lord Templeman rejected the idea that there was any 'pure principle' that any party deriving any benefit from a conveyance must accept any burden in the same conveyance[12] and said:

> 'It does not follow that any condition can be rendered enforceable by attaching it to a right nor does it follow that every burden imposed by a conveyance may be enforced by depriving the covenantor's successor in title of every benefit which he

---

8   [1957] Ch 169.
9   [1908] 2 Ch 665.
10   At p 182.
11   [1994] 2 AC 310.
12   As suggested by Sir Robert Megarry V-C in *Tito v Waddell (No 2)* [1977] Ch 106.

enjoyed there under. The condition must be relevant to the exercise of the right. In *Halsall v Brizell* there were reciprocal benefits and burdens enjoyed by the users of the roads and sewers. In the present case clause 2 of the 1960 conveyance imposes reciprocal benefits and burdens of support but clause 3 which imposed an obligation to repair the roof is an independent provision. In *Halsall v Brizell* the defendant could, at least in theory, choose between enjoying the right and paying his proportion of the cost or alternatively giving up the right and saving his money. In the present case the owners of Walford House could not in theory or in practice be deprived of the benefit of the mutual rights of support if they failed to repair the roof.'

26-12 In *Thamesmead Town Ltd v Allotey*,[13] the Court of Appeal referred to Lord Templeman's decision in *Rhone v Stephens* and pointed to two preconditions for the enforceability of a positive covenant against the covenantor's successor in title. First, the condition of discharging the burden must be relevant to the exercise of the rights which enable the benefit to be obtained. Secondly, successors in title must have the opportunity to choose whether to take the benefit or, having taken it, to renounce it, even if only in theory, and thereby to escape the burden and that the successors in title can be deprived of the benefit if they fail to assume the burden.[14]

By reserving an estate rentcharge under the Rentcharges Act 1977

26-13 A common method of enforcing positive freehold covenants is by an estate rentcharge.

RENTCHARGES

26-14 In broad terms, a rentcharge is an annual or periodical payment which is secured on land and which is payable to someone who is not entitled to the reversion to the land charged with its payment.[15] A rentcharge is thus different from rent payable, where the relationship of landlord and tenant exists, which at common law is called a rent service.[16]

---

13 (1998) 30 HLR 1052 at p 1059, [1998] 3 EGLR 7.

14 See also *Wilkinson v Kerdene Ltd* [2013] EWCA Civ 44.

15 As a result of the Norman Conquest, all land is held from the Crown. The grant of freehold thus created the relationship of 'lord and tenant' in the same way as the grant of a term of years. Before 1290, there was no limit to the number of intervening tenures between the Crown and the tenant in occupation. (The process of creating new tenures is referred to as subinfeudation.) Because, historically, land was the only real form of capital wealth, a person selling land would take payment by way of a continuing obligation to perform services. The statute of *Quia Emptores* 1290 put an end to subinfeudation on the grant of freeholds. No new tenures in fee simple could be created, save by the Crown, and every conveyance of land in fee simple would operate as a transfer of the fee simple and would not create the relationship of lord and tenant. It was thus no longer possible for a grantor to reserve services on a conveyance of freehold land in fee simple and no rent reserved on a conveyance of freehold land in fee simple after 1290 can be a rent service. Rentcharges thus arose as a result of the statute of *Quia Emptores* 1290.

16 Thus if L grants a lease to T at £50 per annum, L has a rent service. If A charges his fee simple estate with the payment of £50 per annum to B, B has a rent charge.

26-15   The Rentcharges Act 1977[17] had the effect of abolishing rentcharges for the future, save for certain exceptions. Not all rentcharges simply provided a source of pure income profit to the rent owner. Some provided a useful device for circumventing the rule that the burden of positive covenants does not run with freehold land.[18] Thus, the 1977 Act did not abolish those rentcharges which were 'covenant-supporting' and which enabled positive covenants to be directly enforceable against successors in title. Such rentcharges facilitate the recovery of service charges in relation to freehold property.

26-16   Section 1 of the Rentcharges 1977 Act provides as follows:

'For the purposes of this Act "rentcharge" means any annual or other periodic sum charged on or issuing out of land, except –

(a)   rent reserved by a lease or tenancy, or

(b)   any sum payable by way of interest.'

26-17   A rentcharge created on or after 22 July 1977[19] will only be valid if it is an 'estate rentcharge' as defined by section 2(4) of the Rentcharges Act 1977. Section 2 of the 1977 Act provides:

'(1)   Subject to this section, no rentcharge may be created whether at law or in equity after the coming into force of this section.

(2)   Any instrument made after the coming into force of this section shall, to the extent that it purports to create a rentcharge the creation of which is prohibited by this section, be void.

(3)   This section does not prohibit the creation of a rentcharge –

...

(c)   which is an estate rentcharge;

...

(4)   For the purposes of this section "estate rentcharge" means (subject to subsection (5) below) a rentcharge created for the purpose –

(a)   of making covenants to be performed by the owner of the land affected by the rentcharge enforceable by the rent owner against the owner for the time being of the land; or

(b)   of meeting, or contribution towards, the cost of the performance by the rent owner of covenants for the provision of services, the carrying out of maintenance or repairs, the effecting of insurance or the making of any payment by him for the benefit of the land affected by the rentcharge or for the benefit of that and other land.

(5)   A rentcharge of more than a nominal amount shall not be treated as an estate rentcharge for the purposes of this section unless it represents a payment for

17   Which implemented the recommendation of the Law Commission in its 1975 *Report on Rentcharges* (Law Com No 68).
18   See, for example, the Law Commission's Report, para 48.
19   The date when the 1977 Act came into force.

213

the performance by the rent owner of a such covenant as is mentioned in subsection (4)(b) above which is reasonable in relation to that covenant.'

26-18   Section 3 of the Rentcharges Act 1977 provides for all other rentcharges (but not estate rentcharges) to be extinguished after a maximum period of 60 years.

26-19   The above provisions thus provide for two types of estate rentcharge:

1   a nominal rentcharge,[20] which will not assist in making the burden of positive covenants run unless it is also accompanied by a right of re-entry (section 4(a)); and

2   a 'service charge' type payment (section 4(b)).

26-20   In practice, many estate rentcharges fall within both section 4(a) and (b).

26-21   Type 2 rentcharges above are most commonly found in residential development schemes, holiday parks, industrial developments and retail parks where freehold units are sold off, but common parts are retained and maintained by a management company. Estate rent charges thus commonly deal with matters such as the repair and maintenance of estate roads, drainage systems and landscaped areas.

26-22   The type 2 variable estate rentcharge can only cover the cost of:

1   providing services;

2   carrying out maintenance or repairs;

3   effecting insurance; or

4   making payment for the benefit of the land affected. (This will include matters such as the payment of rates.[21])

Enforcement of rentcharges

26-23   Rentcharges are the most effective method of enforcing positive freehold covenants but they can still prove to be relatively cumbersome in practice. A

---

20 The object of restricting estate rentcharges to a nominal amount and an amount which is reasonable in relation to the covenanted services is to prevent the exemptions from being used as a way of creating substantial rentcharges which were intended to be abolished. However, rentcharges created for these purposes which existed before 22 August 1977 (one month after the Act was passed: see s 18(1)) will be exempt, regardless of the amount of the rentcharge. Thus, a pre-existing rentcharge which provides for a high level of payment if covenants are not performed, but which reduces to a lower or nominal sum if covenants are performed, will not be extinguished by the 1977 Act.

21 See *Orchard Trading Estate Management Ltd v Johnson Security Ltd* [2002] EWCA Civ 406.

rentcharge will be recoverable against 'the owner for the time being of the land'[22] and there are essentially four remedies available to the owner of a rent charge:

1 A common law action in debt for the money.

2 Distress – either pursuant to a power created by the instrument creating the rentcharge or pursuant to section 121(2), (5), (7) of the Law of Property Act 1925 (once the sum is 21 days in arrear).[23]

3 A right of re-entry – unless the instrument creating the rentcharge expresses a contrary intention, a rentcharge can be supported by a right of re-entry if the relevant sum is unpaid for 40 days.[24]

4 Demise – subject to the instrument creating the rentcharge expressing no contrary indication, if the rent (or any part of it) is 40 days in arrear, the rentcharge owner may demise the land to a trustee for a term of years on trust to raise the money which is outstanding by creating a mortgage, receiving the income or any other reasonable means.[25]

26-24 The principles set out in Chapter 2, above, relating to the interpretation of contracts apply to the interpretation of rentcharges as they do to other forms of service charges. The contractual provisions governing the payment of rentcharges tend to be simpler and shorter than most service charge provisions found in leases. It is sometimes provided that recovery of a charge is subject to a condition precedent requiring prior consent or agreement to the works to be given. Such conditions must be complied with.[26]

Creation of estate rentcharges

26-25 As explained above, to be valid, a rent charge must be an 'estate rentcharge' within section 2(4) of the 1977 Act. The date of the creation of the estate rentcharge is the relevant date for determining whether it has been validly created.[27] A legal rentcharge must be created by deed:[28] an equitable rentcharge may be created by contract or by signed writing.[29]

26-26 There have been very few reported cases relating to estate rentcharges and, until *Orchard Trading Estate Management Ltd v Johnson Security Ltd*,[30] which is considered below, there was no reported case which considered rentcharges under the 1977 Act.

---

22 Rentcharges Act 1977, s 2(4).
23 Note, however, the proposals contained in the Tribunals, Courts and Enforcement Act 2007 (which is not currently in force) which would appear to abolish the remedy of distress for rentcharges. See **44-04** below.
24 Law of Property Act 1925, ss 121(3), (5), (7).
25 Law of Property Act 1925, ss 121(4), (5), (7).
26 See **16-19** to **16-21**.
27 *Smith Brothers Farms Ltd v Canwell Estate Co Ltd* [2012] EWCA Civ 237.
28 Law of Property Act 1925, s 52.
29 Law of Property Act 1925, s 53.
30 [2002] EWCA Civ 406.

26-27 In the case of a variable type 2 rentcharge, it is not clear what happens where an item of expenditure which does not fall within the scope of section 2(4)(b) is included. In *Orchard Trading*, it was argued that a variable rentcharge was void and of no effect where it purported to include matters which could not legitimately be included in a rentcharge by reason of section 2(4)(b). The Court of Appeal, however, declined to decide this issue, having held that, in that case, all items claimed did in fact fall within section 2(4)(b).[31]

26-28 The wording of section 2(2) could be said to require all items within a single rentcharge to fall within section 2(4)(b) as it provides that 'Any instrument made after the coming into force of this section shall, to the extent that it purports to create a rentcharge the creation of which is prohibited by this section, be void'. However, it is considered that a court would be reluctant to adopt such a strict interpretation and the better view is that non-qualifying items could be severed to leave the remainder of a provision valid.

26-29 In *Smith Brothers Farms Ltd v The Canwell Estate Co Ltd*,[32] it was argued that no valid 'estate rentcharge' had been created because the services to which the rentcharge related were not 'for the benefit' of the land, as required by section 2(4)(b).

26-30 Canwell Estate Company Ltd was the owner of a registered estate rentcharge and brought proceedings against Smith Brothers, the owner of freehold agricultural land on the Canwell Estate, for the recovery of arrears of service charge contributions towards the upkeep of roads on the estate. Canwell owned the roads and amenity areas on the estate and Smith Brothers had a right of way over some, but not all, of the estate roads. It was being asked to pay 18.26% of the cost of maintaining those roads over which it did not have a right of way and 90% of the costs of those roads over which a right of way existed.

26-31 Smith Brothers argued that the estate rentcharge was not valid because the services to which the rentcharge related were not 'for the benefit' of its land, in that they included maintaining and repairing roads over which they had no right of way. In relation to this point, Mummery LJ said:[33]

> 'Much has been said on the defendant's behalf about the lack of benefit that it derives from the contributions it is asked to make towards the upkeep of all the roads on the Estate. I note, however, that the emphasis in sub-section (4)(b) is not on the kind or quantum of benefit actually obtained by the particular land affected by the rentcharge in return for contributions to the cost of performing the covenants: the emphasis is on the *performance* of the covenants for the provision of services etc and whether that performance is for the benefit of the land affected, *or of that land and other land* [my emphasis].'

---

31 See paras 26 and 27.
32 [2012] EWCA Civ 237.
33 At para 36.

26-32   He concluded:[34]

> 'Taking s.4(2)(b) first, the error in the defendant's approach is, in my view, in its undue emphasis on the words "for the benefit of the land affected by the rentcharge" which leads to a wrongly formulated question in this case: what benefit does the defendant's land obtain from costs incurred in maintaining and repairing roads over which the defendant has no right of way? It is natural for the defendant to ask what it is being asked to pay for, but the question must properly reflect the purpose, structure and language of the contribution scheme for the Estate underlying the payment claimed.
>
> First, the opening words of s.2(4) require attention to be paid to the *purpose* for which the rentcharge was created. The requirement is that the rentcharge was created "for the purpose ... of contributing towards, the cost of the performance of covenants by the rent owner for the provision of services [etc] for the benefit of the land affected by the rentcharge or for the benefit of that and other land" In my view, the rentcharge in the 1990 Transfer was created for that permitted service-charge purpose, as distinct from the pure income profit purpose, which is prohibited and nullified by the 1977 Act.
>
> Secondly, the focus is on the overall beneficial purpose of the rentcharge for the Estate, not on specific, direct benefit for particular pieces of land affected. It is sufficient that the purpose of the rentcharge is the performance of a covenant that will benefit the land affected directly or indirectly.
>
> Thirdly, the concluding words of s.2(4)(b) are important. The beneficial purpose of the covenant does not have to be directed solely to the defendant's land. It is sufficient for the beneficial purpose of the covenant to be for that *"and other land"* [my emphasis]. That is the case here, the other land being other parts of the Estate that benefit from the performance of the covenant.'

26-33   This decision will be of particular assistance to estate owners who require a contribution to be made by all occupiers in respect of communal services, which may benefit the estate generally, but not necessarily an individual unit. As the Court of Appeal found, an estate rentcharge may be validly created for the purposes of subsection (4)(b), even if it is not solely for, or even directly for, the benefit of the covenantor's land.

Reasonableness

26-34   Unlike leasehold service charges, there are no equivalent statutory provisions to the Landlord and Tenant Act 1985, etc. which require the rent owner to provide estimates and demands.[35] There is also no equivalent of section 19 of the 1985 Act. Some element of control is imposed indirectly by section 2(5) of the 1977 Act and, accordingly, the 'reasonableness' of the sums claimed under an estate rentcharge cannot be ignored completely. However, it seems unlikely that courts will give as broad an interpretation to section 2(5) as has been taken to section 19 of the 1985 Act.

---

34   At paras 54–58.
35   See Chapter 29 below.

26-35   The question of reasonableness was considered in *Orchard Trading Estate Management Ltd v Johnson Security Ltd.*[36] However, this case concerned a dispute about the validity of a variable rentcharge limited to expenditure on the performance of covenants rather than general issues concerning the reasonableness of costs. The decision the court reached in relation to how far section 2(5) imposes any reasonableness requirement is not entirely clear.

Orchard Trading Estate Management Ltd v Johnson Security Ltd

26-36   The Orchard Trading Estate was a small industrial estate comprising 15 units. Orchard Trading Estate Management Ltd was incorporated as a non profit-making company to administer the estate and to provide services to the industrial units. Services were provided in consideration of the payment by the owners of the units of a nominal and a variable rentcharge (i.e. type 1 and type 2 discussed above). The company owned parts of the estate, such as roadways and service areas, which were necessary to enable it to administer the estate. The estate sewerage system broke down and expensive repair costs were incurred. This led to proceedings being commenced by the company against five of the unit owners. The defendant, one such owner, argued that the variable rentcharge which had been created was void and that by reason of section 2(5), a rentcharge must only provide for the payment of a reasonable sum in respect of the performance of the relevant covenant and that the sum sought by the company was not reasonable.

26-37   The Court of Appeal thus considered two key issues, namely:

1   Whether it was a requirement that all of the items of expenditure fell within section 2(4)(b) in order for an estate rentcharge to be valid or whether non-qualifying items could be severed to leave the remainder valid?[37]

2   Whether the amount which was recoverable as an estate rentcharge was limited by a reasonableness requirement.

26-38   As explained above, the Court of Appeal declined to decide the first issue, but did consider whether it was possible only to recover 'reasonable' sums because of section 2(5).[38]

26-39   At first instance, HH Judge Weeks QC found that section 2(5) had a very narrow scope and was aimed at preventing the rentcharge owner from recovering no more than he had actually expended. In the Court of Appeal, Peter Gibson LJ appeared to endorse this view and said:[39]

'[the defendant] contends that the Judge was wrong to hold that s.2(5) was necessarily satisfied if no more than 100% of the total expenditure was recoverable; that, he says, is not sufficient for compliance with s.2(5). He submits that it is necessary

36   [2002] EWCA Civ 406.
37   The issue discussed at **26-27** above.
38   See **26-17** above.
39   At paras 28–30.

that the items for which expenditure may be charged and the level of expenditure on those items are limited by a requirement of reasonableness, and that is missing from the Deed, with the result that the variable rentcharge is invalid.

Again I am not able to agree. It is important to bear in mind that on this appeal we are concerned not with whether any item charged was reasonable in amount but with the validity of the rentcharge. As Mummery LJ pointed out in the course of the argument, s.2(5) is an anti-avoidance provision, designed to prevent a requirement by the rent owner that the owner of the land charges should make a payment unrelated or disproportionate to the performance of covenants within s.2(4)(b). If, for example, a fixed sum was required which was far in excess of what would be reasonable for the performance of the covenant, that rentcharge would be invalidated. As Mr Morgan QC, appearing with Mr Cousins for Orchard, rightly put it, one measures the price of the rentcharge against the promise of the performance of the covenants. A rentcharge of a fixed sum may satisfy s.2(5) as being reasonable even if it is on the high side for a particular year. But in the present case we are concerned with a variable rentcharge which is measured and limited by the expenditure by Orchard in the performance of its covenants. Like the Judge I cannot see how that can be said to be unreasonable in relation to the covenant. In particular I cannot accept that the absence of an express limitation of reasonableness in the Deed renders the rentcharge void.

It may be that in any event a term of reasonableness is to be implied, as Johnson itself contends ... That does not fall for decision in the present case.'

26-40 Following *Orchard Trading*, it can be said that section 2(5) requires only that the rentcharge holder recovers the sum he actually and properly spent and nothing more. There are accordingly parallels between this decision and the approach of the court in a leasehold context to matters such as expenditure by the landlord on insurance.[40] There does not appear to be any requirement to the effect that it must be reasonable to spend money on a particular item or that money spent on a particular item must be reasonable. This is in direct contrast to the way in which section 19 of the 1985 Act has been interpreted.[41]

26-41 The Court of Appeal again considered the requirement of reasonableness imposed by section 2(5) in *Smith Brothers Arms Ltd v The Canwell Estate Co Ltd*.[42] The facts of this case are set out at **26-29** to **26-30** above. It was also argued in this case that no valid 'estate rentcharge' had been created because the sum which was sought to be recovered was not reasonable because (i) the costs did not represent costs incurred in Canwell's performance of covenants for the benefit of the defendant's land; or, in relation to those roads where it did have a right of way, (ii) it was not reasonable in relation to the performance of the covenant. In relation to this argument, Mummery LJ said:[43]

'Similarly I note that the emphasis in sub-section (5) on what represents a "reasonable" payment is not on the kind or quantum of benefit actually obtained

---

40 See, for example, *Havenridge Ltd v Boston Dyers Ltd* [1994] 2 EGLR 73 (**10-11** to **10-14** above).
41 See Chapter 29.
42 [2012] EWCA Civ 237.
43 At paras 37–39.

by the particular land owner in return for contribution to the cost of the services provided: the emphasis is on whether the payment of more than a nominal amount under the rent charge represents what is reasonable for the *performance* of the covenants by the rent owner.

The Law Commission's explanatory comment on its draft of subsection (5) is helpful:–

> "Subsection (5) is designed to ensure that the amount of any 'estate rentcharge' created in the future shall not exceed an amount reasonably necessary for the purpose for which the rentcharge is created. If the sole purpose falls within subsection (4)(a), a rentcharge of nominal amount only is required. If the rentcharge is created wholly or partly for the purpose set out in subsection (4)(b), it will fail if the amount is unreasonably large in relation to the anticipated expenditure on the part of the rent owner."

As indicated in that note and in the draftsman's careful choice of words in subsection (4)(b) and (5), it is necessary, in deciding whether the requirements for the creation of an estate rentcharge are satisfied, to consider the reasonableness of the amount of the contribution sought to be recovered from the landowner in the context of the *purpose* for which the rentcharge was created.'

26-42 Later in his judgment, Mummery LJ[44] referred to the distinction between section 2(4)(b), which defines an 'estate rentcharge' by reference to a legitimate purpose which is not caught by the general prohibition of pure income profit rentcharges, and of section 2(5), an anti-avoidance provision, not a definition section, which provides that, in the specified circumstances, a rentcharge of more than a nominal amount is 'not to be treated as' an estate rentcharge for the purposes of section 2. He then referred to *Orchard Trading* and said:[45]

> 'As was indicated in Orchard, its aim is to prevent the circumvention of the general prohibition on the creation of rentcharges for pure income profit by means of rentcharges for more than nominal amounts that are not reasonable, having regard to the rent owner's performance of the covenant.
>
> In my judgment, it does not follow that the validity of a rentcharge depends on the reasonableness of the amount calculated from time to time for the service charges. If the rent charge is created for the legitimate purpose of contributing to the cost of the performance of a covenant for the benefit of the defendant's land, it is valid from the outset once and for all and it stays valid as a registered estate rentcharge. However, at the point when the rent owner seeks to recover payment of a contribution to the costs from an owner of the land affected, the rentcharge cannot be relied on ("shall *not be treated as* a rentcharge") and "will fail" (using the words of the explanatory note of the Law Commission), if the payment sought by the rent owner against the landowner is not reasonable in relation to the performance of the covenant. In those circumstances the registered estate rentcharge does not automatically cease to be an estate rentcharge or cease to be valid: it simply becomes unavailable to the rent owner as a means of recovering a particular contribution to costs that are not reasonable in relation to the performance of the covenant.'

---

44 At paras 52 *et seq.*
45 At para 59.

Apportionment of rentcharges

26-43　Where a freehold plot which is subject to an estate rentcharge is subdivided, the rentcharge may be apportioned.[46] If the rentcharge owner consents to an agreed apportionment, then he will be bound by the apportionment and will thereafter be entitled to pursue the new owner for an apportioned part and enforce the balance of the original estate rentcharge against the property retained.[47] If the rentcharge owner has not consented, there will only be an equitable apportionment and the rent charge owner will remain free to enforce payment out of any of the property on which the rentcharge was originally imposed.

26-44　In the absence of agreement to an apportionment, the owner of land affected by a rentcharge can seek an order from the Secretary of State apportioning the rentcharge under sections 4 and 5 of the 1977 Act. Section 4 is concerned with the procedure for making an application and requires the suggested apportionment to be given to the Secretary of State.[48] Section 5 provides that, where the Secretary of State is satisfied that he is in a position to do so, a draft order for apportionment of the rentcharge will be made. This is served on the estate rentchage owner, who is entitled to make objections (usually within a period of 21 days) following which an apportionment order is made. A right of appeal to the Upper Tribunal is given by section 6 of the 1977 Act.

26-45　Sections 8 to 10 of the 1977 Act provide a mechanism for the redemption of rentcharges on payment of an equivalent capital sum to the owner of the rentcharge or into court.

ESTATE MANAGEMENT SCHEMES

26-46　When tenants have enfranchised, either pursuant to the Leasehold Reform Act 1967 or the Leasehold Reform, Housing and Urban Development Act 1993, leasehold covenants which protect the character and standards of an estate and which were formerly enforced by a common landlord may be lost. Accordingly, provision was made by section 19 of the 1967 Act and Part 1, Chapter VI of the 1993 Act for the retention of management powers of a common landlord of an estate for the common benefit of the owners and occupiers of properties within the estate. These are known as 'estate management schemes'.

26-47　No new application for a 1967 Act estate management scheme is possible after 31 July 1976 and, save in certain limited circumstances, it has

---

46　Law of Property Act 1925, s 70 provides that 'A release from a rent charge of part of the land charged therewith does not extinguish the whole rent charge, but operates only to bar the right to recover any part of the rentcharge out of the land released, without prejudice to the rights of any persons interested in the land remaining unreleased, and not concurring in or confirming the release.'

47　See also the Law of Property Act 1925, s 77, which makes provision for implied covenants where part of land affected by a rentcharge is transferred.

48　See the Rentcharges Regulations 1978 (SI 1978/16).

not been possible to make a new application for a 1993 Act estate management scheme since 1 April 1999.

26-48 For a more detailed explanation of these schemes see *Hague on Leasehold Enfranchisement.*[49]

COMMONHOLD

26-49 Part I of the Commonhold and Leasehold Reform Act 2002, which came into force on 27 September 2004, together with the Commonhold Regulations 2004[50] (as amended by the Commonhold (Amendment) Regulations 2009[51]) and the Commonhold (Land Registration) Rules 2004[52] establish a new form of land ownership in England and Wales. The commonhold scheme essentially provides for unit holders within a commonhold building or other development to be the members of a private company which will own the registered freehold estate in commonhold land of the common parts of the building or the estate. The common parts of the relevant property will be managed for the benefit of all unit holders by the commonhold association. How this is done is governed by the articles of association of the commonhold association and by the above legislation.[53]

26-50 Commonhold creates its own unique scheme and gives rise to its own set of problems. To date, very few commonhold schemes have been established and problems are not commonly encountered in practice.

49 Radevsky and Greenish (5th edn, 2009).
50 SI 2004/1829.
51 SI 2009/2363.
52 SI 2004/1830.
53 For a more detailed explanation of commonhold see Fetherstonhaugh, Sefton and Peters, *Commonhold* (2003).

PART IV

Statutory regulation of service charges

CHAPTER 27

Introduction

27-01 Almost every aspect of the recovery of service charges from residential tenants is now regulated by statute. The most important statutory provisions are found in sections 18 to 30 of the Landlord and Tenant Act 1985, but the Landlord and Tenant Act 1987 and the Commonhold and Leasehold Reform Act 2002 both contain numerous sections supplementing the core regulatory sections of the 1985 Act.

27-02 This part of the book begins by dealing with the definitions which govern the application of the statutory regulation by reference both to the types of properties and leases included and the nature of the sums which comprise service and administration charges, such as to trigger the application of the statutory regulation.[1]

27-03 The relevant statutory provisions are then dealt with under three general headings. First, consideration is given, in Chapter 29, to the provisions which regulate the substantive amount of service charges by reference to the criterion of reasonableness, principally section 19 of the 1985 Act, but also the provisions of the 2002 Act regulating administration charges, and section 20C of the 1985 Act, which governs recoverability of legal costs. The jurisdiction of the LVT to make determinations as to what service charges are payable by a tenant under section 27A of the 1985 Act is also considered in this section.

27-04 The next section considers the detailed provisions concerning the provision of information to tenants by landlords (found principally in sections 21 to 23 of the 1985 Act, but also sections 47 and 48 of the 1987 Act and in amendments introduced by the 2002 Act). These chapters cover the information which must be included in or provided with service charge demands made by landlords and the entitlement of tenants to seek further information from their landlord as to the calculation of the service charges demanded from them.[2]

---

1   Chapter 28.
2   Chapters 32 to 35.

27-05 Chapters 30 and 31 deal with what may be termed procedural requirements imposed on landlords. The most significant of these are the detailed requirements for consultation in respect of qualifying works or long-term agreements imposed by section 20 of the 1985 Act and the regulations promulgated under that section. Also considered under this heading is the 18-month time limit for service charge demands imposed by section 20B of the 1985 Act.

27-06 This part of the book concludes by considering the potential application of the Unfair Terms in Consumer Contracts Regulations 1999[3] to provisions in residential leases relating to the recovery of service charges, the statutory trust imposed upon service charge contributions by section 42 of the 1987 Act and, briefly, the detailed provisions of the Housing Act 1985 which apply in the case of public sector tenants when exercising the right to buy.

APPLICATION TO CROWN LAND

27-07 By virtue of section 172(1) of the Commonhold and Leasehold Reform Act 2002,[4] the following statutory provisions now apply to Crown land as they do to other property (including the amendments to these provisions introduced by the 2002 Act itself):

(a) sections 18 to 30B of (and the Schedule to) the Landlord and Tenant Act 1985 (service charges, insurance and managing agents),

(b) Part 2 of the Landlord and Tenant Act 1987 (appointment of manager by leasehold valuation tribunal),

(c) Part 4 of the Landlord and Tenant Act 1987 (variation of leases),

(d) sections 46 to 49 of the Landlord and Tenant Act 1987 (information to be furnished to tenants),

(e) Part 1, Chapter 5 of the Leasehold Reform, Housing and Urban Development Act 1993 (management audit),

(f) section 81 of the Housing Act 1996 (restriction on termination of tenancy for failure to pay service charge etc.),

(g) section 84 of (and Schedule 4 to) that Act (right to appoint surveyor).

27-08 By section 172(2) of the 2002 Act, land is Crown land if there is, or has at any time been, an interest or estate in the land:

(a) comprised in the Crown Estate,

---

3   SI 1999/2083.
4   In force from 30 September 2003; Commonhold and Leasehold Reform Act 2002 (Commencement No 2 and Savings) (England) Order 2003 (SI 2003/1986), art 2; Commonhold and Leasehold Reform Act 2002 (Commencement No 2 and Savings) (Wales) Order 2004 (Welsh SI 2004/669), art 2.

(b)   belonging to Her Majesty in right of the Duchy of Lancaster,

(c)   belonging to the Duchy of Cornwall, or

(d)   belonging to a government department or held on behalf of Her Majesty for the purposes of a government department.

27-09   The Crown is, however, exempted from any criminal liability for failure to comply with any duty imposed by or by virtue of any of sections 21 to 23A of, or any of paragraphs 2 to 4A of the Schedule to, the Landlord and Tenant Act 1985, although the High Court may declare any such failure without reasonable excuse to be unlawful.[5]

---

5   Commonhold and Leasehold Reform Act 2002, s 172(3).

CHAPTER 28

Application of the statutory regulations

DEFINITION OF 'SERVICE CHARGE'

28-01   The provisions contained in the Landlord and Tenant Act 1985 discussed in this chapter apply only to service charges as defined by section 18 of the Act. The principal definition is as follows:

> '"service charge" means an amount payable by a tenant of a dwelling as part of or in addition to the rent –
>
> (a)   which is payable, directly or indirectly, for services, repairs, maintenance, improvements or insurance or the landlord's costs of management, and
>
> (b)   the whole or part of which varies or may vary according to the relevant costs.'

28-02   The reference to improvements was added to the definition of a service charge by section 159 and Schedule 9, paragraph 7 of the Commonhold and Leasehold Reform Act 2002.[1] The definition is broad and will include the vast majority of the sums which a landlord might expect to incur in the course of managing a residential property.

'DWELLING'

28-03   As originally enacted, sections 18 to 30 of the Landlord and Tenant Act 1985 only applied to flats. However, section 41 of the Landlord and Tenant Act 1987 substituted the word 'dwelling' in section 18(1) of the 1985 Act. In this context, the word dwelling is defined to mean a building or part of a building occupied or intended to be occupied as a separate dwelling, together with any yard, garden, outhouses and appurtenances belonging to it or usually enjoyed

---

1   With effect in England from 30 September 2003 and in Wales from 31 March 2004. See Commonhold and Leasehold Reform Act 2002 (Commencement No 2 and Savings) (England) Order 2003 (SI 2003/1986), art 2 and Commonhold and Leasehold Reform Act 2002 (Commencement No 2 and Savings) (Wales) Order 2004 (Welsh SI 2004/669), Sch 2, para 2.

with it.[2] It is this definition which prevents the provisions of the 1985 Act from applying to leases of commercial premises.

28-04 This is a broad definition and is, therefore, capable of applying to almost all residential properties. The definition does not require that the tenant be in occupation of the premises in question and, accordingly, a tenant who has sub-let his property is not excluded from relying on the statutory regulation.[3]

Holiday homes

28-05 It seems that the definition in section 18 of the Landlord and Tenant Act 1985 applies to premises let as holiday homes, although the point is not entirely free from doubt. In *King v Udlaw*,[4] the Lands Tribunal decided that the definition in section 18 did not include bungalows on a holiday park which the tenants were not permitted under the terms of the relevant leases to use as a permanent residence. It was agreed that the bungalows possessed all the amenities necessary for residential accommodation. The President held, however, that the authorities, as to the meaning of 'dwelling' in other statutes,[5] demonstrated that 'dwelling', where it appears in legislation conferring protection on tenants, conveyed its ordinary meaning of the occupier's home, unless there was something in the context of the legislation to suggest that it should not be so limited. It was considered that there was nothing in the context of sections 18 to 30 of the Landlord and Tenant Act 1985 which would suggest that the protection should be extended to premises that are not a person's home.

28-06 Conversely, in *Phillips v Francis*,[6] HH Judge Griggs (sitting as a High Court Judge) declined to follow *King v Udlaw* and held that the definition of dwelling in the Landlord and Tenant Act 1985 did apply to holiday chalets. It was considered that the definition in section 38 of the 1985 Act did not contain any limitation to the effect that a dwelling must be the tenant's principal or main home. The rationale of the regulation of service charges in the 1985 Act was not the same as that of legislation conferring security of tenure on residential tenants. The purpose was to enable residential tenants to challenge unreasonable service charges and there was no reason to limit that purpose to premises used as a main home. Accordingly, the word dwelling in the context of the 1985 Act was held to apply to holiday lets.[7]

---

2   Landlord and Tenant Act 1985, s 38.
3   *Oakfern Properties Ltd v Ruddy* [2007] Ch 335.
4   [2008] 2 EGLR 99.
5   Primarily, *Uratemp Ventures Ltd v Collins* [2002] 1 AC 301, where the House of Lords considered the meaning of the phrase 'dwelling-house' in the Housing Act 1988, s 1(1).
6   [2010] 2 EGLR 31.
7   See also *Tingdene Holiday Parks Ltd v Cox* [2011] UKUT 310 (LC), a decision in relation to chalets which were demised as holiday homes. The LVT had decided (in earlier proceedings relating to the same site) that the Landlord and Tenant Act 1985, ss 18–30 did, indeed, apply and there was no appeal against that decision.

Leases of more than one dwelling/mixed use premises

28-07 A person may be 'the tenant of a dwelling' so that a sum payable by him is a service charge within section 18, even though his tenancy includes other property or more than one dwelling. The statutory definition does not mean 'the tenant of the dwelling and nothing else'.[8] In *Oakfern Properties Ltd v Ruddy*,[9] the Court of Appeal confirmed this interpretation of section 18. In that case, the premises in question consisted of a building which was divided into units for commercial and residential use. The upper floors of the building, which comprised 24 separate residential flats, were let on a long lease to a company, which sublet the flats to individual tenants. Under the headlease, the mesne landlord was obliged to pay the freeholder a maintenance charge, and, under the subleases, each subtenant was obliged to pay the mesne landlord one twenty-fourth of that maintenance charge. One of the subtenants applied to the LVT for a determination under section 27A of the Landlord and Tenant Act 1985, on the grounds that the maintenance charged was unreasonable. On a preliminary issue, the LVT determined that the maintenance charge was a service charge in accordance with section 18 and the sub-tenant had *locus standi* to make the application under section 27A. This was upheld on appeal to the Lands Tribunal. The Court of Appeal agreed and held that, whilst a mesne landlord who was tenant of a building comprising a number of dwellings together with common parts was not a tenant of 'a building ... occupied or intended to be occupied as a separate dwelling', he was a tenant of 'part of a building occupied or intended to be occupied as a separate dwelling' as required by section 38 of the Landlord and Tenant Act 1985. Such a person was a 'tenant of a dwelling' for the purposes of section 18(1) of the Act and an amount payable by him was a 'service charge' within the meaning of section 18(1). Accordingly, the maintenance charge levied by the freehold owner on the mesne landlord was a service charge for the purposes of section 27A.

28-08 The Court of Appeal recognised that this construction is capable of leading to anomalies (an example referred to in submissions was a shopping centre which happened to include a janitor's flat; sums payable under a headlease of the whole would be service charges within section 18). However Jonathan Parker LJ (who gave the only substantive judgment) concluded that he could 'find no satisfactory reason for construing the definition of "dwelling" in section 38 so as to exclude a tenant from the definition merely because whilst he is the tenant of a dwelling which extends only to part of a building, he is also the tenant of other parts of the building'.

28-09 The effect of the decision in *Oakfern* is that, in a situation where management of a block rests with the freehold owner, with the freeholder entitled to recover management costs under a headlease of the whole or part of the block and the headlease owner, in turn, entitled to recover a proportion of the costs from a number of sub-tenants of individual units, both the headlessee and

---

8   *Heron Maple House v Central Estates* [2002] 1 EGLR 35.
9   [2007] Ch 335.

the subtenants are entitled to challenge the sums demanded by the freeholder pursuant to sections 18 to 30 of the Landlord and Tenant Act 1985. This result is to be welcomed. The alternative would entitle the subtenants to rely on the provisions of the 1985 Act to limit the sums payable by them to the mesne landlord (even though he is not responsible for incurring the relevant costs), but the mesne landlord would remain liable to the freehold owner for the full amount claimed from him, pursuant to the terms of the headlease.

28-10 A different conclusion was reached by the LVT on the different facts of *Buckley v Bowerbeck Properties Ltd.*[10] There, the premises consisted of a ground floor with a permitted use under the lease as consulting rooms for medical or dental practitioners and a basement with a permitted use as a private residential flat. The landlord argued that the tenancy was not residential, so the premises were not a dwelling within the meaning of section 38, which, in turn, meant that the disputed charges were not service charges within the meaning of section 18(1). The LVT agreed, distinguishing *Oakfern* on the facts and holding that, given that the two parts of the premises in question were connected internally, had a common doorbell and were connected in a number of ways under the lease, such that they could not be occupied separately, then, on balance, the residential part was not separate for the purposes of section 38 and, therefore, the tenant was not a tenant of a dwelling, as required by section 18(1). *Buckley* is not, however, binding authority and may not be followed. The case appears to have turned on the somewhat unusual configuration of the premises in question. However, if applied generally, the reasoning of the tribunal would appear to lead to the surprising result that, whilst a headleasee of mainly commercial premises can rely upon the regulations in the 1985 Act if a small part of the premises comprised in the headlease is residential (provided the residential part is sufficiently separate), the tenant of a house, only a part of which is used for business purposes, cannot.

RELEVANT COSTS

28-11 A sum due under a lease is only a service charge within section 18 if the whole or part of it varies or may vary according to the relevant costs. The relevant costs are the costs or estimated costs incurred or to be incurred by or on behalf of the landlord, or a superior landlord, in connection with the matters for which the service charge is payable.[11] It follows from this that any sum, the amount of which is fixed by the terms of the lease without reference to actual costs incurred by a landlord, is not a service charge within section 18,[12] although it may now be an administration charge within Schedule 11, paragraph 1(3) of the Commonhold and Leasehold Reform Act 2002.[13]

10 [2009] 1 EGLR 43.
11 Section 18(2).
12 *Coventry City Council v Cole* [1994] 1 WLR 398, decided under the materially identical definition of service charges contained in the Housing Act 1985, s 621A.
13 See **29-53** to **29-57** below.

28-12   Given the variety of potential mechanisms via which leases can provide for the recovery of expenditure on the part of a landlord, the requirement of variability consequent on actual or estimated expenditure can raise difficult questions of construction. It is sufficient for the purposes of the section 18 definition that part of the sum said to constitute services charges varies in accordance with expenditure. Thus in *Longmint v Marcus*,[14] it was held that management fees calculated as 15% of the management expenditure were service charges, because they varied in accordance with relevant costs, even though the percentage was fixed by the lease.

28-13   On the other hand, sums which are fixed by the lease cannot be service charges within section 18, even if those sums are intended to and do reflect a proportion of the actual management costs. So, in *Home Group v Lewis*,[15] a number of tenants under agreements described as assured non-shorthold tenancies were obliged to pay to the landlord a fixed monthly sum described as a service charge. The landlord was expressly required to provide services and the agreement made provision for the landlord to increase the rent and service charge after the first year of the term. The landlord served notices each year, increasing the sums payable by the tenant,[16] and the service charge element was calculated by estimating the costs of providing the services for the forthcoming service charge year, including a management fee. Once fixed, the service charge was not varied during the course of the year, depending on the money actually expended. It was held that the service charge element of the rent did not fall within section 18 because there was no link in the terms of the agreement between the expenditure of the landlord and the amount of the service charge. Although the landlord took into account his anticipated expenditure in calculating the proposed service charge, there was nothing in the agreement which dictated this. Accordingly the level of the service charge was a result of a decision of the landlord and not directly linked to the level of expenditure.[17]

28-14   Similarly in *Minister Chalets v Irwin Park Residents Association*,[18] leases of chalets on a holiday park provided for the payment of a fixed site fee by the tenant. The fee could, however, be increased by notice given by the landlord to include an additional amount to be 'determined (in default of agreement) from time to time by the Landlord's valuer (whose opinion shall be final and absolutely binding on the Tenant) as ... shall amount to the fair site fees value of the ... Site'. The landlord was under an obligation to maintain the estate. When the chalets were sold on long leases, interested parties were given documents

14   [2004] 3 EGLR 171.
15   [2008] EWLands LRX_176_2006, HH Judge Huskinson.
16   In accordance with the applicable provisions for increase of rent in the Housing Act 1988.
17   See also *Chand v Calmore Area Housing Association Ltd* [2008] EWLands LRX_170_2007 and *Arnold v Britton* [2012] EWHC 3451 (Ch). The latter case turned on the proper construction of ambiguous provisions relating to a tenant's obligation to pay a sum in respect of services. Having concluded that, correctly construed, the leases in question provided for payment of a fixed annual sum of £90, Morgan J went on to conclude that the sum was not, therefore, a service charge within s 18. Permission to appeal against the decision of Morgan J has been granted by the Court of Appeal but, at the time of writing, the appeal has not been heard.
18   [2001] EWLands LRX_28_2000.

which stated that 'an annual charge is raised for the general upkeep of the park and services supplied' and made reference to additional charges in respect of insurance and water and sewage costs. Site fees, insurance and water rates were billed to tenants annually and increased each year. It was held that the site fees were not service charges within section 18 because there was nothing in the lease itself to suggest that site fees were related to the cost of services or that any increase in site fees is payable according to any increase in such cost. It is not sufficient for the purposes of section 18 that charges should be payable for services. It is necessary also that those charges should vary according to the costs incurred in providing the services.

28-15   The sometimes fine distinction between sums which are not directly referable to landlord's expenditure (as in *Home Group v Lewis*) and those which are and, as a result, are subject to the whole panoply of the regulations discussed below is well illustrated by *Re Southern Housing Group*.[19] This case concerned two tenancy agreements, one assured and one assured shorthold, which both made provision for the recovery of a service charge. The agreements specified a figure for the service charge, but also, unlike in *Home Group v Lewis,* set out, by reference to a number of schedules, the proportion of the service charge attributable to the services provided by the landlord. The landlord was entitled to vary the service charge calculation by serving notice. The President of the Upper Tribunal (Lands Chamber) held that the sums were within section 18. He explained that:[20]

> 'The difference between the provisions of the tenancy agreements in *Home Group and Chand v Calmore Area Housing Ltd* and those of the leases in the present cases is that in the former there was nothing in the agreements indicating that any altered rent was to be calculated in any particular manner, or linking an alteration in rent (including service charge) with an alteration in the costs of providing any relevant services; whereas in each of the present cases there is provision enabling the landlord to vary the service charge but imposing a limit to any increase by reference to the costs of providing the services.'

28-16   It is not a legitimate approach, however, to break down a service charge reserved by a lease into its component parts and assess whether each of the elements of the total charge is itself a service charge. Therefore, the LVT had jurisdiction to consider whether the rent payable by a management company pursuant to a lease of the common parts of a development was payable under section 27A because it comprised part of a service charge within section 18. The common parts rent, though itself a fixed annual sum, was a part of the expenditure incurred by the management company in providing the relevant services and it was sufficient for the purposes of section 18 that the total sum varied according to the relevant costs.[21]

---

19   [2011] L&TR 7.
20   At para 17.
21   *Warwickshire Hamlets Ltd v Gedden* [2010] UKUT 75.

28-17   In an important decision,[22] the Court of Appeal has determined that sums charged to tenants in their capacity as shareholders of a management company do not fall within the definition in section 18 and are accordingly exempt from the requirements of the Landlord and Tenant Act 1985. In that case, the freehold of a block of 104 flats was owned by a company incorporated with the express purpose of owning and managing the block. Each of the flats was let on a long lease containing provisions for the recovery of service charges from the tenant and each tenant was a shareholder in the freehold company. Under its articles of association, the company was entitled to require its members to contribute to its reserves and funds at such time, in such amounts and in such manner as the members approved by ordinary resolution passed in general meeting from time to time. Over the years the company established several funds by seeking contributions from its members under this provision. The funds were used to pay for legal costs but also to maintain and repair the block. One of the tenant shareholders refused to pay a contribution claimed under the articles of association and sought to defend a claim brought against him by relying upon his rights under the Landlord and Tenant Act 1985. His defence was dismissed and the Court of Appeal rejected his appeal because of:

> 'the crucial legal distinction between the liability of a tenant to the landlord under a lease containing service charge provisions, and the liability of the member of a company, in which all the tenants are shareholders, to the company under separate contracts made in and pursuant to the Articles to establish and recover contributions to a Recovery Fund. The two kinds of legal relationship can co-exist between the same parties, but they are different relationships incurred in different capacities and they give rise to different enforceable legal obligations. A defence to one of the claims is not necessarily available as a defence to the other legally separate claim.'[23]

28-18   It followed that the sum demanded from the tenant in his capacity as shareholder was not a service charge within section 18. The Court of Appeal expressly left open the question of whether the company was entitled to apply the sums claimed as a contribution from its shareholders to sums said to be due under the lease by way of service charges.

28-19   An ever increasing number of freehold and management companies are comprised of tenant shareholders, a trend which is encouraged by the right to manage legislation pursuant to which tenants can form a company to acquire the right to manage their block. It would be unfortunate if the detailed requirements of the Landlord and Tenant Act 1985 could be circumvented simply by issuing demands for contributions from tenant shareholders under the articles of association, although whether this is possible in any particular case will turn on the provisions of a company's articles and memorandum of association. It is possible that the danger is more apparent than real, because any abuses could be prevented by majority control by the shareholder tenants.

---

22   *Morshead Mansions Ltd v Di Marco* [2008] EWCA Civ 1371.
23   *Per* Mummery LJ at para 30.

28-20   The decision in *Morshead* provides a mechanism by which landlord companies comprised of tenant shareholders might avoid the consequences of a failure to comply with the statutory regulation. As will be seen,[24] the tribunals and courts have adopted a rigorous approach to, for example, compliance with the consultation requirements imposed by section 20 of the Landlord and Tenant Act 1985. If a landlord failed to consult on a major works project with the result that the tenants contribution is capped, a levy on shareholders may be the only route by which the landlord can avoid insolvency, since a landlord in this position is unlikely to have any source of income other than service charge contributions. Nevertheless, demanding the sums from the lessees in their alternative capacity as shareholders would, on the face of it, enable a landlord to disregard wholesale the valuable statutory protection conferred on tenants by the provisions discussed in this chapter. That said, if the directors engaged in a general practice of issuing demands to lessee shareholders with the intention of avoiding statutory regulation, they may well be susceptible to being removed from office (by an appropriate majority of the shareholders) or to other company law remedies, full consideration of which is outside of the scope of this work.

OVERHEADS

28-21   The definition of relevant costs includes anticipated future expenditure and expenditure incurred by a superior landlord (where relevant).[25] By section 18(3)(a), it is stated that 'costs includes overheads'. The word 'overheads' is not defined and does not appear anywhere else in the Landlord and Tenant Act 1985. Accordingly, the intended effect of this provision is unclear, but it is thought that it may have been included to establish that any charges levied by a landlord in respect of his own time spent on managing the property are regulated by the 1985 Act, even though they do not represent actual expenditure incurred.

28-22   The Court of Appeal has held that where a lease permits the recovery by the landlord of management costs, the landlord is entitled to include in the service charge the costs of employing a managing agent which is a company owned by the landlord provided the arrangement was not 'a complete sham'.[26] The sums charged in relation to the managing agent, however, will be subject to the requirement that they are 'reasonably incurred' and that the service is provided to a 'reasonable standard' imposed by section 19 of the Landlord and Tenant Act 1985.[27]

---

24   See Chapter 30.
25   Section 18(2).
26   *Skilleter v Charles* (1992) 24 HLR 421, applied in *Country Trade Ltd v Noakes* [2011] UKUT 407 (LC), HH Judge Gerald. See **8-08** to **8-10** above.
27   See **29-04** to **29-17** below.

LANDLORD

28-23   By section 30, 'landlord' includes any person who has a right to enforce payment of a service charge. This definition makes it clear that a management company (which does not hold any interest in the reversion) is caught by the definition where it is given responsibility for providing the services and the corresponding right to claim payment under the terms of the lease in question. It is clear that, in appropriate circumstances, both the freehold owner and a management company can fulfil the definition of landlord in section 30 where both are entitled to enforce payment of a sum which is a service charge under section 18.[28]

TENANT

28-24   Section 18 only applies to a sum payable by a tenant and, accordingly, a licensee is not entitled to take advantage of the protection conferred by the Landlord and Tenant Act 1985. No general definition of tenant is provided by the 1985 Act and, therefore, general common law principles will apply in assessing whether a landlord and tenant relationship exists. However, the word 'tenant' in the 1985 Act is expressly defined to include a statutory tenant and, where the dwelling or part of it is sublet, the subtenant.[29] Furthermore, the entitlement to apply for a determination as to whether a service charge is payable extends to a tenant who has assigned the lease, but who remains contractually liable to pay the service charge for the period of his interest in the lease.[30]

GENERAL EXCEPTIONS

28-25   By section 26, sections 18 to 25 do not apply to a service charge payable by a tenant of a local authority, a National Park authority, or a new town corporation, unless the tenancy is a long tenancy,[31] in which case sections 18 to 24 apply, but section 25 (offence of failure to comply[32]) does not. Furthermore, the same provisions do not apply to a service charge payable by the tenant of a dwelling, the rent of which is registered under Part IV of the Rent Act 1977, unless the amount registered is entered as a variable amount in accordance with section 71(4) of that Act.

---

28   *Cinnamon Ltd v Morgan* [2001] EWCA Civ 1616, per Chadwick LJ considering the *obiter* remarks of Beldam LJ in *Berrycroft Management Co Ltd v Sinclair Garden Investments (Kensington) Ltd* [1997] 1 EGLR 47.
29   Section 30.
30   *Re Sarum Properties Ltd's Application* [1999] 2 EGLR 131.
31   For these purposes, a long tenancy is a tenancy of a type specified in s 26(2), most notably any tenancy for a term certain exceeding 21 years.
32   See **33-25** to **33-32** below.

CHAPTER 29

Substantive limitations on residential service charges

THE REQUIREMENT OF REASONABLENESS: SECTION 19 OF THE LANDLORD AND TENANT ACT 1985

29-01   The single most important limitation on residential service charges is the overriding requirement provided by section 19 which states:

'(1)   Relevant costs shall be taken into account in determining the amount of a service charge payable for a period –

(a)   only to the extent that they are reasonably incurred, and

(b)   where they are incurred on the provisions of services or the carrying out of works, only if the services or works are of a reasonable standard;

and the amount payable shall be limited accordingly.'[1]

29-02   The Landlord and Tenant Act 1985 does not attempt to provide any general definition of the concept of reasonableness and, given the variety of situations and types of costs to which the test applies, it is inevitably a flexible concept. However, the case law demonstrates that a number of significant principles have developed in the application of the test.

29-03   The reasonableness test under section 19(1) has two distinct elements. First, the costs must be reasonably incurred. Secondly, the services or works in respect of which the costs are incurred must be of a reasonable standard.

Reasonably incurred

29-04   Under the first limb, the question is not whether the costs are 'reasonable' but whether they were 'reasonably incurred'. This involves consideration of two separate matters:[2]

---

1   For the meaning of 'relevant costs' and other terms used in section 19, see Chapter 28 above.
2   *Forcelux Ltd v Sweetman* [2001] 2 EGLR 173, *per* Mr PR Francis FRICS at para 40.

'First, the evidence, and from that whether the landlord's actions were appropriate and properly effected in accordance with the requirements of the lease, the RICS Code and the 1985 Act. Second, whether the amount charged was reasonable in the light of that evidence. This second point is particularly important as, if that did not have to be considered, it would be open to any landlord to plead justification for any particular figure, on the grounds that the steps it took justified the expense, without properly testing the market ... [the term] "reasonably incurred" ... cannot be a licence to charge a figure that is out of line with the market norm.'

29-05 It follows that a landlord must be able to justify both the *decision* to incur the costs in issue as being reasonable in the circumstances and also that the *amount* of costs actually incurred were reasonable, bearing in mind any available evidence as to the market price for the work which was done. In *Forcelux*, therefore, the Lands Tribunal determined that, whilst the landlord's 'policies and procedures for appointing contractors' to carry out internal redecoration could not be criticised, the costs incurred in carrying out the work were in excess of the appropriate market rate and, therefore, unreasonable under section 19.

29-06 The two-stage approach to a determination as to whether costs were reasonably incurred was also employed in *Veena SA v Cheong*.[3] In that case, the Lands Tribunal had to consider, amongst other things, an appeal against a determination by the LVT that the costs of employing a full-time porter at a Mayfair property containing seven flats were unreasonable. The Tribunal[4] explained the approach as follows:

'The question is not solely whether costs are "reasonable" but whether they were "reasonably incurred", that is to say whether the action taken in incurring the costs and the amount of those costs were both reasonable. The question in this part of the appeal is whether [the landlord] acted reasonably in employing a full-time porter and a part-time cleaner and, if so, whether the amounts charged for those services were reasonable. Both parts of the question must be answered affirmatively for [the landlord] to succeed.'

29-07 The Tribunal went on to hold that the landlord had not acted reasonably in employing a full-time porter and a part-time cleaner, because a part-time cleaner would have provided an adequate service at a cheaper cost to the tenants. It is also clear from this decision that the fact that a particular service is contemplated by the terms of the lease does not automatically make it a reasonable decision to incur costs in respect of that item.

29-08 Sometimes, however, it will prove difficult to separate the reasonableness of the decision to carry out works from the reasonableness of the cost of the works, since the landlord's decision-making process will be closely tied to the overall cost of the project. This is well illustrated by *Wandsworth LBC v Griffin*.[5] In that case, the landlord council replaced the flat roof of a block of flats with

---

3   [2003] 1 EGLR 175.
4   PH Clarke FRICS.
5   [2000] 2 EGLR 106.

a pitched roof and metal-framed windows with uPVC double-glazed units. In deciding to carry out the replacements rather than short term repairs, the council relied on cost-in-use calculations ('CIU') that indicated that the replacement works offered better value for money over the life of the buildings, assumed to be 60 years. The council then sought to recover the costs of doing so from its tenants, two of whom applied to the LVT. The tenants argued that it was not disputed that repairs would have been sufficient to make good the windows and roof for at least 14 years and that it was unreasonable for the council to base its decisions on calculations over a period of 40 years or more. The LVT decided that the decision to carry out the works was unreasonable and that accordingly the costs were not reasonably incurred in accordance with section 19. The council appealed and the Lands Tribunal allowed the appeal, finding that the use of the CIU was a legitimate tool when considering which alternative method of repair was appropriate. The question for the tribunal was whether the landlord had prepared the CIU in a reasonable manner by employing long-term assumptions as to the cost effectiveness of the replacements. The tribunal considered that the council had acted reasonably:

> 'The disputed costs were incurred by the [landlord] in their capacity as local authority landlords of block 7, which forms part of an estate, constructed as a single estate, and managed as such ever since. The [tenants'] lease requires them to pay only a small proportion of the [landlord's] expenditure on one of the blocks on that estate. Against that background, it is, in my opinion, entirely artificial to suggest that, in deciding whether elements of such expenditure were reasonably incurred, no account is to be taken of the interests of either the … landlords or of the other residents in the estate.'

29-09   Although the cases of *Veena SA v Cheong* (full-time porter) and *Wandsworth v Griffin* (replacement of roof and windows) deal with very different subject matter, the principle which emerges is that a landlord, whilst not obliged to adopt the cheapest method of providing a service, is not unfettered in his choice of alternative methods. The criterion of reasonableness requires consideration of whether a cheaper method of providing the service would have been sufficiently adequate for the needs of the tenant for whose benefit the service is provided, such that the additional cost is objectively reasonable. It may also be a relevant consideration in assessing whether the method of providing the service is reasonable, whether the landlord would have chosen the method adopted if he were to bear the costs himself.[6]

29-10   It follows that a landlord is not obliged to adopt the cheapest method of repair, provided that a more expensive scheme is, viewed objectively, reasonable and, furthermore, that a landlord may take its own interests into account in

---

6   *Hyde Housing Association Ltd v Williams* [2000] EWLands LRX_53_1999) and see also *Scottish Mutual Assurance Plc v Jardine Public Relations* [1999] EWHC 276 (TCC), a case relating to commercial premises, but where the wording of a lease entitling the landlord to recover as service charges sums which were reasonably and properly incurred. The duration of the remaining term of the tenant's lease was relevant in considering whether it was reasonable to require the tenant to contribute to long term repairs as opposed to short-term patch repairs. See **4-17** to **4-27** above.

making decisions as to the appropriate method of performing its obligations under the lease. If, however, the works could have been carried out at the cost of a third party and, therefore, at no cost to the tenants, it would be unreasonable for the landlord to have incurred the costs.[7] On the other hand, the fact that funding for the works has been provided by a third party will not necessarily mean that recovery from the tenants is unreasonable. The question of whether possible third-party funding means that any expenditure on the part of the landlord has been unreasonably incurred will depend on whether, on a proper analysis of the funding arrangement, recovery from the tenants would amount to 'double recovery' of the landlord's expenditure.[8]

29-11 It would seem that any professional advice received by a landlord in deciding to incur costs will be relevant in assessing the reasonableness of the decision. In *Fernandez v Shanterton Second Management Co Ltd*,[9] it was held that it would have been reasonable for a landlord to incur costs in pursuing a claim for arrears of service charge if the legal advice received had been in favour of that course, even if the advice turned out to be incorrect.

29-12 A related issue is whether the LVT has jurisdiction to consider whether a landlord has acted reasonably in deciding to carry out a major programme of works, rather than phasing the works over a period of time so as to spread the cost to the tenants. In *Garside v RYFC Ltd*,[10] the Upper Tribunal concluded that the consideration of whether costs were reasonably incurred under section 19(1) could include whether or not it was reasonable for the landlord to decide to carry out all of the necessary works at the same time. In that case, it was accepted by the tenants that the work was necessary and the cost of the work was reasonable. However, it was argued that the issue as to when the works were carried out fell within the first limb of the test identified in *Forcelux* and *Veena*. The Upper Tribunal agreed saying:

> 'there is nothing in the 1985 Act to limit the ambit of what is reasonable in this context so as to exclude considerations of financial impact. In my judgment, giving the expression "reasonable" a broad, common sense meaning in accordance with [*Ashworth Frazer Ltd v Gloucester City Council* [2001] 1 WLR 2180], the financial impact of major works on lessees through service charges and whether as a consequence works should be phased is capable of being a material consideration when considering whether the costs are reasonably incurred for the purpose of section 19(1)(a).'[11]

29-13 This decision sits uneasily with the earlier decisions of the Lands Tribunal in *Southend-on-Sea Borough Council v Skiggs*.[12] In that case, the landlord successfully appealed a decision of the LVT which laid down a timetable

---

7   *Continental Property Ventures Inc v White* [2006] 1 EGLR 85.
8   *Craighead v Homes for Islington Ltd* [2010] UKUT 47.
9   [2007] EWLands LRX_153_2006.
10 [2011] UKUT 367.
11 Per HH Judge Alice Robinson at para 14.
12 [2006] EWLands LRX_110_2005.

for payments to be made by tenants. The Lands Tribunal held, it is considered correctly, that neither section 27A nor section 19 conferred any jurisdiction on the LVT to defer payment of service charges found to be payable, on the grounds of hardship on the part of the tenants or otherwise. To a similar effect is the decision in *Parker v Parham.*[13]

29-14   *Southend v Skiggs* was cited to the Upper Tribunal in *Garside* but was distinguished on the following basis:[14]

> 'It is important to make clear that liability to pay service charges cannot be avoided simply on the grounds of hardship, even if extreme. If repair work is reasonably required at a particular time, carried out at a reasonable cost and to a reasonable standard and the cost of it is recoverable pursuant to the relevant lease then the lessee cannot escape liability to pay by pleading poverty. As the Lands Tribunal made clear in *Southend-on-Sea Borough Council v Skiggs* LRX/110/2005 (a decision on section 27A of the 1985 Act), the LVT cannot alter a tenant's contractual liability to pay. That is a different matter from deciding whether a decision to carry out works and charge for them in a particular service charge year rather than to spread the cost over several years is a reasonable decision and thus the costs reasonably incurred for the purpose of section 19(1)(a) of the 1985 Act.'

29-15   There is a very fine distinction between the LVT determining, on the one hand, that a service charge is payable, but nevertheless purporting to delay time for payment by the tenant[15] and, on the other hand, a decision that it was unreasonable for the landlord to take a decision to carry out a major works project without spreading the cost (as in *Garside*). However, it appears that the LVT is entitled to scrutinise the reasonableness of the decision of the landlord not to phase works so as to spread the cost, but, if satisfied that the costs were reasonably incurred, the LVT has no jurisdiction to extend time for payment, but is bound by the provisions in the lease. The effect of *Garside,* however, would appear to be that section 19(1) can, in appropriate circumstances, be relied upon to oblige a landlord to phase a major programme of works so as to spread the cost to the tenants. In practical terms, it is difficult to see a meaningful distinction between this result and the discretion to extend time for payment on the basis of financial hardship said to be illegitimate in both *Skiggs* and *Garside*.

29-16   As noted above, it was held in *Garside* that financial hardship caused to tenants was a relevant factor in considering the reasonableness of the landlord's decision to incur all of the costs at the same time. It is to be hoped that this approach will be limited to cases of one-off major works causing a significant increase in service charge liability since, otherwise, every decision of a landlord to incur costs in providing services could be open to scrutiny on the grounds of the ability of the tenants to pay for the service. If it is unreasonable for a landlord not to phase a scheme of works on the basis that this will cause financial hardship to the tenants, it is difficult to resist the conclusion that the considerations of

13 [2003] EWLands LRX_35_2002, a case decided under the now repealed s 19(2B).
14 [2011] UKUT 367 at para 20.
15 As per the LVT decision in *Skiggs*, which was reversed by the Lands Tribunal.

financial hardship should not also be relevant to the reasonableness of decisions to provide other services. That would seem to be an unwarranted extension of the limitation that costs must be 'reasonably incurred' imposed by section 19(1). It must always be kept in mind that if a landlord decided not to carry out works or provide other services on the grounds that some of his tenants could not afford to pay for them, he may well thereby be in breach of covenants in the lease which require him to provide that service or do those works actionable at the suit of other tenants who can afford to pay.

29-17   It is, however, clearly established that whether or not a tenant will benefit directly from the services or works in question is irrelevant, provided that he is obliged to pay for them under his lease.[16]

Relevance of the RICS Residential Code

29-18   The RICS has published a 'Service Charge Residential Management Code'. The 2nd Edition of the Code, effective from 6 April 2009, has been approved by the Secretary of State under section 87 of the Leasehold Reform, Housing and Urban Development Act 1993 and sets out very helpful guidance as to best practice for landlords and managing agents of residential properties.[17] The Residential Code is not, in any sense, formally incorporated into the Landlord and Tenant Act 1985 and a failure on the part of a landlord to comply with the code in any material respect should not automatically lead to the conclusion that costs have been 'unreasonably incurred'. Nevertheless, the Residential Code is frequently referred to in practice and may be relied upon by the LVT or Upper Tribunal as part of the assessment as to whether or not a landlord has acted reasonably in incurring costs.[18]

Burden of proof under section 19

29-19   There is no operative presumption either way as to whether or not a claimed sum is reasonable.[19] However, issues sometimes arise as to where the burden of proof lies in establishing the reasonableness of a sum claimed. Tenants often seek to argue that a sum claimed is 'too high', bearing in mind the work which it represents. The LVT will have difficulty in assessing such claims in the absence of comparative evidence as to what a market rate for the same quality of works might have been. In *Schilling v Canary Riverside Development Ptd Ltd*,[20] HH Judge Rich QC said of the burden of proof under section 19:

---

16   *Billson v Tristrem* [2000] L&TR 220.
17   See **1-17**ff. above.
18   See, for example, *Forcelux v Sweetman*, [2001] 2 EGLR 173 at 177A; *Wilkins v Forestcliff Management Ltd* (LVT/SC1007/002/00); *Jones v Vigilcivil Ltd* (LVT/SC/007/124/01).
19   *Yorkbrook Investments v Batten* (1986) 52 P&CR 51; *Regent Management Ltd v Jones* [2010] UKUT 369 (LC).
20   [2005] EWLands LRX_26_2005 at para 15.

'If the landlord is seeking a declaration that a service charge is payable he must show not only that the cost was incurred but also that it was reasonably incurred to provide services or works of a reasonable standard, and if the tenant seeks a declaration to the opposite effect, he must show that either the cost or the standard was unreasonable.'

29-20 The LVT is not, however, obliged to simply accept the landlord's case if the tenant fails to adduce any proper evidence as to reasonableness. In *Country Trade Ltd v Marcus Noakes*,[21] the Upper Tribunal provided some helpful guidance as to how the LVT should approach these issues:[22]

'It is not ... the effect of the ... authorities that the LVT must accept the evidence of the landlord without deduction if there is no countervailing evidence from the tenant. The evidence required in these types of service charge disputes is quite different from the sort of complex largely non-factual evidence and issues addressed in [other areas].

The LVT does not have to suspend judgment or belief and simply accept the landlord's evidence. It is entitled to robustly scrutinise the evidence adduced by the landlord (and, of course, the tenant) which, after examination, it is entitled to accept or reject on grounds of credibility. The course of scrutiny is not just looking through the invoices or other documents, but identifying issues of concern and asking the landlord's (or tenant's) witnesses for explanations and observations. It is not necessary for each and every invoice to be minutely examined, but sufficient for them to be dealt with on a sample basis. It is only once this process has been gone through that the LVT will be able to reach any decision on the credibility of witnesses which will be based on the answers given and any other available evidence.

...

[T]he LVT is entitled to apply a robust, common sense approach and make appropriate deductions based on the available evidence (such as it is) from the amounts claimed always bearing in mind that it must explain its reasons for doing so. The circumstances in which it may do so will depend on the nature of the issues raised and service charge items in dispute, and will always be a question of fact and degree. In some instances, such as insurance premiums, it will be very difficult for the LVT to disallow the landlord's claim in the absence of any comparative or market evidence to the contrary. In other cases, such as gardening, cleaning or such like, the position might be different where the nature and complexity of the work is fairly straightforward. It is only where the issue is finely balanced that resort need be had to the burden of proof.'

29-21 However, whilst the LVT, as a specialist tribunal, is entitled to use its own knowledge and experience to test the evidence before it, there are limits to this principle. As the Lands Tribunal explained in *Arrowdell Ltd v Coniston Court (North) Hove Ltd*:[23]

21 [2011] UKUT 407 (LC).
22 Per HH Judge Gerald at paras 14–17.
23 [2007] RVR 39. See also *A2 Housing Group v Taylor* [2007] EWLands LRX_36_2006.

'there are three inescapable requirements. Firstly, as a tribunal deciding issues between the parties, it must reach its decision on the basis of evidence that is before it. Secondly, it must not reach a conclusion on the basis of evidence that has not been exposed to the parties for comment. Thirdly, it must give reasons for its decision.'

29-22   It follows that there is no general principle that, in order successfully to challenge the reasonableness of service charges, a tenant must always adduce evidence that the same works or service was not at a market rate. However, a tenant is still well advised to provide comparative market evidence, where available, to rebut the landlord's case as to the reasonableness of the sums claimed. This is particularly so given that the burden of proof in establishing that costs were unreasonably incurred will often rest with the tenant.

Evidence of market level of costs

29-23   If tenants seek to adduce evidence that the same services could have been provided at a lower cost, care must be taken to ensure that any comparables relied on by the tenants are on a like for like basis.[24] Where a landlord had, for reasons accepted as legitimate by the LVT, chosen to provide all services via a single provider across its portfolio of properties, it was irrelevant that the tenants might have been able to provide some of those services at a cheaper rate.[25] A landlord is entitled to take into account its own interest in dealing with a single contractor, providing the cost to the tenant is not out of line with market norms. In *A2 Housing Group v Taylor*,[26] it was said:

> 'In considering whether the amount charged for the single contract was reasonable it is necessary to ensure that the market has been properly tested. In my judgment that market is defined by reference to the suppliers capable of complying with the specification for a single contract for all of the appellant's estates and not by reference to the suppliers of individual services to individual estates. The two markets are not the same and the LVT was not comparing like with like when it said that the tender for the single contract should not be out of line with the market for local suppliers. In my opinion the appellant properly tested the market for a single contract. It appointed independent advisers to help prepare the specification and tender, it invited ten contractors to bid, it received two compliant bids and negotiated with the successful bidder to amend the specification and to achieve an overall reduction in cost of more than 50 per cent.

> I conclude that the charges under the single contract with ISS were reasonably incurred for the purposes of section 19(1) of the Landlord and Tenant Act 1985.'

---

24 See *Forcelux v Sweetman* [2001] 2 EGLR 173 at p 177C–D; *A2 Housing Group v Taylor* [2007] EWLands LRX_36_2006.
25 *A2 Housing Group v Taylor* [2007] EWLands LRX_36_2006.
26 *Ibid.*

Impact of historic neglect on the part of the landlord

29-24   Tenants frequently argue that works to their building are only necessary (or that the costs of the necessary works has increased) due to historic neglect on the part of their landlord in failing to carry out works earlier, to a proper standard or at all. This argument has been summarised as the principle that:

> 'A stitch in time ... can save nine; the landlord can, as it were, recover the cost of the timely one stitch but, if he fails to make that one stitch, he cannot later pass on the cost of the nine which would have become necessary'.[27]

29-25   In *Wandsworth v Griffin*,[28] it was said that, to the extent that costs are incurred as a result of past neglect on the part of the landlord, they cannot be said to be 'reasonably incurred' under section 19.

29-26   This approach has now, however, been rejected. In *Continental Property Ventures Inc v White*,[29] the President of the Lands Tribunal accepted that the reasoning employed in *Griffin* had 'superficial attractiveness' but continued:[30]

> 'the "relevant costs" that, by section 19(1)(a), are limited to what is "reasonably incurred" are defined by s. 18(2) as the "costs ... incurred ... by the landlord ... in connection with the matters for which the service charge is payable". Those matters include "repairs maintenance etc". The question of what the costs of repairs is does not depend upon whether the repairs ought to have been allowed to accrue. The reasonableness of incurring costs for their remedy cannot, as a matter of natural meaning, depend upon how the need for remedy arose.'

29-27   It is submitted that this reasoning is correct as a matter of the interpretation of the relevant sections, but also for policy reasons. The approach adopted in *Griffin*, taken to its logical conclusion, would mean that a new landlord might, through no fault of his own, be debarred from recovering the costs incurred in remedying defects arising due to neglect on the part of his predecessor in title.

29-28   Accordingly, historic neglect has no bearing on the question of reasonableness under section 19. That does not mean, however, that it is irrelevant in deciding what is 'payable' by the tenant in an application brought under section 27A. This is because neglect by a landlord in providing services will often amount to a breach of the landlord's covenants under the relevant lease. In such cases, the tenant might well have a claim for damages for breach of covenant which, in appropriate circumstances, could include the amount by which his future service charge liability is increased as a result of the breach, as well as any other foreseeable loss. Under section 27A, the LVT has jurisdiction to consider any right on the part of the tenant to set off such a claim for damages

---

27   *Loria v Hammer* [1989] 2 EGLR 249 at p 258F, *per* Mr John Lindsay QC sitting as a Deputy Judge of the High Court, Chancery Division.
28   [2000] 2 EGLR 106 at p 110G.
29   [2007] L&TR 4.
30   At para 11.

against his service charge liability.[31] Accordingly, the LVT will be entitled to consider whether costs are payable by the tenant in view of any claim he may have to set off against those costs a claim for damages for breach of covenant by the landlord. As HH Judge Rich QC (sitting in the Lands Tribunal) explained in *Continental v White*:[32]

> 'there can be no doubt that breach of the landlord's covenant to repair would give rise to a claim in damages. If the breach were to result in further disrepair, imposing a liability upon the lessee to pay service charge, that is part of what may be claimed by way of damages. At least to the extent that it would, as was held by the Court of Appeal in *Filross Securities Ltd v Midegely* (Peter Gibson, Aldhous and Potter LJJ, 21 July 1998), give rise to an equitable set-off within the rules laid down in *Hanak v Green* [1958] 2 Q.B. 9 and, as such, constitute a defence. This would not mean that the costs incurred for the "nine stitches" had not been reasonably incurred. It would, however, mean that there would be a defence to their recovery. What the LVT was engaged upon was determining whether these costs were "payable" within the meaning of section 27A. They held that they were not, because they had not been reasonably incurred. That, in my judgment, was a mistaken reason. But the conclusion at which they arrived, upon their findings of fact, was none the less correct'.

29-29 In many cases, the distinction between historic neglect, on the one hand, meaning costs were not reasonably incurred and, on the other, that the tenant has an equitable set-off against the sums claimed, will make little difference in practice. The difference will, however, be significant, where the breach of covenant was committed by a predecessor in title to the landlord seeking to recover the costs of remedial work since the tenants' claim for damages would lie against the landlord who failed to act in breach of covenant and will not, therefore, amount to a reason why the costs claimed are not 'payable' within section 27A.[33]

Apportionment/allocation of costs

29-30 The question of apportionment of service charge costs between tenants has been considered in detail above.[34] However, it is necessary to consider whether a residential tenant is entitled to challenge a landlord's apportionment of relevant costs as being unreasonable under section 19. The authorities suggest that this is not permissible since questions of apportionment of costs do not involve consideration of whether costs are 'reasonably incurred'.

29-31 In *Schilling v Canary Riverside*,[35] the tenants' lease obliged them to pay a fixed percentage of an estate charge and a different fixed percentage of a car

---

31 See further **42-02** to **42-12** above as to the LVT's jurisdiction to consider set-off claims under s 27A.
32 [2007] L&TR 4 at para 14.
33 See *Edlington Properties Ltd v Fenner* [2006] 1 WLR 1583.
34 See Chapter 21.
35 [2005] EWLands LRX_26_2005.

park charge. The tenants considered that the allocation of relevant costs to the two charges by the landlord was unfair and sought to challenge this under section 19. The Lands Tribunal found that section 19 did not extend to such matters saying:[36]

> 'Any submission which [counsel for the tenants] could make depended upon construing the limitation of recoverable service charges under s.19(1)(a) of the Act of 1985 as requiring a reasonable apportionment of costs which have been reasonably incurred. In the Applicants' statement of case it was asserted that "a service charge must be reasonable under section 19 of the 1985 Act". That is not what the Section provides. Costs are to be taken into account "only to the extent that they are reasonably incurred", but if reasonably incurred they fall to be apportioned in accordance with the terms of the lease, except if excluded by a failure to consult or otherwise under for example ss.20B and 20C. The foundation of the Applicants' challenge therefore falls away'.

29-32   The LVT does not have a general discretion under section 19 to determine whether a service charge demanded from a tenant is reasonable and, therefore, must give effect to the terms of the lease, however unreasonable the result, providing the relevant costs were reasonably incurred in respect of works done to a reasonable standard.[37] This is subject to the potential application of the Unfair Terms in Consumer Contracts Regulations 1999, considered in detail below.[38] It follows that the LVT must give effect to any fixed percentage specified in the lease and, also, to any mechanism contained in the lease regarding the allocation or apportionment of the cost of services.

29-33   This limitation appears to be a lacuna in the protection afforded to residential tenants. Many modern leases of flats within large developments require tenants to pay a different percentage of costs relating to different headings of service charge expenditure. Thus, for example, a tenant might be required to pay a small percentage of the landlord's costs in maintaining the external common parts of a large estate, a larger percentage of the costs of maintaining the block within which his flat is located and, perhaps, a different percentage for maintenance of, say, a car park structure. A tenant in this position would seem to have no redress under section 19 if his landlord chose to include costs of benefit to the whole estate within the block charge, with the result that the tenant pays a higher percentage. It may be that a tenant will be entitled to challenge such a decision in an application under section 27A on the basis that a proper construction of the terms of the lease requires the expenditure to be placed within a particular category of expenditure with the appropriate percentage. However, the terms of the lease may not be sufficiently clear or may leave the decision to the discretion of the landlord. In such circumstances, the tenant may be left without an effective means of challenging the landlord's decision.

---

36 At para 19. See also *Re Rowner Estates Ltd* [2007] EWLands LRX_3_2006 where the Lands Tribunal (A J Trott FRICS) cited and approved this quote.
37 *Billson v Tristrem* [2000] L&TR 220.
38 At Chapter 37.

Works done to a reasonable standard

29-34   The issue of whether works were carried out to a reasonable standard has received relatively little attention in the reported cases. It seems likely that the two-stage approach derived from *Forcelux*, described above, subsumes considerations as to the reasonable cost of the works within the second stage. It is difficult to see how the cost of works which are not done to a reasonable standard could be said to have been 'reasonably incurred' in the sense that the level of the costs is reasonable in accordance with market norms. It appears that issues regarding the quality of the work carried out are therefore generally addressed when considering the amount of the costs charged in connection with the question of whether those costs are 'reasonably incurred'.

29-35   Where there is a finding that works were not done or a service was not provided to a reasonable standard, in appropriate circumstances the LVT may (and in practice frequently will) make a deduction in the amount claimed to reflect the deficient quality of the works or service, rather than simply disallowing recovery of the whole cost of the works.[39]

Payments on account: Section 19(2)

29-36   Section 19(1) deals only with the reasonableness of costs already incurred by the landlord. Section 19(2) creates a similar jurisdiction in respect of anticipated expenditure. Section 19(2) states:

> 'Where a service charge is payable before the relevant costs are incurred, no greater amount than is reasonable is so payable, and after the relevant costs have been incurred any necessary adjustment shall be made by repayment, reduction or subsequent charges or otherwise.'

29-37   There is limited authority as to the correct approach to be adopted to challenges to on-account payments, but it is thought that the majority of the principles discussed above will be equally relevant under section 19(2).[40] It is likely that the landlord will be required to identify some rational basis for the amount demanded on account, whether by reference to a management plan setting out anticipated expenditure or estimates based on expenditure in previous years. It is unlikely to be considered reasonable to include an arbitrary figure in a demand for an on-account payment, even though there will inevitably be some degree of uncertainty as to what the actual expenditure may be.[41] The existence of

---

39   *Yorkbrook Investments v Batten* (1986) 52 P&CR 51.

40   *Southall Court (Residents) Ltd v Tiwari* [2011] UKUT 218.

41   See, by way of analogy, *Princes House Ltd v Distinctive Clubs Ltd* [2007] EWCA Civ 374, a case concerning commercial premises and not, therefore, within s 19(2), but where the court considered the obligations on a landlord under a clause which required the landlord to prepare 'a reasonable estimate of the amount of the Service Rent payable by the Tenant during each Accounting Year'. See **18-05** above.

a reserve fund and the sums contained in it is a relevant consideration in assessing the reasonableness of on-account demands.

29-38   The reference in section 19(2) to an 'adjustment' being made by 'repayment, reduction or subsequent charges' is unclear and there is no time limit provided for any such adjustment to be effected. It appears that what was intended by this provision is that the landlord should give effect to any determination as to the reasonableness of advance charges by making appropriate reductions in future demands, once costs have been incurred. On the face of it, however, the provision might be interpreted as conferring on the LVT jurisdiction to order the landlord to make a repayment to the tenant of any advance payments found to be unreasonable, after the relevant costs are incurred, but there do not appear to be any reported cases where the provision has been interpreted in this way. It would be surprising if the effect of section 19(2) were to confer jurisdiction on the LVT to order the landlord to make a repayment, since there is no equivalent jurisdiction in the case of sums demanded after relevant costs have been incurred.

29-39   It would appear that a determination as to the reasonableness of anticipated expenditure under section 19(2) would not preclude a tenant from seeking a further determination once the costs have been incurred and the actual expenditure is therefore known.

GRANT-AIDED WORKS

29-40   Where relevant costs are incurred or are to be incurred in the carrying out of works in respect of which a grant has been or is to be paid under section 523 of the Housing Act 1985 (assistance for provision of separate service pipe for water supply), under any provision of Part I of the Housing Grants, Construction and Regeneration Act 1996 (grants, etc. for renewal of private sector housing) or any corresponding earlier enactment, or under article 3 of the Regulatory Reform (Housing Assistance) (England and Wales) Order 2002 (power of local housing authorities to provide assistance), the amount of the grant shall be deducted from the cost of the works and the amount of the service charge payable shall be reduced accordingly.[42]

29-41   In any case where relevant costs are incurred or are to be incurred on the carrying out of works which are included in the external works specified in a group repair scheme within the meaning of Part I of the Housing Grants, Construction and Regeneration Act 1996 and the landlord participated or is participating in that scheme as an assisted participant, the amount which, in relation to the landlord, is the balance of the cost determined in accordance with section 69(3) of the Housing Grants, Construction and Regeneration Act 1996 shall be deducted from the costs and the amount of the service charge payable shall be reduced accordingly.[43]

---

42 Landlord and Tenant Act 1985, s 20A(1).
43 Landlord and Tenant Act 1985, s 20A(2).

29-42   The effect of these provisions is largely self-explanatory. They require the landlord to give credit to the tenants in respect of grants received under the specified schemes when calculating the service charges payable. It has been suggested[44] that these provisions, whilst sensible, do not go far enough because they are not of general application and a section simply requiring the landlord to credit the service charge account with any grant received from any source would be preferable. However, it is difficult to imagine a lease drafted in such a way which would permit a landlord to recover sums from the tenants which have not actually been spent by him because works have been paid for by public grant. Furthermore, it is likely that seeking to include expenditure which has, in fact, been funded by a public grant would amount to double recovery and would, almost certainly therefore, mean that the sum included in service charge demands was unreasonable in accordance with section 19.[45] Accordingly, it seems likely that both the existing provisions of section 20A and any more general replacement for them will be of very limited application in practice.

LIMITS ON THE COSTS INCURRED IN CONNECTION WITH PROCEEDINGS: SECTION 20C

29-43   The vast majority of residential service charge disputes are conducted before the LVT, which has no general costs jurisdiction.[46] Accordingly, landlords will frequently seek to recover their expenditure on legal fees from tenants through the service charge account. Whether, as a matter of construction, the terms of any particular lease will enable the landlord to do so has been considered above.[47]

29-44   Where the landlord is entitled to include legal fees as part of the service charge, a tenant may make an application under section 20C of the Landlord and Tenant Act 1985. That section provides that a tenant may make an application for an order that all or any of the costs incurred or to be incurred by the landlord in connection with proceedings before a court, residential property tribunal or LVT, or the Upper Tribunal, or in connection with arbitration proceedings, are not to be regarded as relevant costs to be taken into account in determining the amount of any service charge payable by the tenant or any other person or persons specified in the application. The court or tribunal to which the application is made may make such order on the application as it considers just and equitable in the circumstances.[48]

29-45   Where the proceedings in respect of which the costs in issue have been incurred are ongoing, the application should be made to the court, LVT or the

---

44 Sheriff, *Service Charges for Leasehold, Freehold and Commonhold* (2007) at para 9.129.
45 See *Craighead v Homes for Islington Ltd* [2010] UKUT 47 (LC), where the tribunal accepted the argument that, in principle, double recovery of this nature would be unreasonable, but found on the facts of that case that this had not happened due to the nature of the public grant in issue.
46 Commonhold and Leasehold Reform Act 2002, Sch 12, para 10.
47 See Chapter 11.
48 Section 20C(3).

Upper Tribunal before which the proceedings are taking place, or (where the proceedings have been concluded) to any county court or any LVT.[49]

29-46 The vast majority of section 20C applications are made to the LVT during the course of ongoing proceedings about service charges and relate to the costs incurred by the landlord in those proceedings. However, that is not the only situation in which section 20C can be invoked and, in particular, it is notable that the wording of the section is sufficiently wide for a tenant to rely on it in relation to the landlord's costs of proceedings against another tenant. Thus tenant A can apply for an order preventing the landlord from including in relevant costs the costs incurred in proceedings brought by or against tenant B. It should also be noted that, whilst the section is most commonly invoked to limit recovery of legal fees, it in fact applies to any 'costs incurred … in connection with the proceedings' and accordingly appears to extend to fees of other professionals such as surveyors and any other costs such as travel costs, providing, of course, the provisions of the lease would otherwise permit these items to be included in the service charge.

29-47 Section 20C confers a very broad discretion as to the circumstances in which it will be appropriate to make an order and the terms of any order. However, some principles as to the exercise of that discretion have emerged. It should be kept in mind that, in addition to the considerations set out below, even where no order is made under section 20C, tenants will still be entitled to contend that costs included in the service charge were unreasonable in whole or in part under section 19.

29-48 Where there has been previous litigation resulting in a costs order in favour of a tenant, the landlord should be precluded from recovering his costs from the tenant via the service charge because the landlord should not 'get through the back door what has been refused by the front'.[50] Accordingly, it has been suggested that where a court makes an award of costs in a case concerning a service charge dispute, it should, at the same time, make an appropriate order under section 20C to avoid its costs order being subverted.[51]

29-49 The only principle upon which the discretion (to make an order under section 20C) should be exercised is to have regard to what is just and equitable in all the circumstances. The circumstances include the conduct and circumstances of all parties, as well as the outcome of the proceedings in which they arise. There is no general rule, or even any presumption, that a landlord should be unable to recover costs incurred in proceedings before the LVT by way of service charge, or even that he should be able to do so only if the tenant has acted unreasonably.[52]

---

49 Section 20C(2).
50 *Iperion Investments v Broadwalk House Residents Ltd* [1995] 2 EGLR 47.
51 *Tenants of Langford Court v Doren Ltd* [2001] EWLands LRX_37_2000, *per* HH Judge Rich QC.
52 *Ibid.*

However, it has also been said that the primary consideration that the LVT should keep in mind is that the power to make an order under section 20C should be used only to ensure that the right to claim costs as part of the service charge is not used in circumstances that make its use unjust. The purpose of section 20C is to give an opportunity to ensure fair treatment as between landlord and tenant in circumstances where, even though costs have been reasonably and properly incurred by the landlord, it would be unjust that the tenants or some particular tenant should have to pay them.[53] However, it must also be kept in mind that an order under section 20C deprives the landlord of a contractual entitlement to recover costs and, accordingly, care must be taken to ensure that section 20C does not, itself, become an instrument of oppression.[54]

29-50   The cases decided under the section suggest that the outcome of the proceedings in which the costs were incurred will usually be the most significant factor in determining what order, if any, to make under section 20C. In *Schilling v Canary Riverside Estate Management Ltd,*[55] the Lands Tribunal determined that tenants who succeeded in their appeal were entitled to an order under section 20C, even though neither side had behaved unreasonably. However, there is no rule that costs should 'follow the event' and the question is always what is just and equitable in the circumstances.[56] A lack of consultation by the landlord prior to making an application for a determination is a relevant consideration in the exercise of the discretion.[57] Any offers of settlement, compliance with directions made during the course of proceedings and offers or refusal of mediation may all be taken into account. It may also be a relevant factor that the landlord is comprised of lessee shareholders and, accordingly, may have no source of income other than the service charge.[58]

29-51   The power to make 'such order' as considered to be just and equitable includes the power to make an order providing that the costs should not form part of the service charges of a particular tenant, whilst being recoverable from the remainder of the tenants. Accordingly, it is possible in appropriate circumstances for the court or LVT to order that, whilst some of the tenants should remain obliged to contribute to the costs, one or more of the other tenants in the same block should not be so obliged.[59] There is also scope for making orders that a

---

53 *Tenants of Langford Court v Doren Ltd* [2001] EWLands LRX_37_2000, *per* HH Judge Rich QC.
54 *Ibid.*
55 2008 WL 4385539, 15 October 2008.
56 See, for example, *Solitaire Property Management Company Ltd v Holden* [2012] UKUT 86 (LC) where the Upper Tribunal considered it was just and equitable to make a s 20C order as regards the costs of an appeal, even though the landlord brought the appeal and succeeded on the majority of grounds of appeal.
57 *Ibrahim v Dovecorn Reversions Ltd* (2001) 82 P&CR 28.
58 *Iperion Investments v Broadwalk House Residents Ltd* [1995] 2 EGLR 47.
59 *Volosinovici v Corvan (Properties) Ltd* (Lands Tribunal, unreported, 25 October 2007, LRX/27/2006).

specified percentage of the landlord's costs cannot be recovered via the service charge.[60]

ADMINISTRATION CHARGES

Introduction

29-52 Many leases entitle the landlord to levy charges against the tenant in specific circumstances, such as fees for registering notice of assignment of the lease or granting consent to alterations. Leases often also contain provisions relating to one-off 'default' payments, such as fees for preparing a notice pursuant to section 146 of the Law of Property Act 1925, late payment fees or interest. Neither of these types of charges fall within the definition of service charge provided in section 18 of the Landlord and Tenant Act 1985[61] and, accordingly, were unregulated until the coming into force of section 158 of the Commonhold and Leasehold Reform Act 2002 and Schedule 11 to that Act.[62] These provisions regulate the recovery of administration charges from tenants of dwellings in a similar, though not identical, manner to the regulation of service charges, discussed above.[63]

Definition of 'administration charge' and 'variable administration charge'

29-53 By Schedule 11, paragraph 1 to the Commonhold and Leasehold Reform Act 2002, administration charge means:

'an amount payable by a tenant of a dwelling as part of or in addition to the rent which is payable, directly or indirectly –

(a) for or in connection with the grant of approvals under his lease, or applications for such approvals,

(b) for or in connection with the provision of information or documents by or on behalf of the landlord or a person who is party to his lease otherwise than as landlord or tenant,

(c) in respect of a failure by the tenant to make a payment by the due date to the landlord or a person who is party to his lease otherwise than as landlord or tenant, or

60 See, for example, *Maryland Estates Ltd v Lynch* (Lands Tribunal, unreported, 5 February 2003, LRX/57/1999) where the landlord was debarred from recovering 50% of its costs despite succeeding in the proceedings, because the confusing way in which accounts were prepared had contributed to the tenants pursuing the case.
61 As discussed in Chapter 28 above.
62 On 30 September 2003 in England (Commonhold and Leasehold Reform Act 2002 (Commencement No 2 and Savings) (England) Order 2003 (SI 2003/1986), art 2) and 31 March 2004 in Wales (Commonhold and Leasehold Reform Act 2002 (Commencement No 2 and Savings) (Wales) Order 2004 (Welsh SI 2004/669), art 2).
63 See **29-04** to **29-42**.

(d)   in connection with a breach (or alleged breach) of a covenant or condition in his lease.'

29-54   Schedule 11, therefore, applies to an amount payable by a tenant of a dwelling[64] which is payable directly or indirectly in respect of the matters listed. This language indicates that the amount payable could include sums claimed in respect of the charges of a third party. The four matters included are largely self-explanatory and the definition has attracted little attention in the reported cases. The four matters listed would appear to catch the majority of potential charges commonly levied by landlords. It should not be assumed, however, that every sum demanded by a landlord from his tenant will be within this definition. For example, in *Mehson Property Co Ltd v Pellegrino*,[65] the Upper Tribunal held that a sum demanded by a landlord in return for entering into a deed of variation did not constitute an administration charge since it did not fall within any of subparagraphs (a)–(d). One potential issue, which does not appear as yet to have been decided by the Upper Tribunal, is whether a sum charged by a landlord on the registration of a notice of assignment is caught by the definition. Many long leases of residential properties do not require the landlord's consent to underletting or assignment, but do require the tenant to give notice to the landlord, with the payment of a fee. It might be argued that any such charge does not fall within subparagraph (a) (or any of the other subparagraphs) on the grounds that the landlord is not, in any sense, granting an approval.

29-55   Schedule 11, paragraph 1(2) defines a 'variable administration charge' as follows:

'an administration charge payable by a tenant which is neither –

(a)   specified in his lease, nor

(b)   calculated in accordance with a formula specified in his lease.'

29-56   The 2002 Act does not provide any definition of 'a formula' and there is some uncertainty as to precisely what is meant by this wording. The distinction between fixed and variable administration charges is relevant to the remedies available to the tenant, as discussed below. As will be seen, a tenant is entitled to challenge the reasonableness of a variable administration charge, but in respect of fixed charges, may only seek to vary the terms of the lease. Accordingly, the intention appears to have been that a variable administration charge would be a sum which is dependent upon a decision taken by the landlord as to the amount to demand. By contrast, a fixed administration charge would be specified by the lease. If that interpretation is correct, then a variable administration charge is closely analogous to a service charge and the jurisdiction as to the reasonableness of such a charge under Schedule 11, paragraph 2 is the equivalent of the requirement of reasonableness imposed on service charges under section 19 of the Landlord and Tenant Act 1985.

---

64   See **28-03** to **28-10** above for detailed discussion of this phrase in the Landlord and Tenant Act 1985, s 18.
65   [2009] UKUT 119 (LC).

29-57 It is suggested that interest which a landlord is entitled to charge on overdue payments would fall within paragraph 1(c).[66] This is potentially significant protection, since leases often entitle a landlord to charge onerous rates of interest to defaulting tenants. However, it has been suggested by the LVT, it is considered correctly, that where the lease specifies the rate of interest payable on overdue sums, this constitutes a formula for the calculation of the charge and the interest is, therefore, a fixed rather than a variable administration charge.[67] Accordingly, the tenant's remedy is not an assessment of reasonableness, but the variation of the lease to alter the rate of interest which the landlord is entitled to charge.

Entitlement to challenge administration charges

29-58 Schedule 11, paragraph 2 provides that a variable administration charge is payable only to the extent that the amount of the charge is reasonable. Given the analogy between variable administration charges and service charges mentioned at **29-56** above, it seems likely that many of the principles discussed at **29-04** to **29-42** above in relation to the reasonableness of service charges under section 19(1) of the Landlord and Tenant Act 1985 will equally be relevant when considering the reasonableness or otherwise of administration charges under this provision.

29-59 There is, however, an important difference of principle. Section 19 requires the LVT to consider whether the service charge in question has been reasonably incurred. Schedule 11, paragraph 2 simply provides that the administration charge must be reasonable. It would appear, therefore, that the LVT need only focus on the amount of the sum actually charged and need not focus on the reasonableness of the landlord's decision-making process, although it must be doubtful whether this distinction will make much practical difference to the outcome in most cases.[68]

29-60 Schedule 11, paragraph 5 contains almost identical provisions to section 27A in respect of service charges. Thus, an application may be made to an LVT for a determination whether an administration charge is payable and, if it is, as to:

(a)   the person by whom it is payable;

(b)   the person to whom it is payable;

(c)   the amount which is payable;

---

66   The LVT has accepted on a number of occasions (e.g. *Fleming Way (Thamesmead) Management Co Ltd v Stevens* (Leasehold Valuation Tribunal, unreported, 24 May 2011, LON/00AD/LSC/2011/0089) that contractual interest falls within the definition of administration charge, although the point does not appear to have been considered by the Upper Tribunal.
67   *Farthing Court (Greenford) Middlesex Ltd v Shepherds Bush Housing Group* (Leasehold Valuation Tribunal, unreported, 21 January 2011, LON/00AJ/LSC/2010/0386).
68   For an example of a case in which the Upper Tribunal upheld the LVT's determination that an administration charge (in respect of granting consent to assignment) was unreasonable, see *Holding & Management (Solitaire) Ltd v Norton* [2012] L&TR 15.

(d)   the date at or by which it is payable; and

(e)   the manner in which it is payable.

29-61   This entitlement arises whether or not any payment has been made[69] and the jurisdiction conferred on an LVT is in addition to any jurisdiction of a court in respect of the matter.[70] No application under subparagraph (1) may be made in respect of a matter which:

(a)   has been agreed or admitted by the tenant;

(b)   has been, or is to be, referred to arbitration pursuant to a post-dispute arbitration agreement to which the tenant is a party;

(c)   has been the subject of determination by a court; or

(d)   has been the subject of determination by an arbitral tribunal, pursuant to a post-dispute arbitration agreement.[71]

29-62   The tenant is not to be taken to have agreed or admitted any matter by reason only of having made any payment.[72] An agreement by the tenant of a dwelling (other than a post-dispute arbitration agreement) is void in so far as it purports to provide for a determination (a) in a particular manner, or (b) on particular evidence, of any question which may be the subject matter of an application under subparagraph (1).[73]

29-63   One difference between the jurisdiction under Schedule 11, paragraph 5 and section 27A of the Landlord and Tenant Act 1985 should be noted, however. There is no equivalent provision in Schedule 11 to section 27A(3), which provides that a party may apply for a determination as to whether, if costs were incurred, a service charge would be payable. Accordingly, it has been held that the LVT does not have jurisdiction to determine whether anticipated variable administration charges would be payable.[74]

29-64   As noted above, Schedule 11, paragraph 2 only applies to variable administration charges and there is no equivalent jurisdiction in respect of fixed charges. However, by Schedule 11, paragraph 3, any party to a lease of a dwelling may apply to the LVT for an order varying the lease in such manner as is specified in the application, on the grounds that –

'(a)   any administration charge specified in the lease is unreasonable, or

(b)   any formula specified in the lease in accordance with which any administration charge is calculated is unreasonable.'

---

69   Schedule 11, para 5(2).
70   Paragraph 5(3).
71   Paragraph 5(4).
72   Paragraph 5(5).
73   Paragraph 5(6).
74   *Drewett v Bold* [2006] EWLands LRX_90_2005.

29-65   If the grounds on which the application was made are established to the satisfaction of the tribunal, it may make an order varying the lease in such manner as is specified in the order. The variation specified in the order may be either the variation specified in the application or such other variation as the tribunal thinks fit. The tribunal may, instead of making an order varying the lease in such manner as is specified in the order, make an order directing the parties to the lease to vary it in such manner as is so specified. The tribunal may, by order, direct that a memorandum of any variation of a lease effected by virtue of this paragraph be endorsed on such documents as are specified in the order. Any such variation of a lease shall be binding, not only on the parties to the lease for the time being, but also on other persons (including any predecessors in title), whether or not they were parties to the proceedings in which the order was made.

29-66   This jurisdiction is potentially wide ranging, particularly given that it expressly provides that any variation is binding on predecessors and successors in title. There is no limitation in the language of the statute which would suggest that a landlord is not equally entitled to apply for the increase of a non-variable administration charge where it is unreasonably small. Again, there is no guidance as to how the question of whether a charge or formula is 'unreasonable' in this context and there is a dearth of authority on the point.

Other provisions relating to administration charges

29-67   Schedule 11, paragraph 4 contains analogous provisions to section 21B of the Landlord and Tenant Act 1985 as regards service charge demands.[75] A demand for payment of an administration charge must be accompanied by a summary of rights and obligations of tenants of dwellings in relation to administration charges. The prescribed form of the summary is provided by the Administration Charges (Summary of Rights and Obligations) (England) Regulations 2007.[76]

29-68   Schedule 11, paragraphs 10 and 11 contain amendments to sections 47 and 48 of the Landlord and Tenant Act 1987,[77] so that demands for administration charges must contain the information required by section 47 and, furthermore, that administration charges are not payable until the requirements of these sections are met.

---

75   Discussed at **33-01** to **33-06** below.
76   SI 2007/1258.
77   See **32-07** to **32-18** below.

CHAPTER 30

Consultation requirements

INTRODUCTION

30-01   The consultation requirements imposed by section 20 of the Landlord and Tenant Act 1985 are, together with the general requirement of reasonableness under section 19, the most significant statutory provisions for the regulation of the recovery of service charges. The effect of these provisions is to limit the amount which a landlord is entitled to recover from a tenant in respect of a programme of major works or a qualifying long-term agreement. Unless the landlord either complies with the somewhat cumbersome requirements or obtains dispensation under section 20ZA,[1] the contribution of each tenant will be capped at £250 in relation to qualifying works, and £100 in respect of a qualifying long-term agreement. Any resulting shortfall in the sums recoverable will almost certainly fall to be met by the landlord. As Lewison J has observed:

> 'The relevant provisions of the Landlord and Tenant Act 1985 do not prohibit a landlord from entering into whatever contract he pleases for the carrying out of works or the supply of services. They merely prevent him from passing on the cost of the works or services to the lessees unless he has satisfied the statutory requirements about price, quality and consultation. As between the landlord and the contractor or service provider, the landlord remains liable on his contract.'[2]

30-02   The consequences for a landlord failing to comply with the requirements are, therefore, potentially serious. Indeed in *Zuckerman v Calthorpe*,[3] the Upper Tribunal accepted an argument on the part of tenants claiming new long leases of flats under the Leasehold Reform, Housing and Urban Development Act 1993 that the management difficulties caused by the consultation requirements had a measureable impact on the value of the landlord's reversionary interest.

---

1   See **30-42**ff. below.
2   *Paddington Basin Developments Ltd v West End Quay Estate Management Ltd* [2010] 1 WLR 2735 at para 27.
3   [2010] 1 EGLR 187.

30-03 There has been some judicial disagreement as to the legislative purpose behind the consultation requirements. As will be seen below,[4] this issue is of particular significance in terms of the approach to be adopted in considering whether the landlord should be granted dispensation from compliance with the requirements of section 20. On the one hand, it has been suggested that section 20 serves a free-standing purpose of providing transparency and accountability going above and beyond the aim of ensuring that tenants do not pay more than they should in respect of works carried out or agreements entered into by their landlord.[5] The authoritative view, however, is now provided by Lord Neuberger, giving the judgment of the majority of the Supreme Court in *Daejan Investments Ltd v Benson*.[6] His Lordship said:[7]

> 'It seems clear that sections 19 to 20ZA are directed towards ensuring that tenants of flats are not required (i) to pay for unnecessary services or services which are provided to a defective standard, and (ii) to pay more than they should for services which are necessary and are provided to an acceptable standard. The former purpose is encapsulated in section 19(1)(b) and the latter in section 19(1) (a). The following two sections, namely sections 20 and 20ZA appear to me to be intended to reinforce, and to give practical effect to, those two purposes. This view is confirmed by the titles to those two sections, which echo the title of section 19.'

30-04 The Supreme Court has therefore rejected the suggestion that sections 20 and 20ZA of the 1985 Act are intended to achieve transparency and accountability as ends in themselves. As Lord Neuberger also remarked, the sections are not concerned with public law issues or public duties.[8]

THE ORIGINAL SECTION 20 REQUIREMENTS

30-05 Section 20, as originally enacted,[9] imposed a set of requirements for consultation in relation to qualifying works, which obliged the landlord to obtain estimates and consult with tenants before commencing the works. The Commonhold and Leasehold Reform Act 2002 substituted a new section 20 with effect from 31 October 2003 (in England) and 31 March 2004 (in Wales).[10]

---

4   At **30-50**ff.
5   See *Paddington Basin Developments Ltd v West End Quay Management Ltd* [2010] EWHC 833, *per* Lewison J at para 26 and *Daejan Investments Ltd v Benson* [2013] UKSC 14, *per* Lord Wilson paras 103–109.
6   [2013] UKSC 14.
7   *Ibid*, at para 42.
8   *Ibid*, at para 52.
9   For a detailed legislative history of s 20 and its statutory precursors, see the dissenting judgment of Lord Wilson in *Daejan Investments Ltd v Benson* [2013] UKSC 14. See also **1-12**ff. above.
10 Commonhold and Leasehold Reform Act 2002, s 151; Commonhold and Leasehold Reform Act 2002 (Commencement No 2 and Savings) (England) Order 2003 (SI 2003/1986), art 3(1); Commonhold and Leasehold Reform Act 2002 (Commencement No 2 and Savings) (Wales) Order 2004 (SI 2004/669), art 2(d).

30-06   The original section 20 continues to apply in the following cases:[11]

(a)   where qualifying works were begun before 31 October 2003;

(b)   where the landlord gave or displayed the notice required in respect of qualifying works under the original section 20 before 31 October 2003;

(c)   where, in relation to qualifying works which are to be carried out under a contract which was to be entered into on or after 31 October 2003 and is for a period of 12 months or less, the landlord gave notice in the Official Journal of the European Union in accordance with the Public Works Contracts Regulations 1991,[12] the Public Services Contracts Regulations 1993[13] or the Public Supply Contracts Regulations 1995[14] before 31 October 2003; and

(d)   where, under an agreement entered into by or on behalf of the landlord or a superior landlord before 31 October 2003, qualifying works were carried out at any time in the period starting on 31 October 2003 and ending two months after that date.[15]

30-07   The original section 20 provided that where relevant costs,[16] incurred on the carrying out of any qualifying works, exceeded the relevant limit, then the excess was not to be taken into account in determining the amount of a service charge, unless the relevant requirements had been either complied with, or dispensed with by the court. This section applied even where the tenancy under which the relevant service charge is payable was of more than one dwelling or included other property.[17]

30-08   Section 20(2) defined 'qualifying works' to mean works (whether on a building or on any other premises), the costs of which the tenant by whom the service charge is payable may be required to contribute to under the terms of his lease. The relevant limit was whichever is the greater of £50 multiplied by the number of flats in the building or £1,000.[18] The Secretary of State has power to prescribe different amounts by order.

30-09   From 1 September 1988,[19] the requirements of the original section 20 as to consultation differ depending on whether the tenant in question was

---

11   Commonhold and Leasehold Reform Act 2002 (Commencement No 2 and Savings) (England) Order 2003 (SI 2003/1986), art 3(2)–(7); Commonhold and Leasehold Reform Act 2002 (Commencement No 2 and Savings) (Wales) Order 2004 (SI 2004/669), art 2(d)(i)–(vi).
12   SI 1991/2680.
13   SI 1993/3228.
14   SI 1995/201.
15   In Wales, the relevant date is in each case 31 March 2004 and not 31 October 2003.
16   See s 18; **28-11**ff. above.
17   *Heron Maple House Ltd v Central Estates Ltd* [2002] 1 EGLR 35.
18   The limits originally in force were £25 and £500 respectively, but these were doubled with effect from 1 September 1988 by the Service Charge (Estimates and Consultation) Order 1988 (SI 1988/1285).
19   The date on which the 1987 Act came into force.

represented by a recognised tenants' association ('RTA').[20] In relation to such of the tenants concerned[21] who are not represented by a tenants' association, the relevant requirements are set out in section 20(4) as follows:

(a)   At least two estimates for the works must be obtained, one of them from a person wholly unconnected with the landlord.

(b)   A notice accompanied by a copy of the estimates must be given to each of the tenants concerned or displayed in one or more places where it is likely to come to the attention of all of those tenants. The landlord must provide copies of the actual estimates obtained and not just a summary.[22] Having the documents available for inspection in a place where a tenant has the ability to see the documents if he makes an effort to do so is not sufficient for these purposes; the requirement envisages that documents are displayed in a sufficiently convenient and obvious place that they will come to the attention of the tenant straight away.[23]

(c)   The notice must describe the works to be carried out and invite observations on them and on the estimates and must state the name and address[24] in the UK of the person to whom the observations may be sent and the date by which they are to be received.

(d)   The date stated in the notice must not be less than one month after the date on which the notice is given or displayed.

(e)   The landlord must have regard to any observations received in pursuance of the notice and, unless the works are urgently required, they must not be begun earlier than the date specified in the notice.

30-10   In relation to any of the tenants concerned who are represented by an RTA, the requirements, pursuant to the original section 20(5) are:

(a)   The landlord must give the secretary of the association a notice containing a detailed specification of the works and specifying a reasonable period within which the association may propose to the landlord the names of one or more persons from whom estimates for the works should, in its view, be obtained by the landlord.

(b)   At least two estimates for the works must be obtained, one of them from a person wholly unconnected with the landlord.

(c)   A copy of each of the estimates must be given to the secretary of the association.

---

20 See Chapter 34 below.
21 Meaning all of the tenants who may be required under the terms of their leases to contribute to the costs of the works in question by payment of service charges: s 20(8).
22 *Richmond Housing Partnership v Smith* LRX/10/2005; *Islington LBC v Abel-Malek* [2008] 1 L&TR 2.
23 *M & M Savant Ltd v Brown* [2008] EWLands LRX_26_2006.
24 Meaning a person's place of abode or place of business or, in the case of a company, its registered office: s 38.

(d)   A notice must be given to each of the tenants concerned who are represented by the association, which must –

(i)   briefly describe the works to be carried out;

(ii)   summarise the estimates;

(iii) inform the tenant that he has a right to inspect and take copies of a detailed specification of the works to be carried out and of the estimates;

(iv)   invite observations on those works and the estimates; and

(v)   specify the name and address in the UK of the person to whom the observations may be sent and the date by which they are to be received.

(e)   The date stated in the notice must be not less than one month after the date on which the notice is given.

(f)   If any tenant to whom the notice is given so requests, the landlord must afford him reasonable facilities for inspecting a detailed specification of the works to be carried out and the estimates, free of charge, and/or taking copies of them on payment of such reasonable charge as the landlord may determine. It is expressly provided that the requirement to make available facilities for inspection free of charge does not preclude the landlord from treating any costs incurred as part of his management costs.[25]

(g)   The landlord must have regard to any observations received in pursuance of the notice and, unless the works are urgently required, they must not be begun earlier than the date specified in the notice.

30-11   The landlord is obliged to have regard to observations made by a tenant or RTA, but the Act gives no guidance as to how this duty is to operate in practice. The landlord is plainly not obliged to adopt any observations, but it would seem that, equally, he is not entitled to disregard them altogether. A landlord may be required to explain why he has not adopted any suggestions made by the tenants and it is probable that the duty extends to considering any observations in good faith. However, it is likely to be difficult for a tenant to establish that a landlord has failed in this duty since the statutory wording suggests that it will be sufficient if a landlord who rejects observations can satisfy the LVT that this decision was within the ambit of what a reasonable landlord in his position might have done, even if other landlords might have reached a different conclusion.

30-12   Under the original section 20(9), the court (rather than the LVT) had jurisdiction to dispense with all or any of the requirements set out above. The court's jurisdiction was limited and the power of dispensation could only be exercised where the court was satisfied that the landlord has acted reasonably.[26] Accordingly, in *Martin v Maryland Estates*,[27] the Court of Appeal held that the

25   Section 20(7).
26   See *Daejan Investments Ltd v Benson* [2013] UKSC 14, *per* Lord Wilson at paras 105–106.
27   [1999] L&TR 30.

discretion to dispense had never arisen since the landlord had not acted reasonably in not consulting tenants about substantial additional work not included in an earlier notice and estimates.

THE CURRENT SECTION 20 REQUIREMENTS

30-13   The new sections 20 and 20ZA came into force on 31 October 2003 in England and 31 March 2004 in Wales, together with the Service Charges (Consultation Requirements) (England) Regulations 2003[28] and the Service Charges (Consultation Requirements) (Wales) Regulations 2004[29] ('the Consultation Regulations').

Qualifying works

30-14   As under the original section 20, the new section 20 limits the tenants' contribution to the cost of 'qualifying works', unless the requirements of the Consultation Regulations are met or dispensed with under section 20ZA. By section 20ZA(2), the phrase 'qualifying works' is defined broadly to mean works on a building or any other premises. The term 'works' is not itself defined. In *Paddington Walk Management Ltd v Peabody Trust*,[30] it was held that window cleaning did not fall within the definition since 'Works on a building comprise matters that one would naturally regard as being "building works"'.[31]

30-15   Section 20 applies to qualifying works if the relevant costs[32] exceed 'an appropriate amount'.[33] The appropriate amount is set by the Secretary of State by regulations[34]and currently the appropriate amount is an amount that results in the relevant contribution of any tenant being more than £250.[35] Relevant contribution means the amount which the tenant may be required under the terms of his lease to contribute (by the payment of service charges) to relevant costs incurred on carrying out the works.[36]

30-16   The effect of these provisions is that a landlord must comply with the consultation requirements in respect of any works which will result in any of the tenants obliged by their lease to contribute to the cost of the works contributing more than £250. If the landlord fails to comply and is unable to obtain dispensation

28   SI 2003/1987.
29   SI 2004/684.
30   [2010] L&TR 6.
31   *Per* HH Judge Marshall QC at para 92.
32   See s 18; **28-11**ff. above.
33   Section 20(3).
34   Section 20(5).
35   Service Charges (Consultation Requirements) (England) Regulations 2003 (SI 2003/1987), art 6; Service Charges (Consultation Requirements) (Wales) Regulations 2004 (SI 2004/684), art 6.
36   Section 20(2).

under section 20ZA, then each tenant's contribution to the works will be capped at £250.

30-17 If only one tenant's contribution exceeds £250, the consultation requirements will still apply and a failure to consult will have the effect of limiting that tenant's contribution to £250. However, this will have no effect on the service charge contributions of other tenants, whose individual liabilities will not in any case exceed the statutory cap of £250.

30-18 The Act does not provide any guidance as to how one programme of works is to be divided from another for the purpose of applying the £250 per tenant threshold. It may be that a landlord decides to carry out a programme of repair or redecoration consisting of a number of potentially distinct elements. To what extent is a landlord entitled to divide the work into parcels with the effect that none exceeds the threshold requiring consultation, although, taken together, the cost of the programme would trigger consultation requirements? A related issue is whether a landlord must conduct a fresh consultation exercise if it appears that the cost of the project will exceed the original estimates provided to tenants.

30-19 In *Martin v Maryland Estates Ltd*,[37] the landlord had conducted a consultation process under the original section 20, providing two estimates and indicating an intention to carry out works in accordance with the lower of those estimates at a total cost of £8,165 plus VAT. During the course of the works being carried out, inspections revealed that the property was in a significantly worse condition than had been appreciated. As a result, it was decided that additional works at a cost of £7,318 plus VAT were necessary. The landlord made a deliberate decision not to engage in a further section 20 consultation before carrying out the additional works. The leaseholders contended that they were not liable to contribute to the additional works above the statutory cap of £1,000. The judge held that the cap applied to the whole of the works and not just to the additional works and rejected the landlord's application for dispensation on the basis that the landlord had not acted reasonably. The Court of Appeal rejected the landlord's appeal on both points. As to whether the cap applied to the whole of the works or only the additional works, Robert Walker LJ said:

> 'It seems to me that since Parliament has not attempted to spell out any precise test, a commonsense approach is necessary. The judge was influenced by the fact that all the works were covered by one contract. That would not to my mind always be a decisive factor but, on the particular facts of this case, that was the right approach. The legislative purpose of the limit is to provide a triviality threshold rather than to build into every contract a margin of error which may in some cases, including this case, simply duplicate a contingency sum which has already been provided for.'

---

37 [1999] L&TR 30. See also *Mihvilovic v Leicester City Council* [2010] UKUT 22 (LC) where the LVT 'disaggregated' a programme of works into its constituent elements and concluded that the cost of two of the four elements did not cross the s 20 threshold. The Upper Tribunal upheld an appeal against this decision, but only on procedural grounds.

30-20   This guidance remains good law in relation to the old section 20, where those provisions remain in force. The proper approach to this issue under the current section 20 must, however, be reconsidered in light of the decision of the Chancellor in *Phillips v Francis.*[38] In that case, the landlord of a holiday site containing more than 150 chalets let on 999-year leases carried out a programme of substantial works of improvement involving a number of elements which might have been regarded as separate qualifying works for section 20 purposes. The cost of the total project resulted in each of the chalet tenants being obliged to contribute significantly more than the £250 threshold but the landlord did not carry out any form of consultation. The tenants challenged the sums demanded on various grounds including the failure to consult. In the County Court, the judge referred to the decision in *Martin v Maryland* and identified the correct approach as involving three steps. First, it was necessary to consider whether the items of expenditure incurred by the landlord constituted qualifying works. Secondly, applying the considerations referred to in *Martin v Maryland*, could any of the items which were qualifying works be grouped together as one or more sets of qualifying works? Thirdly, the 'triviality threshold' of £250 per tenant should be applied to any relevant set of qualifying works. Only where the total cost of the relevant set of qualifying works resulted in a tenant contributing more than £250 would section 20 apply. The judge, applying this approach, identified certain of the works carried out by the landlord as qualifying works, leaving others which fell under the £250 threshold.

30-21   The tenants appealed, contending that the judge was wrong not to have recognised all of the qualifying works as being a single set. The Chancellor upheld the appeal on the basis that the judge's approach to identifying qualifying works had been wrong, since the approach in *Martin v Maryland* was inappropriate following the amendments to section 20. The Chancellor said:

> 'The distinction between that case and this is the change in the legislation. The limit then was by reference to the cost of the works; the limit now is by reference to the amount of the contribution. The consultation requirements then were the provision to the tenants of at least two estimates of the cost of the works; now it is a notice by the landlord to the tenants of his intention to carry out qualifying works and to describe them in general terms. Thus the emphasis has shifted from identifying and costing the works before they start to notifying an intention to carry out the works and limiting the amount of the individual contributions sought to pay for them after their completion. Accordingly, I see nothing in the present legislation which requires the identification of one or more sets of qualifying works. If the works are qualifying works it will be for the landlord to assess whether they will be on such a scale as to necessitate complying with the consultation requirements or face the consequence that he may not recoup the cost from the tenants' contributions. As the contributions are payable on an annual basis then the limit is applied to the proportion of the qualifying works carried out in that year. Under this legislation there is no "triviality threshold" in relation to qualifying works; all the qualifying works must be entered into the calculation unless the landlord is prepared to carry any excess cost himself.'

---

38   [2012] EWHC 3650 (Ch). This followed the earlier decision that the relevant parts of the Landlord and Tenant Act 1985 applied to the holiday site: [2010] 2 EGLR 31. See **25-06** above.

30-22   The Chancellor concluded, therefore, that the judge at first instance had applied the wrong tests. Having concluded that certain of the works carried out by the landlord were 'qualifying works' within the statutory definition, he said:

> 'Accordingly, all of [the qualifying works] should be brought into the account for computing the contribution and then applying the limit. It may be that they should be spread over more than one year, thereby introducing another limit. With that exception, the provisions relating to this service charge do not require any identification of "sets of qualifying works" or the avoidance of "excessive fragmentation".'

30-23   This reasoning appears somewhat circular and, furthermore, offers no real guidance to landlords as to how to determine when individual items of expenditure will be grouped together to arrive at an aggregate cost which would trigger the section 20 requirements. The apparent circularity arises since the triviality threshold of £250 refers to an individual tenant's contribution to the cost of the 'qualifying works'. Accordingly, it is difficult to see how the distinction which the Chancellor sought to draw between the cost of the works (under the old section 20) and the amount of the tenant's contribution (under the new section 20) operates in practice, and what principled distinction can be drawn between those two methods of applying the threshold. The amount of the relevant contribution can only be assessed by first identifying what the qualifying works are, whether as a matter of fact they comprise a single unitary scheme or a series of separate projects, and then what they cost. Once an item of expenditure is found to constitute qualifying works then the only remaining question is whether any individual tenant's contribution to that item of expenditure exceeds £250. It is suggested that in amending the threshold requirement and attaching the threshold not to the cost of works, but to the level of contribution, it is unlikely to have been Parliament's intention to change the entire basis of the consultation rules. It is more likely that the legislative purpose of this amendment was simply to ensure that the application of section 20 should be determined by reference to the amount contributed by an individual tenant rather than the total cost of the 'qualifying works'.[39]

30-24   It follows that it is presently unclear as to how section 20 operates where a landlord intends to carry out a series of distinct works as part of a programme of improvements. Assume that in one service charge year a landlord decides, for example, to replace some of the windows in a block and also to re-surface the communal car park. The works are carried out at different times in the year by different contractors and neither set of works results in any tenant being obliged to contribute more than £250 to the cost. It is suggested that each project should be regarded as qualifying works in its own right and no section 20 consultation should be required for either. The approach suggested by the Chancellor would appear to lead to the result that such distinct items of expenditure should (even

---

39   This change in focus is understandable, in light of the fact that a single threshold for works costs, irrespective of the size of the block in respect of which the works are undertaken, and irrespective of the number of tenants contributing, is arbitrary and unworkable, and a focus on the level of individual contributions appears much more workable.

though each of itself amounts to qualifying works) be aggregated or 'brought into the account for computing the contribution'. Whilst it is accurate to say that the new section 20 does not refer to sets of qualifying works, neither does it envisage the aggregation of items which, taken separately, would fulfil the definition of qualifying works to arrive at a total contribution. Rather, it is suggested that the proper approach is first to identify, on a *Maryland*-common sense basis, whether one is dealing with a single set of works or a number of sets of works. The threshold applies to the tenant's contribution to the cost of the qualifying works and, therefore, it remains the case that it is the cost of the works which governs the application of the threshold.

30-25   Another difficult aspect of this decision is the reference by the Chancellor to works being spread over more than one year.[40] Where a single programme of works spans more than one service charge year, the Chancellor seemed to be saying[41] that it is only the cost of those works in any particular year which must be considered in order to determine whether the contribution of any tenant exceeds £250. The difficulty with this is that this is not what section 20 provides. Moreover, it is possible (albeit unusual) for a lease to provide a service charge period which is longer or shorter than a year.

30-26   The facts of *Phillips v Francis* were different from *Martin v Maryland Estates*. In *Phillips*, the question was how (if at all) to divide a programme of works into 'sets' of qualifying works to which the triviality threshold should be applied. In *Martin v Maryland*, the court was concerned with a programme of works to which the consultation rules applied, which was extended in scope (and therefore cost) during the works, to take account of additional defects which were discovered. It is not clear how the Chancellor's reasoning would apply to this latter situation. On one view, any additional 'qualifying works' would require consultation (or dispensation), even if they are undertaken as part of a programme of works for which the consultation was followed. While nothing in *Phillips v Francis* appears directly to call into question the potential argument that further works carried out within a consulted-upon scheme of major works should be recoverable as being a mere variation of the scheme, the language used by the Chancellor, which appears to suggest that the landlord must set out a comprehensive list of works or bear the risk of non-recovery, may found an argument that variations entailing additional works, and hence costs, might also now be challengeable.

30-27   As the law stands therefore, the only safe course for landlords intending to incur expenditure in respect of matters which amount to qualifying works is to embark on a section 20 consultation whenever the total amount of expenditure on qualifying works in a given service charge year may result in any tenant being obliged to contribute more than £250. This is so even where the expenditure to be incurred relates to apparently unconnected items and the items, considered separately, would not result in any tenant contributing more than £250. It remains

---

40 See **30-22** above.
41 Although this was, strictly, *obiter*.

to be seen how *Phillips v Francis* will be applied by the LVT and the Upper Tribunal and whether it will survive the scrutiny of the Court of Appeal.[42]

Qualifying long-term agreements

30-28   The new provisions extend the scope of consultation to qualifying long-term agreements ('QLTAs'). A QLTA is, subject to the exceptions set out below, any agreement entered into by or on behalf of the landlord or a superior landlord for a term of more than 12 months.[43]

30-29   In an important decision on the scope of the definition of a QLTA, *Paddington Walk Management Ltd v Peabody Trust*,[44] the court considered whether an agreement 'for an initial period of one year from 1 June 2006 [to] continue on a year-to-year basis with the right to termination by either party on giving three months' written notice at any time' fell within the definition. HH Judge Marshall QC concluded that such an agreement was not an agreement for a term of more than 12 months, reasoning as follows:

> 'In my judgment an agreement for a year certain and then from year-to-year to continue subject to not being terminated is not "an *agreement* for a term of *more* than 12 months" (emphasis added) within the meaning of this part of the statute. … the structure of the Act is that the definition of qualifying long-term agreement is to apply to a contract in which the tenants would definitely have to contribute in respect of a period of more than 12 months.
>
> In my judgment the whole flavour of the provisions extending to these agreements is "long-term". I cannot see how a periodic contract for, for example, a month and thereafter from month to month, could be regarded as long term as a matter of impression, even though on [counsel for the tenant's] analysis it would be caught. What seems to me to be the deciding factor is the length of the commitment. A line has to be drawn somewhere, and it has been drawn at a commitment which exceeds 12 months. A commitment of 12 months only is on the non-qualifying side of the "long term" line.'

30-30   It follows that an agreement is only a QLTA if, at the outset, the fixed term exceeds 12 months and the possibility of the contractual arrangements continuing for a longer period, subject to one of the parties giving notice terminating the agreement, is irrelevant.

30-31   If an agreement is made by a landlord (within the extended definition of that term under the Landlord and Tenant Act 1985) for a term exceeding 12 months, then it is a QLTA, regardless of whether a consultation would be a

---

42 It is understood that an application for permission to appeal has been made to the Court of Appeal, but at the time of writing, the application has not been determined.

43 Section 20ZA(2).

44 [2010] L&TR 6.

difficult or a futile exercise. An agreement cannot be a QLTA as against some parties but not others.[45]

30-32   In *Paddington Basin Developments Ltd v West End Quay Estate Management Ltd*,[46] it was held that a QLTA is not limited to an agreement with a provider of a single service, but can include an agreement to provide numerous different services.

30-33   An agreement is not a qualifying long-term agreement:

(a)   if it is a contract of employment;

(b)   if it is a management agreement made by a local housing authority, and –

    (i)   a tenant management organisation, or

    (ii)   a body established under section 2 of the Local Government Act 2000;

(c)   if the parties to the agreement are –

    (i)   a holding company and one or more of its subsidiaries, or

    (ii)   two or more subsidiaries of the same holding company; or

(d)   if –

    (i)   when the agreement is entered into, there are no tenants of the building or other premises to which the agreement relates, and

    (ii)   the agreement is for a term not exceeding five years.[47]

30-34   In *Paddington Walk Management Ltd v Peabody Trust*,[48] it was argued that the exception created by article 3(1)(d) of the Consultation Regulations (the 'no tenants' exception) applied because, at the time the agreements were entered into by the landlord, although leases had been granted, no tenants were in occupation. This argument was rejected since the phrase 'tenants of the building' could not be construed as meaning 'occupying residential tenants'. Accordingly, it was sufficient that leases had been granted, even though no tenants had moved in for the landlord to be required to comply with the Consultation Regulations.

30-35   An agreement entered into by or on behalf of the landlord or a superior landlord before 31 October 2003 is not a QLTA, notwithstanding that more than 12 months of the term remained unexpired on that date.[49] Nor is an agreement for a term of more than 12 months entered into, by or on behalf of the landlord or a superior landlord, which provides for the carrying out of qualifying works for which public notice has been given before 31 October 2003.[50]

---

45   *Paddington Basin Developments Ltd v West End Quay Estate Management Ltd* [2010] 1 WLR 2735.
46   *Ibid.*
47   Consultation Regulations 2003, art 3(1).
48   [2010] L&TR 6.
49   Consultation Regulations 2003, art 3(2).
50   Consultation Regulations 2003, art 3(3).

30-36   Where section 20 applies to a QLTA, the amount that the tenant can be required to contribute by way of service charge to relevant costs incurred under the QLTA is limited to £100 in respect of each accounting period.[51] For these purposes, 'accounting period' means the period beginning with the relevant date and ending with the date that falls 12 months after the relevant date. In the case of the first accounting period, the relevant date is either:

(a)   if the relevant accounts are made up for periods of 12 months, the date on which the period that includes 31 October 2003[52] ends; or

(b)   if the accounts are not so made up, 31 October 2003.

30-37   In the case of subsequent accounting periods, the relevant date is the date immediately following the end of the previous accounting period.[53]

30-38   Where more than one individual dwelling is demised by a single lease, the financial cap is £100 per year per dwelling and not £100 in total. The 'relevant contribution of a tenant' in article 4 of the Consultation Regulations is what he is paying as a 'service charge', which is (by definition) a charge in relation to a 'separate dwelling'.[54] Consequently, although article 4 relates to the payment of 'a tenant of a dwelling', it is directed to the payment he is making in relation to each separate dwelling (even if he is the tenant of several other 'dwellings' which are subject to the same service charge regime).[55]

The consultation requirements

30-39   The consultation requirements are set out in the four schedules to the Consultation Regulations. These are reproduced in full in the Appendix, to which reference should be made for the full details. Precisely which requirements must be complied with depends on whether the consultation relates to qualifying works or to a QLTA and on other factors as follows:

(a)   Schedule 1 applies to QLTAs other than those for which a public notice under European Union public procurement regulations is required. This schedule is, therefore, applicable to private landlords proposing to enter into a QLTA.

(b)   Schedule 2 applies to QLTAs for which a public notice under EU public procurement regulations is required. This schedule will only apply to landlords which are public bodies proposing to enter into a QLTA.

(c)   Schedule 3 sets out more limited consultation requirements that are applicable to qualifying works carried out pursuant to the terms of a QLTA that has previously been the subject of consultation.

51   Section 20(1), (2), (5) and (7) and Consultation Regulations, art 4(1).
52   The date when the Regulations came into force. In Wales, this should be substituted with 31 March 2004.
53   Consultation Regulations, art 4(2)–(4).
54   See the definition of 'dwelling' in the Landlord and Tenant Act 1985, s 38. See **28-03**ff. above.
55   *Paddington Walk Management Ltd v Peabody Trust* [2010] L&TR 6.

(d)   Schedule 4, Part 1 applies to qualifying works where there is no QLTA in place, but public notice under EU public procurement regulations is required. This schedule only applies to landlords which are public bodies proposing to carry out qualifying works.

(e)   Schedule 4, Part 2 applies to qualifying works where there is no QLTA in place in respect of the works. This will ordinarily be the schedule which applies to private landlords proposing to carry out qualifying works.

30-40   All of the schedules contain detailed provisions requiring the landlord to serve various notices and proposals, permit inspections, obtain estimates and have regard to observations made in response. All of the detailed requirements must be complied with if the landlord is to avoid the statutory cap imposed as a consequence for failure to comply, since section 20 does not contain any test of material or substantial compliance. The extent to which the landlord has complied with the requirements, even though the consultation was deficient in some more or less minor respect, will plainly be relevant to the question of dispensation, considered at **30-42** below.

30-41   Although the detailed requirements differ between the schedules, they follow the same broad approach. In *Daejan Investments Ltd v Benson,*[56] the Supreme Court adopted the following four stage summary of the requirements under Schedule 4, Part 2 (qualifying works, private landlord, no QLTA):

'Stage 1: Notice of intention to do the works

Notice must be given to each tenant and any tenants' association, describing the works, or saying where and when a description may be inspected, stating the reasons for the works, specifying where and when observations and nominations for possible contractors should be sent, allowing at least 30 days. The landlord must have regard to those observations.

Stage 2: Estimates

The landlord must seek estimates for the works, including from any nominee identified by any tenants or the association.

Stage 3: Notices about estimates

The landlord must issue a statement to tenants and the association, with two or more estimates, a summary of the observations, and its responses. Any nominee's estimate must be included. The statement must say where and when estimates may be inspected, and where and by when observations can be sent, allowing at least 30 days.[57] The landlord must have regard to such observations.

Stage 4: Notification of reasons

Unless the chosen contractor is a nominee or submitted the lowest estimate, the landlord must, within 21 days of contracting, give a statement to each tenant and

56   [2013] UKSC 14 at para 12.
57   See *Peverel Properties Ltd v Hughes* [2013] L&TR 6, for the requirements to invite observations and to specify the date by which such observations should be sent.

the association of its reasons, or specifying where and when such a statement may be inspected.'

Dispensation

30-42 By section 20ZA(1), the LVT may dispense with all or any of the consultation requirements in relation to any qualifying works or qualifying long-term agreements, if satisfied that it is reasonable to do so. By contrast with the position under the old section 20,[58] it is not a pre-condition to dispensation that the landlord has acted reasonably. The tribunal only has to be satisfied that it is reasonable to dispense with the requirements. In considering whether or not it is reasonable to do so, the primary consideration for the LVT is whether or not prejudice has been caused to the tenants as a result of the particular failure on the part of the landlord.

The test for dispensation

30-43 In the important case of *Daejan Investments Ltd v Benson,*[59] the Supreme Court considered the proper approach to applications for dispensation. It was held that in order to justify refusing a request for dispensation the LVT must be satisfied that prejudice had been caused to the tenants as a result of a failure to comply with the consultation requirements. Significantly, by a bare majority, it was also held that the failure to consult would not in itself amount to sufficient prejudice unless the tenants could also show that the outcome, in terms of the works carried out or the recoverable costs, would have been different had full consultation taken place.

30-44 Prior to the litigation in the *Benson* case, it was established that prejudice to the tenants is the primary consideration in deciding whether or not it is reasonable to grant dispensation. In *Camden LBC v Leaseholders of 37 Flats at 30–40 Grafton Way,*[60] the Lands Tribunal[61] concluded:

> 'The principal consideration for the purpose of any decision on retrospective dispensation must, in our judgment, be whether any significant prejudice has been suffered by a tenant as a consequence of the landlord's failure to comply with the requirement or requirements in question. An omission may not prejudice a tenant if it is small, or if, through material made available in another context and the opportunity to comment on it, it is rendered insignificant. Whether an omission does cause significant prejudice needs to be considered in all the circumstances. If significant prejudice has been caused we cannot see that it could ever be appropriate to grant dispensation.'

58 See *Martin v Maryland Estates Ltd* [1999] 2 EGLR 53, discussed at **30-19** above.
59 [2013] UKSC 14.
60 [2008] EWLands LRX_185_2006, approved by Gross LJ in the Court of Appeal in *Daejan Investments Ltd v Benson* [2011] EWCA Civ 38, but according to the majority of the Supreme Court in *Benson*, whilst *Grafton Way* might have been rightly decided, it was for the wrong reasons: [2013] UKSC 14, *per* Lord Neuberger at para 76.
61 N J Rose FRICS.

30-45 The Lands Tribunal went on to hold that the tenants had suffered prejudice as a result of the landlord's failure to supply estimates. The fact that the tenants had been deprived of the opportunity to examine and comment upon the estimates was in itself significant prejudice and the extent to which the tenants would have taken advantage of that opportunity, had it been given to them, was a matter of pure speculation and, therefore, irrelevant.

30-46 This approach was approved by the Court of Appeal in *Benson*, but was rejected by the Supreme Court. *Benson* concerned a block of shops and seven flats, five of which were let to tenants who were liable to pay service charges and were also members of an RTA. The landlord identified a need to carry out major works which constituted qualifying works under section 20 and, therefore, the requirements of Schedule 4, Part 2 of the Consultation Regulations applied. In July 2005, the landlord sent the tenants a stage 1 notice of intention. The landlord then obtained four tenders for the works, all of which were priced in excess of £400,000. The landlord, however, only supplied one of these tenders to the tenants before it attempted to serve a stage 2 notice, in June 2006. The tenants objected that all of the tenders had not been supplied. A second purported stage 2 notice was served at the end of July, but the priced tenders were not supplied to the tenants until August. By this time, the landlord had notified the tenants that it had awarded the contract to its preferred contractor (which was one of the two most competitive tenders) so that the consultation process was at an end. The tenants applied for a determination of the amount payable by them under section 27A. The LVT determined that the landlord had failed to comply with the section 20 procedure and dismissed the landlord's application for dispensation under section 20ZA. Accordingly, each tenant's contribution was capped at £250. The Upper Tribunal dismissed the landlord's appeal.

30-47 On appeal to the Court of Appeal, the landlord raised three issues of principle. First, the landlord argued that the Upper Tribunal had erred in holding that the financial effects of granting or refusing dispensation were irrelevant. Secondly, the Upper Tribunal was wrong to hold that the nature of the landlord was relevant; that Daejan was a corporate landlord was irrelevant and did not justify the LVT adopting a more rigorous approach to non-compliance with the Consultation Regulations. Thirdly, the Upper Tribunal had erred in law or, alternatively, had reached a conclusion no reasonable tribunal could have reached with regard to the question of whether the tenants had suffered prejudice flowing from Daejan's failure to comply with the Consultation Regulations. The landlord argued that it was for the tenants to prove such prejudice and, regardless of where the burden of proof lay, there was none.

30-48 The Court of Appeal held that the financial effects of a decision to refuse dispensation were irrelevant to the discretion under section 20ZA(1). If the LVT were obliged to consider the financial impact on the landlord of a decision not to grant dispensation, this would inevitably lead to a situation where the higher the service charge, the more likely dispensation would be granted, a potential outcome which Gross LJ described as 'curious'.

30-49   As regards the issue of prejudice, Gross LJ expressly agreed with the observations made in the *Grafton Way* case, quoted at **30-44** above. His Lordship stressed that significant prejudice to the tenants is a consideration of the first importance in exercising the dispensatory discretion under section 20ZA(1) and continued:

> 'In many cases, a landlord could readily assert that further consultation would have made no difference. Disproving such assertions would inevitably give rise to an invidious exercise in speculation, quite apart from difficulties of proof (if and in so far as a burden rests on the tenants in this regard: see below). While there will no doubt be some instances where a landlord may demonstrate that a failure to comply with the consultation requirements was, on the facts, such as to make no difference and to give rise to no prejudice to the tenants, arguments of this nature need careful scrutiny; there would otherwise be a risk of undermining the purpose of the statutory scheme'.[62]

30-50   The Supreme Court, by a majority of three to two,[63] upheld the landlord's appeal. Lord Neuberger, with whom Lord Clarke and Lord Sumption agreed, began by considering the purpose behind the consultation requirements. In the earlier case of *Paddington Basin*, Lewison J had identified two distinct statutory purposes lying behind the regulation of service charges:

> 'there are two separate strands to the policy underlying the regulation of service charges. Parliament gave two types of protection to tenants. First, they are protected by section 19 from having to pay excessive and unreasonable service charges or charges for work and services that are not carried out to a reasonable standard. Second, even if service charges are reasonable in amount, reasonably incurred and are for work and services that are provided to a reasonable standard, they will not be recoverable above the statutory maximum if they relate to qualifying works or a qualifying long term agreement and the consultation process has not been complied with or dispensed with. It follows that the consultation provisions are imposed for an additional reason; namely, to ensure a degree of transparency and accountability when a landlord decides to undertake qualifying works or enter into a qualifying long term agreement.'[64]

30-51   Lord Neuberger, however, focused on the former of these two purposes. He rejected the view that section 20 consultation was introduced for the purposes of providing transparency and accountability as objectives independent of the substantive outcome of the amount payable by tenants. Rather, his Lordship said that sections 19 to 20ZA of the 1985 Act are directed towards ensuring that tenants of flats are not required:

(i)   to pay for unnecessary services or services which are provided to a defective standard, and

---

62 [2011] EWCA Civ 38 at para 73. For a case decided on the basis of the principles set out by the Court of Appeal in *Benson*, before judgment was delivered by the Supreme Court, see *Stenau Properties Ltd v Leek* [2012] L&TR 22.
63 Lord Hope and Lord Wilson dissenting.
64 See also **30-03** above.

(ii) to pay more than they should for services which are necessary and are provided to an acceptable standard.

30-52 The consultation requirements are intended to reinforce and to give practical effect to those two purposes.[65]

30-53 This focus on the purpose of consultation being directed to the substance of the works rather than to procedural transparency and accountability informed the majority's approach to the type of prejudice which is relevant when considering dispensation. Accordingly, Lord Neuberger rejected the view that dispensation should be refused solely because of the seriousness of the breach or departure from the consultation requirements, in the absence of evidence of substantive prejudice to the tenants. To adopt that approach would elevate the consultation requirements to an end in themselves rather than a means to the end of ensuring that tenants do not pay more than they should. It followed that:

> 'In a case where it was common ground that the extent, quality and cost of the works were in no way affected by the landlord's failure to comply with the Requirements [of consultation], I find it hard to see why dispensation should not be granted (at least in the absence of some very good reason): in such a case the tenants would be in precisely the position that the legislation intended them to be – i.e. as if the Requirements had been complied with.'[66]

30-54 It had been argued on behalf of the tenants that requiring them to prove substantive prejudice to support opposition to dispensation would place an unfair burden on them. The majority accepted that the factual burden of identifying relevant substantive prejudice would be on the tenants, but went on to say that the LVT should be sympathetic to tenants and:

> 'if the tenants show that, because of the landlord's non-compliance with the Requirements, they were unable to make a reasonable point [about the proposed works] which, if adopted, would have been likely to have reduced the costs of the works or to have resulted in some other advantage, the LVT would be likely to proceed on the assumption that the point would have been accepted by the landlord. Further, the more egregious the landlord's failure, the more readily an LVT would be likely to accept that the tenants had suffered prejudice.'[67]

30-55 The majority did, however, reject the landlord's argument (which was also run in the Upper Tribunal and the Court of Appeal) that the LVT ought to take account of the financial consequences to the landlord of not granting a dispensation.[68] However, Lord Neuberger went on to comment that 'such consequences are often inversely reflective of the relevant prejudice to the tenants, which is, as already mentioned, centrally important'. Therefore, whilst financial prejudice to a landlord is not, itself, a factor which the LVT ought to

65 *Daejan Investments Ltd v Benson* [2013] UKSC 14 at paras 42–45.
66 *Ibid*, at para 45.
67 *Ibid*, at para 67.
68 *Per* Lord Neuberger at para 51.

rely upon, it was acknowledged that in practice, in applying the test laid down by the majority decision, the landlord is unlikely to be prejudiced financially unless the tenants are able to show that they have suffered prejudice of similar financial magnitude.[69]

30-56 In their dissenting judgments, Lords Hope and Wilson adopted a different approach, based on their alternative view as to the statutory purpose behind sections 20 and 20ZA. Lord Wilson perceived in the legislative history a deliberate policy decision to elevate consultation requirements to the status of a free-standing obligation unconnected with substantive considerations of the quality of the work done or the cost to the tenants.[70] The minority of the Supreme Court in *Benson* on this basis preferred the approach adopted in the *Grafton Way* case as approved by the Court of Appeal.

Attaching conditions to dispensation

30-57 An important aspect of the decision of the Supreme Court in *Benson* was the unanimous confirmation that the LVT has an almost unfettered jurisdiction to attach conditions to the grant of dispensation. In *Benson*, the landlords had, prior to the original LVT determination, offered to make a concession of £50,000 against the sums demanded from the tenants in order to compensate for any perceived prejudice. The LVT rejected that proposal and the Court of Appeal doubted whether the LVT had jurisdiction to attach conditions in this way.

30-58 The Supreme Court confirmed that the LVT did in fact have power to attach conditions to the grant of dispensation.[71] Under section 20ZA(1) the LVT has power to grant dispensation on such terms as it thinks fit. This includes, where appropriate, the power to order that the landlord pays the costs incurred by the tenant in opposing an application for dispensation, even though the LVT does not have any general jurisdiction to award costs.[72] Lord Neuberger considered that the power to award costs as a condition for granting dispensation from the consultation requirements was analogous to the power of the courts to require tenants to pay costs as a condition for obtaining relief from forfeiture, where the landlord has acted reasonably.[73] However, in the forfeiture context, where the landlord behaves unreasonably, he will not be entitled to his costs.[74] Similarly, therefore, it is to be expected that tenants who behave unreasonably in resisting

---

69 *Ibid.* See also para 74, where Lord Neuberger considered that the approach endorsed by the majority ought to ensure that the tenants do not receive a windfall.

70 *Ibid*, at paras 103–107.

71 See paras 53–64 of the judgment of Lord Neuberger.

72 Under the Commonhold and Leasehold Reform Act 2002, Sch 12, para 10, the LVT can only award a limited amount of costs (currently £500) where an application is dismissed on the ground that it is frivolous vexation or an abuse of process or where the applicant has acted frivolously, vexatiously, abusively, disruptively or otherwise unreasonably in connection with the proceedings.

73 See *Egerton v Jones* [1939] 2 KB 702.

74 See, e.g. *Howard v Fanshawe* [1895] 2 Ch 581. Indeed, the landlord might even, as in that case, find himself paying the tenant's costs.

a dispensation application should not expect payment of their costs to be made a condition of dispensation.

30-59   The jurisdiction to attach conditions is an important tool for the LVT. As Lord Neuberger pointed out, if the LVT is limited to a binary choice of granting or not granting dispensation, either decision is capable of causing injustice. His Lordship gave the example of a case where a landlord carries out works costing £1 million but failed to comply with the requirements to a small extent and the tenants establish that the works may have cost £25,000 more as a result of the failure to comply. The LVT could, in such a case, grant dispensation on condition that the landlord reduces the costs recoverable by £25,000. This additional flexibility is to be welcomed, but it is suggested that the LVT must be alive to the risk that landlords might seek to 'buy off' the consultation requirements. Applying the *Benson* test literally, even wanton disregard by a landlord for the statutory consultation requirements is not enough to refuse dispensation unless the tenants can show that they have suffered prejudice. A landlord could proceed in the knowledge that the tenants would have to object to payment, oppose dispensation, establish relevant prejudice and then quantify the value of that prejudice before the landlord's position would be affected. That said, whilst the requirements themselves are clearly onerous and cumbersome for landlords,[75] a landlord who takes a calculated decision not to engage with the process for no apparent reason (such as urgency) runs the risk that the tenants will be able to establish that the failure has caused prejudice to them and in such a case, it seems that the flexibility in the Supreme Court's approach will allow the LVT to lean in favour of the tenants when considering the evidence and arguments they rely upon to show that the landlord's failure has caused prejudice.[76]

30-60   The decision in *Benson* undoubtedly represents an important shift of the balance under sections 20 and 20ZA in favour of landlords. Lord Neuberger summarised the majority judgment as follows:

> 'All in all, it appears to me that the conclusions which I have reached, taken together, will result in (i) the power to dispense with the Requirements being exercised in a proportionate way consistent with their purpose, and (ii) a fair balance between (a) ensuring that tenants do not receive a windfall because the power is exercised too sparingly and (b) ensuring that landlords are not cavalier, or worse, about adhering to the Requirements because the power is exercised too loosely.'

30-61   Tenants who wish to oppose an application for dispensation will now be required to identify what difference would have resulted if the landlord had in fact complied with consultation requirements. It remains to be seen how the LVT will give effect to this requirement in practice. It is notable that Lord Neuberger emphasised that the LVT should be sympathetic to tenants when considering

---

75 Especially as interpreted by the Chancellor in *Phillips v Francis* [2012] EWHC 3650 (Ch) above.

76 See *per* Lord Neuberger at para 67 and see **30-54** above.

arguments about prejudice.[77] He also indicated that 'once the tenants have shown a credible case for prejudice, the LVT should look to the landlord to rebut it'. In practical terms, the effect of *Benson* is that tenants must now identify what representations as to, for example, the scope of the works or the identity of the contractors, they might have made if they had been allowed an opportunity and what impact this might have had on the outcome of the process if the landlord had elected to adopt those suggestions.[78] It would seem, however, that the burden on the tenants will not be as heavy as might appear since the LVT is entitled to assume that any reasonable points which the tenants can identify as being ones that they would have made, given the chance, would have been adopted by the landlords.

30-62 It is suggested that the shift of emphasis away from technical compliance towards assessment of the substantive outcome is to be welcomed. It is difficult to see any real justification for severely prejudicing the landlord in terms of the sums recoverable in the absence of any substantive prejudice to the tenants arising from a failure to consult. The *Grafton Way* approach, as adopted by the Court of Appeal and the minority in the Supreme Court, is evidently capable of giving rise to a significant windfall in favour of tenants. There remains a forceful body of judicial opinion that the consultation requirements were intended to have an independent purpose of transparency and accountability over and above the role of supporting the substantive limitations on service charges identified by Lord Neuberger. However, that is now of academic concern only. The approach of the tribunals which will decide whether dispensation should be granted in any case must, now, follow the decision of the majority in the Supreme Court. This requires a focus on the substantive purpose of the provisions, as explained above.

30-63 There is legitimate reason for concern that landlords will now be rather more willing to deliberately ignore consultation requirements, wholly or in part, in the knowledge that not only will the tenants have to establish that the outcome might have been different, but also that the LVT may be persuaded to permit the landlord effectively to buy off the tenants' consultation entitlement by making a discount against the sums recoverable. Nevertheless, it is considered that the risk is a relatively small one as compared to the apparent injustice of the tenant avoiding contractual obligations to pay sums due to the landlord on the basis of technical and procedural omissions and in the absence of substantive prejudice.

---

77 See **30-55** above.
78 As Lord Neuberger emphasised at para 46, the decision as to which contractors to engage and at what cost remains that of the landlord: the Consultation Regulations merely require the landlord to consult and observe. The decision-making power remains with the landlord. However, in practice, a failure to listen and observe comments by the tenants during the process might well provide evidence for the tenants of unreasonableness under s 19.

CHAPTER 31

Time limit for demands: Section 20B

31-01 Leases often include provisions specifying when demands for payment must be made by a landlord.[1] However, statute now imposes a time limit of 18 months for making demands for the payment of service charges. The obvious purpose is to prevent a landlord making a demand for payment a long time after incurring the expenditure to which the demand relates.

31-02 Section 20B(1) of the Landlord and Tenant Act 1985[2] states that if any of the relevant costs taken into account in determining the amount of any service charge were incurred more than 18 months before a demand for payment of the service charge is served on the tenant, then the tenant shall not be liable to pay so much of the service charge as reflects the costs so incurred. This is a significant provision because a failure to comply will mean that expenditure which is not demanded in time will become altogether irrecoverable. It is, therefore, essential to ensure that valid and accurate demands for all expenditure the landlord will seek to recover are served within 18 months, particularly as it has been decided that a subsequent corrective demand, made out of time, cannot without more be treated as dating back to an earlier demand for less, made within time, so as to enable the landlord to recover an additional contribution.[3]

31-03 The limitation does not apply, however, if within the period of 18 months beginning with the date when the relevant costs in question were incurred, the tenant was notified in writing that those costs had been incurred and that he would subsequently be required under the terms of his lease to contribute to them by the payment of a service charge.[4] Therefore, a landlord who knows that he has incurred costs which he will seek to recover by way of service charge but cannot, for some reason, serve a demand in respect of those costs within 18 months of the date they were incurred by him, can serve a notice under section 20B(2), notifying the tenant that costs to which he will be required to contribute have been incurred.

1   See **16-15** to **16-18**.
2   Which was inserted into the 1985 Act by the Landlord and Tenant Act 1987, s 41, Sch 2, para 4.
3   *Paddington Walk Management Ltd v Peabody Trust* [2010] L&TR 6.
4   Section 20B(2).

31-04   Care must be taken, however, to ensure that any notice purporting to comply with section 20B(2) provides sufficient information to the tenant to avoid the effect of section 20B(1). The requirements of a valid notice under section 20B(2) were discussed at length by Morgan J in *Brent London Borough Council v Shulem B Association Ltd.*[5] The straightforward facts of that case were as follows. The landlord carried out extensive repairs works to blocks of flats and, in February 2006, after the works had been completed, sent each tenant a letter informing them that the actual cost of the works had not yet been calculated, referred to an attached schedule setting out the amount which it estimated each tenant would have to contribute to the works by way of service charge, but warned that the actual costs might be greater than those shown in the schedule. In December 2006, the landlord sent each tenant a second letter notifying them of the actual cost of the works and the amount which they would have to contribute by way of service charge, which was less than the estimated amount set out in the schedule attached to the earlier letter. It was common ground that the relevant costs had been incurred more than 18 months before the December letter but that most of the costs had been incurred less than 18 months before the February letter. The tenant did not pay and applied to strike out the claim made by the landlord to recover the sum demanded on the basis that recovery was precluded by section 20B(1). That application was refused on the ground that the February letter satisfied section 20B(2). Morgan J allowed the tenant's appeal, holding that the February letter was not a valid demand for payment in accordance with the requirements of the lease and so could not, itself, satisfy section 20B(1) and, furthermore, it did not purport to state what the actual costs were and warned that they might be greater than the estimated costs which were referred to and so could not be a valid notice under section 20B(2).

31-05   A valid notification under section 20B(2) must state a figure for the costs that the landlord has actually incurred and reference to an estimate will not be sufficient.[6] A landlord who knows that it has incurred costs, but does not know the precise amount of the expenditure within 18 months, should specify a figure for costs which it is content to have as a limit on the cost ultimately recoverable.[7] A landlord is entitled to 'err on the side of caution' and, if a landlord states that its actual costs were £x, that will be a valid notification in writing for the purposes of section 20B(2), even though the landlord knows that it may turn out that the costs will be somewhat less than £x. The landlord would not then be prevented by section 20B(1) from recovering a lesser amount if it turns out the actual expenditure is lower.

---

5   [2011] 1 WLR 3014.
6   [2011] 1 WLR 3014 at para 57 and see also *Islington LBC v Abdel-Malek* [2008] L&TR 2, where the Lands Tribunal rejected an argument that the reference in section 20B to relevant costs as defined by section 18 meant that it was legitimate for notice under section 20B(2) to refer to costs which the landlord anticipated would be incurred in the future. For a case where letters were held to be valid notice under s 20B(2), see *Jean-Paul v The Mayor and Burgesses of the London Borough of Southwark* [2011] UKUT 178 (LC).
7   *Brent LBC v Shulem B Association Ltd* [2011] EWHC 1663 (Ch) at para 58.

31-06   Whilst this interpretation offers a practical solution for the landlord faced with the apparently intractable problem of not knowing the precise amount of the expenditure incurred within 18 months, it is potentially open to abuse if taken to logical extremes. Morgan J did not purport to offer any guidance as to what would be the result if a landlord included a wholly unrealistic figure in a section 20B(2) notice, whether such a notice would be valid and, indeed, how a tribunal or court could assess whether the figure mentioned was realistic. There must be a danger that landlords will not make any genuine attempt to assess their expenditure, but simply give notice of inflated 'long-stop' sums. Such an approach would appear to undermine one of the purposes of section 20B, which is to enable tenants to make proper provision for future service charge bills.

31-07   However, this is unlikely to be a problem in the vast majority of cases. It must be relatively rare that a landlord can legitimately say that expenditure has been 'incurred' for the purposes of section 20B,[8] but not be able to say what the amount of that expenditure is 18 months later. Furthermore, it seems likely that a purported section 20B(2) notice, which bears no resemblance to the expenditure actually incurred, would be held to be invalid. The reasoning adopted by Morgan J would not obviously be applicable to a landlord who, for example, adopted a practice of serving notices each year, stating that non-existent expenditure had been incurred as a fall-back position. To take advantage of the approach suggested by Morgan J, a landlord would still have to satisfy the court or tribunal that the sums specified in the notice had been incurred by the time the notice under section 20B(2) was given, even if the exact sum could not be quantified at the time of the notice.

31-08   In addition to specifying the actual expenditure incurred, the notice for the purposes of section 20B(2) must tell the tenant that he will subsequently be required, under the terms of his lease, to contribute to those costs by the payment of a service charge. It is not necessary for the notice to tell the tenant what proportion of the cost will be passed on to him or what the resulting service charge demand will be.[9]

COSTS 'INCURRED'

31-09   It is often of critical importance for the operation of the time limit imposed by section 20B to ascertain the date when the relevant costs were 'incurred' by the landlord. The Landlord and Tenant Act 1985 does not provide any guidance as to how this date is to be fixed. Ordinarily, it will not be difficult to ascertain when a particular cost was incurred by the landlord; this will not always be the case. For example, if a managing agent is retained on a yearly contract, but paid monthly, is the whole of the management fee incurred at the start of the

---

8   See **31-09** to **31-12**.
9   *Brent LBC v Shulem B Association Ltd* [2011] EWHC 1663 (Ch) at para 65.

year or is a part of the fee incurred each month? Similarly, in a contract for major works, are the costs incurred when a contract is signed, on the dates that staged payments are made or when a certificate of completion is served and the final payment becomes due? These issues are likely to be of particular significance where balancing payments are in issue and so it becomes necessary to identify the date on which sums demanded on account are exhausted.

31-10 Perhaps surprisingly, the issue of the date on which costs have been incurred has received relatively little attention in the reported cases under section 20B. In *Jean-Paul v The Mayor and Burgesses of the London Borough of Southwark*,[10] the President of the Upper Tribunal said:

> 'In my judgment ... costs are only "incurred" by the landlord within the meaning of section 20B when payment is made. There is clearly a distinction between incurring liability (i.e. an obligation to pay) and incurring costs, and it is the latter formulation that is used in the provision.'

31-11 In *O M Property Management Ltd v Burr*,[11] part of the relevant costs under a service charge comprised gas bills. Due to a mistake, the management company was billed for gas by the wrong utility company, EDF, and settled the bills received. After a number of years, the correct supplier, Total Energy and Gas, pointed this out and requested payment of a higher amount due to a misreading of a gas meter. EDF returned the payments it had received from the management company and Total reduced its charges by 20%, but this left a balance of just over £100,000 which was included in the sum demanded from tenants by way of service charge. An issue arose as to the application of section 20B, given that the gas had been supplied a number of years before the demand which related to the cost of that gas was served. The management company argued that the sums were not incurred for the purposes of section 20B until the invoice to Total was paid. The Lands Tribunal agreed, holding that, while liability to pay may be incurred when something is used, a liability does not become a cost until the cost is expended or becomes payable. Therefore, as a matter of interpretation of section 20B, 'costs' are 'incurred' either on the presentation of an invoice or on payment. Whether a particular cost is incurred on the presentation of an invoice or on payment will depend upon the facts of a particular case.

31-12 It would appear, therefore, that a landlord only incurs a cost for these purposes when money changes hands or an invoice is presented for payment, but there is, as yet, no authority identifying which of those two alternatives should be adopted. The logic of the decisions referred to above would suggest that it is usually the date of payment that is relevant, rather than the date an invoice is received. In any case, entering into a contract for the provision of a service (with payment deferred) does not involve incurring relevant costs.

10 [2011] UKUT 178 (LC).
11 [2012] L&TR 17.

DEMANDS FOR ON-ACCOUNT PAYMENTS

31-13   Section 20B(1) has no application to demands for payments on account of anticipated future expenditure. Accordingly, when a lease permits a landlord to demand on-account payments against estimated expenditure and such payments are made, but the actual expenditure of the landlord does not exceed the amount of the on-account payments so that no demand for a balancing payment needs to be or is, in fact, made, section 20B has no application.[12] The LVT is bound by the decision in *Gilje v Charlgrove* to this effect.[13]

31-14   Matters become rather more complicated where the estimated budget is exceeded and the actual expenditure is more than the sums demanded from the tenants by way of on-account payments, so that the landlord issues a demand for a balancing payment. Section 20B(1) will apply to demands for balancing payments in such circumstances. However, the balancing charge reflects costs incurred by the landlord after the sums demanded on account have been exhausted. Accordingly, the 18-month time limit for the balancing demands only begins to run from the date on which the landlord's actual expenditure exceeded the amount of the on-account payments demanded.[14]

31-15   In some cases, therefore, it will be necessary to undertake what will often be a relatively complicated accounting process to find out whether any part of the relevant costs included in a balancing demand are debarred under section 20B. The first step is to ascertain the total sum demanded on account by the landlord. It will then be necessary to look at the landlord's detailed records to see the date on which items of expenditure were incurred[15] and on what date the total expenditure incurred by the landlord exceeded the sums demanded on account. Given that there is no all-encompassing definition to assist in identifying the date on which expenditure was incurred, this is a potentially difficult exercise to undertake, particularly in the case of larger developments and where there are long-term agreements in place for the provision of services.

31-16   It has been suggested that, when identifying the point in time at which the advance payments have been used up, it is appropriate to take the costs reasonably incurred and not (if different) actual expenditure.[16] Whilst there is logic to this approach, it will, most likely, further and unnecessarily complicate

---

12   *Gilje v Charlgrove Securities Ltd (No 2)* [2002] 1 EGLR 41, followed in *Redendale Ltd v Modi* [2010] UKUT 346 (LC) and *Paddington Walk Management Ltd v Peabody Trust* [2010] L&TR 89. The same conclusion was reached in *Brennan v St Pauls Court Ltd* [2010] UKUT 403 (LC), albeit with some reservations expressed as to the 'strange' effect that 'if the landlord takes the precaution of ensuring that he gets in enough credit so that he never needs to issue a demand (unless something goes seriously wrong) he will have little need to worry about "old costs" or section 20B'.
13   *Solitaire Property Management Co Ltd v Holden* [2012] UKUT 86 (LC).
14   *Holding & Management (Solitaire) Ltd v Sherwin* [2010] UKUT 412 (LC); [2011] 1 EGLR 29.
15   See **31-09** to **31-12** as to the meaning of 'incurred'.
16   *Holding & Management (Solitaire) Ltd v Sherwin* [2010] UKUT 412 (LC); [2011] 1 EGLR 29 at para 28.

matters. For one thing, there could not be a determination on section 20B until all other issues of recoverability and reasonableness had been considered, so additional hearings would be inevitable. In any event, this approach is not necessarily justified by the wording of section 20B(1). That section requires that a demand is served within 18 months of the relevant costs being incurred. A particular element of the charge has still been incurred and constitutes part of the relevant costs within the statutory definition,[17] even if it is unreasonable or irrecoverable for some other reason.

EFFECT OF INVALID DEMANDS

31-17   A potentially difficult point is whether service of a demand which is invalid for some other reason stops time running for the purpose of section 20B. As in Chapters 32 and 33, there are various statutory requirements which must be satisfied in order for a demand for payment of service charges to be valid.[18] Assume a landlord serves an otherwise valid demand for service charges within 18 months of the date the expenditure underlying the demand was incurred, but the demand is not accompanied by a summary of rights and obligations in accordance with section 21B of the Landlord and Tenant Act 1985 or fails to specify a valid name and address of the landlord for the purposes of section 47 of the Landlord and Tenant Act 1987. The landlord does not realise his mistake for 18 months, when he serves a fresh demand accompanied by a valid summary. Is the landlord precluded by section 20B from relying on the demand?

31-18   In *Hymers v MacIntyre*,[19] the LVT determined that a landlord had failed to comply with the requirements of section 47 in that demands served on the tenant did not contain the address of the landlord. The LVT then went on to hold that if and when compliant demands were served, the landlord would be debarred by section 20B from recovering costs incurred more than 18 months prior to the fresh demands. The same conclusion was tentatively reached as regards non-compliance with section 21B in *Oliver v London Development Property Co Ltd*.[20] There, the LVT found that a landlord had not enclosed a summary of rights and obligations with demands for payment of service charges so that no sum was currently payable by the tenant. The LVT, although accepting that, given this conclusion, the issue did not strictly arise, went on to express the view that:

> 'a demand under section 20B probably means a demand that complies with section 21B so that, if the [landlord] were now to serve demands which complied with section 21B, costs incurred more than 18 months prior to the new service would not be recoverable under section 20B.'

---

17   Section 18; see **28-11** to **28-20** above.
18   For example, section 21B (including summary of rights and obligations); see **33-01** to **33-19** below. Landlord and Tenant Act 1987, s 47 (landlord's name and address); see **32-07** to **32-18** below.
19   Leasehold Valuation Tribunal, unreported, 29 November 2006, MAN/00CK/LSC/2006/0014.
20   Leasehold Valuation Tribunal, unreported, 16 May 2012, LON/00AM/LSC/2011/0719.

31-19 The authors would respectfully suggest that these decisions should not be followed and that a failure to comply with section 21B or section 47 of the Landlord and Tenant Act 1987 should not mean that no demand has been served for the purposes of section 20B. First, the effect of both section 21B and section 47 is not expressed to be that the demand which is served is invalid. Both sections merely entitle the tenant to withhold payment until there has been compliance. If the approach adopted by the LVT in the cases quoted above is followed, this would have the result that, in many cases, the effect of section 21B and section 47 would be rendered absolute and the service charges demanded would become irrecoverable, contrary to the clear intention of Parliament in providing that the effect of a failure to comply only suspends and does not extinguish the landlord's entitlement to recover the sums.

31-20 Secondly, the purpose of the 18-month time limit imposed by section 20B was identified in *Gilje v Charlgrove* as follows:

> 'the policy behind section 20B of the Act is that the tenant should not be faced with a bill for expenditure, of which he or she was not sufficiently warned to set aside provision. It is not directed at preventing the lessor from recovering any expenditure on matters, and to the extent, of which there was adequate prior notice.'[21]

31-21 A demand which does not comply with section 21B or section 47 of the 1987 Act will still fulfil these purposes. Accordingly, it is not easy to identify any justification for saying that, if a landlord does not rectify a failure to comply by service of a fresh, compliant demand within 18 months of the date the costs were incurred, he should be barred from recovering the sums under section 20B.

31-22 There is some support for the above view in *Amourgam v Valepark Properties Ltd.*[22] In that case, HH Judge Huskinson held that the requirements of section 21B applied to demands served after the section came into force, even though the expenditure making up the sums demanded was incurred before that date. The learned judge went on to say that the relevant disputed items would become payable by the tenant once a demand which complied with section 21B was served, even though the expenditure was incurred well over 18 months prior to the decision. More significantly, however, in a recent appeal to the Upper Tribunal, it was argued that a demand which failed to comply with section 47 was incapable of satisfying section 20B. This argument was rejected. The tenant relied on dicta of Morgan J in *Brent LBC v Shulem B Association Limited*[23] to the effect that a demand under section 20B must be a 'valid' demand. However, as noted by the President of the Upper Tribunal (Lands Chamber), the invalidity with which the court was concerned in *Shulem* was contractual invalidity and therefore not one which was capable of retrospective correction, as is the case with a failure

---

21 *Per* Etherton J at para 278.
22 [2011] UKUT 261.
23 [2011] EWHC 1663 (Ch).

to comply with section 47.[24] Therefore, it was held that a demand which did not satisfy the requirements of section 47(1) was, nevertheless, sufficient to comply with section 20B.

24 See s 47(2).

CHAPTER 32

Rights to information about the landlord

32-01 A tenant will not be in a position effectively to challenge the sums demanded from him by his landlord (either on the basis that they are not properly recoverable in accordance with the terms of the lease or pursuant to the substantive statutory limitations on the sums recoverable) unless he has sufficient information as to how those sums have been calculated. It is rare for leases to make any requirement as regards information or the form of a demand, aside from sometimes requiring certification by a surveyor or accountant.[1] In order to meet this difficulty, statute now confers on tenants of dwellings a number of rights to information on tenants, some of which have automatic sanctions for non-compliance and others depending on a request being made by a tenant.

32-02 Significant reforms have been proposed to the tenants' entitlement to seek information regarding the constituent elements of a service charge. At the time of writing, these changes have not been brought into effect and, given the amount of time that has elapsed since the legislation implementing the reform was drafted, it is doubtful whether they will, in fact, be implemented. This section first summarises the various provisions conferring entitlement to be given or to seek information relating to service charges, then discusses each of these in turn, before considering the unimplemented reforms.

LANDLORD'S IDENTITY

32-03 By section 1 of the Landlord and Tenant Act 1985, any tenant of a dwelling may make a written request for the landlord's name and address to (a) any person who demands, or the last person who received, rent payable under the tenancy, or (b) any other person for the time being acting as agent for the landlord, in relation to the tenancy. A person in receipt of such a demand must supply the tenant with a written statement of the landlord's name and address within the period of 21 days beginning with the day on which he receives

---

1   See Chapter 17 above.

the request. It is a criminal offence, punishable on conviction by a fine not exceeding level 4 on the standard scale to fail to comply with a valid request without reasonable excuse.[2]

32-04   By section 2, where a tenant is supplied under section 1 with the name and address of his landlord and the landlord is a body corporate, he may make a further written request to the landlord for the name and address of every director and of the secretary of the landlord. Again, the landlord is required to supply the tenant with a written statement of the information requested within the period of 21 days beginning with the day on which he receives the request. A request under section 2 is deemed to be duly made to the landlord if it is made to (a) an agent of the landlord, or (b) a person who demands the rent of the premises concerned and any such agent or person to whom such a request is made shall forward it to the landlord as soon as may be. A failure to comply is again an offence punishable at the same level.

32-05   These provisions were presumably intended to address the situation where a tenant did not know the identity of his landlord due to the employment of professional managing agents, who demanded and accepted rent and service charges. It is little encountered in practice, however, having largely been superseded by the provisions discussed below, which do not depend on any request being made by the tenant.

32-06   Of more use to tenants is the requirement imposed on landlords by section 3, which applies where there has been an assignment of the interest of a landlord in premises consisting of or including a dwelling. The new landlord must give notice in writing of the assignment and of his name and address to the tenant not later than the next day on which rent is payable under the tenancy or, if that is within two months of the assignment, the end of that period of two months. Again, failure to comply is a criminal offence.[3]

SERVICE CHARGE DEMANDS TO DISCLOSE LANDLORD'S NAME AND ADDRESS FOR SERVICE: SECTION 47

32-07   Section 47 of the Landlord and Tenant Act 1987 provides:

> '(1)   Where any written demand is given to a tenant of premises to which this Part applies, the demand must contain the following information, namely –
>
> (a)   the name and address of the landlord, and
>
> (b)   if that address is not in England and Wales, an address in England and Wales at which notices (including notices in proceedings) may be served on the landlord by the tenant.

---

2   Section 1(2).
3   Section 3(3).

(2)   Where –

(a)   a tenant of any such premises is given such a demand, but

(b)   it does not contain any information required to be contained in it by virtue of subsection (1),

then (subject to subsection (3)) any part of the amount demanded which consists of a service charge or an administration charge ("the relevant amount") shall be treated for all purposes as not being due from the tenant to the landlord at any time before that information is furnished by the landlord by notice given to the tenant.'

32-08   This is an important protection for tenants because the liability to pay service charges (and any other sum included in a demand) is suspended unless the demand contains the name and address of their landlord.

32-09   It is important to note that, in the Landlord and Tenant Act 1987, the word 'landlord' is defined differently to the 1985 Act. Whilst 'landlord' in the context of Landlord and Tenant Act 1985 is capable of including a party other than the landlord who is entitled to recover the service charge (e.g. a management company),[4] by section 61 of the 1987 Act, 'landlord' means:

'the immediate landlord or, in relation to a statutory tenant, the person who, apart from the statutory tenancy, would be entitled to possession of the premises subject to the tenancy'.

32-10   It would appear, therefore, that including the name and address of a management company, but not the landlord (properly so called in the sense of the party owning the interest in the premises, immediately in reversion on the lease), does not satisfy section 47 of the 1987 Act, even where it is the management company and not, for example, the freehold owner that is entitled to demand payment of service charges.[5] Conversely, however, it is considered that where service charges are payable to a management company which is not the landlord, section 47(2) will not preclude the management company from recovering the service charges because it provides only that the service charge is not due to 'the landlord'. There is no obvious policy reason for this distinction and it is considered that it is more likely to be a legislative omission.

ADDRESS FOR SERVICE OF NOTICES: SECTION 48

32-11   By section 48 of the Landlord and Tenant Act 1987:

'(1)   A landlord of premises to which this Part applies shall by notice furnish the tenant with an address in England and Wales at which notices (including notices in proceedings) may be served on him by the tenant.

---

4   See **28-23** above.
5   *Shah v Erdogan* (1997) 1 L&T Rev, Issue 3, D40.

(2) Where a landlord of any such premises fails to comply with subsection (1), any rent, service charge or administration charge otherwise due from the tenant to the landlord shall (subject to subsection (3)) be treated for all purposes as not being due from the tenant to the landlord at any time before the landlord does comply with that subsection.'

32-12   Again, the consequences of a failure to comply with this requirement are apparently serious because any liabilities of the tenant as regards rent, service charges and administration charges under the lease are suspended until there has been compliance. Accordingly, the landlord's remedies for non-payment (most obviously a claim in debt or forfeiture of the lease[6]) will not be available. The wording of the section ('treated for all purposes as not being due from the tenant') would appear to dictate that the landlord will not be entitled to charge interest on any sums which would otherwise be payable until section 48 has been complied with.[7]

32-13   However, it is clear that a failure to comply with either section 47 or section 48 does not extinguish the landlord's entitlement to recover the sums included in the demand altogether, but merely suspends the obligation to pay pending compliance.[8]

32-14   Furthermore, the requirements of sections 47 and 48 can be satisfied in a variety of ways, as there is no prescribed form in which the required information must be given. Section 47 requires that the information is given in the demand. If it is not, then the next question is when, if at all, the 'information is furnished by notice given by the landlord to the tenant'. This wording mirrors the requirements of section 48 and, accordingly, it would seem that, if the information has been given for the purposes of section 48, it must also have been furnished by notice for the purposes of section 47. It is, therefore, suggested that the principles in the decided cases as to when proper information has been provided for the purposes of section 48 are equally applicable to the question of when information has been furnished to the tenant under section 47. Where the correct information is not contained in a demand, but is provided at some later stage, the landlord may encounter difficulties as regards the application of the 18-month time limit under section 20B.[9]

32-15   There is, however, an important distinction between the two sections. Whereas section 48 merely requires that the landlord furnish his tenant with an address at which notices may be served upon him, section 47 requires that a demand contains the name and address of the landlord. Accordingly, whilst giving the address of an agent at which notices may be served may satisfy section

---

6   See Chapters 40 and 45 respectively.
7   Where service charges are payable to a management company rather than the landlord, the position will be the same as under s 47. See **32-10** above.
8   *Dallhold Estates (UK) Ltd v Lindsey Trading Inc* [1992] 1 EGLR 88 and [1994] 1 EGLR 93. As to the potential application of the 18-month time limit imposed by s 20B, where the initial demand does not comply, see **31-17** to **31-22** above.
9   See fn 8 above.

48, this will not suffice for the purposes of section 47. In *Beitov Properties Ltd v Martin*,[10] the Upper Tribunal noted this distinction and explained:[11]

> 'the purpose of the requirement in (a) to provide the address (as well as the name) of the landlord is not solely for the purpose of providing the tenant with an address at or through which he can communicate with the landlord. That is clear because (b) provides that, if the landlord's address is not in England and Wales, an address in England and Wales must be given at which notices may be served on the landlord by the tenant. Thus even if the landlord's address is not in England and Wales it still has to be given (and a further address provided for the service of notices). The purpose of the requirement in section 47 to include in any demand the name and address of the landlord, in my judgment, is to enable a tenant to know who his landlord is, and a name alone may not be sufficient for this purpose. To provide an address at which the landlord can be found assists in the process of identification.

> …

> The address of the landlord for the purpose of section 47(1) thus seems to me to be the place where the landlord is to be found. In the case of an individual this would be his place of residence or the place from which he carries on business. In the case of a company it would be the company's registered office or the place from which it carries on business. If there is more than one place of residence or place from which business is carried on, then, depending on the facts, it may be that any one of such addresses will do.'

32-16   In *Rogan v Woodfield Building Services Ltd*,[12] the Court of Appeal held that section 48 was satisfied because the landlord's name and address was stated in the lease itself, without any indication that he could not be communicated with at that address. Provided the name and address is communicated to the tenant in writing, which it is if it is stated in the lease or tenancy agreement, there is no need for a separate notice.

32-17   Even where the landlord has changed since the grant of the lease, any written notification of the landlord's name and address will suffice for section 48 of the Landlord and Tenant Act 1987. In deciding that the information contained in a notice requiring possession under section 21 of the Housing Act 1988 satisfied section 48, Judge LJ commented:

> 'The notice required by Section 48(1) is not very onerous. The tenant must be told of an address in England and Wales at which he may serve notices on the Landlord: no more, no less. Oral notification is insufficient: the notice must be in writing'.[13]

---

10   [2012] UKUT 133 (LC).
11   At paras 9 and 11.
12   [1995] 1 EGLR 72.
13   *Drew Morgan v Hamid-Zadeh* [1999] 2 EGLR 13 at p 14H–K. See also *Marath v MacGillivray* (1996) 28 HLR 484, information in notice under the Housing Act 1988, s 20 sufficient even though notice invalid for purposes of s 20.

32-18   However, the written communication relied upon by the landlord must be such that it would have communicated to a reasonable recipient that the address referred to is one at which notices may be served on him by the landlord.[14] Simply stating an address in correspondence will not, therefore, comply with section 48, unless the context indicates that a reasonable recipient would have understood this to be a notification of the landlord's address for the service of notices. The restrictions on the recovery of sums imposed by both sections 47 and 48 do not apply when, by virtue of an order of any court or tribunal, there is in force an appointment of a receiver or manager whose functions include the receiving of rent, service charges or (as the case may be) administration charges from the tenant.[15]

---

14 *Glen International Ltd v Triplerose Ltd* [2007] EWCA Civ 388, where the Court of Appeal held that a reference to an address in correspondence by the landlord's agents did not meet this requirement.
15 Sections 47(3) and 48(3).

CHAPTER 33

Rights to information about the service charges

SUMMARY OF RIGHTS AND OBLIGATIONS TO ACCOMPANY SERVICE CHARGE DEMANDS: SECTION 21B

33-01   Section 21B(1) of the Landlord and Tenant Act 1985 requires that a demand for the payment of a service charge must be accompanied by a summary of the rights and obligations of tenants of dwellings in relation to service charges. A tenant may withhold payment of a service charge which has been demanded from him if subsection (1) is not complied with in relation to the demand.[1] Where a tenant withholds a service charge under this section, any provisions of the lease relating to non-payment or late payment of service charges do not have effect in relation to the period for which he so withholds it.[2]

33-02   The requirements as to the form and content of the summary are prescribed by the Secretary of State by statutory regulation ('the Regulation').[3] This power was exercised in England with effect from 1 October 2007 and in Wales from 30 November 2007.[4]

33-03   Accordingly, any demand for the payment of service charges served after these dates must be accompanied by a summary in the form prescribed by the Regulations, even where the relevant expenditure was incurred before the Regulations came into force.[5]

33-04   The content of the summary is set out in paragraph 3 of the Regulations and consists of a statement of 12 paragraphs notifying the tenant of his rights, amongst other things, to apply to the LVT for a determination of the amount

1   Section 21B(3).
2   Section 21B(4).
3   Section 21B(2), (5) and (6).
4   The Service Charges (Summary of Rights and Obligations, and Transitional Provision) (England) Regulations 2007 (SI 2007/1257) and the Service Charges (Summary of Rights and Obligations, and Transitional Provision) (Wales) Regulations 2007 (Welsh SI 2007/3160). However, the requirements do not apply where the lease is not a long lease within the Landlord and Tenant Act 1985, s 26 and the landlord is a local authority, a National Park Authority or a new town corporation.
5   *V J Amourgam v Valepark Properties* [2011] UKUT 261 (LC).

payable, to request a summary of the expenditure making up the demand and to consultation under section 20. Neither section 21B nor the regulations contains any saving provision in the case of a summary which is substantially to the same effect as the prescribed form and, accordingly, it appears that the exact wording of the statement in the regulations must be used to comply with the section. Indeed, it has been held that including a copy of the statutory instrument (which, itself, contains the prescribed form in a schedule), rather than a document which comprises only the prescribed statement and heading, does not comply.[6] The summary must be legible in a typewritten or printed form of at least ten point, and must contain the title 'Service Charges – Summary of tenants' rights and obligations'.[7]

33-05   Section 21B requires that the demand is accompanied by the prescribed summary. Accordingly, it is irrelevant if the tenant already has a copy or that the summary is provided shortly after the demand is served. In *Tingdene Holiday Parks v Cox*,[8] it was held that a summary sent 11 days after a demand did not accompany the demand for the purposes of section 21B(1).

33-06   Again, however, the effect of section 21B is merely suspensory. The sums contained in the demand become payable as soon as a copy of the demand is accompanied by the summary. In the meantime, however, the tenant is entitled to withhold payment and the landlord cannot seek to enforce payment by any means provided for in the lease.[9]

SUMMARY OF RELEVANT COSTS

33-07   At present, there are no requirements that a demand for the payment of service charges contains any particular information as to how the sums demanded have been calculated or as to the costs incurred by the landlord in respect of which the demand is made, save in so far as the form and contents of a demand are specified by the lease.[10]

33-08   In many cases, therefore, demands provide very little information to enable a tenant to assess whether the demand is legitimate. Section 21 of the Landlord and Tenant Act 1985 partially addresses this issue by conferring on a tenant the right to make a written request requiring the landlord to supply him with a written summary of the costs incurred in a specified period. If the relevant accounts are made up for periods of 12 months, the request can be in respect of the costs incurred in the last such period ending not later than the date of the request. If the accounts are made up by reference to a different period, then the

---

6   *Tingdene Holiday Parks v Cox* [2011] UKUT 261 (LC).
7   Paragraph 3.
8   See fn 6 above.
9   See, however, potential difficulties arising in respect of the 18-month time limit under s 20B, discussed at **31-17** to **31-22**.
10 See Chapter 20.

request can be made as regards costs incurred in the period of 12 months ending with the date of the request.[11] The entitlement is to request a summary of the relevant costs[12] in relation to the service charges payable or demanded as payable in that or any other period.

33-09   The effect of the somewhat convoluted language employed in section 21(1) is that, where accounts are prepared on an annual basis (as in the vast majority of leases), the tenant is entitled to request a summary of the relevant costs incurred in the completed service charge year immediately preceding the date of the request. If a different accounting period is employed, the request can be made in respect of the 12 months prior to the date of the request, even if this does not coincide with the accounting period. In such a case, the landlord will be obliged to adjust any accounts in order to provide a summary spanning two or more accounting periods.

33-10   A request under section 21(1) is deemed to be duly served on the landlord if it is served on:

(a)   an agent of the landlord named as such in the rent book or similar document, or

(b)   the person who receives the rent on behalf of the landlord,

and a person on whom a request is so served shall forward it as soon as may be to the landlord.[13]

33-11   The landlord must comply with a request for a summary within one month of the date of the request or within six months of the end of the accounting period which is the subject of the request, whichever is the later.[14]

33-12   The landlord's summary must set out the costs in a way which shows how they have been or will be reflected in demands for service charges and, in addition, must summarise each of the following items, namely:

(a)   any of the costs in respect of which no demand for payment was received by the landlord within the relevant accounting period;

(b)   any of the costs in respect of which –

   (i)   a demand for payment was so received, but

   (ii)   no payment was made by the landlord within that period; and

(c)   any of the costs in respect of which –

   (i)   a demand for payment was so received, and

   (ii)   payment was made by the landlord within that period.

---

11   Section 21(1).
12   See **28-11** to **28-20** above.
13   Section 21(3).
14   Section 21(4).

33-13   The summary must also specify the aggregate of any amounts received by the landlord down to the end of the period on account of service charges in respect of relevant dwellings and still standing to the credit of the tenants of those dwellings at the end of that period.[15]

33-14   Section 21(5A) defines the phrase 'relevant dwelling' to mean a dwelling whose tenant is either:

(a)   the person by or with the consent of whom the request was made; or

(b)   a person whose obligations under the terms of his lease to pay service charges are the same as the corresponding obligations of the person mentioned in (a).

33-15   A failure to refer to any sum standing to the credit of the tenants of relevant dwellings (even where there is none) is a breach by the landlord because it cannot be assumed from the failure to refer to it in the summary that there is no such sum.[16]

33-16   The effect of this definition is that the tenant is entitled to be told which of the other tenants within the premises covered by the service charge regime to which he is obliged to contribute have made contributions during the accounting period in question and what balance of the contributions is still held by the landlord. A simpler mechanism to achieve this result might have been to impose an obligation on the landlord to provide a statement of any sums held to the credit of the statutory trust created by section 42 of the 1987 Act[17] and a breakdown of how that trust fund has been accumulated.

33-17   In addition, the summary provided by the landlord must state whether any of the costs relate to works in respect of which a grant has been or is to be paid under section 523 of the Housing Act 1985 (assistance for provision of separate service pipe for water supply) or any provision of Part I of the Housing Grants, Construction and Regeneration Act 1996 (grants, etc. for renewal of private sector housing) or any corresponding earlier enactment.[18] The summary must also state whether any of the costs relate to works which are included in the external works specified in a group repair scheme, within the meaning of Part I, Chapter II of the Housing Grants, Construction and Regeneration Act 1996 or any corresponding earlier enactment, in which the landlord participated or is participating as an assisted participant.[19]

33-18   Of wider significance is the requirement imposed by section 21(6) that if the service charges are payable by the tenants of more than four dwellings, the summary shall be certified by a qualified accountant as:

---

15 Section 21(5).
16 *R v Marylebone Magistrates Court ex parte Westminster City Council* (2000) 32 HLR 266.
17 See Chapter 36.
18 Section 21(5).
19 Section 21(5)(b).

(a)   in his opinion, a fair summary complying with the requirements of subsection (5); and

(b)   being sufficiently supported by accounts, receipts and other documents which have been produced to him.

33-19   A person is a qualified accountant for these purposes if he is eligible for appointment as a statutory auditor under Part 42 of the Companies Act 2006 and is not disqualified by reason of being an officer, employee or partner of the landlord or, where the landlord is a company, of an associated company, a person who is a partner or employee of any such officer or employee, an agent of the landlord who is a managing agent for any premises to which any of the costs covered by the summary in question relate, or an employee or partner of any such agent.[20] Where the landlord is a local authority, National Park authority or a new town corporation:

(a)   the persons who have the necessary qualification include members of the Chartered Institute of Public Finance and Accountancy; and

(b)   subsection (4)(b) (disqualification of officers and employees of landlord) does not apply.[21]

Right to inspect supporting documents

33-20   Where a tenant, or the secretary of an RTA,[22] has obtained a summary of relevant costs of the type referred to in section 21(1), the tenant, or the secretary with the consent of the tenant, may, within six months of obtaining the summary, require the landlord in writing to afford him reasonable facilities for inspecting the accounts, receipts and other documents supporting the summary, and for taking copies or extracts from them.[23] This right arises even if the summary was not provided pursuant to a request under section 21(1).

33-21   Following a valid request under section 22(2) (which, as with a request under section 21, is duly served on the landlord if it is served on (a) an agent of the landlord named as such in the rent book or similar document, or (b) the person who receives the rent on behalf of the landlord[24]), the landlord is obliged to make such facilities available to the tenant or secretary for a period of two months beginning not later than one month after the request is made.[25] The facilities for inspection must be made available to the tenant free of charge, but the landlord is entitled to impose a reasonable charge in respect of the taking of copies of extracts.[26] However, the obligation to provide facilities for inspection

20   Section 28(1)–(5)(a).
21   Section 28(6).
22   See Chapter 34.
23   Section 22(1) and (2).
24   Section 22(3).
25   Section 22(4).
26   Section 22(5).

free of charge does not preclude the landlord from including any costs incurred as part of his management costs.[27] This would, of course, be subject to the terms of the lease permitting the recovery of such costs as part of the service charge and the general requirements of section 19.

Information held by a superior landlord

33-22   In some cases, the tenant's immediate landlord is not the party who incurs the relevant costs ultimately recoverable from the tenant as service charges. In such cases, the immediate landlord would not be in a position to comply with sections 21 and 22. Section 23 addresses this situation by providing that if a request under section 21 relates in whole or in part to relevant costs incurred by or on behalf of a supervisor landlord, and the landlord to whom the request is made is not in possession of the relevant information, he shall in turn make a written request for the relevant information to the person who is his landlord (and so on, if that person is not himself the superior landlord). The superior landlord is then under an obligation to comply with that request within a reasonable time and the immediate landlord shall then comply with the tenant's or secretary's request, or that part of it which relates to the relevant costs incurred by or on behalf of the superior landlord, within the time allowed by section 21 or such further time, if any, as is reasonable in the circumstances.[28]

33-23   Furthermore, if a request under section 22 for facilities to inspect supporting accounts, etc. relates to a summary of costs incurred by or on behalf of a superior landlord, then the landlord to whom the request is made must forthwith inform the tenant or secretary of that fact and of the name and address of the superior landlord and it is provided that section 22 shall then apply to the superior landlord as it applies to the immediate landlord.[29]

33-24   The assignment of a tenancy does not affect the validity of a request made under section 21, 22 or 23 before the assignment; but a person is not obliged to provide a summary or make facilities available more than once for the same dwelling and for the same period.[30] Accordingly, a landlord remains obliged to comply with requests for information even after the assignment of his interest in the property, but only if the request was validly made before the assignment.

Sanctions for failure to comply with requests under sections 21 to 23

33-25   Somewhat surprisingly, given the context, criminal sanctions apply to anyone who fails to comply with the requirements of sections 21 to 23. This

27 Section 22(6).
28 Section 23(1).
29 Section 23(2).
30 Section 24.

seems rather draconian and it must be doubtful whether the vast majority of residential tenants would be prepared to lay a private prosecution against their landlord. The police are rarely, if ever, likely to pursue such matters, although local housing authorities can pursue prosecutions under these provisions.[31]

33-26   Nevertheless, it is a summary offence for a person to fail, without reasonable excuse, to perform a duty imposed on him by section 21, 22 or 23 and a person committing such an offence is liable on conviction to a fine not exceeding level 4 on the standard scale.[32] At the time of writing, the maximum fine is £2,500.[33] It is not an abuse of process to pursue a prosecution under section 25, even where the alleged breach by the landlord could be said to be trivial or technical.[34]

33-27   Liability for offences created by the Landlord and Tenant Act 1985 is extended, in certain circumstances, to directors and other officers of corporate landlords. Where an offence under the Act has been committed by a body corporate and is proved to have been committed with the consent or connivance of a director, manager, secretary or other similar officer of the body corporate, or a person purporting to act in any such capacity, or to be attributable to any neglect on the part of such an officer or person, he, as well as the body corporate, is guilty of an offence.[35] Furthermore, where the affairs of a body corporate are managed by its members, these provisions (section 33(1)) also apply in relation to the acts and defaults of a member in connection with his functions of management, as if he were a director of the body corporate.[36]

33-28   There is very little authority as to what will amount to a reasonable excuse under section 25. However, the decision of the Court of Appeal in *Taber v Macdonald and Clockscreen Holdings Ltd*[37] offers some useful guidance on the scope of sections 21 to 25. There, a tenant made a request under section 21 and the landlord complied by providing a certified summary of relevant costs. The tenant then made a request under section 22 for facilities to inspect the underlying documents. The landlord provided copies of all documentation relating specifically to the tenant's property, but refused to show the tenant documents pertaining to an item referred to as a 'composite labour charge'. It appears (the report is not altogether clear on the point) that this charge consisted of sums expended by the landlord in respect of the tenant's property, but also in respect of other properties owned by the landlord. The landlord did not disclose to the tenant any material supporting these charges. The magistrates dismissed

---

31   Section 34.
32   Section 25.
33   Criminal Justice Act 1991, s 17.
34   *R v Marylebone Magistrates Court ex parte Westminster City Council* (2000) 32 HLR 266. In that case, it was also held that the correct way to challenge the decision of a magistrate under s 25 is by way of case stated pursuant to the Magistrates' Court Act 1980, s 111 and not by way of judicial review.
35   Section 33(1).
36   Section 33(2).
37   (1999) 31 HLR 73.

the private prosecution on the basis that the landlord was not obliged by section 22 to provide facilities for inspecting documentation relating to other properties.

33-29 The Court of Appeal disagreed with this reasoning, holding that the obligation imposed by section 22 is wider than the view adopted by the magistrates. Whilst the reasoning is not entirely clear, it seems that the court formed the view that the tenant was entitled to see any documents supporting the relevant costs,[38] even if those documents related to other properties owned by the landlord.

33-30 Perhaps of more general significance are the observations made by Roch LJ to the effect that the fact the landlord cannot produce adequate records to support the sums demanded from the tenant is not, of itself, an offence under sections 22 and 25. His Lordship said:

> 'sections 21 and 22 are not concerned with the adequacy of the landlord's accounts or system of accounting. A landlord who cannot produce receipts and vouchers, which would normally exist to support a summary, will probably, in the absence of reasonable excuse, be held to be in breach of sections 22 and 25. However, if the landlord satisfies the Magistrates that he has produced such accounts, receipts and documents as he has, the fact that those items are inadequate to support the summary properly in terms of the keeping of proper accounts does not amount to an offence under section 22. Section 22 and section 25 are concerned with the wilful and inexcusable failure of a landlord to produce documents which he has. The remedies for the absence of proper receipts and documents are to be found elsewhere. The landlord will be unable later in other proceedings to produce further documents without running the risk of being prosecuted for perjury committed before the Magistrates. The absence of proper documents may also result in a complaint against the accountant who has certified the summary being made to his or her professional body.'

33-31 Although apparently *obiter*, these remarks provide a useful guide to the scope of sections 21 to 25. They are not intended as a tool for the forensic examination of the landlord's records, but rather as a mechanism for a tenant to obtain such information as the landlord has. Whether the accounts and underlying documents are accurate and support the sums demanded by the landlord is a question for the LVT in the context of, for example, an application under section 27A and not for the Magistrates Court to determine in the context of a prosecution under section 25.

33-32 In *Taber*, it was held that the landlord had a reasonable excuse for not disclosing the documents relating to the composite labour charge. The lease in question contained a provision enabling the parties to refer any matter in dispute to arbitration. The tenant had not disputed the charge when it was levied and had paid the sum demanded without challenging it or seeking to refer the landlord's claim to arbitration. The Court of Appeal accepted that this offered the landlord a reasonable excuse for not making available for inspection all of

---

38 See **28-11** to **28-20**.

the documents supporting the summary of relevant costs, because the tenant's remedy was to pursue an arbitration and he did not avail himself of it. With respect, that reasoning seems overly generous to the landlord if it is adopted generally. The whole purpose of sections 21 to 25 is to enable the tenant to obtain information about the charges demanded which must, in part, be so that he can assess whether there is any basis for challenging the charge in the first place. A failure to refer the matter to arbitration seems to have no bearing on whether or not it was reasonable for the landlord to refuse to disclose supporting documentation, particularly where requests had been made within the time limits specified in the 1985 Act. If this reasoning were taken to its logical conclusion, it could deprive the rights in sections 21 to 25 of any substance because it might always be argued that a tenant had another remedy (e.g. making an application under section 27A), which could have been pursued instead of seeking to inspect the supporting documents.

Reform

33-33 Sections 21 to 23 have been substituted by sections 152 to 154 of the Commonhold and Leasehold Reform Act 2002. However, the relevant provisions have not, at the time of writing, been brought into force (save in relation to the power to make regulations).[39] If and when it is brought into force, the new section 21 would oblige landlords to supply to each tenant by whom service charge is payable a written statement of account within six months after the end of an accounting period, as defined. The statement must deal with the following matters:

'(a) service charges of the tenant and the tenants of dwellings associated with his dwelling,

(b) relevant costs relating to those service charges,

(c) the aggregate amount standing to the credit of the tenant and the tenants of those dwellings –

(i) at the beginning of the accounting period, and

(ii) at the end of the accounting period, and

(d) related matters.'

33-34 The written statement must be accompanied by a certificate of a qualified accountant that, in the accountant's opinion, the statement of account deals fairly with the matters with which it is required to deal and is sufficiently supported by accounts, receipts and other documents which have been produced to him, and a summary of the rights and obligations of tenants of dwellings in relation to service charges. The Secretary of State is given power to make regulations

---

39 Commonhold and Leasehold Reform Act 2002 (Commencement No 1 Savings and Transitional Provisions) (England) Order 2002 (SI 2002/1912); Commonhold and Leasehold Reform Act 2002 (Commencement No 1 Savings and Transitional Provisions) (Wales) Order 2002 (Welsh SI 2002/3012).

governing the form and content of the written statement of account. A proposed new section 21A would entitle a tenant to withhold payment of a service charge if the requirements of the new section 21 are not complied with by the landlord.

33-35 The new section 21 would, accordingly, give the tenant an automatic entitlement to receive a statement of account without having to make a written request as is the case under the current section 21. Even in the absence of regulations prescribing the information to be contained in the written statement of account, it can be seen that the information required by the new section 21 will be more comprehensive than that presently required to be contained in a summary following a request by the tenant under the current section 21. Section 154 of the Commonhold and Leasehold Reform Act 2002 would also introduce a new section 22 which contains similar provisions to the current section 22, entitling the tenant to inspect or take copies of accounts, receipts or other documents relevant to the matters which must be dealt with in a statement of account. A new section 23 (contained in Schedule 10, paragraph 1 to the 2002 Act) would entitle a landlord to request a superior landlord to supply to him the information which must be included in a written statement of account required by the new section 21. A new section 23A[40] deals with the effect of a change of landlord and amendments to section 25[41] would mean that breach of any of the duties imposed by the new sections 21 to 23A is a criminal offence.

RIGHTS RELATING TO INFORMATION ABOUT INSURANCE

33-36 Section 30A of the 1985 Act gives effect to the Schedule to the Act which contains detailed provisions relating specifically to information about the insurance of residential dwellings. The Schedule confers on tenants of dwellings the rights, amongst other things, to obtain a written summary of the insurance, to inspect a copy of any insurance policy and to notify the insurer of potential claims.

33-37 As with other rights to information, it is a summary offence for a person to fail, without reasonable excuse, to perform a duty imposed on him as regards the supply of a summary or facilities for inspection of a policy by or by virtue of any of paragraphs 2 to 4A. A person committing such an offence is liable on conviction to a fine not exceeding level 4 on the standard scale. Again, whilst the criminal liability attaching to non-compliance certainly means landlords and managing agents must take seriously their duties under these provisions, it is dubious that criminal sanctions are the most effective way to ensure compliance.[42]

33-38 The rights conferred by the Schedule do not apply to a tenant of a local authority, a National Park authority or a new town corporation unless the tenancy

---

40 Contained in the Commonhold and Leasehold Reform Act 2002, Sch 10, para 2.
41 Commonhold and Leasehold Reform Act 2002, Sch 10, para 4.
42 See **33-25** above.

is a long tenancy,[43] in which case all of the rights apply, but the criminal sanctions imposed by paragraph 6 for non-compliance do not.[44]

Summary of relevant insurance policy

33-39   Under paragraph 2 of the Schedule, where a service charge is payable by the tenant of a dwelling which consists of or includes an amount payable directly or indirectly for insurance, the tenant may, by notice in writing, require the landlord to supply him with a written summary of the insurance for the time being effected in relation to the dwelling. If the tenant is represented by an RTA[45] and the tenant consents, the notice may be served by the secretary of the association instead of the tenant and may require the summary to be supplied to the secretary of the association. A notice under paragraph 2 of the Schedule is duly served on the landlord if it is served on an agent of the landlord named as such in the rent book or similar document, or the person who receives the rent on behalf of the landlord. A person on whom a notice is so served is obliged to forward it as soon as may be to the landlord.[46]

33-40   The landlord must comply with a notice under paragraph 2 by supplying to the tenant or the secretary of the RTA (as the case may require), within a period of 21 days beginning with the day on which he receives the notice, a summary of the insurance for the time being in effect, which summary must include:

(a)   the insured amount or amounts under any relevant policy;

(b)   the name of the insurer under any such policy; and

(c)   the risks in respect of which the dwelling or (as the case may be) the building containing it is insured under any such policy.[47]

33-41   The phrase 'the insured amount or amounts' is defined to mean, in relation to a relevant policy, in the case of a dwelling other than a flat, the amount for which the dwelling is insured under the policy and, in the case of a flat, the amount for which the building containing it is insured under the policy and, if specified in the policy, the amount for which the flat is insured under it.[48]

33-42   The landlord may, instead of providing a summary, supply copies of every relevant insurance policy within 21 days.[49] In a case where two or more buildings are insured under any relevant policy, the summary or copy supplied by

---

43   Meaning, in summary, a lease exceeding 21 years; see Landlord and Tenant Act 1987, s 59(3).
44   Schedule, para 9.
45   See Chapter 34.
46   Schedule, para 2(3).
47   Schedule, para 2(4).
48   Schedule, para 2(5). The definition of flat is to be found in the Landlord and Tenant Act 1987, s 60. Section 30A and the Schedule were added to the Landlord and Tenant Act 1985 Act by the Landlord and Tenant Act 1987, s 43 and, accordingly, the definitions set out in the Landlord and Tenant Act 1987, s 60 apply to these provisions.
49   Schedule, para 2(6).

the landlord need only be of such parts of the policy as relate to the dwelling and, if the dwelling is a flat, to the building containing it. Throughout the Schedule, the phrase 'relevant policy' means, in relation to a dwelling, any policy of insurance under which the dwelling is insured (being, in the case of a flat, a policy covering the building containing it).[50]

Inspection of insurance policy

33-43 Under paragraph 3 of the Schedule, a tenant may, by notice in writing, require his landlord to afford him reasonable facilities for inspecting any relevant policy or associated documents and for taking copies of or extracts from them, or to take copies of or extracts from any such policy or documents and either send them to him or afford him reasonable facilities for collecting them (as the tenant specifies).[51] Again, this right can be exercised by the secretary of an RTA[52] and a notice is valid if served on the landlord's agent or a person authorised to collect rent.[53] The landlord must comply with the request within 21 days.[54]

33-44 Where the landlord is required to afford facilities for inspecting documents, he must do so free of charge, but he may treat as part of his costs of management any costs incurred by him in doing so.[55] Furthermore, the landlord may make a reasonable charge for doing anything else in compliance with a requirement imposed by a notice under paragraph 3.[56]

33-45 The right of inspection is limited to the 'relevant policy', which has a limited meaning where it appears in paragraph 3. In this paragraph of the Schedule, 'relevant policy' is defined so that it includes a policy of insurance under which the dwelling was insured for the period of insurance immediately preceding that current when the notice is served (being, in the case of a flat, a policy covering the building containing it).[57] The intention behind this varied definition is somewhat unclear, but it would appear to restrict the right of inspection to the insurance policy which is in force at the time the request is made and the policy for the immediately preceding 'period of insurance', which phrase is not defined. The right of inspection does, however, extend to 'associated documents', which means accounts, receipts or other documents which provide evidence of payment of any premiums due under a relevant policy in respect of the period of insurance which is current when the notice is served or the period of insurance immediately preceding that period.[58]

---

50 Schedule, para 1.
51 Schedule, para 3(1).
52 Schedule, para 3(2).
53 Schedule, para 3(3).
54 Schedule, para 3(4).
55 Schedule, para 3(5).
56 Schedule, para 3(6).
57 Schedule, para 3(7).
58 Schedule, para 3(7).

33-46   Paragraph 4 of the Schedule imposes obligations on superior landlords to supply summaries and facilities for inspection when it is they and not the immediate landlord who has put in place the insurance for the dwelling in question, whether in whole or in part. Paragraph 4A applies where a landlord or superior landlord disposes of his interest in the property without complying with a duty owed under paragraph 2 or 4 of the Schedule. If the landlord or superior landlord is, despite the disposal, still in a position to discharge the duty to any extent, he remains responsible for discharging it to that extent. If the other person is in a position to discharge the duty to any extent, he is responsible for discharging it to that extent and, where this is the case, references to the landlord or superior landlord in paragraphs 2 to 4 are to, or include, the other person so far as is appropriate to reflect his responsibility for discharging the duty to that extent, but, in connection with its discharge by that person, paragraphs 2(4) and 3(4) apply as if the reference to the day on which the landlord receives the notice were to the date of the disposal of the former landlord or superior landlord's interest.[59] On the other hand, the assignment of a tenancy by the tenant does not affect any duty imposed by virtue of any of paragraphs 2 to 4A; but a person is not required to comply with more than a reasonable number of requirements imposed by any one person.[60]

Tenant's right to notify insurer of potential claim

33-47   Paragraph 7 of the Schedule contains an unusual, but potentially very useful, mechanism for the tenant to notify the insurer directly of a potential claim under the insurance and thereby extend the time the landlord has to make a claim. It does not enable a tenant to make a direct claim under the policy (although this might sometimes be possible depending on the precise terms of the policy), but it will allow time for the tenant to seek to persuade the landlord to make a claim. If the landlord refuses to do so, this will make it difficult for the landlord to assert that it was not possible to make a claim under the policy if he subsequently seeks to recover, by way of service charge, the cost of works which might have been covered by the insurance.

33-48   So, where it appears to the tenant that damage has been caused to the dwelling or, if the dwelling is a flat, to the dwelling or to any other part of the building containing it in respect of which a claim could be made under the terms of a policy of insurance, and it is a term of that policy that the person insured under the policy should give notice of any claim under it to the insurer within a specified period, the tenant may, within that specified period, serve on the insurer a notice in writing stating that it appears to him that damage has been caused and describing briefly the nature of the damage.[61]

59   Schedule, para 4A.
60   Schedule, para 5.
61   Schedule, para 7(2).

33-49 Where any such notice is served on an insurer by a tenant in relation to any such damage and the period specified in the policy for the notification of a claim would expire earlier than the period of six months beginning with the date on which the notice is served, the policy in question shall have effect as regards any claim subsequently made in respect of that damage by the person insured under the policy, as if for the specified period there were substituted that period of six months.[62]

33-50 Accordingly, if the tenant gives notice of a possible claim within the time specified by the policy for making a claim, the time for the making of a claim by the insured (usually, of course, the landlord) is extended for six months from the date of service of the notice. Where the tenancy of a dwelling to which this paragraph applies is held by joint tenants, a single notice under this paragraph may be given by any one or more of those tenants.[63] The Secretary of State is given power[64] to make regulations which prescribe the form of notices under this paragraph and the particulars which such notices must contain, but, at the time of writing, no such regulations have been made and, accordingly, there is no particular form for a notice under these provisions.

Right to challenge landlord's choice of insurer

33-51 Paragraph 8 of the Schedule applies where a tenancy of a dwelling requires the tenant to insure the dwelling with an insurer nominated or approved by the landlord.[65] The tenant or landlord may apply to a county court or LVT for a determination whether the insurance which is available from the nominated or approved insurer for insuring the tenant's dwelling is unsatisfactory in any respect or the premiums payable in respect of any such insurance are excessive. No such application may be made in respect of a matter which:

(a) has been agreed or admitted by the tenant;

(b) under an arbitration agreement to which the tenant is a party, is required to be referred to arbitration; or

(c) has been the subject of determination by a court or arbitral tribunal.

33-52 On an application under paragraph 8, the court or tribunal may make an order requiring the landlord to nominate or approve such other insurer as is specified in the order, or an order requiring him to nominate or approve another insurer who satisfies such requirements in relation to the insurance of the dwelling as are specified in the order. An agreement by the tenant of a dwelling (other than an arbitration agreement) is void in so far as it purports to provide for

---

62 Schedule, para 7(3).
63 Schedule, para 7(4).
64 Schedule, para 7(5).
65 This right should not be confused with rights in relation to insurance on tenants under long leases of houses conferred by the Commonhold and Leasehold Reform Act 2002, s 164. See **33-53** to **33-58** below.

a determination in a particular manner, or on particular evidence, of any question which may be the subject of an application under paragraph 8.

Rights of tenants under long leases of houses as regards insurance

33-53 Section 164 of the Commonhold and Leasehold Reform Act 2002 confers on a tenant under a long lease[66] of 'a house'[67] specific rights as regards insurance.[68] The section applies where the lease requires the tenant to insure the house with an insurer nominated or approved by the landlord ('the landlord's insurer').[69] The section discharges the tenant's obligation to effect the insurance with the landlord's insurer if:

(a) the house is insured under a policy of insurance issued by an authorised insurer;

(b) the policy covers the interests of both the landlord and the tenant;

(c) the policy covers all the risks which the lease requires to be covered by insurance provided by the landlord's insurer;

(d) the amount of the cover is not less than that which the lease requires to be provided by such insurance; and

(e) the tenant complies with section 164(3).[70]

33-54 By section 164(10), 'authorised insurer', in relation to a policy of insurance, means a person who may carry on in the United Kingdom the business of effecting or carrying out contracts of insurance of the sort provided under the policy, without contravening the prohibition imposed by section 19 of the Financial Services and Markets Act 2000.

33-55 In order to take advantage of this exemption, the tenant must, by section 164(3), give a notice of cover to the landlord before the end of the period of 14 days beginning with the relevant date and, if (after that date) he has been requested to do so by a new landlord, must have given a notice of cover to him within the period of 14 days beginning with the day on which the request was given.

---

66 As defined in the Commonhold and Leasehold Reform Act 2002, ss 76 and 77.
67 As defined in the Leasehold Reform Act 1967, Pt 1. This definition has been the subject of a great deal of authority and a full exposition is outside the scope of this work. For detailed treatment see Radevsky and Greenish, *Hague on Leasehold Enfranchisement* (5th edn, 2009), Ch 2.
68 The section came into force on 28 February 2005 in England and 31 May 2005 in Wales; see Commonhold and Leasehold Reform Act 2002 (Commencement No 5 and Saving and Transitional Provisions) Order 2004 (SI 2004/3056) and Commonhold and Leasehold Reform Act 2002 (Commencement No 2 and Savings) (Wales) Order 2004 (SI 2004/669).
69 Section 164(1).
70 Section 164(2).

33-56   The relevant date means, if the policy has not been renewed, the day on which it took effect or, if it has been renewed, the day from which it was last renewed. A person is a new landlord on any day if he acquired the interest of the previous landlord under the lease on a disposal made by him during the period of one month ending with that day.[71]

33-57   In order to comply with this requirement, the notice given by the tenant must specify:

(a)   the name of the insurer;

(b)   the risks covered by the policy;

(c)   the amount and period of the cover; and

(d)   such further information as may be prescribed.[72]

33-58   The notice of cover must be in the prescribed form[73] and may be sent by post.[74] If it is sent by post, it may be sent to the landlord at the last address furnished for the purpose of section 48 of the Landlord and Tenant Act 1987 or, if no such address has been furnished by the landlord, at the address given for the purpose of section 47 of the 1987 Act,[75] unless the tenant has been notified by the landlord of a different address in England and Wales at which he wishes to be given any such notice.[76]

71 Section 164(4).
72 Section 164(5).
73 For the prescribed form of notice see, in England, Leasehold Houses (Notice of Insurance Cover) (England) Regulations 2004 (SI 2004/3097) as amended by the Leasehold Houses (Notice of Insurance Cover) (England) (Amendment) Regulations 2005 (SI 2005/177) and, in Wales, the Leasehold Houses (Notice of Insurance Cover) (Wales) Regulations 2005 (Welsh SI 2005/1354).
74 Section 164(6).
75 Section 164(7) and (8); and see **32-07** to **32-18** as to the Landlord and Tenant Act 1987, ss 47 and 48.
76 Section 164(9).

CHAPTER 34

Recognised tenants' associations

34-01 The Landlord and Tenant Act 1985 introduced organisations of tenants known as recognised tenants' associations ('RTAs'). RTAs are given various rights which are more extensive than those afforded to individual tenants, although many of the entitlements which were the preserve of RTAs have subsequently been extended to individual tenants by reforms introduced by the Commonhold and Leasehold Reform Act 2002. Nevertheless, RTAs retain exclusive rights in respect of the consultation process under section 20, a specific right of consultation as regards managing agents and the right to appoint a surveyor to conduct an audit.

FORMATION AND RECOGNITION OF AN RTA

34-02 Section 29(1) of the Landlord and Tenant Act 1985 states that an RTA is an association of qualifying tenants (whether with or without other tenants), which is recognised for the purposes of the provisions of the 1985 Act relating to service charges either:

(a) by notice in writing given by the landlord to the secretary of the association; or

(b) by a certificate of a member of the local rent assessment committee panel.

34-03 A notice given under subsection (1)(a) may be withdrawn by the landlord by notice in writing, given to the secretary of the association not less than six months before the date on which it is to be withdrawn.[1] A certificate given under subsection (1)(b) may be cancelled by any member of the local rent assessment committee panel.[2]

34-04 There is provision for regulations to be made by the Secretary of State dealing with:

---

1 Section 29(2).
2 Section 29(3).

(a)   the procedure which is to be followed in connection with an application for, or for the cancellation of, a certificate;

(b)   the matters to which regard is to be had in giving or cancelling such a certificate;

(c)   the duration of such a certificate; and

(d)   any circumstances in which a certificate is not to be given.

34-05   At the time of writing, no such regulations have been made.

34-06   A number of tenants are qualifying tenants for these purposes if each of them may be required under the terms of his lease to contribute to the same costs by the payment of a service charge.[3] However, it is not possible to form a legitimate association which incorporates tenants from more than one block of flats, even if they have a common landlord. Accordingly, where a certificate was granted by a rent assessment panel in respect of an association comprising tenants of five blocks of flats (which had previously comprised a row of eight terraced houses), the court quashed the decision to grant the certificate on a judicial review brought by the landlord.[4]

34-07   Otherwise, there is little statutory guidance as to how an RTA should be constituted and what factors the rent assessment panel will take into account in deciding whether or not to grant a certificate if the landlord does not recognise the association voluntarily.[5] However, the Residential Property Tribunal Service has published guidance[6] as to how an application for recognition can be made and the criteria that will be applied in deciding whether to grant a certificate. This includes consideration of whether the association's rules are fair and democratic as regards membership, subscriptions and voting.

RIGHTS OF AN RTA

34-08   An RTA is entitled to exercise various rights conferred on tenants by the Landlord and Tenant Act 1985, considered elsewhere in this chapter. Thus, an RTA has the right to seek a summary of relevant costs and inspect the underlying documents under sections 21 and 22[7] and also information about insurance under

---

3   Section 29(4). For an example of a case where the sums payable by tenants was not a service charge within s 18 and so a certificate recognising a tenants association should not have been issued, see *Minister Chalets v Irwin Park Residents Association* [2001] EWLands LRX_28_2000.

4   *R v London Rent Assessment Panel ex parte Trustees of Henry Smith's Charity Kensington Estate* (1988) 20 HLR 103.

5   It has been held that a decision by the rent assessment committee to issue a certificate of recognition is an administrative and not a judicial decision – see *Minister Chalets v Irwin Park Residents Association* [2001] EWLands LRX_28_2000.

6   Available online at www.justice.gov.uk/tribunals/residential-property/guidance.

7   See **33-07** to **33-24**.

the Schedule to the Act.[8] In addition, an RTA has more extensive rights under the section 20 consultation procedure.[9]

34-09 There are, however, two rights which are now conferred exclusively on RTAs. First, under section 30B, an RTA may at any time serve a notice on the landlord requesting him to consult the association on matters relating to the appointment or employment by him of a managing agent for any relevant premises. In section 30B, 'landlord' means the immediate landlord of the tenants represented by the association or a person who has a right to enforce payment of service charges payable by any of those tenants.[10] Premises (whether a building or not) are relevant premises in relation to an RTA if any of the tenants represented by the association may be required under the terms of their leases to contribute by the payment of service charges to costs relating to those premises.[11] A 'managing agent', in relation to any relevant premises, means an agent of the landlord appointed to discharge any of the landlord's obligations to the tenants represented by the RTA in question which relate to the management by him of those premises.[12]

34-10 The scope of the right to consultation depends on whether or not the landlord already employs a managing agent. If an agent is already employed, then when an RTA serves notice under section 30B(1) the landlord must, within one month beginning with the date of service of the notice, serve on the association a notice specifying the landlord's obligations to the tenants represented by the association which the managing agent is required to discharge on his behalf and a reasonable period within which the association may make observations on the manner in which the managing agent has been discharging those obligations and on the desirability of his continuing to discharge them.[13]

34-11 If no managing agent is employed by the landlord when a notice is served, the landlord must, before appointing a managing agent, serve on the association a notice specifying the name of the proposed managing agent, the landlord's obligations to the tenants represented by the association which it is proposed that the managing agent should be required to discharge on his behalf and a period of not less than one month beginning with the date of service of the notice within which the association may make observations on the proposed appointment.[14]

34-12 In either case, a landlord who has been served with a notice by an association under section 30B(1) must, so long as he employs a managing agent for any relevant premises, serve on that association, at least once in every five years, a notice specifying any change occurring since the date of the last notice

8 See **33-36** to **33-46**.
9 See Chapter 30.
10 Section 30B(8).
11 Section 30B(8).
12 Section 30B(8).
13 Section 30B(3).
14 Section 30B(2).

served by him on the association under this section in the obligations which the managing agent has been required to discharge on his behalf. The notice must also specify a reasonable period within which the association may make observations on the manner in which the managing agent has discharged those obligations since that date and on the desirability of his continuing to discharge them. The landlord must also, whenever he proposes to appoint any new managing agent for any relevant premises, serve on the RTA a notice specifying the same matters.[15] A notice under section 30B(1) only ceases to have effect once it is withdrawn by the RTA[16] or the interest of the landlord in receipt of the notice becomes vested in a new landlord.[17]

34-13   The rights of the RTA under these provisions are limited to consultation and the RTA cannot oblige the landlord to appoint or dismiss a particular managing agent. The landlord is only obliged to have regard to any observations made by the RTA pursuant to the consultation notices. These rights are, therefore, of limited value, but a landlord who disregards a notice or ignores reasonable observations made by the RTA may face additional difficulties in justifying the reasonableness of the charges incurred by the managing agents in the event that these are challenged.[18]

34-14   The second right which can only be exercised by an RTA is the right to appoint a surveyor under section 84 of the Housing Act 1996. This section provides that the RTA may appoint a surveyor[19] for the purposes of this section to advise on any matters relating to, or which may give rise to, service charges payable to a landlord by one or more members of the association. The process of appointment is simple. The RTA simply gives the landlord a notice stating the name and address of the surveyor, the duration of his appointment and the matters in respect of which he is appointed.[20] The appointment only ceases when the RTA gives the landlord a further notice to that effect.[21]

34-15   The surveyor appointed under this provision has extensive rights to access documents and inspect the premises. Those rights are conferred by Schedule 4 to the 1996 Act and largely mirror the rights of an auditor under the similar process under Chapter V of the 1993 Act.[22] Thus, by Schedule 4, paragraph 3, the surveyor has a right to require the landlord or any other relevant person to afford him reasonable facilities for inspecting any documents, sight of which is reasonably required by him for the purposes of his functions, and to afford him reasonable facilities for taking copies of or extracts from any such documents. The time limit within which the landlord must comply with any request by the

---

15 Section 30B(4).
16 Section 30B(5).
17 Section 30B(6).
18 Under the Landlord and Tenant Act 1985, s 19; see Chapter 29 above.
19 Who must be a qualified surveyor as defined by the Leasehold Reform, Housing and Urban Development Act 1993, s 78(4)(a); s 84(2).
20 Section 84(3).
21 Section 84(4).
22 See Chapter 35.

surveyor to provide such facilities is only one week.[23] This is, therefore, a simple and efficient mechanism by which the RTA can obtain detailed information about the costs underlying the service charges. The surveyor is also given the right to inspect, on request, the common parts of the relevant premises, but no time limit is given as to the date by which the landlord must afford access.[24] The rights given to the surveyor under Schedule 4, paragraphs 3 and 4 can be enforced against the landlord by applying for a court order under paragraph 5 and an order made on an application by the surveyor may be made in general terms or may require the landlord or other person to do specific things, as the court thinks fit.[25]

23 Schedule 4, para 3(4).
24 Schedule 4, para 4. Presumably, if the landlord failed to afford access within a reasonable time, the landlord would be in breach of this duty.
25 Schedule 4, para 5(4).

CHAPTER 35

Right to a management audit

35-01   Chapter V of the Leasehold Reform, Housing and Urban Development Act 1993 confers on tenants under long leases of dwellings the right to a management audit.

SCOPE OF THE RIGHT CONFERRED ON TWO OR MORE QUALIFYING TENANTS

35-02   Two or more qualifying tenants of dwellings held on leases from the same landlord have the right to have an audit carried out on their behalf which relates to the management of the relevant premises and any appurtenant property by or on behalf of the landlord.[1]

35-03   A tenant is a qualifying tenant of a dwelling for the purposes of Chapter V if:

(a)   he is a tenant of the dwelling under a long lease other than a business lease; and

(b)   any service charge[2] is payable under the lease.[3]

35-04   A lease is a long lease if:

(a)   it is a lease falling within section 7(1)(a) to (c) of the 1993 Act; or

(b)   it is a shared ownership lease (within the meaning of section 7), whether granted in pursuance of Part V of the Housing Act 1985 or otherwise.[4]

---

1   Leasehold Reform, Housing and Urban Development Act 1993, s 76(1).
2   Service charge has the same meaning as in the Landlord and Tenant Act 1985, s 18(1): s 84. See **28-01**ff. above.
3   Section 77(1).
4   Section 77(2).

35-05 By section 7, a lease is a long lease if:

(a) it is granted for a term of years certain exceeding 21 years, whether or not it is (or may become) terminable before the end of that term by notice given by or to the tenant or by re-entry, forfeiture or otherwise;

(b) it is a lease for a term fixed by law under a grant with a covenant or obligation for perpetual renewal (other than a lease by sub-demise from one which is not a long lease) or a lease taking effect under section 149(6) of the Law of Property Act 1925 (leases terminable after a death or marriage or the formation of a civil partnership); or

(c) it is a lease granted in pursuance of the right to buy conferred by Part V of the Housing Act 1985 or in pursuance of the right to acquire on 'rent to mortgage' terms conferred by that Part of that Act.

35-06 However, no dwelling shall have more than one qualifying tenant at any one time.[5] Accordingly, where a dwelling is, for the time being, let under two or more leases falling within the definition of long lease, any tenant under any of those leases which is superior to that held by any other such tenant shall not be a qualifying tenant of the dwelling for the purposes of Chapter V. Where a dwelling is, for the time being, let to joint tenants under a lease falling within the definition of a long lease, the joint tenants shall be regarded for the purposes of Chapter V as jointly constituting the qualifying tenant of the dwelling.[6] A person can, however, be (or be among those constituting) the qualifying tenant of each of two or more dwellings at the same time, whether he is a tenant of those dwellings under one lease or under two or more separate leases.[7]

35-07 The right to a management audit can be exercised where the relevant premises consist of, or include, two dwellings let to qualifying tenants of the same landlord, by either or both of those tenants, and where the relevant premises consist of or include three or more dwellings let to qualifying tenants of the same landlord, by not less than two-thirds of those tenants.[8]

35-08 Where the right is exercised by two or more qualifying tenants on behalf of two or more qualifying tenants, 'the relevant premises' means so much of the building or buildings containing the dwellings let to those tenants and any other building or buildings as constitutes premises in relation to which management functions are discharged in respect of the costs of which common service charge contributions are payable under the leases of those qualifying tenants. 'Appurtenant property' means so much of any property not contained in the relevant premises as constitutes property in relation to which any such management functions are discharged.[9]

---

5 Section 77(3).
6 Section 77(4).
7 Section 77(5).
8 Section 76(2).
9 Section 76(3).

SCOPE OF THE RIGHT CONFERRED ON A SINGLE QUALIFYING TENANT

35-09   Chapter V also confers on a single qualifying tenant of a dwelling the right to have an audit carried out on his behalf which relates to the management of the relevant premises and any appurtenant property by or on behalf of the landlord. That right is exercisable by a single qualifying tenant of a dwelling where the relevant premises contain no other dwelling let to a qualifying tenant apart from that let to him.[10]

35-10   In relation to an audit on behalf of a single qualifying tenant, 'the relevant premises' means so much of the building containing the dwelling let to him and any other building or buildings as constitutes premises in relation to which management functions are discharged in respect of the costs of which a service charge is payable under his lease (whether as a common service charge contribution or otherwise). 'Appurtenant property' means so much of any property not contained in the relevant premises as constitutes property in relation to which any such management functions are discharged.[11]

THE AUDITOR

35-11   The audit to which tenants are entitled under Chapter V is an audit carried out for the purpose of ascertaining the extent to which the obligations of the landlord, which are owed to the qualifying tenants of the constituent dwellings and involve the discharge of management functions in relation to the relevant premises or any appurtenant property, are being discharged in an efficient and effective manner and the extent to which sums payable by those tenants by way of service charges are being applied in an efficient and effective manner.[12] In determining whether those obligations are being discharged in an efficient and effective manner, regard shall be had to any applicable provisions of any code of practice for the time being approved by the Secretary of State under section 87.[13]

35-12   A management audit under Chapter V must be carried out by a person who is qualified for appointment in accordance with section 78(4) and who (where the relevant premises consist of or include two dwellings let to qualifying tenants of the same landlord) is appointed by either or both of the qualifying tenants of the constituent dwellings, or (where the relevant premises consist of or include three or more dwellings let to qualifying tenants of the same landlord) by not less than two-thirds of the qualifying tenants of the constituent dwellings.[14]

10   Section 76(5).
11   Section 76(6).
12   Section 78(1).
13   Section 78(2) and see **1-17** above as regards codes of practice.
14   Section 78(3).

35-13   A person is qualified for appointment as an auditor if:

(a)   he has the necessary qualification (within the meaning of section 28(1) of the Landlord and Tenant Act 1985 (meaning of 'qualified accountant'[15])) or is a qualified surveyor;

(b)   he is not disqualified from acting (within the meaning of that subsection); and

(c)   he is not a tenant of any premises contained in the relevant premises.[16]

35-14   A person is a qualified surveyor if he is a fellow or professional associate of the Royal Institution of Chartered Surveyors or of the Incorporated Society of Valuers and Auctioneers or satisfies such other requirement or requirements as may be prescribed by regulations made by the Secretary of State.[17] The auditor may appoint such persons to assist him in carrying out the audit as he thinks fit.[18]

EXERCISE OF THE RIGHT TO A MANAGEMENT AUDIT

35-15   The right is exercised by giving notice to the landlord under section 80. A notice given under section 80 must be given to the landlord by the auditor and must be signed by each of the tenants on whose behalf it is given.[19] Any such notice must state the full name of each of the tenants and the address of the dwelling of which he is a qualifying tenant, state the name and address of the auditor and specify any documents or description of documents:

(i)   which the landlord is required to supply to the auditor under section 79(2)(a)(i) of the 1993 Act; or

(ii)   in respect of which he is required to afford the auditor facilities for inspection or for taking copies or extracts under any other provision of section 79(2) of the 1993 Act.

35-16   If the auditor proposes to carry out an inspection under section 79(4), the notice must state the date on which he proposes to carry out the inspection.[20] Any specified date must be a date falling not less than one month nor more than two months after the date of the giving of the notice.[21] A notice is duly given under section 80 to the landlord of any qualifying tenants if it is given to a person who receives, on behalf of the landlord, the rent payable by any such tenants. A person to whom such a notice is given shall forward it as soon as may be to the landlord.

---

15 Landlord and Tenant Act 1985, s 28(1).
16 Section 78(4).
17 Section 78(5).
18 Section 78(6).
19 Section 80(2).
20 Section 80(3).
21 Section 80(4).

RIGHTS OF THE AUDITOR TO ACCESS RECORDS

35-17   Section 79(2) confers on the auditor a right to require the landlord:

(i)   to supply him with such a summary as is referred to in section 21(1) of the Landlord and Tenant Act 1985 (request for summary of relevant costs) in connection with any service charges payable by the qualifying tenants of the constituent dwellings;[22] and

(ii)   to afford him reasonable facilities for inspecting or taking copies of or extracts from, the accounts, receipts and other documents supporting any such summary.

35-18   The auditor also has a right to require the landlord or any relevant person to afford him reasonable facilities for inspecting any other documents, sight of which is reasonably required by him for the purpose of carrying out the audit, and a right to require the landlord or any relevant person to afford him reasonable facilities for taking copies of or extracts from any documents falling within this description.[23] In this context, 'relevant person' means a person (other than the landlord) who is charged with responsibility for the discharge of any such obligations as are mentioned in section 78(1)(a), or for the application of any such service charges as are mentioned in section 78(1)(b) or has a right to enforce payment of any such service charges.[24]

35-19   The rights conferred on the auditor are exercisable in relation to the landlord, by means of a notice under section 80 and, in relation to any relevant person, by means of a notice given to that person at (so far as is reasonably practicable) the same time as a notice under section 80 is given to the landlord. The auditor shall also be entitled, on giving notice in accordance with section 80, to carry out an inspection of any common parts comprised in the relevant premises or any appurtenant property.[25]

35-20   The landlord or, as the case may be, any relevant person must, where facilities for the inspection of any documents are required, make those facilities available free of charge. Where any documents are required to be supplied or facilities for the taking of copies or extracts are required, the landlord or, as the case may be, relevant person is entitled to supply those documents or make those facilities available on payment of such reasonable charge as he may determine.[26] However, the requirement imposed on the landlord to make any facilities available free of charge shall not be construed as precluding the landlord from treating as part of his costs of management any costs incurred by him in connection with making those facilities so available.[27]

---

22   See **35-02** to **35-08** above.
23   Section 79(2).
24   Section 79(7).
25   Section 79(4).
26   Section 79(5).
27   Section 79(6).

PROCEDURE FOLLOWING GIVING OF NOTICE UNDER SECTION 80

35-21   Where the landlord is given a notice under section 80, within the period of one month beginning with the date of the giving of the notice, he must supply the auditor with any document specified and afford him any facilities specified in the notice.[28]

35-22   In the case of every other document or description of documents specified in the notice under section 80(3)(c)(ii), the landlord must either afford the auditor facilities for inspection or, as the case may be, for taking copies or extracts in respect of that document or those documents, or give the auditor a notice stating that he objects to doing so for such reasons as are specified in the notice. If a date is specified in the notice for the carrying out of an inspection, the landlord must either approve the date or propose another date.[29] Any date so proposed by the landlord must be a date falling not later than the end of the period of two months beginning with the date of the giving of the notice under section 80.[30] Similar duties are imposed on a relevant person in receipt of a notice.[31]

35-23   If, by the end of the period of two months beginning with the date of the giving of the notice to the landlord or the relevant person, the landlord or, as the case may be, a relevant person has failed to comply with any requirement of the notice, the court may, on the application of the auditor, make an order requiring the landlord or, as the case may be, the relevant person to comply with that requirement within such period as is specified in the order.[32] The court shall not make an order on such an application in respect of any document or documents, unless it is satisfied that the document or documents falls or fall within section 79(2)(a) or (b).[33] Any application for an order under this subsection must be made before the end of the period of four months beginning with the date of the giving of that notice.[34]

35-24   Section 82 imposes obligations on superior landlords to comply with notices served by an auditor where the information necessary to comply is in the possession of the superior landlord. Section 83(1) and (2) deal with the position where a landlord disposes of his interest in the property before complying with a notice under section 80. By section 80(2), if the landlord is, despite any such disposal, still in a position to discharge obligations arising out of the service of the notice, he shall remain responsible for so discharging them, but otherwise the person acquiring his interest shall be responsible for so discharging them to the exclusion of the landlord. Where a notice under section 80 has been served

---

28 Section 81(1)(a).
29 Section 81(1)(b).
30 Section 81(2).
31 Section 81(3).
32 Section 81(4).
33 Section 81(5).
34 Section 81(7).

on behalf of a qualifying tenant or tenants, that tenant or those tenants are not permitted to serve a further notice for a period of 12 months.[35]

35-25 Despite the apparently wide-ranging nature of the right to a management audit, it would seem to be little used in practice. There are, perhaps, a number of reasons for this. First, these provisions do not confer rights which are not contained elsewhere. All of the information which the landlord can be obliged to provide to an auditor can be secured directly by tenants without the need to involve an auditor who, of course, will need to be paid for his services. Furthermore, these provisions do not confer any remedy in the event that the audit reveals management failings. Whilst a report of an auditor might be used to support an application under section 27A for a determination that the service charges are not payable or an application for the appointment of a new managing agent under the Landlord and Tenant Act 1987, it will usually be simpler for the tenants to proceed straight to an application to the LVT without first obtaining an audit for which they will presumably have to pay professional fees. In the absence of a remedy directly enforceable under Chapter V and given the many other, cheaper routes by which tenants can obtain both information and scrutiny of management practices, the right to a management audit will rarely be an attractive option.

---

35 Section 83(5).

CHAPTER 36

Statutory trust of service charge funds

36-01   Section 42 of the Landlord and Tenant Act 1987 imposes a statutory trust in respect of all payments made by tenants of dwellings towards service charges. This provides important protection for residential tenants for two main reasons. First, it means that any service charge contributions will be protected in the event that the landlord or management company holding the fund becomes insolvent. Property held on trust does not form part of a bankrupt's estate[1] or part of the property of a company available to creditors on insolvency.[2] Secondly, the landlord and any agent are subject to the general duties of trustees and may be liable for breach of trust if the money is misappropriated or not properly safeguarded or invested.[3] There are also implications as to the limitation period, if any, applicable to any action by the tenant to recover sums which may have been improperly applied by the landlord in breach of the statutory trust.[4]

OPERATION OF THE STATUTORY TRUST

36-02   Section 42 applies where either the tenants of two or more dwellings may be required under the terms of their leases to contribute to the same costs, or the tenant of a dwelling may be required, under the terms of his lease, to contribute to costs to which no other tenant of a dwelling may be required to contribute by the payment of service charges. The protection was extended to a single tenant by the Commonhold and Leasehold Reform Act 2002, with effect from 31 May 2005.

---

1   Section 283(3)(a).
2   Insolvency Act 1986, ss 145 (corporate insolvency) and 283(3)(a) (individual bankruptcy).
3   See, for example, *Warwickshire Hamlets Ltd v Gedden* [2010] UKUT 75, where the Upper Tribunal declined to overturn a decision by the LVT that the use of sums paid to a management company by tenants by way of service charge to pay a debt owed by the management company to the freeholder involved the conversion to its own use of trust monies held by the management company as a trustee under the statutory trust.
4   See further as to limitation periods, **42-21** to **42-34**.

36-03 'Service charge' bears the same meaning as in section 18 of the Landlord and Tenant Act 1985, except that it does not include a service charge payable by the tenant of a dwelling, the rent of which is registered under Part IV of the Rent Act 1977, unless the amount registered is, in pursuance of section 71(4) of that Act, entered as a variable amount. The statutory trust does not apply to an exempt landlord, which, in this instance, includes most public authority landlords.[5]

36-04 By section 42(2), any sums paid to the payee by the contributing tenants or the sole contributing tenant, by way of relevant service charges, and any investments representing those sums, shall (together with any income accruing thereon) be held by the payee either as a single fund or, if he thinks fit, in two or more separate funds. 'The payee' means the landlord or other person to whom any such charges are payable by those tenants, or that tenant, under the terms of their leases, or his lease.[6] The funds established in accordance with section 42(2) are referred to as the trust fund.[7]

36-05 The operative provision establishing the trust is section 42(3), which states:

> 'The payee shall hold any trust fund –
>
> (a)   on trust to defray costs incurred in connection with the matters for which the relevant service charges were payable (whether incurred by himself or by any other person), and
>
> (b)   subject to that, on trust for the persons who are the contributing tenants for the time being, or the person who is the sole contributing tenant for the time being.'

36-06 The effect of these provisions is that the money paid by the tenant in respect of service charges is automatically held on trust for the purpose for which the money was paid and, subject to that, to be held for the contributing tenants 'for the time being'. This phrase demonstrates that the fund is not to be held on behalf of the tenants who have paid over the years, but for those who are contributing tenants at the time when any issue as to beneficial ownership of the trust fund arises. Furthermore, the effect of this provision is that, where actual expenditure exceeds the sum collected by the landlord on account, the surplus cannot be used to defray other costs not identified by the landlord at the time the on-account payments were collected.[8] Whether any such surplus must be returned to the tenants or dealt with by way of a credit on future demands depends on the proper construction of the terms of the lease. Section 42 only applies where sums are actually paid by the contributing tenants and, accordingly, the fact that the landlord (or manager appointed to perform the landlord's functions under the

---

5   Section 42(1). The full list of exempt landlords is set out in the Landlord and Tenant Act 1987, s 58.

6   Section 42(1).

7   *Ibid.*

8   *St Mary's Mansions Ltd v Limegate Investment Co Ltd* [2003] HLR 24, *per* Ward LJ at para 35.

Landlord and Tenant Act 1987) will hold sums on trust when collected has no bearing on whether a defence by way of set-off is available to a tenant in a claim for arrears of service charge.[9]

36-07   The statutory trust takes precedence over the terms of any express or implied trust created by a lease, so far as inconsistent with the provisions of section 42, other than an express trust created before the coming into force of the section or, in the case of the lease of the sole contributing tenant, before the extension of the application of the section to such tenants by the commencement of Schedule 10, paragraph 15 to the Commonhold and Leasehold Reform Act 2002.[10]

36-08   The contributing tenants are to be treated as entitled to such shares in the residue of any such fund, as are proportionate to their respective liabilities to pay service charges, or the sole contributing tenant shall be treated as so entitled to the residue of any such fund.[11] This section is likely to be of only limited application, however, because specific provision is made for distribution of the trust fund on the termination of the lease of a contributing tenant, as set out below. It seems, therefore, that this provision could only apply if the relevant premises were destroyed and not rebuilt, although it may be of assistance if, at any stage, it becomes necessary to calculate for some reason to what proportion of the trust fund each tenant is entitled. It should be noted that the calculation is by reference to the respective liabilities of the contributing tenants and not to their actual contribution. Accordingly, the payee would be entitled to deduct from any sum due to a contributing tenant any amount by which he is in arrears.

36-09   On the termination of the lease of any of the contributing tenants, the tenant is not entitled to any part of any trust fund and (except where subsection (7) applies) any part of any such fund which is attributable to relevant service charges paid under the lease shall, accordingly, continue to be held on the trusts referred to in subsection (3).[12]

36-10   On the termination of the lease of the last of the contributing tenants, or of the lease of the sole contributing tenant, any trust fund shall be dissolved as at the date of the termination of the lease, and any assets comprised in the fund immediately before its dissolution shall, if the payee is the landlord, be retained by him for his own use and benefit and, in any other case, be transferred to the landlord by the payee.[13]

36-11   The tenant is not entitled, therefore, to the return of any sum contributed to the trust fund, either on the termination of his lease or where all of the relevant

9   *Maunder Taylor v Blaquiere* [2003] 1 WLR 379.
10   Section 42(9).
11   Section 42(4).
12   Section 42(5).
13   Section 42(6).

leases have expired.[14] This may appear a surprising result, but it should be kept in mind that the primary object of the trust is to defray costs of management and that any demand for a payment on account or contribution to a reserve fund must be reasonable.[15] It is unlikely to be reasonable to issue demands for significant on-account payments when the leases are about to expire and, accordingly, it would be unusual for there to be significant sums held on trust where all of the leases of contributing tenants have expired. More difficult questions might arise in the case of termination by, for example, forfeiture,[16] but, given the level of statutory protection, forfeiture of long residential leases is rare and shorter leases do not often require significant contribution to service charge expenditure.

36-12   Furthermore, it is expressly provided that these provisions have effect in relation to any of the contributing tenants, or the sole contributing tenant, subject to any express terms of his lease (whenever it was granted) which relate to the distribution, either before or (as the case may be) at the termination of the lease, of amounts attributable to relevant service charges paid under its terms (whether the lease was granted before or after the commencement of section 42).[17]

36-13   The Secretary of State has power to make regulations as to the permitted investment of trust funds.[18] The statutory instruments enacted under this provision[19] provide that service charge funds can only be placed in interest-bearing accounts with banks, building societies, friendly societies and credit unions, as authorised under Part 4 of the Financial Services and Markets Act 2000.

PROPOSED REFORM

36-14   Section 156 of the Commonhold and Leasehold Reform Act 2002 contains new sections 42A and 42B which, if implemented, would further regulate the manner in which service charge funds are held by landlords and others. The proposed new sections were amended (following a consultation conducted in 2007 by the Department of Communities and Local Government[20]) by Schedule 12 of the Housing and Regeneration Act 2008. However, the proposed new

---

14 Contrast the decision in *Brown's Operating System Services Ltd v Southwark Roman Catholic Diocesan Corp* [2008] 1 P&CR 7 in relation to a lease of non-residential premises to which these provisions do not apply. See **22-19** above.
15 Section 19(2).
16 See Chapter 45 below and *Brown's Operating System Services Ltd v Southwark Roman Catholic Diocesan Corp* [2008] 1 P&CR 7; *Secretary of State for the Environment v Possfund (North West) Ltd* [1997] 2 EGLR 56.
17 Section 42(8).
18 Section 42(5).
19 Service Charge Contributions (Authorised Investments) Order 1988 (SI 1988/1284), as amended by the Financial Services and Markets Act 2000 (Consequential Amendments and Repeals) Order 2001 (SI 2001/3649).
20 See *Commonhold and Leasehold Reform Act 2002 – a consultation paper on regular statements of account and designated client accounts*, available at http://www.communities.gov.uk/documents/housing/pdf/regularstatementaccounts.pdf.

sections have not, at the time of writing, been brought into force, save for the purpose of making regulations.

36-15 As originally drafted in section 156 of the 2002 Act, section 42A would have required that any sum standing to the credit of a trust fund must be held by the payee in a designated account with a relevant financial institution and that no other funds should be held in the same account. This would have meant that a separate bank account had to be maintained in respect of each separate service charge regime, with obvious advantages of clarity for tenants wanting to know the balance of the sums standing to the credit of contributing tenants and also tracing how service charge contributions have been applied by the payee.

36-16 However, these requirements have been somewhat watered down by the amendments made following consultation and, if and when the new section 42A is brought into force, whilst it will still oblige the payee to hold funds in a designated account with a relevant financial institution, the designated account can contain sums standing to the credit of one or more other trust funds, though not other funds. The effect would be that landlords and managing agents who manage more than one set of service charge regimes can place all of the funds received in the same bank account. It would, however, remain a requirement that service charge funds are not mixed with other assets of the payee including sums received in connection with commercial service charges, even when these are received from commercial tenants within the same development. This is because the definition of 'trust fund', which is the phrase employed in section 42A, only applies to sums paid by contributing tenants, which means only tenants of dwellings.[21]

36-17 The proposed section 42A would, if implemented, confer on a tenant and any RTA the right, exercisable by notice served on the payee, to inspect documents evidencing that the principal requirements of the section and any regulations made thereunder are being complied with. Any of the contributing tenants, or the sole contributing tenant, would be entitled to withhold payment of a service charge if he has reasonable grounds for believing that the payee has failed to comply with the duty imposed on him by subsection (1) and any provisions of his tenancy relating to non-payment or late payment of service charges do not have effect in relation to the period for which he so withholds it.[22] The section provides for regulations to be made specifying:

(a) the circumstances in which a contributing tenant who has reasonable grounds for believing that the payee has not complied with a duty imposed on him by the regulations may withhold payment of a service charge;

(b) the period for which payment may be so withheld; and

(c) the amount of service charge that may be so withheld.[23]

---

21 Section 42(1) and (2).
22 Section 42A(9).
23 Section 42A(9A).

36-18   At the time of writing, no such regulations have been made. Section 42B would make it a criminal offence to fail, without reasonable excuse, to comply with a duty imposed by section 42A.

CHAPTER 37

Unfair Terms in Consumer Contract Regulations 1999

37-01   The Unfair Contract Terms Act 1977, which applies only to exclusion clauses, does not apply to a clause excluding a tenant's right to set off against service charges any claim he may have against his landlord for breach of covenant.[1] This is because the obligation to pay service charges to a management company which has responsibility for the repair and maintenance of a development is an integral part of a lease and, therefore, a provision relating to the creation of an interest in land within the meaning of Schedule 1, paragraph 1(b) to the 1977 Act. It follows that a provision excluding the tenant's right of set off is exempt from the requirement of reasonableness imposed by section 3 of that Act.

37-02   However, it has been confirmed that the Unfair Terms in Consumer Contract Regulations 1999[2] ('the Regulations') do apply to contracts which relate to interests in land.[3] A full explanation of the Regulations is beyond the scope of this work. However, as the Regulations are capable of applying to service charge provisions in leases, a brief explanation of their operation is merited.

37-03   The Regulations only apply to contracts made between a seller or supplier and a consumer.[4] A consumer means any natural person who is acting for purposes which are outside his trade, business or profession.[5] This definition is unlikely to cause much difficulty in the context of residential service charges, since the vast majority of tenants who are individuals rather than companies will not be acting in a professional or business capacity. The definition of seller or supplier is also broad, being any legal or natural person acting for purposes relating to his trade, business or profession, whether publicly or privately owned.[6] A local authority is a seller or supplier when it grants tenancies in pursuance of its public law housing duties.[7]

1   *Unchained Growth III Plc v Granbyvillage (Manchester) Management Co Ltd* [2010] 1 WLR 739.
2   SI 1999/2083.
3   *R (Khatun) v Newham LBC* [2005] QB 37.
4   Regulation 4(1).
5   Regulation 3(1).
6   *Ibid.*
7   *R (Khatun) v Newham LBC* [2005] QB 37.

37-04   By regulation 5, it is provided that:

> 'A contractual term which has not been individually negotiated shall be regarded as unfair if, contrary to the requirement of good faith, it causes a significant imbalance in the parties' rights and obligations arising under the contract, to the detriment of the consumer.'

37-05   By regulation 5(2), it is provided that 'a term shall always be regarded as not having been individually negotiated where it has been drafted in advance and the consumer has therefore not been able to influence the substance of the term'. It is likely that the majority of service charge provisions in residential leases will fall within the scope of this regulation.

37-06   Each element of regulation 5 has been the subject of analysis in case law arising in a diverse range of circumstances. Reference should be made to specialist works for detailed treatment.

37-07   Regulation 8 provides that an unfair term in a contract shall not be binding on the consumer, but the contract shall continue to bind the parties if it is capable of continuing in existence without the unfair term. Accordingly, a finding that a provision in a lease relating to service charges is unfair would result in the landlord being unable to rely on that term.

37-08   Also of potential relevance in service charge disputes is regulation 7(2), which states:

> 'If there is any doubt about the meaning of a written term, the interpretation which is most favourable to the consumer shall prevail'.

37-09   There will, therefore, generally be an obligation on the LVT or the court to resolve any ambiguity in the meaning of service charge provisions in residential leases in favour of the tenant.[8]

37-10   Given the large degree of statutory protection available to residential tenants, it may be that tenants would rarely need to rely on the additional protection conferred by the Regulations in relation to service charges. Furthermore, the Regulations are not retrospective in effect and, accordingly, do not apply to contracts made prior to the date on which they came into force, 1 October 1999.[9]

37-11   However, as we have seen, the LVT has no general jurisdiction to interfere with the terms of a lease when considering reasonableness under section 19.[10] The Regulations might sometimes prove to be the only method by which

---

8   But see **2-52** to **2-54** above as to the limited relevance of presumptions in the task of construing service charge provisions.
9   Regulation 1 and see the decision of the LVT in *Knight v Notting Hill Home Ownership* (LON/00AN/LSC/2007/0153).
10 See **29-32**.

a tenant faced with unfair service charge provisions can obtain a remedy. There is, though, something of a dearth of reported cases dealing with the application of the Regulations in service charge disputes, certainly above the level of the LVT. It appears that the LVT does have jurisdiction to consider the effect of the Regulations on the issue of whether service charges are payable in an application under section 27A of the Landlord and Tenant Act 1985. It has been suggested, however, that where an issue is raised as to the applicability of the Regulations, the LVT must consider whether it should exercise that jurisdiction or encourage one of the parties to issue court proceedings for a declaration.[11]

37-12 In *Canary Riverside PTE Ltd v Schilling*,[12] the tenants sought to rely upon the Regulations in connection with an application under section 27A. The LVT indicated that it had jurisdiction to apply the Regulations, whereupon the landlord issued proceedings in the High Court seeking a declaration that the LVT either had no jurisdiction or should not be permitted to try the issue under the Regulations. As a result, the tenant withdrew the objection based on the Regulations and the LVT made a determination of the service charges payable without reference to the Regulations. The LVT did, however, consider the application of the Regulations in connection with various applications made by the parties in relation to costs. The LVT rejected a submission on the part of the landlord that its jurisdiction under section 27A did not extend to consideration of the Regulations.

37-13 The LVT also rejected the landlord's contention that service charge provisions amounted to 'core terms' which are not subject to the requirement of fairness, being subject to an exemption under regulation 6(2) which provides:

'(2) In so far as it is in plain intelligible language, the assessment of fairness of a term shall not relate –

(a) to the definition of the main subject matter of the contract, or

(b) to the adequacy of the price or remuneration, as against the goods or services supplied in exchange.'

37-14 In *Canary Riverside PTE Ltd v Schilling*, the LVT found that service charge provisions did not fall within this exemption, saying:[13]

'Reg.6(2)(b) excludes "the adequacy of the price", as against the services, from being a factor in the assessment of fairness. Here, however, the assessment of fairness does not relate to "adequacy" – the reasonableness of the costs incurred will fall for consideration under s.19(1) of the 1985 Act. Instead, the assessment of fairness relates to incidence, ie that liability for the costs in question, whatever their "adequacy", is one-sided, in that a landlord can recover its costs from tenants but not vice versa. The point should also be made that, with service charges generally,

11 *Canary Riverside PTE Ltd v Schilling* [2005] EWLands LRX_65_2005.
12 [2005] EWLands LRX_65_2005.
13 LON/00BG/LSL/2004/0064 at para 50.

the consumer-tenant may not be regarded as paying a "price or remuneration" agreed in the provisions of the underlease (within reg.6(2)(b)) but merely as reimbursing costs incurred.'

37-15   On appeal to the Lands Tribunal,[14] in relation to the costs issues, HH Judge Michael Rich QC considered the LVT's jurisdiction under the Regulations. The judge said:[15]

'The LVT, although, as I think, entitled to decide whether a term is not binding because unfair, has no jurisdiction thereupon to make a determination whether the lease shall continue in existence without the alleged unfair term. It may well therefore regard it as convenient, if other proceedings are brought to determine whether service charge is payable under a term said not to be binding because unfair, to adjourn an application within its jurisdiction, pending such determination.

I can see no basis, however, for saying that the LVT lacks jurisdiction to determine any issue not expressly the subject of some other tribunal's exclusive jurisdiction, if determination of that issue is essential, to determining whether "a service charge is payable." That is the issue which s.27A gives the LVT jurisdiction to determine. That must include any issue necessary for or incidental to such determination. I therefore agree with the LVT that they did have jurisdiction to determine the issue of the effect of the 1999 Regulations, although I think they might have been wiser to encourage the Landlords ... to seek a declaration from the Court.'

37-16   Accordingly, in deciding whether or not to exercise its jurisdiction, the LVT must consider whether it is the appropriate forum to determine issues arising in connection with the Regulations. In one case,[16] the LVT declined to exercise its jurisdiction to consider the fairness of terms in a standard lease used by a local authority in around 10,000 cases, on the basis that the wide-ranging implications of any decision meant that the matter should be determined by the court.

37-17   In *Schilling*, the LVT, having accepted jurisdiction under the Regulations, went on to hold that provisions entitling the landlord to recover costs incurred in proceedings before the tribunal were unfair because, in the absence of a reciprocal right for the tenant to recover his costs from the landlord, such provisions caused a significant imbalance in the parties' rights and obligations arising under the lease. However, that decision was overturned on appeal to the Lands Tribunal. HH Judge Rich QC concluded that the LVT was correct to hold that the exemption in regulation 6(2) did not apply to the clause in question, since it was not the amount the tenant was required to pay which was said to be unfair but rather the requirement to make payment at all. Accordingly, the clause in issue did not relate to the adequacy of the price or remuneration within regulation 6(2)(b).

14 [2005] EWLands LRX_65_2005.
15 [2005] EWLands LRX_65_2005, at paras 44 and 45.
16 *London Borough of Camden v O'Hara* (Leasehold Valuation Tribunal, unreported, 26 April 2010, LON 00AG/LSC/2009/0607). Contrast *Haddo Leaseholders Association v The Mayor and Burgesses of the London Borough of Camden* (Leasehold Valuation Tribunal, unreported, 19 January 2009, LON/00AG/LSC/2007/0465) where the LVT accepted jurisdiction in similar circumstances, but concluded that the terms in issue were not unfair under the Regulations.

However, he went on to conclude that, taking into account the bargain contained in the lease as a whole, the entitlement to recover management costs, including, in appropriate cases, legal fees, did not cause any significant imbalance between the parties and was not contrary to the requirements of good faith.[17]

37-18 However, the LVT has, on occasion, been prepared to hold that service charges are not recoverable by a landlord because the terms of a lease contravene the requirement of fairness set out in the Regulations. Thus, in *Rye v Longmint Ltd*,[18] the LVT held that a provision in a lease, which apparently entitled the landlord to recover 'one quarter plus one third' of the cost of providing an entry phone system, where the lease was of a basement flat which did not use the system and where each of the other three flats in the building were obliged to pay a third of the costs, was unfair pursuant to the Regulations and, accordingly, was not binding on the tenant in accordance with regulation 8(1). On appeal, however, the Lands Tribunal held that, on a proper construction of the lease, the tenant was not under any obligation to contribute to the cost of the entry phone system. Accordingly, the issue of the application of the Regulations did not arise.

37-19 In *Subramaniam v Stadium Housing Association*,[19] the LVT disallowed recovery of elements of a service charge payable by a tenant of a registered social landlord under the terms of an assured shorthold tenancy on the basis that the obligation to contribute to the sums in question breached regulation 5. The LVT was strongly influenced by the personal circumstances of the tenant, who had been homeless and had little option but to accept the terms presented to him. Perhaps of wider significance was the LVT's determination that a unilateral right on the part of the landlord to alter the services to be provided also breached regulation 5 and was accordingly unenforceable.[20]

---

17 See also *Solitaire Property Management Co Ltd v Holden* [2012] UKUT 86, where the Upper Tribunal concluded that a provision entitling the landlord to employ funds collected as a reserve fund to be utilised to make good a 'temporary deficiency' in the service charge accounts was not unfair under reg 5.

18 Leasehold Valuation Tribunal, unreported, 20 June 2005, LON 00AH/LIS/2004/0093.

19 Leasehold Valuation Tribunal, unreported, 29 August 2009, LON/00AE/LSC/2007/0292.

20 For contractual provisions conferring a right on the landlord to vary the services, see **3-04**ff. above. See also *Sherwin v Holding & Management (Solitaire) Ltd* (Leasehold Valuation Tribunal, unreported, 28 February 2009, BIR/00CQ/LIS/2008/0006) (provision entitling landlord to backdate variation in percentage of total costs payable by tenant unfair).

CHAPTER 38

Public sector tenants: Right to buy leases

INTRODUCTION

38-01   There are a number of provisions regulating aspects of service charge recovery which apply only to public sector tenants. The scheme of these provisions to a large degree mirrors the provisions of the Landlord and Tenant Act 1985 and the Landlord and Tenant Act 1987, discussed in Chapters 28 to 33 above, but there are some significant differences. In order to decide what provisions (if any) apply to service charges levied by public authority landlords, careful analysis of the nature of the landlord and the lease in question is required.

SECURE TENANCIES

38-02   In general terms, tenancies, other than 'long tenancies' granted to tenants occupying a dwelling as their only or principal residence by local authorities, development corporations, housing action trusts, some housing co-operatives and some statutory bodies in pursuance of housing functions, will be secure tenancies.[1] A tenancy can cease to be 'secure' if, for example, the tenant ceases to use the dwelling as his only or principal home. There are a variety of different categories of secure tenancy which are based partly on the capacity of the landlord (whether it is a local authority, housing action trust or the Commission for New Towns) and on the length of the term. A full treatment of this complex topic is outside of the scope of this work. This section deals, in brief terms, with the principal statutory provisions affecting secure tenants, but with the caveat that it is vital, when considering the applicability of these provisions, to first ascertain exactly which of the various types of secure tenancy is in issue.

THE RIGHT TO BUY

38-03   A number of the provisions referred to in this section apply where a public sector tenant exercises the 'right to buy'. The qualifications for the right to buy are too complex to set out in full, but they depend on:

1   See the Housing Act 1985, ss 79–81.

(a)   the status of the landlord (whether it is a local authority, housing action trust, etc.);

(b)   the status of the tenant (who must have a residence qualification); and

(c)   the dwelling.

38-04   The 'right to buy' entitles qualifying secure tenants to acquire the freehold or leasehold of the dwelling in which they reside on certain conditions. Where the landlord itself owns a leasehold interest, then the right is to acquire a leasehold interest. The service charge aspects can, in this context, relate to both freehold and leasehold right to buy premises.

38-05   The right to buy is exercised by notice served by the tenant. Assuming the landlord accepts that the tenant has established his right to buy, the landlord has to serve a counter notice which must include certain information. This includes special information about service charges[2] and also (in respect of flats only) about improvements.[3] There are statutory terms for the conveyance or lease, set out in Schedule 6 to the Housing Act 1985. In addition, various other statutory provisions give the purchaser of the freehold or the tenant of the new lease some, but by no means all, of the protection which the Landlord and Tenant Act 1985 confers on private sector tenants.

REASONABLENESS OF SERVICE CHARGES FOR FREEHOLDS

38-06   Section 47 of the Housing Act 1985 is similar, although not identical, to section 19 of the Landlord and Tenant Act 1985.[4] By section 45 of the Housing Act 1985, it applies where:

(a)   the tenant has acquired the freehold from a public sector authority, which remains liable to carry out works or services; and

(b)   the conveyance enables the authority to recover service charges from the purchaser.

Section 181 provides for any disputes to be decided by the county court.

38-07   Section 47 provides for reasonableness of freehold service charges in three ways:

'(1)   Relevant costs shall be taken into account in determining the amount of a service charge payable for a period –

(a)   only to the extent that they are reasonably incurred, and

(b)   where they are incurred on the provision of services or the carrying out of works, only if the services or works are of a reasonable standard;

and the amount payable shall be limited accordingly.

2   Housing Act 1985, s 125A.
3   Housing Act 1985, s 125B.
4   See **32-07** to **32-18** above.

(2)   Where the service charge is payable before the relevant costs are incurred, no greater amount than is reasonable is so payable and after the relevant costs have been incurred any necessary adjustment shall be made by repayment, reduction of subsequent charges or otherwise.'

38-08   Section 47(3) contains a provision analogous to section 27A of the Landlord and Tenant Act 1985, which makes void provisions for deciding particular aspects of reasonableness otherwise than by arbitration. Section 47(4)[5] specifically requires money paid by way of two different types of grant (for works of improvement, repair or conversion) to be deducted from the service charge costs.

38-09   An important difference between the protection afforded under section 47 and that given to private sector tenants is the absence of any equivalent to the consultation requirements mandated by section 20 of the Landlord and Tenant Act 1985.[6] Accordingly, those provisions will apply to right to buy leases (since these will be long leases and fall within the qualifying criteria of the 1985 Act), but not to the freehold equivalent. There is also no equivalent of the 18-month time limit created by section 20B of the Landlord and Tenant Act 1985, nor of the entitlement of a tenant to apply for an order that costs incurred by the landlord are disregarded in assessing the relevant costs conferred by section 20C of the 1985 Act.

INFORMATION AS TO RELEVANT COSTS OF FREEHOLD SERVICE CHARGES

38-10   By section 48 of the Housing Act 1985:

'(1)   The payer may require the payee in writing to supply him with a written summary of the costs incurred –

(a)   if the relevant accounts are made up for periods of twelve months, in the last such period ending not later than the date of the request, or

(b)   if the accounts are not so made up, in the period of twelve months ending with the date of the request,

and which are relevant to the service charges payable or demanded as payable in that or any other period.'

38-11   The payee is required to respond with the summary by the later of one month from the request or six months from the end of the accounting period covered by the statement, whichever is the later.[7] The requirements as to the

---

5   Added by the Housing and Planning Act 1986, s 24(1)(i) and Sch 5.
6   See Chapter 30 above.
7   Housing Act 1985, s 48(2).

content of the statement are rather less clearly defined than in the private sector equivalent.[8] Apart from stating whether grants have been or are to be paid for works of improvement, repair or conversion (which must be deducted from the relevant costs under section 47 (4)), the summary need only 'set out those costs in a way showing how they are or will be reflected in demands for service charges.'[9] The summary must be certified by a qualified accountant as being 'in his opinion a fair summary complying with this requirement and as being sufficiently supported by accounts, receipts and other documents which have been produced to him'.[10] Section 51 sets out details of who can give a valid certificate.

38-12   Section 48(4) confers on a right to buy purchaser the right, within six months of receipt of the summary under section 48(3), to inspect accounts, receipts, etc. and to take copies. These are to be made available for a period of two months beginning one month after the request for inspection. No mention is made of the cost of taking copies or making the accounts, etc. available for inspection, as, in the equivalent provision, section 22 of the Landlord and Tenant Act 1985. Section 48(5) permits the request for either a summary or for inspection to be served on the person who receives the service charge and that person is obliged to pass on the request to the 'payee'. Section 48(6) provides that a disposal of the dwelling does not invalidate any request, but there is no obligation to provide the summary or permit inspection more than once for the same house and for the same period.

38-13   Section 50 of the Housing Act 1985 provides for a fine, not exceeding level 4 on the standard scale, if a person fails, without reasonable excuse, to comply with the obligations imposed by section 48. The criminal liability has, however, only very limited potential application since, by section 50(2), the sanction does not apply where the payee is a local authority, a new town corporation or the Welsh Ministers. This is likely to include the majority of landlords on whom the duties under section 48 are imposed. Section 51 defines who is entitled to certify the summary of costs required under section 48(3) as a person who is eligible for appointment as a company auditor and who is not disqualified by being associated with the landlord. However, the persons who are disqualified are limited by section 51(6), which says that members of the Chartered Institute of Public Finance and Accountancy are qualified and such a person is not disqualified by virtue of being an employee of the payee, where the payee is a local authority, new town corporation or the Welsh Ministers.

INFORMATION TO BE PROVIDED ON THE EXERCISE OF THE RIGHT TO BUY

38-14   Section 125 of the Housing Act 1985 sets out the information which a landlord is required to include in its counter-notice when a tenant serves notice

8   Landlord and Tenant Act 1985, s 21.
9   Housing Act 1985, s 48(3).
10 *Ibid.*

seeking to exercise the right to buy. The purpose of the counter-notice (which must be given by the authority within eight weeks for a freehold and 12 weeks for a leasehold) is to give financial details of how much the tenant has to pay and the discount to which he is entitled. The notice must, by section 125(3), state what provisions the landlord considers should be contained in the conveyance or lease. As regards service charge, the most significant provision is section 125(4), which states:

> 'Where the notice states provisions which would enable the landlord to recover from the tenant –
>
> (a)   service charges, or
>
> (b)   improvement contributions,
>
> the notice shall also contain the estimates and other information required by section 125A (service charges) or 125B (improvement contributions).'

38-15   The notice must also, by section 125(4A), give details of 'any structural defects known to the landlord affecting the dwelling-house or the building in which it is situated or any other building over which the tenant will have rights under the conveyance or lease'. Any such information is likely to give the tenant advance warning of the need for major works to be funded through future service charge contributions.

38-16   Under section 125A of the Housing Act 1985, the landlord is obliged to give to a tenant exercising the right to buy an estimate of service charges for each of the following five years and the aggregate figure. This enables the tenant, when considering the offer to buy, to do so with full knowledge of material financial commitments for a reasonably long time in the future. The landlord's notice in respect of a house must include:

> 'the landlord's estimate of the average annual amount (at current prices) which would be payable in respect of each head of charge in the reference period and ... the aggregate of those estimated amounts.'[11]

38-17   Where the premises in question consist of a flat, the landlord's notice must include the estimates of service charges and repairs, 'including works for the making good of structural defects' referred to in section 125A(3), as well as information concerning a loan for service charge purposes. The estimates required by section 125A(3) within the reference period of five years are:

> 'for works in respect of which the landlord considers that costs may be incurred in the reference period –
>
> (a)   for works itemised in the notice, estimates of the amount (at current prices) of the likely cost of, and of the tenant's likely contribution in respect of, each item, and the aggregate amounts of those estimated costs and contributions, and

11   Section 125A(1).

> (b)   for works not so itemised, an estimate of the average annual amount (at current prices) which the landlord considers is likely to be payable by the tenant.'

38-18   The effect of these provisions in respect of both flats and houses is that the tenant intending to buy must be given information, based on current figures, of the maximum service charge costs for the next five years. Schedule 6, paragraph 16B to the Housing Act 1985 provides that the tenant's liability for service charges is restricted in accordance with these estimates. Thus, where a lease of a flat requires the tenant to pay service charges in respect of repairs (including works for the making good of structural defects), his liability in respect of costs incurred in the initial period of the lease is restricted as follows:

1   He is not required to pay in respect of works itemised in the estimates contained in the landlord's notice under section 125 any more than the amount shown as his estimated contribution in respect of that item, together with an inflation allowance.[12]

2   He is not required to pay in respect of works not so itemised at a rate exceeding –

> (a)   as regards parts of the initial period falling within the reference period for the purposes of the estimates contained in the landlord's notice under section 125, the estimated annual average amount shown in the estimates;

> (b)   as regards parts of the initial period not falling within that reference period, the average rate produced by averaging over the reference period all works for which estimates are contained in the notice;

together, in each case, with an inflation allowance.[13]

38-19   The initial period of the lease for the purpose of this paragraph begins with the grant of the lease and ends five years after the grant, except that:

(a)   if the lease includes provision for service charges to be payable in respect of costs incurred in a period before the grant of the lease, the initial period begins with the beginning of that period; and

(b)   if the lease provides for service charges to be calculated by reference to a specified annual period, the initial period continues until the end of the fifth such period beginning after the grant of the lease.[14]

38-20   In addition to giving estimates of anticipated service charges, the landlord's counter-notice must, under section 125B, include information concerning improvements in the case of flats, but not houses. The landlord must give itemised estimates of those works for which the landlord considers improvements may be made within the five year 'reference period'. The estimates

---

12   Schedule 6, para 16B(2).
13   Schedule 6, para 16B(3).
14   Schedule 6, para 16B(4).

must give details of the works and the likely cost (at current prices) and the tenant's likely contribution for each item and the aggregate of those costs. The notice must also refer the tenant to Schedule 6, paragraph 16C and the statement therein to the effect that the tenant 'is not required to make any payment in respect of works for which no estimate was given in the landlord's notice under section 125'. It follows that, if the landlord's counter-notice fails to mention improvements at all, the tenant has no obligation to pay for any improvements within the first five years following the exercise of the right to buy.

38-21 Section 125C defines the reference period during which the service charges and charges for improvements in right to buy cases are frozen, subject only to inflation. The period begins on 'such date not more than six months after the notice is given as the landlord may reasonably specify as being a date by which the conveyance will have been made or the lease granted'. The reference period ends 'five years after that date, or where the notice specifies that the conveyance or lease will provide for a service charge or improvements to be calculated by reference to a specified annual period, with the end of the fifth such period beginning after that date'.

LOANS FOR SERVICE CHARGES

38-22 Section 450 of the Housing Act 1985 contains provisions relating to loans for repairs or improvement to flats. The reference to improvements was added by Schedule 9 to the Commonhold and Leasehold Reform Act 2002. Under section 450A, the Secretary of State may make regulations to permit a tenant who has exercised the right to buy the lease of a flat (the entitlement does not extend to the purchase of a freehold) and whose landlord is the housing authority who granted the lease or another housing authority, to call for a loan to contribute to service charge costs or improvements payable during the first ten years of the lease. The relevant regulations are the Housing (Service Charge Loans) Regulations 1992.[15] The regulations provide that:

(a) the right to a loan arises only in respect of so much of a service charge to which section 450A applies as –

    (i) exceeds £1,500 less the amount of any service charge already demanded under the lease in respect of the same accounting period as that charge, and

    (ii) does not exceed £20,000 less the amount of any outstanding loan which has been made in pursuance of the right to a loan under regulation 2; and

(b) does not arise unless the amount thus qualifying for a loan itself exceeds £500.

---

15 SI 1992/1708, amended by the Housing (Service Charge Loans) (Amendment) (England) Regulations 2000 (SI 2000/1963).

38-23   The loan is made by an advance, in the case of a housing association landlord or, in any other case, by leaving outstanding the service charges for which the loan is to be made.[16] The loan is only in relation to service charges for repairs or improvements and does not, therefore, cover other services such as cleaning, lighting or gardening.

TERMS OF LEASES AFTER THE EXERCISE OF THE RIGHT TO BUY

38-24   Schedule 6, paragraphs 16A and 16B to the Housing Act 1985 set out the limit on service charges payable for a five-year period by reference to the information provided in the landlord's counter-notice in the manner described above. Schedule 6 also covers matters which are to be included in the conveyance or lease following the exercise of the right to buy. Paragraphs 1 to 7 cover both freeholds and leaseholds, while paragraphs 8 to 10 deal only with conveyances of freeholds. Paragraph 12 provides that a lease is to be for 125 years (or five days less than the landlord's interest, if that interest is shorter) and paragraph 11 states that the rent is not to exceed £10 per annum.

38-25   The important parts of Schedule 6 for the purpose of service charges are paragraphs 14 and 15. Paragraph 14 (which applies only to flats) sets out implied obligations on the part of the landlord:

(a)   to keep in repair the structure and exterior of the dwelling-house and of the building in which it is situated (including drains, gutters and external pipes) and to make good any defect affecting that structure;

(b)   to keep in repair any other property over or in respect of which the tenant has rights by virtue of this Schedule; and

(c)   to ensure, so far as practicable, that services which are to be provided by the landlord and to which the tenant is entitled (whether by himself or in common with others) are maintained at a reasonable level and to keep in repair any installation connected with the provision of those services.

38-26   Under paragraph 14(4), a County Court may make an order excluding or modifying these implied covenants if it appears to the court that it is reasonable to do so. Paragraph 15 applies where the landlord itself holds a leasehold interest. It implies a covenant by the landlord to pay the head rent and observe the head lease covenants, save to the extent that the tenant is liable to do so.

---

16 Regulations 2(2), 5(2).

PART V

Remedies

CHAPTER 39

Introduction

39-01 In this part, consideration is given to the remedies available to a landlord and tenant in circumstances where the tenant is, or is alleged to be, in arrears of service charge or where there is, for any other reason, a dispute about the tenant's liability to pay. The remedies available to a freeholder in respect of freehold service charges are dealt with in Chapter 26 above.

SUMMARY OF THE AVAILABLE REMEDIES

39-02 The remedies available to the landlord are as follows:

1   Debt claim against an existing or former tenant.

2   Debt claim against a guarantor or a party who has provided an authorised guarantee agreement.

3   Determination from the LVT under section 27A of the Landlord and Tenant Act 1985 (residential leases only).

4   Distress.

5   Service of notice under section 6 of the Law of Distress Amendment Act 1908.

6   Forfeiture.

7   Declaratory relief.

8   Deduction from rent deposit and action to require the tenant to replenish.

9   Withholding of services.

10   Bankruptcy/winding-up.

11   Variation of the lease under section 35 of the Landlord and Tenant Act 1987 (residential leases only).

39-03 The remedies and defences available to the tenant are as follows:

1   Set-off.

2   Declaratory relief.

3   Determination from the LVT under section 27A of the Landlord and Tenant Act 1985 (residential leases only).

4   Remedies available to a tenant who has overpaid service charge (exercise of a contractual right to reimbursement, set-off, restitution and breach of trust).

5   Relief from forfeiture.

6   Remedies in relation to information, inspection of documents and assistance (residential leases only).

7   Application for variation of the lease under Part IV of the Landlord and Tenant Act 1987 (residential leases only).

8   Application for the appointment of a manager or receiver.

9   Remedies available to a former tenant who discharges the arrears of an assignee (indemnities and overriding leases).

CHAPTER 40

Landlord's remedies: Debt claim against an existing or former tenant

40-01   The most straightforward means by which a landlord may recover arrears of service charge is by obtaining judgment on the debt by court action.

40-02   In the case of residential leases, service charge liability may be the subject of a separate determination by the LVT pursuant to section 27A of the Landlord and Tenant Act 1985. In such cases, it will still be necessary for the landlord to obtain judgment from the court in respect of any arrears before taking enforcement action, albeit that it will no longer be open to the tenant to dispute the existence of the arrears. The jurisdiction under section 27A of the Landlord and Tenant Act 1985 is considered separately in Chapter 42.

40-03   In order for the landlord to bring a successful claim in debt against an existing or former tenant in respect of service charge arrears, the following conditions will need to be satisfied:

1   There must be arrears of service charge outstanding under the lease.

2   The proposed defendant(s) must currently be liable under the lease or a licence to assign to make payment of the arrears in question.

3   The landlord must be the person presently entitled to sue for those arrears.

4   Where the claim is brought against a former tenant, the notice requirements in section 17 of the Landlord and Tenant (Covenants) Act 1995 must first have been satisfied.

5   The proposed defendant(s) must not presently be immune from legal process under one or other of the statutory insolvency regimes.

6   The defendant must not have a valid defence of set-off against the claim.

7   The claim must have been brought before the expiry of the relevant limitation period.[1]

---

1   The expiry of the relevant limitation period does not operate to extinguish the landlord's contractual right to claim the relevant sum, but operates as a bar to the landlord's right to bring an action to recover the debt. It is accordingly a potential defence which is available to the tenant and, unless such a defence is taken, will not prevent the landlord from recovering the debt.

EXISTENCE OF THE ARREARS

40-04   In order to bring a debt claim against an existing or former tenant, there must be arrears of service charge due under the lease. The arrears may comprise interim or final service charge or a combination of the two. Where the lease provides for contractual interest to be paid on arrears of service charge, the landlord may include this interest in the claim. If the lease does not expressly provide for interest to be paid on arrears of service charge, none will be payable as a matter of contract. However, in any claim for judgment on outstanding arrears, the landlord will be entitled to seek statutory interest under section 69 of the County Courts Act 1984 or section 35A of the Senior Courts Act 1981, as the case may be.

40-05   There will often be a dispute as to whether there are, in fact, arrears of service charges. Common defences relied on by tenants to a claim for arrears are set out below:

1   The contractual or statutory pre-conditions for recovery of interim or final service charge have not yet been complied with.[2]

2   The tenant has, in fact, already paid the arrears and the landlord has failed to give proper credit for the sums paid by the tenant.

3   Some or all of the services, the cost of which the landlord now seeks to recover, are beyond the scope of the services which the landlord is obliged to provide under the lease and, accordingly, the tenant is not obliged to contribute towards them.[3]

4   Contrary to an express or implied term of reasonableness,[4] some or all of the relevant costs were not reasonably incurred, are not reasonable in the amount, or works or other services were not carried out to a reasonable standard.[5]

5   Some or all of the service charges are now either statue barred under the Limitation Act 1980 (see **40-51** below) or, in the case of residential leases, are barred by section 20B of the Landlord and Tenant Act 1985.[6]

6   The tenant has a right of set off against the landlord which is equal to or in excess of the arrears of service charge (see **40-49** to **40-50** below).

7   By reason of an express or implied representation made by the landlord, the landlord is now estopped from recovering the arrears.[7]

8   The service charge provisions in the lease are unfair within the meaning of the Unfair Terms in Consumer Contract Regulations 1999 (see Chapter 37 above).

---

2   Contractual pre-conditions are discussed in Part III above; statutory pre-conditions are discussed in Part IV above.
3   Services are discussed in Part II above.
4   Contractually implied terms of reasonableness are discussed at **2-97** to **2-121** above. Statutorily implied terms of reasonableness are discussed in Chapter 29.
5   See **29-34** to **29-35** above.
6   See Chapter 31 above.
7   *Central London Property Trust Ltd v High Trees House Ltd* [1947] KB 130. See also *Swanston Grange (Luton) Management Ltd v Langley-Essen* [2008] L&TR 20.

40-06   One form of defence which is not open to the tenant is an allegation that the landlord has failed to mitigate his losses (e.g. by forfeiting the lease and then re-letting to a third party).[8] This is because a claim for arrears of service charge, just like a claim for arrears of rent, is a claim in debt, so the ordinary rules relating to mitigation of loss which apply to a damages claim have no application.

40-07   Where the existence of the arrears is in dispute, the matter will ultimately have to be resolved by the court. As the claimant in the action, the burden of proof will rest with the landlord.[9]

PARTIES WHO MAY BE SUED FOR THE ARREARS

40-08   Where the landlord seeks to recover arrears of service charge, it is first necessary to identify the potential defendant or defendants to the claim, being the party or parties who are presently liable under the lease to make payment of the arrears. The potential candidates will include the existing tenant and, where applicable, one or more of the previous tenants. (Guarantors and parties who have given an authorised guarantee agreement are dealt with separately in Chapter 41 below). In addition to establishing liability under the lease, the landlord should also consider whether any separate liability arises under a direct covenant contained in a licence to assign.

40-09   Where the lease is no longer vested in the original tenant, it is essential to distinguish between leases to which the provisions of the Landlord and Tenant (Covenants) Act 1995 apply and those which were granted before[10] the coming into force of that Act on 1 January 1996.[11]

Leases granted before 1996 (to which the Landlord and Tenant (Covenants) Act 1995 does not apply)

40-10   At common law, the original tenant will remain liable on the covenants contained in the lease, even after the lease has been assigned, as a matter of privity of contract.[12] Accordingly, the original tenant will remain liable for arrears of service charge which accrue due after the assignment of the lease. There are, however, three exceptions to this principle:

(i)   Absent some express provision in the lease, an original tenant will not be liable for service charges which accrue due during any statutory continuation of the lease under section 24 of the Landlord and Tenant Act 1954.[13]

---

8   See *Reichman v Beveridge* [2006] EWCA Civ 1659.
9   See **29-19** above for discussion of the burden of proof in the context of applications under the Landlord and Tenant Act 1985, s 27A.
10   Or were granted pursuant to a contract or court order made before the coming into force of the Act.
11   See s 1(3). Prior to 1996, the position was governed by the Law of Property Act 1925, ss 141 and 142.
12   *Walker's Case* (1587) 3 Co rep 22a; *Auriol v Mills* (1790) 4 Term Rep 94.
13   *City of London Corp v Fell* [1993] 3 WLR 1164; *Herbert Duncan v Cluttons* [1993] QB 589.

(ii)   An original tenant of a lease to which the provisions of section 145 of the Law of Property Act 1922 apply (perpetually renewable leases) is only liable to pay arrears which have accrued due whilst the lease was vested in either himself or his personal representatives.[14]

(iii) At common law, the obligations of an original tenant cannot be varied or increased by a subsequent agreement between the landlord and an assignee of the lease without the consent of the original tenant.[15] Similarly, section 18(2) of the Landlord and Tenant (Covenants) Act 1995 (which applies to all leases irrespective of the date of grant) provides that a former tenant is not liable under a covenant to pay any amount in respect of the covenant to the extent that the amount is referable to any relevant variation of the tenant covenants of the tenancy. A variation of the tenant covenants is a relevant variation if either the landlord has, at the time of the variation, an absolute right to refuse to allow it, or the landlord would have had such a right but for a variation of the tenant covenants at or after the assignment.[16] It follows that if, after the assignment of the lease, the landlord and the assignee vary its terms so as to give rise to a greater service charge liability than would otherwise have arisen, the original tenant will not be liable for the increase.

40-11   At common law, an assignee of the lease will not be liable for any arrears of service charge which accrued due prior to the assignment of the lease to him.[17] Nor will the assignee be liable for any arrears of service charge which accrue due after he himself has assigned the lease.[18] However, an assignee will remain liable, notwithstanding any further assignment of the lease, for any arrears of service charge which accrued due whilst the lease remained vested in him.

40-12   Accordingly, where the lease has been the subject of one or more assignments, there may be more than one party who is liable for the same service charge arrears. In such cases, the landlord has a choice: he may elect to proceed against the original tenant or the relevant assignee or both of them.[19] Neither the original tenant nor an assignee can escape liability on the ground that the landlord could equally have sued the other; nor can either of them insist that the landlord exhausts his remedies elsewhere before proceeding against them.[20]

40-13   However, although the landlord can obtain judgment against both the original tenant and the assignee, he cannot actually obtain payment from both

---

14   Law of Property Act 1922, Sch 15, para 11.
15   *Friends Provident Life Office British Railway Board* [1995] 2 EGLR 55. In that case, it was held that where the lease had been varied after assignment so as to increase the rent, the original tenant was liable to pay rent at the old rather than the new rate.
16   Section 18(4).
17   *Parry v Robinson Wyllie Ltd* [1987] 2 EGLR 133; *Wharfland Ltd v South London Co-operative Building Co Ltd* [1995] 2 EGLR 21.
18   *Paul v Nurse* (1828) 8 B&C 486.
19   *Onslow v Corrie* (1817) 2 Madd 330.
20   *Norwich Union Life Insurance Society Ltd v Low Profile Fashions Ltd* (1992) 64 P&CR 187 at p 192.

parties,[21] not least because payment of the arrears by one of them will result in the other being discharged from liability.

40-14   Where part only of the demised premises has been assigned, the position may be more complicated, but the applicable principles are as follows:

1   The assignment of part only of a lease does not itself create two separate tenancies.[22]

2   The effect of the assignment is to sever the covenants of the lease so that liability for performance of the covenants is apportioned as between the two parts. Thus, each tenant will be liable to repair their respective parts[23] and each will be liable for only a proportionate part of the rent.[24] The proportion of the rent for which each is liable is that which the court considers is fairly attributable to the relevant part.[25] By analogy with the common law rules relating to severance of the reversion,[26] it is considered that the proportion fairly attributable to each part will fall to be ascertained by reference to the values of each part. It is considered that, even where a service charge is not reserved as rent, liability for payment of service charge would be apportioned in like manner, although arguably it might be more appropriate, in some cases, to apportion service charges by reference to the value of the services received by each of the severed parts of the premises.

3   It is open to the assignor and assignee of part to agree as between themselves how the rent (including service charge which is reserved as such) is to be apportioned between them and any such agreement will be binding on their respective successors, but not does not bind the landlord unless he was a party to that agreement.[27] In default of agreement with the landlord, the apportionment of rent (including service charge reserved as such) may be determined by the court[28] or by the Secretary of State on an application under section 20 of the Landlord and Tenant Act 1927. Service charges which are not reserved as rent fall outside the scope of these statutory provisions, but it is considered that it would be open to either the assignee or the assignor to obtain declaratory relief from the court, applying the common law principle referred to above.

Leases granted on or after 1 January 1996 (to which the Landlord and Tenant (Covenants) Act 1995 applies)

40-15   Where the provisions of the Landlord and Tenant (Covenants) Act 1995 apply, following an assignment of the lease (otherwise than in breach of covenant

21   *House Property and Investment Company Ltd v Bernardout* [1948] 1 KB 314.
22   *Lester v Ridd* [1990] 2 QB 430.
23   *Stevenson v Lombard* (1802) 2 East 575 at p 580.
24   *Lester v Ridd* [1990] 2 QB 430.
25   *Lester v Ridd* [1990] 2 QB 430.
26   See Co Litt 148c *Swansea Corp v Thomas* (1882) 10 QBD 48.
27   Law of Property Act 1925, s 190(3); *Bliss v Collins* (1822) 5 B&Ald 876.
28   *Whitham v Bullock* [1939] 2 KB 81.

or by operation of law[29]), the original tenant will automatically be released from liability on the covenants in the lease.[30] Accordingly, the original tenant will not have any liability under the lease in respect of arrears of service charge which accrue due after the assignment. However, in appropriate circumstances,[31] a tenant may be required to enter into an authorised guarantee agreement, as a condition of the provision of the landlord's consent to the assignment and he will thereafter be subject to an equivalent liability as guarantor (claims against guarantors are dealt with in Chapter 41 below). The original tenant will not, however, be relieved of liability in respect of any arrears of service charge which accrued due under the lease whilst the lease was vested in him.[32]

40-16   An assignee of the lease will not be liable to pay any arrears of service charge which accrued due prior to the assignment of the lease.[33] However, an assignee will be liable to pay arrears of service charge which accrued due whilst the lease is vested in him[34] and will not escape that liability by a further assignment of the lease. An assignee of the lease will not, however, be liable for any arrears of service charge that accrue due after the date on which he himself assigns the lease.[35]

40-17   Upon an assignment of part only of the demised premises, section 3 of the Landlord and Tenant (Covenants) Act 1995 provides for the burden of the tenant covenants to pass to an assignee whether of the whole or part only of the demised premises.[36] Accordingly, an assignee of part of the demised premises will inherit a liability to pay the whole of the service charge for the demised premises. Although there will not generally be an automatic statutory apportionment of the covenant to pay service charge, provision is made in sections 9 and 10 of the Landlord and Tenant (Covenants) Act 1995 for the assignor and assignee to apply to fix an apportionment so as to bind the landlord.

40-18   Section 25 of the Landlord and Tenant (Covenants) Act 1995 contains anti-avoidance provisions which prevent the parties from contracting out of the effect of the Act.[37]

---

29 Section 11(1).
30 Section 5(1).
31 Section 16(3) provides that the circumstances are: (a) by virtue of a covenant against assignment (whether absolute or qualified) the assignment cannot be effected without the consent of the landlord under the tenancy or some other person; (b) any such consent is given subject to a condition (lawfully imposed) that the tenant is to enter into an agreement guaranteeing the performance of the covenant by the assignee; and (c) the agreement is entered into by the tenant in pursuance of that condition.
32 Section 24(1).
33 Section 23(1).
34 By virtue of s 3(1).
35 Section 5(1).
36 Subject, however, to the exceptions contained in s 3(2)(a), namely: (i) where the relevant covenants did not bind the assignor (s 3(2)(a)(i)); or (ii) they fall to be complied with in relation to any demised premises not comprised in the assignment (s 3(2)(a)(ii)). For the meaning of 'demised premises not comprised in the assignment' in the context of covenants to pay money, see the Landlord and Tenant (Covenants) Act 1995, s 28(3).
37 See the discussion of s 25 in *Avonridge Property Co Ltd v Mashru* [2005] UKHL 70.

LICENCES TO ASSIGN

40-19   As well as liability arising under the lease, both the original tenant and an assignee may have assumed a separate and potentially more extensive contractual liability in a licence to assign. Thus in both *Lyons & Co Ltd v Knowles*[38] and *Estates Gazette Ltd v Benjamin Restaurants Ltd*,[39] it was held that the terms of the licence to assign had created a separate contractual obligation on the part of the assignee to perform the covenants in the lease and that obligation remained enforceable even after the assignee had himself assigned on the lease.

DISTINCTION BETWEEN PERSONAL LIABILITY AND THE RIGHT TO FORFEIT FOR ARREARS

40-20   For the reasons set out above, it will not always be the case that the current tenant is personally liable for the full amount of the outstanding arrears of service charge in circumstances where arrears accrued prior to the assignment of the lease.[40] In relation to leases to which the Landlord and Tenant (Covenants) Act 1995 does not apply,[41] the landlord will be entitled to forfeit the lease for any arrears which have accrued, even if the lease has been assigned and some (or even all) of the arrears accrued before the assignment.[42] However, in relation to leases granted on or after 1 January 1996, to which the 1995 Act applies, it is not entirely clear whether the right of forfeiture survives in respect of arrears which accrued prior to an assignment of the term. Section 23(1) of the Act provides that a tenant 'shall not have any liability' under a covenant in the lease in relation to any time falling before the assignment of the lease to him. Section 23(3) preserves the landlord's remedy of forfeiture for a landlord who takes an assignment of the reversion where the breach occurred before the assignment of the reversion, but there is no equivalent provision governing the landlord's right of forfeiture where the breach occurred before an assignment of the lease to the current tenant.

PARTY WHO IS ENTITLED TO SUE FOR THE ARREARS

40-21   In order to ascertain in whom the right to sue for service charge arrears is presently vested, it is again necessary to distinguish between cases to which the provisions of the Landlord and Tenant (Covenants) Act 1995 applies and those where they do not.[43]

Leases granted before 1996 (to which the Landlord and Tenant (Covenants) Act 1995 does not apply)

40-22   By section 141 of the Law of Property Act 1925, the rent reserved by a lease and the benefit of every covenant having reference to the subject matter

---

38   [1943] KB 366.
39   [1995] 1 All ER 129.
40   See **40-10** to **40-17** above.
41   See **40-09** above.
42   *Bennett v Herring* (1857) 3 CB (NS) 370; *Parry v Robinson Wyllie Ltd* [1987] 2 EGLR 133.
43   See **40-09** above.

of the lease passes to an assignee of the reversion.[44] Section 141 of the Law of Property Act 1925 will enable an assignee of the reversion to recover not only the service charge which accrues due after the assignment, but also those arrears which had accrued due before the assignment.[45] The assignor of the reversion correspondingly loses the right to recover arrears of service charge upon the assignment of the lease.[46]

40-23 The assignment of part only of the reversion does not sever the lease, which remains a single estate.[47] In the case of any lease made after 1 January 1882,[48] section 140 of the Law of Property Act 1925 provides that the benefit of all covenants, conditions and rights of re-entry are apportioned and annexed to the severed parts.[49] Section 140 of the Law of Property Act 1925 is not prescriptive as to the manner of the apportionment, but it is considered that apportionment is likely to be effected by reference to the values of the apportioned parts or (if more appropriate), the value of the services enjoyed by each of the apportioned parts.

Leases granted on or after 1 January 1996 (to which the Landlord and Tenant (Covenants) Act 1995 applies)

40-24 By section 3(1) of the Landlord and Tenant (Covenants) Act 1995, the benefit of a tenant's covenant to pay service charge passes to the assignee on an assignment of the reversion. However, in contrast to the position at common law, the assignee of the reversion does not acquire the right to sue for arrears of service charge that accrued due prior to the assignment.[50] In order for the assignee to sue for such arrears, the assignor's continuing right to do so must be expressly

---

44 However, where the demised premises includes a dwelling, an assignee of the reversion will need to comply with the requirements of the Landlord and Tenant Act 1987, ss 47 and 48 before issuing proceedings to recover service charge arrears. See **32-07** above.
45 *Flight v Bentley* (1835) 7 Sim 149; *Re King, Robinson v Gray* [1963] Ch 459; *London & County (A&D) Ltd v Wilfred Sportsman Ltd* [1971] Ch 764.
46 *Re King, Robinson v Gray* [1963] Ch 459.
47 *Jelley v Buckman* [1974] QB 488.
48 Where the lease was entered into before 1 January 1882 and the reversion severed before 1 January 1926, the common law rules apply (by which the right to receive the rent and to have the other covenants in the lease performed (including payment of service charge where it is not reserved as rent) is apportioned between the severed parts, in accordance with their respective values). See the Law of Property Act 1925, s 140(3).
49 Law of Property Act 1925, s 40 provides as follows: 'Notwithstanding the severance by conveyance, surrender, or otherwise of the reversionary estate in any land comprised in a lease, and notwithstanding the avoidance or cesser in any other manner of the term granted by a lease as to part only of the land comprised therein, every condition or right of re-entry, and every other condition contained in the lease, shall be apportioned, and shall remain annexed to the severed parts of the reversionary estate as severed, and shall be in force with respect to the term whereon each severed part is reversionary, or the term in the part of the land as to which the term has not been surrendered, or has not been avoided or has not otherwise ceased, in like manner as if the land comprised in each severed part, or the land as to which the term remains subsisting, as the case may be, had alone originally been comprised in the lease.'
50 Section 23(1).

assigned to the assignee.[51] An assignment of the right to sue for the pre-assignment arrears will often be incorporated into the transfer of the reversion itself, but it is capable of being separately assigned.

40-25 Where part only of the reversion is assigned, the applicable principles are as follows:

1   There is no automatic statutory apportionment of the benefit of the tenant covenants of the lease 'except to the extent that they fall to be complied with in relation to any such premises'.[52]

2   However, even where there is no automatic statutory apportionment of the benefit of the covenant to pay service charge, provision is made in sections 9 and 10 of the Landlord and Tenant (Covenants) Act 1995 for the assignor and assignee of the reversion to apply to fix an apportionment so as to bind the tenant.

SECTION 17 OF THE LANDLORD AND TENANT (COVENANTS) ACT 1995

40-26 Where a landlord seeks to recover arrears of service charge against a former tenant, the landlord must comply with the requirements of section 17 of the Landlord and Tenant (Covenants) Act 1995 which applies to all leases, irrespective of the date of grant.

40-27 Section 17 provides that a former tenant is not liable to pay any amount in respect of a 'fixed charge' payable under a covenant in a lease unless, within a period of six months beginning on the date when the charge becomes due, the landlord[53] serves notice on him, in the prescribed form[54] or in a form substantially to the same effect,[55] informing him:

(a)   that the charge is now due; and

(b)   that, in respect of the charge, the landlord intends to recover from the former tenant such amount as is specified in the notice and (where payable) interest calculated on such basis as is so specified.

40-28 A 'fixed charge' for the purposes of section 17 expressly includes service charges.[56] For the purposes of section 17 of the Landlord and Tenant

---

51   The right to do so is preserved by s 23(2).
52   Section 3(3)(b). The meaning of the expression 'except to the extent that they fall to be complied with in relation to any such premises' is defined in the Landlord and Tenant (Covenants) Act 1995, s 28(3).
53   The definition of landlord in s 17(6) extends to a management company with whom the original tenant had covenanted to pay service charge.
54   Section 27(1). The prescribed form is contained in the Landlord and Tenant (Covenants) Act 1995 (Notices) Regulations 1995 (SI 1995/2964).
55   Section 27(4).
56   As defined in the Landlord and Tenant Act 1985, s 18, disregarding the words 'of a dwelling' in that section – s 17(6)(b).

(Covenants) Act 1995, it matters not whether service charge is reserved in the lease as rent.

40-29   Section 17(4) provides that, where a landlord has served a notice under section 17(2), the amount (exclusive of interest) which the former is liable to pay in respect of the fixed charge in question shall not exceed the amount specified in the notice unless:

(a)   his liability in respect of the charge is subsequently determined to be for a greater amount;

(b)   the notice informed him of the possibility that that liability would be so determined; and

(c)   within the period of three months beginning with the date of the determination, the landlord serves on him a further notice, informing him that the landlord intends to recover that greater amount from him (plus interest, where payable).

40-30   Paragraph 4 of the explanatory note to the prescribed forms of section 17 notice suggests that service charge which has been ascertained on a budget or interim basis, but not yet determined for year-end purpose, is an example of the form of fixed charge to which section 17(4) of the Landlord and Tenant (Covenants) Act 1995 might apply.[57] However, in *Scottish & Newcastle v Raguz (No 2)*,[58] a case concerning a rent review, the House of Lords held that section 17(4) of the Landlord and Tenant (Covenants) Act 1995 had 'largely misfired'[59] and that a landlord was only ever required to serve notice in accordance with section 17(2) once the payment had become contractually due.

40-31   Following *Scottish & Newcastle Plc v Raguz (No 2)*, it would seem that all that is required of a landlord when seeking to recover a service charge is to serve notice in accordance with section 17(2) of the Landlord and Tenant (Covenants) Act 1995 within six months of the service charge (whether interim or final) becoming contractually due under the lease. It is not necessary for a landlord to serve any further notice in accordance with section 17(4) of the Landlord and Tenant (Covenants) Act 1995 to protect his right to recover an, as yet, undetermined year-end service charge.

TENANT INSOLVENCY

40-32   A landlord's right to recover arrears of service charge by action is restricted in cases where the tenant is insolvent. The applicable restrictions depend on the insolvency regime to which the tenant is subject.

---

57   See the Landlord and Tenant (Covenants) Act 1995 (Notices) Regulations 1995 (SI 1995/2964).
58   [2008] 1 EGLR 27.
59   *Per* Lord Hoffmann at para 13.

Administration

40-33   Where an application for an administration order has been made in respect of a corporate tenant, or notice of intention to appoint an administrator has been filed with the court, a landlord may not institute or continue any legal process (including a claim to recover arrears of service charge) without the permission of the court.[60] Once the tenant is in administration, the landlord may not institute or continue any legal process (including a claim to recover arrears of service charge) without the permission of the court or the consent of the administrator.[61]

40-34   However, where the administrator uses the demised premises for the purposes of the administration, rent is payable as an expense of the administration and, if the administrators fail to make payment, the landlord may apply to the court for an order compelling them to do so.[62] By contrast, a landlord has no right to compel the administrators to pay arrears of rent which accrued due prior to the administration.[63] It is considered that these principles apply equally to service charges whether or not reserved as rent in the lease.

Liquidation

40-35   Where a corporate tenant is in voluntary liquidation, a landlord may sue for arrears of service charge, but, on an application by the liquidator or any contributor or creditor, the court has the power to stay the proceedings.[64]

40-36   Where a winding up petition has been presented, but a winding up order has not yet been made, a landlord is at liberty to issue and pursue proceedings for the recovery of service charge arrears. However, on an application by the liquidator or any contributor or creditor, the court has the power to stay the proceedings.[65]

40-37   Once a winding up order has been made or a provisional liquidator appointed, proceedings may not be issued or continued against the tenant without leave of the court.[66] Any proceedings issued without leave of the court are a nullity.[67] In the case of a simple debt claim for arrears, it is most unlikely that leave would be sought or granted for the simple reason that the company's insolvency would make recovery of the debt very unlikely.

---

60   Insolvency Act 1986, s 8 and Sch B1, para 44.
61   Insolvency Act 1986, s 8 and Sch B1, para 43.
62   *Goldacre (Offices) Ltd v Nortel Networks UK Ltd* [2009] EWHC 3389.
63   *Leisure (Norwich) II Ltd v Luminar Lava Ignite Ltd* [2012] EWHC 951 (Ch).
64   Insolvency Act 1986, ss 112(1) and 126.
65   Insolvency Act 1986, s 126.
66   Insolvency Act 1986, s 130(3).
67   *Re National Employers Mutual General Insurance Association Ltd* [1995] 1 BCLC 232.

40-38 Arrears of service charge which accrued due before the winding up of a corporate tenant must be proved for by the landlord in the liquidation. Rent and service charges[68] (whether or not reserved as rent) which accrue after the winding up has commenced may qualify as an expense of the liquidation[69] and, as such, rank above the claims of other creditors and the liquidator's remuneration.[70]

Bankruptcy

40-39 In cases of bankruptcy of an individual tenant, where a bankruptcy petition has been presented, but a bankruptcy order has not yet been made, a landlord is at liberty to issue and pursue proceedings for the recovery of arrears of service charges. However, on an application by the liquidator or any contributor or creditor, the court has the power to stay the proceedings.[71]

40-40 Once a bankruptcy order has been made, proceedings may not be issued or continued against the tenant without leave of the court.[72] In contrast to the position on a winding up, proceedings issued without leave of the court are not a nullity and leave may be granted retrospectively.[73] In the case of a simple debt claim for arrears, it is most unlikely that leave would be sought or granted.

40-41 Arrears of service charge which accrued due before the making of a bankruptcy order must be proved for by the landlord in the bankruptcy. However, once a trustee in bankruptcy is appointed, the lease vests in him[74] and the landlord may sue the trustee in bankruptcy for any arrears of service charge that accrue due whilst the lease remains vested in him.[75] Service charge which accrues due after the bankruptcy order has been made may, in any event, qualify as an expense of the bankruptcy and, as such, rank above the claims of other creditors and the trustee in bankruptcy's remuneration.[76]

---

68 *Re Linda Marie Ltd* [1989] BCLC 46.
69 In order to qualify as an expense of the litigation, the rent and service charge must qualify under the Insolvency Rules 1986 (SI 1986/1925), r 4.218(3)(a) (expenses incurred in preserving, realising or getting in any of the assets of the company) or 4.218(3)(m) (necessary disbursements), as to which see *Re Linda Marie Ltd* [1989] BCLC 46; *Re HH Realisations Ltd* [1976] 2 EGLR 51 and *Re Lundy Granite Co ex parte Heaven* (1871) 6 Ch App.
70 *Re Toshoku Finance UK Plc* [2002] UKHL 6.
71 Insolvency Act 1986, s 285. See *Sharples (Christina) v Places for People Homes Ltd* [2011] EWCA Civ 813.
72 Insolvency Act 1986, s 285(3)(b).
73 *Re Saunders* [1997] Ch 60.
74 Insolvency Act 1986, s 306.
75 The trustee in bankruptcy is entitled to be indemnified out of the bankrupt's assets: *Wilson v Wallani* (1879–80) LR 5 Ex D 155.
76 In order to qualify as an expense of the litigation, the rent and service charge must qualify under the Insolvency Rules 1986 (SI 1986/1925), r 6.224(1)(a) (expenses incurred in preserving, realising or getting in any of the assets of the company) or 6.224(1)(m) (necessary disbursements). By analogy to the position where a corporate tenant is in liquidation, see *Re Linda Marie Ltd* [1989] BCLC 46; *Re HH Realisations Ltd* [1976] 2 EGLR 51; *Re Lundy Granite Co* (1870–71) LR 6 Ch App 462.

Voluntary arrangements

40-42   Where service charge arrears are caught by a company or individual voluntary arrangement, a landlord will be bound by its terms.[77] A voluntary arrangement may restrict a landlord's ability to recover both existing arrears of service charge and future service charge.[78] The landlord will likewise be prevented from recovering service charge arrears whilst a moratorium is in force under section 1A (small companies) or section 253 (individuals) of the Insolvency Act 1986.

Debt relief order

40-43   Where service charge arrears have been designated as a qualifying debt for the purposes of a debt relief order made under section 251 of the Insolvency Act 1986, the landlord may not sue for those arrears during the one year moratorium imposed by section 251H. Moreover, if proceedings have already been issued by the landlord to recover the arrears by the time of the making of the debt relief order, the court has power to stay those proceedings.[79]

Receivership

40-44   The appointment of a receiver,[80] in respect of either an individual or a corporate tenant, does not affect the tenant's liability to pay rent and service charge and, in default of payment, a landlord can sue for the arrears in the ordinary way.

SET-OFF

40-45   There are two forms of set-off which may be maintained by a tenant in answer to a landlord's claim for arrears of service charge, namely common law recoupment and equitable set-off. These two forms of set-off are considered below.

Common law recoupment

40-46   Where a landlord is in breach of his repairing obligations in the lease and the tenant incurs expenditure carrying out the necessary repairs to remedy the breach, the tenant is entitled to recoup his expenditure from future rents

---

77   Insolvency Act 1986, ss 5 (companies) and 260 (individuals).
78   *Thomas v Ken Thomas Ltd* [2007] BLR 429; *Re Cancol Ltd* [1996] 1 All ER 37.
79   Section 251G(3).
80   Whether appointed under the Law of Property Act 1925, s 109, an administrative receiver appointed under the Insolvency Act 1986 or a court appointed receiver under the Senior Courts Act 1981, s 37.

payable by him to the landlord.[81] The same principle applies where money is paid by the tenant at the request of the landlord in respect of some obligation owed by the landlord in relation to the demised premises.[82] In order for the tenant to exercise a right of recoupment, the following conditions must be satisfied:

1   The money must actually have been paid by the tenant and the quantum of expenditure must have been either acknowledged by the landlord or otherwise be beyond dispute.[83]

2   In cases where the tenant carries out works to remedy the landlord's breach of repairing obligations, notice of the breach must first have been given to the landlord.[84]

40-47   Where available, a common law right of recoupment is unaffected by an assignment of the reversion. Accordingly, a tenant is entitled to set off expenditure incurred before an assignment of the reversion against rent which accrues due after the assignment[85] (this is to be contrasted with the position in relation to equitable set-off, see **40-50** below).

40-48   Where service charge is reserved as rent, it is considered that the common law right of recoupment is likewise available to the tenant. Whether the right extends to enable the tenant to recoup out of service charges which are not reserved as rent in the lease is, in the absence of authority on the point, rather less clear and in the absence of any direct authority on the point, it is considered that the right of recoupment would not apply, such right being limited to rent which issues out of the land itself and is an incident of the ownership of the reversion.[86]

Equitable set-off

40-49   Subject to the exceptions set out at **40-50** below, a tenant may exercise a right of set-off[87] against the landlord's claim for service charge (whether or not reserved as rent in the lease), provided that the cross claim arises under the lease itself, directly from the relationship of landlord and tenant or out of an agreement for lease.[88] The tenant may, therefore, set off a claim for damages for breach of

---

81 *Taylor v Beal* (1591) Cro Eliz 222. This entitlement provides a defence to the claim rather than operating as a cross-claim. The sums paid by the tenant are treated as the rent which would otherwise have been due.

82 *British Anzani (Felixstowe) Ltd v International Marine Management (UK) Ltd* [1980] QB 137 at p 147.

83 *British Anzani (Felixstowe) Ltd v International Marine Management (UK) Ltd* [1980] QB 137.

84 *Lee-Parker v Izzet* [1971] 1 WLR 1688.

85 *Taylor v Beale* (1591) Cro Eliz 222; *Lee Parker v Izzet* [1971] 1 WLR 1688.

86 See *Edlington Properties Ltd v J H Fenner & Co Ltd* [2006] 1 WLR 1583.

87 Which operates as a cross-claim and not as a defence to payment.

88 *British Anzani (Felixstowe) Ltd v International Marine Management (UK) Ltd* [1980] QB 137. See *Continental Property Ventures Inc v White* [2006] 1 EGL. 85, where the Lands Tribunal held that under the Landlord and Tenant Act 1985, s 27A, the LVT has to consider a tenant's set off argument in order to determine whether a service charge is payable under a lease of a dwelling.

the landlord's repairing obligations, breach of the covenant for quiet enjoyment or of any of the landlord's other obligations under the lease. The tenant's cross claim may be liquidated or unliquidated,[89] but the liability must be immediate rather than contingent.[90] The right of set-off is equitable in character and, accordingly, may be refused in circumstances where the tenant does not come to court with clean hands.[91]

40-50 A right of equitable set-off is not exercisable in the following circumstances:

1   Where the tenant's claim arose prior to an assignment of the reversion, it may not be set off against arrears of rent or service charge which accrued due after the assignment.[92]

2   A right of set-off may be excluded by the terms of the lease. However, clear words are needed to exclude the tenant's right of set-off, because of the presumption that neither party to the lease intends to abandon remedies which arise by operation of law.[93] Thus, a covenant to pay rent or service charge 'without any deduction' does not exclude the tenant's equitable right of set-off.[94] By contrast, a covenant to pay rent 'without any deduction or set off whatsoever' was held to exclude the tenant's right of equitable set-off.[95] Where the terms of the lease do exclude equitable set-off, the relevant term cannot be impeached under the Unfair Contract Terms Act 1977.[96]

3   A tenant's claim for damages against the landlord may not be set off against a claim brought by a manager appointed under the Landlord and Tenant Act 1987 to recover arrears of service charge.[97]

4   Once an RTM company has acquired the right to manage pursuant to the provisions of Part II, Chapter 1 of the Commonhold and Leasehold Reform Act 2002, service charges must be paid by the tenant to the RTM company and not the landlord.[98] If a tenant wrongly pays service charge to the landlord rather than the RTM company, the tenant will not be entitled to set off the payment made to the landlord against the RTM company's claim for arrears of service charge.[99]

---

89 This is in contrast to common law recoupment where only actual expenditure may be set-off – see **40-46** above.
90 *Sloan Stanley Estate Trustees v Barribal* [1994] 2 EGLR 8.
91 *Televantos v McCulloch* [1991] 1 EGLR 123.
92 *Edlington Properties Ltd v J H Fenner & Co Ltd* [2006] 1 WLR 1583.
93 *Connaught Restaurants Ltd v Indoor Leisure Ltd* [1994] 1 WLR 501, *per* Waite LJ at p 505.
94 *Connaught Restaurants Ltd v Indoor Leisure Ltd* [1994] 1 WLR 501.
95 *Electricity Supply Nominees Ltd v IAF Group Ltd* [1993] 2 EGLR 95. See also *Star Rider Ltd v Inntrepreneur Pub Co* [1998] 1 EGLR 53.
96 *Electricity Supply Nominees Ltd v IAF Group Ltd* [1993] 2 EGLR 95.
97 *Maunder Taylor v Blacquiere* [2003] 1 WLR 379.
98 Commonhold and Leasehold Reform Act 2002, s 96.
99 *Wilson v Lesley Place (Maidstone) RTM Co Ltd* [2010] UKUT 139.

LIMITATION

40-51   There are several potential limitation periods under the Limitation Act 1980 which may be applicable to a claim to recover arrears of service charge:

1   Where service charge is reserved as rent in the lease, proceedings for recovery of arrears must be issued within six years of the date on which the arrears fell due under the lease.[100]

2   Where a service charge is not reserved as rent in the lease and the lease is made by deed, proceedings to recover arrears of service charge will be an action on a specialty for the purposes of section 8 of the Limitation Act 1980 and, accordingly, the proceedings must be issued within 12 years of the date on which the arrears accrued due under the lease.

3   Where service charge is not reserved as rent in the lease and the lease is not made by deed,[101] the landlord's claim will be an action founded on a simple contract for the purposes of section 5 of the Limitation Act 1980 and, as such, must be brought within six years of the date on which the arrears fell due under the lease.

4   Where the landlord's cause of action arises under a licence to assign, as opposed to the lease, then, unless the licence to assign is itself made by deed, the landlord's claim will be an action on a simple contract for the purposes of section 6 of the Limitation Act 1980 and must, therefore, be brought within six years from the date on which the arrears fell due under the lease. If the licence to assign is by deed, the claim will be an action on a specialty and will, therefore, be subject to the 12-year limitation period in section 8 of the Limitation Act 1980.

40-52   In each of the above cases, the limitation period will run from the date on which the service charge fell due under the lease. It will, therefore, be important to establish exactly when, as a matter of construction of the relevant lease, the service charge becomes contractually due.

40-53   Although a landlord may be prevented from maintaining an action to recover arrears of service charge once the relevant limitation period has expired, that does not prevent the landlord from setting up those arrears as an equitable set-off against any claim that might be brought by the tenant against the landlord. Thus, in *Filross Securities Ltd v Midgeley*,[102] it was held that a landlord was entitled to set off arrears of rent against the tenant's claim for breach of the landlord's repairing obligations and covenant for quiet enjoyment, even though a claim for the rent would, by then, have been statute-barred.

---

100 Limitation Act 1980, s 19.
101 A lease need not be made by deed if it is a lease taking effect in possession for a term not exceeding three years (whether or not the tenant is given power to extend the term) at the best rent which can be reasonably obtained without taking a fine: Law of Property Act 1925, s 54(2).
102 [1998] 3 EGLR 43.

CHAPTER 41

Landlord's remedies: Debt claim against a guarantor or a party who has entered into an authorised guarantee agreement

41-01   Where there are doubts about the tenant's and, where applicable, any former tenant's[1] ability to satisfy a money judgment, a landlord may wish to bring a claim against a guarantor or a party who has entered into an authorised guarantee agreement. Where such a right exists, the landlord has a choice: he may sue the tenant, the guarantor or both. The guarantor cannot insist that the landlord exhaust his remedies against the tenant and any former tenant who remains liable before proceeding against the guarantor.[2]

41-02   There are two types of guarantee to which consideration is given in this section, namely:

(i)   An ordinary guarantee given by a third party usually, but not necessarily, within the lease itself.

(ii)   An authorised guarantee agreement for the purposes of section 16 of the Landlord and Tenant (Covenants) Act 1995.[3]

---

1   The liability of a former tenant is dealt with at **40-08** to **40-18** above.
2   *Norwich Union Life Insurance Society Ltd v Low Profile Fashions Ltd* (1992) 64 P&CR 187 at p 192.
3   By s 16(2), an agreement is an authorised guarantee agreement if: (a) under it, the tenant guarantees the performance of the relevant covenant to any extent by the assignee; (b) it is entered into in the circumstances set out in subsection (3); and (c) its provisions conform with subsections (4) and (5). The circumstances in subsection (3) to which subsection (2) refers are: (a) by virtue of a covenant against assignment (whether absolute or qualified) the assignment cannot be effected without the consent of the landlord under the tenancy or some other person; (b) any such consent is given subject to a condition (lawfully imposed) that the tenant is to enter into an agreement guaranteeing the performance of the covenant by the assignee; and (c) the agreement is entered into by the tenant in pursuance of that condition. Subsection (4) provides that an agreement is not an authorised guarantee agreement to the extent that it purports: (a) to impose on the tenant any requirement to guarantee in any way the performance of the relevant covenant by any person other than the assignee; or (b) to impose on the tenant any liability, restriction or other requirement (of whatever nature) in relation to any time after the assignee is released from that covenant by virtue of the Landlord and Tenant (Covenants) Act 1995.

367

SUMMARY OF THE REQUIREMENTS FOR BRINGING A DEBT CLAIM AGAINST A GUARANTOR

41-03   In order for the landlord to bring a successful claim in debt against a guarantor in respect of service charge arrears, the following conditions will need to be satisfied:

1   There must be arrears of service charge outstanding under the lease.

2   The landlord must be the person presently entitled to sue on the guarantee.

3   The guarantor must be liable under the guarantee to make the relevant payment.

4   Where the claim is brought against a guarantor of a former tenant, the notice requirements in section 17 of the Landlord and Tenant (Covenants) Act 1995 must first have been satisfied.

5   The guarantor must not be immune from legal process under one or other of the statutory insolvency regimes.

6   The guarantor must not have a right of set-off which is equal to, or exceeds, the landlord's claim.

7   The claim must have been brought before the expiry of the relevant limitation period.[4]

41-04   These requirements are considered below.

EXISTENCE OF THE ARREARS

41-05   There must be outstanding arrears of service charge (whether interim or final) and/or interest payable on those arrears outstanding before a landlord may maintain a claim against a guarantor. A guarantor may seek to advance one or more of the arguments summarised at **40-05** above in answer to the landlord's claim for arrears.[5]

PARTY WHO IS ENTITLED TO SUE ON THE GUARANTEE

41-06   A guarantee is enforceable as a matter of contract as between the original parties. The benefit of a guarantee runs with the reversion and it is, therefore, enforceable by an assignee of the reversion, even without an express assignment of the benefit of the guarantee.[6]

---

4   The expiry of the relevant limitation period does not operate to extinguish the landlord's contractual right to claim the relevant sum, but operates as a bar to the landlord's right to bring an action to recover the debt. It is accordingly a potential defence which is available to the tenant and, unless such a defence is taken, will not prevent the landlord from recovering the debt.

5   Which mirror those set out at **40-05** above for a claim against a tenant.

6   *P&A Swift Investments v Combined English Stores Group Plc* [1989] AC 632. In the case of leases granted after 1 January 1996, the Landlord and Tenant (Covenants) Act 1995, s 3 expressly provides that the benefit of a guarantee passes on an assignment of the reversion.

LIABILITY OF THE GUARANTOR

41-07   In order to ascertain whether the guarantor is liable to make payment of the arrears of service charge, it is necessary to consider the following issues:

1   Whether, as a matter of construction of the guarantee, non-payment of service charge by the tenant triggers a liability on the part of the guarantor to make an equivalent payment to the landlord.

2   If so, whether the arrears in question accrued due during a period for which the guarantor has agreed to be liable under the guarantee.

3   If so, whether any subsequent variation of the lease which has been guaranteed has resulted in the guarantor being released in whole or in part from his obligations under the guarantee.

Construction of the guarantee

41-08   A covenant of guarantee may consist of a covenant of guarantee (properly so-called), a covenant of indemnity or both, depending on its terms. Under a covenant of guarantee, the guarantor is obliged to see that the tenant performs his obligations under the lease. The liability of the guarantor is, therefore, a secondary one and the guarantor will only be liable if the tenant is himself liable.[7] Under a covenant of indemnity, the guarantor assumes primary liability to the landlord and his liability does not, therefore, depend on the tenant also being liable.[8]

41-09   Although covenants of guarantee fall to be strictly construed,[9] a well-drafted covenant of guarantee will ensure that non-payment of service charge by the existing tenant triggers an obligation, whether primary or secondary, on the part of the guarantor to make payment.

Duration of the guarantee

41-10   At common law, the duration of the guarantor's liability is simply a matter of construction of the relevant covenant of guarantee. In the absence of clear words, the guarantor's liability will be limited to the contractual term of the lease and will not extend so as to include any statutory continuation of the lease pursuant to Part II of the Landlord and Tenant Act 1954.[10] Similarly, absent clear words, the guarantor's obligations will be limited to those arising under the lease and will not include supplementary agreements (e.g. a rent deposit deed[11] or an

---

7   *Patterson v Guardians of The Belford Union* [1856] 1 HN 523. Thus, if the tenant is able to escape liability (e.g. on the grounds that the obligations in question are void or otherwise unenforceable), the guarantor will likewise escape liability. C.f. *Moschi v Lep Air Services* [1973] AC 331.

8   *Associated Dairies v Pearce* [1983] 1 EGLR 45.

9   *Ibid.*

10   *Junction Estates v Cope* (1974) 27 P&CR 482; *A Plesser & Co v Davis* (1983) 267 EG 1039.

11   *Jaskel v Sophie Nursery Products* [1993] EGCS 42.

agreement to surrender[12]). A covenant of guarantee may be expressed to relate to part only of the contractual term of the lease (e.g. for so long as the lease remains vested in a particular tenant[13]).

41-11   However, in cases of 'new' leases for the purposes of the Landlord and Tenant (Covenants) Act 1995,[14] the contractual provisions in the covenant of guarantee may be abrogated by the provisions of the Act. In such cases, the assignment of lease results in the release of the assigning tenant of his obligations under the lease[15] and, by section 24(2) of the Landlord and Tenant (Covenants) Act 1995, the guarantor of that tenant is likewise released from liability. The anti-avoidance provisions in section 25 of the Landlord and Tenant (Covenants) Act 1995 ensure that the provisions of section 24(2) prevail over any provision to the contrary in the covenant of guarantee itself.[16] However, although the guarantor will not be liable in respect of any breach of the tenant covenants which occurs after the assignment of the lease, he will not escape liability in respect of any breach which occurred before the assignment.[17]

41-12   Similarly, where the guarantee in question is an authorised guarantee agreement within the meaning of section 16 of the Landlord and Tenant (Covenants) Act 1995, the duration of the guarantor's liability is limited to the period in which the lease is vested in the immediate assignee[18] and, therefore, expires if there is a further assignment.

41-13   Irrespective of whether the provisions of the Landlord and Tenant (Covenants) Act 1995 apply to the lease, a guarantee will cease when the lease is determined by notice to quit[19] or by forfeiture[20] or surrender, albeit that liability for breaches which occurred prior to the determination of the lease will remain.[21]

41-14   Different principles apply where the lease has been disclaimed following insolvency of the tenant. The disclaimer of the lease brings to an end the obligations arising under the lease as regards the tenant, but does not automatically do so as regards any guarantor,[22] including a guarantor under an authorised guarantee agreement.[23] Accordingly, the liability of the guarantor will continue after the disclaimer of the lease, unless and until the landlord retakes possession of the premises.[24]

---

12 *BSE Trading Ltd v Hands* [1996] EGCS 99.
13 *Johnsey Estates v Webb* [1990] 1 EGLR 82.
14 See **40-09** above.
15 Section 5; see **40-15** above.
16 *K/S Victoria Street v House of Fraser (Stores Management) Ltd* [2011] 2 P&CR 15, approving *Good Harvest Partnership v Centaur Services* [2011] Ch 426.
17 Section 24(1).
18 Section 16(4).
19 *Tayleur v Wildin* (1867–68) LR 3 Ex 303.
20 *Apus Properties v Douglas Farrow & Co* [1989] 2 EGLR 265.
21 *Ibid.*
22 *Hindcastle Ltd v Barbara Attenborough Associates Ltd* [1996] 1 All ER 737.
23 *Doleman v Shaw* [2009] Bus LR 1175.
24 *Hindcastle Ltd v Barbara Attenborough Associates Ltd* [1996] 1 All ER 737.

Release by variation of the lease

41-15   The variation of a lease without the consent of a guarantor will, in appropriate cases, result in the guarantor being released from his obligations under the guarantee. In order to determine whether and to what extent a release has occurred, it is necessary to consider:

(i)   the common law rules;

(ii)   the terms of the lease and, in particular, any anti-release clause; and

(iii)   where applicable, the effect of the provisions of section 18 of the Landlord and Tenant (Covenants) Act 1995.

41-16   At common law, any variation of the terms of the lease, without the guarantor's consent, will result in the guarantor being released from liability, unless it is self-evident, without a factual enquiry, that the alteration is unsubstantial or one which cannot be prejudicial to the guarantor.[25] Thus, in *West Horndon Industrial Park Ltd v Phoenix Timber Group Plc*,[26] the imposition of additional burdens on the original tenant in respect of the rent payable on review, insurance liability and repairing obligations in a licence to assign was held to have released the guarantor. However, whether the principle that a variation of the terms of the lease discharges the guarantor applies where the covenant is or includes one of indemnity[27] is a matter which is unclear on the authorities.[28]

41-17   In light of the position at common law, it is common for leases to contain an express provision to the effect that variation, waiver or modification of any of the terms of the lease will not result in the release of the guarantor. In *Selous Street Properties v Oronel Fabrics*,[29] an anti-release clause of this kind was held to be effective to preserve the guarantor's liability in circumstances where a subsequent variation of the lease would otherwise have released him from liability. However, an apparent anti-release clause will not always have that effect. The following principles can be distilled from the decided cases:

---

25   *Holme v Brunskill* (1877) 3 QBD 495.

26   [1995] 20 EG 137; see also *Holme v Brunskill* (1877) 3 QBD 495; *Selous Street Properties v Oronel Fabrics* [1984] 1 EGLR 50; *Howard de Walden Estates v Pasta Place Ltd* [1995] 1 EGLR 79.

27   See **41-08** above.

28   In *Way v Hearn* (1862) 11 CB (NS) 774 and *Wilson v Zealandia Soap & Candle Trading Co Ltd* [1927] GIR 120, it was held that a contract of indemnity is not discharged by an agreement under which the principal is given additional time to satisfy the obligation indemnified. It has been suggested that, by parity of reasoning, other types of variation of the principal contract will not result in the indemnifier being discharged; see O'Donovan and Philips, *The Modern Contract of Guarantee*, (2nd edn, 2010) at para 7-70. However, support for the contrary view is to be found in the first instance decision of Cresswell J in *Marubeni Hong Kong and South China Ltd v The Government of Mongolia* [2004] EWHC 472 (Comm); see also *Credit Suisse v Allerdale BC* [1995] 1 Lloyd's Rep 315; *Coal Distributors Ltd v National Westminster Bank* (unreported, 4 February 1981). Pending an authoritative decision on the point, the matter remains open to argument.

29   [1984] 1 EGLR 50.

(i)   The wording of the anti-release clause must be sufficiently clear to prevent a release at common law.[30] More recently, in *Triodos Bank NV v Dobbs*,[31] the Court of Appeal held that an anti-release clause will only be effective if, as a matter of construction, the variations or modifications are within 'the general purview' of the original guarantee.

(ii) Moreover, the power to pre-authorise variations to the lease is subject to one important limitation. The court limits the power to vary so as 'to distinguish between the true variation of an existing obligation and the entering of what is in fact a different obligation, even though it might purport to be no more than a variation'.[32] The former is permissible, the latter is not.

41-18   Section 18 of the Landlord and Tenant (Covenants) Act 1995, which applies to both 'old' and 'new' tenancies for the purposes of the Act, provides additional protection to two classes of guarantor, namely:

(i)   a former tenant who has entered into an authorised guarantee agreement on assignment of the lease;[33] and

(ii) a guarantor of the former tenant whose liability has, for any reason, not been discharged by any relevant variation of the tenant covenants effected after the assignment of the lease.[34]

41-19   In either case, the guarantor is expressly relieved from liability to pay any amount under the guarantee 'to the extent that the amount is referable to any relevant variation of the tenant covenants of the tenancy effected after the assignment'.[35] Section 18(4) of the Landlord and Tenant (Covenants) Act 1995 defines 'relevant variations' as variations which a landlord had, at the time of the variation, an absolute right to refuse or which he would have had an absolute right to refuse but for a variation which has taken place since the former tenant assigned the lease. However, the provisions of section 18 of the Landlord and Tenant (Covenants) Act 1995 do not apply where the variation of the tenant covenants was effected before the Act came into force on 1 January 1996.[36]

41-20   The statutory limitation imposed by section 18 of the Landlord and Tenant (Covenants) Act 1995 supplements (rather than replaces) the protection

---

30 In *West Horndon Industrial Park Ltd v Phoenix Timber Group Plc* [1995] 1 EGLR 77, the guarantor covenanted to perform the tenant's obligations 'notwithstanding any other act or thing whereby but for this provision the guarantor would have been released', but these words were held to be insufficiently clear to prevent a release. See also *Howard de Walden Estates v Pasta Place Ltd* [1995] 1 EGLR 79 where the intended anti-release clause was held to be insufficiently clear.
31 [2005] 2 CLC 95.
32 *Triodos Bank NV v Dobbs* [2005] 2 CLC 95, *per* Longmore LJ at p 105C.
33 Section 18(1).
34 Section 18(3).
35 Section 18(2) and (3).
36 Section 18(5).

afforded by the common law.[37] Accordingly, it is only if the guarantor has not been released altogether at common law that it is necessary to consider whether his liability has been capped by section 18 of the Landlord and Tenant (Covenants) Act 1995.

41-21   The terms of section 18 of the Landlord and Tenant (Covenants) Act 1995 are not limited to cases in which the variation was made without the guarantor's consent. Accordingly, it would seem that the statutory limitation is applicable even where the guarantor has expressly consented to it.[38]

SECTION 17 OF THE LANDLORD AND TENANT (COVENANTS) ACT 1995

41-22   The provisions of section 17 of the Landlord and Tenant (Covenants) Act 1995 apply to guarantors in two situations:

(i)   where the guarantor is a former tenant who has given an authorised guarantee agreement;[39] or

(ii)   where a party has agreed to guarantee the performance by a former tenant of the tenant's covenants in the lease.[40]

41-23   In either case, the landlord will need to have served notice under section 17 of the Landlord and Tenant (Covenants) Act 1995 before issuing proceedings to recover the relevant arrears. The requirements for notices given under section 17 of the Landlord and Tenant (Covenants) Act 1995 are discussed at **40-27** above.

41-24   However, the provisions of section 17 of the Landlord and Tenant (Covenants) Act 1995 are of no application to a guarantee, which is not an authorised guarantee agreement, of the current (as opposed to former) tenant's performance of the obligations arising under the lease.

---

37 This is made explicit by the words in parenthesis in s 18(3). Although there are no equivalent words in either s 18(1) or (2), it is considered that the common law rules also apply to authorised guarantee agreements because s 16(8) expressly provides that 'the rules of law relating to guarantees (and in particular those relating to the release of sureties) are, subject to its terms, applicable in relation to any authorised guarantee agreement as in relation to any other guarantee agreement.'

38 The express consent might take the form of an effective anti-release clause in the guarantee or a specific consent following a request by the landlord and the tenant prior to entering into the variation. There are far reaching anti-avoidance provisions in the Landlord and Tenant (Covenants) Act 1995, s 25 which would appear to make it impossible to avoid this result. C.f. *Avonridge Property Co Ltd v Mashru* [2005] UKHL 70.

39 Section 17(1)(a).

40 Section 17(3).

INSOLVENCY OF THE GUARANTOR

41-25   The restrictions on the landlord's right to bring and pursue an action in debt against a party who is insolvent are discussed at **40-32** to **40-44** above.

SET-OFF

41-26   A guarantor is entitled to rely on any cross claim or defence which is available to the tenant.[41] Accordingly, providing the terms of the guarantee do not contain an express exclusion of the right,[42] a guarantor will be entitled to rely on a defence of set-off which the tenant would be entitled to raise against the landlord's claim for service charge. The tenant's defence of set-off is discussed at **40-45** to **40-50** above.

LIMITATION

41-27   Where the guarantee is contained in a deed, whether within the lease itself or in a separate instrument, a claim for moneys due under the guarantee will be an action on a specialty and, therefore, subject to the 12-year limitation period in section 8 of the Limitation Act 1980. If the guarantee is not contained in a deed, the limitation period will be the six-year period for actions on a simple contract imposed by section 5 of the Limitation Act 1980.

41-28   The question of when a cause of action accrues against a guarantor is a matter of construction of the guarantee. The terms of the guarantee may make the guarantor liable as soon as the tenant defaults, but it is possible for the guarantor's liability to arise later (e.g. following service of a written demand).

---

41 *Hyundai Shipbuilding and Heavy Industries Co Ltd v Pournaras* [1978] 2 Lloyds Rep 502.
42 Clear and unequivocal words are required to achieve this effect: *Port of Tilbury (London) Ltd v Stora Enso Transport and Distribution Ltd* [2009] EWCA Civ 16. Substantially, the same principles apply in relation to exclusion of the tenant's right of set-off: see **40-50** above.

CHAPTER 42

Applications to the LVT: Section 27A of the Landlord and Tenant Act 1985 (residential leases only)

42-01   Section 27A of the Landlord and Tenant Act 1985 confers jurisdiction on the LVT to determine the extent to which service charges are, or would be payable, under a lease of a dwelling.[1] The jurisdiction is available to both landlord and tenant (whether intermediate or occupational[2]). A determination under section 27A may be sought merely for the purposes of resolving a dispute as to liability or as a precursor to the exercise of one of the substantive remedies discussed elsewhere in this chapter.[3]

JURISDICTION OF THE LVT

42-02   The LVT's primary jurisdiction in respect of residential service charge disputes is now contained in section 27A of the 1985 Act, which came into force from 30 September 2003 (in England) and 31 March 2004 (in Wales). The new section 27A replaced the repealed sections 19(2A) to (3) and 31A to 31C of the 1985 Act.[4] The old sections have no continuing relevance, save that they continue to apply in relation to any application made to the LVT under section 19(2A) or (2B) of the 1985 Act, or any proceedings relating to a service charge transferred to the LVT by a County Court, before the coming into force of the new section 27A.

42-03   Section 27A provides:

---

1   A 'dwelling' is defined in the Landlord and Tenant Act 1985, s 38 as 'a building or part of a building occupied or intended to be occupied as a separate dwelling together with any yard, garden, outhouses and appurtenances belonging to it or usually enjoyed with it.' See **28-03** to **28-10** above.

2   *Ruddy v Oakfern Properties Ltd* [2007] Ch 335.

3   A determination under the Landlord and Tenant Act 1985, s 27A would satisfy the requirements of the Housing Act 1996, s 81 for the purposes of forfeiture. See **45-51** to **45-63** below.

4   Commonhold and Leasehold Reform Act 2002, ss 155 and 180; Commonhold and Leasehold Reform Act 2002 (Commencement No 2 and Savings) (England) Order 2003 (SI 2003/1986), art 2(c) and Sch 2, para 6; Commonhold and Leasehold Reform Act 2002 (Commencement No 2 and Savings) (Wales) Order 2004 (SI 2004/669), art 2(c) and Sch 2, para 6.

'(1) An application may be made to a leasehold valuation tribunal for a determination whether a service charge is payable and, if it is, as to –

    (a)   the person by whom it is payable,

    (b)   the person to whom it is payable,

    (c)   the amount which is payable,

    (d)   the date at or by which it is payable, and

    (e)   the manner in which it is payable.

(2)   Subsection (1) applies whether or not any payment has been made.'

42-04   The LVT's jurisdiction under section 27A is far broader than under the old provisions of section 19(2A) to (3). Consequently, many of the difficult jurisdictional issues which previously arose are no longer of concern and authorities relating to limits on the LVT's jurisdiction under the old provisions are of no continuing relevance, save for any applications issued prior to 30 September 2003 (if indeed any such applications remain unresolved). Accordingly, this chapter does not consider the jurisdiction under the previous law.

42-05   It is now clear that the LVT may consider an application as to whether a service charge is payable regardless of whether or not any payment has been made.[5] The LVT does not, however, have jurisdiction to make an order requiring a landlord to make a repayment to a tenant when it finds there has been an overpayment, even where the lease makes express provision for repayment.[6] It follows that a tenant who succeeds in establishing on an application under section 27A that he has made overpayments to his landlord would, assuming the landlord does not voluntarily repay the sums or credit the tenant's account, be obliged to issue court proceedings to secure repayment.[7]

42-06   The LVT does not have any jurisdiction under section 27A as regards sums due under the lease which do not fall within the definition of a service charge. Accordingly, it would not be entitled to consider a claim for damages by a landlord or claims relating to ground rent. Furthermore, the LVT does not have jurisdiction to give a tenant time to pay the service charges which it determines are payable and such charges remain payable on the dates and in the manner provided for in the lease.[8]

42-07   The question for the LVT in an application under section 27A is whether service charges are payable by the tenant. Accordingly, the LVT plainly has jurisdiction to interpret the terms of the lease to assess whether the landlord is entitled

---

5   Section 27A(2), reversing the effect of the decision of the Court of Appeal in *Daejan Properties Ltd v London Leasehold Valuation Tribunal* [2001] 3 EGLR 28, under s 19(2A).

6   *Warrior Quay Management Co Ltd v Joachim* [2006] EWLands LRX_42_2006.

7   See **47-12** to **47-37** below.

8   *Southend-on-Sea Borough Council v Skiggs* [2006] 2 EGLR 87, but contrast the approach of the Upper Tribunal to the timing of payments in considering the question of reasonableness under s 19(1) in *Garside v RYFC Ltd* [2011] UKUT considered in further detail at **29-12** above.

to claim the sums said to be payable by the tenant. In *Ruddy v Oakfern Properties Ltd,*[9] Jonathan Parker LJ said:

> 'In my judgment there is no justification for implying any restriction in the entirely general words of section 27A of the 1985 Act.'

42-08   Furthermore, the LVT has jurisdiction to determine a claim by a tenant for damages for breach of covenant on the part of the landlord, but only to the extent that the claim constitutes a defence by way of set-off to a service charge in respect of which the LVT's jurisdiction under section 27A has been invoked.[10] There is no reason in principle why the jurisdiction to consider a claim for damages should not extend to determining a claim for loss of amenity or loss of health arising from breach of a repairing covenant on the part of the landlord.[11]

42-09   The Upper Tribunal has, however, urged the LVT to exercise restraint in the exercise of the extended jurisdiction under section 27A. In *Canary Riverside PTE Ltd v Schilling,*[12] it was said, in connection with the jurisdiction of the LVT to consider the application of the Unfair Terms in Consumer Contracts Regulations 1999:[13]

> '42. ... s. 27A of the Act of 1985, inserted by s.155 of the Act of 2002 provides, without limitation that "an application may be made to the leasehold valuation tribunal for a determination whether a service charge is payable". [Counsel for the landlord] raised both before the LVT and before this Tribunal a number of examples of issues which it would hardly be appropriate for the LVT to undertake to determine, at least if another more appropriate tribunal was seized of the matter. This, however does not mean that Parliament has not also given the LVT jurisdiction to determine such issues.

> 43. No doubt, if a party to proceedings before a LVT takes proceedings for the determination of such an issue before what the LVT accepts is a more appropriate court, the LVT will, as it did in the course of the Service Charges application adjourn its proceedings pending such determination. It has power so to do under its inherent jurisdiction to regulate its own procedure. That this would be a reasonable and proper course if an issue were raised, to take [counsel for the landlord]'s examples, as to voidability for mistake, forgery or misrepresentation, I do not doubt. Such matters are better determined under Court procedures and by judges, rather than by specialist tribunals, encouraged to adopt comparatively informal procedures.

> 44. I should take the same view where the LVT has jurisdiction to determine only one aspect of a matter better determined as a whole. The LVT, although, as I think,

9   [2007] Ch 335 at p 352.
10 Where the cross-claim exceeds the service charges claimed by the landlord, the LVT's jurisdiction extends only to determining whether the cross-claim extinguishes the service charges which would otherwise be due.
11 *Continental Property Ventures Inc v White* [2006] 1 EGLR 85, *per* HHJ Michael Rich QC at p 87K–M.
12 [2005] EWLands LRX_65_2005.
13 Considered in detail in Chapter 37 above.

entitled to decide whether a term is not binding because unfair, has no jurisdiction thereupon to make a determination whether the lease shall continue in existence without the alleged unfair term. It may well therefore regard it as convenient, if other proceedings are brought to determine whether service charge is payable under a term said not to be binding because unfair, to adjourn an application within its jurisdiction, pending such determination.

45. I can see no basis, however, for saying that the LVT lacks jurisdiction to determine any issue not expressly the subject of some other tribunal's exclusive jurisdiction, if determination of that issue is essential, to determining whether "a service charge is payable." That is the issue which s. 27A gives the LVT jurisdiction to determine. That must include any issue necessary for or incidental to such determination. I therefore agree with the LVT that they did have jurisdiction to determine the issue of the effect of the 1999 Regulations, although I think they might have been wiser to encourage the Landlords to follow the course which they had adopted in regard to the Service Charges application, and to seek a declaration from the Court.'

42-10   This urge for restraint was repeated by the same judge in *Continental Property Ventures Inc v White*,[14] in connection with the LVT's jurisdiction to consider damages claims made by tenants by way of set-off.[15]

42-11   The expanded jurisdiction under section 27A includes jurisdiction to consider claims that a landlord has waived the right to enforce covenants in a lease or is estopped from doing so. It seems that the LVT would not, however, be entitled to determine the question of whether or not a landlord has waived the right to forfeit the lease, since that has no bearing on the question of whether a service charge is payable, only on the remedies available to the landlord in respect of non-payment by the tenant.[16]

42-12   Under section 27A(7), the jurisdiction of the LVT in respect of any matter by virtue of section 27A is in addition to any jurisdiction of a court in respect of the matter.

---

14 [2006] 1 EGLR 85.
15 In addition, the Upper Tribunal has allowed a number of appeals from decisions of the LVT on the ground that the LVT has taken points of its own volition without allowing the parties the opportunity to make submissions on the points or to adduce evidence in relation to them: see, for example, *Wales & West Housing Association Ltd v Paine* [2012] UKUT 372 (LC), *Beitov Properties Ltd v Martin* [2012] UKUT 133 (LC), *Fairhold Mercury Ltd v Merryfield RTM Co Ltd* [2012] UKUT 311 (UC) and *Birmingham City Council v Keddie* [2012] UKUT 323 (LC). In the last of these cases, the Member of the Upper Tribunal said that where the parties have not asked the LVT to rule on a particular matter, it lacked jurisdiction to consider it. The applicant sought to challenge the cost of the replacement of certain windows. However, the LVT went on to decide that the landlord should not have replaced the windows at all. This was not a question which either party wanted the tribunal to consider.
16 See *Swanston Grange (Luton) Management Ltd v Langley-Essen* [2008] L&TR 20 in the context of claims for a determination under the Commonhold and Leasehold Reform Act 2002, s 168 that the tenant is in breach of covenant, before serving a s 146 notice.

PROHIBITION ON CONTRACTING OUT

42-13   Section 27A(4) provides that:

'No application under subsection (1) or (3) may be made in respect of a matter which –

(a)   has been agreed or admitted by the tenant,

(b)   has been, or is to be, referred to arbitration pursuant to a post-dispute arbitration agreement to which the tenant is a party,

(c)   has been the subject of determination by a court, or

(d)   has been the subject of determination by an arbitral tribunal pursuant to a post-dispute arbitration agreement.'

42-14   However, it is expressly provided that the tenant is not to be taken to have agreed or admitted any matter by reason only of having made any payment.[17] Section 27A(4) must, however, be considered alongside section 27A(6), which states that:

'(6) An agreement by the tenant of a dwelling (other than a post-dispute arbitration agreement) is void in so far as it purports to provide for a determination –

(a)   in a particular manner, or

(b)   on particular evidence,

of any question which may be the subject of an application under subsection (1) or (3).'

42-15   Section 38 of the 1985 Act provides that 'arbitration agreement', 'arbitration proceedings' and 'arbitral tribunal' have the same meaning as in Part I of the Arbitration Act 1996; and 'post-dispute arbitration agreement', in relation to any matter, means an arbitration agreement made after a dispute about the matter has arisen.

42-16   The net effect of these provisions is that the jurisdiction of the LVT cannot be ousted by a provision in a lease to the effect that disputes are to be resolved by expert determination, most commonly in practice by the landlord's surveyor.[18] However, the jurisdiction under section 27A can be excluded where the parties agree to refer a particular dispute to arbitration or a matter has been agreed or admitted by the tenant. The critical distinction is therefore between a mechanism contained in the lease which provides for a determination of the service charge liability and an agreement made at some later date after a dispute has arisen.

42-17   The 1985 Act does not provide any limitation as to the form of an agreement or admission which will exclude the LVT's jurisdiction under section

---

17   Section 27A(5).
18   See Chapter 17 above.

27A(4). Accordingly, it would appear that an oral agreement would suffice, though there are obvious evidential difficulties in proving an oral acceptance of a particular matter by the tenant.

42-18   The intention underlying section 27A(6) is plainly to avoid excluding the jurisdiction of the LVT. However, in practice the application of this subsection to provisions in leases requiring the certification of service charges is far from straightforward. As discussed above,[19] many leases contain provisions requiring service charge accounts to be certified, often as a pre-condition to liability on the part of the tenant. There may be a difficult question as to whether such provisions provide for a determination of a particular matter in a way which falls foul of section 27A(6).

42-19   To the extent that a lease purports to make a determination of, for example, the landlord's surveyor, conclusive as to the tenant's liability for service charges, the LVT, by virtue of section 27A(6), retains jurisdiction to review that determination. In *London Borough of Brent v Shulem B Association Limited*,[20] Morgan J considered a clause which obliged a tenant to contribute a 'due proportion' of the cost of providing various services 'such proportion in case of difference to be settled by the surveyor for the time being of the lessor whose decision shall be final'. He said:

> 'It may be that this reference to the finality of the surveyor's decision is no longer contractually effective in view of section 27A(6). I did not hear specific argument on that point.'

42-20   It is suggested that Morgan J's approach is the correct approach to the application of section 27A(6). If it were otherwise, a provision of this nature would effectively exclude the LVT's jurisdiction to determine the amount of service charge payable by the tenant under section 27A(1). This conclusion potentially creates difficulties where the lease makes the certification of the sum due from the tenant a precondition to liability,[21] but it is suggested that section 27A(6) does not render altogether void the requirement of a certification or determination by a surveyor as a pre-condition to liability on the part of the tenant. In such circumstances, the determination made by the surveyor remains liable to a challenge by the tenant via an application to the LVT under section 27A(1).

LIMITATION PERIODS FOR SECTION 27A APPLICATIONS

42-21   There is considerable uncertainty as to whether any limitation period applies to an application brought by either a landlord or a tenant for a determination under section 27A and, if so, what the relevant period is. The Limitation Act 1980 sets out a number of potentially applicable time limits, which are framed

---

19   See Chapter 17 above.
20   [2011] 1 WLR 3014.
21   As to which, see Chapter 17 above.

by reference to the cause of action relied upon. The LVT and Upper Tribunal have considered the potential application of several of these provisions, but none of these sections contains language which is readily applicable to a section 27A determination.

42-22   As discussed below, it would appear that the applicable limitation period, if any, varies depending on whether or not it is the tenant or the landlord who makes the application for a determination under section 27A.[22] Although there is a distinct lack of higher authority, the current position appears to be, in summary, that there is no limitation period where the tenant makes the application, but, where a landlord makes an application, the limitation period is either six years or 12 years, depending on whether or not the lease in question is made by deed and whether or not the service charges are reserved as rent. Where the lease is made by deed and the service charge is not reserved as rent, the limitation period is 12 years, otherwise the limitation period for an application by the landlord is six years.

Potential for the Limitation Act 1980 to apply

42-23   All of the sections of the 1980 Act discussed here limit the period during which 'an action' of the specified type can be commenced. By section 38, this phrase is defined as including 'any proceeding in a court of law'. In *Hillingdon LBC v ARC Ltd*,[23] the Court of Appeal held that the Lands Tribunal constituted a court of law for the purposes of section 9 of the 1980 Act. The decision was made in the context of an application for the assessment of compensation due to a party under compulsory purchase legislation and is not, therefore, authority for the proposition that section 9 applies to an application under section 27A. However, the case does establish that the Lands Tribunal (now the Upper Tribunal) is a court of law for the purposes of the 1980 Act. Potter LJ reasoned:

> 'the Lands Tribunal has judicial rather than essentially administrative characteristics. As the judge observed, it has judicial powers and functions within a specialised and defined jurisdiction for the purpose of resolving disputes involving the valuation of interests in land. It also has procedural rules appropriate to a court of law. Further, in this context, it determines the amount of the liability of an acquiring authority.'

42-24   This reasoning is equally applicable to the LVT when exercising its jurisdiction under section 27A of the 1985 Act. Accordingly, the provisions of

22 It should be remembered that applications regularly come before the LVT after a transfer from the County Court when, usually, the landlord has issued a claim for forfeiture or a money judgment and the claim is defended by the tenant on the ground that the service charge forming the basis of the landlord's claim is disputed. In those cases, it might be said that there is no 'application' made under s 27A, but in this section this situation is considered to be, in effect, an application by a landlord since the landlord instigated the initial court proceedings which have caused the question of whether service charges are payable to be referred to the LVT. The usual practice is for the LVT to designate the landlord as the applicant in these circumstances.

23 [1998] 3 WLR 754.

the 1980 Act are, in principle, capable of applying to an application made under that section.[24]

Application made by landlord

42-25 There are four potentially applicable limitation periods under the 1980 Act where a landlord makes an application for a determination under section 27A:

1   Section 9 – sum payable under an enactment

This section provides that an action to recover any sum recoverable by virtue of any enactment shall not be brought after the expiration of six years from the date on which the cause of action accrued. By analogy with other legislation where an application is required to quantify a sum due to the applicant and section 9 has been held to apply, it has been argued that this period should apply to an application made by a landlord under section 27A,[25] the reasoning being that the application under section 27A is a necessary precondition to a claim to recover service charges by a landlord and, accordingly, the sums determined to be payable on such an application are payable under an enactment. The LVT has, however, rejected this argument. It is considered that this is correct as the LVT merely quantifies a sum which is due under contractual provisions in a lease, so that any sum found to be payable is not recoverable 'by virtue of any enactment'.[26]

2   Section 5 – action founded on simple contract

Section 5 states that an action founded on simple contract shall not be brought after the expiration of six years from the date on which the cause of action accrued. It appears that this limitation period will apply where a landlord makes an application for a determination in respect of service charges payable under a lease which is not made by deed.[27] The majority of service charge disputes concern long leases which are invariably, and by necessity, made by deed, thus, this limitation period is only likely to apply to a minority of cases.

3   Section 8 – action on a specialty

Section 8 provides that an action upon a specialty shall not be brought after the expiration of 12 years from the date on which the cause of action accrued. A specialty, for these purposes, includes documents under seal or

---

24 See *Warwickshire Hamlets Ltd v Gedden* [2010] UKUT 75 (LC); *Al Gailani v St George's Wharf* (LON/00AY/LSC/2010/02) at para 9.

25 *Hillingdon LBC v ARC* [1998] 3 WLR 754 (compulsory purchase); *Re Farmizer (Products) Ltd* [1997] 1 BCLC 589 (proceedings under the Insolvency Act 1986, s 124).

26 See *Al Gailani v St George's Wharf* (LON/00AY/LSC/2010/02); *Re 3, 12, 23 and 29 St Andrew's Square* (LON/00AW/LSL/2003/0027).

27 See *Re 3, 12, 23 and 29 St Andrew's Square* (LON/00AW/LSL/2003/0027).

deeds.[28] An application by a landlord for determination of service charges payable under a lease made by deed would be an action on a specialty and accordingly the limitation period is 12 years.[29] This is because the application for a determination is generally the first step in the process of enforcing the covenants in the lease. It is considered, however, that the purpose for which the landlord seeks the determination is irrelevant in determining the applicable limitation period. As we have seen, an application to the LVT is 'an action' within the meaning of section 8. The only basis on which the LVT can determine that service charges are payable on such an application is pursuant to the covenants in the lease. Accordingly, it is suggested that, whatever the reason for seeking the determination, the application, when made by a landlord, is an action upon a specialty.

4   Section 19 – action to recover rent

Section 19 of the 1980 Act states that no action shall be brought in respect of arrears of rent, after the expiration of six years from the date on which the arrears became due. In many leases, sums due by the tenant in respect of service charges are reserved as rent.[30] Where this is so, an application by a landlord under section 27A would appear to be caught by this shorter limitation period of six years, rather than the 12-year period under section 8, even where the lease is made by deed since section 8(2) provides that the 12-year period for an action on a specialty does not affect any shorter period of limitation prescribed by any other provision of the 1980 Act. It might be objected that, as we have seen, the LVT has no jurisdiction to order the tenant to make a payment of service charges and this applies even where the sum is reserved as rent. However, by analogy with the position under section 8, which was adopted in the *St Andrew's Square* case,[31] it would appear that section 19 does apply where service charges are reserved as rent, as the application for a determination is a necessary step in the process of recovering the arrears.

Application by tenant

42-26   None of the provisions discussed above apply to an application under section 27A made by a tenant. This is because a tenant making an application for a determination is not, in any sense, seeking to enforce his own covenant to pay service charges. The application cannot, therefore, realistically be considered to be an action on the lease, regardless of whether the lease is a specialty or the service charges are reserved as rent.[32]

---

28 See McGee, *Limitation Periods* (6th edn, 2010) para 4.013; *Aiken v Stewart Wrightson Members' Agency Ltd* [1995] 3 All ER 449 at p 459.
29 See *Re 3, 12, 23 and 29 St Andrew's Square* (LON/00AW/LSL/2003/0027) at para 26.
30 See **45-37** to **45-41** below.
31 LON/00AW/LSL/2003/0027, see above at fn 25.
32 See *Re 3, 12, 23 and 29 St Andrew's Square* (LON/00AW/LSL/2003/0027) at para 26; *Al Gailani v St George's Wharf* (LON/00AY/LSC/2010/02).

42-27 It has been suggested that a limitation period of six years should be applied to an application by a tenant under section 5, on the basis that the tenant's application is restitutionary. It is well-established that the six-year limitation period for an action on a simple contract applies to a claim for restitution of over-payments.[33] As we have seen,[34] if a tenant succeeds in obtaining a determination that he has overpaid service charges, he would be obliged to issue proceedings in the County Court to recover the overpayments. The basis of any such claim is discussed in further detail below, but, in essence, it would be a claim for restitution based on a mistake of law (i.e. that the payments were lawfully due to the landlord) when the LVT has subsequently determined they are not. The LVT has, on at least one occasion,[35] held that, as a result, the limitation period applicable to an application by a tenant is six years under section 5, since the application is a precursor to a claim in restitution. However, in *St George Wharf v Al-Gailani*,[36] a differently constituted LVT rejected this approach on the basis that an application under section 27A might be made for other reasons than as a precursor to a restitutionary claim (for example, to pave the way for an application for the appointment of a new manager or to base an equitable right of set-off against future actions by a landlord). Accordingly, the LVT considered that it was not appropriate to base the determination of the applicable limitation period on a prediction as to the future actions of the tenant following any determination. The point does not appear to have been considered in detail above the level of the LVT, however, and therefore remains open as a matter of authority.

42-28 If it is appropriate to apply a six-year limitation period in anticipation of a restitutionary claim by a landlord, it is then necessary to consider when time might start to run. This issue is considered in detail at **47-34** to **47-36** below. In brief, however, it would appear that time would not, in any case, start to run for the purposes of a restitutionary claim until the LVT has made a determination that there have been overpayments, so that the tenant has 'discovered' his mistake in making the payments for the purposes of section 32 of the 1980 Act.

42-29 An alternative approach was adopted by the Upper Tribunal in *Warwickshire Hamlets Ltd v Gedden*.[37] In that case, HHJ Huskinson (having noted that 'there is no specific provision in the Limitation Act which appears directly applicable to an application under section 27A') went on to hold that section 21(1) of the 1980 Act applied. This section provides:

> 'No period of limitation prescribed by this Act shall apply to an action by a beneficiary under a trust, being an action –
>
> (a)   in respect of any fraud or fraudulent breach of trust to which the trustee was a party or privy; or

---

33 *Deutsche Morgan Grenfell Group Plc v IRC* [2005] EWCA Civ 78 and see **47-12** to **47-37** below.
34 See **42-05** above.
35 *Royal Borough of Kensington & Chelsea v Mezziani* (LON/00AW/LSC/2009/0246).
36 *Al Gailani v St George's Wharf* (LON/00AY/LSC/2010/02).
37 [2010] UKUT 75 (LC).

(b)   to recover from the trustee trust property or the proceeds of trust property in the possession of the trustee, or previously received by the trustee and converted to his use.'

42-30   As discussed above,[38] service charges are held on trust for the tenants pursuant to section 42 of the 1987 Act. Accordingly, where a landlord has misappropriated service charge funds for its own use, this section would apply so that there is no limitation period. Therefore, where, as in *Warwickshire v Gedden*,[39] a landlord uses service charge funds not to provide services to the tenants but to settle debts it owed to a third party, the trust money had been appropriated to the landlord's use and accordingly, section 21(1) applied so that there was no limitation period.

42-31   The facts in *Gedden* were, however, somewhat unusual and it seems unlikely that, where the relevant costs are simply determined to be unreasonable under section 19 or irrecoverable for some other reason (for example, due to a failure to follow consultation requirements), this could lead to the conclusion that the funds had been converted to the use of the landlord. It might be argued that, whenever the landlord settles a debt to a third party using service charge funds which are subsequently determined not to be payable, he has converted the funds to his own use since, otherwise, the debt would fall to be settled from the landlord's own pocket. That would appear to be an unwarranted extension of section 21(1), however, since, at the point of payment, the landlord would have no way of knowing that the service charges would subsequently be determined not to be payable on the basis of unreasonableness or otherwise. It is submitted that the application of section 21(1) in service charge cases should be limited to (thankfully rare) cases of fraud or otherwise deliberate misapplication of trust funds on the part of the landlord.

Regulation of stale applications under LVT's procedural rules[40]

42-32   The apparent absence of any limitation period applicable in the case of an application made by a tenant is unsatisfactory, since there are obvious policy reasons in favour of preventing tenants from seeking to challenge service charges paid many years earlier.[41] Nevertheless, it is difficult to see how any of the provisions of the 1980 Act can apply to an application by a tenant under section 27A.

---

38   See Chapter 36.
39   [2010] UKUT 75 (LC).
40   At the time of writing, the Ministry of Justice has completed a consultation on the new procedural rules for the First Tier Tribunal (Property Chambers) into which the LVT is to be subsumed in July 2013. However, the rules have not yet been published.
41   See the concerns expressed by the Court of Appeal in this regard in the context of the old jurisdiction under s 19(3A) in *R v London Leasehold Valuation Tribunal ex parte Daejan Properties Ltd* [2002] HLR 25 at paras 18–19.

The LVT may, however, be in a position to regulate applications relating to historic service charges pursuant to regulation 11 of its procedural rules.[42]

42-33   Regulation 11 states:

> 'Subject to paragraph (2), where –
>
> (a)   it appears to a tribunal that an application is frivolous or vexatious or otherwise an abuse of process of the tribunal; or
>
> (b)   the respondent to an application makes a request to the tribunal to dismiss an application as frivolous or vexatious or otherwise an abuse of the process of the tribunal,
>
> the tribunal may dismiss the application, in whole or in part.'

42-34   The regulation goes on to provide a structure which must be followed before an application is dismissed on this basis. It seems possible that, if a tenant seeks to challenge service charges which have been paid many years previously, the application might be liable to be struck out as vexatious.[43] This might be the case where, for example, the tenant has never previously sought to challenge the sums now disputed and/or a determination would serve no useful purpose. Any such application of regulation 11 would, however, be highly fact sensitive and it is suggested that the LVT should be slow to accede to applications made by landlords on this basis for reasons of convenience, rather than on the basis that the application is genuinely vexatious.

---

42 Leasehold Valuations Tribunals (Procedure) (England) Regulations 2003 (SI 2003/2099); Leasehold Valuations Tribunals (Procedure) (Wakes) Regulations 2004 (SI 2004/681). See *Re 3, 12, 23 and 29 St Andrew's Square* (LON/00AW/LSL/2003/0027) at para 26.
43 This approach was suggested by the LVT in See *Re 3, 12, 23 and 29 St Andrew's Square* (LON/00AW/LSL/2003/0027) at para 26. Contrast, however, the comments of the Court of Appeal in *R v London Leasehold Valuation Tribunal ex parte Daejan Properties Ltd* [2002] HLR 25, discouraging extensive use of procedural regulations in this manner.

CHAPTER 43

Landlord's remedies: Distress

43-01   The law of distress enables a landlord, without prior sanction from the court, to seize or impound chattels located on the demised premises and, eventually, to sell them to satisfy outstanding arrears of rent (which includes service charge reserved as such).

43-02   The law of distress is archaic and arcane and provision has been made in the Tribunals, Courts and Enforcement Act 2007 for its abolition and, in the case of commercial leases, replacement by a new scheme known as 'Commercial Rent Arrears and Recovery'. However, more than five years on from its enactment, the relevant provisions of the Tribunals, Courts and Enforcement Act 2007 have not been brought into force.

43-03   There are a number of significant limitations on a landlord's right to levy distress which mean that it will rarely be appropriate for a landlord to recover service charge arrears by means of distress. In particular:

1   If service charge is not reserved as rent, then service charge arrears may not be recovered by distress.

2   Distress may only be levied in respect of an amount that is certain.[1] Accordingly, save where service charge is paid by way of fixed contribution, service charge arrears may not be recovered by distress unless and until the arrears have been either agreed by the tenant or otherwise ascertained. In *Concorde Graphics Ltd v Andromeda Investments SA,*[2] the lease provided for the tenant to pay a 'rateable or due proportion' of the landlord's costs of services 'such proportion in the case of difference to be settled by the landlord's surveyor whose decision shall be final and binding on the parties'. It was held that until such time as the tenant's proportion of costs had been validly ascertained in accordance with the dispute resolution mechanism in the lease, the landlord was not entitled to distrain for the arrears.

---

1   *Ex parte Voisey* (1882) 21 Ch D 442.
2   [1983] 1 EGLR 53.

In residential leases, the landlord's right to recover service charge is subject to an implied limitation that costs are recoverable only to the extent that they are reasonable.[3] A commercial lease may well contain either an express or implied term to the same effect.[4] If a landlord sought to distrain for arrears of service charge without a binding determination (or agreement by the tenant) as to the amount due, the landlord would risk being faced with an argument that the charges (or some part of them) were unreasonably incurred, with the result that the distress levied for such charges was unlawful.

3   Distress is not available to recover arrears that accrued due prior to the assignment of the lease to the current tenant.[5]

4   A landlord is not entitled to levy distress if the tenant has a valid equitable[6] set-off against the landlord's claim for rent (e.g. for breach of the landlord's repairing obligations).[7]

5   Subject to certain exceptions,[8] the Law of Distress Amendment Act 1908 provides certain subtenants,[9] lodgers and persons with no beneficial interest in any tenancy of the premises with the means to acquire immunity from distress.[10]

6   Distress may not be levied without leave of the court where:

    (a)   The demised premises are let on a protected or statutory tenancy within the meaning of the Rent Act 1977,[11] a protected occupancy or statutory tenancy within the meaning of the Rent (Agriculture) Act 1976[12] or an assured tenancy within the meaning of the Housing Act 1988.[13] Where the landlord applies for leave, the tenant may oppose the application on the ground that there is a reasonable *bona fide* dispute as to the amount due.[14] The court also has power to suspend leave to levy distress on terms that the tenant pays a stipulated amount towards the arrears.[15]

    (b)   An administration application has been made in respect of the tenant or a notice of intention to appoint an administrator has been filed,[16]

3   Landlord and Tenant Act 1985, s 19: see Chapter 29 above.
4   See **2-97** to **2-121** above.
5   *Wharfland Ltd v South London Co-operative Building Co Ltd* [1995] 2 EGLR 21.
6   A legal set-off will not suffice for this purpose: *Fuller v Happy Shopper Markets Ltd* [2001] 1 WLR 1681.
7   *Eller v Grovecast Investments Ltd* [1995] QB 272; *Fuller v Happy Shopper Markets Ltd* [2001] 1 WLR 1681. Equitable set off is discussed at **40-49** and **40-50** above.
8   Law of Distress Amendment Act 1908, s 4.
9   The subtenants protected are those who pay a full market rent in instalments no less frequent than quarterly: s 1(a).
10   Section 1.
11   Section 147.
12   Section 8.
13   Section 19.
14   *Townsend v Charlton* [1922] 1 KB 700.
15   *Metropolitan Properties Co v Purdy* [1940] 1 All ER 188; *Blanket v Palmer* [1940] 1 All ER 524.
16   Insolvency Act 1986, Sch B1, para 43.

compulsory winding up of a corporate tenant has commenced[17] or a moratorium under Part 1 of the Insolvency Act 1986 is in force.

(c)   The debtor is, at the relevant time, performing a period of whole-time service with the reserve or auxiliary forces.[18]

(d)   The demised premises are subject to a restraint order under the Proceeds of Crime Act 2002.[19]

7   Leave of the tenant's administrator is required before distress may be levied against a tenant in administration.[20]

8   Distress is not available against the goods of the Crown, whether the Crown is the tenant or not.[21]

9   Distress may be levied against chattels only; fixtures are immune from distress.[22] There are certain prescribed classes of chattels which are, in any event, immune from distress.[23]

10   Distress is not available where the landlord has elected to forfeit the lease.[24] It should also be noted that, save in cases to which the provisions of section 210 of the Common Law Procedure Act 1852 would apply,[25] the levying of distress will waive any accrued right to forfeit the lease.[26] The remedies of distress and forfeiture are usually mutually exclusive.

43-04   Where, notwithstanding the above restrictions, the landlord is prima facie entitled to levy distress for the purpose of recovering arrears of service charge, consideration will need to be given by the landlord to the considerable body of substantive and procedural law associated with the exercise of a right of distress. The latter is beyond the scope of this book and reference should be made to specialist works.[27]

---

17 Insolvency Act 1986, s 128(1).
18 Reserve Auxiliary Forces (Protection of Civil Interests) Act 1951, ss 2 and 3.
19 Section 58(1) and (2).
20 Insolvency Act 1986, Sch B1, para 43.
21 *Secretary of State for War v Wynee* [1905] 2 KB 845.
22 *Simpson v Hartopp* (1744) Willes 512.
23 For example, chattels subject to trade privilege, chattels in actual use and perishables, certain crops and wild animals. See *Woodfall: Landlord and Tenant*, Vol 1, Ch 9.
24 *Jones v Carter* (1846) 15 M&W 718; *Franklin v Carter* (1845) 1 CB 750; *Bridges v Smyth* (1829) 5 Bing 410; *Serjeant v Nash Field & Co* [1903] 2 KB 304.
25 See **45-82** below.
26 *Cotesworth v Spokes* (1861) 10 CBNS 103.
27 See *Woodfall: Landlord and Tenant*, Vol 1, Ch 9; Tanney and Travers, *Distress for Rent* (2000).

CHAPTER 44

Landlord's remedies: Service of notice under section 6 of the Law of Distress Amendment Act 1908

44-01 Section 6 of the Law of Distress Amendment Act 1908 provides as follows:

'6. To avoid distress

In cases where the rent of the immediate tenant of the superior landlord is in arrear it shall be lawful for such superior landlord to serve upon any under tenant or lodger a notice (by registered post addressed to such under tenant or lodger upon the premises) stating the amount of such arrears of rent, and requiring all future payments of rent, whether the same has already accrued due or not, by such under tenant or lodger to be made direct to the superior landlord giving such notice until such arrears shall have been duly paid, and such notice shall operate to transfer to the superior landlord the right to recover, receive, and give a discharge for such rent.'

44-02 Accordingly, in cases where a headlease reserves service charge as additional rent (but not otherwise) and the premises have been sublet, a landlord may serve notice on the subtenant requiring him to pay the rent due under the sublease (including service charge if it has been reserved as rent in the sublease) directly to the landlord until such time as the headlease arrears have been discharged. Although the 1908 Act is otherwise concerned with the law of distress (see Chapter 43 above), the heading of section 6 makes clear that a notice served under that section is a means of *avoiding the need to levy distress* and the restrictions associated with a landlord's right to levy distress do not apply to section 6.[1]

44-03 Service of notice under section 6 of the 1908 Act operates as a statutory assignment of the head tenant's right to receive the rent from the subtenant.[2] Payment of the sublease rent to the superior landlord discharges the subtenant's obligation under the sublease and the subtenant is not, therefore, vulnerable to a claim by his immediate landlord in respect of the arrears so paid. However, notice under section 6 will only entitle the superior landlord to receive the sublease rent until such time as the arrears of rent (and service charge reserved as such)

1   *Wallrock v Equity and Law Life Assurance Society* [1942] 2 KB 82.
2   *Wallrock v Equity and Law Life Assurance Society* [1942] 2 KB 82.

due at the time of service of the notice have been discharged. Accordingly, if, after service of a section 6 notice, further arrears fall due under the head lease, the superior landlord will need to serve a further section 6 notice in respect of the later arrears.

44-04 The provisions of the Law of Distress Amendment Act 1908, including section 6, are due to be abolished by the Tribunals, Courts and Enforcement Act 2007.[3] However, the relevant provisions of the Tribunals, Courts and Enforcement Act 2007 have not yet come into force.

---

3   Schedule 14, para 20.

CHAPTER 45

Landlord's remedies: Forfeiture

45-01   Forfeiture is the means by which a landlord may bring a lease to a premature end, usually, but not necessarily,[1] following breach by the tenant of one or more of the obligations contained in the lease. A landlord's right to forfeit a lease is subject to numerous restrictions and, in particular, to the right of a tenant, subtenant and mortgagee to apply for relief from forfeiture.

45-02   In practice, forfeiture performs two functions for the landlord. First, forfeiture will, in certain circumstances, enable the landlord to bring the lease to an end altogether. By this means, the landlord may rid himself of a troublesome tenant and potentially achieve a valuable windfall by obtaining early vacant possession of the demised premises. Secondly, even if forfeiture is avoided by the tenant or relief from forfeiture is granted, the threat of the termination of the lease will often provide a landlord with a method of applying meaningful pressure on the tenant or indeed the tenant's mortgagee to discharge the outstanding service charge arrears.

45-03   The law of forfeiture is not without its critics. It is seen by many is being archaic, arcane and long overdue for reform.[2] Nevertheless, it remains the case that there are no immediate plans to effect such reform.

SUMMARY OF REQUIREMENTS FOR FORFEITURE FOR NON-PAYMENT OF SERVICE CHARGE

45-04   In summary, in order for a landlord to forfeit for non-payment of service charge, the following conditions must be satisfied:

---

1   A lease may entitle a landlord to forfeit the lease upon the occurrence of a particular event (e.g. insolvency of the tenant or guarantor), which event may not itself amount to a breach of the lease.
2   In 2006, the Law Commission, in its report, *Termination of Tenancies for Tenant Default* (Law Com 303, 2006), stated, at para 1.3: 'The law of forfeiture is in urgent need of reform … It is complex, it lacks coherence, and it can lead to injustice. The time has come for its abolition and its replacement by a simpler, more coherent statutory scheme based on what is appropriate and proportionate in the circumstances.'

(a) One or more instalments of service charge, whether interim or final, must have accrued due from the tenant.

(b) The tenant must not have a right of set-off, exercisable against the landlord in respect of the service charge claim, which is equal to or in excess of the amount of the service charge and, where applicable, accrued interest due from the tenant.[3]

(c) Unless the obligation to pay service charge is expressed as a condition, the lease must contain a proviso for re-entry which enables the landlord to forfeit for non-payment of service charge, any additional grace period specified in the proviso for re-entry must have elapsed and any other conditions specified in the proviso for re-entry must have been complied with.

(d) The right to forfeit for non-payment of the arrears in question must not have been waived at any time prior to the exercise of the right of re-entry.

(e) The landlord must have taken any necessary preliminary steps, including (where applicable) service of a notice under section 146 of the Law of Property Act 1925, and ensured that none of the other restrictions on the right to forfeit continue to apply.

(f) The landlord must then exercise the right to forfeit in a permissible manner and, where the landlord does so by means of court proceedings in respect of a residential lease, the landlord must comply with the requirements of paragraph 2.4 of CPR Practice Direction 55A.

45-05 Even if the above requirements are met and the lease is successfully terminated, a tenant, subtenant or mortgagee may apply for relief from forfeiture.

EXISTENCE OF ARREARS

45-06 In order for a landlord to forfeit for non-payment of service charge, the tenant must be in arrears of one or more instalments of service charge due under the lease. The arrears may comprise interim or final service charge or a combination of the two. Subject to the terms of the proviso for re-entry, a landlord will usually also be entitled to forfeit a lease for failure to pay contractual interest due on arrears of service charge.

45-07 There will often be a dispute as to whether there are, in fact, arrears of service charges at the relevant time. An existing or former tenant may, for example, advance one or more of the arguments referred to at **40-05** above, which will need to be resolved in order to determine whether the right to forfeit for the arrears of service charges has, indeed, arisen.

45-08 A landlord will not be entitled to forfeit the lease for non-payment of service charge in circumstances where the tenant has a right of set-off against the landlord for an amount which is equal to or greater than the amount of the

---

3   See **40-49** and **40-50** above.

service charge arrears. A tenant's right of set off against service charge arrears is considered at **40-49** and **40-50** above.

PROVISO FOR RE-ENTRY

45-09 A landlord may forfeit a lease for breach of a condition regardless of whether the lease contains a proviso for re-entry. A lease may only be forfeited for breach of a covenant (which is not also a condition) if the lease contains a proviso for re-entry.[4]

45-10 An obligation may be a condition of the lease if either:

(a)   the lease contains express words to that effect; or

(b)   an intention to create a condition can be inferred from the document as a whole.[5]

45-11 Absent express words, it is considered that it will rarely, if ever, be the case that a covenant to pay service charge will be a condition of the lease. Accordingly, in the vast majority of cases, a landlord will only be entitled to forfeit a lease for non-payment of service charge if the lease in question contains a proviso for re-entry. A modern, well-drafted lease will always contain such a proviso. By contrast, a lease which was made orally or informally between parties who have not instructed lawyers may not.

45-12 A proviso for re-entry must be expressly created, there is no scope for the implication of a proviso for re-entry. It is a question of construction whether a proviso for re-entry is sufficiently widely drafted to enable the landlord to forfeit for the breach or other triggering event in question. Provisos for re-entry fall to be strictly construed[6] and, where there are doubts, they are to be resolved against the landlord.[7] However, a modern, well-drafted lease will invariably contain a proviso for re-entry which enables the landlord to re-enter following breach of the tenant's obligation to pay service charge.

45-13 A proviso for re-entry will not usually provide for the landlord to re-enter immediately upon the tenant's failure to pay service charge. It is more common to find that the landlord's right to forfeit for non-payment of rent and service charge is expressed to arise a specific number of days or working days after the due date. Any attempt by the landlord to effect forfeiture of the lease, whether by peaceable re-entry or by proceedings, prior to the expiry of any such grace period, will be unlawful and ineffective.

45-14 It will occasionally also be the case that the proviso for re-entry, itself, imposes further contractual pre-conditions to the exercise of a right of re-entry

4   *Doe d Wilson v Phillips* (1824) 2 Bing 13.
5   *Bashir v Commissioner of Lands* [1960] AC 44.
6   *Croft v Lumley* (1858) 6 HL Cas 672.
7   *Doe d Abdy v Stevens* (1823) 3 B&Ad 299.

(e.g. service of a warning notice on the tenant or the tenant's mortgagee). If so, these too fall to be complied with before forfeiting the lease.

45-15 In the case of tenancies of agricultural holdings within the meaning of the Agricultural Holdings Act 1986, a proviso for re-entry must not be drafted in terms which would enable the landlord to forfeit without giving at least one month's notice of the forfeiture to the tenant. A proviso for re-entry which offends this principle is void.[8]

Prior demand at common law

45-16 Where service charge is reserved as rent (but not otherwise), a landlord will need to ascertain whether the proviso for re-entry excludes the need for a formal demand at common law, prior to the exercise of a right of re-entry. A modern, well-drafted lease will invariably do so by including the words 'whether or not formally demanded' or some other equivalent formulation. But if the lease does not exclude the requirement to make formal demand at common law, then, unless the conditions set out in section 210 of the Common Law Procedure Act 1852 are made out,[9] the landlord will be required to follow the common law procedure before exercising a right of re-entry.[10]

WAIVER

45-17 A landlord with an accrued right to forfeit a lease is put to an election. The landlord may either affirm the lease or, alternatively, treat it as being at an end, but may not do both.[11]

45-18 If the landlord elects to affirm the lease, the right to forfeit for non-payment of the service charge in question will be waived and, therefore, lost, albeit

---

8   *Parry v Million Pigs Ltd* [1981] 2 EGLR 1. See further, *Woodfall: Landlord and Tenant* Vol 2 at para 21.155.

9   Common Law Procedure Act 1832, s 210 provides that a formal demand at common law is unnecessary in all cases between landlord and tenant when one half year's rent is in arrear and no sufficient distress is to be found on the demised premises, or any part thereof, countervailing the arrears and the landlord has power to re-enter for non-payment thereof.

10 A formal demand at common law must be made: (i) by the landlord or an authorised agent in person (*Toms v Wilson* (1862) 32 LJQB 33; affirmed (1863) 32 LJQB 382); (ii) on the last day on which the forfeiture could be saved (*Doe d Dixon v Roe* (1849) 7 CB 134) (accordingly, the demand must be made on the last day of any grace period stated in the proviso for re-entry); (iii) at a convenient time before sunset (Co Lit 202a.) and continued until sunset (*Wood and Chiver's Case* (1573) 4 Leon 179); (iv) absent contrary provision in the lease, upon the land and at the most notorious place on it (Cole, Ejec 413); and (v) for precisely the amount then payable, not a penny more and not a penny less (*Fabian and Windsor's Case* (1589) 1 Leon 305). If the landlord fails to make an effective demand at common law, any subsequent attempt to forfeit the lease by the landlord will be invalid and of no effect.

11 *Kammins Ballrooms Co Ltd v Zenith Investments (Torquay) Ltd* [1971] AC 850.

the landlord will still be able to maintain a debt claim and obtain judgment on the arrears. By contrast, if the landlord elects to forfeit the lease by issuing court proceedings or effecting peaceable re-entry,[12] this operates as a final election to determine the lease. From and after that point, the landlord is no longer at risk of waiving the right to forfeit by acceptance of rent or service charge or otherwise.[13]

45-19   The significance of a waiver of a landlord's right to forfeit will vary depending on whether the breach is:

(a)   a 'once and for all' breach, or, alternatively,

(b)   a continuing breach.

45-20   In the former case, waiver of the right to forfeit will effectively preclude the landlord from forfeiting for that breach at all. In cases of the latter, the right to forfeit for the breach arises afresh with each new day. Moreover, an act of waiver (in relation to a continuing breach) does not even necessitate the service of a fresh notice under section 146 of the Law of Property Act 1925.[14] Waiver of the right to forfeit for a continuing breach will rarely have any significant consequences. However, the right to forfeit for non-payment of service charge is a 'once and for all' breach.[15] That is so even if the proviso for re-entry entitles the landlord to forfeit 'if and whenever' the rent (or service charge) is in arrear.[16]

45-21   Waiver of the right to forfeit for non-payment of service charge will occur where the landlord, with knowledge of the breach, acts in a manner which unequivocally recognises the continued existence of the lease,[17] providing that recognition is then communicated in some way to the tenant.[18]

Landlord's knowledge

45-22   Where the breach in question is non-payment of a service charge, the issue of the landlord's knowledge of the breach is unlikely to present many difficulties since the landlord, or his managing agent,[19] will almost always know that the service charge has not been paid.

---

12   See **45-75** below.
13   *Jones v Carter* (1846) 15 M&W 718.
14   *Penton v Barnett* [1898] 1 QB 276.
15   *London & County (A&D) Ltd v Wilfred Sportsman Ltd* [1971] Ch 764.
16   *Ibid.*
17   *Matthews v Smallwood* [1910] 1 Ch 777 at p 786; *Central Estates (Belgravia) Ltd v Woolgar (No 2)* [1972] 1 WLR 1048 at p 1054.
18   *Scarfe v Jardine* (1882) 7 App Cas 345 at p 360.
19   The knowledge need not be personal to the landlord. It is sufficient if the knowledge is acquired by an employee with a duty to report the matter to the landlord (*Metropolitan Properties Co Ltd v Cordery* (1980) 39 P&CR 10). Accordingly, where rent is habitually paid to a managing agent, knowledge of a tenant's failure to pay service charge would almost certainly be imputed to the landlord.

Conduct amounting to recognition of the continued existence of the lease

45-23   The right to forfeit may be waived by acceptance of rent.[20] Although not authoritatively settled, the same is almost certainly true where rent is demanded by the landlord.[21] It is, however, necessary to pay careful attention to the scope of this principle:

1   If the landlord demands or accepts payment of rent which accrued due after the right to forfeit for a particular breach arose, then, provided that the landlord had knowledge of his right to forfeit for that breach on the date the rent fell due, a demand for or acceptance of the rent will undoubtedly waive the right to forfeit. The legal effect of demanding or accepting rent cannot be avoided by doing so on a 'without prejudice basis'.[22] Similarly, a provision in the lease to the effect that demand for or acceptance of rent will not amount to waiver will not be effective to prevent waiver from occurring.[23]

2   By contrast, where the rent in question accrued due before the right to forfeit for the breach had arisen, the demand for or acceptance of that rent will not amount to waiver of the right to forfeit, even if the demand for or acceptance of rent occurred after the right to forfeit arose.

3   There is presently some uncertainty about whether waiver occurs when –

    (a)   there is a breach of covenant giving rise to a right to forfeit;

    (b)   some time later, rent falls due;

    (c)   the landlord later becomes aware of the breach and his right to forfeit after the rent falls due; and

    (d)   the landlord then accepts that rent.

This point was considered (albeit *obiter*) in *Osibanjo v Seahive Investments Ltd*.[24] Mummery LJ expressed the view that the right to forfeit would not be waived in such circumstances; Rix LJ expressed the opposite view and Smith LJ did not express an opinion on this issue. It is considered that the

---

20   *Doe d Gatehouse v Rees* (1838) 4 Bing NC 384; *Central Estates (Belgravia) Ltd v Woolgar (No 2)* [1972] 1 WLR 1048; *Expert Clothing Service & Sales Ltd v Hillgate House Ltd* [1986] Ch 340.

21   In *Segal Securities Ltd v Thoseby* [1963] 1 QB 887, a first instance decision, it was held that a demand for rent had the same effect as acceptance of it. In both *Expert Clothing Service & Sales Ltd v Hillgate House Ltd* [1986] Ch 340 and *Greenwood Reversions Ltd v World Environmental Foundation Ltd* [2009] L&TR. 2, the Court of Appeal said it was prepared to assume that a demand for rent had the same effect, but specifically declined to decide the point. In *Thomas v Ken Thomas Ltd* [2006] EWCA Civ 1504, Neuberger LJ referred to a subsequent demand for rent as being one of the 'classic ways in which a landlord can waive the right to forfeit'. Given the now long standing practice of first instance courts to treat demand for rent as waiving an antecedent right, it is considered that it is unlikely that the position would be reversed by the Court of Appeal.

22   *Croft v Lumley* (1858) 5 E&B 648 at p 682.

23   *Expert Clothing Service & Sales Ltd v Hillgate House Ltd* [1986] Ch 340.

24   [2008] EWCA Civ 1282.

view expressed by Rix LJ is to be preferred. It is difficult to see any reason of law or policy why it should matter whether the landlord's knowledge of the right to forfeit occurred before or after the rent fell due, provided that the landlord acquired the requisite knowledge by the time of the demand for or acceptance of rent.

4   Where a tenant fails to pay rent and a guarantor is required to make payment pursuant to the guarantee, there is no waiver of any accrued right to forfeit the lease, since the guarantor's payment is not a payment of rent.[25]

45-24   Where the lease in question reserves a service charge as additional rent, then a service charge is to be treated as rent for all purposes, including waiver of the right to forfeiture. Accordingly, the principles discussed at **45-23** above in relation to rent would apply in exactly the same way.

45-25   Where a service charge is not reserved as rent, the special principles applicable to demands for and acceptance of rent discussed above do not apply. The court is required to look at all the circumstances of the case and to decide whether the act relied upon as amounting to waiver was so unequivocal that, when considered objectively, it could only be regarded as having done consistently with the continued existence of the lease.[26] Applying that test, where a landlord with knowledge that the tenant is in breach demands or accepts service charge which accrued due after the date on which the right to forfeit arose, it is considered that this would amount to a recognition of the continued existence of the lease and, accordingly would have the effect of waiving the landlord's right to forfeit.

45-26   Other examples of conduct amounting to waiver of an antecedent right to forfeit include:

(i)   Commencing proceedings for the recovery of rent or service charge which accrued due after the right to forfeit arose.[27] Whilst there is no authority to this effect, it would seem all but certain that the issue of proceedings in the LVT for a determination of the reasonableness of subsequent service charges pursuant to section 27A of the Landlord and Tenant Act 1985 would have the same effect.[28]

(ii)   Exercising other contractual rights under the lease (e.g. a right of access for repair[29] or an option contained in the lease[30]). It is considered that the grant of consent (e.g. for alterations, assignment or subletting) would have the same effect.

25 *London & County (A&D) Ltd v Wilfred Sportsman Ltd* [1971] Ch 764.
26 *Expert Clothing Service & Sales Ltd v Hillgate House Ltd* [1986] Ch 340.
27 *Dendy v Nicholl* (1858) 4 CB (NS) 376.
28 An application for a determination in relation to the service charge arrears for which the landlord seeks to forfeit will not waive the right to forfeit for those arrears because under the Housing Act 1996, s 81, such a determination is a necessary pre-condition to exercising the right of forfeiture. See **45-51** below.
29 *Doe d Rutzen v Lewis* (1836) 5 A&E 277.
30 *First Penthouse Ltd v Channel Hotels and Properties (UK) Ltd* [2004] EWCA Civ 1072.

(iii) Suing on other covenants in the lease (e.g. an injunction to restrain a breach).[31]

(iv) Save in circumstances where section 210 of the Common Law Procedure Act 1852 applies,[32] levying distress will waive the right to forfeit.[33]

(v) Offering to buy the tenant's lease.[34]

45-27   By contrast, service of a notice under section 146 of the Law of Property Act 1925 is not an act of waiver, since service of the notice is a preliminary act of forfeiture.[35]

Waiver in circumstances where statutory restrictions on the exercise of a right of re-entry still apply

45-28   It is considered that there is presently some uncertainty as to whether a right to forfeit which has arisen under the lease, but, by reason of some statutory prohibition, has not yet become exercisable, is capable of being waived by the landlord. This problem arises in three contexts:

1   Section 81 of the Housing Act 1996 provides that a landlord of premises which have been let as a dwelling may not forfeit the lease unless and until the amount of the arrears has been admitted by the tenant or alternatively determined by the court, the LVT or an arbitral tribunal (and a further 14 days has expired). The provisions of section 81 of the Housing Act 1996 are dealt with at **45-51** to **45-63** below.

2   Section 146 of the Law of Property Act 1925 provides that a right of re-entry or forfeiture shall not be enforceable until notice in accordance with the section has been served on the tenant and a reasonable time for compliance with the notice has expired. The provisions of section 146 of the Law of Property Act 1925 are dealt with at **45-34** to **45-38** below.

3   Section 167 of the Commonhold and Leasehold Reform 2002 Act provides that a landlord under a long lease of a dwelling may not exercise a right of re-entry or forfeiture for failure by a tenant to pay an amount consisting of rent, service charges or administration charges (or a combination of them) ('the unpaid amount') unless either –

    (a)   the unpaid amount exceeds the prescribed sum (currently £350[36]), or

---

31 *Wheeler v Keeble (1914) Ltd* [1920] 1 Ch 27.
32 See **45-82** below.
33 *Ward v Day* (1863–64) 4 B&S 337.
34 *Bader Properties Ltd v Linley Property Investments Ltd* (1968) 19 P&CR 620.
35 *Church Commissioners for England v Nodjoumi* (1986) 51 P&CR 155.
36 Rights of Re-entry and Forfeiture (Prescribed Sum and Period) (England) Regulations 2004 (SI 2004/3086) and the Rights of Re-entry and Forfeiture (Prescribed Sum and Period) (Wales) Regulations 2005 (SI 2005/1352).

(b)   the unpaid amount consists of, or includes, an amount which has been payable for more than a prescribed period (currently three years[37]).

45-29   All three sections, therefore, impose a statutory moratorium on the exercise of a right of re-entry which, at least for the purposes of the lease, has arisen, pending compliance with statutory conditions. The question which arises is whether a landlord may waive the right to forfeit during the period of the statutory moratorium. The point is potentially of real importance where a landlord wishes to forfeit for non-payment of arrears of service charge, but has undertaken some act which recognises the continued existence of the lease, since the right to forfeit for those arrears arose under the lease.

45-30   Surprisingly, there does not appear to be any decided case in which this issue has been directly considered (although there are a number of cases where the courts have held that a right to forfeit has been waived by a landlord prior to the service of a section 146 notice without any argument on this point).[38] The matter must, therefore, be approached from first principles.

45-31   Arguably, the landlord is put to an election (as to whether to forfeit or affirm the lease) as soon as the right to forfeit *accrues* under the lease.[39] If so, the landlord may be taken to have made his election even before he has complied with the obligations imposed by section 146 of the 1925 Act, section 81 of the Housing Act 1996 and section 167 of the Commonhold and Leasehold Reform Act 2002. This is because compliance with these statutory requirements is expressed to be a pre-condition to the *exercise* of an accrued right to forfeit the lease.

45-32   On the other hand, the doctrine of election is concerned with the requirement to choose between existing, but inconsistent, rights.[40] Given that the landlord will not be entitled to lawfully forfeit the lease until such time as the various statutory preconditions to the exercise of that right have been complied with, it is

---

37   Rights of Re-entry and Forfeiture (Prescribed Sum and Period) (England) Regulations 2004 (SI 2004/3086) and the Rights of Re-entry and Forfeiture (Prescribed Sum and Period) (Wales) Regulations 2005 (SI 2005/1352).

38   See, for example, *Van Haarlam v Kasner* [1992] 2 EGLR 59. See, however, an apparent view to the contrary in *Woodfall: Landlord and Tenant,* Vol 1 at para 17.098.1. However, the various authorities cited in support of the proposition that rent accepted during the currency of a section 146 notice cannot waive the right of forfeiture, relate to continuing breaches (as to which, see **45-20** above). It is not, therefore, considered that this statement in *Woodfall* supports the general proposition that the landlord's election does not arise until the expiry of a section 146 notice.

39   The right to forfeit the lease accrues once the tenant is in breach and once any grace period prescribed by the proviso for re-entry has elapsed.

40   *Motor Oil Hellas (Corinth) Refineries SA v Shipping Corporation of India (The Kanchenjunga)* [1990] 1 Lloyds Rep 392 at p 397. In Lord Diplock's classic statement of the law of waiver by election in *Kammins Ballrooms Co Ltd v Zenith Investments (Torquay) Ltd* [1971] AC 850 at p 882, waiver by election was said to arise 'in a situation where a person *is entitled* to alternative rights inconsistent with one another' (emphasis supplied). The need for the element of choice was also emphasised by Clarke J in *Lexington Insurance Co v Multinacional de Seguros SA* [2009] Lloyds Rep IR 1.

equally arguable that, prior to that time, the landlord does not yet have a choice to make and is correspondingly not yet put to his election.

45-33   Pending authoritative guidance from the courts on this issue, the counsel of perfection is for landlords to assume that that the right to forfeit may be waived at any time after it has arisen.

GENERAL RESTRICTIONS ON THE EXERCISE OF THE RIGHT TO FORFEIT

45-34   There are a number of important restrictions on the exercise of a landlord's right to forfeit a lease. Some restrictions apply only to certain residential leases: these are considered separately at **45-50** to **45-73** below.

Section 146 of the Law of Property Act 1925

45-35   In cases to which section 146(1) of the Law of Property Act 1925 applies, before taking steps to enforce a right of re-entry or forfeiture against the tenant, a landlord must serve a notice in accordance with the section and allow a reasonable time to expire following service of the notice.

When does the landlord need to serve a section 146 notice?

45-36   A landlord will not be required to serve a notice under section 146 of the Law of Property Act 1925 in all cases. The orthodox view is that a section 146 notice need only be served by the landlord prior to the exercise of a right of re-entry for non-payment of service charge in circumstances where the lease in question does *not* reserve service charge as rent.

45-37   Whether or not a service charge is reserved as further or additional rent is a question of construction of the lease. The default position is that service charge will *not* be treated as rent.[41] If, however, a lease contains an express provision that a service charge is or is deemed to be rent or additional rent, then the service charge will be treated as such for all purposes, including forfeiture.[42] The relevant deeming provision is usually contained in the *reddendum* of the lease, but it will still be effective if it is contained elsewhere in the lease.[43]

45-38   Doubt has, however, been cast on the orthodox view, at least in so far as it relates to leases to which section 81 of the Housing Act 1996 applies (premises let as a dwelling), by the Court of Appeal's decision in *Freeholders of 69 Marina,*

---

41   *Khar v Delmounty Ltd* (1998) 75 P&CR 232.
42   *Escalus Properties Ltd v Robinson* [1996] 2 QB 231.
43   *Escalus Properties Ltd v Robinson* [1996] 2 QB 231.

St Leonards-on-Sea v Oram.[44] In that case, the LVT made a determination under section 27A of the Landlord and Tenant Act 1985. In later proceedings before the County Court, the landlord recovered the costs of the earlier proceedings by relying on a tenant's covenant to pay costs incurred by the landlord incidental to the preparation and service of a section 146 notice. The decision to award the landlord his costs of the earlier proceedings was upheld on appeal. Sir Andrew Morritt, who gave the leading judgment in the Court of Appeal, noted that the definition of service charge in section 18 of the Landlord and Tenant Act 1985 included service charges which had been reserved as rent and that the requirements of section 81 of the Housing Act 1996 had to be met[45] even before the landlord serves a section 146 notice. He concluded:[46]

> 'Subsections (2) and (4A) [of the Housing Act 1996] plainly recognise that the s.146 procedure is applicable in the case of re-entry or forfeiture in the case of non-payment of a service charge. Given that the definition of service charge includes "an amount … payable as a part of … the rent", the evident intention is that the s.146 procedure, as modified, is to be applicable in cases of non-payment of a service charge *even when such charge is recoverable as part of the rent.*

> There is no doubt that the Freeholders incurred costs in the repair of the common parts of the Building in performance of their obligation under clause 4(1). That, in turn, created a liability on the tenants, including the Lessees, to reimburse the Freeholders for those costs under clause 1(b). The amount of that liability comes within the definition of service charge in s.18 Landlord and Tenant Act 1985 but cannot be enforced except in accordance with the terms of s.81 Housing Act 1996 and, in the case of a long lease, as defined, in accordance with the provisions of s.168 Commonhold and Leasehold Reform Act 2002. Each of those sections requires the amount of the tenant's liability to have been finally determined by the Leasehold Valuation Tribunal. *Moreover each of those sections requires or recognises that even when so determined the enforcement of that liability is subject to the provisions of s.146 even if the lease treats it as an additional rent recoverable as such. In short the enforcement of the liability of the tenants under clause 1(b) required first the determination of the Tribunal and second a s.146 notice.*' (Emphasis added.)

45-39   The views expressed by Sir Andrew Morritt in *Freeholders of 69 Marina, St Leonards-on-Sea v Oram* are surprising and contrary to the long established view that the requirements of section 146 of the Law of Property Act 1925 do not apply where a landlord seeks to forfeit for non-payment of rent. It is considered that the decision is open to doubt in this regard for the following reasons:

1   As Nourse LJ explained in *Escalus Properties Ltd v Robinson*, where the lease provides that service charge is or is deemed to be additional rent, service charge then acquires 'all the attributes of rent'.[47]

---

44   [2011] EWCA Civ 1258.
45   See **45-51** below.
46   At paras 12 and 18.
47   [1996] 2 QB 231 at pp 243–244.

2   Section 146(11) of the Law of Property Act specifically excludes forfeiture for non-payment of rent from the ambit of the section.[48]

3   Neither section 18 of the Landlord and Tenant Act 1985 nor section 81 of the Housing Act 1996 imposes any obligation on the landlord to serve a section 146 notice before forfeiting for non-payment of service charge reserved as rent.

4   On the contrary, section 81(4A) of the Housing Act 1996, provides that the references in section 81 to 'the exercise of a right of re-entry or forfeiture *include* the service of a notice under section 146(1) of the Law of Property Act 1925' (emphasis added). The wording of section 81(4A) implicitly recognises that a right of re-entry or forfeiture for the purposes of section 81(1) of the Housing Act 1996 may be exercised otherwise than by service of a section 146 notice.

5   It is not, in any event, essential to the operation of either section 18 of the Landlord and Tenant Act 1985[49] or section 81 of the Housing Act 1996 that there should be an obligation on a landlord to serve a notice under section 146 of the Law of Property Act 1925 prior to forfeiting for non-payment of service charges which have been reserved as rent. Moreover, in cases where service charge is reserved as rent, section 81 of the Housing Act 1996 will still prevent the landlord from forfeiting (whether by the issue or proceedings or peaceable re-entry) until the requirements of the section are met.

6   In *Khar v Delmounty Ltd*,[50] the Court of Appeal confirmed that the jurisdiction to grant relief from forfeiture under section 146(2) of the Law of Property Act 1925 to an immediate tenant[51] may only be exercised where service charge is *not* reserved as rent. Where service charge is reserved as rent, relief may only be granted under the court's equitable jurisdiction (in the High Court) or pursuant to sections 138 and 139 (in the County Court).[52] Accordingly, if *Freeholders of 69 Marina, St Leonards-on-Sea v Oram* is correct, then, where service charge is reserved as rent, the requirement to service notice in section 146(1) of the Law of Property Act does apply, but the jurisdiction to grant relief in section 146(2) does not. This would be a curious result.

45-40   It has been suggested that, because the *dicta* of Nourse LJ in *Escalus Properties v Robinson* and section 146(11) of the Law of Property Act 1925 appear not to have been specifically drawn to the Court of Appeal's attention in *Freeholders of 69 Marina, St Leonards-on-Sea v Oram*, the decision is *per*

---

48   In *Khar v Delmounty Ltd* (1998) 75 P&CR 232, the Court of Appeal confirmed that the effect of the Law of Property Act 1925, s 146(11) was to exclude altogether cases of non-payment of rent from the ambit of the section.
49   Or indeed to any of the other sections dealing with service charge in the Landlord and Tenant Act 1985 to which the definition in s 18 relates.
50   (1998) 75 P&CR 232; (1998) 75 P&CR 232.
51   The position is different where relief is claimed by a subtenant. In such cases, the jurisdiction arises under the Law of Property Act 1925, s 146 (4).
52   Relief from forfeiture is considered at **45-79** to **45-126** below.

incuriam.[53] However, it might be questioned whether this would have been relevant to the court's decision, which related to the interrelation between sections 18 of the Landlord and Tenant Act 1985 and section 81 of the Housing Act 1996 and the effect of these sections on the requirement to serve a section 146 notice in all cases. If that is right (and the decision was not *per incuriam*), it will be binding on any judge at first instance. Therefore, although the court's reasoning may be open to question, the counsel of perfection for a landlord seeking to forfeit a residential lease for non-payment of service charge which has been reserved as rent is:

(a) to obtain an agreement or determination for the purposes of section 81 of the Housing Act 1996, and, thereafter,

(b) to serve a section 146 notice on the tenant before taking steps to forfeit the lease.

45-41 In the case of leases to which section 81(1) of the Housing Act 1996 does not apply (i.e. a lease of premises *not* let as a dwelling or premises to which one of the exclusions in subsection (4) applies[54]), the orthodox view undoubtedly prevails and there is accordingly no need to serve a notice under section 146 of the Law of Property Act 1925 where service charge has been reserved as rent in the lease.

Cases where a section 146 notice must be served

45-42 Where section 146(1) of the Law of Property Act 1925 applies, notice in accordance with the section must be served on the tenant. It is not possible to contract out of the requirement to serve a section 146 notice in the lease.[55]

45-43 A valid section notice must:

(i) specify the particular breach complained of;

(ii) if the breach is capable of remedy, require the lessee to remedy the breach; and

(iii) in any case, require the lessee to make compensation in money for the breach.

45-44 A section 146 notice must be sufficiently clear to enable the tenant to understand with reasonable certainty those matters about which the landlord complains;[56] failure to do so will render the intended notice invalid. It is usual,

---

53 This has been suggested in a recent article, Dovar 'Reservations on Forfeiture' L&T Review 2012, 16(1) at pp 23–26.
54 The following tenancies are excluded from the ambit of s 81: (a) a tenancy to which the Landlord and Tenant Act 1954, Pt II applies (business tenancies); (b) a tenancy of an agricultural holding within the meaning of the Agricultural Holdings Act 1986 in relation to which that Act applies; or (c) a farm business tenancy within the meaning of the Agricultural Tenancies Act 1995.
55 Section 146(12). Any provision in a lease which purports to do so will be void.
56 *Jolly v Fox* [1916] 1 AC 1; *Fletcher v Nokes* [1897] 1 Ch 271; *Re Serle* [1898] 1 Ch 652.

although not essential, for the landlord to set out the service charge provisions in the lease within the notice itself. Landlords frequently also include a running statement of account in the section 146 notice, either within the body of the notice itself or as an annex. Again, this is good practice, but probably not essential. Provided that the contents of the section 146 notice, as a whole, communicate to the tenant that he is in arrears of the service charge payable under the relevant clause or clauses of the lease and specify the amount of the arrears, the first of the above requirements will be satisfied.

45-45 Breach of a covenant to pay service charge is a remediable breach and, accordingly, the section 146 notice must require the tenant to remedy the breach.

45-46 Although the third requirement (compensation) is expressed in apparently mandatory terms, it has been held that failure to do so does not render a section 146 notice invalid.[57]

45-47 The requirements for service of a section 146 notice are as follows:

1 A section 146 notice must be served on the current tenant – a former tenant will not suffice.[58] If there is more than one tenant, the section 146 notice must be served on all of them.[59]

2 There is no requirement for the landlord to serve a section 146 notice on the tenant's mortgagee, even where the mortgagee is, by then, in possession of the premises.[60] However, it is right to note that, as a matter of practice rather than obligation, landlords frequently do so in the hope that the mortgagee will either discharge the arrears itself or apply pressure on the tenant to do so.[61]

3 Section 196 of the Law of Property Act 1925[62] applies to section 146 notices. Accordingly, a section 146 notice must be in writing and may be served –

  (a) by leaving it at the lessee's last known abode or place of business in the United Kingdom;

  (b) by affixing it or leaving it on the land or any house or building comprised in the lease;[63]

  (c) by posting it by registered post or recorded delivery addressed to the tenant by name at the last known abode or place of business in the

---

57 *Lock v Pearce* [1893] 2 Ch 271; *Civil Service Co-operative Society v McGrigor's Trustee* [1923] 2 Ch 347; *Rugby School (Governors) v Tannahill* [1935] 1 KB 87; *Egerton v Esplanade Hotels (London) Ltd* [1947] 2 All ER 88; *Hoffman v Fineberg* [1949] Ch 245.
58 *Old Grovebury Manor Farm v W Seymour Plant Sales & Hire Ltd (No 2)* [1979] 1 WLR 1397; *Fuller v Judy Properties Ltd* [1992] 1 EGLR 75.
59 *Blewett v Blewett* [1936] 2 All ER 188.
60 *Smith v Spaul* [2003] QB 983.
61 But see CPR Practice Direction 55A, para 2.4 for the need to serve proceedings on a mortgagee.
62 As amended by the Recorded Delivery Act 1962.
63 It has been held that service is effected if the notice is left with some person at the premises and there are reasonable grounds for the landlord to suppose that it will be passed on to the tenant: *Cannon Brewery Co v Signal Press Ltd* (1928) 44 TLR 486.

United Kingdom – provided that the letter is not then returned unde-livered. Where service is effected by this means, service is deemed to have occurred at the time at which the letter would in the ordinary course be expected to be delivered.

4   The provisions of section 196 of the Law of Property Act 1925 are per-missive rather than restrictive.[64] It follows that a section 146 notice can be served by other means. Given the potential importance of service of a section 146 notice and the propensity of certain tenants to deny receipt, landlords would be well advised to adopt a means of service which can be easily proved in evidence.

5   Where section 81 of the Housing Act 1996 applies,[65] a landlord must not serve the section 146 notice until either –

(a)   the service charge arrears have been admitted by the tenant; or

(b)   the arrears have been determined by the court, the LVT or an arbitrator and a further period of 14 days has elapsed since the final[66] determina-tion was made.

The provisions of section 81 of the Housing Act 1996 are discussed at **45-51** below.

45-48   In addition to service of the section 146 notice itself, a landlord must allow a reasonable period of time for the tenant to remedy the breach before taking any further steps to forfeit the lease. What will constitute a reasonable period of time depends on the nature of the breach. Where the breach is a failure to pay service charge, it is considered that only a comparatively short period need be allowed. The period in question should be sufficiently long to enable the tenant to effect the payment by one or other of the modern methods of payment.

Where the tenant is insolvent

45-49   Further restrictions on the landlord's ability to forfeit apply where the tenant is subject to one of the insolvency regimes:

1   A landlord may not commence or continue forfeiture proceedings or effect peaceable re-entry if either –

(a)   an administration application in respect of the tenant has been made or notice of intention to appoint an administrator has been filed with the court, without the permission of the court; or

(b)   where the tenant is in administration, without the permission of the court or the consent of the administrators.[67]

---

64 But see the *obiter* comments of Arnold J in *E.ON UK Plc v Gilesport Ltd* [2012] EWHC 2172 (Ch) at para 54.
65 That is, to premises let as a dwelling.
66 As defined in the Housing Act 1996, s 81(3) – see **45-55** below.
67 Insolvency Act 1986, s 8 and Sch B1, paras 43 and 44.

2   The landlord may not commence or continue forfeiture proceedings if either –

(a)   a winding up order has been made; or

(b)   a provisional liquidator has been appointed,

except by the permission of the court and subject to such terms as the court may impose.[68] It has not yet been settled by authority whether the landlord is entitled to forfeit by peaceable re-entry in these circumstances. Where an application for leave is made, permission will be granted if the tenant company has no defence[69] and the court will generally make an order for possession without the need for the landlord to issue fresh forfeiture proceedings.[70]

3   A landlord may not commence or continue forfeiture proceedings or effect peaceable re-entry during the currency of an interim order under section 252 of the Insolvency Act 1986 (in respect of an individual) or a moratorium under section 1A of that Act.

4   Where the tenant has been made bankrupt, then, unless service charge is reserved as rent, a landlord may not forfeit by court proceedings without leave of the court.[71] However, a landlord may still forfeit by peaceable re-entry without permission of the court, irrespective of whether service charge has been reserved as rent.[72]

5   Where a debt relief order under Part 7A of the Insolvency Act 1986 is in place and service charge is not reserved as rent in the lease, a landlord may not forfeit a lease by court proceedings.[73]

Restrictions on the right to forfeit residential leases

45-50   There are a number of restrictions on the landlord's right to forfeit which apply only in relation to certain residential leases. These are considered below.

---

68   Insolvency Act 1986, s 130(2).
69   *General Share & Trust Co v Wetley Brick & Pottery Co* (1882) 20 Ch D 260.
70   *Re Blue Jeans Sales Ltd* [1988] 2 EGLR 57.
71   Insolvency Act 1986, s 285(3); *Sharples v Places for People Homes Ltd* [2011] EWCA Civ 813.
72   Peaceable re-entry is not a 'security' for the purposes of the Insolvency Act 1986, s 383(2) and does not therefore require permission of the court: *Re Lomax Leisure* [2000] Ch 502.
73   The moratorium does not prevent proceedings for forfeiture on account of non-payment of rent (where the rent is a specified qualifying debt) because such proceedings are seeking a 'remedy in respect of the debt' and are not proceedings 'for the debt': *Godfrey v A2 Dominion Homes Ltd* [2011] EWCA Civ 813.

Section 81 of the Housing Act 1996

45-51   Section 81 of the Housing Act 1996[74] provides that:

'(1)   A landlord may not, in relation to premises let as a dwelling,[75] exercise a right of re-entry or forfeiture for failure by a tenant to pay a service charge or administration charge unless –

(a)   it is finally determined by (or on appeal from) a leasehold valuation tribunal or by a court, or by an arbitral tribunal in proceedings pursuant to a post-dispute arbitration agreement, that the amount of the service charge or administration charge is payable by him, or

(b)   the tenant has admitted that it is so payable.'

45-52   Although section 81(1) refers to any 'premises let as a dwelling', there are a number of important exclusions in section 81(4), namely:

(a)   a tenancy to which Part II of the Landlord and Tenant Act 1954 (business tenancies) applies;[76]

(b)   a tenancy of an agricultural holding within the meaning of the Agricultural Holdings Act 1986 in relation to which that Act applies;[77] or

(c)   a farm business tenancy within the meaning of the Agricultural Tenancies Act 1995.[78]

45-53   It follows that if the premises in question are mixed residential and commercial user (e.g. ground floor shop and residential upper parts), the lease, being one to which Part II of the Landlord and Tenant Act 1954 applies,[79] would fall outside the scope of section 81 of the Housing Act 1996.

45-54   Where section 81 of the Housing Act 1996 applies, a landlord may not exercise a right of re-entry or forfeiture by virtue of subsection (1)(a) until after the end of the period of 14 days beginning with the day after that on which

---

74   The modern Housing Act 1996, s 81 is the result of amendments made by the Commonhold and Leasehold Reform Act 2002, ss 167 and 170, which came into force on 28 February 2005 in England and 31 March 2005 in Wales.

75   'Dwelling' is defined in the Landlord and Tenant Act 1985, s 38 as meaning 'a building or part of a building occupied or intended to be occupied as a separate dwelling, together with any yard, garden, outhouses and appurtenances belonging to it or usually enjoyed with it.'

76   Landlord and Tenant Act 1954, Pt II applies to 'any tenancy where the property comprised in the tenancy is or includes premises which are occupied by the tenant and are so occupied for the purposes of a business carried on by him or for those and other purposes': s 23.

77   'Agricultural holding' is defined in s 1 as meaning 'the aggregate of the land (whether agricultural land or not) comprised in a contract of tenancy which is a contract for an agricultural tenancy, not being a contract under which the land is let to the tenant during his continuance in any office, appointment or employment held under the landlord.'

78   A 'farm business tenancy' is defined in the Agricultural Tenancies Act 1995, s 1 as meaning a tenancy which meets the business and agriculture conditions set out in that section and is not otherwise excluded by s 2.

79   Landlord and Tenant Act 1954, Pt II applies to 'any tenancy where the property comprised in the tenancy is or includes premises which are occupied by the tenant and are so occupied for the purposes of a business carried on by him or for those and other purposes': s 23.

the final determination is made.[80] This additional 14 days beyond the date of admission or final determination is easily overlooked. If proceedings are issued or peaceably re-entry is effected within this 14 day period, the forfeiture will be invalid.

45-55   A 'final determination' for the purposes of section 81 of the Housing Act 1996 occurs:[81]

(a)   if a decision that it is payable is not appealed against or otherwise challenged, at the end of the time for bringing an appeal or other challenge; or

(b)   if such a decision is appealed against or otherwise challenged and not set aside in consequence of the appeal or other challenge, at the time when the appeal or other challenge is disposed of by either –

   (i)   the determination of the appeal or other challenge and the expiry of the time for bringing a subsequent appeal (if any), or

   (ii)   by its being abandoned or otherwise ceasing to have effect.

45-56   The reference in section 81(1) of the Housing Act 1996 to 'the exercise of a right of re-entry or forfeiture include[s] the service of a notice under section 146(1) of the Law of Property Act 1925'. It follows that where service charge is not reserved as rent, the landlord may not even serve notice under section 146 of the Law of Property Act 1925 until the period to which section 81(1) of the Housing Act 1996 refers has expired.

45-57   Prior to the decision of the Court of Appeal in *Freeholders of 69 Marina, St Leonards-on-Sea v Oram*,[82] it was thought that the effect of section 81 of the Housing Act 1996, in cases where service charge is reserved as rent in the lease, was merely to prevent the landlord from issuing forfeiture proceedings or effecting peaceable re-entry[83] until the requirements of the section had been met. However, in *Freeholders of 69 Marina, St Leonards-on-Sea v Oram*, the Court of Appeal appeared to hold that a landlord must serve a section 146 notice, even if service charge is reserved as rent in the lease.[84] If this decision is right, then section 81 of the Housing Act 1996 operates in exactly the same way regardless of whether service charge is or is not reserved as rent.

45-58   Where section 81 of the Housing Act 1996 does apply, a landlord cannot escape the effect of the moratorium on forfeiture by waiting for the tenant to issue proceedings and claiming forfeiture by way of a counterclaim.[85]

---

80   Section 81(2).
81   Sections 81(3) and 81(3A).
82   [2011] EWCA Civ 1258.
83   Forfeiture by peaceable re-entry is not, in any event, now available where premises are let as a dwelling: Protection from Eviction Act 1977, s 2.
84   The decision on this point is open to criticism for the reasons set out at **45-39** above.
85   *Mohammadi v Anston Investments Ltd* [2004] HLR 8.

45-59   In *Mohammadi v Anston Investments Ltd*,[86] May LJ expressed a tentative view that the court ought to give effect to section 81, even where the tenant had not specifically pleaded this as a defence. This conclusion is, perhaps, not surprising. Section 81 imposes a complete embargo on the exercise of a landlord's right of re-entry until such time as the requirements of the section have been complied with. Accordingly, regardless of the nature of the tenant's pleaded case, it does not appear to be open to the court to make an order for possession whilst the section 81 embargo remains in place.

45-60   The absence of statutory guidance as to the meaning of 'determination' has led to difficulty. In particular, there is doubt as to whether judgment in default of a defence amounts to a determination for the purposes of section 81. The issue is an important one in the context of service charge, since it is by no means uncommon for tenants to fail to defend proceedings to recover service charge.

45-61   In *Southwark LBC v Tornaritis*,[87] HH Judge Cox held that a determination for the purposes of (the unamended) section 81 of the Housing Act 1996 included default judgment. By contrast, in *Hillbrow (Richmond) v Alogaily*,[88] HH Judge Rose declined to follow *Southwark LBC v Tornaritis* and held that a default judgment is not a final determination for the purposes of section 81 of the Housing Act 1996 (as amended). In reaching this view, HH Judge Rose was plainly influenced by the fact that a default judgment was a procedural process and did not involve any kind of analysis of, or adjudication upon, the merits of the claim.

45-62   This issue was again considered in *Church Commissioners for England v Koyale Enterprises*.[89] Having considered both of the decisions referred to above, HH Judge Dight held that a judgment in default was a determination for the purposes of section 81 of the Housing Act 1996, giving the following reasons for his conclusion:

(i)   There was nothing in the statutory background or the wording of section 81 which compels the court to reach the conclusion that a default judgment is not a determination for the purposes of the section.

(ii)   There is high authority[90] to the effect that a default judgment is binding on the parties and constitutes *res judicata* in respect of the matter directly decided.

(iii)   The buffer or breathing space which section 81 was enacted to provide is not defeated by construing a default judgment as a determination.

86   *Mohammadi v Anston Investments Ltd* [2004] HLR 8.
87   [1999] CLY 3744.
88   [2006] CLY 2707.
89   [2012] 21 EG 96.
90   In the form of the decisions of the Privy Council in *New Brunswick Railway Co v British and French Trust Corp Ltd* [1939] AC 1 and the Court of Appeal in *Pugh v Cantor Fitzgerald International* [2001] EWCA Civ 307.

(iv) It would be all but impossible to have a meaningful trial on the merits in circumstances where the tenant had failed to advance the case against the landlord.

(v) The alternative construction would involve the landlord in disproportionate delay and expenditure, even where the amounts in question where small and would correspondingly unnecessarily increase the burden on the court.

45-63 Although the decision in *Church Commissioners for England v Koyale Enterprises* is a County Court decision (and is not therefore binding), it is considered that the decision is correct and likely to be followed in future cases.

Failure to pay small amount or for the prescribed period: Section 167 of the Commonhold and Leasehold Reform Act 2002

45-64 Section 167 of the Commonhold and Leasehold Reform 2002 Act provides that a landlord under a long lease[91] of a dwelling[92] may not exercise a right of re-entry or forfeiture for failure by a tenant to pay an amount consisting of rent, service charges or administration charges[93] (or a combination of them) ('the unpaid amount') unless:

(a) the unpaid amount exceeds the prescribed sum (currently £350[94]); or

(b) the unpaid amount consists of or includes an amount which has been payable for more than a prescribed period (currently three years[95]).

---

91 By the Commonhold and Leasehold Reform Act 2002, s 166(7), a 'long lease' has the meaning given to it in ss 76 and 77 of that Act. Section 76 provides that a lease is a long lease if: (a) it is granted for a term of years certain exceeding 21 years, whether or not it is (or may become) terminable before the end of that term by notice given by or to the tenant, by re-entry or forfeiture or otherwise; (b) it is for a term fixed by law under a grant with a covenant or obligation for perpetual renewal (but is not a lease by subdemise from one which is not a long lease); (c) it takes effect under the Law of Property Act 1925, s 149(6) (leases terminable after a death or marriage or the formation of a civil partnership); (d) it was granted in pursuance of the right to buy conferred by the Housing Act 1985, Pt 5 or in pursuance of the right to acquire on rent to mortgage terms conferred by that Part of that Act; (e) it is a shared ownership lease (within the meaning of s 76(3)), whether granted in pursuance of that Part of that Act or otherwise, where the tenant's total share is 100%; or (f) it was granted in pursuance of that Part of that Act as it has effect by virtue of the Housing Act 1996, s 17 (the right to acquire).
92 By the Commonhold and Leasehold Reform Act 2002, s 166(7), a 'dwelling' has the same meaning as it does in the Landlord and Tenant Act 1985, s 38, namely 'a building or part of a building occupied or intended to be occupied as a separate dwelling, together with any yard, garden, outhouses and appurtenances belonging to it or usually enjoyed with it.'
93 As defined in the Commonhold and Leasehold Reform Act 2002, Sch 11, Pt 1.
94 Rights of Re-entry and Forfeiture (Prescribed Sum and Period) (England) Regulations 2004 (SI 2004/3086) and the Rights of Re-entry and Forfeiture (Prescribed Sum and Period) (Wales) Regulations 2005 (SI 2005/1352).
95 *Ibid.*

45-65   If the unpaid amount includes a default charge, it is to be treated for these purposes as reduced by the amount of the charge and, for this purpose, default charge means an administration charge payable in respect of the tenant's failure to pay any part of the unpaid amount.[96]

45-66   However, section 167 of the Commonhold and Leasehold Reform Act 2002 does not apply to:

(a)   a tenancy to which Part 2 of the Landlord and Tenant Act 1954 (business tenancies) applies;[97]

(b)   a tenancy of an agricultural holding within the meaning of the Agricultural Holdings Act 1986 in relation to which that Act applies;[98] or

(c)   a farm business tenancy within the meaning of the Agricultural Tenancies Act 1995.[99]

45-67   Section 167 of the Commonhold and Leasehold Reform Act 2002 is designed to prevent a landlord from forfeiting a residential lease for a relatively insignificant sum. However, in practice, it is unlikely to be worth the landlord's while issuing forfeiture proceedings for an amount which is less than £350.

No forfeiture without leave of the court where an enfranchisement claim has been made

45-68   Where the tenant has made a claim to acquire the freehold or an extended lease of the premises pursuant to the provisions of the Leasehold Reform Act 1967,[100] or a claim for collective enfranchisement under the Leasehold Reform, Housing and Urban Development Act 1993,[101] a landlord may not bring proceedings for possession of the premises without the leave of the court.

Section 16 of the Landlord and Tenant Act 1954

45-69   Where the provisions of Part 1 of the Landlord and Tenant Act 1954 apply to the lease,[102] then, unless service charge is reserved as rent, the court may

---

96   Commonhold and Leasehold Reform Act 2002, s 167(3).
97   Landlord and Tenant Act 1954, Pt II applies to 'any tenancy where the property comprised in the tenancy is or includes premises which are occupied by the tenant and are so occupied for the purposes of a business carried on by him or for those and other purposes' (s 23).
98   'Agricultural holding' is defined in s 1 as meaning 'the aggregate of the land (whether agricultural land or not) comprised in a contract of tenancy which is a contract for an agricultural tenancy, not being a contract under which the land is let to the tenant during his continuance in any office, appointment or employment held under the landlord.'
99   A 'farm business tenancy' is defined in the Agricultural Tenancies Act 1995, s 1 as meaning a tenancy which meets the business and agriculture conditions set out in that section and is not otherwise excluded by s 2 of that Act.
100   Leasehold Reform Act 1967, Sch 3, para 4(1).
101   Leasehold Reform, Housing and Urban Development Act 1993, Sch 3, para 7.
102   Landlord and Tenant Act 1954, s 2 (residential long tenancies at low rent).

not make an order for possession on the grounds of forfeiture at any time when there is less than seven months remaining before the expiry of the contractual term of the lease.[103]

Residential tenancies with security of tenure

45-70   Further restrictions on a landlord's right to forfeit apply where the lease or tenancy is protected by one of the residential statutory schemes. In particular:

1   Where the tenancy is a regulated or protected tenancy within the meaning of the Rent Act 1977, the contractual tenancy may be forfeited by means of court proceedings, but the landlord would then need to establish one of the statutory grounds to terminate the statutory tenancy which arises in its place.[104] Failure to pay service charge is amongst the discretionary grounds[105] on which the court can terminate a tenancy.

2   An assured tenancy within the meaning of the Housing Act 1988 cannot be terminated by forfeiture.[106] Instead, the landlord must serve notice under section 8 of the Housing Act 1988 and establish one of the statutory grounds for termination in Schedule 2 or, alternatively, serve notice under section 21 of the Housing Act 1988. Failure to pay service charge is amongst the discretionary grounds.[107] A tenancy will, however, only remain an assured tenancy for so long as the tenant is occupying the property as his only or principal home.[108] Accordingly, a tenancy which has ceased to be an assured tenancy will again be susceptible to forfeiture.

3   Where a fixed-term secured tenancy within the meaning of the Housing Act 1985 contains a proviso for re-entry, the court may make an order akin to forfeiture under section 82(3). However, the effect of doing so is to give rise to a periodic tenancy under section 86 of the Housing Act 1985. In order to actually obtain possession of a secure tenancy, a landlord must service notice under section 83 of the Housing Act 1985 and establish one of the grounds in Schedule 2. Failure to pay service charge is amongst the discretionary grounds on which the court can terminate a tenancy.[109] A tenancy will, however, only remain a secure tenancy for so long as the tenant is occupying the property as his only or principal home.[110] Accordingly, a tenancy which has ceased to be a secure tenancy will, again, be susceptible to forfeiture.

---

103   Landlord and Tenant Act 1954, s 16.
104   Rent Act 1977, s 2(1)(a).
105   Rent Act 1977, Sch 15.
106   *Artesian Residential Investments Ltd v Beck* [1999] 2 EGLR 30.
107   Grounds 10 and 11 (where service charge is reserved as rent) and Ground 12 otherwise.
108   Housing Act 1988, s 1(1)(a).
109   Schedule 2, Ground 1.
110   Housing Act 1985, ss 79–81.

Sections 166 and 168(1) of the Commonhold and Leasehold Reform Act 2002 do not apply to forfeiture for non-payment of service charge

45-71   Section 166 of the Commonhold and Leasehold Reform Act 2002 pro-vides that a tenant under a long lease of a dwelling is not liable to pay rent unless and until the landlord has served him with notice in accordance with the section. However, section 166(7) provides that 'rent' for the purposes of the section does not include service charge within the meaning of section 18 of the Landlord and Tenant Act 1985. Accordingly, irrespective of whether service charge is reserved as rent in the lease, the provisions of section 166 of the Commonhold and Lease-hold Reform Act 2002 do not apply to service charge.[111]

45-72   Section 168 of the Commonhold and Leasehold Reform Act 2002 pro-vides that a landlord may not serve a notice under section 146 of the Law of Property Act 1925 on a tenant under a long lease of a dwelling unless either:

(a)   the breach has been admitted by the tenant; or

(b)   determined in proceedings before the court, the LVT or an arbitrator and a further 14 days has elapsed.

45-73   However, section 169(7) expressly provides that nothing in section 168 affects the service of a notice under section 146 of the Law of Property Act 1925 in respect of a failure to pay service charge. It follows that, whilst a landlord must obtain a determination or an admission under section 81 of the Housing Act 1996[112] before serving a notice under section 146 of the Law of Property Act 1925, which alleges non-payment of service charge, it is not necessary for the landlord to additionally obtain a determination under section 168 of the Com-monhold and Leasehold Reform Act 2002.[113]

EXERCISE OF THE RIGHT TO FORFEIT

45-74   A landlord may exercise an accrued right to forfeit a lease by effecting peaceable re-entry or by obtaining an order from the court.

Peaceable re-entry

45-75   Although the most common means of effecting peaceable re-entry is for the landlord to enter the premises and change the locks, that is not the only means

---

111   This is because the definition of service charge in the Landlord and Tenant Act 1985, s 18 applies to all forms of service charge whether or not reserved as rent.
112   See **45-51**.
113   In *Glass v McCready* [2009] UKUT 136, the Upper Tribunal left open the question as to whether the court, LVT or an arbitrator would nevertheless have jurisdiction under the Commonhold and Leasehold Reform Act 2002, s 168 to make a determination that a tenant was in arrears of service charge if an application were made. HH Judge Huskinson, in any event, concluded that it would be open to the LVT to treat an application made under the Commonhold and Leasehold Reform Act 2002, s 168 as being an application under the Housing Act 1996, s 81 where the breach alleged is non-payment of service charge.

by which peaceable re-entry may be achieved. The constituent requirements of peaceable re-entry are as follows:

(i) the landlord must manifest an intention to forfeit[114] the lease by some positive act which is communicated to the tenant;[115] and

(ii) the landlord must subjectively hold an intention to forfeit at the time that the positive act is undertaken.[116]

45-76   Section 2 of the Protection from Eviction Act 1977 imposes a prohibition on peaceable re-entry in respect of premises let as a dwelling at a time when any person is lawfully residing at the premises or part of them. This prohibition extends to premises which are mixed residential/commercial premises.[117] In such cases, forfeiture must be effected by way of court proceedings. Even where peaceable re-entry is available, care must be exercised to ensure that an offence under section 6 of the Criminal Law Act 1977 is not committed in the process.[118]

Forfeiture by court proceedings

45-77   Forfeiture may also be effected by the issue and service[119] of proceedings in which possession of the grounds of forfeiture is claimed by the landlord – albeit that the landlord will not know whether the forfeiture has been effective until judgment is given by the court.

45-78   Where a landlord seeks to forfeit a residential lease, the Particulars of Claim must give the name of any person known to be entitled to relief and the landlord must file additional copies of the Claim Form and the Particulars of Claim to enable the court to serve the proceedings on any such party.[120] Failure to do so will provide grounds for setting aside any possession order obtained.

RELIEF FROM FORFEITURE

45-79   Even where the landlord has successfully forfeited the lease for non-payment of service charge (or is in the process of doing so), a tenant, subtenant or mortgagee may still apply for relief from forfeiture.

---

114 *Arnsby v Woodward* (1827) 6 B&C 519; *Roberts v Davey* (1833) 4 B&Ad 664; *Baylis v Le Gros* (1858) 4 CB (NS) 537.
115 *Jones v Carter* (1846) 15 M&W 718; *Canas Property Co Ltd v KL Television Services Ltd* [1970] 2 QB 433; *London & County (A&D) Ltd v Wilfred Sportsman Ltd* [1971] Ch 764.
116 Thus, if a tenant who is in arrears vacates and the landlord changes the locks to keep out trespassers, this will not amount to peaceable re-entry: *Relvok Properties v Dixon* (1972) 25 P&CR 1.
117 *Patel v Pirabakaran* [2006] 1 WLR 3112.
118 A criminal offence will be committed if violence is used in order to gain entry if there is some person physically present on the premises who is opposed to the entry.
119 Merely issuing the proceedings is not enough – they must be served on the tenant: *Canas Property Co Ltd v KL Television Services Ltd* [1970] 2 QB 433.
120 CPR Practice Direction 55A, para 2.4.

45-80   The nature and scope of the court's jurisdiction to grant relief from forfeiture will depend on whether or not a service charge is reserved as rent, whether the application for relief is made to the High Court or the County Court and whether the application for relief is made by an immediate tenant, a subtenant or a mortgagee. The five different forms of application for relief from forfeiture are discussed below.

Cases where service charge is reserved as rent – application for relief made by an immediate tenant in the High Court

45-81   Where service charge is reserved as rent, section 146 of the Law of Property Act 1925 does not apply.[121] In such cases, the court instead retains an equitable jurisdiction to grant relief from forfeiture, which has been recognised by statute in sections 210 to 212 of the Common Law Procedure Act 1852 and section 38(1) of the Senior Courts Act 1981.[122]

45-82   An application for relief from forfeiture must be made by the current tenant and, where there are joint tenants, by all of them.[123] The principles to be applied by the court in deciding whether to grant relief from forfeiture for non-payment of service charge (reserved as rent) are as follows:

1   It has been said that the landlord's proviso for re-entry is merely a security for the rent.[124] Accordingly, save in exceptional circumstances, relief from forfeiture will be granted as a matter of course if the tenant has or will, within a fixed time, discharge the arrears of rent[125] or service charges.[126] The fact that the tenant is insolvent by the time the application for relief is determined does not itself justify a departure from the general rule.[127] However, a landlord will not be permitted to profit from the forfeiture. Accordingly, where a landlord has received monies by reason of his being in possession of the premises in the period leading up to the hearing of the tenant's application for relief from forfeiture (e.g. from a new tenant), the tenant will be entitled to set those sums off against the sum which the tenant would otherwise have been required to pay as a condition of relief.[128]

2   Save where section 212 of the Common Law Procedure Act 1852 applies (see subparagraph 3 below), the general rule referred to in subparagraph 1

121 Law of Property Act 1925, s 146(11).
122 Senior Courts Act 1981, s 38(1) provides that: 'In any action in the High Court for the forfeiture of a lease for non-payment of rent, the court shall have power to grant relief against forfeiture in a summary manner, and may do so subject to the same terms and conditions as to the payment of rent, costs or otherwise as could have been imposed by it in such an action immediately before the commencement of the Act.'
123 *Gill v Lewis* [1956] 2 QB 1 at p 13.
124 *Wadman v Calcraft* (1804) 10 Ves 67; *Howard v Fanshawe* [1895] 2 Ch 581; *Inntrepreneur v Langton* [2000] 1 EGLR 34.
125 *Gill v Lewis* [1956] 2 QB 1 at p 13.
126 *Khar v Delmounty Ltd* (1998) 75 P&CR 232.
127 *Re Brompton Securities (No 2)* [1988] 3 All ER 677.
128 *Bland v Ingrams Estates Ltd (No 2)* [2002] Ch 177.

above is not an inflexible one. In exceptional circumstances, the court may consider other breaches and other circumstances when considering whether or not to grant relief. For example, in *Tryfonos v D Landau & Son*,[129] relief was refused in circumstances where one of the joint lessees was serving a prison sentence for arson, both lessees were insolvent, there were grave breaches of the covenant to repair and the landlords were well advanced in negotiations to dispose of the premises elsewhere. But genuinely exceptional circumstances will be required before the court will depart from the general rule. In *Gill v Lewis*,[130] relief from forfeiture was granted to a tenant notwithstanding that he had been convicted of having carried out two indecent assaults at the demised premises.

Where the tenant has delayed in making his application for relief from forfeiture and the grant of relief would prejudice the landlord or a third party who has acquired rights in the meantime, relief will be more readily refused.[131] In *Silverman v AFCO (UK)*,[132] relief was refused in circumstances where the landlord had reasonably and not precipitously re-let the property. By contrast, if the landlord re-lets in full knowledge of the tenant's relief application, this will almost certainly not result in relief being refused.[133] If the landlord himself has reasonably altered his position by other means, relief may be refused to a tenant who has delayed before making his application for relief.[134]

3   If rent is six months' in arrear and the tenant pays the arrears[135] and costs prior to the trial of the landlord's forfeiture proceedings, the tenant will automatically obtain relief (by means of a stay of the landlord's proceedings) under section 212 of the Common Law Procedure Act 1852. Even if there would otherwise have been exceptional circumstances, the court has no power to refuse relief.

4   An application for relief from forfeiture must be made promptly:

      (a)   Section 210 of the Common Law Procedure Act 1852 provides that where a landlord obtains an order for possession from the court in circumstances where rent is at least six months in arrear and there is no sufficient distress to be found at the demised premises, the tenant must make his application for relief from forfeiture within six months of the date on which the landlord executes the order for possession. The

---

129   (1961) 181 EG 405.
130   [1956] 2 QB 1.
131   The knowledge of the third party may also be a relevant consideration: see, for example, *Bank of Ireland Home Mortgages Ltd v South Lodge Developments* [1996] 1 EGLR 91 at p 94.
132   [1988] 1 EGLR 51.
133   *Lovelock v Margo* [1963] 2 QB 787.
134   In *Stanhope v Haworth* (1886) 3 TLR 34, relief was refused in circumstances where the landlord had expended considerable sums of money taking over the operation of the tenant's colliery. See also *Public Trustee v Westbrook* [1965] 3 All ER 398.
135   In *Thomas v Ken Thomas Ltd* [2006] EWCA 1504, Neuberger LJ expressed the view (*obiter*) that the arrears to which section 212 of the Common Law Procedure Act 1852 refers are limited to those arrears upon which the forfeiture was based and would not include arrears of rent in respect of which the right to forfeit has already been waived.

time limit is strict and if the tenant fails to make the application for relief in time, the court has no jurisdiction to grant relief. Section 210 of the Common Law Procedure Act 1852 is, however, merely a long-stop date by which the application for relief must be made. It does not follow that an application for relief made within the six-month period could not founder on the grounds of delay.[136]

(b)   In cases where section 210 of the Common Law Procedure Act 1852 does not apply, which is to say cases where there are less than six months' rent in arrear or where forfeiture is effected by peaceable re-entry, there is no strict time limit for applications for relief from forfeiture, but it is generally thought that the court will take the six-month time limit imposed by section 210 as a guide.[137]

45-83   The principles applied by the court when determining the terms on which relief from forfeiture on the grounds of non-payment of service charge (reserved as rent) are as follows:

1   The court will invariably require payment of the arrears to be paid within a time specified by the court (if they have not already been discharged by the time of the hearing) as a condition of granting relief from forfeiture. Any period fixed for payment of the arrears must be within the immediately foreseeable future so that the court can say with a sufficient degree of certainty that the arrears will be paid.[138] It will not necessarily be enough for the tenant to assert that he will discharge the arrears within a fixed time; where there are doubts about the tenant's financial strength, the tenant may need to adduce evidence to demonstrate his ability to pay.[139]

2   The tenant will also be required to pay any contractual or statutory interest payable on the arrears of rent.[140]

3   The tenant will ordinarily be required to pay the landlord's costs of the forfeiture action or peaceable re-entry,[141] as the case may be, and of the relief application, in addition to the arrears. Where costs are so ordered, they will be taxed on an indemnity basis.[142] The court will usually require the tenant to pay the landlord's costs, however, it retains a discretion to do otherwise. If the landlord has acted unreasonably in pursuing the forfeiture action or lost on certain issues, the court may deprive the landlord of some or all of his costs[143] and, in appropriate cases, the landlord may even be

---

136   *Gill v Lewis* [1956] 2 QB 1 at p 13.
137   *Thatcher v C H Pearce & Sons (Contractors) Ltd* [1968] 1 WLR 748.
138   *Inntrepreneur Pub Co (CPC) Ltd v Langton* [2000] 1 EGLR 34, *per* Arden J.
139   *Ibid.*
140   *Bland v Ingrams Estates Ltd (No 2)* [2002] Ch 177.
141   *Ibid.*
142   *Ibid.*
143   *Grangeside Properties Ltd v Collingwoods Securities Ltd* [1964] 1 WLR 139 (where the tenants were required to pay two thirds of the landlord's costs); *Segal Securities Ltd v Thoseby* [1963] 1 QB 887 (in which Sachs J held that, although the forfeiture action had succeeded, the landlord has acted unreasonably in pursuing it and made no order as to costs).

ordered to pay the tenant's costs.[144] In particular, where the landlord unsuc-
cessfully opposes the tenant's application for relief from forfeiture, he may
be required to pay the cost associated with that opposition.[145]

4   Where relief on payment of the arrears, interests and costs would not put the
landlord back into the position he would have been in absent the forfeiture,
the court may impose further terms. Thus, in *Soteri v Psylides*,[146] the Court
of Appeal held that it was appropriate to have regard to the fact that the
forfeiture had resulted in a loss of the landlord's right to implement a rent
review and ordered that relief from forfeiture be made conditional upon
the rent review being implemented retrospectively.[147] It is considered that
it would be open to the court to make payment of a service charge, which
would otherwise have fallen due between the date of forfeiture (whether by
the issue of proceedings or peaceable re-entry) and the hearing of the relief
application, a condition of relief being granted.[148]

45-84   Where relief is granted under section 212 of the Common Law Procedure Act 1852, the effect is to avoid the forfeiture altogether, with the result
that the lease and any subleases carved out of it continue without interruption.
Where relief is granted pursuant to section 38(1) of the Senior Courts Act 1981,
relief when granted is retrospective in effect.[149] Accordingly, the lease and any
sublease carved out of it are reinstated and the tenant will not be liable to pay
mesne profits in respect of the period between the date of the forfeiture and the
grant of relief.[150]

Cases where service charge is reserved as rent – application for relief made in the County Court

45-85   The County Court is a creature of statute and accordingly has no equitable or inherent jurisdiction to grant relief from forfeiture.[151] The County Court's

144 *House Property & Investment Co Ltd v James Walker Goldsmith & Silversmith Ltd* [1947] 2
All ER 789; *Belgravia Insurance Co Ltd v Meah* [1964] 1 QB 436; *Woodtrek v Jezek* (1982)
261 EG 571.
145 *Howard v Fanshawe* [1895] 2 Ch 581; *Abbey National Building Society v Maybeech Ltd*
[1985] Ch 190.
146 [1991] 1 EGLR 138.
147 *Soteri Psylides* was cited with approval in *Bland v Ingrams Estates Ltd (No 2)* [2002] Ch 177.
148 In practice, landlords often stop demanding payment of service charge once proceedings have
been issued or peaceable re-entry has been effected. This may present a problem for the landlord if, by the time relief is granted, it is too late for the landlord to demand and then recover
service charge for the relevant period. This would be the case where some or all of the service
charge in question has fallen foul of the 18-month bar in section 20B of the Landlord and
Tenant Act 1985 or where the lease makes time of the essence for making service charge
demands. It is considered that it would be open to the court to overcome any hardship to the
landlord by making payment of the service charge arrears which would otherwise have been
demanded a condition of relief.
149 *Dendy v Evans* [1910] 1 KB 263.
150 *Ibid.*
151 *Di Palma v Victoria Square Property Co* [1986] Ch 150.

power to grant relief from forfeiture for non-payment of rent (including non-payment of service charge reserved as rent[152]) is exhaustively conferred and regulated by sections 138 and 139 of the County Courts Act 1984.

45-86   Where the landlord seeks to forfeit the lease by means of court proceedings, rather than peaceable re-entry, the County Court's jurisdiction to grant relief is as follows:

1   If the tenant pays into court not less than five clear days before the return day of the landlord's forfeiture proceedings all the rent in arrear and the costs of the action, then the action ceases automatically under section 138(2) of the County Courts Act 1984 without the need for the tenant to be granted a new lease. There are two important restrictions on the application of section 138(2). First, the automatic cessation of the proceedings does not occur if the landlord is proceeding in the same action to enforce a right of re-entry or forfeiture on any other ground as well as non-payment of rent, or to enforce any other claim as well as the right of re-entry or forfeiture and the claim for arrears of rent.[153] Secondly, section 138(2) likewise does not apply where the arrears and costs are discharged by someone other than the tenant.[154] In *Thomas v Ken Thomas Ltd*,[155] Neuberger LJ expressed the view, albeit *obiter*, that 'all the rent in arrear' for the purposes of section 138 of the County Courts Act 1984 was limited to the arrears on which the forfeiture was based and, therefore, did not include arrears in respect of which the right to forfeit had been waived. The point is potentially one of real significance, given that the difference between the arrears on which the forfeiture is based and the total arrears may be substantial.

2   If the landlord's proceedings do not cease under section 138(2) of the County Courts Act 1984 and the court is satisfied at trial that the landlord is entitled to forfeit the lease, section 138(3) provides that the court shall order possession of the land to be given to the landlord at the expiration of such period, not being less than four weeks from the date of the order, as the court thinks fit, unless, within that period, the tenant pays into court or to the landlord all the rent in arrear[156] and the costs of the action. However, the court has power to extend the period specified under section 138(3) at any time prior to the date on which the landlord recovers possession of the land pursuant to an order made under that subsection.[157] The power to extend time may be exercised even where the period initially specified has expired or where the landlord has applied for a warrant of possession of the land.[158] If the tenant pays the arrears and costs within the period specified

---

152   *Escalus Properties Ltd v Robinson* [1995] 2 EGLR 23.
153   Section 138(6).
154   *Matthews v Dobbins* [1963] 1 WLR 227.
155   [2006] EWCA Civ 1504.
156   In this context, all rent in arrear will include the arrears at the date of the order rather than the date on which the forfeiture was effected: *Maryland Estates Ltd v Bar-Joseph* [1999] 1 WLR 83.
157   Section 138(4).
158   Section 138(9).

under section 138(3) (or any period of extension), the tenant will, thereafter, continue to occupy under the existing lease.[159]

3   If the tenant does not pay the arrears and costs within the period specified under section 138(3) (or any period of extension), the landlord may proceed to enforce the order for possession. However, even once the possession order has been enforced, the tenant may still apply for relief under section 138(9A) of the County Courts Act 1984 at any time up to six months after the date on which the landlord recovers possession and 'the court may, if it thinks fit, grant to the lessee such relief, subject to the terms and conditions, as it thinks fit'. There is no automatic entitlement to be granted relief from forfeiture on payment of arrears and costs under section 138(9A), relief is a matter of discretion for the court. The principles to be applied in the exercise of that discretion are the same as those set out at **45-82** above.

45-87   Where the landlord has forfeited the lease by means of peaceable re-entry, rather than court proceedings, the tenant may apply for relief within six months of the date of the landlord's re-entry.[160] If an application for relief is made, the County Court may grant the tenant such relief as could have been granted by the High Court.[161] Accordingly, the principles to be applied are those summarised at **45-82** and **45-83** above.

Cases where service charge is not reserved as rent – High Court and County Court

45-88   Where the service charge is not reserved as rent, the jurisdiction of both the High Court and the County Court to award relief from forfeiture to a tenant (subtenant's and mortgagees are dealt with separately at **45-101** to **45-122** below) is exclusively contained in section 146(2) of the Law of Property Act 1925.

45-89   Section 146(2) of the Law of Property Act 1925 provides that:

'Where a lessor is proceeding, by action or otherwise, to enforce a right of re-entry or forfeiture for breach of covenant or condition in a lease, the lessee may, in the lessor's action, if any, or in any action brought by himself, apply to the court for relief; and the court may grant or refuse relief, as the court, having regard to the proceedings and conduct of the parties, and to all the other circumstances, thinks fit, and in case of relief it may grant it on such terms, if any, as to costs, expenses, damages, compensation, penalty, or otherwise, including the granting of an injunction to restrain any like breach in the future, as the court, in the circumstances of each case, thinks fit.'

45-90   An application for relief from forfeiture under section 146(2) of the Law of Property Act 1925 may be made by the tenant or by a party with a specifically

---

159 Section 138(3).
160 Section 139(2).
161 Section 139(2).

enforceable agreement for lease.[162] Where there are joint tenants, all of them must join in the application for relief from forfeiture.[163]

45-91   An application for relief from forfeiture under section 146(2) of the Law of Property Act 1925 may be made at any time whilst the landlord 'is proceeding, by action or otherwise, to enforce a right of re-entry or forfeiture'. It follows that:

1   An application for relief may be made at any time after service of the land-lord's notice under section 146(1) of the Law of Property Act 1925 and may, therefore, be issued before the landlord has issued any forfeiture proceedings or effected physical re-entry.[164] A tenant would be entitled to apply for relief from forfeiture even after a possession order has been made, provided that it has not yet been enforced (see below).

2   Once the landlord has obtained an order for possession on the grounds of forfeiture and executed it, the tenant's right to apply for relief from forfeiture under section 146(2) of the Law of Property Act 1925 is lost and the court has no power to grant relief.[165] In such circumstances, the tenant's only recourse would be to apply to set aside[166] or appeal the possession order.[167]

45-92   However, the position is otherwise where the landlord recovers possession by peaceable re-entry, rather than court proceedings. A landlord who peaceably re-enters without a court order is still proceeding to enforce his right of re-entry and the jurisdiction to grant relief under section 146(2) of the Law of Property Act 1925 continues.[168] There is no long-stop date by which a tenant must make an application for relief under section 146(2) of the Law of Property Act 1925, following peaceable re-entry by the landlord, but it is considered that the court would be likely take the six-month time limit in section 210 of the Common Law Procedure Act 1852 (see **45-82**) as a guide when considering whether to refuse relief on the grounds of delay.

45-93   It has been said that section 146(2) of the Law of Property Act 1925 confers 'the widest discretion' on the court to grant relief[169] and the section itself requires the court to have regard to 'the proceedings and conduct of the parties, and to all the other circumstances'. It might, therefore, be thought that section 146(2) afforded greater scope for the court to look beyond the service charges arrears for which the landlord forfeited than would be the case if the service charge were reserved as rent (where payment of the arrears, interest and costs

---

162   Section 146(5); *High Street Investments Ltd v Bellshore Property Investments Ltd* (1997) 73 P&CR 143.
163   *Fairclough & Sons v Berliner* [1931] 1 Ch 60.
164   *Parkwood Transport v 15 Beauchamp Place* (1978) 36 P&CR 112.
165   *Billson v Residential Apartments Ltd* [1992] 2 AC 494.
166   Where the possession order was made, in the absence of the tenant, at a first hearing under CPR, r 55.8, the application to set aside should be made under CPR, r 3.1(2)(m) (rather than CPR, r 39.3): *Forcelux Ltd v Martin Ewan Binnie* [2009] EWCA Civ 854.
167   *Rexhaven v Nurse* (1996) 28 HLR 241.
168   *Billson v Residential Apartments Ltd* [1992] 2 AC 494.
169   *Chapman Empire Theatre v Ultrans* [1961] 1 WLR 817.

will almost always result in relief being granted – see **45-82** above). However, in
Khar v Delmounty Ltd,[170] the Court of Appeal held that the principles to be applied
under section 146(2) of the Law of Property Act 1925 are not materially different
to those applicable in cases of non-payment of rent. In that case, the tenants had
applied for relief and had paid the full amount of the service charge arrears on
which the forfeiture had been based into their solicitors' account in readiness for
payment to the landlord. The judge at first instance held that, although it would
undoubtedly have been appropriate to grant relief had the service charge been
reserved as rent, the jurisdiction under section 146(2) of the Law of Property Act
1925 called for a broader balancing exercise and he held that, having regard to
the tenants history of poor payment and the intervention of a third party interest,
relief should be refused. The Court of Appeal allowed the tenants' appeal and
Lord Woolf MR said as follows:

> '[the judge] exercised that discretion by reference to a list of specific factors set out
> in Woodfall on Landlord & Tenant Volume 1 Paragraph 17.166. The editors cite
> Shiloh Spinners v. Harding and other authorities. All the matters relied on by the
> judge, such as wilful breach, the conduct of the parties, delay, relative hardship,
> third party rights, are relevant, but, in his evaluation of the specific factors,
> the judge contrasted breach of the covenant to pay rent with breaches of other
> covenants in such a way as to obscure the substantial similarity between a covenant
> to pay rent and a covenant to pay a maintenance charge: they are both covenants
> to pay money, secured by the right of forfeiture. In the case of such covenants, the
> proper approach is, in general, to grant relief on terms that the sums due are paid.
> If payment is made, the forfeiture provision has served its purpose, the essentials
> of the bargain have been secured and it is fair and just to prevent the landlord from
> exercising his legal right to forfeit the lease. The discretion in section 146(2) affects
> different kinds of covenant. An important factor in the exercise of the discretion
> is the nature of the covenant broken. Not all covenants are of the same nature or,
> if breached, have the same consequences. The purpose of the forfeiture provision
> in relation to the maintenance charge and to the ground rent, is to reinforce the
> obligation to pay and to ensure that the landlord receives payment of the sum due
> and not to obtain a benefit (*e.g.* the residue of the term of the lease worth a six
> figure sum), unreasonably disproportionate to the damage suffered by the landlord
> as a result of the failure to pay the sum.
>
> In our judgment, it is not correct in this context to contrast in this way the rent
> cases with cases of breaches of other covenants. If the breach of a covenant, other
> than payment of rent, relates to non payment of a periodic liquidated sum, such as
> a maintenance charge, considerations affecting relief in a case of non payment of
> rent are applicable.'

45-94   Accordingly, the principles to be applied when determining whether to
accede to an application for relief from forfeiture for non-payment of service
charges which are not reserved as rent are those summarised at **45-82** above.

45-95   In other contexts, it has been held that relief may be granted on terms
that do not require the breach in question to be remedied immediately or even

170 (1998) 75 P&CR 232.

at all.[171] However, having regard to the dicta of the Court of Appeal in *Khar v Delmounty Ltd*,[172] it is considered that the tenant will be required to discharge the service charge arrears and any accrued contractual or statutory interest as a condition of relief. These requirements are discussed in greater detail at **45-83** above.

45-96 The tenant will also be required to pay the landlord's costs. The land-lord has a statutory right in section 146(3) of the Law of Property Act 1925 to recover 'all reasonable costs and expenses properly incurred by the [landlord] in the employment of a solicitor and surveyor or valuer, or otherwise, in refer-ence to any breach giving rise to a right of re-entry or forfeiture which, at the request of the [tenant], is waived by the [landlord], or from which the [tenant] is relieved'. The costs of preparation and service of a section 146 notice are not recoverable under section 146(3), because those costs arise, not from the breach, but from the requirement in section 146(1) to serve notice.[173] It might, therefore, be arguable that costs incurred by the landlord in obtaining a determination under section 81 of the Housing Act 1996[174] prior to service of a section 146 notice would likewise be outside the scope of the jurisdiction under section 146(3) of the Law of Property Act 1925.

45-97 However, the court will ordinarily make payment of the landlord's costs of the forfeiture a condition of relief.[175] The court is entitled to and usually does include both the costs associated with the preparation and service of a section 146 notice and those incurred in obtaining a determination under section 81 of the Housing Act 1996 as part of the overall costs payable by the tenant as a condi-tion of relief. Despite the criticism expressed in *Billson v Residential Apartments Ltd*,[176] there is authority for such costs to be ordered on an indemnity basis.[177] In *Patel v K&J Restaurants Ltd*,[178] Lloyd LJ considered the various authorities and expressed the view that there is a 'general principle' that an applicant for relief from forfeiture should pay the landlord's costs on the indemnity basis.[179]

45-98 Although the conditions of relief will usually be limited to a require-ment that the tenant pay the arrears, interest and the landlord's costs, the court has a discretion to impose further conditions. Thus, in *Soteri v Psylides*,[180] the Court of Appeal held that it was appropriate to have regard to the fact that the

---

171 *Westminster (Duke) v Swinton* [1948] 1 KB 524; *Associated British Ports v C H Bailey Plc* [1990] 2 AC 703.
172 (1998) 75 P&CR 232.
173 *Skinners' Co v Knight* [1891] 2 QB 542, a case concerning the equivalent provisions in the Conveyancing and Law of Property Act 1881, s 14.
174 See **45-51** above.
175 *Quilter v Mapleson* (1882) 9 QBD 672; *Egerton v Jones* [1939] 2 KB 702; *Factors (Sundries) Ltd v Miller* [1952] 2 All ER 630.
176 [1992] 1 AC 494, *per* Lord Templeman at p 541.
177 *Bland v Ingrams Estates Ltd (No 2)* [2002] Ch 177; *Forcelux Ltd v Binnie* [2009] EWCA Civ 1077.
178 [2011] L&TR 1211.
179 At para 104.
180 [1991] 1 EGLR 138.

forfeiture had resulted in a loss of the landlord's right to implement a rent review and ordered that relief from forfeiture be made conditional upon the rent review being implemented retrospectively. In *Khar v Delmounty Ltd*,[181] the Court of Appeal had regard to the following facts:

(i)   the tenants had a long history of failing to pay service charges;

(ii) the landlord had had to issue numerous sets of proceedings to recover arrears; and

(iii) the tenants lived abroad and were embroiled in a matrimonial dispute which meant that they were unable to agree joint instructions in relation to the flat.

45-99   Accordingly, the Court of Appeal ordered that relief from forfeiture be granted on terms that the tenants' lease be sold (after the expiry of a short tenancy which the landlord had granted to a third party in the interim) and that the net proceeds of sale, following payment of the arrears to the landlord, be paid to the tenants.

45-100   When relief is granted to the tenant under section 146(2) of the Law of Property Act 1925, whether forfeiture was effected by peaceable re-entry or court proceedings, the effect of granting relief is to restore the tenant's lease as if it had never been forfeited[182] and any derivative interests (e.g. a sublease or mortgage) are restored.[183] The tenant will not, therefore, be liable to pay mesne profits[184] in respect of the period between the forfeiture and the grant of relief.[185]

Cases where the party applying for relief is a subtenant

45-101   Subject to two exceptions,[186] forfeiture of a lease will result in the destruction of any subleases which have been carved out of it.[187] A subtenant will, therefore, need to apply for relief from forfeiture to preserve his continuing interest in the premises.

45-102   The law in relation to relief from forfeiture granted to a subtenant is undeniably complex. There is a multiplicity of materially different jurisdictions under which relief may be granted to a subtenant and the same facts will not

---

181   (1998) 75 P&CR 232.
182   *Dendy v Evans* [1910] 1 KB 263; *Meadows v Clerical, Medical and General Life Assurance Society* [1980] 1 All ER 454; *Liverpool Properties Ltd v Oldbridge Investments Ltd* (1985) 276 EG 1352 and *Ivory Gate Ltd v Spetale* [1998] 2 EGLR 43.
183   *Dendy v Evans* [1910] 1 KB 263.
184   Mesne profits are calculated by reference to the market rent for the premises. This may be greatly in excess of the passing rent under the lease, especially in the case of long residential leases which reserve only a ground rent or peppercorn rent.
185   *Escalus Properties Ltd v Robinson* [1996] 2 QB 321.
186   If a subtenancy is lawful at the time of forfeiture, protected and statutory tenancies under the Rent Act 1977, s 137 and assured tenancies under the Housing Act 1988, s 18 survive the forfeiture of the head lease.
187   *Great Wester Railway v Smith* (1876) 2 Ch D 235.

necessarily lead to the same outcome under each. Moreover, the nature of the relief granted will, again, depend on the jurisdiction under which it is granted.

45-103 Where service charge is reserved as rent in the lease and the application for relief is made in the High Court, the position is as follows:

1   A subtenant may apply for relief under section 212 of the Common Law Procedural Act 1852 if the requirements of section 210 of that Act are satisfied (see **45-82** above). If a subtenant complies with the requirements of section 212 of the Common Law Procedure Act 1852, the forfeiture proceedings brought by the landlord against the intermediate landlord are stayed with the result that both the head lease and the sublease are preserved. It follows that the subtenant will, thereafter, continue to occupy under the terms of his existing sublease.

2   Where forfeiture was effected by proceedings rather than peaceable re-entry, a subtenant may apply for relief under section 38(1) of the Senior Courts Act 1981, which applies to subtenants by virtue of section 38(2).[188] Where relief was granted under the court's equitable jurisdiction (prior to the enactment of section 38(1) of the Senior Courts Act 1981), relief took the form of restoration of the head lease in the head lease tenant which, in turn, restored the sublease in the subtenant.[189] However, it is considered that the wording of section 38(2) of the Senior Courts Act 1981 indicates that the effect of the grant of relief is to vest the land in the subtenant on the terms of the head lease.[190] Accordingly, from and after the grant of relief under section 38(1) of the Senior Courts Act 1981, the subtenant will occupy under the terms of the head lease, rather than the terms of the former sublease.

3   Where forfeiture was effected by peaceable re-entry (with the result that the provisions of section 38(1) of the Senior Courts Act 1981 do not apply), a subtenant may apply for relief under the court's inherent jurisdiction. The effect of relief is to reinstate the head lease and, with it, the sublease.[191]

4   A subtenant may also apply for relief under section 146(4) of the Law of Property Act 1925 provided that the landlord has not already executed an order for possession (see **45-91** above). Section 146(4) expressly provides that relief is available to a subtenant of part only of the premises demised by the head lease. If relief is granted under section 146(4) of the Law of Property Act 1925, the subtenant will thereafter occupy as the forfeiting landlord's immediate tenant under the terms of a new lease vested in him by the court (the terms of which will not necessarily be identical to either those contained in the head lease or the original sublease).

45-104 Where service charge is reserved as rent and the application for relief is made in the County Court, the position is as follows:

---

188   *Escalus Properties Ltd v Robinson* [1996] QB 231.
189   *Dendy v Evans* [1910] 1 KB 263.
190   See also *Escalus Properties Ltd v Robinson* [1996] QB 231 at p 246.
191   *Escalus Properties Ltd v Robinson* [1996] QB 231 at p 251.

1   A subtenant may obtain relief from forfeiture under sections 138(2) and (5) of the County Courts Act 1984 (see **45-86** above).[192] The effect of relief granted under section 138(2) of the County Courts Act 1984 is to put a stop to the landlord's forfeiture proceedings with the result that both the head lease and the sublease are preserved. It would appear that the grant of relief to a subtenant under section 138(2) of the County Courts Act 1984 has the effect of restoring both the head lease and the sublease derived out of it.[193]

2   Additionally, a subtenant may, at any time up to six months after the date on which the landlord recovers possession of the premises, apply for relief under section 138(9C) of the County Court's Act 1984. Section 138(9C) provides that an application for relief 'may be made by a person with an interest under a lease of the land derived (whether immediately or otherwise) from the lessee's interest therein in like manner as if he were the lessee; and on any such application the court may make an order which (subject to such terms and conditions as the court thinks fit) vests the land in such a person, as lessee of the lessor, for the remainder of the term of the lease under which he has any such interest as aforesaid, or for any lesser term.' It follows that from and after the grant of relief, the subtenant will occupy under the terms of a new lease vested in him by the court as the forfeiting landlord's immediate tenant.

3   If the landlord forfeited by peaceable re-entry, rather than court proceedings, a subtenant may apply for relief up to six months after the date of the landlord's re-entry. If an application for relief is made, the County Court may grant the tenant such relief as could have been granted by the High Court[194] and sections 138(9B) and (9C) of the County Courts Act 1984 apply.[195] Accordingly, from and after the grant of relief, the subtenant will occupy under the terms of a new lease vested in the court as the forfeiting landlord's immediate tenant.

4   A subtenant may also apply for relief under section 146(4) of the Law of Property Act 1925 provided that the landlord has not already executed an order for possession (see **45-91** above).

45-105 Where service charge is *not* reserved as rent, irrespective of whether the application for relief is made in the High Court or the County Court, the position is as follows:

1   A subtenant can apply for relief under section 146(4) of the Law of Property Act 1925 (see **45-103**, subparagraph 4 above).

2   Following the decision of the Court of Appeal in *Escalus Properties Ltd v Robinson*,[196] it is now open to a subtenant to apply for relief under section

---

192 County Courts Act 1984, s 140; *United Dominions Trust v Shellpoint Trustees Ltd* [1993] 25 HLR 503.
193 *United Dominions Trust v Shellpoint Trustees Ltd* [1993] 25 HLR 503 at p 508.
194 Section 139(2).
195 Section 139(3).
196 [1996] QB 231.

146(2) of the Law of Property Act 1925.[197] It is clear less clear whether a sub-tenant of part only of the premises demised by the head lease can likewise apply for relief under section 146(2) of the Law of Property Act 1925.[198] It is considered that it is also unclear whether relief granted to a subtenant under section 146(2) of the Law of Property Act 1925 is by means of –

(a) an order restoring the head lease to the head tenant (which correspondingly restores the sublease to the subtenant[199]); or

(b) an order vesting the head lease directly in the hands of the subtenant (this point is considered further at **45-116** below).

45-106 In any case, where the subtenant seeks relief on terms which result in the reinstatement of the head lease in the head tenant (as opposed to the vesting of a lease in the subtenant himself), a subtenant must either bring the head tenant[200] to the hearing of the relief application or be able to show good cause for not doing so.[201] This is because the reinstatement of the head lease in the head lease tenant will mean that the latter is once again subject to the obligations arising under it.

45-107 A subtenant who qualifies under sections 212 of the Common Law Procedure Act 1852 or the provisions of section 138(2) and (5) of the County Courts Act 1984, should undoubtedly avail himself of the opportunity to obtain automatic, rather than merely discretionary, relief. These provisions are respectively discussed at **45-82** and **45-86** above.

45-108 Where service charge is reserved as rent and the subtenant applies under the court's inherent jurisdiction, relief is within the discretion of the court, but

197 In *Escalus Properties Ltd v Robinson* [1996] QB 231 it was held that a mortgagee by sub-demise was a lessee for the purposes of the Law of Property Act 1925, s 146(2) because the definition of 'lessee' in the Law of Property Act 1925, s 146(5)(b) includes 'an original or derivative under-lessee, and persons deriving title under the lessees'. A subtenant must likewise be entitled to apply for relief under s 146(2).

198 As a matter of language, the definition of 'lessee' in s 146(5)(b) appears to be broad enough to embrace a subtenant of part. In *GMS Syndicate Ltd v Gary Elliott Ltd* [1982] Ch 1, the court granted relief from forfeiture to an immediate tenant in respect of part only of the demised premises, albeit it that the form of relief granted was predicated upon a finding that there had been forfeiture in relation to part only of the demised premises. In support of the alternative view, it is notable that, whereas the Law of Property Act 1925, s 146(4) contains express words extending the jurisdiction to include a subtenant of part, there are no equivalent words in s 146(2) and the difference in the wording of the two subsections might be said to suggest that s 146(2) only applies to subtenants of the whole. It is also notable that in *Burt v Gray* [1891] 2 QB 98, it was held that the Conveyancing Act 1881, s 14(3), which contains a similar definition of 'lessee' to that contained in the Law of Property Act, s 146(5)(b), did not extend to a subtenant of part.

199 *Dendy v Evans* [1910] 1 KB 263.

200 In the case of leases to which the provisions of the Landlord and Tenant (Covenants) Act 1995 do not apply (i.e. those granted before 1 January 1996), the subtenant should bring both the original tenant and the current tenant because, as is explained at **45-103**, subparagraph 2 above, the restoration of the head lease will result in both being once again liable on the covenants in the lease. Where the provisions of the Landlord and Tenant (Covenants) Act 1995 do apply (i.e. leases granted after 1 January 1996), only the current tenant need be brought to court.

201 *Hare v Elms* [1893 1 QB 604.

absent exceptional circumstances, payment of the arrears, interest and costs will generally result in relief being granted to the subtenant (see **45-83** above).

45-109 In *Belgravia Insurance Co Ltd v Meah*,[202] it was held by the Court of Appeal that, in cases of non-payment of rent, an application by a subtenant or mortgagee for relief under section 146(4) of the Law of Property Act 1925 falls to determined by reference to the same principles as would apply if the application were being made under section 38(1) of the Senior Courts Act 1981.[203] Accordingly, absent exceptional circumstances, relief will be granted as a matter of course if the subtenant pays the arrears, interest and costs.[204]

45-110 However, as the Court of Appeal was at pains to point out in *Belgravia Insurance Co Ltd v Meah*,[205] different principles apply where the breach in question is otherwise than non-payment of rent.[206] Where service charge is not reserved as rent, it falls to be considered by reference to the principles applicable to all other breaches of covenant. In contrast to the general approach in cases of non-payment of rent, relief under section 146(4) of the Law of Property Act 1925 is not granted as a matter of course where the subtenant has or is willing to remedy the breach. The decided cases make clear that relief under section 146(4) of the Law of Property Act 1925 is to be exercised sparingly because it involves forcing the landlord into a direct contractual relationship with a person whom the landlord has never accepted as his tenant.[207] In considering whether or not to grant relief, the court will consider the conduct of the subtenant,[208] the likely consequences of granting relief[209] and will assess the proportionality between the hardship to the landlord if relief is given and the hardship to the tenant if relief is refused.[210] Applying these principles, an application for relief might fail even where the subtenant was willing and able to pay the service charge arrears, interest and costs.

45-111 It is not easy to see any reason of policy why a subtenant who applies for relief from forfeiture based on non-payment of service charge which is reserved as rent should be in a materially better position than a subtenant who applies

---

202 [1964] Ch 436.
203 The equitable jurisdiction was, at that time, contained in and preserved by the Judicature Act 1925, s 46.
204 However, where the subtenant is a subtenant of part only of the premises demised by the head lease, the subtenant may only be required to pay an apportioned part of the arrears: *Chapman Empire Theatre (1955) Ltd v Ultrans Ltd* [1961] 1 WLR 817.
205 [1964] Ch 436.
206 *Ibid.* at p 433.
207 *Creery v Summersell* [1949] Ch 751; *Fivecourts Ltd v J R Leisure Development Co Ltd* [2001] L&TR 47; *Duarte v Mount Cook* [2001] 33 EG 87.
208 *Hurt v Whaley* [1918] 1 KB 448 (whether the subtenant is himself in breach of the sublease); *Imray Oakshette* [1897] 2 QB 218 (whether the subtenant had properly investigated the landlord's title).
209 *Gray v Bonsall* [1904] 1 KB 601 (whether the subtenant is willing to remedy any breaches of the head lease); *Creery v Summersell* [1949] Ch 751 (whether the subtenant is willing to accept and will be able to perform the obligations in the head lease); *Factors (Sundries) Ltd v Miller* [1952] 2 All ER 360 (whether the subtenant will acquire any security of tenure at the expiry of the sublease).
210 *Duarte v Mount Cook* [2001] 33 EG 87.

for relief from forfeiture based on non-payment of service charge which is not reserved as rent. Although not yet tested in the courts, it would seem arguable that, by analogy with the approaches taken in *Khar v Delmounty Ltd*[211] and *Belgravia Insurance Co Ltd v Meah*,[212] the approach should be the same in all service charge cases (irrespective of whether service charge happens to be reserved as rent) so that, absent exceptional circumstances, relief should be granted on payment of the arrears, interest and costs.

45-112 Where the court does grant relief under section 146(4) of the Law of Property Act 1925, it does by means of an order vesting a new lease in the applicant. The court has a wide discretion as to the terms of the new lease but the following principles can be derived from the decided cases:

1   The terms of the new lease will usually be no less onerous than those imposed under the former head lease.[213]

2   If the head lease reserved a rent which is higher than the sublease, a subtenant may be required to pay the higher of the two.[214] However, the mere fact that market values have increased since the grant of the sublease will not ordinarily justify an increase in the rent payable under the new lease.[215]

3   The court may restrict relief to part only of the premises originally demised.[216]

4   However, the court may not vest a new lease under section 146(4) of the 1925 Act which has a longer contractual term than the head lease.[217]

45-113 One important difference between relief granted under section 146(4) of the Law of Property Act 1925 and relief granted under section 146(2) of the Law of Property Act, or under one of the jurisdictions available to the High Court, is that relief is not retrospective and takes effect only from the date of the order. There are a number of important consequences of this:

1   A landlord will be entitled to remain in possession of the premises between the date of peaceable re-entry and the determination of the relief application and will be entitled to retain any money derived from the premises during this period.[218]

2   If the landlord has forfeited by court proceedings rather than peaceable re-entry, the subtenant will be liable for *mesne profits* between the date of the proceedings and the date of the order. This may be a matter of real impor-

---

211   (1998) 75 P&CR 232, discussed at **45-93** above.
212   [1964] Ch 436.
213   *Gray v Bonsall* [1904] 1 KB 601; *Creery v Summersell* [1949] Ch 751.
214   *Cholmeley's School Highgate v Sewell* [1894] 2 QB 906.
215   *Ibid.*
216   *Gray v Bonsall* [1904] 1 KB 601.
217   *Fryer v Ewart* [1902] AC 187.
218   *Official Custodian for Charities v Mackey* [1985] Ch 168. The position is different where relief is granted retrospectively. In such cases, the court will be astute to ensure that the landlord does not profit from the forfeiture: *Bland v Ingrams Estates Ltd (No 2)* [2002] Ch 177.

tance because *mesne profits* will be calculated by reference to the market rent of the premises, rather than the passing rent[219] under the sublease.[220]

45-114 Another important difference is that, whereas the grant relief under section 146(2) of the Law of Property Act 1925 automatically revives all derivative interests,[221] when relief is granted under section 146(4) of the Law of Property Act 1925, the grant of the new lease does not revive the interest of persons who had previously derived their title from the applicant.[222]

45-115 If relief is granted under section 146(4) of the Law of Property Act 1925, the subtenant will also be required to pay the landlord's costs of the forfeiture as a condition of relief. The requirements in relation to costs are discussed at **45-83**, subparagraph 4 above.

45-116 For the reasons set out above, a subtenant has no guarantee that relief will be granted under section 146(4) of the Law of Property Act 1925. This fact, together with the fact that the terms of any new lease which is granted may well be less favourable than those previously enjoyed under the sublease, a subtenant may find it preferable to apply for relief under section 146(2) of the Law of Property Act 1925. However, it is considered that the nature of the relief which the court may grant to a subtenant under section 146(2) of the Law of Property Act 1925 is presently unclear. In *Escalus Properties Ltd v Robinson*,[223] the Court of Appeal held that a subtenant and mortgagee by subdemise are within the definition of lessee in section 146(5)(b) of the Law of Property Act 1925, and are, therefore, each entitled to apply for relief under section 146(2) of the Law of Property Act 1925, the Court of Appeal did not, however, clarify the form of relief which would be granted. Relief, when granted to either a subtenant or mortgagee by subdemise could take the form of:

(a)   an order restoring the head lease to the head tenant (which correspondingly restores the sublease to the subtenant[224]); or

(b)   an order vesting the head lease directly in the hands of the subtenant.

45-117 If relief takes the form of subparagraph (a) above, both subtenant and any mortgagee would avoid having to enter into any direct contractual relationship with the landlord. Moreover, this would mean that the subtenant or mortgagee would be in a stronger position when applying for relief under section 146(2) of the Law of Property Act 1925 than they would when applying under section 146(4), because the argument that a landlord should not be forced into a contractual relationship with a stranger would not apply (see **45-110** above). The potential disadvantage of this form of relief is that it involves reinstating the head lease in the head lease

---

219   The passing rent will often be substantially lower than the market rent, especially in residential long leases which tend to reserve a ground rent or peppercorn rent only.
220   *Escalus Properties Ltd v Robinson* [1996] 2 QB 321.
221   *Dendy v Evans* [1910] 1 KB 263.
222   *Hammersmith & Fulham LBC v Top Shops Centres Ltd* [1990] Ch 237.
223   [1996] 2 QB 321.
224   *Dendy v Evans* [1910] 1 KB 263.

tenant who, by definition, has already defaulted on his obligations under the head lease and who may well do so again in the future. This presents less of a problem from the point of view of a mortgagee because, following the grant of relief, the latter will be able to exercise the mortgagee's remedies[225] to ensure that the obligations under the head lease are properly performed. By contrast, a subtenant who merely obtains an order restoring the head lease will have to assume the risk that the head tenant will again default in the future.

45-118 It is considered that it is arguable that the jurisdiction under section 146(2) of the Law of Property Act 1925 is broad enough to enable the court to grant relief on terms that the head lease be directly vested in the subtenant or mortgagee, as the case may be. In the case of a subtenant, for the reasons set out in the previous paragraph, relief on such terms would provide a more long-term solution for both the forfeiting landlord and the subtenant. It is, however, considered that it would be a matter for the court's discretion as to whether relief should take the form of restoration of the head lease in the head lease tenant or alternatively a vesting of the head lease in the subtenant or mortgagee.

45-119 Similarly, if the subtenant applies for relief under both section 146(2) and (4) of the Law of Property Act 1925, the court has a discretion as to which jurisdiction should be exercised.[226]

45-120 Where service charge is reserved as rent and an application for relief is brought by a subtenant under section 138(9C) or 139(2) of the County Court Act 1984, the court:

> 'may make an order which (subject to such terms and conditions as the court thinks fit) vests the land in such a person, as lessee of the lessor, for the remainder of the term of the lease under which he has any such interest as aforesaid, or for any lesser term.'

45-121 The jurisdiction under section 138(9C) of the County Courts Act 1984 enables the court to make a vesting order in favour of the subtenant. Although there is very little judicial guidance on the nature and extent of this jurisdiction, the terms of the new lease appear to be matters which are in the court's discretion. It would, therefore, seem likely that the court would be guided by the authorities on the terms of a new lease granted under section 146(4) of the Law of Property Act 1925 (see **45-112** above).

Cases where the party applying for relief is a mortgagee

45-122 Subject to two exceptions,[227] forfeiture of a lease will result in the destruction of any interests which have been carved out of it, including a mort-

---

225 For example, possession, sale and appointment of a receiver.
226 *Escalus Properties Ltd v Robinson* [1996] 2 QB 321.
227 If a subtenancy is lawful at the time of forfeiture, protected and statutory tenancies under the Rent Act 1977, s 137 and assured tenancies under the Housing Act 1988, s 18 survive the forfeiture of the head lease.

gage.[228] Accordingly, provision is made in section 146 of the Law of Property Act 1925 for a mortgagee to apply for relief from forfeiture so as to preserve its security.

45-123 A mortgagee by subdemise, a mortgagee by way of legal charge[229] and an equitable mortgagee who has the right to call for the execution of a legal charge[230] are all in the same position as a subtenant as regards relief. The jurisdiction to grant relief and the applicable principles are, therefore, the same as set out at **45-101** to **45-122** above.

45-124 A mortgagee's right to relief under section 146(4) of the Law of Property Act is unaffected by the disclaimer of the lease by the tenant's trustee in bankruptcy.[231]

45-125 Where relief is granted by means of the vesting of a new lease in the mortgage,[232] the new lease is subject to the mortgage by way of substituted security and is, accordingly, subject to the mortgagor's equity of redemption.[233]

45-126 It has been held that the holder of a charge under the Charging Orders Act 1979 has sufficient interest to obtain relief under section 138(9C) of the County Courts Act 1984.[234] By contrast, the holder of such a charge has no direct right to relief in the High Court, but has an equitable right to compel the defaulting tenant to seek relief for his benefit.[235]

No relief from forfeiture without court order

45-127 It has been held in the County Court,[236] it is considered correctly, that discretionary relief from forfeiture[237] may only be granted by the court and that it is not open to the parties to agree as between themselves that the tenant should have relief. If the landlord and the tenant wish to compromise forfeiture proceedings on terms that the latter is given relief, it is considered that the parties should jointly apply to the court for an appropriate order.

---

228 *Great Western Railway Co v Smith* (1876) 2 Ch D 235.
229 *Grand Junction Ltd v Bates* [1954] 2 QB 160. This is because a mortgagee by legal charge is entitled to the same protection powers and remedies as if a subterm, less by one day than the term vested in the mortgagor, had been created in its favour: Law of Property Act 1925, s 87(1).
230 *Re Good's Lease* [1954] 1 All ER 275.
231 *Barclays Bank v Prudential Assurance* [1998] 1 EGLR 44.
232 Under the Law of Property Act 1925, s 146(4) or under the County Courts Act 1984, s 138(9C).
233 *Chelsea Estates Investment Co Ltd v Marche* [1955] Ch 328.
234 *Croydon (Unique) Ltd v Wright* [2001] Ch 767.
235 *Bland v Ingrams Estates Ltd (No 2)* [2002] Ch 177.
236 *Zestcrest Ltd v County Hall Green Ventures* [2011] EGLR 9.
237 As opposed to automatic relief under the County Courts Act 1984, s 138(2) or (5) or the Common Law Procedure Act 1852, s 212.

CHAPTER 46

Miscellaneous landlord's remedies

DECLARATORY RELIEF

46-01   Where a tenant is in arrears of service charge, the landlord will most commonly issue proceedings claiming judgment on the arrears and/or forfeiture of the lease. However, it remains open to either party to the lease to claim declaratory relief from the court as to the extent of the tenant's service charge liability. The court's jurisdiction to grant declaratory relief is now to be found in rule 40.20 of the CPR.[1] Declaratory relief may be sought on its own or in addition to some other form of relief.

46-02   Declaratory relief is a discretionary remedy and not, therefore, available as of right. In determining whether to grant declaratory relief, the court will take into account justice to the claimant, justice to the defendant, whether the declaration would serve a useful purpose and whether there are any other special reasons why the court should or should not grant the declaration.[2]

46-03   In cases where there is a genuine and subsisting dispute between the landlord and the tenant as to whether the tenant is or would be liable to pay service charge in particular circumstances, it is likely that the court would be prepared to resolve that dispute by way of appropriate declaratory relief.

46-04   In the case of residential leases, declaratory relief may be sought under section 27A of the Landlord and Tenant Act 1985[3] or section 81 of the Housing Act 1996,[4] but the existence of these specific statutory jurisdictions does not preclude the court from granting declaratory relief pursuant to the general power under rule 40.20 of the CPR in an appropriate case.

---

1   CPR, r 40.20 simply provides: 'The court may make binding declarations whether or not any other remedy is claimed.'
2   *Financial Services Authority v Rourke* [2002] CP 14, *per* Neuberger J; see also *Wembley Stadium Ltd v Wembley (London) Ltd* [2007] EWHC 756 (Ch).
3   See Chapter 42 above.
4   See **45-51** above.

DEDUCTION FROM RENT DEPOSIT AND ACTION TO REQUIRE THE TENANT TO REPLENISH

46-05   It is common, particularly in commercial leases, for a deposit to be paid by the tenant to the landlord or management company (in tripartite leases) as security for the performance of the tenant's obligations under the lease. A deposit is sometimes paid even where the tenant has also provided a guarantor. The terms on which the deposit is held are sometimes set out in the lease itself or, alternatively, in a separate contract or deed.

46-06   It will be a question of construction of the relevant document whether, and in what circumstances, the landlord may have recourse to the deposit if the tenant fails to pay service charges. The terms of the deposit will often provide that, where a deduction is made by the landlord following a failure by the tenant to observe the tenant covenants in the lease, the tenant falls under a specific duty to replenish the amount of the deposit within a specified number of days after any deduction. In such circumstances, if the tenant then fails to replenish the deposit, the landlord may sue for specific performance of the obligation to do so. The terms of the deposit may also provide that breach of one of the obligations relating to the deposit will afford the landlord with a right to forfeit the lease.

46-07   In appropriate cases, a landlord may be able to have recourse to a deposit to discharge arrears of service charge, even where the tenant is insolvent.[5]

WITHHOLDING OF SERVICES

46-08   It is not uncommon for leases to provide that the landlord's obligation to provide services is subject to payment of the service charge by the tenant. It will be a question of construction in each case as to whether such a provision has the effect of making the tenant's obligation to pay a condition precedent to the performance of services by the landlord. It will not necessarily be the case that a landlord will be justified in withholding services where a tenant has not paid and a landlord may be putting itself at risk if it refused to perform its obligations because a tenant had not paid its service charge. This issue is discussed more fully at **2-15** and **2-16** above.

BANKRUPTCY/WINDING UP OF THE TENANT

46-09   Although a full treatment of the law of personal and corporate insolvency is beyond the scope of this book, it is right to note that where there are arrears of service charge in excess of £750,[6] those arrears may properly form the

---

5   *Obaray v Gateway (London) Ltd* [2001] L&TR 20.
6   £750 is the threshold amount for the purposes of both bankruptcy (Insolvency Act 1986, s 267(4)) and winding up of companies (Insolvency Act 1986, s 123(1)).

subject matter of a statutory demand served on an individual[7] or corporate tenant.[8] If, three weeks[9] after service of the statutory demand, the tenant has neither paid the arrears nor applied to set the statutory demand aside, the landlord will be able to present a bankruptcy petition[10] or winding up petition,[11] as the case may be.

46-10 The threat of bankruptcy or winding up is a means by which the landlord may apply pressure on the tenant to discharge the arrears. However, if the tenant is ultimately made bankrupt or wound up, the landlord will rank as an unsecured creditor in the bankruptcy or liquidation and is correspondingly not certain to recover the full amount of the arrears.

VARIATION OF THE LEASE UNDER PART IV OF THE LANDLORD AND TENANT ACT 1987 (LONG RESIDENTIAL LEASES ONLY)

46-11 Where difficulties arise in relation to the recoverability of service charges, not because of a failure by the tenant to comply with the service charge provisions in the lease, but because the lease itself contains inadequate or defective machinery, the problem may be overcome by means of an application to the LVT to vary the lease under section 35 or 37 of the Landlord and Tenant Act 1987. Applications under sections 35 and 37 of the Landlord and Tenant Act 1987 are discussed in Chapter 24 above.

---

7   Insolvency Act 1986, s 268.
8   Insolvency Act 1986, s 123(1).
9   The period is the same whether the tenant is an individual (Insolvency Act 1986, s 268(1)) or a
    company (Insolvency Act 1986, s 123(1)).
10 Insolvency Act 1986, s 267.
11 Insolvency Act 1986, ss 122 and 124.

CHAPTER 47

Tenants' remedies and defences

SET-OFF

47-01   A tenant may be entitled to raise the defence of set-off, whether by way of common law recoupment or equitable set-off, in answer to a landlord's claim for arrears of service charge. If the tenant's right of set-off is for an amount which is equal to or in excess of the landlord's claim for service charge, the tenant will avoid liability altogether. The principles applicable to common law recoupment and equitable set-off are discussed respectively at **40-46** and **40-49** above.

DECLARATORY RELIEF

47-02   Just as a landlord is entitled to seek declaratory relief from the court as to the extent of the tenant's service charge liability, a tenant may similarly obtain a declaration as to the extent, if any, of his liability for the arrears in question. The applicable principles are discussed at **46-01** to **46-09** above.

DETERMINATION FROM THE LVT UNDER SECTION 27A OF THE LANDLORD AND TENANT ACT 1985

47-03   Section 27A of the Landlord and Tenant Act 1985 confers jurisdiction on the LVT to determine the extent to which a service charge is, or would be, payable under a lease of a dwelling.[1] The jurisdiction is available to both landlord and tenant (whether intermediate or occupational).[2] A determination under section 27A may be sought merely for the purposes of resolving a dispute as to liability or as a precursor to the exercise of one of the substantive remedies discussed elsewhere in this chapter. The nature and extent of the jurisdiction under section 27A of the Landlord and Tenant Act 1985 is discussed in Chapter 42 above.

---

1   A 'dwelling' is defined in the Landlord and Tenant Act 1985, s 38 as 'a building or part of a building occupied or intended to be occupied as a separate dwelling together with any yard, garden, outhouses and appurtenances belonging to it or usually enjoyed with it'.
2   *Ruddy v Oakfern Properties Ltd* [2007] Ch 335.

REMEDIES AVAILABLE TO A TENANT WHO HAS OVERPAID SERVICE CHARGE

47-04   In this section, consideration is given to the remedies available to a tenant who has paid service charges to the landlord in excess of his contractual liability under the lease. An overpayment of service charge may occur for a variety of reasons and can be divided into the following categories:

Category 1: Payment of on account or interim service charge which exceeds the tenant's year-end liability.

Category 2: Overpayment because of some clerical or administrative error on the part of the tenant.

Category 3: Payment of the full amount demanded by the landlord in circumstances where some or all of the amount paid is not contractually due from the tenant (e.g. because it falls foul of an express or implied term of reasonableness,[3] is statute-barred,[4] or represents the costs of providing services for which the tenant is not liable to contribute under the lease). This category of overpayment may be broken down into a number of sub-categories:

    (i) Cases where the tenant is wholly ignorant that he is not liable to pay all or part of the sum demanded by the landlord at the time the payment is made.

    (ii) Cases where the tenant believes that he is not liable to pay the full amount, but pays on the understanding that, once a final determination has been made (e.g. by a court, the LVT or an arbitrator), any overpayment will be reimbursed to him.

    (iii) Cases where the tenant believes that he is not liable to pay the full amount, but pays in the belief that, once there has been a final determination (e.g. by a court, the LVT or an arbitrator), the landlord will be obliged to reimburse any overpayment. Here, there is no agreement with the landlord that reimbursement will take place (as in (ii) above), there is merely a subjective belief on the tenant's part that the landlord will be legally obliged to reimburse any overpayment once it has been finally determined.

    (iv) Cases where the tenant believes that he is not liable to make the payment, but decides to pay anyway in order to bring the dispute with the landlord to an end.

47-05   The tenant's remedies in respect of the above categories of overpayment are discussed below.

Reliance on express contractual provisions in the lease

47-06   The lease will often make express provision for what is to happen in the event that the budget or interim service charge exceeds the tenant's proportion of

---

3   Contractually implied terms of reasonableness are discussed at **2-97** to **2-121** above. Statutorily implied terms of reasonableness are discussed in Chapter 29.

4   See **40-51** above.

the landlord's actual costs (Category 1 overpayments). Leases generally provide that any excess is to be reimbursed to the tenant or, alternatively, to be applied by the landlord towards the tenant's liability for the following year to be credited to a reserve fund. The relevant provisions in the lease may be broad enough to encompass certain Category 3 overpayments as well.

47-07   Where the lease does contain contractual provisions which dictate how overpayments are to be treated, these will be determinative to the exclusion of the alternative remedies discussed below.[5]

Reliance on an express or implied agreement to reimburse arising at the time of payment

47-08   Where there is a dispute about the tenant's liability to pay the amount demanded by the landlord, the parties may expressly, or by their conduct, agree that payment will be made in full in the first instance, but on terms that, once a determination has been made by a court, LVT or in arbitration, as the case may be, any overpayment will be reimbursed to the tenant. A payment made pursuant to an agreement of this kind (Category 3(ii) above) may be recovered by the tenant pursuant to the agreement.[6] Thus, in *Nurdin & Peacock Plc v D B Ramsden & Co Ltd*,[7] the tenant was able to recover an overpayment of rent in circumstances where the payment had been expressed to be made by the tenant on terms that any overpayment would be repaid if the tenant later persuaded the court that it was not liable for the full amount and the payment was then accepted by the landlord without demur.[8]

47-09   However, whilst it is clear that an agreement to reimburse overpayments may be created by conduct, as well as express words, there must, nevertheless, be a clear, bi-lateral agreement to that effect. The mere fact that the tenant makes the payment whilst purporting to reserve his existing rights or makes it under cover of a letter labelled 'without prejudice' will not of itself be sufficient to give rise to an agreement to reimburse.[9]

Set-off against future rent and service charge

47-10   If there has been an overpayment of historic service charge, the tenant's claim for restitution of the overpayment (which is discussed further at **47-12** below) may be set off against the tenant's future liability, whether for payment of rent or service charge. In *Fuller v Happy Shopper Markets Ltd*,[10] it was held that

---

5   *Williams v Southwark LBC* (2001) 33 HLR 22.
6   *Woolwich Equitable Building Society v Inland Revenue Commissioners* [1993] AC 70, *per* Lord Goff at pp 165–166.
7   [1999] 1 WLR 1249.
8   [1999] 1 WLR 1249 at p 1267.
9   *Woolwich Equitable Building Society v Inland Revenue Commissioners* [1993] AC 70.
10 [2001] 1 WLR 1249.

there is a sufficient connection between the tenant's restitutionary cross claim and the landlord's claim for later rents to enable the tenant to exercise a right of equitable set-off and that there was no need for the tenant to have made a prior demand for restitution of the overpayment before doing so.

47-11   However, there are two important limitations on the tenant's right to set off overpayments against future liability for rent or service charge:

1   Set-off will not be available where there is a clear contractual provision excluding the tenant's right of set-off. Provisions which seek to exclude the tenant's right of set-off are discussed at **40-49** and **40-50** above.

2   A claim in restitution will only lie against the party to whom the overpayments were made. It follows that where the landlord to whom the overpayments have been made transfers the reversion, the tenant will not be able to set off historic overpayments against arrears of rent or service charge which accrue due after the assignment of the reversion. Similarly, where the landlord to whom the overpayments were made loses the right to recover later instalments of service charge in favour of a manager appointed under the Landlord and Tenant Act 1987 or an RTM company which has acquired the right to manage under the Commonhold and Leasehold Reform Act 2002,[11] the tenant will not be able to set off the overpayments against his future service charge liability. In such cases, the tenant would have to pursue the overpaid landlord separately.

3   Like any other equitable remedy, a right of set-off may be lost if the tenant is guilty of inequitable conduct.[12]

Restitution

47-12   Prior to the decision in *Kleinwort Benson Ltd v Lincoln CC*,[13] money paid under a mistake of law, as opposed to one of fact, was not recoverable by the paying party. Thus, in *IVS Enterprises Ltd v Chelsea Cloisters Management Ltd*,[14] overpayments of service charge due under a contract for the provision of satellite television services were found to be irrecoverable because the mistake was as to the underlying liability to pay which, on the law as it then stood, did not found a restitutionary claim. However, in *Kleinwort Benson Ltd v Lincoln CC*,[15] the House of Lords held that money paid under a mistake of law could be recovered in just the same way as money paid under a mistake of fact, by means of a claim for unjust enrichment. Their Lordships held that there were three essential ingredients to such a claim:[16]

1   The paying party must have been mistaken in some respect when he made the payment.

11 *Wilson v Lesley Place (Maidstone) RTM Co Ltd* [2010] UKUT 139.
12 *Televantos v McCulloch* (1991) 19 EG 18.
13 [1999] 2 AC 349.
14 [1994] EG 14 (CS).
15 [1999] 2 AC 349.
16 *Per* Lord Hope at p 407H.

2   The mistake must have caused the paying party to make the payment.

3   The payment must not have been due to the payee.

47-13   Applying the test in *Kleinwort Benson Ltd v Lincoln CC*[17] to the categories of service charge overpayment listed at **47-04** above, the position is as follows:

1   Category 1 and Category 3(ii) and (iv) overpayments do not qualify because the payments were not mistaken. Category 3(iii) overpayments would likewise fail the second limb of the test because the payments were made, not because of a mistake, but because the tenant had reached agreement with the landlord that any overpayments would be reimbursed.

2   Category 2 and Category 3(i) payments undoubtedly do satisfy the test and would be recoverable by the overpaying tenant.

3   It might have been thought that Category 3(iii) overpayments would not satisfy the test because the tenant was not mistaken about his liability to pay when the payment was made. However, in *Nurdin & Peacock v Ramsden*,[18] Neuberger J held that the relevant mistake need not be a mistake as to the underlying liability to pay and that a mistaken belief that the landlord would be obliged to reimburse the tenant if the latter's contentions about his liability were ultimately upheld at trial would, itself, be a mistake which would entitle the tenant to restitution of the overpayment. If the payment is made in circumstances where the tenant harbours doubts about his liability to pay, but is *not* operating under the misapprehension that the landlord will be obliged to reimburse him if the tenant is vindicated at trial, there is presently some uncertainty in the law as to the ability of the tenant to recover the overpayment.[19] However, if the tenant can show that he believed that it was more likely than not that he was liable to make the payment at the time it was made, it is likely that the tenant will be entitled to recover it.[20]

47-14   Restitution is not available where the lease expressly provides for what is to happen in the event of overpayment. Thus, where the lease contains an express

---

17 [1999] 2 AC 349.

18 [1999] 1 WLR 1249 at p 1272.

19 In *Kleinwort Benson Ltd v Lincoln CC* [1999] 2 AC 349 at p 410C, Lord Hope appeared to express doubt about whether a payment made by a party who is uncertain about his legal liability to pay may be recovered. However, in *Deutsche Morgan Grenfell Group v IRC* [2006] UKHL 49 at paras 64 and 65, Lord Hope clarified that a degree of doubt was not necessarily incompatible with mistake and stated that, provided that the paying party would not have made the payment had he been aware of the true legal position, the payment may still be recovered. Lord Hoffmann thought that such payments should always be regarded as payment made under a mistake and expressed the view that the question of recoverability should turn whether the paying party should be regarded as having undertaken the risk that he did not owe the money (paras 26 and 27). Lord Brown considered that, once the paying party reaches the stage where he realises that he has 'a worthwhile claim' that he should not have to pay, any mistake has been 'discovered' and the payment is not then recoverable as a payment made under a mistake (paras 165–176).

20 *Marine Trade SA v Pioneer Freight Futures Co Ltd BVI* [2009] EWHC 2656 (Comm), *per* Flaux J at paras 76 and 77.

provision that, if the interim service charge paid by the tenant exceeds his final or year-end service charge liability, the excess is to be credited against the tenant's service charge liability for the following year (i.e. Category 1 overpayments),[21] the tenant will not be able to recover the excess by means of a claim in restitution.[22]

47-15 Moreover, even where the test in *Kleinwort Benson Ltd v Lincoln CC* is satisfied such that the tenant is *prima facie* entitled to recover the overpayment, the claim may, nevertheless, be barred by one or more of the defences discussed below.

Innocent change of position

47-16 In *Lipkin Gorman v Karpnale Ltd*,[23] the House of Lords recognised a broad defence of 'innocent change of position'. The exact nature and parameters of this defence is the subject of some debate[24] and were, in any event, said to be likely to evolve on a case-by-case basis. However, it is clear that if A makes a payment to B under a mistake of fact or law[25] and then B, acting in good faith, pays the money or part of it over to a third party under a transaction which would not otherwise have taken place, B will be able to set up a defence of innocent change of position against any restitutionary claim which might later be brought against him by A. The defence of innocent change of position operates *pro tanto*. Accordingly, if B has been overpaid by £1,000 and then pays £500, in good faith, to a third party, A will still be entitled to recover £500 from B.

47-17 The decided cases provide the following refinements of the general principle:

1   Although there are a number of references in Lord Goff's speech in *Lipkin Gorman v Karpnale Ltd*[26] to the defence's role in avoiding 'inequity', it is clear that the defence falls to be applied by reference to the principles discussed below, rather than as an exercise of a general discretion.[27]

2   With the exception of cases where the defendant's change in position precedes receipt of the payment (see subparagraph 4 below), there is no need

---

21 The effect of contractual provisions of this kind is discussed at **47-06** above.
22 *Williams v Southwark LBC* (2001) 33 HLR 22.
23 [1991] 2 AC 548.
24 See Virgo, *The Principles of the Law of Restitution* (2nd edn, 2006), Ch 24, section 3; Burrows, *The Law of Restitution* (3rd edn, 2010), Ch 21, section 2; Goff and Jones, *The Law of Unjust Enrichment* (8th edn, 2010), Ch 27.
25 *Kleinwort Benson Ltd v Lincoln CC* [1999] 2 AC 349.
26 [1991] 2 AC 548 at p 582.
27 In *Lipkin Gorman v Karpnale Ltd* [1991] 2 AC 548 at p 578, Lord Goff made clear that the court does not have *carte blanche* to reject a claim in restitution 'simply because it thinks it is unfair or unjust in the circumstances to grant recover'. Similarly, in *Scottish Equitable Plc v Derby* [2001] EWCA Civ 369 at para 34, Robert Walker LJ warned that: 'The court must proceed on the basis of principle, not sympathy, in order that the defence of change of position should not ... disintegrate into a case by discretionary analysis of the individual facts, far removed from principle.'

for the change in the defendant's position to be in reliance upon receipt of the payment.[28]

3   However, although reliance is not necessary, the change in position must be causally linked to receipt of the payment. Accordingly, where the change of position consists of expenditure incurred by the defendant, the expenditure must be *extraordinary*.[29] In other words, the party seeking to set up the defence of innocent change of position must prove that, *but for* the relevant payment, the expenditure would not have been incurred.[30]

4   Payment of an existing debt will not generally be regarded as extraordinary expenditure since the receiving party would ultimately have had to repay the debt anyway.[31] However, the defence of innocent change of position is available to a defendant who changes his position in anticipation of receipt of the particular payment.[32]

5   The defence of innocent change of position is not available to a defendant who has acted in bad faith.[33] The latter will include dishonesty on the part of the recipient, but is 'also capable of embracing a failure to act in a commercially acceptable way and sharp practice of a kind that falls short of outright dishonesty'.[34] Accordingly, where the recipient knows that the payer has made a mistake, the defence of change of position cannot be maintained.[35]

6   Whether the defence of change of position is available to a recipient who ought to have known or discovered that the payment was made in error is a moot point. It has been held in a number of cases that bad faith does not extend to negligence on the part of the recipient.[36] However, in *Niru Battery Manufacturing Co v Milestone Trading Ltd (No 1)*, Moore-Bick J suggested that, where the recipient has grounds for believing that the payment was made in error and fails to make appropriate enquiries of the payer, the defence of change of position may not be available.[37]

---

28 In *Scottish Equitable Plc v Derby* [2001] EWCA Civ 369, Robert Walker LJ stated that a concession to that effect had been rightly made by counsel in the case.
29 *Dextra Bank & Trust Co Ltd v Bank* [2001] UKPC 50, *per* Lord Goff at para 38.
30 *Scottish Equitable Plc v Derby* [2001] EWCA Civ 369 at para 31.
31 *Ibid.*
32 *Dextra Bank & Trust Co Ltd v Bank* [2001] UKPC 50; *Commerzbank AG v Gareth Price-Jones* [2005] Lloyds Rep 298.
33 *Niru Battery Manufacturing Co v Milestone Trading Ltd (No 1)* [2002] EWHC 1425 (Comm); affirmed [2003] EWCA Civ 1446.
34 *Niru Battery Manufacturing Co v Milestone Trading Ltd (No 1)* [2002] EWHC 1425 (Comm) at para 135.
35 *Ibid.*
36 *Abou-Rahmah v Abacha* [2006] EWCA Civ 1492; *Dextra Bank & Trust Co Ltd v Bank* [2001] UKPC 50; *Niru Battery Manufacturing Co v Milestone Trading Ltd (No 1)* [2002] EWHC 1425 (Comm).
37 [2002] EWHC 1425 (Comm) at para 135. See also *Criterion Properties plc v Stratford UK Properties LLC* [2002] EWCA Civ 1883 and *Commerzbank AG v Gareth Price-Jones* [2005] Lloyds Rep 298 where the degree of fault on the part of the recipient was treated by the court as being a relevant factor in deciding whether the defence was available.

47-18   There is a surprising dearth of authority dealing with the availability of the defence of innocent change of position to a landlord who has been paid an amount by way of service charge that exceeds the tenant's liability. It is, however, apparent from the judgment of Neuberger J in *Nurdin & Peacock v Ramsden*[38] that there is no reason in principle why a landlord would not be entitled to set up the defence of innocent change of position in answer to a claim for restitution of the overpaid service charge.[39]

47-19   Applying the general principles summarised at **47-17** above, it is suggested that the question might be approached in this way:

1   Where the landlord has, in fact, expended the sum overpaid by tenant (e.g. by purchasing materials, paying insurance policies or paying the contractors' and other professionals' fees incurred by the landlord in the provision of the services required by the lease), this expenditure would, in principle, be capable of amounting to an innocent change of position by the landlord.

2   However, the landlord would need to demonstrate that the expenditure was 'extraordinary'. There must, therefore, be a sufficient connection between the landlord's receipt (or expectation of receipt) of the overpayment and the assumption by the landlord of a liability to pay the relevant third party. Given that the assumption of the liability to pay the third party occurs in performance of the landlord's duties under the lease, it will often be difficult for the landlord to establish the requisite causal link. The court will need to be persuaded that, if the tenant had not paid the full amount demanded by the landlord, the landlord would not simply have incurred the relevant liability anyway and, in due course, sued the tenant for any unpaid service charges. However, if the landlord can prove that, if the tenant had not paid the full amount, he would not have incurred the relevant liability at all or, alternatively, would have incurred a liability at a lower level (e.g. by providing a less expensive form of service), the expenditure incurred by the landlord in discharging that liability might constitute extraordinary expenditure for these purposes. It may, therefore, be that RTM companies, managers appointed under the Landlord and Tenant Act 1987 and other landlords who have no independent source of funds (e.g. enfranchisement companies[40]) will find it easier to establish

---

38   [1999] 1 WLR 1249 at p 1264. See also *R (on the application of Daejan Properties Ltd) v London Leasehold Valuation Tribunal* [2001] EWCA Civ 1095, where the Court of Appeal commented that a tenant's prospects of successfully obtaining restitution of excess service charge would be 'slender' (*per* Simon Brown LJ at para 11).

39   But see **47-20** below for a discussion of the effect of the Landlord and Tenant Act 1985, s 19(2) in relation to residential leases.

40   Where tenants exercise the right to collective enfranchisement under the Leasehold Reform, Housing and Urban Development Act 1993, Ch I, the freehold is generally transferred to a nominee purchaser company as a representative body for the tenants. This company will become the landlord for the purposes of the relevant flat leases, but, unlike most ordinary landlords, it will have no independent source of income and its ability to provide the landlord's services under the lease will, in most cases, be completely dependent on prompt payment of service charge by the tenants.

that the relevant expenditure was extraordinary than ordinary landlords with independent means.

3   The landlord will also need to establish that he did not act in bad faith in relation to the overpayment. Where the landlord subjectively knows that the tenant has paid more than the amount properly due under the lease, the landlord will undoubtedly fail the bad faith test.[41] If the landlord does not know for certain that the tenant has overpaid, but has grounds for suspecting that that is the case, then applying the dicta of Moore-Bick J in *Niru Battery Manufacturing Co v Milestone Trading Ltd (No 1)*,[42] the landlord is at risk of failing the bad faith test if the landlord does not then make enquiries of the tenant. Category 2 overpayments (clerical error at the time of payment) may well require the landlord to make enquiries of the tenant. The landlord might also fail the bad faith test if his conduct in relation to the payment is found by the court to be 'sharp' or commercially unacceptable.[43] If, for example, the landlord exerted pressure on the tenant[44] (e.g. by threatening forfeiture proceedings) to make the payment and was later unable to point to at least an arguable basis for contending that the tenant was liable to do so, it is considered that the landlord would be at risk of a finding of bad faith.

47-20   It has been suggested that the defence of innocent change of position is not available where the tenant's claim for restitution is brought under section 19(2) of the Landlord and Tenant Act 1985.[45] Section 19(2), which applies to leases of dwellings,[46] provides that:

'Where a service charge is payable before the relevant costs are incurred, no greater amount than is reasonable is so payable, *and after the relevant costs have been incurred any necessary adjustment shall be made by repayment, reduction or*[47] *subsequent charges or otherwise.*' (emphasis added)

47-21   The italicized words of section 19(2) of the Landlord and Tenant Act 1985 might be thought to afford the tenant with a specific statutory right to restitution of certain overpayments of service charge. If so, the question which then arises is whether the defence of innocent change of position is available to defeat such a claim.

47-22   It is considered that the obligation imposed by section 19(2) of the Landlord and Tenant Act 1985 does not extend beyond requiring the landlord to

---

41   *Niru Battery Manufacturing Co v Milestone Trading Ltd (No 1)* [2002] EWHC 1425 (Comm) at para 135.
42   [2002] EWHC 1425 (Comm) at para 135; see **47-17** above.
43   *Niru Battery Manufacturing Co v Milestone Trading Ltd (No 1)* [2002] EWHC 1425 (Comm) at para 135.
44   Where the tenant is a private residential tenant without ready access to legal advice, the tenant's case may be said to be stronger than where the tenant is a commercial tenant.
45   See 'Service charges, *Daejan* and claims in restitution', *Conveyancer and Property Lawyer* (2003).
46   Landlord and Tenant Act 1985, s 18(1).
47   It is considered that the word 'or' is a drafting error and should instead read 'of'.

make some form of appropriate adjustment in the event that the interim service charge paid by the tenant is in excess of his year-end service charge liability. Accordingly, the scope of the statutory right conferred by section 19(2) of the Landlord and Tenant Act 1985 appears to be limited to Category 1 overpayments. Moreover, it is clear that section 19(2) of the Landlord and Tenant 1985 Act does not necessarily entitle the tenant to restitution. The section expressly contemplates that the adjustment may, instead, be by way of a credit towards the tenant's service charge liability for the following year.[48]

Estoppel

47-23   The defence of estoppel is, in principle, available to a defendant to a restitutionary claim.[49] The constituent elements of the defence are as follows:

1   There must have been an express or implied representation by the claimant that the defendant was entitled to treat the money as his own. Sometimes a representation to that effect may be implied from the payment itself in the light of the surrounding circumstances.[50]

2   The defendant must have relied to his detriment on the claimant's representation. In appropriate circumstances, detrimental reliance may include paying the money away to a third party to whom the defendant is indebted.[51] However, the defendant will need to establish a sufficient causal connection between the claimant's representation and the defendant's detrimental reliance.[52]

3   The circumstances must be such that it would be unjust for the defendant to be made to give restitution of the money paid. It has been held that the defence of estoppel is not available where the claimant's mistaken payment has been primarily caused by the defendant's fault.[53]

47-24   In *Avon CC v Howlett*,[54] the Court of Appeal held that, unlike innocent change of position, the defence of estoppel does not generally operate *pro tanto*. Accordingly, if A pays B £1,000 and B then spends £500 of it in reliance upon A's representation that the money is B's to spend and retains the other £500, A would be estopped from recovering any of the money and B would obtain a windfall of £500. However, in *Avon CC v Howlett*, the Court of Appeal recognised that, exceptionally, the defence of estoppel might operate *pro tanto* where it would be unconscionable for the defendant to retain the balance of the money.[55]

---

48   The words 'or otherwise' in s 19(2) indicate that there may be still other means by which the landlord may make an appropriate adjustment.
49   *United Overseas Bank v Jiwani* [1976] 1 WLR 964.
50   *National Westminster Bank Plc v Somer International (UK) Ltd* [2001] EWCA Civ 970; *Holt v Markham* [1923] 1 KB 504.
51   *Deutsche Bank v Beriro & Co* (1895) 73 LT 669.
52   *United Overseas Bank v Jiwani* [1976] 1 WLR 964.
53   *Larner v London County Council* [1949] QB 683, *per* Denning LJ at p 689.
54   [1983] 1 WLR 605.
55   [1983] 1 WLR 605, *per* Slade LJ at p 624; *per* Eveleigh LJ at p 611.

This unconscionability exception has been applied in a number of subsequent cases where the defendant would otherwise have obtained a substantial windfall[56] and it has been suggested that, in practice, the unconscionability exception effectively swallows up the rule.[57]

47-25 Applying the above principles to the position of a landlord who has been paid an amount by way of service charge that exceeds the tenant's liability, it is suggested that the question might be approached in this way:

1   Although a question of fact in each case, payment of service charge (without protest) by the tenant may well amount to an implied representation that the landlord is entitled to treat the money as his own.

2   If the tenant has made the relevant representation and the landlord then expends the money (e.g. by purchasing materials, paying insurance policies or paying the contractors' and other professionals' fees incurred by the landlord in the provision of the services required by the lease), this would, in principle, be capable of amounting to detrimental reliance. However, the landlord will need to establish the necessary causal link between the representation and the detrimental reliance. Substantially, the same issues arise in relation to causation as those discussed at **47-19**, subparagraph 2 above in the context of innocent change in position.

3   The landlord will need to establish that the circumstances are such as to make it inequitable for the landlord to be required to give restitution of the overpayment. It is considered that the court has a greater element of discretion than it does in the context of an innocent change of position defence (which will generally only be refused if the landlord is guilty of bad faith). The court would be entitled to look at the conduct of both parties and to consider the relative fault. In particular, if the landlord is at fault for the overpayment (e.g. because the landlord has misconstrued the lease or failed to comply with contractual or statutory pre-conditions of recovery), the landlord may have difficulty in persuading the court that it would be inequitable for him to be required to give restitution of the overpayment. It is, therefore, considered that the landlord may find it more difficult to establish the defence of estoppel than innocent change of position.

Policy restrictions: Judgments, payments after legal process, compromise and submission to an honest claim

47-26 There are certain recognised situations in which, for reasons of policy, a restitutionary claim will not lie. It is perhaps open to question whether these situations should be properly regarded as defences to a restitutionary claim or whether they are limitations on the underlying right to restitution. However, in practice, a restitutionary claim will fail in the following circumstances.

---

56   *National Westminster Bank Plc v Somer International (UK) Ltd* [2001] EWCA Civ 970; *Scottish Equitable Plc v Derby* [2001] EWCA Civ 369.
57   See Burrows, *The Law of Restitution* (3rd edn, 2011) at p 557.

47-27   First, where money is paid pursuant to a court order or judgment, the payment cannot be recovered unless and until the order or judgment is successfully appealed or set aside.[58] Although there is no authority on this point, it is considered that this principle would likewise prevent a tenant from recovering a payment made following a determination made by the LVT under section 27A of the Landlord and Tenant Act 1985. Accordingly, even where a subsequent decision of a court or tribunal shows that an earlier decision was wrongly decided, it will not be open to the tenant who paid under the earlier judgment to recover the sum so paid, otherwise than impeaching the judgment itself.

47-28   Secondly, even if where the proceedings have not been finally determined by the court, a payment made after the payee has issued legal proceedings, acting in good faith, for the recovery of the sum paid will not be recoverable.[59] It follows that, where the tenant has made payment of service charge arrears after the landlord has issued proceedings claiming judgment on those arrears, the payment will be irrecoverable unless the tenant is able to demonstrate bad faith on the part of the landlord. The concept of bad faith is discussed at **47-19**, subparagraph 3 above in the context of the defence of innocent change of position.

47-29   Thirdly, where a payment is made as part of a contract of compromise, it will not generally be recoverable.[60] A contract of compromise may be express or implied from conduct. A contract of compromise may be reached both before and after the issue of proceedings.[61] But there must have been some form of dispute between the parties before a contract of compromise can be entered into. Accordingly, a payment made following a simple, but mistaken, demand does not of itself give rise to a contract of compromise (see *Baylis v Bishop of London*).[62]

47-30   Although the courts lean in favour of upholding compromises, a contract of compromise may itself be set aside on the grounds of a shared fundamental mistake,[63] including one of law,[64] as well on the grounds of fraud, duress, undue influence or bad faith.[65]

47-31   It follows from the principles set out above that the mere fact of payment of service charge arrears by the tenant is unlikely to be sufficient to found

58 *Marriot v Hampton* (1797) 7 TR 269.
59 *Hamlets v Richardson* (1833) 9 Bing 644; *Moore v Vestry of Fulham* [1895] 1 QB 399.
60 *Marriot v Hampton* (1797) 7 TR 269. Many payments made pursuant to a contract of compromise will, in any event, fall within Category 3(iv) overpayments (see **47-04** above) which, properly analysed, are not payments made under a mistake.
61 *Brisbane v Dacres* (1813) 5 Taunt 143 at p 160.
62 [1913] 1 Ch 127.
63 *Holmes v Payne* [1930] 2 KB 301.
64 *Brennan v Bolt Burdon* [2004] EWCA Civ 1017. However, although, in principle, a contract of compromise may be set aside on the grounds of a mutual mistake of law, a compromise was said to be 'a matter of give-and-take which ought not lightly to be set aside', *per* Maurice Kay LJ at para 23.
65 *The Universe Sentinel* [1983] AC 366.

a contract of compromise. However, where, for example, the tenant has disputed his liability to pay the service charge in correspondence with the landlord, there may be greater scope for the landlord to argue that the tenant's subsequent payment of all or part of those arrears formed part of an express or implied contract of compromise. If the service charge arrears have been paid under a contract of compromise, the tenant will face the comparatively onerous task of vitiating the contract of compromise on one of the grounds referred to at **47-30** above, if the payment is to be recovered.

47-32   Fourthly, there is at least some support in the authorities[66] for the proposition that money paid in submission to an honest claim is not recoverable. The notion of submission to an honest claim may be broad enough to embrace a payment made in circumstances where proceedings have not yet been issued and where there is no contract of compromise. However, the existence and scope of the concept of submission to an honest claim has been questioned by both the judiciary and academic commentators alike.[67] It is considered that cases in which the defence of submission to an honest claim has been applied are better analysed as examples of payments which were not, in fact, mistakenly made or, alternatively, as cases where restitution is barred under one or more of the policy based restrictions discussed above.

Limitation

47-33   After a period of some uncertainty, it is now clear that a claim for restitution on the grounds of unjust enrichment is subject to the ordinary six-year limitation period for actions on a simple contract in section 5 of the Limitation Act 1980.[68] As a general rule, time starts to run for the purposes of such a claim when the defendant receives the enrichment.[69]

47-34   However, section 32(1)(c) of the Limitation Act 1980 defers the commencement of the limitation period of an action for relief from the consequences of a mistake 'until the plaintiff has discovered the … mistake … or could with reasonable diligence have discovered it'. The provisions of section 32(1)(c) of the Limitation Act 1980, therefore, have the effect of ensuring that the limitation period for the purposes of a claim for restitution of overpaid service charge will not commence until the tenant discovers his mistake or, if earlier, the point at which the mistake could, with reasonable diligence, have been discovered by the tenant.

---

66 *Brisbane v Dacres* (1813) 5 Taunt 143; *Kelly v Solari* (1841) 9 M&W 54 at p 59.
67 *Kleinwort Benson Ltd v Lincoln CC* [1999] 2 AC 349 at pp 382, 385 and 413; *Brennan v Bolt Burdon* [2004] EWCA Civ 1017 at para 62. See also *Goff & Jones: The Law of Restitution* (7th edn, 2006) at para 1-70; Burrows, *The Law of Resitution* (3rd edn, 2011) at p 210.
68 *Re Diplock* [1948] 465; *Westdeutsche Landesbank Girozentrale v Islington LBC* [1994] 4 All ER 890.
69 *Kleinwort Benson v South Tyneside Metropolitan BC* [1994] 4 All ER 972 at p 978; see also *Fuller v Happy Shopper Markets Ltd* [2001] 1 WLR 1681.

47-35 Where an overpayment is made by reason of a clerical error on the part of the tenant (i.e. Category 2 overpayments), the grace period for the purposes of section 32(1)(c) of the Limitation Act 1980 is likely to be short. Where, however, the error stems from a misunderstanding of the terms of the lease or the law (i.e. Category 3(i) overpayments), comparatively subtle questions may arise as to when the tenant ought reasonably to have discovered the error.

47-36 It follows from the absence of any fixed long-stop date for commencement of the limitation period that, in appropriate cases, a claim for restitution of overpaid service charge may extend back to payments made considerably more than six years prior to the issue of proceedings. This presents obvious practical difficulties for the court and litigants alike, given that the evidence relating to such historic claims may no longer be available.[70]

Appropriate forum

47-37 It has been held by the Lands Tribunal in *Warrior Quay Management Co Ltd v Joachim*[71] that the LVT lacks jurisdiction to order a landlord to give restitution of overpaid service charge to the tenant, even if the lease itself makes provision for the landlord to do so. The appropriate forum for the determination of a tenant's claim for restitution of overpaid service charge is, therefore, in all cases the court.

Breach of trust

47-38 It is not uncommon for leases to contain an express provision that a reserve fund or service charges generally are held by the landlord or, alternatively, a management company on trust for the tenants, on terms which oblige the trustee to apply the funds towards the provision of the services required under the lease.

47-39 Where the lease is of a dwelling,[72] section 42 of the Landlord and Tenant Act 1987 provides that service charges are held by the landlord or other party to whom service charge is payable under the lease:

> '(a)   on trust to defray costs incurred in connection with the matters for which the relevant service charges were payable (whether incurred by himself or by any other person), and

---

70   See **29-19** above in relation to the burden of proof regarding disputes concerning dwellings under the Landlord and Tenant Act 1985, s 27A.

71   [2008] EWLands LRX_42_2006.

72   'Dwelling' is defined in section 60 of the Landlord and Tenant Act 1987 as meaning 'a building or part of a building occupied or intended to be occupied as a separate dwelling, together with any yard, garden, outhouses and appurtenances belonging to it or usually enjoyed with it'.

(b)   subject to that, on trust for the persons who are the contributing tenants for the time being, or the person who is the sole contributing tenant for the time being.'[73]

47-40   Where a service charge is held on an express or statutorily implied trust, it must be applied by the trustee for the proper purposes. Thus, in *Warwickshire Hamlets v Gedden*,[74] it was held that, on a true construction of the subject lease, rent due under a head lease of the common parts of a block of flats could not be passed on to the tenants of the flats through the service charge. It was held that the service charges which had been paid by the management company in satisfaction of the rent due under the common parts head lease had been applied in breach of the statutory trust imposed by section 42 of the Landlord and Tenant Act 1987 and was, therefore, recoverable from the management company personally as trustee.[75] It was also held that the provisions of section 21(1)(b) of the Limitation Act 1980[76] applied to such a claim, such that there was no applicable limitation period.

47-41   Where the tenant's complaint is that the landlord or the management company has used service charges for purposes beyond the scope of the services required by the lease, the claim may be brought as a claim for restitution on the grounds of unjust enrichment or for breach of trust, in the alternative. There may be some advantage to the tenant in pleading breach of trust because the defence of innocent change of position (discussed at **47-16** above) would not be available to the trustee in answer to a claim for breach of trust. The defence of estoppel would, in principle, be available to the landlord or management company, but it may prove difficult to make good in circumstances where the starting point for the claim is a breach by defendant of his duties as trustee.

47-42   It has been held that a trustee owes a limited duty of care in the management of the trust fund.[77] In addition, trustees owe a statutory duty of care under the Trustee Act 2000 in relation to certain aspects of the trusteeship, such as the power of investment of the trust fund.[78] The existence of this duty of care might, in an appropriate case, afford a tenant with a separate right of action against the landlord in negligence. However, a full consideration of this issue is beyond the scope of this work.

RELIEF FROM FORFEITURE

47-43   Where the landlord forfeits the lease for non-payment of service charge or is in the process of doing so, a tenant and/or any subtenant wishing to remain

73   Section 42(3). Section 42 is discussed in detail in Chapter 36 above.
74   [2010] UKUT 75 (LC).
75   *Per* HH Judge Huskinson at para 58.
76   Section 21(1)(b) provides that: 'No period of limitation prescribed by this Act shall apply to an action by a beneficiary under a trust, being an action ... (b) to recover from the trustee trust property or the proceeds of trust property in the possession of the trustee, or previously received by the trustee and converted to his use.'
77   *Bartlett v Barclays Bank Trust Co Ltd (Nos 1 and 2)* [1980] 2 WLR 430; [1980] Ch 515.
78   Trustee Act 2000, Sch 1, para 1.

in occupation of demised premises will need to apply for relief from forfeiture. Forfeiture is discussed at **45-01**ff. above. Relief from forfeiture is discussed at **45-79**ff. above.

REMEDIES IN RELATION TO INFORMATION, INSPECTION OF DOCUMENTS AND ASSISTANCE (RESIDENTIAL LEASES ONLY)

47-44   In the case of leases of dwellings,[79] a dispute about service charge may be resolved or clarified by the exercise by tenant or an RTA[80] of one or more the following rights:

1   A tenant or the secretary of an RTA may require the landlord to supply him with a written summary of service charge costs incurred during the relevant 12-month period pursuant to section 21 of the Landlord and Tenant Act 1985. Section 21 of the Landlord and Tenant Act is discussed at **33-08** above.

2   Where a summary under section 21 of the Landlord and Tenant Act 1985 has been obtained, the tenant or the secretary of the RTA may, within six months, require the landlord to afford them reasonable facilities for inspecting and taking copies or extracts of accounts, receipts or other documents supporting the summary pursuant to section 22 of the Landlord and Tenant Act 1985. Section 22 of the Landlord and Tenant Act 1985 is discussed at **33-20** above.

3   A tenant or the secretary of an RTA may require the landlord to supply a written summary of the insurance for the time being effected in relation to the dwelling pursuant to the Schedule, paragraph 2 to the Landlord and Tenant Act 1985 and to provide facilities to enable the insurance to be inspected and copies taken pursuant to the Schedule, paragraph 3 to the Landlord and Tenant Act 1985. These provisions are discussed at **33-39** above.

4   An RTA is entitled to appoint a surveyor under section 84 of the Housing Act 1996 to advise on any matters relating to, or which may give rise to, service charges payable to a landlord by one or more of the members of the association. Section 84 of the Housing Act 1996 is discussed at **33-14** above.

APPLICATION FOR VARIATION OF THE LEASE UNDER PART IV OF THE LANDLORD AND TENANT ACT 1987 (RESIDENTIAL LEASES ONLY)

47-45   As discussed in Chapter 24 above, where difficulties arise in relation to the recoverability of service charge, not because of any failure by the tenant

---

79 'Dwelling' is defined in the Landlord and Tenant Act 1987, s 60 as meaning 'a building or part of a building occupied or intended to be occupied as a separate dwelling, together with any yard, garden, outhouses and appurtenances belonging to it or usually enjoyed with it'.
80 As to which see **34-02** above.

to comply with the service charge provisions in the lease, but because the lease itself contains inadequate or defective machinery, the problem may be overcome by means of an application to the LVT to vary the lease under section 35 or 37 of the Landlord and Tenant Act 1987.

APPLICATION FOR THE APPOINTMENT OF A MANAGER OR RECEIVER

47-46   Where the landlord has historically charged or purported to charge excessive service charges, this may, in an appropriate case, afford the tenant with a right to apply for the appointment of a manager or receiver. Where the provisions of Part II of the Landlord and Tenant Act 1987 apply, an application for the appointment of a manager may be made by a tenant to the LVT. In any other case, an application may be made to the court by one or more of the landlord's tenants for the appointment of a receiver pursuant to section 37 of the Senior Court Act 1981.

Application for the appointment of a manager under Part II of the Landlord and Tenant Act 1987

47-47   An application to the LVT for the appointment of a manager under Part II of the Landlord and Tenant Act 1987 may be made if the following conditions are satisfied:

1   The applicant[81] must be a tenant[82] in a flat contained in premises to which to which Part II of the Landlord and Tenant Act 1987 applies.[83] Part II applies to premises consisting of the whole or part of a building if the building or part contains two or more flats[84] and is not within functional land of a charity.[85]

2   The applicant's tenancy must not be one to which the provisions of Part II of the Landlord and Tenant Act 1954 apply.[86]

---

81   An application may be made jointly by tenants of different flats, even where the flats are in different buildings: s 21(4).
82   Where the tenancy is held by joint tenants, any one or more of them is entitled to make the application: s 21(5).
83   Section 21(1).
84   The term 'flat' is defined in the Landlord and Tenant Act 1987, s 60(1) as meaning a separate set of premises, whether or not on the same floor, which: (i) forms part of a building, and (ii) is divided horizontally from some other part of a building, and is constructed or adapted for use for the purposes of a dwelling.
85   Section 21(3)(b). Functional land of a charity is land occupied by the charity or trustees for it and wholly or mainly used for charitable purpose: s 60(1). The Landlord and Tenant Act 1987, Pt II applies to Crown Land in exactly the same way as it applies to other land: Commonhold and Leasehold Reform Act 2002, s 172.
86   Section 21(7).

3   The applicant's landlord must be neither an exempt landlord[87] nor a resident landlord[88] for the purposes of the Part II of the Landlord and Tenant Act 1987.

The preliminary notice

47-48   Prior to making an application for the appointment of a manager, the tenant must serve a preliminary notice on the landlord and any person other than the landlord by whom obligations relating to the management of the building are owed.[89] The preliminary notice must:

(a)   specify the tenant's name, the address of his flat and an address in England and Wales (which may be the address of the flat) at which the landlord or other person may serve notices, including notices in proceedings on him;[90]

(b)   state that the tenant intends to make an application for an order under section 24 of the Landlord and Tenant Act 1987 in respect of such premises as are specified in the notice, but (if subparagraph (d) below is applicable) he will not do so if the landlord or other person complies with the requirement specified in pursuance of that subparagraph;

(c)   specify the grounds[91] on which the tribunal will be asked to make such an order and the matters[92] which will be relied on by the tenant for the purpose of establishing those grounds;

---

87 An exempt landlord is a landlord who is one of the bodies referred to in s 58(1), namely: a local authority or a joint authority, the Commission for New Towns or a development corporation, an urban development corporation, a housing action trust, the Housing Corporation, the Secretary of State for Wales, a charitable housing trust, a registered housing association or a fully mutual housing association and a joint waste disposal authority.

88 A landlord of any premises is a resident landlord of premises at any time if: (a) those premises are not and do not form part of, a purpose-built block of flats; (b) at that time the landlord occupies a flat contained in the premises as his only or principal residence; and (c) he has so occupied such a flat throughout a period of not less than 12 months ending with that time: s 58(2). A purpose-built block of flats is a building which contained, as constructed, and contains, two or more flats: s 58(3). The resident landlord exception does not apply where at least half the flats in the premises are held on relevant long leases: s 21(3A).

89 Section 22(1).

90 In *Tudor v M25 Group Ltd* [2004] 1 WLR 2319, a case concerning the validity of a notice served under the Landlord and Tenant Act 1987, Pt I, it was held that the requirement to specify the tenants' addresses was directory only and that failure to comply with that requirement did not invalidate the notice. It is considered that the same would apply to a notice served under the Landlord and Tenant Act 1987, s 22.

91 The grounds are those set out in the Landlord and Tenant Act 1987, s 24(2). The grounds are: (a) that the landlord is in breach of obligations owed to the tenants relating to the management of the premises and that it is just and convenient to make an order in all the circumstances of the case; (b) that unreasonable service charge demands have been made and that it is just and convenient to make an order in all the circumstances; and (c) failure to comply with a Code of Practice approved under the Leasehold Reform, Housing and Urban Development Act 1993, s 87 and it is just and convenient to make an order.

92 The 'matters' to which the Landlord and Tenant Act 1987, s 22(2) refers are the particulars. In the case of an application based upon unreasonable service charge, the notice should set out the particulars of the tenant's allegation that the landlord or, where applicable, management company has made or is likely to make unreasonable service charge demands.

(d)   where those matters are capable of being remedied by the landlord or other person, require him, within such reasonable period as may be specified in the notice, to take such steps for the purpose of remedying them as are so specified; and

(e)   contain such information (if any) as may be specified by the Secretary of State.[93]

47-49   The notice must be in writing and it may be sent by post.[94] The LVT may dispense with the requirement to serve a preliminary notice where it is satisfied that it would not be reasonably practicable to serve such a notice on the relevant person.[95] When giving dispensation, the tribunal may direct that such other notices be served or such other steps be taken as it thinks fit. Moreover, even where the tenant has served a defective preliminary notice, the LVT may still decide to make an order appointing a manager.[96]

47-50   Section 23 of the Landlord and Tenant Act 1987 imposes the following restrictions on the timing of an application under section 24:

(i)   Where the preliminary notice under section 22 of the Landlord and Tenant Act 1987 required the landlord or other person to remedy the matters complained of within a specified time, an application for the appointment of a manager may not be issued until after that period has expired.[97]

(ii)   Where the LVT dispensed with the need for service of a preliminary notice, but made directions for service of other notices or the taking of other steps, an application for the appointment of a manager may not be issued until such directions have been complied with.

47-51   In any other case, there are no restrictions on the timing of the application. Where an application under section 24 of the Landlord and Tenant Act 1987 is issued, the application must include a copy of the preliminary notice unless the requirement to serve a preliminary notice has been dispensed with under section 22(3).[98]

Grounds

47-52   The grounds on which the LVT may make an order appointing a manager are set out in section 24(2) of the Landlord and Tenant Act 1987. These grounds include cases where the tribunal is satisfied:

---

93   Section 22(2). No regulations have yet been made.
94   Section 54(1). Accordingly, the provisions in relation to service of notices in the Law of Property Act 1925, s 196 apply to notices served under the Landlord and Tenant Act 1987, s 22.
95   Section 22(3).
96   Section 24(7); *Howard v Midrome* [1991] 1 EGLR 58.
97   Section 23(1)(a).
98   Leasehold Valuations Tribunals (Procedure) (England) Regulations 2003 (SI 2003/2099) and Leasehold Valuation Tribunals (Procedure) (Wales) Regulations 2004 (SI 2004/681), Sch 2.

(i)   that unreasonable service charges[99] have been made, or are proposed or likely to be made; and

(ii) that it is just and convenient to make the order in all the circumstances of the case.[100]

47-53   For the purposes of this ground, a service charge shall be taken to be unreasonable if:

(i)   the amount is unreasonable having regard to the items for which it is payable;

(i)   the items for which it is payable are of an unnecessarily high standard; or

(ii) the items for which it is payable are of an insufficient standard, with the result that additional service charges are or may be incurred.[101]

47-54   The grounds in section 24(2) of the Landlord and Tenant Act 1987 also include cases where the LVT is satisfied:

(i)   that any relevant person[102] has failed to comply with any relevant provision of a code of management practice approved by the Secretary of State under section 87 of the Leasehold Reform, Housing and Development Act 1993; and

(ii) that it is just and convenient to make the order in all the circumstances of the case.[103]

47-55   For present purposes, the relevant code of management is the RICS Residential Code.[104] The latter contains detailed provision as to the manner in which service charges should be collected, treated and applied[105] and the tenant may, therefore, be able to rely on additional matters which would not separately qualify under the ground at section 24(2)(ab) under this ground.

47-56   The LVT may also make an order appointing a manager if it is satisfied that it is just and convenient to make the order in all the circumstances of the case.[106] However, in the context of an application based on unreasonable service

---

99   For the purposes of the Landlord and Tenant Act 1987, s 24, 'service charge' has the meaning attributed by the Landlord and Tenant Act 1985, s 18(1).
100   Section 24(2)(ab).
101   Section 24(2A).
102   'Relevant person' refers back to s 22(1) and, therefore, includes both the landlord and any person other than the landlord by whom obligations relating to the management of the building are owed.
103   Section 24(2)(ac).
104   The Approval of Code of Management Practice (Residential Management) (Service Charges) (England) Order 2009 (SI 2009/512). This second edition of the RICS Residential Code came into force on 6 April 2009. Where the matters of which complaint is made pre-date 6 April 2009, they fall to be considered by reference to the first edition of the code.
105   The principle provisions relating to service charge are to be found in the RICS Residential Code, Pts 4, 6–11 and 21.
106   Section 24(2)(b).

charge, it is considered that this residual discretion is unlikely to add greatly to the grounds referred to above.

47-57   By definition, the effect of an order made under section 24 of the Landlord and Tenant Act 1987 is to deprive the landlord of his legal and contractual right to manage property in his ownership. The making of such an order is, therefore, a serious step that will not be undertaken lightly by the LVT. It is considered that, even where the LVT is satisfied that one or more of the statutory grounds in section 24 of the Landlord and Tenant Act 1987 is made out, it is only where those grounds disclose comparatively serious mismanagement on the part of the landlord that the LVT should go on to exercise its residual discretion to order the appointment of a manager.

The order

47-58   The LVT has a wide discretion as to the terms on which any order under section 24 of the Landlord and Tenant Act 1987 may be made. In particular, the tribunal may make an order:

(a)   appointing a manager to carry out, in relation to any premises to which Part II of the Act applies, such functions in connection with the management of the premises or such functions of a receiver, or both, as the tribunal thinks fit.[107] 'Management' is expressly stated to include the repair, maintenance or insurance of the premises,[108] but implicitly the right to collect service charge from the tenant or tenants;

(b)   which is interlocutory or final in character;[109]

(c)   which is subject to conditions or suspended on terms fixed by the tribunal;[110]

(d)   which relates to premises which are either more or less extensive than the premises specified in the tenant's application;[111]

(e)   which relates not only to premises to which section 21 of the Landlord and Tenant Act 1987 refers, but also, in appropriate cases, to other adjoining land;[112]

(f)   which makes provision with respect to such matters relating to the exercise by the manager of his functions under the order, and such incidental or

---

107   Section 24(1).
108   Section 24(11).
109   Section 24(1).
110   Section 24(6).
111   Section 24(3).
112   In *Cawsand Fort Management Co Ltd v Stafford* [2008] 1 WLR 371, it was held by the Court of Appeal that, provided that there is a causal link or nexus between the functions to be carried out by the manager and the premises defined in section 21(1), the order may be expressed to relate to land beyond the building and its immediate curtilage. Accordingly, the LVT had been entitled to include certain recreational land over which the tenants enjoyed only easements as part of the premises in respect of which a manager was appointed.

ancillary matters, as the tribunal thinks fit.[113] In particular, provision may be made for –

(i)   rights and liabilities arising under contracts to which the manager is not a party to become rights and liabilities of the manager,

(ii)   the manager to be entitled to prosecute claims in respect of causes of action (whether contractual or tortious) accruing before or after the date of his appointment,

(iii) remuneration to be paid to the manager by any relevant person, or by the tenants of the premises in respect of which the order is made, or by all or any of those persons,[114]

(iv) the manager's functions to be exercisable by him either during a specified period or without limit of time.[115]

Position following the making of the order

47-59   A manager appointed under the Landlord and Tenant Act 1987 performs a statutory function and derives his powers from the order rather than the lease and a tenant may not set-off an accrued right of action against the landlord against a 1987 Act appointed manager's claim for service charge.[116]

47-60   The manager is entitled to apply to the LVT at any time for directions in relation to the performance of his duties.[117] Moreover, the tribunal may, on the application of any person interested, vary or discharge the order[118] and it may do so conditionally or unconditionally.[119] However, the tribunal should not vary or discharge an order unless it is satisfied that the variation or discharge will not result in a recurrence of the offending circumstances and that it is just and convenient to do so.[120]

Alternatives to an application for the appointment of a manager under the Landlord and Tenant Act 1987

47-61   The jurisdiction to appoint a manager under the Landlord and Tenant Act 1987 has, in large part, been overtaken by the enactment of the right to manage provisions in Part II of the Commonhold and Leasehold Reform Act

---

113   Section 24(4).
114   Where the proposed manager is a company controlled by the tenants, remuneration may be inappropriate: *Howard v Midrome* [1991] 1 EGLR 58. The LVT's jurisdiction to make provision for the remuneration of the manager does not depend on there being provision within the lease itself which would have enabled the landlord to recover the costs of a manager: *Maunder Taylor v Joshi* [2006] EWLands LRX_107_2005.
115   Section 24(5).
116   *Maunder Taylor v Blaquiere* [2003] 1 WLR 379.
117   Section 24(4).
118   This includes a suspended or conditional order.
119   Section 24(9).
120   Section 24(9A); *Orchard Court Residents' Association v St Anthony's Homes* [2003] 2 EGLR 28.

2002. The latter enables the requisite majority of tenants holding long leases of flats to acquire the right to manage their block without establishing fault on the part of the landlord (see **15-07**, subparagraph 2). For those tenants who meet the qualifying criteria, the exercise of the right to manage under the provisions of Part II of the Commonhold and Leasehold Reform Act 2002 represents a quicker, cheaper and more certain means of divesting an unsatisfactory landlord or management company (as the case may be) of the right to manage the premises.

47-62 It is also right to note that the same outcome could be achieved by acquiring the freehold of the premises under the Leasehold Reform Act 1967 (where the demised premises is a house) or under Chapter I of the Leasehold Reform, Housing and Urban Development Act 1993 (where the demised premises consists of a flat or flats), or by obtaining an acquisition order under Part III of the Landlord and Tenant Act 1987 – albeit that in each case the tenant(s) would incur the associated cost of acquiring the freehold. These jurisdictions are outside the scope of this book and reference should be made to specialist works.[121]

Application for the appointment of a receiver pursuant to section 37 of the Senior Courts Act 1981

47-63 Section 37 of the Senior Courts Act 1981 provides that the High Court may by order (whether interlocutory or final) appoint a receiver, on such terms and conditions as the court thinks fit, in all cases in which it appears to the court to be just and convenient to do so. The jurisdiction under section 37 of the Senior Courts Act 1981 is available in all cases, save where the tenant would qualify to make an application under Part II of the Landlord and Tenant Act 1987.[122]

47-64 The jurisdiction under section 37 of the Senior Courts Act 1981 is sufficiently widely drafted to enable the court to make an order appointing a receiver on the grounds that the landlord had previously charged or proposes to charge the tenant applicant excessive service charge. However, it is considered that it would only be in severe cases that historic overcharging would make it appropriate for the court to appoint a receiver under section 37 of the Senior Courts Act 1981. The court should not, in any event, exercise its jurisdiction to appoint a receiver of a class of property which Parliament has enacted should be managed by a specific body. Thus, in *Parker v Camden LBC*,[123] the court refused, as a matter of principle, to appoint a receiver where the property in question was owned and managed by a local authority pursuant to its obligations under section 111 of the Housing Act 1957.

47-65 The jurisdiction under section 37 of the Senior Courts Act 1981 would also be available in circumstances where the landlord is an absentee and has,

---

121 See *Hague on Leasehold Enfranchisement* (5th edn, 2009); *Woodfall: Landlord and Tenant*, Vol 4.
122 Landlord and Tenant Act 1987, s 21(6); *Stylli v Hamberton Properties* [2002] EWHC 394 (Ch).
123 *Parker v Camden LBC* [1986] Ch 162.

therefore, failed to collect any service charge and failed to perform the services required by the lease.[124]

47-66   The Court's jurisdiction under section 37 of the Senior Courts Act 1981 does not confer power to direct the landlord to remunerate any receiver appointed. Accordingly, a receiver is only likely to take office if the assets of which he is appointed receiver will be sufficient to meet his remuneration,[125] or he has an enforceable indemnity by a party to the litigation capable of meeting his remuneration.[126]

REMEDIES AVAILABLE TO A FORMER TENANT WHO DISCHARGES THE ARREARS OF AN ASSIGNEE

47-67   In this section, consideration is given to the remedies available to a former tenant who has been compelled to discharge arrears of service charge that accrued due after the former tenant had assigned the lease.[127] In such circumstances, a former tenant may bring an indemnity claim against an assignee of the lease and/or claim an overriding lease pursuant to section 19 of the Landlord and Tenant (Covenants) Act 1995.

Claim for an indemnity

47-68   In this context, it is necessary to distinguish between 'old' and 'new' leases for the purposes of the Landlord and Tenant (Covenants) Act 1995.[128]

Leases to which the provisions of the Landlord and Tenant (Covenants) Act 1995 do not apply

47-69   Where the lease was granted prior to 1 January 1996, such that the provisions of the Landlord and Tenant (Covenants) Act 1995 do *not* apply, a former tenant who has been compelled by the landlord to discharge arrears of service charge will be entitled to recover the sum paid out to the landlord from one of the assignees of the lease. The right to be indemnified by an assignee may arise in one of three ways.

47-70   First, the former tenant may be entitled to recover under an express covenant of indemnity. It is common for an assignor of the lease to require the assignee to enter into an express covenant of indemnity in deed by which the lease is assigned. A covenant of this kind will be personal in character and,

---

124 *Hart v Emelkirk* [1983] 1 WLR 1289.
125 This will be so where the lease or leases of the premises enable the receiver to recover his remuneration through the service charge.
126 *Clayhope Properties Ltd v Evans* [1988] 1 WLR 358.
127 The circumstances in which a former tenant may continue to be liable on the covenants of a lease following the assignment of the lease are discussed at **40-10** above.
128 'Old' leases are leases granted before 1 January 1996 or pursuant to a contract entered into before that date: Landlord and Tenant (Covenants) Act 1995, s 1(3). All other leases are 'new' leases.

accordingly, will be enforceable against the immediate assignee, but not a further assignee of the lease.

47-71 Secondly, the following covenants are implied by statute:

1 Where the assignment of the lease is for valuable consideration,[129] the following covenants on the part of the assignee are implied by section 77(1)(C) and (D) of and Schedule 2 to the Law of Property Act 1925:[130]

   (a) On an assignment of the whole of the land comprised in the lease, a covenant that the assignee will pay the rent and perform the tenant's covenants and will indemnify the assignor against a failure to do so.

   (b) On an assignment of part only of the land comprised in the lease, where the rent has been apportioned otherwise than with the landlord's consent,[131] a covenant that the assignee will, at all times from the date of the assignment, pay the apportioned rent and observe and perform the tenant's covenants, other than the covenant to pay the entire rent and will indemnify the assignor against a failure to do so.

2 On an assignment of a lease of registered land, then unless there is an entry on the register negating such implication, the following covenants are implied by section 24 of the Land Registration Act 1925:[132]

   (a) A covenant with the assignor that, during the residue of the term, the assignee and the persons deriving title under him will pay, perform, and observe the rent, covenants, and conditions by and in the registered lease reserved and contained, and on the part of the lessee to be paid, performed, and observed, and will keep the assignor and the persons deriving title under him indemnified against all actions, expenses, and claims on account of the non-payment of the said rent or any part thereof, or the breach of the said covenants or conditions, or any of them.[133]

   (b) Where the assignment is of part only of the land held under the lease, the covenant implied on the part of the assignee by section 24(1) of the Land Registration Act 1925 is limited to the payment of the apportioned rent, if any, and the performance and observance of the covenants by the lessee and conditions in the registered lease so far only as they affect the part assigned.[134]

---

129 This requirement does not mean that the assignee must have paid a premium for the assignment of the lease. An assignment of the lease will be 'for valuable consideration' simply by virtue of the assignee assuming the obligation to pay the rent and perform the other covenants in the lease: *Johnsey Estates Ltd v Lewis and Manley (Engineering) Ltd* (1987) 54 P&CR 296.

130 Law of Property Act 1925, s 77(1)(C) and (D) have been repealed, but their effect in relation to leases to which the provisions of the Landlord and Tenant (Covenants) Act 1995 do not apply is preserved: Landlord and Tenant (Covenants) Act 1995, s 30(3)(a).

131 See **40-41** above.

132 Law of Property Act 1925, s 24 has been repealed, but its effect in relation to leases to which the provisions of the Landlord and Tenant (Covenants) Act 1995 do not apply is preserved: Landlord and Tenant (Covenants) Act 1995, s 30(3)(a).

133 Section 24(1).

134 Section 24(2).

47-72 The party entitled to be indemnified under the statutorily implied covenants may recover not only the sum paid out to the landlord, but also any charges which necessarily and reasonably arise out of the circumstances under which the party charged became responsible.[135] Accordingly, if the former tenant incurred legal costs or otherwise suffered loss as a result of the assignee's non-payment, these too may be recovered under the statutorily implied covenants. A former tenant may even be able to recover his losses under the statutorily implied covenants, even if he had not been legally obliged to make the payment (e.g. where the landlord had lost the right to recover from the former tenant having failed to serve notice under section 17 of the Landlord and Tenant (Covenants) Act 1995).[136] The obligation to indemnify under the statutorily implied covenants subsists for the residue of the term granted by the lease and the covenanting party will, therefore, remain liable even after he himself assigns the lease.[137] However, the statutorily implied covenants only afford a right of action against an *immediate* assignee and do not enable a former tenant who has been made to discharge arrears to recover against a successor to his immediate assignee.

47-73 Thirdly, an original tenant who is required to discharge the current tenant's arrears of service charge is entitled to be indemnified by the current tenant, even if he is not an immediate assignee of the original tenant.[138] This right of action is probably more accurately analysed as a claim in restitution or subrogation. It has also been held that an original tenant may also recover against a surety who has guaranteed the current tenant's performance of the obligations arising under the lease.[139] However, in either case, the right of recovery is limited to the sum paid out to the landlord and, unlike the statutory covenants of indemnity discussed at **47-71** above, does not extend to enable recovery of the original tenant's legal costs or other losses consequential on the default by the current tenant. The original tenant is not entitled to be subrogated to the landlord's right to levy distress for rent[140] or forfeit the lease[141] and the landlord is not entitled to compel an immediate assignee to assign the benefit of a subsequent assignee's covenant of indemnity.[142]

47-74 The provisions of section 17 of the Landlord and Tenant (Covenants) Act 1995[143] do not apply to claims between assignor and assignee. Accordingly,

---

135 *Smith v Howell* (1851) 6 Exch 730; see also *Scottish & Newcastle Plc v Raguz (No 2)* [2008] 1 WLR 2494.

136 In *Scottish & Newcastle Plc v Raguz (No 2)* [2008] 1 WLR 2494, a case concerning statutorily implied indemnity under the Land Registration Act 1925, s 24, the Supreme Court endorsed the view expressed by Lloyd LJ in the Court of Appeal that the indemnity extended to all costs reasonably and fairly incurred which, in principle, might include sums that the indemnified party had not been legally obliged to pay.

137 *Crossfield v Morrison* (1849) 7 CB 286.

138 *Moule v Garrett* (1872) LR 7 Ex 101.

139 *Selous Street Properties Ltd v Oronel Fabrics Ltd* [1984] 1 EGLR 50; *Becton Dickinson v Zwebner* [1989] QB 208.

140 *Re Perkins* [1898] 2 Ch 182.

141 *BSE Trading Ltd v Hands* (1998) 75 P&CR 138.

142 *RPH Ltd v Mirror Group Newspapers Ltd* [1993] 13 EG 113.

143 Landlord and Tenant (Covenants) Act 1995, s 17 is discussed at **40-26** above.

there is no need to serve notices under section 17 of the Landlord and Tenant (Covenants) Act 1995 before bringing a claim under one or more of the indemnities discussed above.[144]

Leases to which the provisions of the Landlord and Tenant (Covenants) Act 1995 apply

47-75   In the case of leases to which the provisions of the Landlord and Tenant (Covenants) Act 1995 apply,[145] each tenant is automatically released from liability under the covenants in the lease from the assignment.[146] Accordingly, unless the tenant is required to enter into an authorised guarantee agreement, he has no need of a right of indemnity against assignees of the lease.

47-76   However, where the assigning tenant is required to enter into an authorised guarantee agreement, he may be required to discharge the arrears of service charge if the assignee fails to pay. If so, the former tenant is entitled to be indemnified by the assignee.[147] Once there is a further assignment of the lease, the former tenant who had entered into the authorised guarantee agreement will then be released from further liability[148] and has no need to be indemnified by subsequent assignees of the lease.

Exercise of the right to take an overriding lease

47-77   Where a former tenant, including a former tenant who has entered into an authorised guarantee agreement, makes full payment[149] of the amount specified by the landlord in a notice served under section 17 of the Landlord and Tenant (Covenants) Act 1995,[150] he is entitled to take an overriding lease of the premises pursuant to section 19 of that Act.

47-78   An overriding lease is a lease of the reversion immediately expectant upon the existing lease, granted for a term equal to the unexpired residue of the existing lease (less three days) and is otherwise on the same terms as the existing lease (excluding only personal covenants and covenants which have ceased to be

---

144   *Fresh (Retail) Ltd v Emsden* [1999] 5 CL 455; *M W Kellogg Ltd v Tobin* [1999] L&TR 513.
145   See **40-09** above.
146   Landlord and Tenant (Covenants) Act 1995, s 3. The operation of the provisions of the Landlord and Tenant (Covenants) Act 1995 is discussed in more detail at **40-15** above.
147   There is an implied term to that effect in every contract of surety: *Alexander v Vane* (1836) 1 M&W 511; *Re Chetwynd's Estate* [1938] Ch 13. The same result might be achieved by bringing a claim in restitution against the assignee: *Moule v Garrett* (1872) LR 7 Ex 101.
148   Landlord and Tenant (Covenants) Act 1995, s 24(2).
149   The right to take an overriding lease is not available to a former tenant who pays part only of the sum demanded by the landlord in the relevant notice under the Landlord and Tenant (Covenants) Act 1995, s 17.
150   See **40-26** above.

binding).[151] A claim for an overriding lease must be made in writing[152] and not later than 12 months after the relevant payment is made.[153]

47-79   Once an overriding lease has been granted to the former tenant, he can take steps to forfeit the lease. Once the lease has been forfeited and vacant possession of the lease has been recovered, the former tenant will be able to exploit the premises himself (e.g. by trading from them if they are commercial premises) or, alternatively, he may assign the overriding lease or grant a sublease for a premium. By one or other of these means, the former tenant may be able to recoup some or all of the amount which he had been required to pay over to the landlord.

---

151 Section 19(2)–(4).
152 Section 19(5)(a).
153 Section 19(5)(b). Provision is made in s 19(6)–(10) for the procedure to be followed once a request for an overriding lease has been made.

APPENDIX

Landlord and Tenant Act 1985 (extract)

Service charges

18. Meaning of "service charge" and "relevant costs".

(1) In the following provisions of this Act "service charge" means an amount payable by a tenant of a [dwelling]¹ as part of or in addition to the rent—

    (a) which is payable, directly or indirectly, for services, repairs, maintenance [, improvements]² or insurance or the landlord's costs of management, and

    (b) the whole or part of which varies or may vary according to the relevant costs.

(2) The relevant costs are the costs or estimated costs incurred or to be incurred by or on behalf of the landlord, or a superior landlord, in connection with the matters for which the service charge is payable.

(3) For this purposes—

    (a) "costs" includes overheads, and

    (b) costs are relevant costs in relation to a service charge whether they are incurred, or to be incurred, in the period for which the service charge is payable or in an earlier or later period.

1   Word substituted by Landlord and Tenant Act 1987, s 41, Sch 2, para 1.
2   Word inserted by Commonhold and Leasehold Reform Act 2002, Sch 9, para 7 (30 March 2004 as SI 2004/669).

19. Limitation of service charges: reasonableness.

(1) Relevant costs shall be taken into account in determining the amount of a service charge payable for a period—

    (a) only to the extent that they are reasonably incurred, and

    (b) where they are incurred on the provisions of services or the carrying out of works, only if the services or works are of a reasonable standard;

    and the amount payable shall be limited accordingly.

(2) Where a service charge is payable before the relevant costs are incurred, no greater amount than is reasonable is so payable, and after the relevant costs have been incurred any necessary adjustment shall be made by repayment, reduction or subsequent charges or otherwise.

[…]¹

[…]²

[(5) If a person takes any proceedings in the High Court in pursuance of any of the provisions of this Act relating to service charges and he could have taken those proceedings in the county court, he shall not be entitled to recover any costs.]³

1   Repealed subject to savings specified in SI 2004/669, Sch 2, para 6 by Commonhold and Leasehold Reform Act 2002, Sch 14 para 1 (30 March 2004: repeal has effect as SI 2004/669 subject to savings specified in SI 2004/669, Sch 2, para 6).
2   Repealed by Housing Act 1996, Sch 19(III), para 1 (1 September 1997: as in SI 1997/1851).
3   Section 19(5) inserted by Landlord and Tenant Act 1987, s 41, Sch 2, para 2(b).

[20. Limitation of service charges: consultation requirements.
(1) Where this section applies to any qualifying works or qualifying long term agreement, the relevant contributions of tenants are limited in accordance with subsection (6) or (7) (or both) unless the consultation requirements have been either—
(a) complied with in relation to the works or agreement, or
(b) dispensed with in relation to the works or agreement by (or on appeal from) a leasehold valuation tribunal.
(2) In this section "relevant contribution", in relation to a tenant and any works or agreement, is the amount which he may be required under the terms of his lease to contribute (by the payment of service charges) to relevant costs incurred on carrying out the works or under the agreement.
(3) This section applies to qualifying works if relevant costs incurred on carrying out the works exceed an appropriate amount.
(4) The Secretary of State may by regulations provide that this section applies to a qualifying long term agreement—
(a) if relevant costs incurred under the agreement exceed an appropriate amount, or
(b) if relevant costs incurred under the agreement during a period prescribed by the regulations exceed an appropriate amount.
(5) An appropriate amount is an amount set by regulations made by the Secretary of State; and the regulations may make provision for either or both of the following to be an appropriate amount—
(a) an amount prescribed by, or determined in accordance with, the regulations, and
(b) an amount which results in the relevant contribution of any one or more tenants being an amount prescribed by, or determined in accordance with, the regulations.
(6) Where an appropriate amount is set by virtue of paragraph (a) of subsection (5), the amount of the relevant costs incurred on carrying out the works or under the agreement which may be taken into account in determining the relevant contributions of tenants is limited to the appropriate amount.
(7) Where an appropriate amount is set by virtue of paragraph (b) of that subsection, the amount of the relevant contribution of the tenant, or each of the tenants, whose relevant contribution would otherwise exceed the amount prescribed by, or determined in accordance with, the regulations is limited to the amount so prescribed or determined.][1]

1   Sections 20–20ZA substituted for s 20 subject to savings specified in SI 2003/1986, art 3(2)–(7) and SI 2004/669, art 2(d)(i)–(vi) by Commonhold and Leasehold Reform Act 2002, Pt 2, s 151 (26 July 2002 in relation to England for the purpose of making regulations as specified in SI 2002/1019, art 2(c); 1 January 2003 in relation to Wales for the purpose of making regulations as specified in SI 2002/3012, art 2(c); 31 October 2003 in relation to England otherwise as specified in SI 2003/1986, art 3(1) and subject to savings in art 3(2)–(7) thereof; 30 March 2004 in relation to Wales otherwise as specified in SI 2004/669, art 2(d) and subject to savings in art 2(d)(i)–(iv) thereof).

[20ZA. Consultation requirements: supplementary.
(1) Where an application is made to a leasehold valuation tribunal for a determination to dispense with all or any of the consultation requirements in relation to any qualifying works or qualifying long term agreement, the tribunal may make the determination if satisfied that it is reasonable to dispense with the requirements.

(2) In section 20 and this section—
"qualifying works" means works on a building or any other premises, and
"qualifying long term agreement" means (subject to subsection (3)) an agreement entered into, by or on behalf of the landlord or a superior landlord, for a term of more than twelve months.

(3) The Secretary of State may by regulations provide that an agreement is not a qualifying long term agreement—
(a) if it is an agreement of a description prescribed by the regulations, or
(b) in any circumstances so prescribed.

(4) In section 20 and this section "the consultation requirements" means requirements prescribed by regulations made by the Secretary of State.

(5) Regulations under subsection (4) may in particular include provision requiring the landlord—
(a) to provide details of proposed works or agreements to tenants or the recognised tenants' association representing them,
(b) to obtain estimates for proposed works or agreements,
(c) to invite tenants or the recognised tenants' association to propose the names of persons from whom the landlord should try to obtain other estimates,
(d) to have regard to observations made by tenants or the recognised tenants' association in relation to proposed works or agreements and estimates, and
(e) to give reasons in prescribed circumstances for carrying out works or entering into agreements.

(6) Regulations under section 20 or this section—
(a) may make provision generally or only in relation to specific cases, and
(b) may make different provision for different purposes.

(7) Regulations under section 20 or this section shall be made by statutory instrument which shall be subject to annulment in pursuance of a resolution of either House of Parliament.][1]

1   Sections 20–20ZA substituted for s 20 subject to savings specified in SI 2003/1986, art 3(2)–(7) and SI 2004/669, art 2(d)(i)–(vi) by Commonhold and Leasehold Reform Act 2002, Pt 2, s 151 (26 July 2002 in relation to England for the purpose of making regulations as specified in SI 2002/1019, art 2(c); 1 January 2003 in relation to Wales for the purpose of making regulations as specified in SI 2002/3012, art 2(c); 31 October 2003 in relation to England otherwise as specified in SI 2003/1986, art 3(1) and subject to savings in art 3(2)–(7) thereof; 30 March 2004 in relation to Wales otherwise as specified in SI 2004/669, art 2(d) and subject to savings in art 2(d)(i)–(iv) thereof).

[20A. Limitation of service charges; grant-aided works.
Where relevant costs are incurred or to be incurred on the carrying out of works in respect of which a grant has been or is to be paid under [section 523 of the Housing Act 1985 (assistance for provision of separate service pipe for water supply) or any provision of Part I of the Housing Grants, Construction and Regeneration Act 1996 (grants, &c. for renewal of private sector housing) or any corresponding earlier enactment][2] [or article 3 of the Regulatory Reform (Housing Assistance) (England and Wales) Order 2002 (power of local housing authorities to provide assistance)][3], the amount of the grant shall be deducted from the costs and the amount of the service charge payable shall be reduced accordingly.

[(2) In any case where—
(a) relevant costs are incurred or to be incurred on the carrying out of works which are included in the external works specified in a group repair scheme, within the meaning of [Part I of the Housing Grants, Construction and Regeneration Act 1996][5], and

(b) the landlord participated or is participating in that scheme as an assisted participant,

the amount which, in relation to the landlord, is [the balance of the cost determined in accordance with section 69(3) of the Housing Grants, Construction and Regeneration Act 1996][6] shall be deducted from the costs, and the amount of the service charge payable shall be reduced accordingly.][4]][1]

1 Section 20A inserted by Housing and Planning Act 1986, s 24(1), Sch 5, para 9(1).
2 Words substituted by Housing Grants, Construction and Regeneration Act 1996, Sch 1, para 11(1) (17 December 1996).
3 Words inserted by Regulatory Reform (Housing Assistance) (England and Wales) Order 2002/1860, Sch 1, para 2 (19 July 2002).
4 Section 20A(2) inserted by Local Government and Housing Act 1989, s 194, Sch 11, para 90.
5 Words substituted by Housing Grants, Construction and Regeneration Act 1996, Sch 1, para 11(2)(a) (17 December 1996).
6 Words substituted by Housing Grants, Construction and Regeneration Act 1996, Sch1, para 11(2)(b) (17 December 1996).

[20B. Limitation of service charges: time limit on making demands.

(1) If any of the relevant costs taken into account in determining the amount of any service charge were incurred more than 18 months before a demand for payment of the service charge is served on the tenant, then (subject to subsection (2)), the tenant shall not be liable to pay so much of the service charge as reflects the costs so incurred.

(2) Subsection (1) shall not apply if, within the period of 18 months beginning with the date when the relevant costs in question were incurred, the tenant was notified in writing that those costs had been incurred and that he would subsequently be required under the terms of his lease to contribute to them by the payment of a service charge.][1, 2, 3, 4]

1 Sections 20B, 20C inserted by Landlord and Tenant Act 1987, s 41, Sch 2, para 4.
2 Act amended by Housing (Consequential Provisions) Act 1985, s 2(3), modified by SI 1988/1283, art 2, Sch, para 7.
3 Section 20B amended by Housing Act 1988, s 79(12).
4 Section 20B(2) modified by SI 1988/1283, art 2, Sch, para 6.

[20C. Limitation of service charges: costs of proceedings.

(1) A tenant may make an application for an order that all or any of the costs incurred, or to be incurred, by the landlord in connection with proceedings before a court [, residential property tribunal][2] or leasehold valuation tribunal, or the [Upper Tribunal][3], or in connection with arbitration proceedings, are not to be regarded as relevant costs to be taken into account in determining the amount of any service charge payable by the tenant or any other person or persons specified in the application.

(2) The application shall be made—

(a) in the case of court proceedings, to the court before which the proceedings are taking place or, if the application is made after the proceedings are concluded, to a county court;

[(aa) in the case of proceedings before a residential property tribunal, to a leasehold valuation tribunal;][2]

(b) in the case of proceedings before a leasehold valuation tribunal, to the tribunal before which the proceedings are taking place or, if the application is made after the proceedings are concluded, to any leasehold valuation tribunal;

(c) in the case of proceedings before the [Upper Tribunal][3], to the tribunal;

(d) in the case of arbitration proceedings, to the arbitral tribunal or, if the application is made after the proceedings are concluded, to a county court.

(3) The court or tribunal to which the application is made may make such order on the application as it considers just and equitable in the circumstances.][1]

1   Substituted subject to savings specified in SI 1997/1851, Sch 1, para 1 by Housing Act 1996, Pt III, s 83(4) (1 September 1997: substitution has effect subject to savings specified in SI 1997/1851, Sch 1, para 1).
2   Amended by Housing Act 2004, Sch 15, para 32 (16 June 2006 as SI 2006/1535).
3   Words substituted by Transfer of Tribunal Functions (Lands Tribunal and Miscellaneous Amendments) Order 2009/1307, Sch 1, para 177 (1 June 2009).

21. Request for summary of relevant costs.

(1) A tenant may require the landlord in writing to supply him with a written summary of the costs incurred—

(a) if the relevant accounts are made up for periods of twelve months, in the last such period ending not later than the date of the request, or

(b) if the accounts are not so made up, in the period of twelve months ending with the date of the request,

and which are relevant costs in relation to the service charges payable or demanded as payable in that or any other period.

(2) If [the tenant is represented by a recognised tenants' association and he][1] consents, the request may be made by the secretary of the association instead of by the tenant and may then be for the supply of the summary to the Secretary.

(3) A request is duly served on the landlord if it is served on—

(a) an agent of the landlord named as such in the rent book or similar document, or

(b) the person who receives the rent on behalf of the landlord;

and a person on whom a request is so served shall forward it as soon as may be to the landlord.

(4) The landlord shall comply with the request within one month of the request or within six months of the end of the period referred to in subsection (1)(a) or (b) whichever is the later.

(5) The summary shall [state whether any of the costs relate to works in respect of which a grant has been or is to be paid under [section 523 of the Housing Act 1985 (assistance for provision of separate service pipe for water supply) or any provision of Part I of the Housing Grants, Construction and Regeneration Act 1996 (grants, &c. for renewal of private sector housing) or any corresponding earlier enactment][3] and][2] set out the costs in a way showing [how they have been or will be reflected in demands for service charges and, in addition, shall summarise each of the following items, namely—][4]

[(a) any of the costs in respect of which no demand for payment was received by the landlord within the period referred to in subsection (1)(a) or (b),

(b) any of the costs in respect of which—

(i) a demand for payment was so received, but

(ii) no payment was made by the landlord within that period, and

(c) any of the costs in respect of which—

(i) a demand for payment was so received, and

(ii) payment was made by the landlord within that period,

and specify the aggregate of any amounts received by the landlord down to the end of that period on account of service charges in respect of relevant dwellings and still standing to the credit of the tenants of those dwellings at the end of that period][4]

[(5A) In subsection (5) "relevant dwelling" means a dwelling whose tenant is either—

(a) the person by or with the consent of whom the request was made, or

(b) a person whose obligations under the terms of his lease as regards contributing to relevant costs relate to the same costs as the corresponding obligations of the person mentioned in paragraph (a) above relate to.][4]

[(5B) The summary shall state whether any of the costs relate to works which are included in the external works specified in a group repair scheme, within the meaning of [Chapter II of Part I of the Housing Grants, Construction and Regeneration Act 1996 or any corresponding earlier enactment][6], in which the landlord participated or is participating as an assisted participant.][5]

(6) [If the service charges in relation to which the costs are relevant costs as mentioned in subsection (1) are payable by the tenants of more than four dwellings][7], the summary shall be certified by a qualified accountant as—

(a) in his opinion a fair summary complying with the [requirements][8] of subsection (5), and

(b) being sufficiently supported by accounts, receipts and other documents which have been produced to him.

In relation to England: for the purposes of making regulations (as inserted by Sch 12 para 2 of the Housing and Regeneration Act 2008 (c. 17)):

[21. Service charge information.
(1) The appropriate national authority may make regulations about the provision, by landlords of dwellings to each tenant by whom service charges are payable, of information about service charges.

(2) The regulations must, subject to any exceptions provided for in the regulations, require the landlord to provide information about–

(a) the service charges of the tenant,

(b) any associated service charges, and

(c) relevant costs relating to service charges falling within paragraph (a) or (b).

(3) The regulations must, subject to any exceptions provided for in the regulations, require the landlord to provide the tenant with a report by a qualified person on information which the landlord is required to provide by virtue of this section.

(4) The regulations may make provision about–

(a) information to be provided by virtue of subsection (2),

(b) other information to be provided (whether in pursuance of a requirement or otherwise),

(c) reports of the kind mentioned in subsection (3),

(d) the period or periods in relation to which information or reports are to be provided,

(e) the times at or by which information or reports are to be provided,

(f) the form and manner in which information or reports are to be provided (including in particular whether information is to be contained in a statement of account),

(g) the descriptions of persons who are to be qualified persons for the purposes of subsection (3).

(5) Subsections (2) to (4) do not limit the scope of the power conferred by subsection (1).

(6) Regulations under this section may–

(a) make different provision for different cases or descriptions of case or for different purposes,

(b) contain such supplementary, incidental, consequential, transitional, transitory or saving provision as the appropriate national authority considers appropriate.

(7) Regulations under this section are to be made by statutory instrument which, subject to subsections (8) and (9)–

(a) in the case of regulations made by the Secretary of State, is to be subject to annulment in pursuance of a resolution of either House of Parliament, and

(b) in the case of regulations made by the Welsh Ministers, is to be subject to annulment in pursuance of a resolution of the National Assembly for Wales.

(8) The Secretary of State may not make a statutory instrument containing the first regulations made by the Secretary of State under this section unless a draft of the instrument has been laid before, and approved by a resolution of, each House of Parliament.

(9) The Welsh Ministers may not make a statutory instrument containing the first regulations made by the Welsh Ministers under this section unless a draft of the instrument has been laid before, and approved by a resolution of, the National Assembly for Wales.

(10) In this section–

"the appropriate national authority"–

(a) in relation to England, means the Secretary of State, and

(b) in relation to Wales, means the Welsh Ministers,

"associated service charges", in relation to a tenant by whom a contribution to relevant costs is payable as a service charge, means service charges of other tenants so far as relating to the same costs.]⁹

In relation to Wales: for the purposes of making regulations (as inserted by s 152 of the Commonhold and Leasehold Reform Act 2002):

[21. Regular statements of account.

(1) The landlord must supply to each tenant by whom service charges are payable, in relation to each accounting period, a written statement of account dealing with—

(a) service charges of the tenant and the tenants of dwellings associated with his dwelling,

(b) relevant costs relating to those service charges,

(c) the aggregate amount standing to the credit of the tenant and the tenants of those dwellings—

(i) at the beginning of the accounting period, and

(ii) at the end of the accounting period, and

(d) related matters.

(2) The statement of account in relation to an accounting period must be supplied to each such tenant not later than six months after the end of the accounting period.

(3) Where the landlord supplies a statement of account to a tenant he must also supply to him—

(a) a certificate of a qualified accountant that, in the accountant's opinion, the statement of account deals fairly with the matters with which it is required to deal and is sufficiently supported by accounts, receipts and other documents which have been produced to him, and

(b) a summary of the rights and obligations of tenants of dwellings in relation to service charges.

(4) The Secretary of State may make regulations prescribing requirements as to the form and content of—

(a) statements of account,

(b) accountants' certificates, and

(c) summaries of rights and obligations,

required to be supplied under this section.

(5) The Secretary of State may make regulations prescribing exceptions from the requirement to supply an accountant's certificate.

(6) If the landlord has been notified by a tenant of an address in England and Wales at which he wishes to have supplied to him documents required to be so supplied under this section, the landlord must supply them to him at that address.

(7) And the landlord is to be taken to have been so notified if notification has been given to—

(a) an agent of the landlord named as such in the rent book or similar document, or

(b) the person who receives the rent on behalf of the landlord;

and where notification is given to such an agent or person he must forward it as soon as may be to the landlord.

(8) For the purposes of this section a dwelling is associated with another dwelling if the obligations of the tenants of the dwellings under the terms of their leases as regards contributing to relevant costs relate to the same costs.

(9) In this section "accounting period" means such period—

(a) beginning with the relevant date, and

(b) ending with such date, not later than twelve months after the relevant date,

as the landlord determines.

(10) In the case of the first accounting period in relation to any dwellings, the relevant date is the later of—

(a) the date on which service charges are first payable under a lease of any of them, and

(b) the date on which section 152 of the Commonhold and Leasehold Reform Act 2002 comes into force,

and, in the case of subsequent accounting periods, it is the date immediately following the end of the previous accounting period.

(11) Regulations under subsection (4) may make different provision for different purposes.

(12) Regulations under this section shall be made by statutory instrument which shall be subject to annulment in pursuance of a resolution of either House of Parliament.][10]

1   Words substituted by Landlord and Tenant Act 1987, s 41, Sch 2, para 5(2).
2   Words inserted by Housing and Planning Act 1986, s 24(1), Sch 5, para 9(2).
3   Words substituted by Housing Grants, Construction and Regeneration Act 1996, Sch 1, para 12(a) (17 December 1996).
4   Words substituted by Landlord and Tenant Act 1987, s 41, Sch 2, para 5(3).
5   Section 21(5B) inserted by Local Government and Housing Act 1989, s 194, Sch 11, para 91(2).
6   Words substituted by Housing Grants, Construction and Regeneration Act 1996, Sch 1, para 12(b) (17 December 1996).
7   Words substituted by Landlord and Tenant Act 1987, s 41, Sch 2, para 5(4)(a).
8   Word substituted by Landlord and Tenant Act 1987, s 41, Sch 2, para 5(4)(b).
9   Substituted by Housing and Regeneration Act 2008, Sch 12, para 2 (1 December 2008: substitution has effect on 12 December 2008 as SI 2008/3068 in relation to England for the purpose of making regulations; not yet in force otherwise).
10   Sections 21–21A substituted for s 21 by Commonhold and Leasehold Reform Act 2002, Pt 2, s 152 (1 January 2003: substitution has effect on 1 January 2003 as SI 2002/3012 in relation to Wales for the purpose of making regulations but is not yet in force otherwise).

[21A. Withholding of service charges.

[(1) A tenant may withhold payment of a service charge if–

(a) the landlord has not provided him with information or a report–

(i) at the time at which, or

(ii) (as the case may be) by the time by which,

he is required to provide it by virtue of section 21, or

(b) the form or content of information or a report which the landlord has provided him with by virtue of that section (at any time) does not conform exactly or substantially with the requirements prescribed by regulations under that section.][2]

(2) The maximum amount which the tenant may withhold is an amount equal to the aggregate of—

(a) the service charges paid by him in the [period to which the information or report][3] concerned would or does relate, and

[(b) amounts standing to the tenant's credit in relation to the service charges at the beginning of that period.][4]

(3) An amount may not be withheld under this section—
    (a) in a case within paragraph (a) of subsection (1), after the [information or report concerned has been provided][5] to the tenant by the landlord, or
    [(b) in a case within paragraph (b) of that subsection, after information or a report conforming exactly or substantially with requirements prescribed by regulations under section 21 has been provided to the tenant by the landlord by way of replacement of that previously provided.][6]
(4) If, on an application made by the landlord to a leasehold valuation tribunal, the tribunal determines that the landlord has a reasonable excuse for a failure giving rise to the right of a tenant to withhold an amount under this section, the tenant may not withhold the amount after the determination is made.
(5) Where a tenant withholds a service charge under this section, any provisions of the tenancy relating to non-payment or late payment of service charges do not have effect in relation to the period for which he so withholds it.[...][7]][1]

1   Sections 21–21A substituted for s 21 by Commonhold and Leasehold Reform Act 2002, Pt 2, s 152 (26 July 2002: substitution has effect on 26 July 2002 as SI 2002/1912 in relation to England for the purpose of making regulations but is not yet in force otherwise).
2   Substituted by Housing and Regeneration Act 2008, Sch 12, para 3(2) (1 December 2008 for the purpose of enabling the Secretary of State to make regulations under Landlord and Tenant Act 1985, s 21; not yet in force otherwise).
3   Words substituted by Housing and Regeneration Act 2008, Sch 12, para 3(3)(a) (1 December 2008 for the purpose of enabling the Secretary of State to make regulations under Landlord and Tenant Act 1985, s 21; not yet in force otherwise).
4   Substituted by Housing and Regeneration Act 2008, Sch 12, para 3(3)(b) (1 December 2008 for the purpose of enabling the Secretary of State to make regulations under Landlord and Tenant Act 1985, s 21; not yet in force otherwise).
5   Words substituted by Housing and Regeneration Act 2008, Sch12, para 3(4)(a) (1 December 2008 for the purpose of enabling the Secretary of State to make regulations under Landlord and Tenant Act 1985, s 21; not yet in force otherwise).
6   Substituted by Housing and Regeneration Act 2008, Sch 12, para 3(4)(b) (1 December 2008 for the purpose of enabling the Secretary of State to make regulations under Landlord and Tenant Act 1985, s 21; not yet in force otherwise).
7   Sections 21–21A substituted for s 21 by Commonhold and Leasehold Reform Act 2002, Pt 2, s 152 (1 January 2003: substitution has effect on 1 January 2003 as SI 2002/3012 in relation to Wales for the purpose of making regulations but is not yet in force otherwise).

[21B. Notice to accompany demands for service charges.
(1) A demand for the payment of a service charge must be accompanied by a summary of the rights and obligations of tenants of dwellings in relation to service charges.
(2) The Secretary of State may make regulations prescribing requirements as to the form and content of such summaries of rights and obligations.
(3) A tenant may withhold payment of a service charge which has been demanded from him if subsection (1) is not complied with in relation to the demand.
(4) Where a tenant withholds a service charge under this section, any provisions of the lease relating to non-payment or late payment of service charges do not have effect in relation to the period for which he so withholds it.
(5) Regulations under subsection (2) may make different provision for different purposes.
(6) Regulations under subsection (2) shall be made by statutory instrument which shall be subject to annulment in pursuance of a resolution of either House of Parliament.][1]

1   Added by Commonhold and Leasehold Reform Act 2002, Pt 2, s 153 (26 July 2002 in relation to England for the purpose of making regulations as specified in SI 2002/1912, art 2(c); 1 January 2003 in relation to Wales for the purpose of making regulations as specified in SI 2002/3012, art 2(c); 1 October 2003 in relation to England otherwise as specified in SI 2007/1256, art 2; 30 November 2007 in relation to Wales otherwise as specified in SI 2007/3161, art 2).

22. Request to inspect supporting accounts &c.

(1) This section applies where a tenant, or the secretary of a recognised tenants' association, has obtained such a summary as is referred to in section 21(1) (summary of relevant costs), whether in pursuance of that section or otherwise.

(2) The tenant, or the secretary with the consent of the tenant, may within six months of obtaining the summary require the landlord in writing to afford him reasonable facilities—

    (a) for inspecting the accounts, receipts and other documents supporting the summary, and

    (b) for taking copies or extracts from them.

(3) A request under this section is duly served on the landlord if it is served on—

    (a) an agent of the landlord named as such in the rent book or similar document, or

    (b) the person who receives the rent on behalf of the landlord,

and a person on whom a request is so served shall forward it as soon as may be to the landlord.

(4) The landlord shall make such facilities available to the tenant or secretary for a period of two months beginning not later than one month after the request is made.

[(5) The landlord shall—

    (a) where such facilities are for the inspection of any documents, make them so available free of charge;

    (b) where such facilities are for the taking of copies or extracts, be entitled to make them so available on payment of such reasonable charge as he may determine.

(6) The requirement imposed on the landlord by subsection (5)(a) to make any facilities available to a person free of charge shall not be construed as precluding the landlord from treating as part of his costs of management any costs incurred by him in connection with making those facilities so available.][1,2,3]

1 Sections 22(5), (6) inserted by Landlord and Tenant Act 1987, s 41, Sch 2, para 6.
2 Act amended by Housing (Consequential Provisions) Act 1985, s 2(3), modified by SI 1988/1283, art 2, Sch, para 7.
3 Section 22 amended by Local Government Act 1985, s 57(7), Sch 13, para 24 (as substituted by Housing (Consequential Provisions) Act 1985, s 4, Sch 2, para 61), Housing Act 1988, s 79(12). Section 22 excluded by SI 1988/1283, art 2, Sch, para 2(d).

23. Request relating to information held by superior landlord.

(1) If a request under section 21 (request for summary of relevant costs) relates in whole or in part to relevant costs incurred by or on behalf of a supervisor landlord, and the landlord to whom the request is made is not is possession of the relevant information—

    (a) he shall in turn make a written request for the relevant information to the person who is his landlord (and so on, if that person is not himself the superior landlord),

    (b) the superior landlord shall comply with that request within a reasonable time, and

    (c) the immediate landlord shall then comply with the tenant's or secretary's request, or that part of it which relates to the relevant costs incurred by or on behalf of the superior landlord, within the time allowed by section 21 or such further time, if any, as is reasonable in the circumstances.

(2) If a request under section 22 (request for facilities to inspect supporting accounts, &c.) relates to a summary of costs incurred by or on behalf of a superior landlord—

    (a) the landlord to whom the request is made shall forthwith inform the tenant or secretary of that fact and of the name and address of the superior landlord, and

    (b) section 22 shall then apply to the superior landlord as it applies to the immediate landlord.[1,2]

1 Act amended by Housing (Consequential Provisions) Act 1985, s 2(3), modified by SI 1988/1283, art 2, Sch, para 7.

2 Section 23 amended by Local Government Act 1985, s 57(7), Sch 13, para 24 (as substituted by Housing (Consequential Provisions) Act 1985, s 4, Sch 2, para 61), Housing Act 1988, s 79(12), excluded by SI 1988/1283, art 2, Sch, para 2(d).

24. Effect of assignment on request.

The assignment of a tenancy does not affect the validity of a request made under section 21, 22 or 23 before the assignment; but a person is not obliged to provide a summary or make facilities available more than once for the same [dwelling][1] and for the same period.[2, 3]

1 Word substituted by Landlord and Tenant Act 1987, s 41, Sch 2, para 7.
2 Act amended by Housing (Consequential Provisions) Act 1985, s 2(3), modified by SI 1988/1283, art 2, Sch, para 7.
3 Section 24 amended by Local Government Act 1985, s 57(7), Sch 13, para 24 (as substituted by Housing (Consequential Provisions) Act 1985, s 4, Sch 2, para 61), Housing Act 1988, s 79(12).

25. Failure to comply with s. 21, 22 or 23 an offence.

(1) It is a summary offence for a person to fail, without reasonable excuse, to perform a duty imposed on him by section 21, 22 or 23.
(2) A person committing such an offence is liable on conviction to a find not exceeding level 4 on the standard scale.[1, 2]

1 Act amended by Housing (Consequential Provisions) Act 1985, s 2(3), modified by SI 1988/1283, art 2, Sch, para 7.
2 Section 25 amended by Local Government Act 1985, s 57(7), Sch 13, para 24 (as substituted by Housing (Consequential Provisions) Act 1985, s 4, Sch 2, para 61), Housing Act 1988, s 79(12).

26. Exception: tenants of certain public authorities.

(1) Sections 18 to 25 (limitation on service charges and requests for information about costs) do not apply to a service charge payable by a tenant of—
    a local authority,
    [a National Park authority,[or][2]][1]
    a new town corporation [...][3]
    [...][3]
unless the tenancy is a long tenancy, in which case sections 18 to 24 apply but section 25 (offence of failure to comply) does not.
(2) The following are long tenancies for the purposes of subsection (1), subject to subsection (3)—
    (a) a tenancy granted for a term certain exceeding 21 years, whether or not it is (or may become) terminable before the end of that term by notice given by the tenant or by re-entry or forfeiture;
    (b) a tenancy for a term fixed by law under a grant with a covenant or obligation for perpetual renewal, other than a tenancy by sub-demise from one which is not a long tenancy;
    (c) any tenancy granted in pursuance of Part V of the Housing Act 1985 (the right to buy) [, including any tenancy granted in pursuance of that Part as it has effect by virtue of section 17 of the Housing Act 1996 (the right to acquire)][4].
(3) A tenancy granted so as to become terminable by notice after a death is not a long tenancy for the purposes of subsection (1), unless—
    (a) it is granted by a housing association which at the time of the grant is [a private registered provider of social housing or][5] [a registered social landlord][6],
    (b) it is granted at a premium calculated by reference to a percentage of the value of the dwelling-house or the cost of providing it, and

(c) at the time it is granted it complies with the requirements of the regulations then in force under section 140(4)(b) of the Housing Act 1980 [or paragraph 4(2)(b) of Schedule 4A to the Leasehold Reform Act 1967][7] (conditions for exclusion of shared ownership leases from Part I of Leasehold Reform Act 1967) or, in the case of a tenancy granted before any such regulations were brought into force, with the first such regulations to be in force.

1   Words inserted by Environment Act 1995, Sch 10, para 25(1) (23 November 1995).
2   Word inserted by Government of Wales Act 1998, Sch 15, para 12 (1 October 1998).
3   Words repealed by Government of Wales Act 1998, Sch 18(IV), para 1 (1 October 1998).
4   Words inserted by Housing Act 1996 (Consequential Amendments) (No 2) Order 1997/627, Sch 1, para 4 (1 April 1997).
5   Words inserted by Housing and Regeneration Act 2008 (Consequential Provisions) Order 2010/866, Sch 2, para 60 (1 April 2010).
6   Words substituted by Housing Act 1996 (Consequential Provisions) Order 1996/2325, Sch 2 para 16(3) (1 October 1996).
7   Words inserted by Housing Act 1988, s 140(1), Sch 17, para 68.

27. Exception: rent registered and not entered as variable.

Sections 18 to 25 (limitation on service charges and requests for information about costs) do not apply to a service charge payable by the tenant of a [dwelling][1] the rent of which is registered under Part IV of the Rent Act 1977, unless the amount registered is, in pursuance of section 71(4) of that Act, entered as a variable amount.[2, 3]

1   Word substituted by Landlord and Tenant Act 1987, s 41, Sch 2, para 8.
2   Act amended by Housing (Consequential Provisions) Act 1985, s 2(3), modified by SI 1988/1283, art 2, Sch, para 7.
3   Section 27 amended by Local Government Act 1985, s 57(7), Sch 13, para 24 (as substituted by Housing (Consequential Provisions) Act 1985, s 4, Sch 2, para 61), Housing Act 1988, s 79(12).

[27A. Liability to pay service charges: jurisdiction.

(1) An application may be made to a leasehold valuation tribunal for a determination whether a service charge is payable and, if it is, as to—
    (a) the person by whom it is payable,
    (b) the person to whom it is payable,
    (c) the amount which is payable,
    (d) the date at or by which it is payable, and
    (e) the manner in which it is payable.
(2) Subsection (1) applies whether or not any payment has been made.
(3) An application may also be made to a leasehold valuation tribunal for a determination whether, if costs were incurred for services, repairs, maintenance, improvements, insurance or management of any specified description, a service charge would be payable for the costs and, if it would, as to—
    (a) the person by whom it would be payable,
    (b) the person to whom it would be payable,
    (c) the amount which would be payable,
    (d) the date at or by which it would be payable, and
    (e) the manner in which it would be payable.
(4) No application under subsection (1) or (3) may be made in respect of a matter which—
    (a) has been agreed or admitted by the tenant,
    (b) has been, or is to be, referred to arbitration pursuant to a post-dispute arbitration agreement to which the tenant is a party,
    (c) has been the subject of determination by a court, or
    (d) has been the subject of determination by an arbitral tribunal pursuant to a post-dispute arbitration agreement.

(5) But the tenant is not to be taken to have agreed or admitted any matter by reason only of having made any payment.

(6) An agreement by the tenant of a dwelling (other than a post-dispute arbitration agreement) is void in so far as it purports to provide for a determination—

(a) in a particular manner, or

(b) on particular evidence,

of any question which may be the subject of an application under subsection (1) or (3).

(7) The jurisdiction conferred on a leasehold valuation tribunal in respect of any matter by virtue of this section is in addition to any jurisdiction of a court in respect of the matter. [...]²]¹

1   Inserted subject to savings specified in SI 2003/1986, Sch 2, para 6 by Commonhold and Leasehold Reform Act 2002, Pt 2, s 155(1) (30 September 2003: insertion has effect as SI 2003/1986 subject to savings specified in SI 2003/1986, Sch 2, para 6).

2   Inserted subject to savings specified in SI 2004/669, Sch 2, para 6 by Commonhold and Leasehold Reform Act 2002, Pt 2, s 155(1) (30 March 2004: insertion has effect as SI 2004/669 subject to savings specified in SI 2004/669, Sch 2, para 6).

28. Meaning of "qualified accountant".

(1) The reference to a "qualified accountant" in section 21(6) (certification of summary of information about relevant costs) is to be a person who, in accordance with the following provisions, has the necessary qualification and is not disqualified from acting.

[(2) A person has the necessary qualification if he is eligible for appointment as a [statutory auditor under Part 42 of the Companies Act 2006]².;]¹

[...]³

(4) The following are disqualified from acting—

[...]⁴

(b) an officer [employee or partner]⁵ of the landlord or, where the landlord is a company, of an associated company;

(c) a person who is a partner or employee of any such officer or employee.

[

(d) an agent of the landlord who is a managing agent for any premises to which any of the costs covered by the summary in question relate;

(e) an employee or partner of any such agent.]⁶

(5) For the purposes of subsection (4)(b) a company is associated with a landlord company if it is (within the meaning of [section 1159 of the Companies Act 2006]⁷) the landlord's holding company, a subsidiary of the landlord or another subsidiary of the landlord's holding company.

[(5A) For the purposes of subsection (4)(d) a person is a managing agent for any premises to which any costs relate if he has been appointed to discharge any of the landlord's obligations relating to the management by him of the premises and owed to the tenants who may be required under the terms of their leases to contribute to those costs by the payment of service charges.]⁸

(6) Where the landlord is a local authority, [National Park authority]⁹ [or a new town corporation]¹⁰ —

(a) the persons who have the necessary qualification include members of the Chartered Institute of Public Finance and Accountancy, and

(b) subsection (4)(b) (disqualification of officers and employees of landlord) does not apply.

1   Substituted by Companies Act 1989 (Eligibility for Appointment as Company Auditor) (Consequential Amendments) Regulations 1991/1997, Sch 1, para 60(a) (1 October 1991).

2   Words substituted subject to savings specified in SI 2008/948, arts 11 and 12 by Companies Act 2006 (Consequential Amendments etc) Order 2008/948, Sch 1(1), para 1 (6 April 2008).

3   Repealed by Companies Act 1989 (Eligibility for Appointment as Company Auditor) (Consequential Amendments) Regulations 1991/1997, Sch 1, para 60(b) (1 October 1991).
4   Repealed by Companies Act 1989 (Eligibility for Appointment as Company Auditor) (Consequential Amendments) Regulations 1991/1997, Sch 1, para 60(c) (1 October 1991).
5   Words substituted by Landlord and Tenant Act 1987, s 41, Sch 2, para 9(2)(a).
6   Section 28(4)(d), (e) inserted by Landlord and Tenant Act 1987, s 41, Sch 2, para 9(2)(b).
7   Words substituted by Companies Act 2006 (Consequential Amendments, Transitional Provisions and Savings) Order 2009/1941, Sch 1, para 64 (1 October 2009).
8   Section 28(5A) inserted by Landlord and Tenant Act 1987, s 41, Sch 2, para 9(3).
9   Words inserted by Environment Act 1995, Sch 10, para 25(2) (23 November 1995).
10   Words substituted by Government of Wales Act 1998, Sch 15, para 13 (1 October 1998).

29. Meaning of "recognised tenants' association".
(1) A recognised tenants' association is an association of [qualifying tenants (whether with or without other tenants)][1] which is recognised for the purposes of the provisions of this Act relating to service charges either—
      (a) by notice in writing given by the landlord to the secretary of the association, or
      (b) by a certificate of a member of the local rent assessment committee panel.
(2) A notice given under subsection (1)(a) may be withdrawn by the landlord by notice in writing given to the secretary of the association not less than six months before the date on which it is to be withdrawn.
(3) A certificate given under subsection (1)(b) may be cancelled by any member of the local rent assessment committee panel.
(4) In this section the "local rent assessment committee panel" means the persons appointed by the Lord Chancellor under the Rent Act 1977 to the panel of persons to act as members of a rent assessment committee for the registration area in which [the dwellings let to the qualifying tenants are situated, and for the purposes of this section a number of tenants are qualifying tenants if each of them may be required under the terms of his lease to contribute to the same costs by the payment of a service charge.][2]
[(5) The Secretary of State may be regulations specify—
      (a) the procedure which is to be followed in connection with an application for, or for the cancellation of, a certificate under subsection (1)(b);
      (b) the matters to which regard is to be had in giving or cancelling such a certificate;
      (c) the duration of such a certificate; and
      (d) any circumstances in which a certificate is not to be given under subsection (1) (b).][3]
(6) Regulations under subsection (5)—
      (a) may make different provisions with respect to different cases or descriptions of case, including different provision for different areas, and
      (b) shall be made by statutory instrument which shall be subject to annulment in pursuance of a resolution of either House of Parliament.[4,5]

1   Words substituted by Landlord and Tenant Act 1987, s 41, Sch 2, para 10(2).
2   Words substituted by Landlord and Tenant Act 1987, s 41, Sch 2, para 10(3).
3   Section 29(5) substituted by Landlord and Tenant Act 1987, s 41, Sch 2, para 10(4).
4   Act amended by Housing (Consequential Provisions) Act 1985, s 2(3), modified by SI 1988/1283, art 2, Sch, para 7.
5   Section 29 amended by Local Government Act 1985, s 57(7), Sch 13, para 24 (as substituted by Housing (Consequential Provisions) Act 1985, s 4, Sch 2, para 61), Housing Act 1988, s 79(12).

30. Meaning of "flat", "landlord" and "tenant".
In the provisions of this Act relating to service charges—
      [...][1]

"landlord" includes any person who has a right to enforce payment of a service charge;

"tenant" includes

(a) a statutory tenant, and

(b) where the [dwelling][2] or part of it is sub-let, the sub-tenant.[3, 4]

1 Definition of 'flat' repealed by Landlord and Tenant Act 1987, ss 41, 61(2), Sch 2, para 11(a), Sch 5.
2 Word substituted by Landlord and Tenant Act 1987, s 41, Sch 2, para 11(b).
3 Act amended by Housing (Consequential Provisions) Act 1985, s 2(3), modified by SI 1988/1283, art 2, Sch, para 7.
4 Section 30 amended by Local Government Act 1985, s 57(7), Sch 13, para 24 (as substituted by Housing (Consequential Provisions) Act 1985, s 4, Sch 2, para 61), Housing Act 1988, s 79(12).

Insurance

[30A. Rights of tenants with respect to insurance.
The Schedule to this Act (which confers on tenants certain rights with respect to the insurance of their dwellings) shall have effect.][1, 2]

1 Section 30A inserted by Landlord and Tenant Act 1987, s 43(1).
2 Act amended by Housing (Consequential Provisions) Act 1985, s 2(3), modified by SI 1988/1283, art 2, Sch, para 7.

Managing agents

[30B. Recognised tenants' associations to be consulted about managing agents.
(1A) A recognised tenants' association may at any time serve a notice on the landlord requesting him to consult the association in accordance with this section on matters relating to the appointment or employment by him of a managing agent for any relevant premises.
(2) Where, at the time when any such notice is served by a recognised tenants' association, the landlord does not employ any managing agent for any relevant premises, the landlord shall, before appointing such a managing agent, serve on the association a notice specifying—

(a) the name of the proposed managing agent;

(b) the landlord's obligations to the tenants represented by the association which it is proposed that the managing agent should be required to discharge on his behalf; and

(c) a period of not less than one month beginning with the date of service of the notice within which the association may make observations on the proposed appointment.

(3) Where, at the time when a notice is served under subsection (1) by a recognised tenants' association, the landlord employs a managing agent for any relevant premises, the landlord shall, within the period of one month beginning with the date of service of that notice, serve on the association a notice specifying—

(a) the landlord's obligations to the tenants represented by the association which the managing agent is required to discharge on his behalf; and

(b) a reasonable period within which the association may make observations on the manner in which the managing agent has been discharging those obligations, and on the desirability of his continuing to discharge them.

(4) Subject to subsection (5), a landlord who has been served with a notice by an association under subsection (1) shall, so long as he employs a managing agent for any relevant premises—

> (a) serve on that association at least once in every five years a notice specifying—
>
> > (i) any change occurring since the date of the last notice served by him on the association under this section in the obligations which the managing agent has been required to discharge on his behalf; and
> >
> > (ii) a reasonable period within which the association may make observations on the manner in which the managing agent has discharged those obligations since that date, and on the desirability of his continuing to discharge them;
>
> (b) serve on that association, whenever he proposes to appoint any new managing agent for any relevant premises, a notice specifying the matters mentioned in paragraphs (a) to (c) of subsection (2).

(5) A landlord shall not, by virtue of a notice served by an association under subsection (1), be required to serve on the association a notice under subsection (4)(a) or (b) if the association subsequently serves on the landlord a notice withdrawing its request under subsection (1) to be consulted by him.

(6) Where—

> (a) a recognised tenants' association has served a notice under subsection (1) with respect to any relevant premises, and
>
> (b) the interest of the landlord in those premises becomes vested in a new landlord,

that notice shall cease to have effect with respect to those premises (without prejudice to the service by the association on the new landlord of a fresh notice under that subsection with respect to those premises).

(7) Any notice served by a landlord under this section shall specify the name and the address in the United Kingdom of the person to whom any observations made in pursuance of the notice are to be sent; and the landlord shall have regard to any such observations that are received by that person within the period specified in the notice.

(8) In this section—

> "landlord", in relation to a recognised tenants' association, means the immediate landlord of the tenants represented by the association or a person who has a right to enforce payment of service charges payable by any of those tenants;
>
> "managing agent", in relation to any relevant premises, means an agent of the landlord appointed to discharge any of the landlord's obligations to the tenants represented by the recognised tenants' association in question which relate to the management by him of those premises; and
>
> "tenant" includes a statutory tenant;

and for the purposes of this section any premises (whether a building or not) are relevant premises in relation to a recognised tenants' association if any of the tenants represented by the association may be required under the terms of their leases to contribute by the payment of service charges to costs relating to those premises.][1, 2]

1 Section 30B inserted by Landlord and Tenant Act 1987, s 44.
2 Act amended by Housing (Consequential Provisions) Act 1985, s 2(3), modified by SI 1988/1283, art 2, Sch, para 7.

Miscellaneous

31. Reserve power to limit rents.

(1) The Secretary of State may by order provide for—

> (a) restricting or preventing increases of rent for dwellings which would otherwise take place, or

(b) restricting the amount of rent which would otherwise be payable on new lettings of dwellings;

and may so provide either generally or in relation to any specified description of dwelling.

(2) An order may contain supplementary or incidental provisions, including provisions excluding, adapting or modifying any provision made by or under an enactment (whenever passed) relating to rent or the recovery of overpaid rent.

(3) In this section—

"new letting" includes any grant of a tenancy, whether or not the premises were previously let, and any grant of a licence;

"rent" includes a sum payable under a licence, but does not include a sum attributable to rates or [council tax or][1] , in the case of dwellings of local authorities [,National Park authorities][2] or new town corporations, to the use of furniture, or the provision of services:

and for the purposes of this section an increase in rent takes place at the beginning of the rental period for which the increased rent is payable.

(4) An order under this section shall be made by statutory instrument which shall be subject to annulment in pursuance of a resolution of either House of Parliament.

1   Words inserted by Local Government Finance (Housing) (Consequential Amendments) Order 1993/651, Sch 1, para 16 (1 April 1993).
2   Words inserted by Environment Act 1995, Sch 10, para 25(3) (23 November 1995).

Supplementary provisions

32. Provisions not applying to tenancies within Part II of the Landlord and Tenant Act 1954.

(1) The following provisions do not apply to a tenancy to which Part II of the Landlord and Tenant Act 1954 (business tenancies) applies—

[sections 1 to 3A][1] (information to be given to tenant),

section 17 (specific performance of landlord's repairing obligations).

(2) Section 11 (repairing obligations) does not apply to a new lease granted to an existing tenant, or to a former tenant still in possession, if the new lease is a tenancy to which Part II of the Landlord and Tenant Act 1954 applies and the previous lease either is such a tenancy or would be but for section 28 of that Act (tenancy not within Part II if renewal agreed between the parties).

In this subsection "existing tenant", "former tenant still in possession" and "previous lease" have the same meaning as in section 14(2).

(3) Section 31 (reserve power to limit rents) does not apply to a dwelling forming part of a property subject to a tenancy to which Part II of the Landlord and Tenant Act 1954 applies; but without prejudice to the application of that section in relation to a sub-tenancy of a part of the premises comprised in such a tenancy.

1   Words substituted subject to savings specified in SI 1996/2212, Sch 1, para 2 by Housing Act 1996, Pt III, s 93(2) (1 October 1996: substitution has effect subject to savings specified in SI 1996/2212, Sch 1, para 2).

33. Liability of directors, &c. for offences by body corporate.

(1) Where an offence under this Act which has been committed by a body corporate is proved—

(a) to have been committed with the consent or connivance of a director, manager, secretary or other similar officer of the body corporate, or a person purporting to act in any such capacity, or

(b) to be attributable to any neglect on the part of such an officer or person, he, as well as the body corporate, is guilty of an offence and liable to be proceeded against and punished accordingly.

(2) Where the affairs of a body corporate are managed by its members, subsection (1) applies in relation to the acts and defaults of a member in connection with his functions of management as if he were a director of the body corporate.[1]

1　Act amended by Housing (Consequential Provisions) Act 1985, s 2(3), modified by SI 1988/1283, art 2, Sch, para 7.

34. Power of local housing authority to prosecute.

Proceedings for an offence under any provision of this Act may be brought by a local housing authority.[1]

1　Act amended by Housing (Consequential Provisions) Act 1985, s 2(3), modified by SI 1988/1283, art 2, Sch, para 7.

35. Application to Isles of Scilly.

(1) This Act applies to the Isles of Scilly subject to such exceptions, adaptations and modifications as the Secretary of State may by order direct.

(2) An order shall be made by statutory instrument which shall be subject to annulment in pursuance of a resolution of either House of Parliament.[1]

1　Act amended by Housing (Consequential Provisions) Act 1985, s 2(3), modified by SI 1988/1283, art 2, Sch, para 7.

36. Meaning of "lease" and "tenancy" and related expressions.

(1) In this Act "lease" and "tenancy" have the same meaning.

(2) Both expressions include—

(a) a sub-lease or sub-tenancy, and

(b) an agreement for a lease or tenancy (or sub-lease or sub-tenancy).

(3) The expressions "lessor" and "lessee" and "landlord" and "tenant", and references to letting, to the grant of a lease or to covenants or terms, shall be construed accordingly.[1]

1　Act amended by Housing (Consequential Provisions) Act 1985, s 2(3), modified by SI 1988/1283, art 2, Sch, para 7.

37. Meaning of "statutory tenant" and related expressions.

In this Act—

(a) "statutory tenancy" and "statutory tenant" mean a statutory tenancy or statutory tenant within the meaning of the Rent Act 1977 or the Rent (Agriculture) Act 1976; and

(b) "landlord", in relation to a statutory tenant, means the person who, apart from the statutory tenancy, would be entitled to possession of the premises.[1]

1　Act amended by Housing (Consequential Provisions) Act 1985, s 2(3), modified by SI 1988/1283, art 2, Sch, para 7.

38. Minor definitions.

In this Act—

"address" means a person's place of abode or place of business or, in the case of a company, its registered office;

["arbitration agreement", "arbitration proceedings" and "arbitral tribunal" have the same meaning as in Part I of the Arbitration Act 1996;[and " post-dispute arbitration agreement", in relation to any matter, means an arbitration agreement made after a dispute about the matter has arisen;][2]][1]

"co-operative housing association" has the same meaning as in the Housing Associations Act 1985;

"dwelling" means a building or part of a building occupied or intended to be occupied as a separate dwelling, together with any yard, garden, outhouses and appurtenances belonging to it or usually enjoyed with it;

"housing association" has the same meaning as in the Housing Associations Act 1985;

"local authority" means a district, county [, county borough]³ or London borough council, the Common Council of the City of London or the Council of the Isles of Scilly and in sections 14(4), 26(1) and 28(6) includes [...]⁴ [the Broads Authority]⁵ [, [a police and crime commissioner, the Mayor's Office for Policing and Crime]⁷ [,]⁸ [...]⁹ [...]¹⁰]⁶ a joint authority established by Part IV of the Local Government Act 1985[, [an economic prosperity board established under section 88 of the Local Democracy, Economic Development and Construction Act 2009, a combined authority established under section 103 of that Act,]¹² an authority established for an area in England by an order under section 207 of the Local Government and Public Involvement in Health Act 2007 (joint waste authorities)]¹¹ [and the London Fire and Emergency Planning Authority]¹³;

"local housing authority" has the meaning given by section 1 of the Housing Act 1985;

"new town corporation" means —

(a) a development corporation established by an order made, or treated as made, under the New Towns Act 1981, [...]¹⁴

[(b) the Homes and Communities Agency so far as exercising functions in relation to anything transferred (or to be transferred) to it as mentioned in section 52(1)(a) to (d) of the Housing and Regeneration Act 2008, [...]¹⁵

[(ba) the Greater London Authority so far as exercising its new towns and urban development functions, or]¹⁵

(c) the Welsh Ministers so far as exercising functions in relation to anything transferred (or to be transferred) to them as mentioned in section 36(1)(a)(i) to (iii) of the New Towns Act 1981;]¹⁴

"protected tenancy" has the same meaning as in the Rent Act 1977;

["registered social landlord" has the same meaning as in the Housing Act 1985 (see section 5(4) and (5) of that Act);]¹⁶

"restricted contract" has the same meaning as in the Rent Act 1977;

"urban development corporation" has the same meaning as in Part XVI of the Local Government, Planning and Land Act 1980.

---

1   Definition inserted subject to savings specified in SI 1997/1851, Sch 1, para 1 by Housing Act 1996, Pt III, s 83(5) (1 September 1997: insertion has effect subject to savings specified in SI 1997/1851, Sch 1, para 1).

2   Words inserted subject to savings specified in SI 2004/669, Sch 2, para 6 by Commonhold and Leasehold Reform Act 2002, Pt 2, s 155(2) (30 March 2004: insertion has effect as SI 2004/669 subject to savings specified in SI 2004/669, Sch 2, para 6).

3   Words inserted by Local Government (Wales) Act 1994, Sch 8, para 7 (1 April 1996).

4   Words repealed by Education Reform Act 1988, ss 231(7), 235(6), 237(2), Sch 13, Pt I.

5   Words inserted by Norfolk and Suffolk Broads Act 1988, ss 23(2), 27(2), Sch 6, para 26.

6   Words inserted by Police and Magistrates' Courts Act 1994, Sch 4, Pt II, para 60 (1 October 1994 for the purposes specified in SI 1994/2025, art 6; 1 April 1995 otherwise).

7   Words substituted by Police Reform and Social Responsibility Act 2011, Sch 16, Pt 3, para 170 (22 November 2012: commenced by an amendment).

8   Words added by Greater London Authority Act 1999, Sch 27, para 53 (3 July 2000).

9   Words repealed by Criminal Justice and Police Act 2001, Sch 7, Pt 5(1), para 1 (1 April 2002 as SI 2002/344).

10 Words repealed by Greater London Authority Act 1999, Sch 34, Pt VIII, para 1 (3 July 2000).
11 Words inserted by Local Government and Public Involvement in Health Act 2007, Sch 13, Pt 2, para 42 (1 April 2008).
12 Words inserted by Local Democracy, Economic Development and Construction Act 2009, Sch 6, para 70 (17 December 2009).
13 Words added by Greater London Authority Act 1999, Sch 29, Pt I, para 44 (3 July 2000).
14 Paras (b) and (c) substituted for para (b) by Housing and Regeneration Act 2008, Sch 8, para 36 (1 December 2008).
15 Added by Localism Act 2011, Sch 19, para 22 (1 April 2012 subject to SI 2012/628, arts 9, 11, 14, 15 and 17).
16 Words substituted by Housing Act 1996 (Consequential Provisions) Order 1996/2325, Sch 2, para 16(4) (1 October 1996).

39. Index of defined expressions.

The following Table shows provisions defining or otherwise explaining expressions used in this Act (other than provisions defining or explaining an expression in the same section):

address	section 38
[arbitration agreement, arbitration proceedings [, arbitral tribunal and post-dispute arbitration agreement][2]	section 38][1]
co-operative housing association	section 38
dwelling	section 38
dwelling-house (in the provisions relating to repairing obligations)	section 16
fit for human habitation	section 10
[...][3]	
housing association	section 38
landlord—	
(generally)	section 36(3)
(in sections 1 and 2)	section 1(3)
(in the provisions relating to rent books)	section 4(3)
(in the provisions relating to service charges)	section 30
(in relation to a statutory tenancy)	section 37(b)
lease, lessee and lessor—	
(generally)	section 36
(in the provisions relating to repairing obligations)	section 16
local authority	section 38
local housing authority	section 38
new town corporation	section 38
protected tenancy	section 38
qualified accountant (for the purposes of section 21(6))	section 28
[registered social landlord][4]	section 38
recognised tenants' association	section 29
relevant costs (in relation to a service charge)	section 18(2)
restricted contract	section 38
service charge	section 18(1)
statutory tenant	section 37(a)
tenancy and tenant—	
(generally)	section 36

(in sections 1 and 2)	section 1(3)
(in the provisions relating to rent books)	section 4(3)
(in the provisions relating to service charges)	section 30
urban development corporation	section 38

1   Entry inserted subject to savings specified in SI 1997/1851, Sch 1, para 1 by Housing Act 1996, Pt III, s 83(6) (1 September 1997: insertion has effect subject to savings specified in SI 1997/1851, Sch 1, para 1).

2   Words substituted subject to savings specified in SI 2004/669, Sch 2, para 6 by Commonhold and Leasehold Reform Act 2002, Pt 2, s 155(3) (30 March 2004: substitution has effect as SI 2004/669 subject to savings specified in SI 2004/669, Sch 2, para 6).

3   Entry repealed by Commonhold and Leasehold Reform Act 2002, Sch 14, para 1 (30 March 2004 as SI 2004/669).

4   Words substituted by Housing Act 1996 (Consequential Provisions) Order 1996/2325, Sch 2, para 16(5) (1 October 1996).

...

SCHEDULE   RIGHTS OF TENANTS WITH RESPECT TO INSURANCE

Construction

[**1.** In this Schedule—

"landlord", in relation to a tenant by whom a service charge is payable which includes an amount payable directly or indirectly for insurance, includes any person who has a right to enforce payment of that service charge;

"relevant policy", in relation to a dwelling, means any policy of insurance under which the dwelling is insured (being, in the case of a flat, a policy covering the building containing it); and

"tenant" includes a statutory tenant.][1, 2]

1   Schedule inserted by Landlord and Tenant Act 1987, s 43(2).

2   Act amended by Housing (Consequential Provisions) Act 1985, s 2(3), modified by SI 1988/1283, art 2, Sch, para 7.

Summary of insurance cover

[**2.**—(1) Where a service charge is payable by the tenant of a dwelling which consists of or includes an amount payable directly or indirectly for insurance, the tenant may [by notice in writing require the landlord][2] to supply him with a written summary of the insurance for the time being effected in relation to the dwelling.

(2) If the tenant is represented by a recognised tenants' association and he consents, the [notice may be served][2] by the secretary of the association instead of by the tenant and may then be for the supply of the summary to the secretary.

(3) A [notice under this paragraph is duly][2] served on the landlord if it is served on—

(a) an agent of the landlord named as such in the rent book or similar document, or

(b) the person who receives the rent on behalf of the landlord;

and a person on [whom such a notice][2] is so served shall forward it as soon as may be to the landlord.

(4) The landlord shall, within [the period of twenty-one days beginning with the day on which he receives the notice,][2] comply with it by supplying to the tenant or the secretary of the recognised tenants' association (as the case may require) such a summary as is mentioned in sub-paragraph (1), which shall include—

(a) the insured amount or amounts under any relevant policy, and

(b) the name of the insurer under any such policy, and

(c) the risks in respect of which the dwelling or (as the case may be) the building containing it is insured under any such policy.

(5) In sub-paragraph (4)(a) "the insured amount or amounts", in relation to a relevant policy, means—

(a) in the case of a dwelling other than a flat, the amount for which the dwelling is insured under the policy; and

(b) in the case of a flat, the amount for which the building containing it is insured under the policy and, if specified in the policy, the amount for which the flat is insured under it.

(6) The landlord shall be taken to have complied with the [notice][2] if, within the period mentioned in sub-paragraph (4), he instead supplies to the tenant or the secretary (as the case may require) a copy of every relevant policy.

(7) In a case where two or more buildings are insured under any relevant policy, the summary or copy supplied under sub-paragraph (4) or (6) so far as relating to that policy need only be of such parts of the policy as relate—

(a) to the dwelling, and

(b) if the dwelling is a flat, to the building containing it.][1]

1 Schedule inserted by Landlord and Tenant Act 1987, s 43(2).
2 Amended by Commonhold and Leasehold Reform Act 2002, Sch 10, para 8 (30 March 2004 as SI 2004/669).

Request to inspect insurance policy etc.
[3 Inspection of insurance policy etc.

(1) Where a service charge is payable by the tenant of a dwelling which consists of or includes an amount payable directly or indirectly for insurance, the tenant may by notice in writing require the landlord—

(a) to afford him reasonable facilities for inspecting any relevant policy or associated documents and for taking copies of or extracts from them, or

(b) to take copies of or extracts from any such policy or documents and either send them to him or afford him reasonable facilities for collecting them (as he specifies).

(2) If the tenant is represented by a recognised tenants' association and he consents, the notice may be served by the secretary of the association instead of by the tenant (and in that case any requirement imposed by it is to afford reasonable facilities, or to send copies or extracts, to the secretary).

(3) A notice under this paragraph is duly served on the landlord if it is served on—

(a) an agent of the landlord named as such in the rent book or similar document, or

(b) the person who receives the rent on behalf of the landlord;

and a person on whom such a notice is so served shall forward it as soon as may be to the landlord.

(4) The landlord shall comply with a requirement imposed by a notice under this paragraph within the period of twenty-one days beginning with the day on which he receives the notice.

(5) To the extent that a notice under this paragraph requires the landlord to afford facilities for inspecting documents—

(a) he shall do so free of charge, but

(b) he may treat as part of his costs of management any costs incurred by him in doing so.

(6) The landlord may make a reasonable charge for doing anything else in compliance with a requirement imposed by a notice under this paragraph.

(7) In this paragraph—

"relevant policy" includes a policy of insurance under which the dwelling was insured for the period of insurance immediately preceding that current when the notice is served (being, in the case of a flat, a policy covering the building containing it), and

"associated documents" means accounts, receipts or other documents which provide evidence of payment of any premiums due under a relevant policy in respect of the period of insurance which is current when the notice is served or the period of insurance immediately preceding that period.][1]

1   Substituted by Commonhold and Leasehold Reform Act 2002, Sch10, para 9 (30 March 2004 as SI 2004/669).

Insurance effected by superior landlord

[**4.**—(1) If [a notice is served][2] under paragraph 2 in a case where a superior landlord has effected, in whole or in part, the insurance of the dwelling in question and the landlord [on whom the notice is served][2] is not in possession of the relevant information—

(a) he shall in turn [by notice in writing require the person who is his landlord to give him the relevant information][2] (and so on, if that person is not himself the superior landlord),

(b) the superior landlord shall comply with [the notice][2] within a reasonable time, and

(c) the immediate landlord shall then comply with the tenant's or [secretary's notice][2] in the manner provided by sub-paragraphs (4) to (7) of paragraph 2 within the time allowed by that paragraph or such further time, if any, as is reasonable in the circumstances.

(2) If, in a case where a superior landlord has effected, in whole or in part, the insurance of the dwelling in question, a [notice under paragraph 3 imposes a requirement relating][2] to any policy of insurance effected by the superior landlord—

(a) the landlord [on whom the notice is served][2] shall forthwith inform the tenant or secretary of that fact and of the name and address of the superior landlord, and

(b) that paragraph shall then apply to the superior landlord in relation to that policy as it applies to the immediate landlord.][1]

1   Schedule inserted by Landlord and Tenant Act 1987, s 43(2).
2   Amended by Commonhold and Leasehold Reform Act 2002, Sch 10, para 10 (30 March 2004 as SI 2004/669).

Effect of change of landlord

[**4A.**—(1) This paragraph applies where, at a time when a duty imposed on the landlord or a superior landlord by virtue of any of paragraphs 2 to 4 remains to be discharged by him, he disposes of the whole or part of his interest as landlord or superior landlord).

(2) If the landlord or superior landlord is, despite the disposal, still in a position to discharge the duty to any extent, he remains responsible for discharging it to that extent.

(3) If the other person is in a position to discharge the duty to any extent, he is responsible for discharging it to that extent.

(4) Where the other person is responsible for discharging the duty to any extent (whether or not the landlord or superior landlord is also responsible for discharging it to that or any other extent)—

(a) references to the landlord or superior landlord in paragraphs 2 to 4 are to, or include, the other person so far as is appropriate to reflect his responsibility for discharging the duty to that extent, but

(b) in connection with its discharge by that person, paragraphs 2(4) and 3(4) apply as if the reference to the day on which the landlord receives the notice were to the date of the disposal referred to in sub-paragraph (1).[...]²]¹

1   Added by Commonhold and Leasehold Reform Act 2002, Sch 10, para 11 (30 September 2003 as SI 2003/1986).
2   Added by Commonhold and Leasehold Reform Act 2002, Sch 10, para 11 (30 March 2004 as SI 2004/669).

Effect of assignment

[**5.** The assignment of a tenancy does not affect any duty imposed by virtue of any of paragraphs 2 to 4A; but a person is not required to comply with more than a reasonable number of requirements imposed by any one person.]¹

1   Words substituted by Commonhold and Leasehold Reform Act 2002, Sch 10, para 12 (30 March 2004 as SI 2004/669).

Offence of failure to comply

[**6.**—(1) It is a summary offence for a person to fail, without reasonable excuse, to perform a duty imposed on him by or by virtue of any of paragraphs 2 to 4A.
(2) A person committing such an offence is liable on conviction to a fine not exceeding level 4 on the standard scale.]¹

1   Words substituted by Commonhold and Leasehold Reform Act 2002, Sch 10, para 13 (30 March 2004 as SI 2004/669).

Tenant's right to notify insurers of possible claim

[**7.**—(1) This paragraph applies to any dwelling in respect of which the tenant pays to the landlord a service charge consisting of or including an amount payable directly or indirectly for insurance.
(2) Where—
> (a) it appears to the tenant of any such dwelling that damage has been caused—
>> (i) to the dwelling, or
>> (ii) if the dwelling is a flat, to the dwelling or to any other part of the building containing it,
> in respect of which a claim could be made under the terms of a policy of insurance, and
> (b) it is a term of that policy that the person insured under the policy should give notice of any claim under it to the insurer within a specified period,

the tenant may, within that specified period, serve on the insurer a notice in writing stating that it appears to him that damage has been caused as mentioned in paragraph (a) and describing briefly the nature of the damage.
(3) Where—
> (a) any such notice is served on an insurer by a tenant in relation to any such damage, and
> (b) the specified period referred to in sub-paragraph (2)(b) would expire earlier than the period of six months beginning with the date on which the notice is served,

the policy in question shall have effect as regards any claim subsequently made in respect of that damage by the person insured under the policy as if for the specified period there were substituted that period of six months.
(4) Where the tenancy of a dwelling to which this paragraph applies is held by joint tenants, a single notice under this paragraph may be given by any one or more of those tenants.
(5) The Secretary of State may by regulations prescribe the form of notices under this paragraph and the particulars which such notices must contain.

(6) Any such regulations—
    (a) may make different provision with respect to different cases or descriptions of case, including different provision for different areas, and
    (b) shall be made by statutory instrument.][1, 2]

1   Schedule inserted by Landlord and Tenant Act 1987, s 43(2).
2   Act amended by Housing (Consequential Provisions) Act 1985, s 2(3), modified by SI 1988/1283, art 2, Sch, para 7.

Right to challenge landlord's choice of insurers

[**8.**—(1) This paragraph applies where a tenancy of a dwelling requires the tenant to insure the dwelling with an insurer nominated [or approved][2] by the landlord.
(2) The tenant or landlord may apply to a county court or leasehold valuation tribunal for a determination whether—
    (a) the insurance which is available from the nominated [or approved][2] insurer for insuring the tenant's dwelling is unsatisfactory in any respect, or
    (b) the premiums payable in respect of any such insurance are excessive.
(3) No such application may be made in respect of a matter which—
    (a) has been agreed or admitted by the tenant,
    (b) under an arbitration agreement to which the tenant is a party is to be referred to arbitration, or
    (c) has been the subject of determination by a court or arbitral tribunal.
(4) On an application under this paragraph the court or tribunal may make—
    (a) an order requiring the landlord to nominate [or approve][2] such other insurer as is specified in the order, or
    (b) an order requiring him to nominate [or approve][2] another insurer who satisfies such requirements in relation to the insurance of the dwelling as are specified in the order.
[...][3]
(6) An agreement by the tenant of a dwelling (other than an arbitration agreement) is void in so far as it purports to provide for a determination in a particular manner, or on particular evidence, of any question which may be the subject of an application under this paragraph.][1]

1   Substituted subject to savings specified in SI 1997/1851, Sch1, para 1 by Housing Act 1996, Pt III, s 83(2) (1 September 1997: substitution has effect subject to savings specified in SI 1997/1851, Sch 1, para 1).
2   Amended by Commonhold and Leasehold Reform Act 2002, Pt 2, s 165 (31 May 2005 as SI 2005/1353).
3   Repealed by Commonhold and Leasehold Reform Act 2002, Sch 14, para 1 (30 March 2004 as SI 2004/669).

Exception for tenants of certain public authorities

[**9.**—(1) Paragraphs 2 to 8 do not apply to a tenant of—
    a local authority,
    [a National Park authority,[or][3]][2]
    a new town corporation [...][4]
    [...][4]
unless the tenancy is a long tenancy, in which case paragraphs 2 to 5 and 7 and 8 apply but paragraph 6 does not.
(2) Subsections (2) and (3) of section 26 shall apply for the purposes of sub-paragraph (1) as they apply for the purposes of subsection (1) of that section.][1]

1   Schedule inserted by Landlord and Tenant Act 1987, s 43(2).
2   Words inserted by Environment Act 1995, Sch 10, para 25(1) (23 November 1995).
3   Word inserted by Government of Wales Act 1998, Sch 15, para 14 (1 October 1998).
4   Words repealed by Government of Wales Act 1998, Sch 18, Pt IV, para 1 (1 October 1998).

Landlord and Tenant Act 1987 (extract)

PART II APPOINTMENT OF MANAGERS BY THE COURT

21. Tenant's right to apply to court for appointment of manager.
(1) The tenant of a flat contained in any premises to which this Part applies may, subject to the following provisions of this Part, apply to [a leasehold valuation tribunal][1] for an order under section 24 appointing a manager to act in relation to those premises.
(2) Subject to subsection (3), this Part applies to premises consisting of the whole or part of a building if the building or part contains two or more flats.
(3) This Part does not apply to any such premises at a time when—
    [(a) the interest of the landlord in the premises is held by–
        (i) an exempt landlord or a resident landlord, or
        (ii) the Welsh Ministers in their new towns residuary capacity,][2]
(b) the premises are included within the functional land of any charity.
[(3A) But this Part is not prevented from applying to any premises because the interest of the landlord in the premises is held by a resident landlord if at least one-half of the flats contained in the premises are held on long leases which are not tenancies to which Part 2 of the Landlord and Tenant Act 1954 (c. 56) applies.][3]
(4) An application for an order under section 24 may be made—
    (a) jointly by tenants of two or more flats if they are each entitled to make such an application by virtue of this section, and
    (b) in respect of two or more premises to which this Part applies;
    and, in relation to any such joint application as is mentioned in paragraph (a), references in this Part to a single tenant shall be construed accordingly.
(5) Where the tenancy of a flat contained in any such premises is held by joint tenants, an application for an order under section 24 in respect of those premises may be made by any one or more of those tenants.
(6) An application to the court for it to exercise in relation to any premises [any jurisdiction][1] to appoint a receiver or manager shall not be made by a tenant (in his capacity as such) in any circumstances in which an application could be made by him for an order under section 24 appointing a manager to act in relation to those premises.
(7) References in this Part to a tenant do not include references to a tenant under a tenancy to which Part II of the Landlord and Tenant Act 1954 applies.

1   Words substituted by Housing Act 1996, Pt III, s 86(2) (1 September 1997 subject to savings specified in SI 1997/1851, Sch 1, para 2).
2   Existing text renumbered as s 21(3)(a)(i) and s 21(3)(a)(ii) inserted by Housing and Regeneration Act 2008, Sch 8, para 38 (1 December 2008).

3   Added by Commonhold and Leasehold Reform Act 2002, Pt 2, s 161 (1 January 2003 as SI
2002/3012, insertion has effect subject to transitional provisions and savings specified in SI
2002/3012, Sch 2).

22. Preliminary notice by tenant.
(1) Before an application for an order under section 24 is made in respect of any
premises to which this Part applies by a tenant of a flat contained in those premises,
a notice under this section must (subject to subsection (3)) be served [by the tenant
on—]¹
        [(i) the landlord, and
        (ii) any person (other than the landlord) by whom obligations relating to the
        management of the premises or any part of them are owed to the tenant under his
        tenancy.]¹
(2) A notice under this section must—
        (a) specify the tenant's name, the address of his flat and an address in England and
        Wales (which may be the address of his flat) at which [any person on whom the
        notice is served]¹ may serve notices, including notices in proceedings, on him in
        connection with this Part;
        (b) state that the tenant intends to make an application for an order under section 24
        to be made by [a leasehold valuation tribunal]² in respect of such premises to which
        this Part applies as are specified in the notice, but (if paragraph (d) is applicable)
        that he will not do so if the [requirement specified in pursuance of that paragraph
        is complied with]¹;
        (c) specify the grounds on which the court would be asked to make such an order
        and the matters that would be relied on by the tenant for the purpose of establishing
        those grounds;
        (d) where those matters are capable of being remedied by [any person on whom the
        notice is served, require him]¹, within such reasonable period as is specified in the
        notice, to take such steps for the purpose of remedying them as are so specified; and
        (e) contain such information (if any) as the Secretary of State may by regulations
        prescribe.
(3) [a leasehold valuation tribunal]² may (whether on the hearing of an application for an
order under section 24 or not) by order dispense with the requirement to serve a notice
under this section [on a person]¹ in a case where it is satisfied that it would not be
reasonably practicable to serve such a notice on the [person]¹, but [a leasehold valuation
tribunal]² may, when doing so, direct that such other notices are served, or such other
steps are taken, as it thinks fit.
(4) In a case where—
        (a) a notice under this section has been served on the landlord, and
        (b) his interest in the premises specified in pursuance of subsection (2)(b) is subject
        to a mortgage, the landlord shall, as soon as is reasonably practicable after receiving
        the notice, serve on the mortgagee a copy of the notice.

1   Amended by Commonhold and Leasehold Reform Act 2002, Pt 2, s 160(2) (1 January 2003 as
SI 2002/3012, modification has effect subject to transitional provisions and savings specified in
SI 2002/3012, Sch 2).
2   Words substituted by Housing Act 1996, Pt III, s 86(2) (1 September 1997 subject to savings
specified in SI 1997/1851, Sch 1, para 2).

23. Application to court for appointment of manager.
(1) No application for an order under section 24 shall be made to [a leasehold valuation
tribunal]¹ unless—

(a) in a case where a notice has been served under section 22, either—
    (i) the period specified in pursuance of paragraph (d) of subsection (2) of that section has expired without the [person required to take steps in pursuance of that paragraph having taken them][2], or
    (ii) that paragraph was not applicable in the circumstances of the case; or
(b) in a case where the requirement to serve such a notice has been dispensed with by an order under subsection (3) of that section, either—
    (i) any notices required to be served, and any other steps required to be taken, by virtue of the order have been served or (as the case may be) taken, or
    (ii) no direction was given by the court when making the order.

[...][3]

1 Words substituted by Housing Act 1996, Pt III, s 86(2) (1 September 1997 subject to savings specified in SI 1997/1851, Sch 1, para 2).
2 Words substituted by Commonhold and Leasehold Reform Act 2002, Pt 2, s 160(3) (1 January 2003 as SI 2002/3012, substitution has effect subject to transitional provisions and savings specified in SI 2002/3012, Sch 2).
3 Repealed by Commonhold and Leasehold Reform Act 2002, Sch 14, para 1 (30 March 2004 as SI 2004/669).

24. Appointment of manager by the court.
(1) [A leasehold valuation tribunal][1] may, on an application for an order under this section, by order (whether interlocutory or final) appoint a manager to carry out in relation to any premises to which this Part applies—
    (a) such functions in connection with the management of the premises, or
    (b) such functions of a receiver,
or both, as the court thinks fit.
(2) [A leasehold valuation tribunal][1] may only make an order under this section in the following circumstances, namely—
    (a) where the court is satisfied—
        (i) that [any relevant person][2] either is in breach of any obligation owed by him to the tenant under his tenancy and relating to the management of the premises in question or any part of them or (in the case of an obligation dependent on notice) would be in breach of any such obligation but for the fact that it has not been reasonably practicable for the tenant to give him the appropriate notice, and
        [...][3]
        (iii) that it is just and convenient to make the order in all the circumstances of the case; or
    [(ab) where the court is satisfied—
        (i) that unreasonable service charges have been made, or are proposed or likely to be made, and
        (ii) that it is just and convenient to make the order in all the circumstances of the case;
    [(aba) where the tribunal is satisfied—
        (i) that unreasonable variable administration charges have been made, or are proposed or likely to be made, and
        (ii) that it is just and convenient to make the order in all the circumstances of the case;
    ][5]
    (ac) where the court is satisfied—
        (i) that [any relevant person][2] has failed to comply with any relevant provision of a code of practice approved by the Secretary of State under section 87 of

the Leasehold Reform, Housing and Urban Development Act 1993 (codes of management practice); and

(ii) that it is just and convenient to make the order in all the circumstances of the case;][4]

(b) where the court is satisfied that other circumstances exist which make it just and convenient for the order to be made.

[(2ZA) In this section "relevant person" means a person—

(a) on whom a notice has been served under section 22, or

(b) in the case of whom the requirement to serve a notice under that section has been dispensed with by an order under subsection (3)of that section.
][2]

[(2A) For the purposes of subsection (2)(ab) a service charge shall be taken to be unreasonable—

(a) if the amount is unreasonable having regard to the items for which it is payable,

(b) if the items for which it is payable are of an unnecessarily high standard, or

(c) if the items for which it is payable are of an insufficient standard with the result that additional service charges are or may be incurred.

In that provision and this subsection "service charge" means a service charge within the meaning of section 18(1) of the Landlord and Tenant Act 1985, other than one excluded from that section by section 27 of that Act (rent of dwelling registered and not entered as variable).][6]

[(2B) In subsection (2)(aba) "variable administration charge" has the meaning given by paragraph 1 of Schedule 11 to the Commonhold and Leasehold Reform Act 2002.][5]

(3) The premises in respect of which an order is made under this section may, if the court thinks fit, be either more or less extensive than the premises specified in the application on which the order is made.

(4) An order under this section may make provision with respect to—

(a) such matters relating to the exercise by the manager of his functions under the order, and

(b) such incidental or ancillary matters,

as the court thinks fit; and, on any subsequent application made for the purpose by the manager, the court may give him directions with respect to any such matters.

(5) Without prejudice to the generality of subsection (4), an order under this section may provide—

(a) for rights and liabilities arising under contracts to which the manager is not a party to become rights and liabilities of the manager;

(b) for the manager to be entitled to prosecute claims in respect of causes of action (whether contractual or tortious) accruing before or after the date of his appointment;

(c) for remuneration to be paid to the manager by [any relevant person][2], or by the tenants of the premises in respect of which the order is made or by all or any of those persons;

(d) for the manager's functions to be exercisable by him (subject to subsection (9)) either during a specified period or without limit of time.

(6) Any such order may be granted subject to such conditions as the court thinks fit, and in particular its operation may be suspended on terms fixed by the court.

(7) In a case where an application for an order under this section was preceded by the service of a notice under section 22, the court may, if it thinks fit, make such an order notwithstanding—

(a) that any period specified in the notice in pursuance of subsection (2)(d) of that section was not a reasonable period, or

(b) that the notice failed in any other respect to comply with any requirement contained in subsection (2) of that section or in any regulations applying to the notice under section 54(3).

(8) The Land Charges Act 1972 and the [Land Registration Act 2002][7] shall apply in relation to an order made under this section as they apply in relation to an order appointing a receiver or sequestrator of land.

(9) [A leasehold valuation tribunal][1] may, on the application of any person interested, vary or discharge (whether conditionally or unconditionally) an order made under this section; and if the order has been protected by an entry registered under the Land Charges Act 1972 or the [Land Registration Act 2002][7], the court may by order direct that the entry shall be cancelled.

[

(9A) The [tribunal][9] shall not vary or discharge an order under subsection (9) on [the application of any relevant person][2] unless it is satisfied—

(a) that the variation or discharge of the order will not result in a recurrence of the circumstances which led to the order being made, and

(b) that it is just and convenient in all the circumstances of the case to vary or discharge the order.][8]

(10) An order made under this section shall not be discharged by [a leasehold valuation tribunal][1] by reason only that, by virtue of section 21(3), the premises in respect of which the order was made have ceased to be premises to which this Part applies.

(11) References in this [Part][2] to the management of any premises include references to the repair, maintenance [, improvement][10] or insurance of those premises.

1   Words substituted by Housing Act 1996, Pt III, s 86(2) (1 September 1997 subject to savings specified in SI 1997/1851, Sch 1, para 2).
2   Amended by Commonhold and Leasehold Reform Act 2002, Pt 2, s 160(4) (1 January 2003 as SI 2002/3012, modification has effect subject to transitional provisions and savings specified in SI 2002/3012, Sch 2).
3   Repealed by Housing Act 1996, Pt III, s 85(2) (24 September 1996).
4   Added by Housing Act 1996, Pt III, s 85(3) (24 September 1996).
5   Amended by Commonhold and Leasehold Reform Act 2002, Sch 11(2), para 8 (30 March 2004 as SI 2004/669).
6   Added by Housing Act 1996, Pt III, s 85(4) (24 September 1996).
7   Words substituted by Land Registration Act 2002, Sch 11, para 20 (13 October 2003).
8   Added by Housing Act 1996, Pt III, s 85(6) (24 September 1996).
9   Substituted by Commonhold and Leasehold Reform Act 2002, Sch 13, para 9 (30 March 2004 as SI 2004/669).
10 Word inserted by Commonhold and Leasehold Reform Act 2002, Sch 9, para 8 (30 March 2004 as SI 2004/669).

24A. Jurisdiction of leasehold valuation tribunal.

(1) The jurisdiction conferred by this Part on a leasehold valuation tribunal is exercisable by a rent assessment committee constituted in accordance with Schedule 10 to the Rent Act 1977 which when so constituted for the purposes of exercising any such jurisdiction shall be known as a leasehold valuation tribunal.

(2) The power to make regulations under section 74(1)(b) of the Rent Act 1977 (procedure of rent assessment committees) extends to prescribing the procedure to be followed in connection with any proceedings before a leasehold valuation tribunal under this Part. . Such regulations are referred to in this Part as "procedure regulations".

(3) Procedure regulations may, in particular, make provision— .

(a) for securing consistency where numerous applications under this Part are or may be brought in respect of the same or substantially the same matters; and .

(b) empowering a leasehold valuation tribunal to dismiss an application, in whole or in part, on the ground that it is frivolous or vexatious or otherwise an abuse of the process of the tribunal.

(4) Any order made by a leasehold valuation tribunal under this Part may, with the leave of the court, be enforced in the same way as an order of the county court. .

(5) No costs incurred by a party in connection with proceedings under this Part before a leasehold valuation tribunal shall be recoverable by order of any court. .

(6) Paragraphs 2, 3 and 7 of Schedule 22 to the Housing Act 1980 (supplementary provisions relating to leasehold valuation tribunals: appeals and provision of information) apply to a leasehold valuation tribunal constituted for the purposes of this section. .

(7) No appeal shall lie to the Lands Tribunal from a decision of a leasehold valuation tribunal under this Part without the leave of the leasehold valuation tribunal concerned or the Lands Tribunal. .

(8) On an appeal to the Lands Tribunal from a decision of a leasehold valuation tribunal under this Part— .

(a) the Lands Tribunal may exercise any power available to the leasehold valuation tribunal in relation to the original matter, and .

(b) an order of the Lands Tribunal may be enforced in the same way as an order of the leasehold valuation tribunal.[1]

1   Repealed by Commonhold and Leasehold Reform Act 2002, Sch 14, para 1 (30 September 2003: 26 July 2002 in relation to England for repeals specified in SI 2002/1912, art 2(b)(ii) and Sch 1; 1 January 2003 in relation to Wales for repeals specified in SI 2002/3012, art 2(b)(ii) and Sch 1; 30 September 2003 in relation to England for repeals specified in SI 2003/1986 art 2(c)(iv) and Sch 1; 30 March 2004 in relation to Wales for repeals specified in SI 2004/669, art 2(c)(iv) and Sch 1; 17 November 2004 for the repeal specified in SI 2004/3056, art 2; 28 February 2005 in relation to England for repeals specified SI 2004/3056, art 3(j)(i)–(iii); 31 May 2005 in relation to Wales for repeals specified in SI 2005/1353, art 2(j)(i)–(iii); not yet in force otherwise).

24B. Leasehold valuation tribunal: application and fees.

(1) The Secretary of State may make provision by order as to the form of, or the particulars to be contained in, an application made to a leasehold valuation tribunal under this Part.

(2) The Secretary of State may make provision by order— .

(a) requiring the payment of fees in respect of any such application, or in respect of any proceedings before, a leasehold valuation tribunal under this Part; and .

(b) empowering a leasehold valuation tribunal to require a party to proceedings before it to reimburse any other party the whole or part of any fees paid by him. .

(3) The fees payable shall be such as may be specified in or determined in accordance with the order subject to this limit, that the fees payable in respect of any one application or reference by the court together with any proceedings before the tribunal arising out of that application or reference shall not exceed £500 or such other amount as may be specified by order of the Secretary of State. .

(4) An order under this section may make different provision for different cases or classes of case or for different areas. .

(5) An order may, in particular, provide for the reduction or waiver of fees by reference to the financial resources of the party by whom they are to be paid or met. .

Any such order may apply, subject to such modifications as may be specified in the order, any other statutory means-testing regime as it has effect from time to time.

(6) An order under this section shall be made by statutory instrument. .

(7) No order altering the limit under subsection (3) shall be made unless a draft of the order has been laid before and approved by a resolution of each House of Parliament. .

(8) Any other order under this section, unless it contains only such provision as is

mentioned in subsection (1), shall be subject to annulment in pursuance of a resolution of either House of Parliament.[1]

1   Repealed by Commonhold and Leasehold Reform Act 2002, Sch 14, para 1 (30 September 2003: 26 July 2002 in relation to England for repeals specified in SI 2002/1912, art 2(b)(ii) and Sch 1; 1 January 2003 in relation to Wales for repeals specified in SI 2002/3012, art 2(b)(ii) and Sch 1; 30 September 2003 in relation to England for repeals specified in SI 2003/1986, art 2(c)(iv) and Sch 1; 30 March 2004 in relation to Wales for repeals specified in SI 2004/669, art 2(c)(iv) and Sch 1; 17 November 2004 for the repeal specified in SI 2004/3056, art 2; 28 February 2005 in relation to England for repeals specified SI 2004/3056, art 3(j)(i)–(iii); 31 May 2005 in relation to Wales for repeals specified in SI 2005/1353, art 2(j)(i)–(iii); not yet in force otherwise).

PART IV VARIATION OF LEASES

Applications relating to flats

35. Application by party to lease for variation of lease.
(1) Any party to a long lease of a flat may make an application to [a leasehold valuation tribunal][1] for an order varying the lease in such manner as is specified in the application.
(2) The grounds on which any such application may be made are that the lease fails to make satisfactory provision with respect to one or more of the following matters, namely—
    (a) the repair or maintenance of—
        (i) the flat in question, or
        (ii) the building containing the flat, or
        (iii) any land or building which is let to the tenant under the lease or in respect of which rights are conferred on him under it;
    [(b) the insurance of the building containing the flat or of any such land or building as is mentioned in paragraph (a)(iii);][2]
    (c) the repair or maintenance of any installations (whether they are in the same building as the flat or not) which are reasonably necessary to ensure that occupiers of the flat enjoy a reasonable standard of accommodation;
    (d) the provision or maintenance of any services which are reasonably necessary to ensure that occupiers of the flat enjoy a reasonable standard of accommodation (whether they are services connected with any such installations or not, and whether they are services provided for the benefit of those occupiers or services provided for the benefit of the occupiers of a number of flats including that flat);
    (e) the recovery by one party to the lease from another party to it of expenditure incurred or to be incurred by him, or on his behalf, for the benefit of that other party or of a number of persons who include that other party;
    (f) the computation of a service charge payable under the lease [;][2]
    [(g) such other matters as may be prescribed by regulations made by the Secretary of State.][2]
(3) For the purposes of subsection (2)(c) and (d) the factors for determining, in relation to the occupiers of a flat, what is a reasonable standard of accommodation may include—
    (a) factors relating to the safety and security of the flat and its occupiers and of any common parts of the building containing the flat; and
    (b) other factors relating to the condition of any such common parts.
[(3A) For the purposes of subsection (2)(e) the factors for determining, in relation to a service charge payable under a lease, whether the lease makes satisfactory provision include whether it makes provision for an amount to be payable (by way of interest or otherwise) in respect of a failure to pay the service charge by the due date.][2]

(4) For the purposes of subsection (2)(f) a lease fails to make satisfactory provision with respect to the computation of a service charge payable under it if—

(a) it provides for any such charge to be a proportion of expenditure incurred, or to be incurred, by or on behalf of the landlord or a superior landlord; and

(b) other tenants of the landlord are also liable under their leases to pay by way of service charges proportions of any such expenditure; and

(c) the aggregate of the amounts that would, in any particular case, be payable by reference to the proportions referred to in paragraphs (a) and (b) would [either exceed or be less than][3] the whole of any such expenditure.

(5) [Procedure regulations under Schedule 12 to the Commonhold and Leasehold Reform Act 2002][1] shall make provision—

(a) for requiring notice of any application under this Part to be served by the person making the application, and by any respondent to the application, on any person who the applicant, or (as the case may be) the respondent, knows or has reason to believe is likely to be affected by any variation specified in the application, and

(b) for enabling persons served with any such notice to be joined as parties to the proceedings.

[(6) For the purposes of this Part a long lease shall not be regarded as a long lease of a flat if—

(a) the demised premises consist of or include three or more flats contained in the same building; or

(b) the lease constitutes a tenancy to which Part II of the Landlord and Tenant Act 1954 applies.][4]

(8) In this section "service charge" has the meaning given by section 18(1) of the 1985 Act.

1   Amended by Commonhold and Leasehold Reform Act 2002, Pt 2, s 163(2) (30 March 2004 as SI 2004/669).
2   Amended by Commonhold and Leasehold Reform Act 2002, Pt 2, s 162 (1 January 2003 as SI 2002/3012, modification has effect subject to transitional provisions and savings specified in SI 2002/3012, Sch 2).
3   Words substituted by Leasehold Reform, Housing and Urban Development Act 1993, Pt I, s 86 (1 November 1993 subject to transitional provisions and savings specified in SI 1993/2134, Sch 1).
4   Section 35(6), (7) substituted by Housing Act 1988, s 119, Sch 13, para 5.

36. Application by respondent for variation of other leases.

(1) Where an application ("the original application") is made under section 35 by any party to a lease, any other party to the lease may make an application to the [tribunal][1] asking it, in the event of its deciding to make an order effecting any variation of the lease in pursuance of the original application, to make an order which effects a corresponding variation of each of such one or more other leases as are specified in the application.

(2) Any lease so specified—

(a) must be a long lease of a flat under which the landlord is the same person as the landlord under the lease specified in the original application; but

(b) need not be a lease of a flat which is in the same building as the flat let under that lease, nor a lease drafted in terms identical to those of that lease.

(3) The grounds on which an application may be made under this section are—

(a) that each of the leases specified in the application fails to make satisfactory provision with respect to the matter or matters specified in the original application; and

(b) that, if any variation is effected in pursuance of the original application, it would be in the interests of the person making the application under this section, or in the interests of the other persons who are parties to the leases specified in that application, to have all of the leases in question (that is to say, the ones specified in that application together with the one specified in the original application) varied to the same effect.

1   Word substituted by Commonhold and Leasehold Reform Act 2002, Pt 2, s 163(3) (30 March 2004 as SI 2004/669).

37. Application by majority of parties for variation of leases.
(1) Subject to the following provisions of this section, an application may be made to [a leasehold valuation tribunal][1] in respect of two or more leases for an order varying each of those leases in such manner as is specified in the application.
(2) Those leases must be long leases of flats under which the landlord is the same person, but they need not be leases of flats which are in the same building, nor leases which are drafted in identical terms.
(3) The grounds on which an application may be made under this section are that the object to be achieved by the variation cannot be satisfactorily achieved unless all the leases are varied to the same effect.
(4) An application under this section in respect of any leases may be made by the landlord or any of the tenants under the leases.
(5) Any such application shall only be made if—
　　(a) in a case where the application is in respect of less than nine leases, all, or all 0but one, of the parties concerned consent to it; or
　　(b) in a case where the application is in respect of more than eight leases, it is not opposed for any reason by more than 10 per cent. of the total number of the parties concerned and at least 75 per cent. of that number consent to it.
(6) For the purposes of subsection (5)—
　　(a) in the case of each lease in respect of which the application is made, the tenant under the lease shall constitute one of the parties concerned (so that in determining the total number of the parties concerned a person who is the tenant under a number of such leases shall be regarded as constituting a corresponding number of the parties concerned); and
　　(b) the landlord shall also constitute one of the parties concerned.

1   Words substituted by Commonhold and Leasehold Reform Act 2002, Pt 2, s 163(4) (30 March 2004 as SI 2004/669).

Orders varying leases

38. Orders [...][1] varying leases.
(1) If, on an application under section 35, the grounds on which the application was made are established to the satisfaction of the [tribunal][2] , the [tribunal][2] may (subject to subsections (6) and (7)) make an order varying the lease specified in the application in such manner as is specified in the order.
(2) If—
　　(a) an application under section 36 was made in connection with that application, and
　　(b) the grounds set out in subsection (3) of that section are established to the satisfaction of the [tribunal][2] with respect to the leases specified in the application under section 36,
the [tribunal][2] may (subject to subsections (6) and (7)) also make an order varying each of those leases in such manner as is specified in the order.
(3) If, on an application under section 37, the grounds set out in subsection (3) of that section are established to the satisfaction of the [tribunal][2] with respect to the leases

503

specified in the application, the [tribunal]² may (subject to subsections (6) and (7)) make an order varying each of those leases in such manner as is specified in the order.

(4) The variation specified in an order under subsection (1) or (2) may be either the variation specified in the relevant application under section 35or 36 or such other variation as the [tribunal]² thinks fit.

(5) If the grounds referred to in subsection (2) or (3) (as the case may be) are established to the satisfaction of the [tribunal]² with respect to some but not all of the leases specified in the application, the power to make an order under that subsection shall extend to those leases only.

(6) [A tribunal]² shall not make an order under this section effecting any variation of a lease if it appears to [the tribunal]² —

> (a) that the variation would be likely substantially to prejudice—
>> (i) any respondent to the application, or
>> (ii) any person who is not a party to the application,
> and that an award under subsection (10) would not afford him adequate compensation, or
> (b) that for any other reason it would not be reasonable in the circumstances for the variation to be effected.

(7) [A tribunal]² shall not, on an application relating to the provision to be made by a lease with respect to insurance, make an order under this section effecting any variation of the lease—

> (a) which terminates any existing right of the landlord under its terms to nominate an insurer for insurance purposes; or
> (b) which requires the landlord to nominate a number of insurers from which the tenant would be entitled to select an insurer for those purposes; or
> (c) which, in a case where the lease requires the tenant to effect insurance with a specified insurer, requires the tenant to effect insurance otherwise than with another specified insurer.

(8) [A tribunal]² may, instead of making an order varying a lease in such manner as is specified in the order, make an order directing the parties to the lease to vary it in such manner as is so specified; and accordingly any reference in this Part (however expressed) to an order which effects any variation of a lease or to any variation effected by an order shall include a reference to an order which directs the parties to a lease to effect a variation of it or (as the case may be) a reference to any variation effected in pursuance of such an order.

(9) [A tribunal]² may by order direct that a memorandum of any variation of a lease effected by an order under this section shall be endorsed on such documents as are specified in the order.

(10) Where [a tribunal]² makes an order under this section varying a lease [the tribunal]² may, if it thinks fit, make an order providing for any party to the lease to pay, to any other party to the lease or to any other person, compensation in respect of any loss or disadvantage that the court considers he is likely to suffer as a result of the variation.

1   Words repealed subject to savings specified in SI 2004/669, Sch 2, para 12 by Commonhold and Leasehold Reform Act 2002, Sch 14, para 1 (30 March 2004: repeal has effect as SI 2004/669 subject to savings specified in SI 2004/669, Sch 2, para 12).
2   Amended by Commonhold and Leasehold Reform Act 2002, Pt 2, s 163(5) (30 March 2004 as SI 2004/669).

39. Effect of orders varying leases: applications by third parties.

(1) Any variation effected by an order under section 38 shall be binding not only on the parties to the lease for the time being but also on other persons (including any predecessors

in title of those parties), whether or not they were parties to the proceedings in which the order was made or were served with a notice by virtue of section 35(5).

(2) Without prejudice to the generality of subsection (1), any variation effected by any such order shall be binding on any surety who has guaranteed the performance of any obligation varied by the order; and the surety shall accordingly be taken to have guaranteed the performance of that obligation as so varied.

(3) Where any such order has been made and a person was, by virtue of section 35(5), required to be served with a notice relating to the proceedings in which it was made, but he was not so served, he may—

(a) bring an action for damages for breach of statutory duty against the person by whom any such notice was so required to be served in respect of that person's failure to serve it;

(b) apply to [a leasehold valuation tribunal][1] for the cancellation or modification of the variation in question.

(4) [A tribunal][1] may, on an application under subsection (3)(b) with respect to any variation of a lease—

(a) by order cancel that variation or modify it in such manner as is specified in the order, or

(b) make such an order as is mentioned in section 38(10) in favour of the person making the application,

as it thinks fit.

(5) Where a variation is cancelled or modified under paragraph (a) of subsection (4)—

(a) the cancellation or modification shall take effect as from the date of the making of the order under that paragraph or as from such later date as may be specified in the order, and

(b) the [tribunal][1] may by order direct that a memorandum of the cancellation or modification shall be endorsed on such documents as are specified in the order;

and, in a case where a variation is so modified, subsections (1) and (2) above shall, as from the date when the modification takes effect, apply to the variation as modified.

1   Amended by Commonhold and Leasehold Reform Act 2002, Pt 2, s 163(6) (30 March 2004 as SI 2004/669).

Applications relating to dwellings other than flats

40. Application for variation of insurance provisions of lease of dwelling other than a flat.

(1) Any party to a long lease of a dwelling may make an application to [a leasehold valuation tribunal][1] for an order varying the lease, in such manner as is specified in the application, on the grounds that the lease fails to make satisfactory provision with respect to any matter relating to the insurance of the dwelling, including the recovery of the costs of such insurance.

(2) Sections 36 and 38 shall apply to an application under subsection (1) subject to the modifications specified in subsection (3).

(3) Those modifications are as follows—

(a) in section 36—

(i) in subsection (1), the reference to section 35 shall be read as a reference to subsection (1) above, and

(ii) in subsection (2), any reference to a flat shall be read as a reference to a dwelling; and

(b) in section 38—

(i) any reference to an application under section 35 shall be read as a reference to an application under subsection (1) above, and

(ii) any reference to an application under section 36 shall be read as a reference to an application under section 36 as applied by subsection (2) above.

[(4) For the purpose of this section, a long lease shall not be regarded as a long lease of a dwelling if—

(a) the demised premises consist of three or more dwellings; or

(b) the lease constitutes a tenancy to which Part II of the Landlord and Tenant Act 1954 applies.][2]

[(4A) Without prejudice to subsection (4), an application under sub-section (1) may not be made by a person who is a tenant under a long lease of a dwelling if, by virtue of that lease and one or more other long leases of dwellings, he is also a tenant from the same landlord of at least two other dwellings.

(4B) For the purposes of subsection (4A), any tenant of a dwelling who is a body corporate shall be treated as a tenant of any other dwelling held from the same landlord which is let under a long lease to an associated company, as defined in section 20(1).][3]

(5) In this section "dwelling" means a dwelling other than a flat.

1 Words substituted by Commonhold and Leasehold Reform Act 2002, Pt 2, s 163(7) (30 March 2004 as SI 2004/669).
2 Section 40(4) substituted by Housing Act 1988, s 119, Sch 13, para 6.
3 Section 40(4A), (4B) substituted by Housing Act 1988, s 119, Sch 13, para 6.

PART V MANAGEMENT OF LEASEHOLD PROPERTY

Service charges

...

[42. Service charge contributions to be held in trust.

(1) This section applies where the tenants of two or more dwellings may be required under the terms of their leases to contribute to the same costs, or the tenant of a dwelling may be required under the terms of his lease to contribute to costs to which no other tenant of a dwelling may be required to contribute, by the payment of service charges; and in this section—

"the contributing tenants" means those tenants and "the sole contributing tenant" means that tenant;

"the payee" means the landlord or other person to whom any such charges are payable by those tenants, or that tenant, under the terms of their leases, or his lease;

"relevant service charges" means any such charges;

"service charge" has the meaning given by section 18(1) of the 1985 Act, except that it does not include a service charge payable by the tenant of a dwelling the rent of which is registered under Part IV of the Rent Act 1977, unless the amount registered is, in pursuance of section 71(4) of that Act, entered as a variable amount;

"tenant" does not include a tenant of an exempt landlord; and

"trust fund" means the fund, or (as the case may be) any of the funds, mentioned in subsection (2) below.

(2) Any sums paid to the payee by the contributing tenants, or the sole contributing tenant, by way of relevant service charges, and any investments representing those sums, shall (together with any income accruing thereon) be held by the payee either as a single fund or, if he thinks fit, in two or more separate funds.

(3) The payee shall hold any trust fund—

(a) on trust to defray costs incurred in connection with the matters for which the relevant service charges were payable (whether incurred by himself or by any other person), and

(b) subject to that, on trust for the persons who are the contributing tenants for the time being, or the person who is the sole contributing tenant for the time being.

(4) Subject to subsections (6) to (8), the contributing tenants shall be treated as entitled by virtue of subsection (3)(b) to such shares in the residue of any such fund as are proportionate to their respective liabilities to pay relevant service charges or the sole contributing tenant shall be treated as so entitled to the residue of any such fund.

(5) If the Secretary of State by order so provides, any sums standing to the credit of any trust fund may, instead of being invested in any other manner authorised by law, be invested in such manner as may be specified in the order; and any such order may contain such incidental, supplemental or transitional provisions as the Secretary of State considers appropriate in connection with the order.

(6) On the termination of the lease of any of the contributing tenants the tenant shall not be entitled to any part of any trust fund, and (except where subsection (7) applies) any part of any such fund which is attributable to relevant service charges paid under the lease shall accordingly continue to be held on the trusts referred to in subsection (3).

(7) On the termination of the lease of the last of the contributing tenants, or of the lease of the sole contributing tenant, any trust fund shall be dissolved as at the date of the termination of the lease, and any assets comprised in the fund immediately before its dissolution shall—

(a) if the payee is the landlord, be retained by him for his own use and benefit, and

(b) in any other case, be transferred to the landlord by the payee.

(8) Subsections (4), (6) and (7) shall have effect in relation to any of the contributing tenants, or the sole contributing tenant, subject to any express terms of his lease (whenever it was granted) which relate to the distribution, either before or (as the case may be) at the termination of the lease, of amounts attributable to relevant service charges paid under its terms (whether the lease was granted before or after the commencement of this section).

(9) Subject to subsection (8), the provisions of this section shall prevail over the terms of any express or implied trust created by a lease so far as inconsistent with those provisions, other than an express trust so created, in the case of a lease of any of the contributing tenants, before the commencement of this section or, in the case of the lease of the sole contributing tenant, before the commencement of paragraph 15 of Schedule 10 to the Commonhold and Leasehold Reform Act 2002.][1]

1 Amended by Commonhold and Leasehold Reform Act 2002, Sch 10, para 15 (31 May 2005 as SI 2005/1353).

[42A. Service charge contributions to be held in designated account.

(1) The payee must hold any sums standing to the credit of any trust fund in a designated account at a relevant financial institution.

(2) An account is a designated account in relation to sums standing to the credit of a trust fund if—

(a) the relevant financial institution has been notified in writing that sums standing to the credit of the trust fund are to be (or are) held in it, and

[(b) any other sums held in the account are sums standing to the credit of one or more other trust funds,][2]

and the account is an account of a description specified in regulations made by the [appropriate national authority][3].

[(2A) The appropriate national authority may by regulations ensure that a payee who holds more than one trust fund in the same designated account cannot move any of those funds to another designated account unless conditions specified in the regulations are met.][4]

507

(3) Any of the contributing tenants, or the sole contributing tenant, may by notice in writing require the payee—

(a) to afford him reasonable facilities for inspecting documents evidencing that subsection (1) is [, or regulations under subsection (2A) are,]⁵ complied with and for taking copies of or extracts from [such documents]⁶ , or

(b) to take copies of or extracts from any such documents and either send them to him or afford him reasonable facilities for collecting them (as he specifies).

(4) If the tenant is represented by a recognised tenants' association and he consents, the notice may be served by the secretary of the association instead of by the tenant (and in that case any requirement imposed by it is to afford reasonable facilities, or to send copies or extracts, to the secretary).

(5) A notice under [subsection (3)]⁷ is duly served on the payee if it is served on—

(a) an agent of the payee named as such in the rent book or similar document, or

(b) the person who receives the rent on behalf of the payee;

and a person on whom such a notice is so served must forward it as soon as may be to the payee.

(6) The payee must comply with a requirement imposed by a notice under [subsection (3)]⁷ within the period of twenty-one days beginning with the day on which he receives the notice.

(7) To the extent that a notice under [subsection (3)]⁷ requires the payee to afford facilities for inspecting documents—

(a) he must do so free of charge, but

(b) he may treat as part of his costs of management any costs incurred by him in doing so.

(8) The payee may make a reasonable charge for doing anything else in compliance with a requirement imposed by a notice under [subsection (3)]⁷.

(9) Any of the contributing tenants, or the sole contributing tenant, may withhold payment of a service charge if he has reasonable grounds for believing that the payee has failed to comply with the duty imposed on him by subsection (1); and any provisions of his tenancy relating to non-payment or late payment of service charges do not have effect in relation to the period for which he so withholds it.

[(9A) Regulations under subsection (2A) may include provision about–

(a) the circumstances in which a contributing tenant who has reasonable grounds for believing that the payee has not complied with a duty imposed on him by the regulations may withhold payment of a service charge,

(b) the period for which payment may be so withheld,

(c) the amount of service charge that may be so withheld;

and the regulations may provide that any provisions of the contributing tenant's tenancy relating to non-payment or late payment of service charge do not have effect in relation to the period for which the payment is so withheld.]⁸

(10) Nothing in this section [or in regulations under subsection (2A)]⁹ applies to the payee if the circumstances are such as are specified in regulations made by the [appropriate national authority]¹⁰.

[(10A) Regulations under this section may–

(a) make different provision for different cases, including different provision for different areas,

(b) contain such supplementary, incidental, consequential, transitional, transitory or saving provision as the appropriate national authority considers appropriate.

(10B) Regulations under this section are to be made by statutory instrument which–

(a) in the case of regulations made by the Secretary of State, is to be subject to annulment in pursuance of a resolution of either House of Parliament, and

(b) in the case of regulations made by the Welsh Ministers, is to be subject to annulment in pursuance of a resolution of the National Assembly for Wales.][11]

(11) In this section—

["the appropriate national authority"–

(a) in relation to England, means the Secretary of State, and

(b) in relation to Wales, means the Welsh Ministers,][12]

"recognised tenants' association" has the same meaning as in the 1985 Act, and

"relevant financial institution" has the meaning given by regulations made by the [appropriate national authority][13];

and expressions used both in section 42 and this section have the same meaning as in that section.][1]

1 Added by Commonhold and Leasehold Reform Act 2002, Pt 2, s 156(1) (26 July 2002 in relation to England for the purpose of making regulations as specified in SI 2002/1912, art 2(c); 1 January 2003 in relation to Wales for the purpose of making regulations as specified in SI 2002/3012, art 2(c); not yet in force otherwise).

2 Substituted by Housing and Regeneration Act 2008, Sch 12, para 12(2)(a) (1 December 2008 for the purpose of enabling the Secretary of State to make regulations under Landlord and Tenant Act 1987, s 42A; not yet in force otherwise).

3 Words substituted by Housing and Regeneration Act 2008, Sch 12, para 12(2)(b) (1 December 2008 for the purpose of enabling the Secretary of State to make regulations under Landlord and Tenant Act 1987, s 42A; not yet in force otherwise).

4 Added by Housing and Regeneration Act 2008, Sch 12, para 12(3) (1 December 2008 for the purpose of enabling the Secretary of State to make regulations under Landlord and Tenant Act 1987, s 42A; not yet in force otherwise).

5 Words inserted by Housing and Regeneration Act 2008, Sch 12, para 12(4)(a) (1 December 2008 for the purpose of enabling the Secretary of State to make regulations under Landlord and Tenant Act 1987, s 42A; not yet in force otherwise).

6 Word substituted by Housing and Regeneration Act 2008, Sch 12, para 12(4)(b) (1 December 2008 for the purpose of enabling the Secretary of State to make regulations under Landlord and Tenant Act 1987, s 42A; not yet in force otherwise).

7 Words substituted by Housing and Regeneration Act 2008, Sch 12, para 12(5) (1 December 2008 for the purpose of enabling the Secretary of State to make regulations under Landlord and Tenant Act 1987, s 42A; not yet in force otherwise).

8 Added by Housing and Regeneration Act 2008, Sch 12, para 12(6) (1 December 2008 for the purpose of enabling the Secretary of State to make regulations under Landlord and Tenant Act 1987, s 42A; not yet in force otherwise).

9 Words inserted by Housing and Regeneration Act 2008, Sch 12, para 12(7)(a) (1 December 2008 for the purpose of enabling the Secretary of State to make regulations under Landlord and Tenant Act 1987, s 42A; not yet in force otherwise).

10 Words substituted by Housing and Regeneration Act 2008, Sch 12, para 12(7)(b) (1 December 2008 for the purpose of enabling the Secretary of State to make regulations under Landlord and Tenant Act 1987, s 42A; not yet in force otherwise).

11 Added by Housing and Regeneration Act 2008, Sch 12, para 12(8) (1 December 2008 for the purpose of enabling the Secretary of State to make regulations under Landlord and Tenant Act 1987, s.42A; not yet in force otherwise).

12 Definition inserted by Housing and Regeneration Act 2008, Sch 12, para 12(9)(a) (1 December 2008 for the purpose of enabling the Secretary of State to make regulations under Landlord and Tenant Act 1987, s 42A; not yet in force otherwise).

13 Words substituted by Housing and Regeneration Act 2008, Sch 12, para 12(9)(b) (1 December 2008 for the purpose of enabling the Secretary of State to make regulations under Landlord and Tenant Act 1987, s 42A; not yet in force otherwise).

[42B. Failure to comply with section 42A.

(1) If a person fails, without reasonable excuse, to comply with a duty imposed on him by or by virtue of section 42A he commits an offence.

(2) A person guilty of an offence under this section is liable on summary conviction to a fine not exceeding level 4 on the standard scale.

(3) Where an offence under this section committed by a body corporate is proved—

> (a) to have been committed with the consent or connivance of a director, manager, secretary or other similar officer of the body corporate, or a person purporting to act in such a capacity, or
>
> (b) to be due to any neglect on the part of such an officer or person,

he, as well as the body corporate, is guilty of the offence and liable to be proceeded against and punished accordingly.

(4) Where the affairs of a body corporate are managed by its members, subsection (3) applies in relation to the acts and defaults of a member in connection with his functions of management as if he were a director of the body corporate.

(5) Proceedings for an offence under this section may be brought by a local housing authority (within the meaning of section 1 of the Housing Act 1985 (c. 68)).][1]

1   Added by Commonhold and Leasehold Reform Act 2002, Pt 2, s 156(1) (26 July 2002 in relation to England for the purpose of making regulations as specified in SI 2002/1912, art 2(c); 1 January 2003 in relation to Wales for the purpose of making regulations as specified in SI 2002/3012, art 2(c); not yet in force otherwise).

PART VI INFORMATION TO BE FURNISHED TO TENANTS

46. Application of Part VI, etc.

(1) This Part applies to premises which consist of or include a dwelling and are not held under a tenancy to which Part II of the Landlord and Tenant Act 1954 applies.

(2) In this Part "service charge" has the meaning given by section 18(1) of the 1985 Act.

[(3) In this Part "administration charge" has the meaning given by paragraph 1 of Schedule 11 to the Commonhold and Leasehold Reform Act 2002.][1]

1   Added by Commonhold and Leasehold Reform Act 2002, Sch 11(2), para 9 (30 March 2004 as SI 2004/669).

47. Landlord's name and address to be contained in demands for rent etc.

(1) Where any written demand is given to a tenant of premises to which this Part applies, the demand must contain the following information, namely—

> (a) the name and address of the landlord, and
>
> (b) if that address is not in England and Wales, an address in England and Wales at which notices (including notices in proceedings) may be served on the landlord by the tenant.

(2) Where—

> (a) a tenant of any such premises is given such a demand, but
>
> (b) it does not contain any information required to be contained in it by virtue of subsection (1),

then (subject to subsection (3)) any part of the amount demanded which consists of a service charge [or an administration charge][1] ("the relevant amount") shall be treated for all purposes as not being due from the tenant to the landlord at any time before that information is furnished by the landlord by notice given to the tenant.

(3) The relevant amount shall not be so treated in relation to any time when, by virtue of an order of any [or tribunal][2], there is in force an appointment of a receiver or manager whose functions include the receiving of service charges [or (as the case may be) administration charges][1] from the tenant.

(4) In this section "demand" means a demand for rent or other sums payable to the landlord under the terms of the tenancy.

1   Amended by Commonhold and Leasehold Reform Act 2002, Sch 11(2), para 10 (30 March 2004 as SI 2004/669).
2   Words inserted by Commonhold and Leasehold Reform Act 2002, Sch 13, para 10 (30 March 2004 as SI 2004/669).

48. Notification by landlord of address for service of notices.
(1) A landlord of premises to which this Part applies shall by notice furnish the tenant with an address in England and Wales at which notices (including notices in proceedings) may be served on him by the tenant.
(2) Where a landlord of any such premises fails to comply with subsection (1), any rent [, service charge or administration charge][1] otherwise due from the tenant to the landlord shall (subject to subsection (3)) be treated for all purposes as not being due from the tenant to the landlord at any time before the landlord does comply with that subsection.
(3) Any such rent [, service charge or administration charge][1] shall not be so treated in relation to any time when, by virtue of an order of any court [or tribunal][2], there is in force an appointment of a receiver or manager whose functions include the receiving of rent [, service charges or (as the case may be) administration charges][1] from the tenant.

1   Amended by Commonhold and Leasehold Reform Act 2002, Sch 11(2), para 11 (30 March 2004 as SI 2004/669).
2   Words inserted by Commonhold and Leasehold Reform Act 2002, Sch 13, para 11 (30 March 2004 as SI 2004/669).

...

PART VII GENERAL

...

53. Regulations and orders.
(1) Any power of the Secretary of State to make an order or regulations under this Act shall be exercisable by statutory instrument and may be exercised so as to make different provision for different cases, including different provision for different areas.
(2) A statutory instrument containing—
    (a) an order made under section 1(5), 25(6), 42(5) or 55, or
    (b) any regulations made [...][1] under section 20(4) [or 35(2)(g)][2] [...][3],
shall be subject to annulment in pursuance of a resolution of either House of Parliament.
[(3) This section does not apply to any power to make regulations under section 42A.][4]

1   Words repealed by Commonhold and Leasehold Reform Act 2002, Sch 14, para 1 (30 March 2004 as SI 2004/669).
2   Words inserted by Commonhold and Leasehold Reform Act 2002, Pt 2, s 162(5) (1 January 2003 as SI 2002/3012, insertion has effect subject to transitional provisions and savings specified in SI 2002/3012, Sch 2).
3   Words repealed by Housing and Regeneration Act 2008, Sch12, para 13(2) (1 December 2008 for the purpose of enabling the Secretary of State to make regulations under Landlord and Tenant Act 1987, s 42A; not yet in force otherwise).
4   Added by Housing and Regeneration Act 2008, Sch 12, para 13(3) (1 December 2008 for the purpose of enabling the Secretary of State to make regulations under Landlord and Tenant Act 1987, s 42A; not yet in force otherwise).

54. Notices.
(1) Any notice required or authorised to be served under this Act—
    (a) shall be in writing; and
    (b) may be sent by post.

(2) Any notice purporting to be a notice served under any provision of Part I or IIIby the requisite majority of any qualifying tenants (as defined for the purposes of that provision) shall specify the names of all of the persons by whom it is served and the addresses of the flats of which they are qualifying tenants.

(3) The Secretary of State may by regulations prescribe—

(a) the form of any notices required or authorised to be served under or in pursuance of any provision of Parts I to III, and

(b) the particulars which any such notices must contain (whether in addition to, or in substitution for, any particulars required by virtue of the provision in question).

(4) Subsection (3)(b) shall not be construed as authorising the Secretary of State to make regulations under subsection (3) varying [any of the periods specified in section 5A(4) or (5), 5B(5) or (6), 5C(4) or (5), 5D(4) or (5) or 5E(3)]¹ (which accordingly can only be varied by regulations under section 20(4)).

1   Words substituted subject to savings specified in SI 1996/2212, Sch 1, para 2 by Housing Act 1996, Sch 6, Pt IV, para 9 (1 October 1996: substitution has effect subject to savings specified in SI 1996/2212, Sch 1, para 2).

55. Application to Isles of Scilly.

This Act shall apply to the Isles of Scilly subject to such exceptions, adaptations and modifications as the Secretary of State may by order direct.

56. Crown land.

(1) [Parts 1 and 3 and section 42 (and so much of this Part as relates to those provisions)]¹ shall apply to a tenancy from the Crown if there has ceased to be a Crown interest in the land subject to it.

[…]²

(3) Where there exists a Crown interest in any land subject to a tenancy from the Crown and the person holding that tenancy is himself the landlord under any other tenancy whose subject-matter comprises the whole or part of that land, [the provisions mentioned in subsection (1)]¹ shall apply to that other tenancy, and to any derivative sub-tenancy, notwithstanding the existence of that interest.

(4) For the purposes of this section "tenancy from the Crown" means a tenancy of land in which there is, or has during the subsistence of the tenancy been, a Crown interest superior to the tenancy, and "Crown interest" means —

(a) an interest comprised in the Crown Estate;

(b) an interest belonging to Her Majesty in right of the Duchy of Lancaster;

(c) an interest belonging to the Duchy of Cornwall;

(d) any other interest belonging to a government department or held on behalf of Her Majesty for the purposes of a government department.

1   Amended by Commonhold and Leasehold Reform Act 2002, Pt 2, s 172(6) (30 March 2004 as SI 2004/669).
2   Repealed by Commonhold and Leasehold Reform Act 2002, Sch 14, para 1 (30 March 2004 as SI 2004/669).

57. Financial provision.

There shall be paid out of money provided by Parliament any increase attributable to this Act in the sums payable out of money so provided under any other Act.

58. Exempt landlords and resident landlords.

(1) In this Act "exempt landlord" means a landlord who is one of the following bodies, namely—

(a) a district, county [, county borough][1] or London borough council, the Common Council of the City of London, [the London Fire and Emergency Planning Authority,][2] the Council of the Isles of Scilly, [a police and crime commissioner, the Mayor's Office for Policing and Crime][3] [...][4] [...][5] [,][6] [...][7] [a joint authority established by Part 4 of the Local Government Act 1985, an economic prosperity board established under section 88 of the Local Democracy, Economic Development and Construction Act 2009 or a combined authority established under section 103 of that Act;][8];

(b) [...][9] a development corporation established by an order made (or having effect as if made) under the New Towns Act 1981;

[(ba) a Mayoral development corporation;][10]

(c) an urban development corporation within the meaning of Part XVI of the Local Government, Planning and Land Act 1980;

[(ca) a housing action trust established under Part III of the Housing Act 1988.][11]

[...][12]

[(dd) the Broads Authority;][13]

[(de) a National Park authority;][14]

[(df) the Homes and Communities Agency;][15]

[(dg) the Greater London Authority so far as exercising its housing or regeneration functions or its new towns and urban development functions;][16]

(e) the [Regulator of Social Housing][17];

[...][18]

(f) a housing trust (as defined in section 6 of the Housing Act 1985) which is a charity;

[(g) a non-profit private registered provider of social housing;

(ga) a registered social landlord;

(gb) a fully mutual housing association which is neither a private registered provider of social housing nor a registered social landlord; or][19]

(h) an authority established under section 10 of the Local Government Act 1985(joint arrangements for waste disposal functions).

[(1ZA) In this Act "exempt landlord", in relation to social housing (within the meaning of Part 2 of the Housing and Regeneration Act 2008), includes a landlord which is a profit-making private registered provider of social housing.][20]

[(1A) In subsection (1)(ga) "registered social landlord" has the same meaning as in the Housing Act 1985 (see section 5(4) and (5) of that Act).

(1B) In subsection (1)(gb) "fully mutual housing association" has the same meaning as in the Housing Associations Act 1985 (see section 1(1) and (2) of that Act).][21]

(2) For the purposes of this Act the landlord of any premises consisting of the whole or part of a building is a resident landlord of those premises at any time if—

(a) the premises are not, and do not form part of, a purpose-built block of flats; and

(b) at that time the landlord occupies a flat contained in the premises as his only or principal residence; and

(c) he has so occupied such a flat throughout a period of not less than 12 months ending with that time.

(3) In subsection (2) "purpose-built block of flats" means a building which contained as constructed, and contains, two or more flats.

1   Words inserted by Local Government (Wales) Act 1994, Sch 8, para 8 (1 April 1996).
2   Words added by Greater London Authority Act 1999, Sch 29, Pt I, para 48 (3 July 2000).
3   Words substituted by Police Reform and Social Responsibility Act 2011, Sch 16, Pt 3, para 176 (22 November 2012: commenced by an amendment).
4   Words repealed by Education Reform Act 1988, ss 231(7), 235(6), 237(2), Sch 13, Pt I.

5   Words repealed by Criminal Justice and Police Act 2001, Sch 7, Pt 5(1), para 1 (1 April 2002 as SI 2002/344).
6   Words inserted by Police Act 1997, Sch 9, para 52 (31 October 1997).
7   Words repealed by Police Reform and Social Responsibility Act 2011, Sch 16, Pt 3, para 176 (22 November 2012 being the date on which Police Reform and Social Responsibility Act 2011, s 1 comes into force).
8   Words substituted by Local Democracy, Economic Development and Construction Act 2009, Sch 6, para 72 (17 December 2009).
9   Words repealed by Housing and Regeneration Act 2008, Sch 16, para 1 (1 December 2008 as SI 2008/3068).
10   Added by Localism Act 2011, Sch 22, para 22 (15 January 2012).
11   Section 58(1)(ca) inserted by Housing Act 1988, s 119, Sch 13, para 7.
12   Repealed by Government of Wales Act 1998, Sch 18, Pt IV, para 1 (1 October 1998).
13   Section 58(1)(dd) inserted by Norfolk and Suffolk Broads Act 1988, ss 21, 23(2), Sch 6, para 28.
14   Added by Environment Act 1995, Sch 10, para 26 (23 November 1995).
15   Added by Housing and Regeneration Act 2008, Sch 8, para 40(b) (1 December 2008).
16   Added by Localism Act 2011, Sch 19, para 23 (1 April 2012 subject to SI 2012/628, arts 9, 11, 14, 15 and 17).
17   Words substituted by Housing and Regeneration Act 2008 (Consequential Provisions) Order 2010/866, Sch 2, para 62(2)(a) (1 April 2010).
18   Repealed by Government of Wales Act 1998, Sch 18, Pt VI, para 1 (1 November 1998).
19   Section 58(1)(g)–(gb) substituted for s 58(1)(g) by Housing and Regeneration Act 2008 (Consequential Provisions) Order 2010/866, Sch 2, para 62(2)(b) (1 April 2010).
20   Added by Housing and Regeneration Act 2008 (Consequential Provisions) Order 2010/866, Sch 2, para 62(3) (1 April 2010).
21   Section 58(1A) and (1B) substituted for s 58(1A) by Housing and Regeneration Act 2008 (Consequential Provisions) Order 2010/866, Sch 2, para 62(4) (1 April 2010).

59. Meaning of "lease", "long lease" and related expressions.
(1) In this Act "lease" and "tenancy" have the same meaning;
and both expressions include—
        (a) a sub-lease or sub-tenancy, and
        (b) an agreement for a lease or tenancy (or for a sub-lease or sub-tenancy).
(2) The expressions "landlord" and "tenant", and references to letting, to the grant of a lease or to covenants or the terms of a lease shall be construed accordingly.
(3) In this Act "long lease" means —
        (a) a lease granted for a term certain exceeding 21 years, whether or not it is (or may become) terminable before the end of that term by notice given by the tenant or by re-entry or forfeiture;
        (b) a lease for a term fixed by law under a grant with a covenant or obligation for perpetual renewal, other than a lease by sub-demise from one which is not a long lease; or
        (c) a lease granted in pursuance of Part V of the Housing Act 1985 (the right to buy).
[, including a lease granted in pursuance of that Part as it has effect by virtue of section 17 of the Housing Act 1996 (the right to acquire)]¹

1   Words inserted by Housing Act 1996 (Consequential Amendments) (No 2) Order 1997/627, Sch 1, para 5 (1 April 1997).

60. General interpretation.
(1) In this Act—
        "the 1985 Act" means the Landlord and Tenant Act 1985;
        ["charitable purposes", in relation to a charity, means charitable purposes whether of that charity or of that charity and other charities;]¹

"common parts", in relation to any building or part of a building, includes the structure and exterior of that building or part and any common facilities within it;

"the court" means the High Court or a county court;

"dwelling" means a building or part of a building occupied or intended to be occupied as a separate dwelling, together with any yard, garden, outhouses and appurtenances belonging to it or usually enjoyed with it;

"exempt landlord" has the meaning given by section 58(1);

"flat" means a separate set of premises, whether or not on the same floor, which—

    (a) forms part of a building, and

    (b) is divided horizontally from some other part of that building, and

    (c) is constructed or adapted for use for the purposes of a dwelling;

"functional land", in relation to a charity, means land occupied by the charity, or by trustees for it, and wholly or mainly used for charitable purposes;

"landlord" (except for the purposes of Part I) means the immediate landlord or, in relation to a statutory tenant, the person who, apart from the statutory tenancy, would be entitled to possession of the premises subject to the tenancy;

"lease" and related expressions shall be construed in accordance with section 59(1) and (2);

"long lease" has the meaning given by section 59(3);

"mortgage" includes any charge or lien, and references to a mortgagee shall be construed accordingly;

"notices in proceedings" means notices or other documents served in, or in connection with, any legal proceedings;

[...]²

"resident landlord" shall be construed in accordance with section 58(2);

"statutory tenancy" and "statutory tenant" mean a statutory tenancy or statutory tenant within the meaning of the Rent Act 1977 or the Rent (Agriculture) Act 1976;

"tenancy" includes a statutory tenancy.

[(1A) In this Act a reference to the Welsh Ministers in their new towns residuary capacity means the Welsh Ministers so far as exercising functions in relation to anything transferred (or to be transferred) to them as mentioned in section 36(1)(a)(i) to (iii) of the New Towns Act 1981.]³

[...]⁴

1   Definition repealed by Charities (Pre-consolidation Amendments) Order 2011/1396, Sch 1, Pt 4, para 42 (14 March 2012 immediately before 2011 c.25).

2   Repealed subject to savings specified in SI 1996/2212, Sch 1, para 2 by Housing Act 1996, Sch 6, Pt IV, para 10 (1 October 1996: repeal has effect subject to savings specified in SI 1996/2212, Sch 1, para 2).

3   Added by Housing and Regeneration Act 2008, Sch 8, para 41 (1 December 2008).

4   Section 60(2) repealed by Housing Act 1988, s 140(2), Sch 18.

Leasehold Reform, Housing and Urban Development Act 1993 (extract)

PART I LANDLORD AND TENANT

Chapter V Tenants' right to management audit

76. Right to audit management by landlord.

(1) This Chapter has effect to confer on two or more qualifying tenants of dwellings held on leases from the same landlord the right, exercisable subject to and in accordance with this Chapter, to have an audit carried out on their behalf which relates to the management of the relevant premises and any appurtenant property by or on behalf of the landlord.

(2) That right shall be exercisable—

(a) where the relevant premises consist of or include two dwellings let to qualifying tenants of the same landlord, by either or both of those tenants; and

(b) where the relevant premises consist of or include three or more dwellings let to qualifying tenants of the same landlord, by not less than two-thirds of those tenants;

and in this Chapter the dwellings let to those qualifying tenants are referred to as "the constituent dwellings".

(3) In relation to an audit on behalf of two or more qualifying tenants—

(a) "the relevant premises" means so much of—

(i) the building or buildings containing the dwellings let to those tenants, and

(ii) any other building or buildings,

as constitutes premises in relation to which management functions are discharged in respect of the costs of which common service charge contributions are payable under the leases of those qualifying tenants; and

(b) "appurtenant property" means so much of any property not contained in the relevant premises as constitutes property in relation to which any such management functions are discharged.

(4) This Chapter also has effect to confer on a single qualifying tenant of a dwelling the right, exercisable subject to and in accordance with this Chapter, to have an audit carried out on his behalf which relates to the management of the relevant premises and any appurtenant property by or on behalf of the landlord.

(5) That right shall be exercisable by a single qualifying tenant of a dwelling where the relevant premises contain no other dwelling let to a qualifying tenant apart from that let to him.

(6) In relation to an audit on behalf of a single qualifying tenant—

(a) "the relevant premises" means so much of—

(i) the building containing the dwelling let to him, and

(ii) any other building or buildings,

as constitutes premises in relation to which management functions are discharged in respect of the costs of which a service charge is payable under his lease (whether as a common service charge contribution or otherwise); and

(b) "appurtenant property" means so much of any property not contained in the relevant premises as constitutes property in relation to which any such management functions are discharged.

(7) The provisions of sections 78 to 83 shall, with any necessary modifications, have effect in relation to an audit on behalf of a single qualifying tenant as they have effect in relation to an audit on behalf of two or more qualifying tenants.

(8) For the purposes of this section common service charge contributions are payable by two or more persons under their leases if they may be required under the terms of those leases to contribute to the same costs by the payment of service charges.

77. Qualifying tenants.

(1) Subject to the following provisions of this section, a tenant is a qualifying tenant of a dwelling for the purposes of this Chapter if—

(a) he is a tenant of the dwelling under a long lease other than a business lease; and

(b) any service charge is payable under the lease.

(2) For the purposes of subsection (1) a lease is a long lease if—

(a) it is a lease falling within any of paragraphs (a) to (c) of subsection (1) of section 7; or

(b) it is a shared ownership lease (within the meaning of that section), whether granted in pursuance of Part V of the Housing Act 1985 or otherwise and whatever the share of the tenant under it.

(3) No dwelling shall have more than one qualifying tenant at any one time.

(4) Accordingly—

(a) where a dwelling is for the time being let under two or more leases falling within subsection (1), any tenant under any of those leases which is superior to that held by any other such tenant shall not be a qualifying tenant of the dwelling for the purposes of this Chapter; and

(b) where a dwelling is for the time being let to joint tenants under a lease falling within subsection (1), the joint tenants shall (subject to paragraph (a)) be regarded for the purposes of this Chapter as jointly constituting the qualifying tenant of the dwelling.

(5) A person can, however, be (or be among those constituting) the qualifying tenant of each of two or more dwellings at the same time, whether he is tenant of those dwellings under one lease or under two or more separate leases.

(6) Where two or more persons constitute the qualifying tenant of a dwelling in accordance with subsection (4)(b), any one or more of those persons may sign a notice under section 80on behalf of both or all of them.

78. Management audits.

(1) The audit referred to in section 76(1) is an audit carried out for the purpose of ascertaining—

(a) the extent to which the obligations of the landlord which—

(i) are owed to the qualifying tenants of the constituent dwellings, and

(ii) involve the discharge of management functions in relation to the relevant premises or any appurtenant property,

are being discharged in an efficient and effective manner; and

(b) the extent to which sums payable by those tenants by way of service charges are being applied in an efficient and effective manner;

and in this Chapter any such audit is referred to as a "management audit".

(2) In determining whether any such obligations as are mentioned in subsection (1)(a) are being discharged in an efficient and effective manner, regard shall be had to any applicable provisions of any code of practice for the time being approved by the Secretary of State under section 87.

(3) A management audit shall be carried out by a person who—

    (a) is qualified for appointment by virtue of subsection (4); and

    (b) is appointed—

        (i) in the circumstances mentioned in section 76(2)(a), by either or both of the qualifying tenants of the constituent dwellings, or

        (ii) in the circumstances mentioned in section 76(2)(b), by not less than two-thirds of the qualifying tenants of the constituent dwellings;

and in this Chapter any such person is referred to as "the auditor".

(4) A person is qualified for appointment for the purposes of subsection (3) above if—

    (a) he has the necessary qualification (within the meaning of subsection (1) of section 28 of the 1985 Act (meaning of "qualified accountant")) or is a qualified surveyor;

    (b) he is not disqualified from acting (within the meaning of that subsection); and

    (c) he is not a tenant of any premises contained in the relevant premises.

(5) For the purposes of subsection (4)(a) above a person is a qualified surveyor if he is a fellow or professional associate of the Royal Institution of Chartered Surveyors or of the Incorporated Society of Valuers and Auctioneers or satisfies such other requirement or requirements as may be prescribed by regulations made by the Secretary of State.

(6) The auditor may appoint such persons to assist him in carrying out the audit as he thinks fit.

79. Rights exercisable in connection with management audits.

(1) Where the qualifying tenants of any dwellings exercise under section 80 their right to have a management audit carried out on their behalf, the rights conferred on the auditor by subsection (2) below shall be exercisable by him in connection with the audit.

(2) The rights conferred on the auditor by this subsection are—

    (a) a right to require the landlord—

        (i) to supply him with such a summary as is referred to in section 21(1) of the 1985 Act (request for summary of relevant costs) in connection with any service charges payable by the qualifying tenants of the constituent dwellings, and

        (ii) to afford him reasonable facilities for inspecting, or taking copies of or extracts from, the accounts, receipts and other documents supporting any such summary;

    (b) a right to require the landlord or any relevant person to afford him reasonable facilities for inspecting any other documents sight of which is reasonably required by him for the purpose of carrying out the audit; and

    (c) a right to require the landlord or any relevant person to afford him reasonable facilities for taking copies of or extracts from any documents falling within paragraph (b).

(3) The rights conferred on the auditor by subsection (2) shall be exercisable by him—

    (a) in relation to the landlord, by means of a notice under section 80; and

    (b) in relation to any relevant person, by means of a notice given to that person at (so far as is reasonably practicable) the same time as a notice under section 80 is given to the landlord;

and, where a notice is given to any relevant person in accordance with paragraph (b) above, a copy of that notice shall be given to the landlord by the auditor.

(4) The auditor shall also be entitled, on giving notice in accordance with section 80, to carry out an inspection of any common parts comprised in the relevant premises or any appurtenant property.

(5) The landlord or (as the case may be) any relevant person shall—

(a) where facilities for the inspection of any documents are required under subsection (2)(a)(ii) or (b), make those facilities available free of charge;

(b) where any documents are required to be supplied under subsection (2)(a)(i) or facilities for the taking of copies or extracts are required under subsection (2)(a)(ii) or (c), be entitled to supply those documents or (as the case may be) make those facilities available on payment of such reasonable charge as he may determine.

(6) The requirement imposed on the landlord by subsection (5)(a) to make any facilities available free of charge shall not be construed as precluding the landlord from treating as part of his costs of management any costs incurred by him in connection with making those facilities so available.

(7) In this Chapter "relevant person" means a person (other than the landlord) who—

(a) is charged with responsibility—

(i) for the discharge of any such obligations as are mentioned in section 78(1) (a), or

(ii) for the application of any such service charges as are mentioned in section 78(1)(b); or

(b) has a right to enforce payment of any such service charges.

(8) In this Chapter references to the auditor in the context of—

(a) being afforded any such facilities as are mentioned in subsection (2), or

(b) the carrying out of any inspection under subsection (4),

shall be read as including a person appointed by the auditor under section 78(6).

80. Exercise of right to have a management audit.

(1) The right of any qualifying tenants to have a management audit carried out on their behalf shall be exercisable by the giving of a notice under this section.

(2) A notice given under this section—

(a) must be given to the landlord by the auditor, and

(b) must be signed by each of the tenants on whose behalf it is given.

(3) Any such notice must—

(a) state the full name of each of those tenants and the address of the dwelling of which he is a qualifying tenant;

(b) state the name and address of the auditor;

(c) specify any documents or description of documents—

(i) which the landlord is required to supply to the auditor under section 79(2) (a)(i), or

(ii) in respect of which he is required to afford the auditor facilities for inspection or for taking copies or extracts under any other provision of section 79(2); and

(d) if the auditor proposes to carry out an inspection under section 79(4), state the date on which he proposes to carry out the inspection.

(4) The date specified under subsection (3)(d) must be a date falling not less than one month nor more than two months after the date of the giving of the notice.

(5) A notice is duly given under this section to the landlord of any qualifying tenants if it is given to a person who receives on behalf of the landlord the rent payable by any such tenants; and a person to whom such a notice is so given shall forward it as soon as may be to the landlord.

81. Procedure following given of notice under section 80.

(1) Where the landlord is given a notice under section 80, then within the period of one month beginning with the date of the giving of the notice, he shall—

(a) supply the auditor with any document specified under subsection (3)(c)(i) of that section, and afford him, in respect of any document falling within section 79(2)(a) (ii), any facilities specified in relation to it under subsection (3)(c)(ii) of section 80;

(b) in the case of every other document or description of documents specified in the notice under subsection (3)(c)(ii) of that section, either—

(i) afford the auditor facilities for inspection or (as the case may be) taking copies or extracts in respect of that document or those documents, or

(ii) give the auditor a notice stating that he objects to doing so for such reasons as are specified in the notice; and

(c) if a date is specified in the notice under subsection (3)(d) of that section, either approve the date or propose another date for the carrying out of an inspection under section 79(4).

(2) Any date proposed by the landlord under subsection (1)(c) must be a date falling not later than the end of the period of two months beginning with the date of the giving of the notice under section 80.

(3) Where a relevant person is given a notice under section 79 requiring him to afford the auditor facilities for inspection or taking copies or extracts in respect of any documents or description of documents specified in the notice, then within the period of one month beginning with the date of the giving of the notice, he shall, in the case of every such document or description of documents, either—

(a) afford the auditor the facilities required by him; or

(b) give the auditor a notice stating that he objects to doing so for such reasons as are specified in the notice.

(4) If by the end of the period of two months beginning with—

(a) the date of the giving of the notice under section 80, or

(b) the date of the giving of such a notice under section 79 as is mentioned in subsection (3) above,

the landlord or (as the case may be) a relevant person has failed to comply with any requirement of the notice, the court may, on the application of the auditor, make an order requiring the landlord or (as the case may be) the relevant person to comply with that requirement within such period as is specified in the order.

(5) The court shall not make an order under subsection (4) in respect of any document or documents unless it is satisfied that the document or documents falls or fall within paragraph (a) or (b) of section 79(2).

(6) If by the end of the period of two months specified in subsection (2) no inspection under section 79(4) has been carried out by the auditor, the court may, on the application of the auditor, make an order providing for such an inspection to be carried out on such date as is specified in the order.

(7) Any application for an order under subsection (4) or (6) must be made before the end of the period of four months beginning with—

(a) in the case of an application made in connection with a notice given under section 80, the date of the giving of that notice; or

(b) in the case of an application made in connection with such a notice under section 79 as is mentioned in subsection (3) above, the date of the giving of that notice.

82. Requirement relating to information etc. held by superior landlord.

(1) Where the landlord is required by a notice under section 80 to supply any summary falling within section 79(2)(a), and any information necessary for complying with the notice so far as relating to any such summary is in the possession of a superior landlord—

(a) the landlord shall make a written request for the relevant information to the person who is his landlord (and so on, if that person is himself not the superior landlord);

(b) the superior landlord shall comply with that request within the period of one month beginning with the date of the making of the request; and

(c) the landlord who received the notice shall then comply with it so far as relating to any such summary within the time allowed by section 81(1) or such further time, if any, as is reasonable.

(2) Where—

(a) the landlord is required by a notice under section 80 to afford the auditor facilities for inspection or taking copies or extracts in respect of any documents or description of documents specified in the notice, and

(b) any of the documents in question is in the custody or under the control of a superior landlord,

the landlord shall on receiving the notice inform the auditor as soon as may be of that fact and of the name and address of the superior landlord, and the auditor may then give the superior landlord a notice requiring him to afford the facilities in question in respect of the document.

(3) Subsections (3) to (5) and (7) of section 81 shall, with any necessary modifications, have effect in relation to a notice given to a superior landlord under subsection (2) above as they have effect in relation to any such notice given to a relevant person as is mentioned in subsection (3) of that section.

83. Supplementary provisions.

(1) Where—

(a) a notice has been given to a landlord under section 80, and

(b) at a time when any obligations arising out of the notice remain to be discharged by him—

(i) he disposes of the whole or part of his interest as landlord of the qualifying tenants of the constituent dwellings, and

(ii) the person acquiring any such interest of the landlord is in a position to discharge any of those obligations to any extent,

that person shall be responsible for discharging those obligations to that extent, as if he had been given the notice under that section.

(2) If the landlord is, despite any such disposal, still in a position to discharge those obligations to the extent referred to in subsection (1), he shall remain responsible for so discharging them; but otherwise the person referred to in that subsection shall be responsible for so discharging them to the exclusion of the landlord.

(3) Where a person is so responsible for discharging any such obligations (whether with the landlord or otherwise)—

(a) references to the landlord in section 81 shall be read as including, or as, references to that person to such extent as is appropriate to reflect his responsibility for discharging those obligations; but

(b) in connection with the discharge of any such obligations by that person, that section shall apply as if any reference to the date of the giving of the notice under section 80 were a reference to the date of the disposal referred to in subsection (1).

(4) Where—

(a) a notice has been given to a relevant person under section 79, and

(b) at a time when any obligations arising out of the notice remain to be discharged by him, he ceases to be a relevant person, but

(c) he is, despite ceasing to be a relevant person, still in a position to discharge those obligations to any extent, he shall nevertheless remain responsible for discharging those obligations to that extent; and section 81 shall accordingly continue to apply to him as if he were still a relevant person.

(5) Where—

(a) a notice has been given to a landlord under section 80, or

(b) a notice has been given to a relevant person under section 79,

then during the period of twelve months beginning with the date of that notice, no subsequent such notice may be given to the landlord or (as the case may be) that person on behalf of any persons who, in relation to the earlier notice, were qualifying tenants of the constituent dwellings.

84. Interpretation of Chapter V.

In this Chapter—

"the 1985 Act" means the Landlord and Tenant Act 1985;

"appurtenant property" shall be construed in accordance with section 76(3) or (6);

"the auditor", in relation to a management audit, means such a person as is mentioned in section 78(3);

"the constituent dwellings" means the dwellings referred to in section 76(2)(a) or (b) (as the case may be);

"landlord" means immediate landlord;;

"management audit" means such an audit as is mentioned in section 78(1);

"management functions" includes functions with respect to the provision of services or the repair, maintenance [, improvement][1] or insurance of property ;

"relevant person" has the meaning given by section 79(7);

"the relevant premises" shall be construed in accordance with section 76(3) or (6);

"service charge" has the meaning given by section 18(1) of the 1985 Act.

1   Word inserted by Commonhold and Leasehold Reform Act 2002, Sch 9, para 10 (30 March 2004 as SI 2004/669).

Chapter VI Miscellaneous

...

Codes of practice

87. Approval by Secretary of State of codes of management practice.

(1) The Secretary of State may, if he considers it appropriate to do so, by order—

(a) approve any code of practice—

(i) which appears to him to be designed to promote desirable practices in relation to any matter or matters directly or indirectly concerned with the management of residential property by relevant persons; and

(ii) which has been submitted to him for his approval;

(b) approve any modifications of any such code which have been so submitted; or

(c) withdraw his approval for any such code or modifications.

(2) The Secretary of State shall not approve any such code or any modifications of any such code unless he is satisfied that arrangements have been made for the text of the code or the modifications to be published in such manner as he considers appropriate for bringing the provisions of the code or the modifications to the notice of those likely to be affected by them (which, in the case of modifications of a code, may include publication of a text of the code incorporating the modifications).

(3) The power of the Secretary of State under this section to approve a code of practice which has been submitted to him for his approval includes power to approve a part of any such code; and references in this section to a code of practice may accordingly be read as including a reference to a part of a code of practice.

(4) At any one time there may be two or more codes of practice for the time being approved under this section.

(5) A code of practice approved under this section may make different provision with respect to different cases or descriptions of cases, including different provision for different areas.

(6) Without prejudice to the generality of subsections (1) and (5)—

    (a) a code of practice approved under this section may, in relation to any such matter as is referred to in subsection (1), make provision in respect of relevant persons who are under an obligation to discharge any function in connection with that matter as well as in respect of relevant persons who are not under such an obligation; and

    (b) any such code may make provision with respect to—

        (i) the resolution of disputes with respect to residential property between relevant persons and the tenants of such property;

        (ii) competitive tendering for works in connection with such property; and

        (iii) the administration of trusts in respect of amounts paid by tenants by way of service charges.

(7) A failure on the part of any person to comply with any provision of a code of practice for the time being approved under this section shall not of itself render him liable to any proceedings; but in any proceedings before a court or tribunal—

    (a) any code of practice approved under this section shall be admissible in evidence; and

    (b) any provision of any such code which appears to the court or tribunal to be relevant to any question arising in the proceedings shall be taken into account in determining that question.

(8) For the purposes of this section—

    (a) "relevant person" means any landlord of residential property or any person who discharges management functions in respect of such property, and for this purpose "management functions" includes functions with respect to the provision of services or the repair, maintenance [, improvement][1] or insurance of such property ;

    (b) "residential property" means any building or part of a building which consists of one or more dwellings let on leases, but references to residential property include—

        (i) any garage, outhouse, garden, yard and appurtenances belonging to or usually enjoyed with such dwellings,

        (ii) any common parts of any such building or part, and

        (iii) any common facilities which are not within any such building or part; and

    (c) "service charge" means an amount payable by a tenant of a dwelling as part of or in addition to the rent—

        (i) which is payable, directly or indirectly, for services, repairs, maintenance [, improvements][1] or insurance or any relevant person's costs of management, and

        (ii) the whole or part of which varies or may vary according to the costs or estimated costs incurred or to be incurred by any relevant person in connection with the matters mentioned in sub-paragraph (i).

(9) This section applies in relation to dwellings let on licences to occupy as it applies in relation to dwellings let on leases, and references in this section to landlords and tenants of residential property accordingly include references to licensors and licensees of such property.

1   Amended by Commonhold and Leasehold Reform Act 2002, Sch 9, para 11 (30 March 2004 as SI 2004/669).

Housing Act 1996 (extract)

PART III LANDLORD AND TENANT

Chapter I Tenants' rights

Forfeiture

81. Restriction on termination of tenancy for failure to pay service charge.
(1) A landlord may not, in relation to premises let as a dwelling, exercise a right of re-entry or forfeiture for failure [by a tenant to pay a service charge or administration charge unless—][1]

>[(a) it is finally determined by (or on appeal from) a leasehold valuation tribunal or by a court, or by an arbitral tribunal in proceedings pursuant to a post-dispute arbitration agreement, that the amount of the service charge or administration charge is payable by him, or

>(b) the tenant has admitted that it is so payable.][1]

[(2) The landlord may not exercise a right of re-entry or forfeiture by virtue of subsection (1)(a) until after the end of the period of 14 days beginning with the day after that on which the final determination is made.][1]

[(3) For the purposes of this section it is finally determined that the amount of a service charge or administration charge is payable—

>(a) if a decision that it is payable is not appealed against or otherwise challenged, at the end of the time for bringing an appeal or other challenge, or

>(b) if such a decision is appealed against or otherwise challenged and not set aside in consequence of the appeal or other challenge, at the time specified in subsection (3A).

(3A) The time referred to in subsection (3)(b) is the time when the appeal or other challenge is disposed of—

>(a) by the determination of the appeal or other challenge and the expiry of the time for bringing a subsequent appeal (if any), or

>(b) by its being abandoned or otherwise ceasing to have effect.][1]

(4) The reference in subsection (1) to premises let as a dwelling does not include premises let on—

>(a) a tenancy to which Part II of the Landlord and Tenant Act 1954 applies (business tenancies),

>(b) a tenancy of an agricultural holding within the meaning of the Agricultural Holdings Act 1986 in relation to which that Act applies, or

>(c) a farm business tenancy within the meaning of the Agricultural Tenancies Act 1995.

[(4A) References in this section to the exercise of a right of re-entry or forfeiture include the service of a notice under section 146(1) of the Law of Property Act 1925 (restriction on re-entry or forfeiture).][1]

[(5) In this section

(a) "administration charge" has the meaning given by Part 1 of Schedule 11 to the Commonhold and Leasehold Reform Act 2002,

(b) "arbitration agreement" and "arbitral tribunal" have the same meaning as in Part 1 of the Arbitration Act 1996 (c. 23) and "post-dispute arbitration agreement", in relation to any matter, means an arbitration agreement made after a dispute about the matter has arisen,

(c) "dwelling" has the same meaning as in the Landlord and Tenant Act 1985 (c. 70), and

(d) "service charge" means a service charge within the meaning of section 18(1) of the Landlord and Tenant Act 1985, other than one excluded from that section by section 27 of that Act (rent of dwelling registered and not entered as variable).][1]

[(5A) Any order of a court to give effect to a determination of a leasehold valuation tribunal shall be treated as a determination by the court for the purposes of this section.][2]

(6) Nothing in this section affects the exercise of a right of re-entry or forfeiture on other grounds.

1   Amended by Commonhold and Leasehold Reform Act 2002, Pt 2, s 170 (31 May 2005 as SI 2005/1353).
2   Added by Commonhold and Leasehold Reform Act 2002, Sch13, para 16 (31 May 2005 as SI 2005/1353).

...

Service charges

...

84. Right to appoint surveyor to advise on matters relating to service charges.

(1) A recognised tenants' association may appoint a surveyor for the purposes of this section to advise on any matters relating to, or which may give rise to, service charges payable to a landlord by one or more members of the association.

The provisions of Schedule 4 have effect for conferring on a surveyor so appointed rights of access to documents and premises.

(2) A person shall not be so appointed unless he is a qualified surveyor.

For this purpose "qualified surveyor" has the same meaning as in section 78(4)(a) of the Leasehold Reform, Housing and Urban Development Act 1993 (persons qualified for appointment to carry out management audit).

(3) The appointment shall take effect for the purposes of this section upon notice in writing being given to the landlord by the association stating the name and address of the surveyor, the duration of his appointment and the matters in respect of which he is appointed.

(4) An appointment shall cease to have effect for the purposes of this section if the association gives notice in writing to the landlord to that effect or if the association ceases to exist.

(5) A notice is duly given under this section to a landlord of any tenants if it is given to a person who receives on behalf of the landlord the rent payable by those tenants; and a person to whom such a notice is so given shall forward it as soon as may be to the landlord.

(6) In this section—

"recognised tenants' association" has the same meaning as in the provisions of the Landlord and Tenant Act 1985 relating to service charges (see section 29 of that Act); and

"service charge" means a service charge within the meaning of section 18(1) of that Act, other than one excluded from that section by section 27 of that Act (rent of dwelling registered and not entered as variable).

...

SCHEDULE 4 RIGHTS EXERCISABLE BY SURVEYOR APPOINTED BY TENANTS' ASSOCIATION

Introductory

1.—(1) A surveyor appointed for the purposes of section 84 has the rights conferred by this Schedule.

(2) In this Schedule—

(a) "the tenants' association" means the association by whom the surveyor was appointed, and

(b) the surveyor's "functions" are his functions in connection with the matters in respect of which he was appointed.

Appointment of assistants

2.—(1) The surveyor may appoint such persons as he thinks fit to assist him in carrying out his functions.

(2) References in this Schedule to the surveyor in the context of—

(a) being afforded any such facilities as are mentioned in paragraph 3, or

(b) carrying out an inspection under paragraph 4,

include a person so appointed.

Right to inspect documents, etc.

3.—(1) The surveyor has a right to require the landlord or any other relevant person—

(a) to afford him reasonable facilities for inspecting any documents sight of which is reasonably required by him for the purposes of his functions, and

(b) to afford him reasonable facilities for taking copies of or extracts from any such documents.

(2) In sub-paragraph (1) "other relevant person" means a person other than the landlord who is or, in relation to a future service charge, will be—

(a) responsible for applying the proceeds of the service charge, or

(b) under an obligation to a tenant who pays the service charge in respect of any matter to which the charge relates.

(3) The rights conferred on the surveyor by this paragraph are exercisable by him by notice in writing given by him to the landlord or other person concerned.

Where a notice is given to a person other than the landlord, the surveyor shall give a copy of the notice to the landlord.

(4) The landlord or other person to whom notice is given shall, within the period of one week beginning with the date of the giving of the notice or as soon as reasonably practicable thereafter, either—

(a) afford the surveyor the facilities required by him for inspecting and taking copies or extracts of the documents to which the notice relates, or

(b) give the surveyor a notice stating that he objects to doing so for reasons specified in the notice.

(5) Facilities for the inspection of any documents required under sub-paragraph (1)(a) shall be made available free of charge.

This does not mean that the landlord cannot treat as part of his costs of management any costs incurred by him in connection with making the facilities available.

(6) A reasonable charge may be made for facilities for the taking of copies or extracts required under sub-paragraph (1)(b).

(7) A notice is duly given under this paragraph to the landlord of a tenant if it is given to a person who receives on behalf of the landlord the rent payable by that tenant.

A person to whom such a notice is so given shall forward it as soon as may be to the landlord.

Right to inspect premises

4.—(1) The surveyor also has the right to inspect any common parts comprised in relevant premises or any appurtenant property.

(2) In sub-paragraph (1)—

"common parts", in relation to a building or part of a building, includes the structure and exterior of the building or part and any common facilities within it;

"relevant premises" means so much of—

(i) the building or buildings containing the dwellings let to members of the tenants' association, and

(ii) any other building or buildings,

as constitute premises in relation to which management functions are discharged in respect of the costs of which service charges are payable by members of the association; and

"appurtenant property" means so much of any property not contained in relevant premises as constitutes property in relation to which any such management functions are discharged.

For the purposes of the above definitions "management functions" includes functions with respect to the provision of services, or the repair, maintenance [, improvement][1] or insurance of property .

(3) On being requested to do so, the landlord shall afford the surveyor reasonable access for the purposes of carrying out an inspection under this paragraph.

(4) Such reasonable access shall be afforded to the surveyor free of charge.

This does not mean that the landlord cannot treat as part of his costs of management any costs incurred by him in connection with affording reasonable access to the surveyor.

(5) A request is duly made under this paragraph to the landlord of a tenant if it is made to a person appointed by the landlord to deal with such requests or, if no such person has been appointed, to a person who receives on behalf of the landlord the rent payable by that tenant.

A person to whom such a request is made shall notify the landlord of the request as soon as may be.

1   Word inserted by Commonhold and Leasehold Reform Act 2002, Sch 9, para 12 (30 March 2004 as SI 2004/669).

Enforcement of rights by the court

5.—(1) If the landlord or other person to whom notice was given under paragraph 3 has not, by the end of the period of one month beginning with the date on which notice was given, complied with the notice, the court may, on the application of the surveyor, make an order requiring him to do so within such period as is specified in the order.

(2) If the landlord does not, within a reasonable period after the making of a request under paragraph 4, afford the surveyor reasonable access for the purposes of carrying out an inspection under that paragraph, the court may, on the application of the surveyor, make an order requiring the landlord to do so on such date as is specified in the order.

(3) An application for an order under this paragraph must be made before the end of the period of four months beginning with the date on which notice was given under paragraph 3 or the request was made under paragraph 4.

(4) An order under this paragraph may be made in general terms or may require the landlord or other person to do specific things, as the court thinks fit.

Documents held by superior landlord

6.—(1) Where a landlord is required by a notice under paragraph 3 to afford the surveyor facilities for inspection or taking copies or extracts in respect of any document which is in the custody or under the control of a superior landlord—

> (a) the landlord shall on receiving the notice inform the surveyor as soon as may be of that fact and of the name and address of the superior landlord, and
>
> (b) the surveyor may then give the superior landlord notice in writing requiring him to afford the facilities in question in respect of the document.

(2) Paragraphs 3 and 5(1) and (3) have effect, with any necessary modifications, in relation to a notice given to a superior landlord under this paragraph.

Effect of disposal by landlord

7.—(1) Where a notice under paragraph 3 has been given or a request under paragraph 4 has been made to a landlord, and at a time when any obligations arising out of the notice or request remain to be discharged by him—

> (a) he disposes of the whole or part of his interest as landlord of any member of the tenants' association, and
>
> (b) the person acquiring that interest ("the transferee") is in a position to discharge any of those obligations to any extent,

that person shall be responsible for discharging those obligations to that extent, as if he had been given the notice under paragraph 3 or had received the request under paragraph 4.

(2) If the landlord is, despite the disposal, still in a position to discharge those obligations, he remains responsible for doing so.

Otherwise, the transferee is responsible for discharging them to the exclusion of the landlord.

(3) In connection with the discharge of such obligations by the transferee, paragraphs 3 to 6 apply with the substitution for any reference to the date on which notice was given under paragraph 3 or the request was made under paragraph 4 of a reference to the date of the disposal.

(4) In this paragraph "disposal" means a disposal whether by the creation or transfer of an estate or interest, and includes the surrender of a tenancy; and references to the transferee shall be construed accordingly.

Effect of person ceasing to be a relevant person

8.—Where a notice under paragraph 3 has been given to a person other than the landlord and, at a time when any obligations arising out of the notice remain to be discharged by him, he ceases to be such a person as is mentioned in paragraph 3(2), then, if he is still in a position to discharge those obligations to any extent he remains responsible for discharging those obligations, and the provisions of this Schedule continue to apply to him, to that extent.

Commonhold and Leasehold Reform Act 2002 (extract)

PART 2 LEASEHOLD REFORM

Chapter 5 Other provisions about leases

Service charges, administration charges, etc.

...

158. Administration charges
Schedule 11 (which makes provision about administration charges payable by tenants of dwellings) has effect.

159. Charges under estate management schemes
(1) This section applies where a scheme under—
    (a) section 19 of the 1967 Act (estate management schemes in connection with enfranchisement under that Act),
    (b) Chapter 4 of Part 1 of the 1993 Act (estate management schemes in connection with enfranchisement under the 1967 Act or Chapter 1 of Part 1 of the 1993 Act), or
    (c) section 94(6) of the 1993 Act (corresponding schemes in relation to areas occupied under leases from Crown),
includes provision imposing on persons occupying or interested in property an obligation to make payments ("estate charges").
(2) A variable estate charge is payable only to the extent that the amount of the charge is reasonable; and "variable estate charge" means an estate charge which is neither—
    (a) specified in the scheme, nor
    (b) calculated in accordance with a formula specified in the scheme.
(3) Any person on whom an obligation to pay an estate charge is imposed by the scheme may apply to a leasehold valuation tribunal for an order varying the scheme in such manner as is specified in the application on the grounds that—
    (a) any estate charge specified in the scheme is unreasonable, or
    (b) any formula specified in the scheme in accordance with which any estate charge is calculated is unreasonable.
(4) If the grounds on which the application was made are established to the satisfaction of the tribunal, it may make an order varying the scheme in such manner as is specified in the order.
(5) The variation specified in the order may be—
    (a) the variation specified in the application, or
    (b) such other variation as the tribunal thinks fit.

(6) An application may be made to a leasehold valuation tribunal for a determination whether an estate charge is payable by a person and, if it is, as to—

    (a) the person by whom it is payable,

    (b) the person to whom it is payable,

    (c) the amount which is payable,

    (d) the date at or by which it is payable, and

    (e) the manner in which it is payable.

(7) Subsection (6) applies whether or not any payment has been made.

(8) The jurisdiction conferred on a leasehold valuation tribunal in respect of any matter by virtue of subsection (6) is in addition to any jurisdiction of a court in respect of the matter.

(9) No application under subsection (6) may be made in respect of a matter which—

    (a) has been agreed or admitted by the person concerned,

    (b) has been, or is to be, referred to arbitration pursuant to a post-dispute arbitration agreement to which that person is a party,

    (c) has been the subject of determination by a court, or

    (d) has been the subject of determination by an arbitral tribunal pursuant to a post-dispute arbitration agreement.

(10) But the person is not to be taken to have agreed or admitted any matter by reason only of having made any payment.

(11) An agreement (other than a post-dispute arbitration agreement) is void in so far as it purports to provide for a determination—

    (a) in a particular manner, or

    (b) on particular evidence,

of any question which may be the subject matter of an application under subsection (6).

(12) In this section—

    "post-dispute arbitration agreement", in relation to any matter, means an arbitration agreement made after a dispute about the matter has arisen, and

    "arbitration agreement" and "arbitral tribunal" have the same meanings as in Part 1 of the Arbitration Act 1996 (c. 23).

...

Insurance

164. Insurance otherwise than with landlord's insurer

(1) This section applies where a long lease of a house requires the tenant to insure the house with an insurer nominated or approved by the landlord ("the landlord's insurer").

(2) The tenant is not required to effect the insurance with the landlord's insurer if—

    (a) the house is insured under a policy of insurance issued by an authorised insurer,

    (b) the policy covers the interests of both the landlord and the tenant,

    (c) the policy covers all the risks which the lease requires be covered by insurance provided by the landlord's insurer,

    (d) the amount of the cover is not less than that which the lease requires to be provided by such insurance, and

    (e) the tenant satisfies subsection (3).

(3) To satisfy this subsection the tenant—

    (a) must have given a notice of cover to the landlord before the end of the period of fourteen days beginning with the relevant date, and

    (b) if (after that date) he has been requested to do so by a new landlord, must have given a notice of cover to him within the period of fourteen days beginning with the day on which the request was given.

(4) For the purposes of subsection (3)—
  (a) if the policy has not been renewed the relevant date is the day on which it took effect and if it has been renewed it is the day from which it was last renewed, and
  (b) a person is a new landlord on any day if he acquired the interest of the previous landlord under the lease on a disposal made by him during the period of one month ending with that day.
(5) A notice of cover is a notice specifying—
  (a) the name of the insurer,
  (b) the risks covered by the policy,
  (c) the amount and period of the cover, and
  (d) such further information as may be prescribed.
(6) A notice of cover—
  (a) must be in the prescribed form, and
  (b) may be sent by post.
(7) If a notice of cover is sent by post, it may be addressed to the landlord at the address specified in subsection (8).
(8) That address is—
  (a) the address last furnished to the tenant as the landlord's address for service in accordance with section 48 of the 1987 Act (notification of address for service of notices on landlord), or
  (b) if no such address has been so furnished, the address last furnished to the tenant as the landlord's address in accordance with section 47 of the 1987 Act (landlord's name and address to be contained in demands for rent).
(9) But the tenant may not give a notice of cover to the landlord at the address specified in subsection (8) if he has been notified by the landlord of a different address in England and Wales at which he wishes to be given any such notice.
(10) In this section—
  "authorised insurer", in relation to a policy of insurance, means a person who may carry on in the United Kingdom the business of effecting or carrying out contracts of insurance of the sort provided under the policy without contravening the prohibition imposed by section 19 of the Financial Services and Markets Act 2000 (c. 8),
  "house" has the same meaning as for the purposes of Part 1 of the 1967 Act,
  "landlord" and "tenant" have the same meanings as in Chapter 1 of this Part,
  "long lease" has the meaning given by sections 76 and 77 of this Act, and
  "prescribed" means prescribed by regulations made by the appropriate national authority.

...

Forfeiture of leases of dwellings

167. Failure to pay small amount for short period
(1) A landlord under a long lease of a dwelling may not exercise a right of re-entry or forfeiture for failure by a tenant to pay an amount consisting of rent, service charges or administration charges (or a combination of them) ("the unpaid amount") unless the unpaid amount—
  (a) exceeds the prescribed sum, or
  (b) consists of or includes an amount which has been payable for more than a prescribed period.
(2) The sum prescribed under subsection (1)(a) must not exceed £500.
(3) If the unpaid amount includes a default charge, it is to be treated for the purposes of subsection (1)(a) as reduced by the amount of the charge; and for this purpose "default

charge" means an administration charge payable in respect of the tenant's failure to pay any part of the unpaid amount.

(4) In this section "long lease of a dwelling" does not include—

(a) a tenancy to which Part 2 of the Landlord and Tenant Act 1954 (c. 56) (business tenancies) applies,

(b) a tenancy of an agricultural holding within the meaning of the Agricultural Holdings Act 1986 (c. 5) in relation to which that Act applies, or

(c) a farm business tenancy within the meaning of the Agricultural Tenancies Act 1995 (c. 8).

(5) In this section—

"administration charge" has the same meaning as in Part 1 of Schedule 11,

"dwelling" has the same meaning as in the 1985 Act,

"landlord" and "tenant" have the same meaning as in Chapter 1 of this Part,

"long lease" has the meaning given by sections 76 and 77 of this Act, except that a shared ownership lease is a long lease whatever the tenant's total share,

"prescribed" means prescribed by regulations made by the appropriate national authority, and

"service charge" has the meaning given by section 18(1) of the 1985 Act.

168. No forfeiture notice before determination of breach

(1) A landlord under a long lease of a dwelling may not serve a notice under section 146(1) of the Law of Property Act 1925 (c. 20) (restriction on forfeiture) in respect of a breach by a tenant of a covenant or condition in the lease unless subsection (2) is satisfied.

(2) This subsection is satisfied if—

(a) it has been finally determined on an application under subsection (4) that the breach has occurred,

(b) the tenant has admitted the breach, or

(c) a court in any proceedings, or an arbitral tribunal in proceedings pursuant to a post-dispute arbitration agreement, has finally determined that the breach has occurred.

(3) But a notice may not be served by virtue of subsection (2)(a) or (c) until after the end of the period of 14 days beginning with the day after that on which the final determination is made.

(4) A landlord under a long lease of a dwelling may make an application to a leasehold valuation tribunal for a determination that a breach of a covenant or condition in the lease has occurred.

(5) But a landlord may not make an application under subsection (4) in respect of a matter which—

(a) has been, or is to be, referred to arbitration pursuant to a post-dispute arbitration agreement to which the tenant is a party,

(b) has been the subject of determination by a court, or

(c) has been the subject of determination by an arbitral tribunal pursuant to a post-dispute arbitration agreement.

...

Crown application

172. Application to Crown

(1) The following provisions apply in relation to Crown land (as in relation to other land)—

(a) sections 18 to 30B of (and the Schedule to) the 1985 Act (service charges, insurance and managing agents),

(b) Part 2 of the 1987 Act (appointment of manager by leasehold valuation tribunal),

(c) Part 4 of the 1987 Act (variation of leases),

(d) sections 46 to 49 of the 1987 Act (information to be furnished to tenants),

(e) Chapter 5 of Part 1 of the 1993 Act (management audit),

(f) section 81 of the Housing Act 1996 (c. 52) (restriction on termination of tenancy for failure to pay service charge etc.),

(g) section 84 of (and Schedule 4 to) that Act (right to appoint surveyor), and

(h) in this Chapter, the provisions relating to any of the provisions within paragraphs (a) to (g), Part 1 of Schedule 11 and sections 164 to 171.

(2) Land is Crown land if there is or has at any time been an interest or estate in the land—

(a) comprised in the Crown Estate,

(b) belonging to Her Majesty in right of the Duchy of Lancaster,

(c) belonging to the Duchy of Cornwall, or

(d) belonging to a government department or held on behalf of Her Majesty for the purposes of a government department.

(3) No failure by the Crown to perform a duty imposed by or by virtue of any of sections 21 to 23A of, or any of paragraphs 2 to 4A of the Schedule to, the 1985 Act makes the Crown criminally liable; but the High Court may declare any such failure without reasonable excuse to be unlawful.

(4) Any sum payable under any of the provisions mentioned in subsection (1) by the Chancellor of the Duchy of Lancaster may be raised and paid under section 25 of the Duchy of Lancaster Act 1817 (c. 97) as an expense incurred in improvement of land belonging to Her Majesty in right of the Duchy.

(5) Any sum payable under any such provision by the Duke of Cornwall (or any other possessor for the time being of the Duchy of Cornwall) may be raised and paid under section 8 of the Duchy of Cornwall Management Act 1863 (c. 49) as an expense incurred in permanently improving the possessions of the Duchy.

(6) In section 56 of the 1987 Act (Crown land)—

(a) in subsection (1), for "This Act" substitute "Parts 1 and 3 and sections 42 to 42B (and so much of this Part as relates to those provisions)", and

(b) in subsection (3), for "this Act" substitute "the provisions mentioned in subsection (1)".

Chapter 6 Leasehold valuation tribunals

173. Leasehold valuation tribunals

(1) Any jurisdiction conferred on a leasehold valuation tribunal by or under any enactment is exercisable by a rent assessment committee constituted in accordance with Schedule 10 to the Rent Act 1977 (c. 42).

(2) When so constituted for exercising any such jurisdiction a rent assessment committee is known as a leasehold valuation tribunal.

174. Procedure

Schedule 12 (leasehold valuation tribunals: procedure) has effect.

175. Appeals

(1) A party to proceedings before a leasehold valuation tribunal may appeal to the [Upper Tribunal][1] from a decision of the leasehold valuation tribunal.

(2) But the appeal may be made only with the permission of—
    (a) the leasehold valuation tribunal, or
    (b) the [Upper Tribunal][1].
[…][2]
(4) On the appeal the [Upper Tribunal][1] may exercise any power which was available to the leasehold valuation tribunal.
(5) And a decision of the [Upper Tribunal][1] on the appeal may be enforced in the same way as a decision of the leasehold valuation tribunal.
[…][3]
(8) No appeal lies from a decision of a leasehold valuation tribunal to the High Court by virtue of section 11(1) of the Tribunals and Inquiries Act 1992 (c. 53).
(9) And no case may be stated for the opinion of the High Court in respect of such a decision by virtue of that provision.
[…][2]

1   Words substituted by Transfer of Tribunal Functions (Lands Tribunal and Miscellaneous Amendments) Order 2009/1307, Sch 1, para 269(a) (1 June 2009).
2   Repealed by Transfer of Tribunal Functions (Lands Tribunal and Miscellaneous Amendments) Order 2009/1307, Sch 1, para 269(b) (1 June 2009).
3   Repealed by Transfer of Tribunal Functions Order 2010/22, Sch 2, para 73 (18 January 2010).

…

SCHEDULE 11 ADMINISTRATION CHARGE

Part 1 Reasonableness of administration charges

Meaning of "administration charge"
1.—(1) In this Part of this Schedule "administration charge" means an amount payable by a tenant of a dwelling as part of or in addition to the rent which is payable, directly or indirectly—
    (a) for or in connection with the grant of approvals under his lease, or applications for such approvals,
    (b) for or in connection with the provision of information or documents by or on behalf of the landlord or a person who is party to his lease otherwise than as landlord or tenant,
    (c) in respect of a failure by the tenant to make a payment by the due date to the landlord or a person who is party to his lease otherwise than as landlord or tenant, or
    (d) in connection with a breach (or alleged breach) of a covenant or condition in his lease.
(2) But an amount payable by the tenant of a dwelling the rent of which is registered under Part 4 of the Rent Act 1977 (c. 42) is not an administration charge, unless the amount registered is entered as a variable amount in pursuance of section 71(4) of that Act.
(3) In this Part of this Schedule "variable administration charge" means an administration charge payable by a tenant which is neither—
    (a) specified in his lease, nor
    (b) calculated in accordance with a formula specified in his lease.
(4) An order amending sub-paragraph (1) may be made by the appropriate national authority.

Reasonableness of administration charges
2. A variable administration charge is payable only to the extent that the amount of the charge is reasonable.

3.—(1) Any party to a lease of a dwelling may apply to a leasehold valuation tribunal for an order varying the lease in such manner as is specified in the application on the grounds that—

(a) any administration charge specified in the lease is unreasonable, or

(b) any formula specified in the lease in accordance with which any administration charge is calculated is unreasonable.

(2) If the grounds on which the application was made are established to the satisfaction of the tribunal, it may make an order varying the lease in such manner as is specified in the order.

(3) The variation specified in the order may be—

(a) the variation specified in the application, or

(b) such other variation as the tribunal thinks fit.

(4) The tribunal may, instead of making an order varying the lease in such manner as is specified in the order, make an order directing the parties to the lease to vary it in such manner as is so specified.

(5) The tribunal may by order direct that a memorandum of any variation of a lease effected by virtue of this paragraph be endorsed on such documents as are specified in the order.

(6) Any such variation of a lease shall be binding not only on the parties to the lease for the time being but also on other persons (including any predecessors in title), whether or not they were parties to the proceedings in which the order was made.

Notice in connection with demands for administration charges

4.—(1) A demand for the payment of an administration charge must be accompanied by a summary of the rights and obligations of tenants of dwellings in relation to administration charges.

(2) The appropriate national authority may make regulations prescribing requirements as to the form and content of such summaries of rights and obligations.

(3) A tenant may withhold payment of an administration charge which has been demanded from him if sub-paragraph (1) is not complied with in relation to the demand.

(4) Where a tenant withholds an administration charge under this paragraph, any provisions of the lease relating to non-payment or late payment of administration charges do not have effect in relation to the period for which he so withholds it.

Liability to pay administration charges

5.—(1) An application may be made to a leasehold valuation tribunal for a determination whether an administration charge is payable and, if it is, as to—

(a) the person by whom it is payable,

(b) the person to whom it is payable,

(c) the amount which is payable,

(d) the date at or by which it is payable, and

(e) the manner in which it is payable.

(2) Sub-paragraph (1) applies whether or not any payment has been made.

(3) The jurisdiction conferred on a leasehold valuation tribunal in respect of any matter by virtue of sub-paragraph (1) is in addition to any jurisdiction of a court in respect of the matter.

(4) No application under sub-paragraph (1) may be made in respect of a matter which—

(a) has been agreed or admitted by the tenant,

(b) has been, or is to be, referred to arbitration pursuant to a post-dispute arbitration agreement to which the tenant is a party,

(c) has been the subject of determination by a court, or

(d) has been the subject of determination by an arbitral tribunal pursuant to a post-dispute arbitration agreement.

(5) But the tenant is not to be taken to have agreed or admitted any matter by reason only of having made any payment.

(6) An agreement by the tenant of a dwelling (other than a post-dispute arbitration agreement) is void in so far as it purports to provide for a determination—

(a) in a particular manner, or

(b) on particular evidence,

of any question which may be the subject matter of an application under sub-paragraph (1).

Interpretation

6.—(1) This paragraph applies for the purposes of this Part of this Schedule.

(2) "Tenant" includes a statutory tenant.

(3) "Dwelling" and "statutory tenant" (and "landlord" in relation to a statutory tenant) have the same meanings as in the 1985 Act.

(4) "Post-dispute arbitration agreement", in relation to any matter, means an arbitration agreement made after a dispute about the matter has arisen.

(5) "Arbitration agreement" and "arbitral tribunal" have the same meanings as in Part 1 of the Arbitration Act 1996 (c. 23).

Part 2 AMENDMENTS OF LANDLORD AND TENANT ACT 1987

7.—The 1987 Act has effect subject to the following amendments.

8. (1) Section 24 (appointment of manager by leasehold valuation tribunal) is amended as follows.

(2) In subsection (2), after paragraph (ab) insert—

"(aba) where the tribunal is satisfied—

(i) that unreasonable variable administration charges have been made, or are proposed or likely to be made, and

(ii) that it is just and convenient to make the order in all the circumstances of the case;".

(3) After subsection (2A) insert—

"(2B) In subsection (2)(aba) 'variable administration charge' has the meaning given by paragraph 1 of Schedule 11 to the Commonhold and Leasehold Reform Act 2002."

9. In section 46 (interpretation of provisions concerning information to be furnished to tenants), insert at the end—

"(3) In this Part 'administration charge' has the meaning given by paragraph 1 of Schedule 11 to the Commonhold and Leasehold Reform Act 2002."

10.—(1) Section 47 (landlord's name and address to be contained in demands for rent etc.) is amended as follows.

(2) In subsection (2), after "service charge" insert "or an administration charge".

(3) In subsection (3), after "service charges" insert "or (as the case may be) administration charges".

11.—(1) Section 48 (notification by landlord of address for service of notices) is amended as follows.

(2) In subsection (2), for "or service charge" substitute ", service charge or administration charge".

(3) In subsection (3)—

(a) for "or service charge" substitute ", service charge or administration charge", and

(b) for "or (as the case may be) service charges" substitute ", service charges or (as the case may be) administration charges".

SCHEDULE 12 LEASEHOLD VALUATION TRIBUNALS: PROCEDURE

1. Procedure regulations
The appropriate national authority may make regulations about the procedure of leasehold valuation tribunals ("procedure regulations").

2. Applications
Procedure regulations may include provision—
(a) about the form of applications to leasehold valuation tribunals,
(b) about the particulars that must be contained in such applications,
(c) requiring the service of notices of such applications, and
(d) for securing consistency where numerous applications are or may be brought in respect of the same or substantially the same matters.

3. Transfers
(1) Where in any proceedings before a court there falls for determination a question falling within the jurisdiction of a leasehold valuation tribunal, the court—
(a) may by order transfer to a leasehold valuation tribunal so much of the proceedings as relate to the determination of that question, and
(b) may then dispose of all or any remaining proceedings, or adjourn the disposal of all or any remaining proceedings pending the determination of that question by the leasehold valuation tribunal, as it thinks fit.
(2) When the leasehold valuation tribunal has determined the question, the court may give effect to the determination in an order of the court.
(3) Rules of court may prescribe the procedure to be followed in a court in connection with or in consequence of a transfer under this paragraph.
(4) Procedure regulations may prescribe the procedure to be followed in a leasehold valuation tribunal consequent on a transfer under this paragraph.

4. Information
(1) A leasehold valuation tribunal may serve a notice requiring any party to proceedings before it to give to the leasehold valuation tribunal any information which the leasehold valuation tribunal may reasonably require.
(2) The information shall be given to the leasehold valuation tribunal within such period (not being less than 14 days) from the service of the notice as is specified in the notice.
(3) A person commits an offence if he fails, without reasonable excuse, to comply with a notice served on him under sub-paragraph (1).
(4) A person guilty of an offence under sub-paragraph (3) is liable on summary conviction to a fine not exceeding level 3 on the standard scale.

5. Pre-trial reviews
(1) Procedure regulations may include provision for the holding of a pre-trial review (on the application of a party to proceedings or on the motion of a leasehold valuation tribunal).
(2) Procedure regulations may provide for the exercise of the functions of a leasehold valuation tribunal in relation to, or at, a pre-trial review by a single member of the panel provided for in Schedule 10 to the Rent Act 1977 (c. 42) who is qualified to exercise them.
(3) A member is qualified to exercise the functions specified in sub-paragraph (2) if he was appointed to that panel by the Lord Chancellor.

6. Parties
Procedure regulations may include provision enabling persons to be joined as parties to proceedings.

7. Dismissal

Procedure regulations may include provision empowering leasehold valuation tribunals to dismiss applications or transferred proceedings, in whole or in part, on the ground that they are—

> (a) frivolous or vexatious, or
>
> (b) otherwise an abuse of process.

8. Determination without hearing

(1) Procedure regulations may include provision for the determination of applications or transferred proceedings without an oral hearing.

(2) Procedure regulations may provide for the determinations without an oral hearing by a single member of the panel provided for in Schedule 10 to the Rent Act 1977.

9. Fees

(1) Procedure regulations may include provision requiring the payment of fees in respect of an application or transfer of proceedings to, or oral hearing by, a leasehold valuation tribunal in a case under—

> (a) the 1985 Act (service charges and choice of insurers),
>
> (b) Part 2 of the 1987 Act (managers),
>
> (c) Part 4 of the 1987 Act (variation of leases),
>
> (d) section 168(4) of this Act, or
>
> (e) Schedule 11 to this Act.

(2) Procedure regulations may empower a leasehold valuation tribunal to require a party to proceedings to reimburse any other party to the proceedings the whole or part of any fees paid by him.

(3) The fees payable shall be such as are specified in or determined in accordance with procedure regulations; but the fee (or, where fees are payable in respect of both an application or transfer and an oral hearing, the aggregate of the fees) payable by a person in respect of any proceedings shall not exceed—

> (a) £500, or
>
> (b) such other amount as may be specified in procedure regulations.

(4) Procedure regulations may provide for the reduction or waiver of fees by reference to the financial resources of the party by whom they are to be paid or met.

(5) If they do so they may apply, subject to such modifications as may be specified in the regulations, any other statutory means-testing regime as it has effect from time to time.

10. Costs

(1) A leasehold valuation tribunal may determine that a party to proceedings shall pay the costs incurred by another party in connection with the proceedings in any circumstances falling within sub-paragraph (2).

(2) The circumstances are where—

> (a) he has made an application to the leasehold valuation tribunal which is dismissed in accordance with regulations made by virtue of paragraph 7, or
>
> (b) he has, in the opinion of the leasehold valuation tribunal, acted frivolously, vexatiously, abusively, disruptively or otherwise unreasonably in connection with the proceedings.

(3) The amount which a party to proceedings may be ordered to pay in the proceedings by a determination under this paragraph shall not exceed—

> (a) £500, or
>
> (b) such other amount as may be specified in procedure regulations.

(4) A person shall not be required to pay costs incurred by another person in connection with proceedings before a leasehold valuation tribunal except by a determination under this paragraph or in accordance with provision made by any enactment other than this paragraph.

11. Enforcement

Procedure regulations may provide for decisions of leasehold valuation tribunals to be enforceable, with the permission of a county court, in the same way as orders of such a court.

Unfair Terms in Consumer Contracts Regulations 1999 (SI 1999/2083)

1. Citation and commencement

These Regulations may be cited as the Unfair Terms in Consumer Contracts Regulations 1999 and shall come into force on 1st October 1999.

2. Revocation

The Unfair Terms in Consumer Contracts Regulations 1994 are hereby revoked.

3. Interpretation

(1) In these Regulations–

"the Community" means the European Community;

"consumer" means any natural person who, in contracts covered by these Regulations, is acting for purposes which are outside his trade, business or profession;

"court" in relation to England and Wales and Northern Ireland means a county court or the High Court, and in relation to Scotland, the Sheriff or the Court of Session;

"Director" means the Director General of Fair Trading;

"EEA Agreement" means the Agreement on the European Economic Area signed at Oporto on 2nd May 1992 as adjusted by the protocol signed at Brussels on 17th March 1993[1];

"Member State" means a State which is a contracting party to the EEA Agreement;

"notified" means notified in writing;

"qualifying body" means a person specified in Schedule 1;

"seller or supplier" means any natural or legal person who, in contracts covered by these Regulations, is acting for purposes relating to his trade, business or profession, whether publicly owned or privately owned;

"unfair terms" means the contractual terms referred to in regulation 5.

[(1A) The references–

(a) in regulation 4(1) to a seller or a supplier, and

(b) in regulation 8(1) to a seller or supplier,

include references to a distance supplier and to an intermediary.

(1B) In paragraph (1A) and regulation 5(6)–

"distance supplier" means–

(a) a supplier under a distance contract within the meaning of the Financial Services (Distance Marketing) Regulations 2004, or

(b) a supplier of unsolicited financial services within regulation 15 of those Regulations; and

"intermediary" has the same meaning as in those Regulations.][2]

543

(2) In the application of these Regulations to Scotland for references to an "injunction" or an "interim injunction" there shall be substituted references to an "interdict" or "interim interdict" respectively.

1 Protocol 47 and certain Annexes to the EEA Agreement were amended by Decision No 7/94 of the EEA Joint Committee which came into force on 1 July 1994, (OJ No L160, 28.6.94, p 1). Council Directive 93/13/EEC was added to Annex XIX to the Agreement by Annex 17 to the said Decision No 7/94.
2 Added by Financial Services (Distance Marketing) Regulations 2004/2095, reg 24(2) (31 October 2004).

4. Terms to which these Regulations apply
(1) These Regulations apply in relation to unfair terms in contracts concluded between a seller or a supplier and a consumer.
(2) These Regulations do not apply to contractual terms which reflect–
  (a) mandatory statutory or regulatory provisions (including such provisions under the law of any Member State or in [EU]¹ legislation having effect in the United Kingdom without further enactment);
  (b) the provisions or principles of international conventions to which the Member States or the Community are party.

1 Word substituted by Treaty of Lisbon (Changes in Terminology) Order 2011/1043, Pt 2, art 6(2)(c) (22 April 2011).

5. Unfair Terms
(1) A contractual term which has not been individually negotiated shall be regarded as unfair if, contrary to the requirement of good faith, it causes a significant imbalance in the parties' rights and obligations arising under the contract, to the detriment of the consumer.
(2) A term shall always be regarded as not having been individually negotiated where it has been drafted in advance and the consumer has therefore not been able to influence the substance of the term.
(3) Notwithstanding that a specific term or certain aspects of it in a contract has been individually negotiated, these Regulations shall apply to the rest of a contract if an overall assessment of it indicates that it is a pre-formulated standard contract.
(4) It shall be for any seller or supplier who claims that a term was individually negotiated to show that it was.
(5) Schedule 2 to these Regulations contains an indicative and non-exhaustive list of the terms which may be regarded as unfair.
[(6) Any contractual term providing that a consumer bears the burden of proof in respect of showing whether a distance supplier or an intermediary complied with any or all of the obligations placed upon him resulting from the Directive and any rule or enactment implementing it shall always be regarded as unfair.
(7) In paragraph (6)–
  "the Directive" means Directive 2002/65/EC of the European Parliament and of the Council of 23 September 2002 concerning the distance marketing of consumer financial services and amending Council Directive 90/619/EEC and Directives 97/7/EC and 98/27/EC; and
  "rule" means a rule made by the Financial Services Authority under the Financial Services and Markets Act 2000or by a designated professional body within the meaning of section 326(2) of that Act.]¹

1 Added by Financial Services (Distance Marketing) Regulations 2004/2095 reg 24(3) (31 October 2004).

6. Assessment of unfair terms

(1) Without prejudice to regulation 12, the unfairness of a contractual term shall be assessed, taking into account the nature of the goods or services for which the contract was concluded and by referring, at the time of conclusion of the contract, to all the circumstances attending the conclusion of the contract and to all the other terms of the contract or of another contract on which it is dependent.

(2) In so far as it is in plain intelligible language, the assessment of fairness of a term shall not relate–

(a) to the definition of the main subject matter of the contract, or

(b) to the adequacy of the price or remuneration, as against the goods or services supplied in exchange.

7. Written contracts

(1) A seller or supplier shall ensure that any written term of a contract is expressed in plain, intelligible language.

(2) If there is doubt about the meaning of a written term, the interpretation which is most favourable to the consumer shall prevail but this rule shall not apply in proceedings brought under regulation 12.

8. Effect of unfair term

(1) An unfair term in a contract concluded with a consumer by a seller or supplier shall not be binding on the consumer.

(2) The contract shall continue to bind the parties if it is capable of continuing in existence without the unfair term.

9. Choice of law clauses

These Regulations shall apply notwithstanding any contract term which applies or purports to apply the law of a non-Member State, if the contract has a close connection with the territory of the Member States.

10. Complaints – consideration by Director

(1) It shall be the duty of the Director to consider any complaint made to him that any contract term drawn up for general use is unfair, unless–

(a) the complaint appears to the Director to be frivolous or vexatious; or

(b) a qualifying body has notified the Director that it agrees to consider the complaint.

(2) The Director shall give reasons for his decision to apply or not to apply, as the case may be, for an injunction under regulation 12 in relation to any complaint which these Regulations require him to consider.

(3) In deciding whether or not to apply for an injunction in respect of a term which the Director considers to be unfair, he may, if he considers it appropriate to do so, have regard to any undertakings given to him by or on behalf of any person as to the continued use of such a term in contracts concluded with consumers.

11. Complaints – consideration by qualifying bodies

(1) If a qualifying body specified in Part One of Schedule 1 notifies the Director that it agrees to consider a complaint that any contract term drawn up for general use is unfair, it shall be under a duty to consider that complaint.

(2) Regulation 10(2) and (3) shall apply to a qualifying body which is under a duty to consider a complaint as they apply to the Director.

12. Injunctions to prevent continued use of unfair terms

(1) The Director or, subject to paragraph (2), any qualifying body may apply for an injunction (including an interim injunction) against any person appearing to the Director or that body to be using, or recommending use of, an unfair term drawn up for general use in contracts concluded with consumers.

(2) A qualifying body may apply for an injunction only where–

(a) it has notified the Director of its intention to apply at least fourteen days before the date on which the application is made, beginning with the date on which the notification was given; or

(b) the Director consents to the application being made within a shorter period.

(3) The court on an application under this regulation may grant an injunction on such terms as it thinks fit.

(4) An injunction may relate not only to use of a particular contract term drawn up for general use but to any similar term, or a term having like effect, used or recommended for use by any person.

13. Powers of the Director and qualifying bodies to obtain documents and information

(1) The Director may exercise the power conferred by this regulation for the purpose of–

(a) facilitating his consideration of a complaint that a contract term drawn up for general use is unfair; or

(b) ascertaining whether a person has complied with an undertaking or court order as to the continued use, or recommendation for use, of a term in contracts concluded with consumers.

(2) A qualifying body specified in Part One of Schedule 1 may exercise the power conferred by this regulation for the purpose of–

(a) facilitating its consideration of a complaint that a contract term drawn up for general use is unfair; or

(b) ascertaining whether a person has complied with–

(i) an undertaking given to it or to the court following an application by that body, or

(ii) a court order made on an application by that body,

as to the continued use, or recommendation for use, of a term in contracts concluded with consumers.

(3) The Director may require any person to supply to him, and a qualifying body specified in Part One of Schedule 1 may require any person to supply to it–

(a) a copy of any document which that person has used or recommended for use, at the time the notice referred to in paragraph (4) below is given, as a pre-formulated standard contract in dealings with consumers;

(b) information about the use, or recommendation for use, by that person of that document or any other such document in dealings with consumers.

(4) The power conferred by this regulation is to be exercised by a notice in writing which may–

(a) specify the way in which and the time within which it is to be complied with; and

(b) be varied or revoked by a subsequent notice.

(5) Nothing in this regulation compels a person to supply any document or information which he would be entitled to refuse to produce or give in civil proceedings before the court.

(6) If a person makes default in complying with a notice under this regulation, the court may, on the application of the Director or of the qualifying body, make such order as the

court thinks fit for requiring the default to be made good, and any such order may provide that all the costs or expenses of and incidental to the application shall be borne by the person in default or by any officers of a company or other association who are responsible for its default.

14. Notification of undertakings and orders to Director

A qualifying body shall notify the Director–

(a) of any undertaking given to it by or on behalf of any person as to the continued use of a term which that body considers to be unfair in contracts concluded with consumers;

(b) of the outcome of any application made by it under regulation 12, and of the terms of any undertaking given to, or order made by, the court;

(c) of the outcome of any application made by it to enforce a previous order of the court.

15. Publication, information and advice

(1) The Director shall arrange for the publication in such form and manner as he considers appropriate, of–

(a) details of any undertaking or order notified to him under regulation 14;

(b) details of any undertaking given to him by or on behalf of any person as to the continued use of a term which the Director considers to be unfair in contracts concluded with consumers;

(c) details of any application made by him under regulation 12, and of the terms of any undertaking given to, or order made by, the court;

(d) details of any application made by the Director to enforce a previous order of the court.

(2) The Director shall inform any person on request whether a particular term to which these Regulations apply has been–

(a) the subject of an undertaking given to the Director or notified to him by a qualifying body; or

(b) the subject of an order of the court made upon application by him or notified to him by a qualifying body;

and shall give that person details of the undertaking or a copy of the order, as the case may be, together with a copy of any amendments which the person giving the undertaking has agreed to make to the term in question.

(3) The Director may arrange for the dissemination in such form and manner as he considers appropriate of such information and advice concerning the operation of these Regulations as may appear to him to be expedient to give to the public and to all persons likely to be affected by these Regulations.

[16. The functions of the Financial Services Authority

The functions of the Financial Services Authority under these Regulations shall be treated as functions of the Financial Services Authority under the [Financial Services and Markets Act 2000][2].][1]

1   Added by Unfair Terms in Consumer Contracts (Amendment) Regulations 2001/1186, reg 2(a) (1 May 2001).
2   Words substituted by Financial Services and Markets Act 2000 (Consequential Amendments and Repeals) Order 2001/3649, Pt 9, art 583 (1 December 2001).

SCHEDULE I QUALIFYING BODIES

Part I

[**1.** The Information Commissioner.]¹

1   Words substituted by Unfair Terms in Consumer Contracts (Amendment) Regulations 2001/1186, reg 2(b) (1 May 2001).

[**2.** The Gas and Electricity Markets Authority.]¹

1   Words substituted by Unfair Terms in Consumer Contracts (Amendment) Regulations 2001/1186, reg 2(b) (1 May 2001).

[**3.** The Director General of Electricity Supply for Northern Ireland.]¹

1   Words substituted by Unfair Terms in Consumer Contracts (Amendment) Regulations 2001/1186, reg 2(b) (1 May 2001).

[**4.** The Director General of Gas for Northern Ireland.]¹

1   Words substituted by Unfair Terms in Consumer Contracts (Amendment) Regulations 2001/1186, reg 2(b) (1 May 2001).

[**5.** [The Office of Communications]².]¹

1   Words substituted by Unfair Terms in Consumer Contracts (Amendment) Regulations 2001/1186, reg 2(b) (1 May 2001).
2   Words substituted by Communications Act 2003 (Consequential Amendments No 2) Order 2003/3182, art 2(2) (29 December 2003).

[**6.** [The Water Services Regulation Authority]².]¹

1   Words substituted by Unfair Terms in Consumer Contracts (Amendment) Regulations 2001/1186, reg 2(b) (1 May 2001).
2   Entry substituted by Unfair Terms in Consumer Contracts (Amendment) and Water Act 2003 (Transitional Provision) Regulations 2006/523, reg 2(2) (1 April 2006).

[**7.** The Rail Regulator.]¹

1   Words substituted by Unfair Terms in Consumer Contracts (Amendment) Regulations 2001/1186, reg 2(b) (1 May 2001).

[**8.** Every weights and measures authority in Great Britain.]¹

1   Words substituted by Unfair Terms in Consumer Contracts (Amendment) Regulations 2001/1186, reg 2(b) (1 May 2001).

[**9.** The Department of Enterprise, Trade and Investment in Northern Ireland.]¹

1   Words substituted by Unfair Terms in Consumer Contracts (Amendment) Regulations 2001/1186, reg 2(b) (1 May 2001).

[**10.** The Financial Services Authority.]¹

1   Words substituted by Unfair Terms in Consumer Contracts (Amendment) Regulations 2001/1186, reg 2(b) (1 May 2001).

Part II

11. Consumers' Association.

SCHEDULE 2 INDICATIVE AND NON-EXHAUSTIVE LIST OF TERMS WHICH MAY BE REGARDED AS UNFAIR

1. Terms which have the object or effect of–

(a) excluding or limiting the legal liability of a seller or supplier in the event of the death of a consumer or personal injury to the latter resulting from an act or omission of that seller or supplier;

(b) inappropriately excluding or limiting the legal rights of the consumer vis-a-vis the seller or supplier or another party in the event of total or partial non-performance or inadequate performance by the seller or supplier of any of the contractual obligations, including the option of offsetting a debt owed to the seller or supplier against any claim which the consumer may have against him;

(c) making an agreement binding on the consumer whereas provision of services by the seller or supplier is subject to a condition whose realisation depends on his own will alone;

(d) permitting the seller or supplier to retain sums paid by the consumer where the latter decides not to conclude or perform the contract, without providing for the consumer to receive compensation of an equivalent amount from the seller or supplier where the latter is the party cancelling the contract;

(e) requiring any consumer who fails to fulfil his obligation to pay a disproportionately high sum in compensation;

(f) authorising the seller or supplier to dissolve the contract on a discretionary basis where the same facility is not granted to the consumer, or permitting the seller or supplier to retain the sums paid for services not yet supplied by him where it is the seller or supplier himself who dissolves the contract;

(g) enabling the seller or supplier to terminate a contract of indeterminate duration without reasonable notice except where there are serious grounds for doing so;

(h) automatically extending a contract of fixed duration where the consumer does not indicate otherwise, when the deadline fixed for the consumer to express his desire not to extend the contract is unreasonably early;

(i) irrevocably binding the consumer to terms with which he had no real opportunity of becoming acquainted before the conclusion of the contract;

(j) enabling the seller or supplier to alter the terms of the contract unilaterally without a valid reason which is specified in the contract;

(k) enabling the seller or supplier to alter unilaterally without a valid reason any characteristics of the product or service to be provided;

(l) providing for the price of goods to be determined at the time of delivery or allowing a seller of goods or supplier of services to increase their price without in both cases giving the consumer the corresponding right to cancel the contract if the final price is too high in relation to the price agreed when the contract was concluded;

(m) giving the seller or supplier the right to determine whether the goods or services supplied are in conformity with the contract, or giving him the exclusive right to interpret any term of the contract;

(n) limiting the seller's or supplier's obligation to respect commitments undertaken by his agents or making his commitments subject to compliance with a particular formality;

(o) obliging the consumer to fulfil all his obligations where the seller or supplier does not perform his,

(p) giving the seller or supplier the possibility of transferring his rights and obligations under the contract, where this may serve to reduce the guarantees for the consumer, without the latter's agreement;

(q) excluding or hindering the consumer's right to take legal action or exercise any other legal remedy, particularly by requiring the consumer to take disputes exclusively to arbitration not covered by legal provisions, unduly restricting the evidence available to him or imposing on him a burden of proof which, according to the applicable law, should lie with another party to the contract.

2. Scope of paragraphs 1(g), (j) and (l)

(a) Paragraph 1(g) is without hindrance to terms by which a supplier of financial services reserves the right to terminate unilaterally a contract of indeterminate duration without notice where there is a valid reason, provided that the supplier is required to inform the other contracting party or parties thereof immediately.

(b) Paragraph 1(j) is without hindrance to terms under which a supplier of financial services reserves the right to alter the rate of interest payable by the consumer or due to the latter, or the amount of other charges for financial services without notice where there is a valid reason, provided that the supplier is required to inform the other contracting party or parties thereof at the earliest opportunity and that the latter are free to dissolve the contract immediately.

Paragraph 1(j) is also without hindrance to terms under which a seller or supplier reserves the right to alter unilaterally the conditions of a contract of indeterminate duration, provided that he is required to inform the consumer with reasonable notice and that the consumer is free to dissolve the contract.

(c) Paragraphs 1(g), (j) and (l) do not apply to:

— transactions in transferable securities, financial instruments and other products or services where the price is linked to fluctuations in a stock exchange quotation or index or a financial market rate that the seller or supplier does not control;

— contracts for the purchase or sale of foreign currency, traveller's cheques or international money orders denominated in foreign currency;

(d) Paragraph 1(l) is without hindrance to price indexation clauses, where lawful, provided that the method by which prices vary is explicitly described.

EXPLANATORY NOTE

These Regulations revoke and replace the Unfair Terms in Consumer Contracts Regulations 1994 (S.I. 1994/3159) which came into force on 1st July 1995.

Those Regulations implemented Council Directive 93/13/EEC on unfair terms in consumer contracts (O.J. No. L95, 21.4.93, p. 29). Regulations 3 to 9 of these Regulations re-enact regulations 2 to 7 of the 1994 Regulations with modifications to reflect more closely the wording of the Directive.

The Regulations apply, with certain exceptions, to unfair terms in contracts concluded between a consumer and a seller or supplier (regulation 4). The Regulations provide that an unfair term is one which has not been individually negotiated and which, contrary to the requirement of good faith, causes a significant imbalance in the parties' rights and obligations under the contract to the detriment of the consumer (regulation 5). Schedule 2 contains an indicative list of terms which may be regarded as unfair.

The assessment of unfairness will take into account all the circumstances attending the conclusion of the contract. However, the assessment is not to relate to the definition of the main subject matter of the contract or the adequacy of the price or remuneration as against the goods or services supplied in exchange as long as the terms concerned are in plain, intelligible language (regulation 6). Unfair contract terms are not binding on the consumer (regulation 8).

The Regulations maintain the obligation on the Director General of Fair Trading (contained in the 1994 Regulations) to consider any complaint made to him about the fairness of any contract term drawn up for general use. He may, if he considers it appropriate to do so, seek an injunction to prevent the continued use of that term or of a term having like effect (regulations 10 and 12).

The Regulations provide for the first time that a qualifying body named in Schedule 1 (statutory regulators, trading standards departments and Consumers' Association) may also apply for an injunction to prevent the continued use of an unfair contract term provided it has notified the Director General of its intention at least 14 days before the application is made (unless the Director General consents to a shorter period) (regulation 12). A qualifying body named in Part One of Schedule 1 (public bodies) shall be under a duty to consider a complaint if it has told the Director General that it will do so (regulation 11).

The Regulations provide a new power for the Director General and the public qualifying bodies to require traders to produce copies of their standard contracts, and give information about their use, in order to facilitate investigation of complaints and ensure compliance with undertakings or court orders (regulation 13).

Qualifying bodies must notify the Director General of undertakings given to them about the continued use of an unfair term and of the outcome of any court proceedings (regulation 14). The Director General is given the power to arrange for the publication of this information in such form and manner as he considers appropriate and to offer information and advice about the operation of these Regulations (regulation 15). In addition the Director General will supply enquirers about particular standard terms with details of any relevant undertakings and court orders.

A Regulatory Impact Assessment of the costs and benefits which will result from these Regulations has been prepared by the Department of Trade and Industry and is available from Consumer Affairs Directorate, Department of Trade and Industry, Room 407, 1 Victoria Street, London SWIH 0ET (Telephone 0171 215 0341). Copies have been placed in the libraries of both Houses of Parliament.

Service Charges (Consultation Requirements) (England) Regulations 2003 (SI 2003/1987)

1. Citation, commencement and application

(1) These Regulations may be cited as the Service Charges (Consultation Requirements) (England) Regulations 2003 and shall come into force on 31st October 2003.

(2) These Regulations apply in relation to England only.

(3) These Regulations apply where a landlord–

(a) intends to enter into a qualifying long term agreement to which section 20 of the Landlord and Tenant Act 1985 applies[1] on or after the date on which these Regulations come into force; or

(b) intends to carry out qualifying works to which that section[2] applies on or after that date.

1   See s 20ZA(2) and regs 3 and 4 of these Regulations.
2   See s 20(3) and reg 6 of these Regulations. For the application of s 20, as originally enacted, in transitional cases, see Commonhold and Leasehold Reform Act 2002 (Commencement No 2 and Savings) (England) Order 2003 (SI 2003/1986), art 3.

2. Interpretation

(1) In these Regulations–

"the 1985 Act" means the Landlord and Tenant Act 1985;

"close relative", in relation to a person, means a spouse or cohabitee, a parent, parent-in-law, son, son-in-law, daughter, daughter-in-law, brother, brother-in-law, sister, sister-in-law, step-parent, step-son or step-daughter of that person;

"cohabitee", in relation to a person, means–

(a) a person of the opposite sex who is living with that person as husband or wife; or

(b) a person of the same sex living with that person in a relationship which has the characteristics of the relationship between husband and wife;

"nominated person" means a person whose name is proposed in response to an invitation made as mentioned in paragraph 1(3) of Schedule 1 or paragraph 1(3) of Part 2 of Schedule 4; and "nomination" means any such proposal;

["public notice" means notice published in the Official Journal of the European Union pursuant to the Public Contracts Regulations 2006;][1]

"relevant period", in relation to a notice, means the period of 30 days beginning with the date of the notice;

"RTB tenancy" means the tenancy of an RTB tenant;

"RTB tenant", in relation to a landlord, means a person who has become a tenant of the landlord by virtue of section 138 of the Housing Act 1985 (duty of landlord to convey freehold or grant lease), section 171A of that Act (cases in which right to buy

553

is preserved), [section 180 of the Housing and Regeneration Act 2008][2] or section 16 of the Housing Act 1996 (right of tenant to acquire dwelling)[3] under a lease whose terms include a requirement that the tenant shall bear a reasonable part of such costs incurred by the landlord as are mentioned in paragraphs 16A to 16D of Schedule 6 to that Act (service charges and other contributions payable by the tenant)[4];

"section 20" means section 20 (limitation of service charges: consultation requirements) of the 1985 Act;

"section 20ZA" means section 20ZA (consultation requirements: supplementary) of that Act;

"the relevant matters", in relation to a proposed agreement, means the goods or services to be provided or the works to be carried out (as the case may be) under the agreement.

(2) For the purposes of any estimate required by any provision of these Regulations to be made by the landlord–

(a) value added tax shall be included where applicable; and

(b) where the estimate relates to a proposed agreement, it shall be assumed that the agreement will terminate only by effluxion of time.

1   Definition substituted by Public Contracts Regulations 2006/5, Sch 7, Pt 1, para 3 (31 January 2006).
2   Words inserted by Housing and Regeneration Act 2008 (Consequential Provisions) (No 2) Order 2010/671, Sch 1, para 34 (1 April 2010: insertion has effect subject to savings and transitional provisions specified in SI 2010/671, Sch 2, paras 2, 5, 6 and 8).
3   Housing Act 1985, s 138 is applied in relation to s 171A by s 171C. Sections 171A and 171C were inserted by Housing and Planning Act 1996, s 8. See also Housing (Extension of Right to Buy) Order 1993 (SI 1993/2240) and Housing (Preservation of Right to Buy) Regulations 1993 (SI 1993/2241). Section 138 is applied in relation to Housing Act 1996, s 16 by s 17 of that Act. See also the Housing (Right to Acquire) Regulations 1997 (SI 1997/619).
4   See also Housing Act 1985, s 139 and Sch 6, Pts 1 and 3. Schedule 6, paras 16A–16D were inserted by the Housing and Planning Act 1986, s 4(4).

3. Agreements that are not qualifying long term agreements

(1) An agreement is not a qualifying long term agreement[1]–

(a) if it is a contract of employment; or

(b) if it is a management agreement made by a local housing authority[2] and–

(i) a tenant management organisation; or

(ii) a body established under section 2 of the Local Government Act 2000 [or section 1 of the Localism Act 2011][3];

(c) if the parties to the agreement are–

(i) a holding company and one or more of its subsidiaries; or

(ii) two or more subsidiaries of the same holding company;

(d) if–

(i) when the agreement is entered into, there are no tenants of the building or other premises to which the agreement relates; and

(ii) the agreement is for a term not exceeding five years.

(2) An agreement entered into, by or on behalf of the landlord or a superior landlord–

(a) before the coming into force of these Regulations; and

(b) for a term of more than twelve months,

is not a qualifying long term agreement, notwithstanding that more than twelve months of the term remain unexpired on the coming into force of these Regulations.

(3) An agreement for a term of more than twelve months entered into, by or on behalf of the landlord or a superior landlord, which provides for the carrying out of qualifying works for which public notice has been given before the date on which these Regulations come into force, is not a qualifying long term agreement.

(4) In paragraph (1)–

"holding company" and "subsidiaries" have the same meaning as in the Companies Act 1985[4];

"management agreement" has the meaning given by section 27(2) of the Housing Act 1985[5]; and

"tenant management organisation" has the meaning given by section 27AB(8) of the Housing Act 1985[6].

1   See the definition Landlord and Tenant Act 1985, s 20ZA(2), inserted by Commonhold and Leasehold Reform Act 2002, s 151.
2   See Landlord and Tenant Act 1985, s 38 and Housing Act 1985, s 1.
3   Words inserted by Localism Act 2011 (Consequential Amendments) Order 2012/961, Sch 1, para 7 (28 March 2012).
4   Definitions of "holding company" and "subsidiary" are in s 736. That section and s 736A were substituted for the original s 736 by Companies Act 1989, s 144(1).
5   Section 27(2) was substituted by SI 2003/940.
6   Section 27AB was inserted by Leasehold Reform, Housing and Urban Development Act 1993, s 132. See also Housing (Right to Manage) Regulations 1994 (SI 1994/627), reg 1(4).

4. Application of section 20 to qualifying long term agreements

(1) Section 20 shall apply to a qualifying long term agreement if relevant costs[1] incurred under the agreement in any accounting period exceed an amount which results in the relevant contribution of any tenant, in respect of that period, being more than £100.

(2) In paragraph (1), "accounting period" means the period–

(a) beginning with the relevant date, and

(b) ending with the date that falls twelve months after the relevant date.

(3) [In][2] the case of the first accounting period, the relevant date is–

(a) if the relevant accounts are made up for periods of twelve months, the date on which the period that includes the date on which these Regulations come into force ends, or

(b) if the accounts are not so made up, the date on which these Regulations come into force.

[(3A) Where–

(a) a landlord intends to enter into a qualifying long term agreement on or after 12th November 2004; and

(b) he has not at any time between 31st October 2003 and 12th November 2004 made up accounts relating to service charges referable to a qualifying long term agreement and payable in respect of the dwellings to which the intended agreement is to relate,

the relevant date is the date on which begins the first period for which service charges referable to that intended agreement are payable under the terms of the leases of those dwellings.][3]

(4) In the case of subsequent accounting periods, the relevant date is the date immediately following the end of the previous accounting period.

1   See Landlord and Tenant Act 1985, s 18(2).
2   Words substituted by Service Charges (Consultation Requirements) (Amendment) (No 2) (England) Regulations 2004/2939, reg 2(a) (12 November 2004).
3   Possible drafting error – reg 4(3A) purportedly inserted but reg 4(3A) already exists and therefore reg 4(3A) is substituted by Service Charges (Consultation Requirements) (Amendment) (No 2) (England) Regulations 2004/2939, reg 2(b) (12 November 2004).

5. The consultation requirements: qualifying long term agreements

(1) Subject to paragraphs (2) and (3), in relation to qualifying long term agreements to which section 20 applies, the consultation requirements for the purposes of that section and section 20ZA are the requirements specified in Schedule 1.

(2) Where public notice is required to be given of the relevant matters to which a qualifying long term agreement relates, the consultation requirements for the purposes of sections 20 and 20ZA, as regards the agreement, are the requirements specified in Schedule 2.

(3) In relation to a RTB tenant and a particular qualifying long term agreement, nothing in paragraph (1) or (2) requires a landlord to comply with any of the consultation requirements applicable to that agreement that arise before the thirty-first day of the RTB tenancy.

6. Application of section 20 to qualifying works

For the purposes of subsection (3) of section 20 the appropriate amount is an amount which results in the relevant contribution of any tenant being more than £250.

7. The consultation requirements: qualifying works

(1) Subject to paragraph (5), where qualifying works are the subject (whether alone or with other matters) of a qualifying long term agreement to which section 20 applies, the consultation requirements for the purposes of that section and section 20ZA, as regards those works, are the requirements specified in Schedule 3.

(2) Subject to paragraph (5), in a case to which paragraph (3) applies the consultation requirements for the purposes of sections 20 and 20ZA, as regards qualifying works referred to in that paragraph, are those specified in Schedule 3.

(3) This paragraph applies where–
> (a) under an agreement entered into, by or on behalf of the landlord or a superior landlord, before the coming into force of these Regulations, qualifying works are carried out at any time on or after the date that falls two months after the date on which these Regulations come into force; or
> (b) under an agreement for a term of more than twelve months entered into, by or on behalf of the landlord or a superior landlord, qualifying works for which public notice has been given before the date on which these Regulations come into force are carried out at any time on or after the date.

(4) Except in a case to which paragraph (3) applies, and subject to paragraph (5), where qualifying works are not the subject of a qualifying long term agreement to which section 20 applies, the consultation requirements for the purposes of that section and section 20ZA, as regards those works–
> (a) in a case where public notice of those works is required to be given, are those specified in Part 1 of Schedule 4;
> (b) in any other case, are those specified in Part 2 of that Schedule.

(5) In relation to a RTB tenant and particular qualifying works, nothing in paragraph (1), (2) or (4) requires a landlord to comply with any of the consultation requirements applicable to that agreement that arise before the thirty-first day of the RTB tenancy.

SCHEDULE I CONSULTATION REQUIREMENTS FOR QUALIFYING LONG TERM AGREEMENTS OTHER THAN THOSE FOR WHICH PUBLIC NOTICE IS REQUIRED

Notice of intention

1.—(1) The landlord shall give notice in writing of his intention to enter into the agreement–
> (a) to each tenant; and
> (b) where a recognised tenants' association[1] represents some or all of the tenants, to the association.

(2) The notice shall–

    (a) describe, in general terms, the relevant matters or specify the place and hours at which a description of the relevant matters may be inspected;

    (b) state the landlord's reasons for considering it necessary to enter into the agreement;

    (c) where the relevant matters consist of or include qualifying works, state the landlord's reasons for considering it necessary to carry out those works;

    (d) invite the making, in writing, of observations in relation to the proposed agreement; and

    (e) specify–

        (i) the address to which such observations may be sent;

        (ii) that they must be delivered within the relevant period; and

        (iii) the date on which the relevant period ends.

(3) The notice shall also invite each tenant and the association (if any) to propose, within the relevant period, the name of a person from whom the landlord should try to obtain an estimate in respect of the relevant matters.

1   See Landlord and Tenant Act 1985, s 29(1), which was amended by the Landlord and Tenant Act 1987, Sch 2, para 10.

Inspection of description of relevant matters

2.—(1) Where a notice under paragraph 1 specifies a place and hours for inspection–

    (a) the place and hours so specified must be reasonable; and

    (b) a description of the relevant matters must be available for inspection, free of charge, at that place and during those hours.

(2) If facilities to enable copies to be taken are not made available at the times at which the description may be inspected, the landlord shall provide to any tenant, on request and free of charge, a copy of the description.

Duty to have regard to observations in relation to proposed agreement

3. Where, within the relevant period, observations are made in relation to the proposed agreement by any tenant or recognised tenants' association, the landlord shall have regard to those observations.

Estimates

4.—(1) Where, within the relevant period, a single nomination is made by a recognised tenants' association (whether or not a nomination is made by any tenant), the landlord shall try to obtain an estimate from the nominated person.

(2) Where, within the relevant period, a single nomination is made by only one of the tenants (whether or not a nomination is made by a recognised tenants' association), the landlord shall try to obtain an estimate from the nominated person.

(3) Where, within the relevant period, a single nomination is made by more than one tenant (whether or not a nomination is made by a recognised tenants' association), the landlord shall try to obtain an estimate–

    (a) from the person who received the most nominations; or

    (b) if there is no such person, but two (or more) persons received the same number of nominations, being a number in excess of the nominations received by any other person, from one of those two (or more) persons; or

    (c) in any other case, from any nominated person.

(4) Where, within the relevant period, more than one nomination is made by any tenant and more than one nomination is made by a recognised tenants' association, the landlord shall try to obtain an estimate–

(a) from at least one person nominated by a tenant; and

(b) from at least one person nominated by the association, other than a person from whom an estimate is sought as mentioned in paragraph (a).

Preparation of landlord's proposals

5.—(1) The landlord shall prepare, in accordance with the following provisions of this paragraph, at least two proposals in respect of the relevant matters.

(2) At least one of the proposals must propose that goods or services are provided, or works are carried out (as the case may be), by a person wholly unconnected with the landlord.

(3) Where an estimate has been obtained from a nominated person, the landlord must prepare a proposal based on that estimate.

(4) Each proposal shall contain a statement of the relevant matters.

(5) Each proposal shall contain a statement, as regards each party to the proposed agreement other than the landlord–

(a) of the party's name and address; and

(b) of any connection (apart from the proposed agreement) between the party and the landlord.

(6) For the purposes of sub-paragraphs (2) and (5)(b), it shall be assumed that there is a connection between a party (as the case may be) and the landlord–

(a) where the landlord is a company, if the party is, or is to be, a director or manager of the company or is a close relative of any such director or manager;

(b) where the landlord is a company, and the party is a partner in a partnership, if any partner in that partnership is, or is to be, a director or manager of the company or is a close relative of any such director or manager;

(c) where both the landlord and the party are companies, if any director or manager of one company is, or is to be, a director or manager of the other company;

(d) where the party is a company, if the landlord is a director or manager of the company or is a close relative of any such director or manager; or

(e) where the party is a company and the landlord is a partner in a partnership, if any partner in that partnership is a director or manager of the company or is a close relative of any such director or manager.

(7) Where, as regards each tenant's unit of occupation and the relevant matters, it is reasonably practicable for the landlord to estimate the relevant contribution attributable to the relevant matters to which the proposed agreement relates, each proposal shall contain a statement of that estimated contribution.

(8) Where–

(a) it is not reasonably practicable for the landlord to make the estimate mentioned in sub-paragraph (7); and

(b) it is reasonably practicable for the landlord to estimate, as regards the building or other premises to which the proposed agreement relates, the total amount of his expenditure under the proposed agreement,

each proposal shall contain a statement of that estimated expenditure.

(9) Where–

(a) it is not reasonably practicable for the landlord to make the estimate mentioned in sub-paragraph (7) or (8)(b); and

(b) it is reasonably practicable for the landlord to ascertain the current unit cost or hourly or daily rate applicable to the relevant matters,

each proposal shall contain a statement of that cost or rate.

(10) Where the relevant matters comprise or include the proposed appointment by the landlord of an agent to discharge any of the landlord's obligations to the tenants which relate to the management by him of premises to which the agreement relates, each proposal shall contain a statement–

(a) that the person whose appointment is proposed–

(i) is or, as the case may be, is not, a member of a professional body or trade association; and

(ii) subscribes or, as the case may be, does not subscribe, to any code of practice or voluntary accreditation scheme relevant to the functions of managing agents; and

(b) if the person is a member of a professional body trade association, of the name of the body or association.

(11) Each proposal shall contain a statement as to the provisions (if any) for variation of any amount specified in, or to be determined under, the proposed agreement.

(12) Each proposal shall contain a statement of the intended duration of the proposed agreement.

(13) Where the landlord has received observations to which (in accordance with paragraph 3) he is required to have regard, each proposal shall contain a statement summarising the observations and setting out the landlord's response to them.

Notification of landlord's proposals

6.—(1) The landlord shall give notice in writing of proposals prepared under paragraph 5–

(a) to each tenant; and

(b) where a recognised tenants' association represents some or all of the tenants, to the association.

(2) The notice shall–

(a) be accompanied by a copy of each proposal or specify the place and hours at which the proposals may be inspected;

(b) invite the making, in writing, of observations in relation to the proposals; and

(c) specify–

(i) the address to which such observations may be sent;

(ii) that they must be delivered within the relevant period; and

(iii) the date on which the relevant period ends.

(3) Paragraph 2 shall apply to proposals made available for inspection under this paragraph as it applies to a description of the relevant matters made available for inspection under that paragraph.

Duty to have regard to observations in relation to proposals

7. Where, within the relevant period, observations are made in relation to the landlord's proposals by any tenant or recognised tenants' association, the landlord shall have regard to those observations.

Duty on entering into agreement

8.—(1) Subject to sub-paragraph (2), where the landlord enters into an agreement relating to relevant matters, he shall, within 21 days of entering into the agreement, by notice in writing to each tenant and the recognised tenants' association (if any)–

(a) state his reasons for making that agreement or specify the place and hours at which a statement of those reasons may be inspected; and

(b) where he has received observations to which (in accordance with paragraph 7) he is required to have regard, summarise the observations and respond to them or specify the place and hours at which that summary and response may be inspected.

(2) The requirements of sub-paragraph (1) do not apply where the person with whom the agreement is made is a nominated person or submitted the lowest estimate.

(3) Paragraph 2 shall apply to a statement, summary and response made available for inspection under this paragraph as it applies to a description of the relevant matters made available for inspection under that paragraph.

SCHEDULE 2 CONSULTATION REQUIREMENTS FOR QUALIFYING LONG TERM AGREEMENTS FOR WHICH PUBLIC NOTICE IS REQUIRED

Notice of intention
1.—(1) The landlord shall give notice in writing of his intention to enter into the agreement–

> (a) to each tenant; and
> (b) where a recognised tenants' association represents some or all of the tenants, to the association.

(2) The notice shall–

> (a) describe, in general terms, the relevant matters or specify the place and hours at which a description of the relevant matters may be inspected;
> (b) state the landlord's reasons for considering it necessary to enter into the agreement;
> (c) where the relevant matters consist of or include qualifying works, state the landlord's reasons for considering it necessary to carry out those works;
> (d) state that the reason why the landlord is not inviting recipients of the notice to nominate persons from whom he should try to obtain an estimate for the relevant matters is that public notice of the relevant matters is to be given;
> (e) invite the making, in writing, of observations in relation to the relevant matters; and
> (f) specify–
>> (i) the address to which such observations may be sent;
>> (ii) that they must be delivered within the relevant period; and
>> (iii) the date on which the relevant period ends.

Inspection of description of relevant matters
2.—(1) Where a notice under paragraph 1 specifies a place and hours for inspection–

> (a) the place and hours so specified must be reasonable; and
> (b) a description of the relevant matters must be available for inspection, free of charge, at that place and during those hours.

(2) If facilities to enable copies to be taken are not made available at the times at which the description may be inspected, the landlord shall provide to any tenant, on request and free of charge, a copy of the description.

Duty to have regard to observations in relation to relevant matters
3. Where, within the relevant period, observations are made, in relation to the relevant matters by any tenant or recognised tenants' association, the landlord shall have regard to those observations.

Preparation of landlord's proposal
4.—(1) The landlord shall prepare, in accordance with the following provisions of this paragraph, a proposal in respect of the proposed agreement.

(2) The proposal shall contain a statement–

> (a) of the name and address of every party to the proposed agreement (other than the landlord); and
> (b) of any connection (apart from the proposed agreement) between the landlord and any other party.

(3) For the purpose of sub-paragraph (2)(b), it shall be assumed that there is a connection between the landlord and a party–

(a) where the landlord is a company, if the party is, or is to be, a director or manager of the company or is a close relative of any such director or manager;
(b) where the landlord is a company, and the party is a partner in a partnership, if any partner in that partnership is, or is to be, a director or manager of the company or is a close relative of any such director or manager;
(c) where both the landlord and the party are companies, if any director or manager of one company is, or is to be, a director or manager of the other company;
(d) where the party is a company, if the landlord is a director or manager of the company or is a close relative of any such director or manager; or
(e) where the party is a company and the landlord is a partner in a partnership, if any partner in that partnership is a director or manager of the company or is a close relative of any such director or manager.
(4) Where, as regards each tenant's unit of occupation, it is reasonably practicable for the landlord to estimate the relevant contribution to be incurred by the tenant attributable to the relevant matters to which the proposed agreement relates, the proposal shall contain a statement of that contribution.
(5) Where–
(a) it is not reasonably practicable for the landlord to make the estimate mentioned in sub-paragraph (4); and
(b) it is reasonably practicable for the landlord to estimate, as regards the building or other premises to which the proposed agreement relates, the total amount of his expenditure under the proposed agreement,
the proposal shall contain a statement of the amount of that estimated expenditure.
(6) Where–
(a) it is not reasonably practicable for the landlord to make the estimate mentioned in sub-paragraph (4) or (5)(b); and
(b) it is reasonably practicable for the landlord to ascertain the current unit cost or hourly or daily rate applicable to the relevant matters to which the proposed agreement relates,
the proposal shall contain a statement of that cost or rate.
(7) Where it is not reasonably practicable for the landlord to make the estimate mentioned in sub-paragraph (6)(b), the proposal shall contain a statement of the reasons why he cannot comply and the date by which he expects to be able to provide an estimate, cost or rate.
(8) Where the relevant matters comprise or include the proposed appointment by the landlord of an agent to discharge any of the landlord's obligations to the tenants which relate to the management by him of premises to which the agreement relates, each proposal shall contain a statement–
(a) that the person whose appointment is proposed–
(i) is or, as the case may be, is not, a member of a professional body or trade association; and
(ii) subscribes or, as the case may be, does not subscribe, to any code of practice or voluntary accreditation scheme relevant to the functions of managing agents; and
(b) if the person is a member of a professional body trade association, of the name of the body or association.
(9) Each proposal shall contain a statement of the intended duration of the proposed agreement.
(10) Where the landlord has received observations to which (in accordance with paragraph 3) he is required to have regard, the proposal shall contain a statement summarising the observations and setting out the landlord's response to them.

Notification of landlord's proposal

5.—(1) The landlord shall give notice in writing of the proposal prepared under paragraph 4–

(a) to each tenant; and

(b) where a recognised tenants' association represents some or all of the tenants, to the association.

(2) The notice shall–

(a) be accompanied by a copy of the proposal or specify the place and hours at which the proposal may be inspected;

(b) invite the making, in writing, of observations in relation to the proposal; and

(c) specify–

(i) the address to which such observations may be sent;

(ii) that they must be delivered within the relevant period; and

(iii) the date on which the relevant period ends.

(3) Paragraph 2 shall apply to a proposal made available for inspection under this paragraph as it applies to a description made available for inspection under that paragraph.

Duty to have regard to observations in relation to proposal

6. Where, within the relevant period, observations are made in relation to the landlord's proposal by any tenant or recognised tenants' association, the landlord shall have regard to those observations.

Landlord's response to observations

7. Where the landlord receives observations to which (in accordance with paragraph 6) he is required to have regard, he shall, within 21 days of their receipt, by notice in writing to the person by whom the observations were made, state his response to the observations.

Supplementary information

8. Where a proposal prepared under paragraph 4 contains such a statement as is mentioned in sub-paragraph (7) of that paragraph, the landlord shall, within 21 days of receiving sufficient information to enable him to estimate the amount, cost or rate referred to in sub-paragraph (4), (5) or (6) of that paragraph, give notice in writing of the estimated amount, cost or rate (as the case may be)–

(a) to each tenant; and

(b) where a recognised tenants' association represents some or all of the tenants, to the association.

SCHEDULE 3 CONSULTATION REQUIREMENTS FOR QUALIFYING WORKS UNDER QUALIFYING LONG TERM AGREEMENTS AND AGREEMENTS TO WHICH REGULATION 7(3) APPLIES

Notice of intention

1.—(1) The landlord shall give notice in writing of his intention to carry out qualifying works–

(a) to each tenant; and

(b) where a recognised tenants' association represents some or all of the tenants, to the association.

(2) The notice shall–

(a) describe, in general terms, the works proposed to be carried out or specify the place and hours at which a description of the proposed works may be inspected;

(b) state the landlord's reasons for considering it necessary to carry out the proposed works;

(c) contain a statement of the total amount of the expenditure estimated by the landlord as likely to be incurred by him on and in connection with the proposed works;

(d) invite the making, in writing, of observations in relation to the proposed works or the landlord's estimated expenditure;

(e) specify–

    (i) the address to which such observations may be sent;

    (ii) that they must be delivered within the relevant period; and

    (iii) the date on which the relevant period ends.

Inspection of description of proposed works

2.—(1) Where a notice under paragraph 1 specifies a place and hours for inspection–

    (a) the place and hours so specified must be reasonable; and

    (b) a description of the proposed works must be available for inspection, free of charge, at that place and during those hours.

(2) If facilities to enable copies to be taken are not made available at the times at which the description may be inspected, the landlord shall provide to any tenant, on request and free of charge, a copy of the description.

Duty to have regard to observations in relation to proposed works and estimated expenditure

3. Where, within the relevant period, observations are made in relation to the proposed works or the landlord's estimated expenditure by any tenant or the recognised tenants' association, the landlord shall have regard to those observations.

Landlord's response to observations

4. Where the landlord receives observations to which (in accordance with paragraph 3) he is required to have regard, he shall, within 21 days of their receipt, by notice in writing to the person by whom the observations were made, state his response to the observations.

SCHEDULE 4 CONSULTATION REQUIREMENTS FOR QUALIFYING WORKS OTHER THAN WORKS UNDER QUALIFYING LONG TERM OR AGREEMENTS TO WHICH REGULATION 7(3) APPLIES

Part I Consultation requirements for qualifying works for which public notice is required

Notice of intention

1.—(1) The landlord shall give notice in writing of his intention to carry out qualifying works–

    (a) to each tenant; and

    (b) where a recognised tenants' association represents some or all of the tenants, to the association.

(2) The notice shall–

    (a) describe, in general terms, the works proposed to be carried out or specify the place and hours at which a description of the proposed works may be inspected;

    (b) state the landlord's reasons for considering it necessary to carry out the proposed works;

    (c) state that the reason why the landlord is not inviting recipients of the notice to nominate persons from whom he should try to obtain an estimate for carrying out the works is that public notice of the works is to be given;

(d) invite the making, in writing, of observations in relation to the proposed works; and

(e) specify–

(i) the address to which such observations may be sent;

(ii) that they must be delivered within the relevant period; and

(iii) the date on which the relevant period ends.

Inspection of description of proposed works

2.—(1) Where a notice under paragraph 1 specifies a place and hours for inspection–

(a) the place and hours so specified must be reasonable; and

(b) a description of the proposed works must be available for inspection, free of charge, at that place and during those hours.

(2) If facilities to enable copies to be taken are not made available at the times at which the description may be inspected, the landlord shall provide to any tenant, on request and free of charge, a copy of the description.

Duty to have regard to observations in relation to proposed works

3. Where, within the relevant period, observations are made in relation to the proposed works by any tenant or the recognised tenants' association, the landlord shall have regard to those observations.

Preparation of landlord's contract statement

4.—(1) The landlord shall prepare, in accordance with the following provisions of this paragraph, a statement in respect of the proposed contract under which the proposed works are to be carried out.

(2) The statement shall set out–

(a) the name and address of the person with whom the landlord proposes to contract; and

(b) particulars of any connection between them (apart from the proposed contract).

(3) For the purpose of sub-paragraph (2)(b) it shall be assumed that there is a connection between a person and the landlord–

(a) where the landlord is a company, if the person, or is to be, a director or manager of the company or is a close relative of any such director or manager;

(b) where the landlord is a company, and the person is a partner in a partnership, if any partner in that partnership is, or is to be, a director or manager of the company or is a close relative of any such director or manager;

(c) where both the landlord and the person are companies, if any director or manager of one company is, or is to be, a director or manager of the other company;

(d) where the person is a company, if the landlord is a director or manager of the company or is a close relative of any such director or manager; or

(e) where the person is a company and the landlord is a partner in a partnership, if any partner in that partnership is a director or manager of the company or is a close relative of any such director or manager.

(4) Where, as regards each tenant's unit of occupation, it is reasonably practicable for the landlord to estimate the amount of the relevant contribution to be incurred by the tenant attributable to the works to which the proposed contract relates, that estimated amount shall be specified in the statement.

(5) Where–

(a) it is not reasonably practicable for the landlord to make the estimate mentioned in sub-paragraph (4); and

(b) it is reasonably practicable for the landlord to estimate, as regards the building or other premises to which the proposed contract relates, the total amount of his expenditure under the proposed contract,

that estimated amount shall be specified in the statement.

(6) Where–

(a) it is not reasonably practicable for the landlord to make the estimate mentioned in sub-paragraph (4) or (5)(b); and

(b) it is reasonably practicable for the landlord to ascertain the current unit cost or hourly or daily rate applicable to the works to which the proposed contract relates,

that cost or rate shall be specified in the statement.

(7) Where it is not reasonably practicable for the landlord to make the estimate mentioned in sub-paragraph (6)(b), the reasons why he cannot comply and the date by which he expects to be able to provide an estimated amount, cost or rate shall be specified in the statement.

(8) Where the landlord has received observations to which (in accordance with paragraph 3) he is required to have regard, the statement shall summarise the observations and set out his response to them.

Notification of proposed contract

5.—(1) The landlord shall give notice in writing of his intention to enter into the proposed contract–

(a) to each tenant; and

(b) where a recognised tenants' association represents some or all of the tenants, to the association.

(2) The notice shall–

(a) comprise, or be accompanied by, the statement prepared in accordance with paragraph 4 ("the paragraph 4 statement") or specify the place and hours at which that statement may be inspected;

(b) invite the making, in writing, of observations in relation to any matter mentioned in the paragraph 4 statement;

(c) specify–

(i) the address to which such observations may be sent;

(ii) that they must be delivered within the relevant period; and

(iii) the date on which the relevant period ends.

(3) Where the paragraph 4 statement is made available for inspection, paragraph 2 shall apply in relation to that statement as it applies in relation to a description of proposed works made available for inspection under that paragraph.

Landlord's response to observations

6. Where, within the relevant period, the landlord receives observations in response to the invitation in the notice under paragraph 5, he shall, within 21 days of their receipt, by notice in writing to the person by whom the observations were made, state his response to the observations.

Supplementary information

7. Where a statement prepared under paragraph 4 sets out the landlord's reasons for being unable to comply with sub-paragraph (6) of that paragraph, the landlord shall, within 21 days of receiving sufficient information to enable him to estimate the amount, cost or rate referred to in sub-paragraph (4), (5) or (6) of that paragraph, give notice in writing of the estimated amount, cost or rate (as the case may be)–

(a) to each tenant; and

(b) where a recognised tenants' association represents some or all of the tenants, to the association.

Part 2 Consultation requirements for qualifying works for which public notice is not required

Notice of intention
1.—(1) The landlord shall give notice in writing of his intention to carry out qualifying works–
> (a) to each tenant; and
> (b) where a recognised tenants' association represents some or all of the tenants, to the association.

(2) The notice shall–
> (a) describe, in general terms, the works proposed to be carried out or specify the place and hours at which a description of the proposed works may be inspected;
> (b) state the landlord's reasons for considering it necessary to carry out the proposed works;
> (c) invite the making, in writing, of observations in relation to the proposed works; and
> (d) specify–
>> (i) the address to which such observations may be sent;
>> (ii) that they must be delivered within the relevant period; and
>> (iii) the date on which the relevant period ends.

(3) The notice shall also invite each tenant and the association (if any) to propose, within the relevant period, the name of a person from whom the landlord should try to obtain an estimate for the carrying out of the proposed works.

Inspection of description of proposed works
2.—(1) Where a notice under paragraph 1 specifies a place and hours for inspection–
> (a) the place and hours so specified must be reasonable; and
> (b) a description of the proposed works must be available for inspection, free of charge, at that place and during those hours.

(2) If facilities to enable copies to be taken are not made available at the times at which the description may be inspected, the landlord shall provide to any tenant, on request and free of charge, a copy of the description.

Duty to have regard to observations in relation to proposed works
3. Where, within the relevant period, observations are made, in relation to the proposed works by any tenant or recognised tenants' association, the landlord shall have regard to those observations.

Estimates and response to observations
4.—(1) Where, within the relevant period, a nomination is made by a recognised tenants' association (whether or not a nomination is made by any tenant), the landlord shall try to obtain an estimate from the nominated person.

(2) Where, within the relevant period, a nomination is made by only one of the tenants (whether or not a nomination is made by a recognised tenants' association), the landlord shall try to obtain an estimate from the nominated person.

(3) Where, within the relevant period, a single nomination is made by more than one tenant (whether or not a nomination is made by a recognised tenants' association), the landlord shall try to obtain an estimate–
> (a) from the person who received the most nominations; or
> (b) if there is no such person, but two (or more) persons received the same number of nominations, being a number in excess of the nominations received by any other person, from one of those two (or more) persons; or
> (c) in any other case, from any nominated person.

(4) Where, within the relevant period, more than one nomination is made by any tenant and more than one nomination is made by a recognised tenants' association, the landlord shall try to obtain an estimate–

    (a) from at least one person nominated by a tenant; and

    (b) from at least one person nominated by the association, other than a person from whom an estimate is sought as mentioned in paragraph (a).

(5) The landlord shall, in accordance with this sub-paragraph and sub-paragraphs (6) to (9)–

    (a) obtain estimates for the carrying out of the proposed works;

    (b) supply, free of charge, a statement ("the paragraph (b) statement") setting out–

        (i) as regards at least two of the estimates, the amount specified in the estimate as the estimated cost of the proposed works; and

        (ii) where the landlord has received observations to which (in accordance with paragraph 3) he is required to have regard, a summary of the observations and his response to them; and

    (c) make all of the estimates available for inspection.

(6) At least one of the estimates must be that of a person wholly unconnected with the landlord.

(7) For the purpose of paragraph (6), it shall be assumed that there is a connection between a person and the landlord–

    (a) where the landlord is a company, if the person is, or is to be, a director or manager of the company or is a close relative of any such director or manager;

    (b) where the landlord is a company, and the person is a partner in a partnership, if any partner in that partnership is, or is to be, a director or manager of the company or is a close relative of any such director or manager;

    (c) where both the landlord and the person are companies, if any director or manager of one company is, or is to be, a director or manager of the other company;

    (d) where the person is a company, if the landlord is a director or manager of the company or is a close relative of any such director or manager; or

    (e) where the person is a company and the landlord is a partner in a partnership, if any partner in that partnership is a director or manager of the company or is a close relative of any such director or manager.

(8) Where the landlord has obtained an estimate from a nominated person, that estimate must be one of those to which the paragraph (b) statement relates.

(9) The paragraph (b) statement shall be supplied to, and the estimates made available for inspection by–

    (a) each tenant; and

    (b) the secretary of the recognised tenants' association (if any).

(10) The landlord shall, by notice in writing to each tenant and the association (if any)–

    (a) specify the place and hours at which the estimates may be inspected;

    (b) invite the making, in writing, of observations in relation to those estimates;

    (c) specify–

        (i) the address to which such observations may be sent;

        (ii) that they must be delivered within the relevant period; and

        (iii) the date on which the relevant period ends.

(11) Paragraph 2 shall apply to estimates made available for inspection under this paragraph as it applies to a description of proposed works made available for inspection under that paragraph.

Duty to have regard to observations in relation to estimates

5. Where, within the relevant period, observations are made in relation to the estimates by a recognised tenants' association or, as the case may be, any tenant, the landlord shall have regard to those observations.

Duty on entering into contract

6.—(1) Subject to sub-paragraph (2), where the landlord enters into a contract for the carrying out of qualifying works, he shall, within 21 days of entering into the contract, by notice in writing to each tenant and the recognised tenants' association (if any)–

    (a) state his reasons for awarding the contract or specify the place and hours at which a statement of those reasons may be inspected; and

    (b) there he received observations to which (in accordance with paragraph 5) he was required to have regard, summarise the observations and set out his response to them.

(2) The requirements of sub-paragraph (1) do not apply where the person with whom the contract is made is a nominated person or submitted the lowest estimate.

(3) Paragraph 2 shall apply to a statement made available for inspection under this paragraph as it applies to a description of proposed works made available for inspection under that paragraph.

EXPLANATORY NOTE

These Regulations, which apply only in relation to England, relate to the amount that tenants can be required to contribute, by the payment of service charges, to relevant costs incurred by landlords in carrying out works or under certain agreements. Unless a landlord complies with prescribed consultation requirements or obtains a dispensation from a leasehold valuation tribunal under section 20(9) of the Landlord and Tenant Act 1985 in respect of all or any of those requirements, his tenants' contributions by way of service charges are limited.

Regulation 3(1) exempts from the consultation requirements applicable to agreements for a term of more than 12 months ("qualifying long term agreements"):

(a)   contracts of employment;

(b)   agreements between a tenant management organisation or an arms length management organisation (a body established under section 2 of the Local Government Act 2000) and a local housing authority under section 27 of the Housing Act 1985 (management agreements);

(c)   agreements between a holding company and any of its subsidiaries or between two or more subsidiaries of the same holding company; and

(d)   agreements for a term of not more than five years relating to buildings or other premises which are untenanted when the agreement is entered into.

Regulation 3(2) provides that an agreement entered into before the coming into force of these Regulations is not a qualifying long term agreement even if more than 12 months of the term of the agreement remain when these Regulations come into force.

Regulation 3(3) provides that an agreement for a term of more than 12 months is not a qualifying long term agreement if it provides for the carrying out of works on a building or any other premises ("qualifying works") for which notice has been published in the Official Journal of the European Union ("the Official Journal") (to comply with EU procurement rules) before these Regulations come into force.

Regulation 4 imposes a limit of £100 in any accounting period (defined in regulation 4(2)) in respect of service charges attributable to the provision of goods or services, or the carrying out of works, under a qualifying long term agreement. That limit will apply unless the landlord complies with the consultation requirements prescribed by regulation 5 or obtains a dispensation from a leasehold valuation tribunal in respect of all or any of those requirements.

Regulation 5 deals with the consultation requirements applicable to qualifying long term agreements. Except in the cases mentioned below, the consultation requirements are those specified in Schedule 1. Where, on or after the coming into force of these Regulations, notice is required to be published in the Official Journal (to comply with EU procurement rules) of goods or services to be provided or works to be carried out under the agreement, the consultation requirements are those set out in Schedule 2. Where a person becomes a tenant as the result of exercising the right to be granted a long lease under section 138 of the Housing Act 1985 (right to buy) (including that section as applied in relation to the preserved right to buy under section 171A of that Act or the right to acquire under section 16 of the Housing Act 1996) the landlord is only required to comply with such of the consultation requirements applicable to the agreement as remain to be complied with after the thirtieth day of that person's tenancy.

Regulation 6 imposes a limit of £250 as regards a tenant's contribution in respect of service charges attributable to qualifying works. That limit will apply unless the landlord complies with the consultation requirements prescribed by regulation 7 or obtains a dispensation from a leasehold valuation tribunal in respect of all or any of those requirements.

Regulation 7 deals with the consultation requirements relevant to qualifying works of the descriptions specified in that regulation. In relation to other qualifying works, the consultation requirements under section 20 of the Landlord and Tenant Act 1985, as it stood immediately before the substitution effected by section 151 of the Commonhold and Leasehold Reform Act 2002, continue to apply by virtue of article 3 of the Commonhold and Leasehold Reform Act 2002 (Commencement No.2 and Savings) (England) Order 2003 (S.I. 2003/1986 (c. 82)).

Paragraph (1) of regulation 7 relates to qualifying works that are the subject of a qualifying long term agreement. Subject to the exception for which paragraph (5) provides ("the paragraph (5) exception"), the consultation requirements are those set out in Schedule 3 to the Regulations.

Paragraphs (2) to (4) relate to qualifying works that are not the subject of a qualifying long term agreement.

Paragraph (2) deals with the consultation requirements in a case to which paragraph (3) applies. Subject to the paragraph (5) exception, the consultation requirements in such a case are those set out in Schedule 3 (the same requirements as apply to qualifying works under qualifying long term agreements).

Paragraph (3) applies where qualifying works are carried out:

(a)   on or after the date that falls two months after the date on which these Regulations come into force under an agreement entered into before these Regulations come into force; or

(b)   under an agreement for more than 12 months where notice of those works was published in the Official Journal before these Regulations come into force.

Paragraph (4) applies to cases to which paragraph (3) does not apply. Where notice of the qualifying works is required to be published in the Official Journal (to comply with EU procurement rules), and subject to the paragraph (5) exception, the consultation requirements are those set out in Part 1 of Schedule 4. Where notice is not required to be published in the Official Journal, and subject to the paragraph (5) exception, the consultation requirements are those set out in Part 2 of Schedule 4.

The paragraph (5) exception applies where a person becomes a tenant as the result of exercising the right to be granted a long lease under section 138 of the Housing Act 1985 (including that section as applied in relation to the preserved right to buy under section 171A of that Act or the right to acquire under section 16 of the Housing Act 1996). In that case, and in relation to that person and particular qualifying works, the landlord is only required to comply with such of the consultation requirements applicable to those works as remain to be complied with after the thirtieth day of that person's tenancy.

A Regulatory Impact Assessment has been prepared in connection with these Regulations. A copy may be obtained from the Office of the Deputy Prime Minister, Leasehold Reform Branch, Zone 2/J6, Eland House, Bressenden Place, London, SW1E 5DU (Tel 020 7944 3462).

Service Charges (Summary of Rights and Obligations, and Transitional Provision) (England) Regulations 2007 (SI 2007/1257)

1. Citation and commencement
These Regulations may be cited as the Service Charges (Summary of Rights and Obligations, and Transitional Provision) (England) Regulations 2007 and shall come into force on the 1st October 2007.

2. Application
(1) Subject to regulation 4, these Regulations apply where, on or after 1st October 2007, a demand for payment of a service charge[1] is served in relation to a dwelling[2].

(2) Subject to paragraph (3) these Regulations apply to dwellings in England which are subject to a lease[3].

(3) These Regulations do not apply where—

(a) the lease is not a long lease within section 26 of the Landlord and Tenant Act 1985; and

(b) the landlord is a local authority, a National Park Authority or a new town corporation.

1   For the meaning of "service charge", see Landlord and Tenant Act 1985, s 18. Section 18 was amended by Landlord and Tenant Act 1987, s 41 and Commonhold and Leasehold Reform Act 2002, s 150.
2   For the meaning of "dwelling", see Landlord and Tenant Act 1985, s 38.
3   For the meaning of "lease", see Landlord and Tenant Act 1985, s 36.

3. Form and content of summary of rights and obligations
Where these Regulations apply the summary of rights and obligations which must accompany a demand for the payment of a service charge must be legible in a typewritten or printed form of at least 10 point, and must contain—

(a) the title "Service Charges — Summary of tenants' rights and obligations"; and

(b) the following statement—

"(1) This summary, which briefly sets out your rights and obligations in relation to variable service charges, must by law accompany a demand for service charges. Unless a summary is sent to you with a demand, you may withhold the service charge. The summary does not give a full interpretation of the law and if you are in any doubt about your rights and obligations you should seek independent advice.

(2) Your lease sets out your obligations to pay service charges to your landlord in addition to your rent. Service charges are amounts payable for services, repairs, maintenance, improvements, insurance or the landlord's costs of management, to the extent that the costs have been reasonably incurred.

(3) You have the right to ask a leasehold valuation tribunal to determine whether you are liable to pay service charges for services, repairs, maintenance, improvements, insurance or management. You may make a request before or after you have paid the service charge. If the tribunal determines that the service charge is payable, the tribunal may also determine—

who should pay the service charge and who it should be paid to;
the amount;
the date it should be paid by; and
how it should be paid.

However, you do not have these rights where—

a matter has been agreed or admitted by you;
a matter has already been, or is to be, referred to arbitration or has been determined by arbitration and you agreed to go to arbitration after the disagreement about the service charge or costs arose; or
a matter has been decided by a court.

(4) If your lease allows your landlord to recover costs incurred or that may be incurred in legal proceedings as service charges, you may ask the court or tribunal, before which those proceedings were brought, to rule that your landlord may not do so.

(5) Where you seek a determination from a leasehold valuation tribunal, you will have to pay an application fee and, where the matter proceeds to a hearing, a hearing fee, unless you qualify for a waiver or reduction. The total fees payable will not exceed £500, but making an application may incur additional costs, such as professional fees, which you may also have to pay.

(6) A leasehold valuation tribunal has the power to award costs, not exceeding £500, against a party to any proceedings where—

it dismisses a matter because it is frivolous, vexatious or an abuse of process; or
it considers a party has acted frivolously, vexatiously, abusively, disruptively or unreasonably.

The [Upper Tribunal][1] has similar powers when hearing an appeal against a decision of a leasehold valuation tribunal.

(7) If your landlord—

proposes works on a building or any other premises that will cost you or any other tenant more than £250, or
proposes to enter into an agreement for works or services which will last for more than 12 months and will cost you or any other tenant more than £100 in any 12 month accounting period,
your contribution will be limited to these amounts unless your landlord has properly consulted on the proposed works or agreement or a leasehold valuation tribunal has agreed that consultation is not required.

(8) You have the right to apply to a leasehold valuation tribunal to ask it to determine whether your lease should be varied on the grounds that it does not make satisfactory provision in respect of the calculation of a service charge payable under the lease.

(9) You have the right to write to your landlord to request a written summary of the costs which make up the service charges. The summary must—

cover the last 12 month period used for making up the accounts relating to the service charge ending no later than the date of your request, where the accounts are made up for 12 month periods; or
cover the 12 month period ending with the date of your request, where the accounts are not made up for 12 month periods.

The summary must be given to you within 1 month of your request or 6 months of the end of the period to which the summary relates whichever is the later.

(10) You have the right, within 6 months of receiving a written summary of costs, to require the landlord to provide you with reasonable facilities to inspect the accounts, receipts and other documents supporting the summary and for taking copies or extracts from them.

(11) You have the right to ask an accountant or surveyor to carry out an audit of the financial management of the premises containing your dwelling, to establish the obligations of your landlord and the extent to which the service charges you pay are being used efficiently. It will depend on your circumstances whether you can exercise this right alone or only with the support of others living in the premises. You are strongly advised to seek independent advice before exercising this right.

(12) Your lease may give your landlord a right of re-entry or forfeiture where you have failed to pay charges which are properly due under the lease. However, to exercise this right, the landlord must meet all the legal requirements and obtain a court order. A court order will only be granted if you have admitted you are liable to pay the amount or it is finally determined by a court, tribunal or by arbitration that the amount is due. The court has a wide discretion in granting such an order and it will take into account all the circumstances of the case.".

1   Words substituted by Transfer of Tribunal Functions (Lands Tribunal and Miscellaneous Amendments) Order 2009/1307, Sch 2, para 119 (1 June 2009).

4. Transitional provision

The following provisions apply where a demand ("the first demand") for the payment of service charges was served prior to 1st October 2007—

(a) the requirements of section 21B(3) and (4) of the Landlord and Tenant Act 1985, as inserted by section 153 of the Act, shall not apply to a further demand for the payment of service charges where the first demand was served before 1st October 2007 in respect of service charges due for payment before 1st October 2007; and

(b) section 21B of the Landlord and Tenant Act 1985 shall apply to a further demand for the payment of service charges where the first demand was served before 1st October 2007 in respect of service charges due for payment on or after 1st October 2007.

EXPLANATORY NOTE

These Regulations prescribe the content of the summary of tenants' rights and obligations relating to service charges, which must accompany any demand for such charges made by a landlord, under section 21B of the Landlord and Tenant Act 1985. The Regulations also make provision for minor matters in respect of the form of the summary.

Regulation 4 provides a transitional provisions relating to demands for service charges sent to tenants prior to 1st October 2007.

A Regulatory Impact Assessment has been prepared in relation to these Regulations. It has been placed in the Library of each House of Parliament and copies may be obtained from the Leasehold and Park Homes Branch of the Department for Communities and Local Government, Zone 2/H10, Eland House, Bressenden Place, London SW1E 5DU (Telephone 020 7944 3463).

Index

References are to paragraph numbers.